Knowledge and Profanation

Intersections

INTERDISCIPLINARY STUDIES IN EARLY MODERN CULTURE

General Editor

Karl A.E. Enenkel (*Chair of Medieval and Neo-Latin Literature
Westfälische Wilhelms-Universität Münster
e-mail: kenen_01@uni_muenster.de*)

Editorial Board

W. van Anrooij (*University of Leiden*)
W. de Boer (*Miami University*)
Chr. Göttler (*University of Bern*)
J.L. de Jong (*University of Groningen*)
W.S. Melion (*Emory University*)
R. Seidel (*Goethe University Frankfurt am Main*)
P.J. Smith (*University of Leiden*)
J. Thompson (*Queen's University Belfast*)
A. Traninger (*Freie Universität Berlin*)
C. Zittel (*University of Stuttgart*)
C. Zwierlein (*Otto-Friedrich-Universität Bamberg*)

VOLUME 63 – 2019

The titles published in this series are listed at *brill.com/inte*

Knowledge and Profanation

Transgressing the Boundaries of Religion in Premodern Scholarship

Edited by

Martin Mulsow
Asaph Ben-Tov

BRILL

LEIDEN | BOSTON

Cover illustration: *Antonii van Dale poliatri Harlemensis De oraculis veterum ethnicorum dissertationes duae, quarum nunc prior agit de eorum origine atque auctoribus; secunda de ipsorum duratione et interitu.* Courtesy the Wellcome Trust – Wellcome Library – catalogue number EPB 19573/B – photo number: L0051050.

Library of Congress Cataloging-in-Publication Data

Names: Mulsow, Martin, editor.
Title: Knowledge and profanation : transgressing the boundaries of religion in premodern scholarship / edited by Martin Mulsow, Asaph Ben-Tov.
Description: Leiden ; Boston : Brill, 2019. | Series: Intersections : interdisciplinary studies in early modern culture, ISSN 1568-1181 ; volume 63 | Includes bibliographical references and index.
Identifiers: LCCN 2019015051 (print) | LCCN 2019018662 (ebook) | ISBN 9789004398931 (Ebook) | ISBN 9789004398924 (hardback : alk. paper)
Subjects: LCSH: Religions—Relations. | Aesthetics—Religious aspects.
Classification: LCC BL410 (ebook) | LCC BL410 .K56 2019 (print) | DDC 201/.5—dc23
LC record available at https://lccn.loc.gov/2019015051

Typeface for the Latin, Greek, and Cyrillic scripts: "Brill". See and download: brill.com/brill-typeface.

ISSN 1568-1181
ISBN 978-90-04-39892-4 (hardback)
ISBN 978-90-04-39893-1 (e-book)

Copyright 2019 by Koninklijke Brill NV, Leiden, The Netherlands.
Koninklijke Brill NV incorporates the imprints Brill, Brill Hes & De Graaf, Brill Nijhoff, Brill Rodopi, Brill Sense, Hotei Publishing, mentis Verlag, Verlag Ferdinand Schöningh and Wilhelm Fink Verlag.
All rights reserved. No part of this publication may be reproduced, translated, stored in a retrieval system, or transmitted in any form or by any means, electronic, mechanical, photocopying, recording or otherwise, without prior written permission from the publisher.
Authorization to photocopy items for internal or personal use is granted by Koninklijke Brill NV provided that the appropriate fees are paid directly to The Copyright Clearance Center, 222 Rosewood Drive, Suite 910, Danvers, MA 01923, USA. Fees are subject to change.

This book is printed on acid-free paper and produced in a sustainable manner.

Contents

Notes on the Editors   VII
Notes on the Contributors   VIII

Introduction   1
   Martin Mulsow and Asaph Ben-Tov

PART 1
The Sacred and the Profane in Art, Literature and Parody

1   Lucian of Samosata on Magic and Superstition   9
     Wolfgang Spickermann

2   Rabbi Lazarus and the Rich Man: A Talmudic Parody of the Late Roman Hell (Yerushalmi Hagigah 2.2, 77d and Sanhedrin 6.9, 23c)   23
     Holger Zellentin

3   Cardinal Gabriele Paleotti's Call for Reform of Christian Art   95
     Karl F. Morrison

4   The Sacred Becomes Profane – The Profane Becomes Sacred: Observations on the Desubstantialisation of Religious Discourse in the Early Modern Age   133
     Andreas Mahler

PART 2
Early Modern European Knowledge about Pagan Religion

5   The Seventeenth Century Confronts the Gods: Bishop Huet, Moses, and the Dangers of Comparison   159
     Martin Mulsow

6   The Eleusinian Mysteries in the Age of Reason   197
     Asaph Ben-Tov

PART 3
Crossing the Boundaries in Biblical Scholarship: Ancient Preconditions and Early Modern Conflict

7   Athens and Jerusalem? Early Jewish Biblical Scholarship and the Pagan World   231
    Azzan Yadin-Israel

8   Richard Simon and the Charenton Bible Project: The Quest for 'Perfect Neutrality' in Interpreting Scripture   253
    John Woodbridge

9   The Devil in the Details: The Case of Hermann Samuel Reimarus (1694–1768)   273
    Ulrich Groetsch

PART 4
Scientific Knowledge and Religion

10   Cry Me a Relic: The Holy Tear of Vendôme and Early Modern Lipsanomachy   299
     Anthony Ossa-Richardson

11   The Powerlessness of the Devil: Scientific Knowledge and Demonology in Clemente Baroni Cavalcabò (1726–1796)   330
     Riccarda Suitner

Index Nominum   357

Notes on the Editors

Asaph Ben-Tov

focuses in his research on the classical tradition and oriental studies in Early Modern Europe. He is the author of *Lutheran Humanists and Greek Antiquity: Melanchthonian Scholarship between Universal History and Pedagogy* (2009) and co-editor of *Knowledge and Religion in Early Modern Europe: Studies in Honor of Michael Heyd* (2013). His biography of the seventeenth-century Orientalist Johann Ernst Gerhard is forthcoming and he is currently completing a broad study of oriental studies in Germany, 1600–1750.

Martin Mulsow

is professor of intellectual history at the University of Erfurt and director of the Gotha Research Centre. From 2005–2008 he was professor of history at Rutgers University, USA. He is member of several German academies and was member of the Institute for Advanced Study in Princeton, the Wissenschaftskolleg in Berlin and the NIAS in Amsterdam. His work on Renaissance philosophy, the history of early modern scholarship and the radical enlightenment received many prizes, among them the prize of the Berlin-Brandenburg Academy of Sciences (2012) and the Anna-Krüger-Prize (2014). He is the author of *Die unanständige Gelehrtenrepublik. Wissen, Libertinage und Kommunikation in der Frühen Neuzeit* (2007), *Prekäres Wissen: Eine andere Ideengeschichte der Frühen Neuzeit* (2012), *Enlightenment Underground: Radical Germany, 1680–1720* (2015) and *Radikale Frühaufklärung in Deutschland 1680–1720* (2018).

The editors wish to thank Maximilian Gutberlet and Enoch Tabak for their valuable assistance in preparing the manuscript for publication.

Notes on the Contributors

Ulrich Groetsch
is Associate Professor of History at the University of North Alabama. He is the author of *Hermann Samuel Reimarus (1694–1768): Classicist, Hebraist, Enlightenment Radical in Disguise* (2015).

Andreas Mahler
is Professor of English Literature at the Freie Universität Berlin. He is co-editor of *Texte zur Theorie der Ideengeschichte* (2014) and of *Handbuch Literatur & Raum* (2017).

Karl F. Morrison
is Professor Emeritus at Rutgers University. Among his many publications are *Understanding Conversion* (1992) and, as a co-editor, *Seeing the Invisible in Late Antiquity and the Early Middle Ages* (2005) and *Studies on Medieval Empathies* (2013).

Anthony Ossa-Richardson
is a Lecturer in Early Modern English Literature at University College London. He is the author of *The Devil's Tabernacle: The Pagan Oracles in Early Modern Thought* (2013) and *A History of Ambiguity* (2019).

Wolfgang Spickermann
is Professor of Ancient History at the University of Graz. Among his publications are *Religionsgeschichte des römischen Germanien*, 2 vols. (2003 and 2008) and, as a co-editor, *Burial Rituals, Ideas of Afterlife, and the Individual in the Hellenistic World and the Roman Empire* (2016).

Riccarda Suitner
is Researcher in Early Modern History at the German Historical Institute in Rome. She has published *Die philosophischen Totengespräche der Frühaufklärung* (2016) and, as editor, *Gli Illuministi e i demoni. Il dibattito su magia e stregoneria dal Trentino all'Europa* (2019).

John Woodbridge
is Research Professor of Church History and the History of Christian Thought at Trinity Evangelical Divinity School, Deerfield, Illinois. He is the author of *The History of Biblical Authority* (1982) and *Revolt in Prerevolutionary France: The Prince de Conti's Conspiracy against Louis XV (1755–1757)* (1995).

Azzan Yadin-Israel
is Professor of Jewish Studies at Rutgers University. He has published *Scripture as Logos: Rabbi Ishmael and the Origins of Midrash* (2004) and *Scripture and Tradition: Rabbi Akiva and the Triumph of Midrash* (2015).

Holger Zellentin
is Lecturer in Classical Rabbinic Judaism at the University of Cambridge. Among his publications are *Rabbinic Parodies of Jewish and Christian Literature* (2011) and *The Qurʾān's Legal Culture: The Didascalia Apostolorum as a Point of Departure* (2013).

Introduction

Martin Mulsow and Asaph Ben-Tov

> *Procul, o procul este, profani.*
> VIRGIL, *Aeneid*, vi.258

∴

'Far hence be souls profane!' exclaims the Sibyl in John Dryden's rendering of the *Aeneid* (1697). Throughout history 'souls profane' have repeatedly ignored this caution and it is with a series of their scholarly representatives that this volume is concerned. As the following studies demonstrate, scholars ranging from the Italian Renaissance to the early nineteenth century, as well as several antique predecessors considered in this volume, had various means by which to profanate and a variety of reasons for doing so. But what is profanation? Taken literally, it is the rendering of that, which is considered sacred *profanum*, i.e. transforming it into an object or person relegated to the sphere from without the sanctuary (*fanum*).[1] Taken less literally, it is a form of de-sacralisation of a text, site, person, tradition, or institution considered by some to be sacred.[2] Following profanation, these, at least in the eyes of the profaner and those who share his or her views, are removed from the sacred sphere. Some profanations are carried out in full acquiescence of sacral authorities. This is the case with the recall of objects, which had under given sacral circumstances acquired sacral status, to their quotidian context. In most cases, however, profanations are not consensual and are marked by struggles with the offended adherents of the sacrality of that which has been banished from the *fanum*. Profanation and hurt feelings usually go hand in hand, and yet it must be stressed that

---

1 See in general Borgeaud P., "Le couple sacré/profane. Genèse et fortune d'un concept 'opératoire' en histoire des religions", *Revue de l'histoire des religions* 211, no. 4 (1994) 387–418; Colpe C., "Heilig (sprachlich)" and "Das Heilige", in *Handbuch religionswissenschaftlicher Grundbegriffe*, vol. 3, edited by H. Cancik, B. Gladigow and K.-H. Kohl (Stuttgart: 1993); Dihle A., "Heilig", in: *Reallexikon für Antike und Christentum*, vol. 13 (Stuttgart: 1987); Schilling R., "Sacrum et profanum. Essay d'interprétation", *Latomus* 30 (1971): 953–969. Classical monographs are Otto R., *The Idea of the Holy* (Oxford: 1923), and Eliade M., *The Sacred and the Profane* (New York: 1959).

2 See especially Agamben G., *Profanations*, trans. Jeff Fort (Cambridge, Mass.: 2007).

profanizers, whether or not intending to hurt others' feelings (some do not, others relish the injury) are not necessarily irreligious. The present volume offers numerous instances of profoundly religious polemicists profanizing other religions *ad majorem Dei gloriam*, as well as sincere adherents of their own religion, whose reflective scholarly undertakings were perceived as profanizing transgressions – occasionally with good reason. In the history of knowledge of religion and profanation unintended consequences often play a decisive role.

Motives for profanation vary. In fact, the very identification of a given utterance or process as profanation, depends on varying sensitivities. This is particularly true in regard to the relation between knowledge of religion and profanation. Can too much knowledge of religion be harmful? Could the profanation of a foreign religion turn out to be a double-edged sword? How much profanating knowledge of other religions could be tolerated in a premodern world? The latter was an urgent early modern concern, since profanating the religions, or confessions, of others was often a thin veil shrouding a profanation of one's own religion or sacred institutions. A further, cardinal point for premodern thinkers concerns comparative approaches to religion. Was it permissible to compare one's own religion or confession to others? Were their claims to exclusiveness not undermined by the equation, implicit in such comparisons? Thirdly, in an age which witnessed a series of contested translations of religious texts, e.g. the Bible, Koran, Patristic texts, and Confucius' *Analects*, the textual handling of the sacred and canonical comes to the fore. Is the very translation of sacred texts into other languages an act of profanation? And finally, should adherents of a religion fear having the recondite inner mechanism of their religion laid bare by excessive rationality? For all these reasons, there exists in all religions a tension-fraught relation to the publication of learned debates about them.[3]

Though each contribution in this volume deals with a given historical case, when viewed as a whole it becomes clear that these case studies intersect and overlap. We assume that there is a continuity between the problem of 'other' religions, the profane in one's own culture, and of cases of transgression and even blasphemy, especially when a reflexive study of external influences plays a role. Which kind of influence was admissible? Which was not? Under what circumstances was a discourse about 'the other' within one's own culture

---

3 Literature on these topics is extensively cited in the contributions of this volume. On the tensions see e.g. Webb E., *The Dark Dove: The Sacred and Secular in Modern Literature* (Seattle: 1975).

permissible? What apologetic strategies were available in the case of controversial borrowings?

Scholars, by the inherent rationale of their trade, tend to compare, translate, explain, and to adduce evidence from other fields of knowledge. An explication of one's dogmas may be conceived as helpful, but it may also be seen as a betrayal of the 'mysteries' of one's religion. Ancient mystery-cults in particular, as Asaph Ben-Tov shows, were difficult for uninitiated contemporaries to understand and more so for curious transgressors centuries later.

When other religions are available for explication, the problem of commixture with 'the other' presents itself – the other culture and religion quickly becomes 'pagan' and 'profane' and a comparative reference to it becomes a transgression. Just as Israelites and ancient Jews viewed the Babylonians, Egyptians, or Greeks and Romans as idolatrous, Romans and Greeks in return often viewed Jews and early Christians as barbarous and impious. Borrowings from one religion to another were dangerous because they threatened to expose affinities, which could be taken as evidence for possible inter-dependence. To this was added a perceived risk of 'contagion', when the unmasking of false pretentions in the one could be transferred to the other. Early Modern scholars, well versed in the literary remains of Graeco-Roman antiquity, were well acquainted with ancient predecessors, 'Pagan', Jewish, and Christian. A particular posthumous resonance was enjoyed since the Renaissance by Lucian of Samosata. Thus Lucian's satirical exposure of false magic and prophecy, discussed here by Wolfgang Spickermann, would later serve as a model for criticizing the prophets of Judaism, Christianity, and Islam.

Despite general commonalities, there are differences which need to be acknowledged. Certain religions, and monotheistic ones in particular, are more adamantly exclusive, whereas others, especially polytheistic religions, have less difficulty with religious translations and syncretism. Foreign gods are included in the local pantheon and assimilated. But even the distinction itself between monotheistic and polytheistic religions simplifies the historical reality. As Azzan Yadin shows, it was often a matter of how well monotheistic elites of different religious cultures were able to come to an agreement with each other. One outcome was a tacit agreement between rabbis and Neo-Platonic philosophers. The world of the Bible and that of 'Paganism' were not necessarily diametrically opposed. This entanglement of the biblical text and its editors in ancient Mediterranean culture was increasingly perceived by less orthodox readers of the Christian canon.

Every culture knows the phenomenon of a conscious desacralization of one's own religion or that of others: blasphemy and profanation. These are moments of protest and conflict, well known to students of the Early Modern period. In his study of ancient predecessors of Early Modern cross religious mockery, Holger Zellentin demonstrates the important role parodies played in Rabbinical literature faced with emerging Christianity and, moving to Elizabethan and early Stuart England, Andreas Mahler discusses the satirical elements in Ben Johnson's plays – two historical examples of profanizing humour used by very different authors in very different circumstances, each, in its own way, exemplifying the role of humour and satire in profanating strategies in a religiously contested context.

It is when spheres collide rather than coexist, that the profane becomes subversive to the holy. When is a certain influence tolerated, when does it become a profanation? When does it become subversive to the foundations of a religion? If Paolo Veronese in his painting of the Last Supper seats fools and monkeys around the table does this mean that he is only accommodating the image for the modern spectator or is he mocking Scripture? In his contribution Karl Morrison shows how the Counter Reformation Catholic Church took measures to avoid such incidents.

The complex issue of religious reflexivity and self-consciousness is crucial here. What were the boundaries of a scholarly study of one's own religion? Is reflection strictly subject to the rules of the religion itself or is it permissible to identify and analyse outside influences? Did the Catholic Church need to fear a 'scientific' scrutiny of relics, and was then profanation inexorable? Anthony Ossa-Richardson's study offers a complex and ambivalent case in point. Viewed from a converse perspective, Riccarda Suitner's study raises the question of how useful or detrimental to religion was an overly critical scrutiny of the Devil's powers in the early eighteenth century.

A key point is the question of whether a comparative approach as such constitutes a profanation. This kind of sensitivity existed, to varying degrees, at different historical points and one can hardly exaggerate how poignantly relevant this issue remains today. Already in Late Antiquity the question of comparison was of great importance and it became ever more explosive in the context of polemics between vying religions. During the Early Modern period, it was for quite some time that biblical commentators making references to Greek and Roman authors were frowned upon, as Ulrich Groetsch shows in his contribution on Hermann Samuel Reimarus. Comparing ancient Israel or early Christianity with the religious practices of Egypt or Babylon was far from innocuous, at least as long as it was not established in advance that the Judaeo-Christian culture possessed temporal, cultural, and epistemic priority. But even cross-references between Early Modern Christian denominations could be problematic. In his contribution John Woodbridge shows how scholars from different Christian confessions strove to develop a more neutral interpretation of the Bible in the age of confessional strife.

It is especially where religious traditions become increasingly reflexive, so our thesis goes, that the problem of the profane becomes more explosive. This is true, e.g. of the centuries which witnessed the simultaneous emergence of Christianity and rabbinical Judaism, the religious upheavals of sixteenth- and seventeenth-century Europe, and the new challenges to religious orthodoxies arising in the eighteenth century. As Martin Mulsow argues for the seventeenth-century, Pierre-Daniel Huet's reference to the Hellenistic-Judaic exaltation of Moses as a cultural hero, or conversely, references to the late antique degradation of Moses as a political villain, in the case of La Mothe Le Vayer, reveal the effective longevity of ancient sensibilities. The example of Reimarus, in fact, illustrates very well how a profanizing reflexivity of biblical commentaries may gradually develop the potential for the biblical criticism of the radical Enlightenment. It is a turning point that happened sometime between the seventeenth and eighteenth century.[4] This is the culmination point where such ideas arrive claiming that rites or beliefs in the Bible were in fact borrowed from ancient Egypt or that Pauline Christianity incorporates ancient mystery cults or Greek theology, while, at the same time, rejecting the sacred nature of the founding document of religious culture – in this case the Bible. It remains to be seen whether such inferences should be judged as overreactions stemming from an awareness of this cultural transfer. During the nineteenth century the 'Bible-Babel-dispute' would provide a further illustration for such patterns of reaction.[5] Indeed since earliest recorded times knowledge of religion has proven too alluring for 'souls profane' to resist, despite the judicious caution from Virgil's Sibyl. This is true especially of the period between the Reformation and the Late Enlightenment on which the present volume concentrates. These Early Modern profanations raise at times more questions for us today than the present collection claims to answer; one thing, however, remains clear: we will not be able to determine the exact level of tolerance of the sacred, also in our own times, in the face of a revelation of its origins, without studying the complex connections between cultural contact, reflexivity, and profanation.

---

4 See Hazard P., *The Crisis of the European Mind 1685–1715*, trans. J. Lewis May (New York: 1963).
5 See Lehmann R. G.: *Friedrich Delitzsch und der Babel-Bibel-Streit* (Fribourg/Göttingen: 1994).

Bibliography

Agamben G., *Profanations*, trans. Jeff Fort (Cambridge, Mass.: 2007).

Borgeaud P., "Le couple sacré/profane. Genèse et fortune d'un concept 'opératoire' en histoire des religions", *Revue de l'histoire des religions* 211, no. 4 (1994) 387–418.

Colpe C., "Heilig (sprachlich)" and "Das Heilige", in *Handbuch religionswissenschaftlicher Grundbegriffe*, vol. 3, edited by H. Cancik, B. Gladigow and K.-H. Kohl (Stuttgart: 1993).

Dihle A., "Heilig", in: *Reallexikon für Antike und Christentum*, vol. 13 (Stuttgart: 1987).

Eliade M., *The Sacred and the Profane* (New York: 1959).

Hazard P., *The Crisis of the European Mind 1685–1715*, trans. J. Lewis May (New York: 1963).

Lehmann R. G., *Friedrich Delitzsch und der Babel-Bibel-Streit* (Fribourg /Göttingen: 1994).

Otto R.: *The Idea of the Holy* (Oxford: 1923).

Schilling R., "Sacrum et profanum. Essay d'interprétation", *Latomus* 30 (1971): 953–969.

Webb E., *The Dark Dove: The Sacred and Secular in Modern Literature* (Seattle: 1975).

PART 1

The Sacred and the Profane in Art, Literature and Parody

∴

CHAPTER 1

Lucian of Samosata on Magic and Superstition

Wolfgang Spickermann

1 Lucian's Life and Work*

Born in Syrian Samosata between 115 and 125 AD, Lucian calls himself an Assyrian in his *Dea Syria*,[1] while elsewhere he refers to himself as 'Syrian' or even 'barbarian'.[2] As a Hellenized Syrian, he could either engage in the ethnography of his own territory, or, following in the footsteps of Herodotus, describe the 'barbarian' rites of Hierapolis in his *Dea Syria* as a tourist from the Hellenic world would see them. In the end, we cannot be sure how to treat the first-person narrator within Lucian's writings, or answer the question of how much fiction and actual biography are interwoven in the texts.[3] It is, however, relatively certain that Lucian was born to a wealthy family in Samosata, situated on the Euphrates in Roman Syria. He received a rhetorical education in Ionia,[4] travelling to Italy and Gaul as an itinerant orator.[5] He visited Antioch in 163/4 to curry favour with the emperor Lucius Verus, who was stationed in the city at the time of his Persian campaign of 161–166 AD. It is possible that Lucian had already been in Samosata in 161/2 AD.[6] Soon after, the confrontation with the oracle prophet Alexander of Abonuteichos took place, as related by Lucian in *Alexander or The False Prophet*. He also recorded the self-immolation of the Pythagorean Cynic Peregrinos in Olympia in 165 AD. Lucian must have been in Athens around this time, probably until the 70s, a time in which he wrote much of his oeuvre. Later on we find him employed in the provincial administration of Egypt,[7] though the *prolalia* (prologue) *Heracles* shows him returning

---

* This contribution is a revised version of my article "Lucian of Samosata on Oracles, Magic and Superstition" in Veit Rosenberger (ed.), *Divination in the Ancient World. Religious Options and the Individual*. Potsdamer Altertumswissenschaftliche Beiträge 46 (Stuttgart: 2013) 139–151, which I have adapted to the topic of this volume.
1 Lucian, *De Dea Syria* 1.8.
2 Lucian, *On the Syrian Goddess*, ed. and trans. L. Lightfoot (Oxford: 2003) 205.
3 Ibid.
4 Lucian, *Bis Accusatus* 27.
5 Ibid., 37; Lucian, *Apologia* 15.
6 Lucian, *On the Syrian Goddess* 208.
7 Lucian, *Apologia* 12.

to rhetorical studies later in life. Since he mentions the apotheosis of Marcus Aurelius in his *Alexander*, he must have died after 180 AD.[8]

It is well-known that Lucian was one of the main figures of the Second Sophistic, although he must still be considered a rather marginal figure. He was, nonetheless, an exponent of an intellectual standard of learning, whose literary discourses were directed at the members of a socio-political elite within the Roman Empire. Research has so far focussed – and focuses still – either on the author's contemporary significance, and – in connection – his function as an agent of a prevailing commitment of cultural identity or on the work's traditionalism, i.e. the recourse to classical models and an ideological retrospection. It has often been claimed that Lucian's work lacks almost any reference to contemporary questions, not commenting at all on phenomena such as 'emperor cult', 'syncretism', or 'astrology'.[9] Lucian's text on astrology, however, deals, as he himself points out, with the art of divination, and criticizes mythological obliquities and superstitions since Homer.[10]

The contemporary significance of his writings is the subject of an ongoing debate. While Josef Delz, James H. Oliver, and Barry Baldwin regard Lucian as a critic of the political, cultural, and social conditions of his time,[11] Jacques Bompaire, Jennifer Hall, and Matthew D. Macleod question the topicality of his writings, and stress, rather, his classicism.[12] Graham Anderson may be viewed, in this context, as propounding a middle position, which I favour.[13]

I think, however, that in Lucian's oeuvre of over eighty texts, it is possible to discern also a moralizing sense in his understanding of *paideia* and the ideal of classic Greek culture characteristic of the Second Sophistic. The *mimesis*, the imitation of classical literature, often serves him as a tool to satirize the

---

8   Nesselrath H.-G., "Lukianos", in Cancik H. – Schneider H. (eds.), *Der Neue Pauly. Enzyklopädie der Antike* (Stuttgart – Weimar: 1999) VII, 493; see now: Baumbach M. – von Möllendorf P., *Ein literarischer Prometheus. Lukian von Samosata und die Zweite Sophistik* (Heidelberg: 2017) 13ff.

9   Caster M., *Lucien et la pensée religieuse de son temps* (Paris: 1984) 175ff.; see Bompaire J., *Lucien écrivain: Imitation et création* (Paris: 1958) 493f.

10 Its authorship is disputed; see Berdozzo F., *Götter, Mythen, Philosophen. Lukian und die paganen Göttervorstellungen seiner Zeit* (Berlin – Boston: 2011) 169ff.

11 Delz J., *Lukians Kenntnis der athenischen Antiquitäten* (Fribourg: 1950). Cf. Oliver J.H., "The actuality of Lucian's *Assembly of the Gods*", *American Journal of Philology* 101 (1980) 304–313; Baldwin, *Studies in Lucian*.

12 Bompaire, *Lucien écrivain*. Cf. Hall J., *Lucian's Satire* (New York: 1981); Macleod M.D., "Lucianic Studies since 1930", in *Aufstieg und Niedergang der Römischen Welt* II, 34.2. (Berlin – New York: 1994) 1362–1421.

13 Anderson G., *The Second Sophistic: A Cultural Phenomenon in the Roman Empire* (London – New York: 1993).

conditions of his own day. In this he was a master as far as the choice and subtlety of his allusions are concerned.[14]

In the following remarks, I will deal firstly with Lucian's *The Lovers of Lies* (*Philopseudes sive Incredulus*) and his text *On Astrology* (*De astrologia*), since these are the central texts for our topic. I will later try to answer the question of what the author understood to be magic and superstition, and where he believed to find it, before concluding with an analysis of his position on this question.

2   Lucian on Magic Practices and Divination

In his text *The Lovers of Lies*, Tychiades, Lucian's *alter ego* in many writings, visits the bedridden Eucrates, who is afflicted by a bout of gout. While there, he meets not only the attending doctor Antigonus, but a number of well-known philosophers, the Peripatetic Cleodemus, the Stoic Dinomachus, and the Platonist Ion. Since Eucrates is on his way to convalescence, and the gout has slid to his feet, a lively discussion unfolds. When Tychiades the Sceptic reveals the philosophers' various, and very abstruse, proposals of healing gout to be superstitious, even ridiculing them, he has, at first, the doctor's support. His rejection culminates in the words:

> I do, said I, not being altogether full of drivel, so as to believe that external remedies, which have nothing to do with the internal causes of the ailments, applied as you say in combination with set phrases and hocus-pocus of some sort, are efficacious and bring on the cure. That could never happen, not even if you should wrap sixteen entire weasels in the skin of the Nemean lion; in fact I have often seen the lion himself limping in pain with his skin intact upon him![15]

In order to prove to Tychiades that magic and witchcraft do indeed have power, the philosophers and the patient relate a number of miraculous tales, all of which are commented on and ridiculed by Tychiades, revealing them all to be rather obvious lies. Even the ghost stories told by late-comer Arignotus, a Pythagorean known as 'The Holy One', and the story of the walking statue of Hippocrates, related by the doctor, do not convince Tychiades. He finally leaves

---

14   Cf. Baumbach – von Möllendorf, *Ein literarischer Prometheus*, 54ff.
15   Lucian, *Philopseudes* 8. Quotes from Lucian are taken from A.M. Harmon's translation for The Loeb Classical Library.

the company when Eucrates starts telling ever more incredible stories in the company of his two young sons. We need not retell these stories here, but what we can say is that foreign magical practices taken from the Babylonians, the Chaldeans, and the Egyptians play a large part. Of the latter two I wish to give two brief examples.

> When I heard all this (sc. a phantom in an uninhabitable house), I took my books – I have a great number of Egyptian works about such matters – and went into the house at bed-time [...]. Standing over me, he made attempts upon me, attacking me from all sides to see if he could get the best of me anywhere, and turning now into a dog, now into a bull or a lion. But I brought into play my most frightful imprecation, speaking the Egyptian language, pent him up in a certain corner of a dark room, and laid him. Then, having observed, where he went down, I slept for the rest of the night.[16]
>
> [Eucrates]: 'When I was living in Egypt during my youth (my father had sent me travelling for the purpose of completing my education), I took it in my head to sail up to Koptos and go from there to the statue of Memnon in order to hear it sound that marvellous salutation to the rising sun. [...] But on the voyage up, there chanced to be sailing with us a man from Memphis, one of the scribes of the temple, wonderfully learned, familiar with all the culture of the Egyptians. He was said to have lived underground for twenty-three years in their sanctuaries, learning magic from Isis.' 'You mean Pancrates', said Arignotus, 'my own teacher, a holy man, clean shaven, in white linen, always deep in thought, speaking imperfect Greek, tall, flat-nosed, with protruding lips and thinnish legs.' 'That self-same Pancrates', he replied, 'and at first I did not know who he was, but when I saw him working all sorts of wonders whenever we anchored the boat, particularly riding on crocodiles and swimming in company with the beasts, while they fawned and wagged their tales, I recognised that he was a holy man, and by degrees, through my friendly behaviour, I became his companion and associate, so that he shared all his secret knowledge with me.'[17]

In this episode Lucian links magic to Egyptian teachings which have been recounted by the philosophers in order to underline the credibility of their cock-and-bull stories. We do find in Lucian, however, a pervasive disdain for

---

16   Ibid., 31.
17   Ibid., 33–34.

Egyptian cult practices and imagery. His discussion of the various episodes mentioned by the philosophers reveals a very thorough knowledge of the current superstitions and magical practices of his time.[18]

His *prolalia* on astrology is, unlike the *Philopseudes*, less a satire or a parody than a sophistic exercise on a serious topic.[19] Lucian discusses both the benefits and the correct application of astrology, as does Cicero in *De divinatione*;[20] he looks into the origins and meaning of Greek mythology and history. Important episodes include the descent of Ulysses into Hades in order to question Tiresias – something Lucian will come back to in relation to his *Necyomanteia*, the journey of the Cynic Menippus into Hades – and the rational application of the story of Phaeton, who could not have been a son of Helios, since, if that were true, he would not have died. Phaeton rather made observations about the course of the sun, but died before he could bring his theories to a conclusion.[21] Among the Egyptians, however, it was common for different people to worship different animals of the Zodiac and to use them in divination so that, for example, those who elected the sign of the bull also worshipped Aries, those who paid homage to the *pisces* would not eat fish, and those who employed the Capricorn for astrological means would not even think of killing a buck. Lucian uses these *topoi*, already known to Herodotus, firstly to explain the animal forms of Egyptian deities, which he mentions on various occasions, and secondly to explain certain customs; the taboo on the eating of fish can also be found in the *Dea Syria*.[22]

Astrology had been around among the 'fringe peoples', the Ethiopians, Egyptians and Libyans for a long time but it took Orpheus for the Greeks to become acquainted with the practice.

> As for the Greeks, they learned not a whit of astrology either from the Aethiopians or from the Aegyptians. It was Orpheus, the son of Oeagrus and Calliope, that first declared these matters upon them, but not all plainly, nor did he bring the science forth unto illucidation but unto ingannation and pious fraude, such being the humour of the man. For he made a harp and exposed his mystic rites in poesy and his theology in song; and the harp, that had seven chords, discoursed the harmony of the errant spheres.[23]

---

18   Jones C.P., *Culture and Society in Lucian* (Cambridge, MA: 1986) 48.
19   Harmon A.M. (ed.), *Lucian, vol. 3*, Loeb Classical Library 130 (Cambridge, MA: 1969) 347.
20   Cicero, *De divinatione* 1. 42.
21   Lucian, *De astrologia* 19.
22   Lucian, *De Dea Syria* 14.
23   Lucian, *De astrologia* 10.

Contrary to common opinion that took Atlas to be the first astrologer, having received his knowledge from the heavens and passing it on to Hercules, who in turn instructed the Greeks,[24] Lucian claims Orpheus as the father of astrology, understanding the seven-chorded harp as a symbol for the heavenly spheres known to Lucian's contemporaries.[25]

Lucian does not deny divination outright.[26] He rather emphasizes ironically its right use.

> Furthermore, astrology is indeed impotent to convert bad into good, or to effect mutation in any of the effluents, yet it is profitable to those that employ it, in so much as the good, when they know that it is to come, delighteth them long beforehand, while the bad they accept readily, for it cometh not upon them unawares, but in virtue of contemplation and expectance is deemed easy and light. That is my opinion in the matter of astrology.[27]

3 Education (*Paideia*), Knowledge and Superstition

With *paideia* and the ideal of classical Greek culture in the Second Sophistic came the devaluation of everything 'barbarous'. This included Egyptian practices. Especially for Pausanias Egyptians and other foreign peoples did not have a notable culture. His *periegesis* may be traced back to two basic principles: 1. the pre-eminence of Athens among mainland Greeks; 2. the pre-eminence of anything mainland-Greek to a) Asia Minor, b) anything Island-Greek, c) Cyrenean Greek, d) Western Greek (here – in a negative sense – especially Sicily), and e) anything 'rest-of-the-world', with a special depreciation of Egypt.[28] According to Christa Frateantonio, the description of (mainland) Greece with a view to these two general principles turns the actual political, economic, cultural, and religious conditions of the Eastern Roman Empire in the second century AD on their heads. It has been viewed as an (anachronistic) archaism, therefore terming Pausanias a 'nostalgic'. Both general principles must be viewed as

---

24 Cicero, *Tusculanae disputationes* 5.3.8; Virgil, *Aeneid* 1.740.
25 Harmon, *Lucian* 354f. note 2.
26 Berdozzo, *Götter, Mythen, Philosophen* 169ff. offers a somewhat different account, owing his purely philological approach.
27 Lucian, *De astrologia* 29.
28 See Pausanias 1.14.2: 'The Greeks who dispute most the Athenian claim to antiquity and the gifts they say they have received from the gods are the Argives, just as among those who are not Greeks the Egyptians compete with the Phrygians.'

programmatic, however, thus *intentionally* turning contemporary conditions upside down – and of course Pausanias knew the realities he subverted all too well for us to find any chance moment in his account. Accordingly, Athens and Greece are not depicted as overly prosperous, but are rather stylized as the medium of 'Homeric land' to 'Holy Land of Hellenism'.[29] While later on Philostratus (c. 170–248 AD) in his *Life of Apollonius* links the Pythagorean philosopher Apollonius of Tyana to Egyptian sages, as well as Babylonian *magoi* and Indian Brahmins (as his teachers) to magic practices, speaking of secret knowledge and a deeper, allegorical sense of the animal forms of Egyptian deities,[30] Lucian simply regards Apollonius as a charlatan, much the same as his teacher Alexander, the 'false prophet', was before him.[31] He summarizes foreign practices *via* the Epicurean Damis in his *Zeus Tragodos*, saying:[32] the Phrygians sacrifice to Men,[33] the Ethiopians to Tag, the Cyllenians to Phales,[34] the Assyrians to a dove,[35] and the Persians to Fire.[36] These have – as do the Gymnosophists – their own religious specialists: the Brahmins among the Indians and the Magoi among the Persians.[37] The Assyrians and Arabs had their own interpreters of religious traditions and fables.[38] The Ethiopians are furthermore the inventors and first practitioners of astrology, which Lucian

---

29 See Frateantonio C., *Religion und Städtekonkurrenz: Zum politischen und kulturellen Kontext von Pausanias Periegese* (Berlin: 2009).

30 Philostratus 1.1f.; 6.4; 6.10.

31 Lucian, *Alexander* 5.16–5.22. Cf. Nesselrath H.-G., "Lukian und die Magie", in Ebner M. – Gzella H. – Nesselrath H.-G. – Ribbat E. (eds.), *Lukian. Die Lügenfreunde oder: der Ungläubige*, SAPERE 3 (Darmstadt: 2001) 153–166, 162 n. 26; 166; see also Baldwin, *Studies in Lucian* 105.

32 Lucian, *Zeus tragodos* 42: Σκύθαι μὲν ἀκινάκῃ θύοντες καὶ Θρᾷκες Ζαμόλξιδι, δραπέτῃ ἀνθρώπῳ ἐκ Σάμου ὡς αὐτοὺς ἥκοντι, Φρύγες δὲ Μήνῃ καὶ Αἰθίοπες Ἡμέρᾳ καὶ Κυλλήνιοι Φάλητι καὶ Ἀσσύριοι περιστερᾷ καὶ Πέρσαι πυρὶ καὶ Αἰγύπτιοι ὕδατι.

33 Cf. Diodorus 3.57.

34 According to Pausanias 6.25.5, Hermes was worshipped in Elean Cyllene in Phallic form. The reference to a Greek city would surprise in this context, it is possible that a city in Asia Minor of the same name is meant. Cf. Coenen J., *Lukian. Zeus tragodos. Überlieferungsgeschichte, Text und Kommentar*, Beiträge zur klassischen Philologie 88 (Meisenheim am Glan: 1977) 124.

35 Cf. Lucian, *De Dea Syria* 54. The esteem in which the dove is held among the Syrian is a classical *topos*, cf. Xenophon, *Anabasis* 1.4.9. Lucian describes the worship of a dove in Hierapolis without explicitly calling her 'divine'. See Lightfoot, *Lucian* 513.

36 Fire appears in Herodotus 1.131 as one of the elements worshipped by the Persians.

37 Brahmins: Lucian, *De Morte Peregrini* 25; 39.5; Lucian, *Toxaris* 34.4; Lucian, *Macrobii* 4.5; Lucian, *Fugitivi* 6.14; 8.1; Persian magoi: Lucian, *Macrobii* 4.7; Babylonian Magoi: *Necyomanteia* 6.

38 Lucian, *Macrobii* 4.3f.

terms the source of mythology.[39] In this context, Lucian stresses the absurdity of foreign peoples' ideas.[40] He employs a number of common clichés in order to separate Greek culture from those of 'fringe peoples'. The sacrificial practices of Assyrians, Lydians, and Scythians are depicted accordingly,[41] the Scythians being further discredited due to their alleged practice of human sacrifices to Artemis.[42] The commonplace of the Scythians eating their dead is also employed with relish when comparing the differences in burial rites: the Greeks burning their dead, the Persians burying them, the Indians glazing, the Scythians eating, and the Egyptians salting them.[43]

The Greeks made use of the magical knowledge of their neighbours. During the *Necyomanteia* – the descent of the itinerant Cynic philosopher Menippus into Hades (modelled along the lines of Ulysses' descent into the Underworld) – he meets the Chaldean Mithrobazanes in Babylon, who is persuaded to prepare the protagonist for his *katabasis* in exchange for an arbitrary sum of money. What follows are a number of purification rites and the donning of the sacred dress, before both men load a boat with all the necessary magical props, cross the marshes of the Euphrates, and dig, as did Ulysses, a sacrificial *fovea* to collect the blood of the sacrificial animals. And then the magician's show starts:

> Meanwhile the magician held a burning torch and no longer muttered in a low tone but shouted as loudly as he could, invoking the spirits, one and all, at the top of his lungs; also the Tormentors, the Furies, 'Hecate, queen of the night, and eery Persephoneia.' With these names he intermingled a number of foreign-sounding, meaningless words of many syllables.[44]

A similar episode is also related by the host Eucrates in *The Lovers of Lies*. In the course of the grape harvest, the earth shook, and he suddenly encountered Hecate, who threatened him with her dogs, larger than elephants. By turning a magic ring set with a cameo, which he had received from an Arab, Hecate's

---

39 Lucian, *De astrologia* 4.
40 Cf. Coenen, *Lukian* 123, who believes that Lucian was following a Sceptic-Academic source.
41 Lucian, *De Sacrificiis* 14.
42 Lucian, *Zeus tragodos* 44; Lucian, *De Sacrificiis* 13; Lucian, *Dialogi Deorum* 3[23].1–18[16].1. This is also a quite common *topos*, cf. Coenen, *Lukian* 129f.
43 Lucian, *De Luctu* 21; cf. Herodotus 3.24; Diodorus 2.14f.; here also Betz H.D., *Lukian von Samosata und das Neue Testament. Religionsgeschichtliche und paränetische Parallelen. Ein Beitrag zum Corpus Hellenisticum Novi Testamenti*, Texte und Untersuchungen zur Geschichte der altchristlichen Literatur 76 (Berlin: 1961) 73.
44 Lucian, *Menippus* 9.

stamping of her serpent's foot creates a rift down to Tartarus, into which she disappears. While Eucrates himself clutched a tree, he can look into Hades:

> Then I saw everything in the Hades, the River of Blazing Fire, and the Lake, and Cerberus, and the dead, well enough to recognise some of them. My father, for instance, I saw distinctly, still wearing the same clothes in which we buried him.[45]

Lucian speaks of another kind of magic known to his contemporaries in his dialogue *Navigium*. Three friends narrate their wishful fantasies to Lucian's alter ego Tychiades, who sneeringly comments on each of them. The first wishes for immense wealth, the second for the power of Alexander the Great, the third – as Eucrates did – for magic rings, with which he would be able to fulfil all his desires.[46] The passage shows the agelessness of wishful thinking, which defies the laws of nature and achieves the unattainable. Tychiades reacts harshly to all these fantasies, denouncing them as unbecoming of a grown man, and reminds his friends that there is no profit in daydreaming, which only serves to make life in the real world much harder than it already is.[47]

The worldliness of his writings is rather characteristic for Lucian's position. His stance with regard to magic may be exemplified by two anecdotes he tells about Demonax, the most revered Cynic philosopher of his day. The first:

> When a fellow claimed to be a sorcerer and to have spells so potent that by their agency he could prevail on everybody to give him whatever he wanted, Demonax said: 'Nothing strange in that! I am in the same business: follow me to the breadwoman's, if you like and you shall see me persuade her to give me bread with a single spell and a tiny charm' – implying that a coin is good as a spell.[48]

Lucian had already mentioned something similar in *The Lovers of Lies*,[49] when Tychiades remarks that, after all, one might actually not have needed the very complicated love magic described before, since twenty drachmas would have been enough to lure Chrysis into her lover's arms.

---

45 Lucian, *Philopseudes* 24.
46 Lucian, Navigium 41–44.
47 Nesselrath, "Lukian und die Magie" 157.
48 Lucian, *Demonax* 23.
49 Lucian, *Philopseudes* 15.

The second episode refers, according to Heinz-Günther Nesselrath, to Herodes Atticus, inconsolable after the death of his beloved son:

> He (Demonax) went to a man who was mourning the death of a son and had shut himself up in the dark, and told him that he was a sorcerer (*magos*) and could raise the boy's shade for him if he would name three men who had never mourned for anyone. When the man hesitated long and was perplexed – I suppose he could not name a single one – Demonax said: 'You ridiculous fellow, do you think then, that you alone suffer beyond endurance, when you see that nobody is unacquainted with mourning?'[50]

In referring to actual magical practices of his times, Lucian denotes magic not only as superfluous but as downright harmful since it makes empty promises to people, evoking only false hope.

The magicians themselves, as said before, were mostly members of 'fringe peoples', and were called by Lucian *magoi*, or, more often and in reference to soothsayers and fortune-tellers, *goes* (charlatans). Lucian directs his satirical criticism mostly at false prophets like Alexander of Abonoteichus or the Cynic Peregrinus (Proteus), to each of whom he dedicated a treatises.

Egyptian Oracles, much criticized by Lucian, were the domain of bull-bodied Apis in Memphis.[51] The ancient practice, reported by Herodotus, of burying the Apis bull after its death and having its priests elect a new one, is ridiculed just as much as the rest of Egyptian religious rituals[52] but the supposed ancestry of Alexander from Ammon and his entire cult are also included in Lucian's extensive criticism of oracles.[53] In his *Dialogues of the Dead* Diogenes pokes fun at the fact that the Greeks added Alexander to the twelve Olympian deities, even dedicating a temple to him. Alexander himself hoped, by having his

---

50   Lucian, *Demonax* 25; Nesselrath, "Lukian und die Magie" 157f.
51   Lucian, *De astrologia* 7, understanding the zodiac sign to be derived from the Apis bull: Lucian, *Deorum Concilium* 10; Lucian, *Zeus tragodos* 42. On the criticism of oracles: Bendlin A., "Vom Nutzen und Nachteil der Mantik: Orakel im Medium von Handlung und Literatur in der Zeit der Zweiten Sophistik", in Elm von der Osten D. – Rüpke J. – Waldner K. (eds.), *Texte als Medium und Reflexion von Religion im römischen Reich*, Potsdamer Altertumswissenschaftliche Beiträge 14 (Stuttgart: 2006) 197ff.; see also Coenen, *Lukian* 91.
52   Herodotus 3,28; Lucian, *De Sacrificiis* 15. The killing of the Apis bull by Cambyses as related in Herodotus may also be found in Lucian, *Contemplantes* 13.
53   Lucian, *Dialogi Mortuorum* 12 [14] a. 13. The oracular deity Ammon is referred to as γόης καὶ ψευδόμαντις (charlatan and false prophet) by Philipp; 11, 12 [14],5; cf. Nesselrath, "Lukian und die Magie" 159 n. 20. On the Libyan origin of the Ammon oracle: Lucian, *De astrologia* 8.

body transferred to Egypt by Ptolemy, to become a second Anubis or Osiris.[54] Following this line of thought, one may here find a general rejection of the whole notion of ruler cults. Alexander the Great stood at the threshold of a long evolution of Hellenistic divinization, a tradition continued by the Roman emperor cult and the conveyance of his body to Alexandria was milked for all it was worth by Ptolemy I. Soter. It is here worth recalling Octavian/Augustus' visit to the grave of Alexander at this point.[55] A mocking of the imperial apotheosis can also be found in the *Peregrinus*, a vulture rising out of the flames and into the heavens, joining those on Mt. Olympus.[56]

With his criticism of magic and superstition Lucian joins a tradition already six hundred years old. The polemical use of the term *magoi* can already be found in Heraclitus,[57] followed by Sophocles, who depicts Tiresias as merely another *magos* looking to his personal gain,[58] the Hippocratic text *De morbo sacro*, which derides the people who see epilepsy as something supernatural, down to Plato, who turns against 'beggar priests and soothsayers' in both *The Republic* and *The Laws*,[59] imposing harsh punishments on malign magic, and on the use of sacrifice and gifts to the gods in order to win their favour for private wishes.[60] Pliny the Elder offers a highly polemical epitome on the origins and history of magic in the thirtieth book of his Natural History, claiming that magic gained such momentum only by incorporating the resources of other arts, such as medicine, religion and astrology. Pliny is frankly surprised that magic, coming from the Persian orient, ever made it this far, so that even emperors like Nero were eager to master it – though the latter's attempts remained futile. However, in Pliny's books we find a number of medicinal recipes against ailments, which we cannot but term 'magical'. Lucian remains in the tradition of consequential rationalism, turning also against

---

54   Lucian, *Dialogi Mortuorum* 13.2f.
55   Suetonius, *Augustus* 18,1. Cf. Bohm C., *Imitatio Alexandri im Hellenismus: Untersuchungen zum politischen Nachwirken Alexanders des Großen in hoch- und späthellenistischen Monarchien* (Tuduv – Munich: 1989); Heuß A., "Alexander der Große und die politische Ideologie im Altertum", *Antike und Abendland* 4 (1954) 65–104.
56   Lucian, *De Morte Peregrini* 39; cf. Pilhofer P., "Anmerkungen", in Pilhofer P. – Baumbach M. – Gerlach J. – Hansen D.U. (eds.), *Lukian. Der Tod des Peregrinos. Ein Scharlatan auf dem Scheiterhaufen*, SAPERE 9 (Darmstadt: 2005) 48–93, 87f. n. 126. Nesselrath, "Lukian und die Magie" 162 regards the vulture as a neo-Pythagorean element; cf. Hall, *Lucian's Satire* 178ff.; sceptical: Jones, *Culture and Society in Lucian* 129. A certain influence must also be attributed to Seneca's *Apocolocyntosis* (The Pumpkinification of Emperor Claudius).
57   Heraclitus, VS 22 B 14.
58   Sophocles, *Oedipus Rex* 387f.
59   Plato, *The Laws* 364b–364c.
60   Ibid., 10f.

contemporaries like Apuleius, who, as we know, was forced to disclaim accusations of using magic.[61]

4 Conclusion

Lucian is entirely focused on the here and now of this world. He precludes any transcendental speculation. The potency of any kind of magical practice is continually disclaimed, astrology may serve to perceive but does not have any actual influence on the world. With his *Lovers of Lies* Lucian turns on those contemporaries who claim to be educated philosophers, though they give great credence to tales of miracles, denoting them as irrational and gullible. All of Lucian's texts reveal a fundamental defense of *paideia*. He shared Pausanias' opinion that the barbarians had no distinct culture of their own. Athens remained the centre of the educated world and was the place from which all cultural impulses originated. Not even the Romans could claim a distinct culture, since they also copied what was Greek.[62] This holds true also for religions. The impulse did not come from Egypt, rather Egypt was influenced by Greece, turning Greek deities into 'dogfaces'. Even astrology, with the invention of which he credits the Ethiopians, did not come to Greece via Ethiopia or Egypt, but was rather revealed to the Greeks by Orpheus himself.[63]

Lucian himself takes an ethic-intellectual stance on religion, rejecting the notions of magic, oracles, superstitions and all-too-exotic deities.[64] He does admit to a certain influence of the stars on the lives and actions of men, admitting to the divinatory function of astrology, which may not convert bad into good, but may well proclaim fate.[65] So Lucian never intended to be an iconoclast as some scholars, like Marcel Caster, believe.[66] In his *Lovers of Lies* Lucian stresses via his alter ego Tychiades that he does not deny the existence

---

61 Nesselrath, "Lukian und die Magie" 163ff.
62 Cf. e.g. Lucian, *Nigrinus* 15.
63 Lucian, *De astrologia* 4–10.
64 On the rejection of magic: Nesselrath, "Lukian und die Magie"; for exotic deities see Spickermann W., "Lukian von Samosata und die fremden Götter", *Archiv für Religionsgeschichte* 11 (2009) 229–261.
65 Lucian, *De astrologia* 28f.; 29,14f.: ἀλλὰ τοὺς χρεωμένους τάδε ὠφελέει τὰ μὲν ἐσθλὰ εἰδότας ἀπιξόμενα πολλὸν ἀπόπροσθεν εὐφρανέει, τὰ δ' φαῦλα εὐμαρέως δέχονται. οὐ γὰρ σφισιν ἀγνοέουσιν ἐπέρχεται, ἀλλ' ἐν μελέτῃ καὶ προσδοκίῃ ῥηίδια καὶ πρηέα ἡγεῖται. τάδε ἀστρολογίης πέρι ἐγὼν ὑπολαμβάνω. Lucian expressedly turns against the doubts voiced by contemporaries as to the practical use of astrology, thus also against Cicero in *De divinatione*.
66 Cf. Hall, *Lucian's Satire* 194ff.; Jones, *Culture and Society in Lucian* 33ff.; Branham R.B., *Unruly Eloquence. Lucian and the Comedy of Traditions*, Revealing Antiquity 2 (Cambridge, MA: 1989) 127ff.; Luchner K., *Philiatroi. Studien zum Thema Krankheit in der griechischen Literatur der Kaiserzeit*, Hypomnemata 156 (Göttingen: 2004) 376.

of the gods, that he venerates them, even going so far as to admit to traditional temple medicine.[67] And the gods, which Tychiades/Lucian worshipped, were the *di indigetes* of the Graeco-Roman religion.[68]

From a modern point of view Lucian was undoubtedly one of most important representatives of the Second Sophistic, and as such he regarded religion and philosophy first as objects of his satires. At first glance he seems to treat superficially rhetorical clashes with the traditional education, the contradictions of the Homeric pantheon, or even with the teachings of the various philosophical 'sects'. Here Lucian tries to restrain himself, his own position remains nebulous, which resulting in the nineteenth-century criticism of him as a nihilist.[69] Religion in particular is profaned, the author takes an outsider's perspective without making his own religious or philosophical position clear, except for the central importance of paideia and its consequences for the individual's life. Lucian here is standing in the tradition of Aristotle's phronesis – proper knowledge cannot be separated from a virtuous practice.[70] In terms of magic and superstition, however, he goes a step further. An educated person, a pepaideumenos, cannot adopt a neutral stance on magical practices; he must condemn them.

Bibliography

Anderson G., *The Second Sophistic: A Cultural Phenomenon in the Roman Empire* (London – New York: 1993).

Baldwin B., *Studies in Lucian* (Toronto: 1973).

Baumbach M. – von Möllendorf P., *Ein literarischer Prometheus. Lukian von Samosata und die Zweite Sophistik* (Heidelberg: 2017).

Bendlin A., "Vom Nutzen und Nachteil der Mantik: Orakel im Medium von Handlung und Literatur in der Zeit der Zweiten Sophistik", in Elm von der Osten D. – Rüpke J. – Waldner K. (eds.), *Texte als Medium und Reflexion von Religion im römischen Reich*, Potsdamer Altertumswissenschaftliche Beiträge 14 (Stuttgart: 2006).

---

67   Lucian, *Philopseudes* 10, 5–11: κωλύει γὰρ οὐδὲν καὶ θεῶν ὄντων ὅμως τὰ τοιαῦτα ψευδῆ εἶναι. ἐγὼ δὲ καὶ θεοὺς σέβω καὶ ἰάσεις αὐτῶν ὁρῶ καὶ ἃ εὖ ποιοῦσι τοὺς κάμνοντας ὑπὸ φαρμάκων καὶ ἰατρικῆς ἀνιστάντες ὁ γοῦν Ἀσκληπιὸς αὐτὸς καὶ οἱ παῖδες αὐτοῦ ἤπια φάρμακα πάσσοντες ἐθεράπευον τοὺς νοσοῦντας […]; *cf.* Luchner, *Philiatroi* 379.

68   This is one of the main topics of the recent book by Berdozzo, *Götter, Mythen, Philosophen* esp. 187f.

69   Cf. Spickermann, *Fremde Götter* 229f.

70   Aristotle, *Nicomachean Ethics* 1140a 24. Cf. Taylor C., *A Secular Age* (Cambridge, MA: 2007) 501. Baumbach – von Möllendorf, *Ein literarischer Prometheus* 71 emphasizes that in Lucian's work there is no real person to come close to the ideal of a comprehensively trained Pepaideumenos.

Berdozzo F., *Götter, Mythen, Philosophen. Lukian und die paganen Göttervorstellungen seiner Zeit* (Berlin – Boston: 2011).

Betz H.D., *Lukian von Samosata und das Neue Testament. Religionsgeschichtliche und paränetische Parallelen. Ein Beitrag zum Corpus Hellenisticum Novi Testamenti*, Texte und Untersuchungen zur Geschichte der altchristlichen Literatur 76 (Berlin: 1961).

Bohm C., *Imitatio Alexandri im Hellenismus: Untersuchungen zum politischen Nachwirken Alexanders des Großen in hoch- und späthellenistischen Monarchien* (Munich: 1989).

Branham R.B., *Unruly Eloquence. Lucian and the Comedy of Traditions*, Revealing Antiquity 2 (Cambridge, MA: 1989).

Bompaire J., *Lucien écrivain: Imitation et création* (Paris: 1958).

Caster M., *Lucien et la pensée religieuse de son temps* (Paris: 1984).

Coenen J., *Lukian. Zeus tragodos. Überlieferungsgeschichte, Text und Kommentar*, Beiträge zur klassischen Philologie 88 (Meisenheim am Glan: 1977).

Delz J., *Lukians Kenntnis der athenischen Antiquitäten* (Fribourg: 1950).

Frateantonio C., *Religion und Städtekonkurrenz: Zum politischen und kulturellen Kontext von Pausanias Periegese* (Berlin: 2009).

Hall J., *Lucian's Satire* (New York: 1981).

Harmon A.M. (ed.), *Lucian, vol. 3*, Loeb Classical Library 130 (Cambridge, MA: 1969).

Heuß A., "Alexander der Große und die politische Ideologie im Altertum", *Antike und Abendland* 4 (1954) 65–104.

Jones C.P., *Culture and Society in Lucian* (Cambridge, MA: 1986).

Luchner K., *Philiatroi. Studien zum Thema Krankheit in der griechischen Literatur der Kaiserzeit*, Hypomnemata 156 (Göttingen: 2004).

Lucian, *On the Syrian Goddess*, ed. and trans. L. Lightfoot (Oxford: 2003).

Macleod M.D., "Lucianic Studies since 1930", in *Aufstieg und Niedergang der Römischen Welt* II, 34.2. (Berlin – New York: 1994) 1362–1421.

Möllendorf P. von, *Auf der Suche nach der verlogenen Wahrheit. Lukians Wahre Geschichten*, Classica Monacensia 21 (Tübingen: 2000).

Nesselrath H.-G., "Lukianos", in Cancik H. – Schneider H. (eds.), *Der Neue Pauly. Enzyklopädie der Antike* (Stuttgart – Weimar: 1999) VII, 493.

Nesselrath H.-G., "Lukian und die Magie", in Ebner M. – Gzella H. – Nesselrath H.-G. – Ribbat E. (eds.), *Lukian. Die Lügenfreunde oder: der Ungläubige*, SAPERE 3 (Darmstadt: 2001) 153–166.

Oliver J.H., "The actuality of Lucian's Assembly of the Gods", *American Journal of Philology* 101 (1980) 304–313.

Pilhofer P., "Anmerkungen", in Pilhofer P. – Baumbach M. – Gerlach J. – Hansen D.U. (eds.), *Lukian. Der Tod des Peregrinos. Ein Scharlatan auf dem Scheiterhaufen*, SAPERE 9 (Darmstadt: 2005) 48–93.

Spickermann W., "Lukian von Samosata und die fremden Götter", *Archiv für Religionsgeschichte* 11 (2009) 229–261.

Taylor C., *A Secular Age* (Cambridge, MA: 2007).

CHAPTER 2

Rabbi Lazarus and the Rich Man: A Talmudic Parody of the Late Roman Hell (Yerushalmi Hagigah 2.2, 77d and Sanhedrin 6.9, 23c)

Holger Zellentin

> Laugh where we must, be candid where we can;
> But vindicate the ways of God to Man.
> ALEXANDER POPE, *An Essay on Man*

⋮

> The tax-collectors and the whores
> are going into the kingdom of God ahead of you
> MATTHEW 21:31

⋮

Visits to the underworld have captivated the human imagination since antiquity.[1] Individuals descend physically or through visions, only to re-emerge and tell the living what they have seen. Gilgamesh, in search of Enkidu, visits

---

* My gratitude for the helpful comments offered by the participants of the 2012 Oxford Seminar on Jewish History and Literature in the Graeco-Roman Period, organized by Martin Goodman, and by the PhD students who made my Advanced Talmud seminar in 2010 the most enjoyable teaching and learning experience: Noah Greenfield, Marina Zilbergerts-Bitzan, Mira Wasserman, and Yoseph Rosen. All translations in this paper, unless otherwise noted, are my own. Hebrew, Aramaic, and Syriac are transliterated ʾ b g d h w z ḥ ṭ y k l m n s ʿ p ṣ q r š s t; Arabic ʾ b t ṯ ǧ ḥ ḵ d ḏ r z s š ṣ ḍ ṭ ẓ ʿ ġ f q k l m n h w y, proper names follow the traditional renderings.

1 On the development of hell see the overviews by Bernstein A.E., *The Formation of Hell: Death and Retribution in the Ancient and Early Christian Worlds* (Ithaca – London: 1993); Goff J. Le, *The Birth of Purgatory* (Chicago: 1984); Brandon S.G.F., *The Judgment of the Dead: An Historical and Comparative Study of the Idea of a Post-Mortem Judgment in the Major Religions* (London: 1967); all useful but slightly dated.

the underworld in one of the earliest preserved Near Eastern examples.[2] What Gilgamesh sees is gloomy, but there is no punishment; the Hebrew Bible likewise lacks such imagery.[3] The idea of hell, broadly construed as a place of postmortem punishment, seems to be attested first in Egyptian,[4] Zoroastrian, and likely Vedic texts.[5] In the Greek and Roman tradition, from Odysseus' depiction of Tantalus' torments, to Plato's elaborate *Myth of Er* and Virgil's *Aeneid*, hell was a mandatory stop on any tour of the realm of the dead.[6]

In all those texts, hell serves as a source of awe and moral instruction, yet at least from classical Greece onwards, and to this day, hell was also a preferred playground for philosophy, poetry, and parody.[7] Aristophanes, for example, turns the punishments for certain wrongdoers into a farcical reckoning with literary crimes. In *The Frogs* Dionysus seeks to visit the underworld, while Heracles is set on dissuading him by depicting the terrible punishments the visitor will have to witness:

> Heracles: 'And next you'll see great snakes
> and savage monsters, in tens of thousands.'
> Dionysus: 'You needn't try to scare me, I'm going to go.'
> Heracles: 'Then weltering seas of filth
> And ever-rippling dung: and plunged therein,
> Whoso has wronged the stranger here on earth,
> Or robbed his boylove of the promised pay,
> Or swinged his mother, or profanely smitten

---

2 The story is preserved on Tablet XII, and unanimously considered secondary to the composition of the main narrative. See e.g. Kovacs M., *The Epic of Gilgamesh* (Stanford: 1989) 117.
3 See Bernstein, *The Formation of Hell* 178–201.
4 The Book of the Dead contains images of souls being destroyed in a sea of fire and many other punishments. See Brandon, *The Judgment of the Dead* 6–48.
5 For an excellent overview see Stausberg M., "Hell in Zoroastrian History", *Numen* 56 (2009) 217–253, who illustrates how Zoroastrian thought in turn developed previous Vedic ideas (ibid., esp. 223).
6 See Homer, *Odyssey* XI.505–XI.600; Plato, *The Republic* 10.607b–10.621d; Virgil, *Aeneid* VI.236–VI.901; for a recent discussion of the Graeco-Roman tradition see Bremmer J., "Tours of Hell: Greek, Jewish, Roman, and Early Christian", in Ameling W. (ed.), *Topographie des Jenseits: Studien zur Geschichte des Todes in Kaiserzeit und Spätantike* (Stuttgart: 2011) 13–34; Bernstein, *The Formation of Hell* 19–130.
7 A parody is an ironic retelling that emphasizes the difference between the imitated text and the parody. Many parodies also contain elements of comical criticism, or satire. See Hutcheon L., *A Theory of Parody: The Teachings of Twentieth-Century Art Forms* (Urbana – Chicago: 2000) xii. On parody and satire in Antiquity and especially in rabbinic literature see Zellentin H., *Rabbinic Parodies of Jewish and Christian Literature* (Tübingen: 2011), esp. 1–21.

His father's cheek, or sworn an oath forsworn,
Or copied out a speech of Morsimus.'[8]

Heracles evokes bathing in filth and faeces as the punishment meted out to some of the Greek stock inmates of hell: those who did injustice to strangers or parents, or took a false oath. Chiastically interwoven among the serious crimes, however, we find rather incongruously the transgressions of withholding the fee of a young male lover, and the perpetuation of the contemptible tragedies of Morsimus (whose writings are now lost).

In similar manner, the heroes and the villains of yore continued to be deployed in parodic missions to hell from classical Greece through the Second Sophistic and beyond. This paper argues that the Palestinian Talmud (henceforth: Yerushalmi), an early fifth century rabbinic compilation, sends its own mythical heroes on a tour of hell in order to engage in satirical parody of Late Roman myth, a parody comparable in its literary playfulness to that of Aristophanes, reckoning in turn with the perceived narrative transgressions of New Testament and patristic literature.

In order to illustrate the Yerushalmi's precise imitation of Christian discourse, it is necessary to consider more broadly how the burgeoning Hellenistic genre of visits to the underworld was integrated into many local cultural matrices. The resulting ecotypification continues to share many standard traits of Hellenistic hell: suffering, punishment for the wicked, and reward for the righteous are of course commonplaces. In addition, we also find variations on one literary motif across of several Late Antique cultures: the post-mortem inversion of social hierarchy. The narrator, onstage in hell or from an omniscient perspective, informs the audience that the fortunes of a rich and a poor man switch after death. The rich man is demoted, while the poor is afforded eternal bliss. Lucian, for example, uses hell to promote poverty and philosophy. In his *Downward Journey*, a poor man, accordingly, embraces his death willingly:

> And by God, I see already that everything is splendid here with you, for that all should have equal rank and nobody be better than his neighbor is more than pleasant, to me at last. And I infer that there is no dunning of debtors here and no paying of taxes, and above all no freezing in winter or falling ill or being thrashed by men of greater consequence. All are

---

8   Aristophanes, *The Frogs* 144–154, trans. J. Henderson, in *Aristophanes* (Cambridge, MA: 2002) IV, 38–41.

at peace, the tables are turned, for we paupers laugh while the rich are distressed and lament.[9]

Lucian's virtuosic literary play with the conventions of hell, much in line with Aristophanes' passage above, is of utmost importance to the Yerushalmi's story, which I shall present as standing in the same literary tradition of parodic post-mortem inversion.[10] Needless to say, the comical elements in Lucian are pervasive. For example, Hermes is suspected of drunkenness by having tasted himself the waters of *lethe*;[11] the cynic philosopher aids in Hermes' tasks;[12] describes the dead newborns as 'green grapes', the old men as 'raisins';[13] and he notices that hapless doctors die along with their patients, unable to cure either their patients or themselves.[14]

Such comical elements, both for Lucian and the Yerushalmi, are employed for the moral improvement of the audience. In Lucian, when a deceased philosopher is questioned why the 'marks' of his soul, the platonic imprint of unrighteous behaviour, have been erased, the philosopher explains: 'I will tell you. For a long time I was a wicked man through ignorance and earned many marks (on my soul) thereby; but no sooner had I begun to be a philosopher than I gradually washed away all the scars from my soul'.[15] In other words, philosophy prepared the man for the afterlife by overcoming his ignorance that lead to injustice; the role of philosophy will be filled by Torah learning in the Yerushalmi.

Similar stories of just deserts, with further examples from Greek, Demotic, and Aramaic literature, will allow us to contextualize the Yerushalmi within its broader Hellenistic and specifically Christian context. We find a closely corresponding vision of just deserts in the Demotic story of Setme Kamwas.[16] Similar visions become an established genre already in the earliest Christian

---

9   See Harmon A.M. (ed.), *Lucian in Seven Volumes* (New York: 1919) 33.
10 On the relevance to Palestinian rabbinic Judaism of Lucian and of the Second Sophistic more broadly, see Zellentin, *Rabbinic Parodies* 16–18; 213–236. Cf. Daniel Boyarin's respective claim for the rabbis of the Sasanian Empire in idem, *Socrates and the Fat Rabbis* (Chicago: 2009) 14; see also the reviews by Becker A., "Positing a 'Cultural Relationship' between Plato and the Babylonian Talmud" *Jewish Quarterly Review* 101 (2011) 255–269; Kiperwasser R., "Rev. of Boyarin, *Socrates and the Fat Rabbis*", *Jewish History* 25 (2011) 377–397.
11 Harmon, *Lucian* 4.
12 Ibid., 5; 7; passim.
13 Ibid., 11.
14 Ibid., 15.
15 Ibid., 47.
16 See Griffith F.L., *Stories of the High Priests of Memphis: The Sethon of Herodotus and the Demotic Tales of Khamuas* (Oxford: 1900) 42–66.

literature, and especially in the story of Lazarus and the Rich man in the Gospel of Luke; both the Demotic and the Christian story are discussed below. Luke's hell especially features prominently in patristic writings; the most extensive patristic treatment of the afterlife may be that of Augustine.[17] The earliest Christian tour of hell is the *Apocalypse of Peter*, which inspired many works throughout late antiquity.[18] The earliest Jewish hell may be contained in the first century BCE *Book of the Watchers*.[19] Martha Himmelfarb suggests that the Jewish so called *Isaiah Fragment* (of uncertain date) and the Christian *Elijah Fragment* (first attested in the fifth century) may well predate and form the basis of the Yerushalmi.[20]

The Yerushalmi's story of a dream vision of the afterlife of a pious Jew from Ashkelon may be the most intriguing Jewish example of the Hellenistic motif of post-mortem social inversion. It is attested (as is common) twice in the Yerushalmi: once in Sanhedrin 6.9 23c, and once in Hagigah 2.2, 77d. My endeavour here is twofold. I first emphasize how much the Yerushalmi's narrative is part of its Hellenistic environs, and how closely its ethic and narrative structure correspond to those of the Late Roman Empire, especially as manifested in the Sayings of the Desert Fathers (*Apophtegmata Patrum*) that were redacted at the same time as the Yerushalmi, equally in the Roman Province of *Palaestina Secunda* under the Theodosian Dynasty.[21] Secondly, I illustrate how the Yerushalmi resists cultural colonization by parodying and satirizing

---

17   See Augustine, *The City of God against the Pagans* (Cambridge, MA: 1972) VII, 2–169 (Book 21); see note 67 below.
18   See Elliot J.K., *The Apocryphal New Testament* (Oxford: 1993) 593–615.
19   Here, Enoch, in his tour of the "other side", sees a deep, dry, and barren valley (26.4f), whose inhabitants are the deceased blasphemers (27.2). See Nickelsburg G.W.E. – VanderKam J.C., *1 Enoch: A New Translation* (Minneapolis: 2004); and now Langlois M., *Le premier manuscrit du livre d'Hénoch: Etude épigraphique et philologique des fragments araméens de 4Q201 à Qumrân* (Paris: 2008).
20   See Himmelfarb M., *Tours of Hell: An Apocalyptic Form in Jewish and Christian Literature* (Philadelphia: 1983) esp. 29–32; 131–139; see note 57 below. For an overview of the historical developments of Jewish and Christian tours of hell see most recently Bremmer, "Tours of Hell"; Himmelfarb M., *Tours of Hell*.
21   On the redaction of the collection see Wortley J., *Book of the Elders: Sayings of the Desert Fathers: The Systematic Collection*, Cistercian Studies Series 240 (Collegeville: 2012) xi–xix. Like the Yerushalmi, the sayings probably reflect much older oral traditions. On the importance of the Sayings of the Desert Fathers for the Babylonian Talmud, see now Siegal M.B.-A., "The Making of a Monk-Rabbi: the Background for the Creation of the Stories of R. Shimon bar Yohai in the Cave", *Zion* 76 (2011) 279–304; eadem, *Literary Analogies in Rabbinic and Christian Monastic Sources*, Ph.D. dissertation (Yale University: 2010). The importance of the Sayings of the Desert Fathers and cognate traditions for Palestinian rabbinic will become clearer in the present essay. Cf. Hezser C., "Apophtegmata Patrum and Apophtegmata of the Rabbis", in *La Narrativa Cristiana Antica. Codici Narrativi*,

specific oral Gospel traditions that can be reconstructed with help of the Gospels (especially Luke, and the respective material in the *Diatessaron*) and their interpretation in the later patristic literature. In the words the Babylonian Talmud (henceforth: Bavli) attributes to the Palestinian rabbis; Jews ate the date – by adopting Christian morals and narratives – but threw away the stone – by discarding specific stories and sayings attributed to Jesus.[22]

To reiterate what I argued elsewhere at length, I locate the historical dialogue that exposed the rabbis to the Gospel passages not so much between rabbis and Church Fathers in an 'academic' setting (without excluding this possibility in specific cases), but rather between Jews and their Christian neighbours in daily informal encounters. The oral culture of Late Antiquity and the shared Aramaic and Greek languages of Palestinian Jews and Christians were conducive to ad hoc religious debate or polemic on a popular level. At the same time, the best way in which we can reconstruct popular Christian readings of relevant Gospel passages is through the patristic literature, which stood in continuous feedback with preaching and popular beliefs.[23] In my view, the rabbis

---

Strutture Formali, Schemi Retorici, Studia Ephemeridia Augustinianum 50 (Rome: 1995) 453–464.

[22] See Bavli Hagigah 15b. Note that the Bavli renders the same saying first attributed to Palestinian rabbis once more as having been reiterated in a modified form by the Babylonian rabbis themselves: 'eating the date, while throwing away the stone' became 'eating the flesh of a pomegranate, while throwing away its peel' (Bavli Hagigah 15b). Dates are common in the Bavli and therefore cannot be the reason for the rephrasing, suggesting that the text points to a slightly less intimate relationship between the Bavli's narratives and those of the Christian Other. Indeed, in my view, the Bavli adopts certain elements of Christian narrative in a more open, though less immediate way than does the Yerushalmi, see Zellentin, *Rabbinic Parodies*, 137–166. In contrast to my own findings, Adiel Schremer deplores the scholarly 'Christianization' of research on rabbinic Judaism, mostly wrestling with the work of Daniel Boyarin; see Schremer A., *Brothers Estranged: Heresy, Christianity, and Jewish Identity in Late Antiquity* (Oxford: 2010) 101–120. Schremer's concerns may partially be justified regarding cavalier assumptions made in the field, yet he pours out the baby with the bath water when seeking entirely to dismiss both Christian influence on rabbinic Judaism and the rabbis' manifold ways of accommodation and resistance. For a nuanced and balanced approach see most recently Schäfer P., *The Jewish Jesus: How Judaism and Christianity Shaped Each Other* (Princeton: 2012).

[23] See a previous illustration of these issues in Zellentin, *Rabbinic Parodies*, 137–236. The rabbis do not, in general, engage in extensive or careful study of the New Testament. At the same time, it seems clear that the rabbis knew, parodied and satirized some Gospel passages that figured prominently in patristic and popular Christian discourse. Burton Visotzky has pointed out that many comparisons between the rabbinic literature and New Testament materials are chronologically inaccurate; see idem, "Prolegomena to the Study of Jewish-Christians in Rabbinic Literature", *AJS Review* 14 (1989) 47–70. This is evidently true for the texts collected in the New Testament in their compositional first century context, which predated the earliest texts of the rabbinic movement by over a century.

are not so much using their knowledge of Christian myth simply to profane it. Rather, they sanctify the Christian narrative of hell, the date's 'flesh', by rabbinizing it. Then, they throw away the date's stone: by populating hell with Christian inmates, the rabbis create a hybrid narrative that inverts the social hierarchy they experienced under Late Roman rule in fifth century Palestine.

1 Shimon ben Shetach in Hell

In order to place the Yerushalmi's story of post-mortem social inversion in its broader Hellenistic and specifically Late Roman context, one should first read it in its own literary and legal rabbinic (henceforth: halakhic) framework. The prevailing tension between the Palestinian rabbis' halakhic narrative and their allusive and tacit engagement with Christian stories generates the Yerushalmi's literary massage.[24] As a result, we cannot ever say that any Talmudic passage is 'about' Christianity; all rabbinic texts are 'about' the rabbis. Rather, I take the Yerushalmi's tacit engagement with aspects of Christianity as evidence of how the rabbis seek to situate themselves vis-à-vis *specific* aspects of ascending Christianity in the Late Roman Empire. The rabbis do not digress from their halakhic enterprise and often allude to their internal or external Others without bestowing the honour of a name upon them.[25]

The two halakhic discussions in which the Yerushalmi places its vision of hell are, on the one hand, the tractate Sanhedrin, on criminal law, or more specifically the 'hanging' of women as practiced by Shimon ben Shetach (which occurs towards the end of our story). On the other hand, the Yerushalmi also places the vision in the tractate Hagigah, on festival offerings in the Jerusalem temple, which actually commences with the rabbis' mystical visit to the heavenly orchard and the apostasy of Elisha Ben Abuya.[26] In Hagigah, Yehuda ben Tabai and Shimon ben Shetach differ on an aspect of the ritual for the Day of

---

The New Testament as a collection of texts, however, is a late Roman creation, and was recreated, interpreted, and translated into various languages every day throughout late Antiquity – including the days of the Yerushalmi. On the Jews under early Byzantine rule see most recently Bonfil R. – Irshai O. – Stroumsa G.G. – Talgam R. (eds.), *Jews in Byzantium: Dialectics of Minority and Majority Cultures* (Leiden: 2011).

24 On the complex relationship between halakhah and rabbinic narrative see now Wimpfheimer B.S., *Narrating the Law: A Poetics of Talmudic Legal Stories* (Philadelphia: 2011).

25 See Zellentin, *Rabbinic Parodies* esp. 21–26.

26 Yerushalmi Hagigah 2.1 77b–c; see Schäfer P., *The Origins of Jewish Mysticism* (Princeton: 2009) 214–221. On the Babylonian development of this story see ibid. 222–242; idem, *The Jewish Jesus* 103–149.

Atonement.[27] After we learn that disagreement about the halakhah increased over time, leading to inner-Jewish schisms and even to excommunications, the narrative surface shifts away from atoning sacrifice and to a discussion about the actual office which Yehuda and Shimon held,[28] the point at which the text of both Yerushalmi tractates – Hagigah and Sanhedrin – converge in discussing the following statement, cited according to the Assis fragment:[29]

> We learned that Yehuda ben Tabai was Patriarch and Shimon ben Shetach was the President of the Court.
> There is one teacher who teaches the opposite (namely that Shimon was Patriarch and Yehuda President of the Court).

In order to clarify the respective office, the Yerushalmi tells two stories in the sequel.[30] Both stories illustrate the distribution of roles between Yehuda and Shimon while continuing to address the themes which underlie the

---

27 Yehuda ben Tabai holds the opinion that the laying of hands on the scapegoat to be slaughtered on the Day of Atonement (see Leviticus 1.4) is not obligatory, whereas Shimon ben Shetach considers it obligatory. The Mishna (Hagigah 2.2) which the Yerushalmi discusses reports that the earliest holders of the office of Patriarch (*nsy'*) and President of the Court (*'b byt dyn*) were all divided on this topic, as equally preserved in Tosefta Hagigah 2.8 (Lieberman 235).

28 The President of the Court was the head of the Jewish judicative as imagined by the rabbis. The Patriarch was the official leader of the Jewish community, recognized by the Roman government from the second century onwards; the office was abolished under the Theodosian dynasty. If the Yerushalmi was indeed redacted around the same time as the abolishment of the patriarchate, then the discussion of two possible patriarchs in the context of a gospel parody in the present story would respond to political circumstances and belong to the youngest parts of the text; our limited understanding of the Yerushalmi's precise redaction history, however, does not yet allow to substantiate or dismiss this possibility.

29 The text here and in the following is based on the Assis fragment; see Assis M., "A Fragment of Yerushalmi Sanhedrin", *Tarbits* 46 (1977) 29–90 [Hebrew]. In the footnotes, I offer the *variae lectiones* from 'Sanhedrin' (i.e. Yerushalmi Sanhedrin 6.9, 23c) and from 'Hagigah' (i.e. Hagigah 2.2, 77d), according to manuscript Leiden and the Venetian *editio princeps*. Assis may be the most important witness for the text itself, yet the Yerushalmi's use of the text in Sanhedrin may be dependent on its use in Hagigah. This possibility is supported by the fact that the Assis fragment of Sanhedrin is often congruent with Hagigah and differs from the two other witnesses of Sanhedrin. On the importance of the Assis fragment see Lieberman S., "On the New Fragments of the Palestinian Talmud", *Tarbits* 46 (1977) 91–96 [Hebrew].

30 The texts imagine the two Jewish officials, Yehuda and Shimon, to have lived in the first century BCE; they are indeed attested as a pair in the opening of Mishna *Pirqe Avot* (1.8). While the Mishna does not discuss any office the two men held, the Tosefta (Hagigah 2.8, Lieberman 235) may be the source of the Yerushalmi's second opinion that Shimon was Patriarch, and Yehuda was President of the Court.

Yerushalmi's halakhic discussion both in Sanhedrin and in Hagigah: sin, punishment and religious schism, be it in the form of witchcraft, heresy, or apostasy. Both stories adopt hagiographical motifs also extant in Christian discourse, and both parody specific gospel passages. The first story, set in Egypt, concerns a lewd disciple with remarkable likeness to (a rabbinically inflected) Jesus, and is told to argue that Yehuda was Patriarch. In order to streamline my argument, I shall discuss the first story after addressing the following, originally subsequent second story, set in Ashkelon, about Shimon's punishment in hell, which ends by establishing that Shimon he was indeed the Patriarch:

> The one who said that Shimon ben Shetach was patriarch: the event in Ashkelon supports him.
> There were two students[31] in Ashkelon,
> Who ate (*'klyn*) like one and drank (*wštyyn*) like one, and laboured in the Torah like one.
> One of them died, and (the townspeople) did not show any piety to him (through mourning and burial rites).
> Then *Son of a Fountain* (or: *Son of a Belly, bryh dm'yyn*), the tax collector (*mwks*) died (*wmyt*), and the entire town stopped working to show piety to him.
> The (remaining) student[32] began to be grieved[33] and said: 'Perhaps, for the Haters of Israel (i.e. Jews[34]), there is no (reward)?'[35]
> (The deceased student) appeared (*'thmy*, i.e. to his friend) in a dream (*bhylm'*)[36], and he said to him: 'Do not despise the sons of your Lord. This one committed (but) one sin and it was nullified (lit. 'he got out of it'), and this one committed (but) one good deed (*tybh*)[37] and it was nullified.'

---

31 Hagigah has 'pious ones'.
32 Hagigah has 'pious one'.
33 *Editio princeps* and manuscript Leiden of Sanhedrin have 'to cry'.
34 The dysphemism for pious Jews, 'haters of Israel,' *sn'yhwn dysr'l*, is common in the Bavli (see e.g. *Berakhot* 4b, 7a, 28a and 32a, *Shabbat* 33a, *Sukkah* 29a, *Yoma* 72b and 75b, Sanhedrin 94a and 105b, and *Avodah Zarah* 4b), and therefore there bears little connotation. In Palestinian rabbinic literature, however, it is much less attested (see e.g. *Wayiqra Rabbah* 25:1); its use here would have given pause to a rabbinic audience less accustomed to it, therefore subtly adding to the apparent sense of inversion of morals in the present story.
35 Sanhedrin and Hagigah have 'Vey! For the Haters of Israel (there is) no (reward)!'.
36 Only Sanhedrin and Hagigah explicate 'in a dream'.
37 Following Hagigah. Here and in the term's repetition, Assis and Sanhedrin have *zkw* 'meritorious deed'.

'And what sin did this student[38] commit?'

'Heaven forbid[39] he ever committed a sin, but one time he first put on the Tefillin of the head and then the Tefillin of the hands.'

'And what good deed did Son of a Fountain, the tax collector, do?'

'Heaven forbid he ever committed a good deed, but once he was walking in the market[40] with bread in his hand …, and it fell (*wnpl*) from him, and it was picked up by a poor man (*mskn*) taking it, but did not say anything to him so that (the poor man) would not blush.'

And some say:[41] He gave a feast (*'ryṣṭwn*) to the magistrates, but they did not eat.[42] He said: 'The poor ones (*msknyyh*) should eat,[43] so (the food) should not be thrown away.'[44]

After a few days, (the student) saw the pious one, his companion, promenading[45] between gardens (*gnyn*), and orchards (*prdsyn*) and fountains (*mbwʿyn dmwyy*).

(The student) also saw the Son of a Fountain, the tax collector, his tongue (*lšwnw*) slavering (*šwtt*) next to a river, wanting to reach the water (*myʾ*), and not reaching it.

And (the student) also saw Mary (*mrym*[46]), the daughter of *Leaves of Onions* (*ʿly bṣlym*)

Rabbi Lazarus (*lʿzr*) bar Yose said: 'She was hanging by the nipples of her breasts.'

Rabbi Yose ben Hanina[47] said: 'The hinge of the door of Gehenna (*dgyhnm*) was resting in her ear.'

(The student) said to them: 'Why is this?'

They said to him: 'Since she fasted (*ṣyymh*) and made it public to her neighbour.'[48]

---

38   Hagigah has 'pious one'.
39   Reading *ḥd* as *ḥs*, according to Hagigah and Sanhedrin.
40   Hagigah has 'once he passed the market'; Sanhedrin is corrupted, perhaps under the influence of Yerushalmi *Terumot* 6.10, 45d.
41   The order of the two possible meritorious deeds is inverted in Sanhedrin and Hagigah.
42   Sanhedrin has 'they did not come'. Hagigah has 'they did not come to eat'.
43   Sanhedrin has 'should come'.
44   *ytlq*, following the Assis fragment and possibly manuscript Leiden (*ytlʾ*) of Hagigah. The *editio princeps* (*ytlwn*) of Hagigah seems corrupted; Sanhedrin has 'so the food does not spoil (*lyqlql*)'.
45   'Promenading' is missing in Sanhedrin.
46   Following Sanhedrin and Hagigah. Assis is conspicuously corrupted, reading only *mʾ*.
47   Following Assis and Hagigah. Sanhedrin does not attribute knowledge about Mary's two punishments to specific sages.
48   'To her neighbour' is missing in Sanhedrin and Hagigah.

And there are some who say: 'Since she fasted one day, and deducted two (sins) for it.'

(The student) said to them: 'Until when will she be like this?'

They said to him: 'Until Shimon ben Shetach comes, and we will lift (*mrymyn*, i.e. the hinge) from (Mary's) ear and put it on his ear, because he said "If I will be made Patriarch, I will kill the witches." But as he was made patriarch, he did not kill the witches. But go (*'yzyl*) and tell (*w'mwr*, i.e. Shimon about the witches and his impending punishment)!'

(The student) said to them: 'He is a great man, and will not believe me (*mhymnty*).'

They said to him: 'He will be very friendly and will believe you. And if he will not believe you, make this sign (*symn'*) in front of him.'

He said to them: 'What will I do?'

They said to him: 'Take out your eye (*'pyq 'ynk*), and it will come on your hand (*ydk*).'

He took out his eye and it came to his hand.

They said to him: 'Return it (*ḥzrh*)!'

He returned it, and it rejoined its companion.

(The student) went and he told (Shimon) the story. He wanted to make the sign before him, and (Shimon) did not let him.

(Shimon) said to him: 'I know (*yd'*) that you are a pious (*ḥsyd'*) man. Even if I think (*ḥšbyt*) in my heart (*blby*), with my mouth (*bpmy*) I will not say.'

At once Shimon ben Shetach went on a day of a rainstorm ([*b*]*ywm sgryr*) and he took with him eighty young men (*gwbryn bḥwryn*), and he gave them eighty clean robes (*lbwšwn nqyyn*) and he placed them in new pots (*bqdryn ḥdth*) and (placed) baskets (*wkpwnwn*) on their hea(ds).[49]

The Assis fragment breaks off here. In the story's sequel, as preserved in the witnesses for both Sanhedrin and Hagigah, Shimon tricks the witches into opening the door of the cave by using a Bacchic incantation. As they ask him how he reached them on such a rainy day, he answers that he walked between the raindrops. The witches magically produce bread, a cooked dish, and wine, as well as meat in the Sanhedrin version; Shimon then lures them with promises of erotic exploits with the eighty young men, annuls their magical powers and crucifies them – doing so in a single day, not quite in line with halakhic precepts concerning capital punishment.

---

49   *Yerushalmi Sanhedrin* (Assis fragment). See note 29 above.

Rather than dedicating much attention to Shimon ben Shetach's office as patriarch right away, the Yerushalmi first tells a story about the disappointment of a pious Jew over the lack of 'piety,' i.e. communal mourning, bestowed upon his study partner after the latter's death. The two rabbinic students had spent their lives dedicated to the study of the Torah, moderating their consumption of food and drink, so the survivor's sense of justice is offended. Even worse, the community engages in excessive pious mourning upon the death of a tax-collector. Not only was that the tax collector likely working for the hostile Roman government, but moreover, the meaning of his name – 'Son of a Belly' or 'Son of a Fountain' – also implies that he was 'accustomed to fill his belly,' as Saul Lieberman put it.[50] Indulging in food or alcohol, he needed a large amount of funds to sustain his habit.[51]

The anger of the pious Jew is understandable: just as Ecclesiastes teaches, there seems to be no reward for piety in this world. The Yerushalmi here emphasizes the lack of just deserts by stringing together its narrative with the Hebrew term *ḥesed*, which denotes the piety of the two study partners as well as the act of mourning. Then, the pious deceased friend appears to his companion in a dream and comforts him that divine justice is, indeed, unfailing. For both the communal 'lack of piety' for the student, and the exuberant mourning for Son of a Fountain, was all guided by a divine scheme, written straight in crooked lines. The deceased student had once inversed the order of putting on his Tefillin, a real, but almost absurdly minute transgression.[52]

---

[50] Lieberman, S., "On Sins and Their Punishment", in Lieberman, S., *Texts and Studies* (New York: 1974) 29–56, 35.

[51] On the realia of alcoholism and the cost of alcohol in Late Antique Palestine see Zellentin, *Rabbinic Parodies* 51–94. The term *m'yn* in Aramaic can designate a womb or intestines; in Hebrew, it designates a spring or a fountain; see Sokoloff M., *A Dictionary of Jewish Palestinian Aramaic of the Byzantine Period* (Ramat Gan: 2002) 322. While the term *bny m'yn* is attested as 'intestines' (ibid. 99); its use as proper name seems intentionally incongruous. Saul Lieberman translates the tax collector's name as 'paunchy one' (idem, "On Sins and Their Punishment" 34). Based on the homophony of *m'yn* and *myn*, notwithstanding the medial *'ayin*, Hugo Gressmann understands the term as 'son of a heretic (*myn*).' The Late Roman Empire, for whom the Yerushalmi likely implied the tax-collector worked, was indeed in the middle of a turn to *mynwt*, to 'heresy,' according to the Yerushalmi (see *Sotah* 9.17, 24c). The reading of the tax collector as an explicit (Christian) heretic, however, should not be understood as an anything else than a possible allusive conotation; idem, *Vom reichen Mann und armen Lazarus: Eine literaturgeschichtliche Studie* (Berlin: 1918) 22. Ultimately, Gressmann's reading simply distracts from the Yerushalmi's main point of gluttony.

[52] The procedure is based on Deuteronomy 6.8 (see also Deuteronomy 11.18 and Exodus 13.16), and seems widely accepted, see Cohen Y., *Tangled up in Text: Tefillin and the Ancient World* (Providence: 2008). While the details of Tefillin are a pervasive topic in

The punishment is appropriately marked by a subtle paradox: the 'lack of piety' the community metes out to the student occurs after the latter's death, when his capabilities of perception would be impaired according to Greek discourse, but not according to the Yerushalmi.[53] Still, the deceased student, by being purged from his one transgression in this world already, now stands completely righteous, and can himself wander between the fountains of paradise.[54]

Son of a Fountain, inversely, inadvertently committed one single good deed in his lifetime. He procured food for the poor on one occasion – the precise nature is disputed – and we learn that the communal mourning of the people was his reward which he received in this world already, marked with the same subtle paradox of post-mortem benefaction that is possibly more difficult to enjoy. Having been fully remunerated, he now awaits hell. The punishment of Son of a Fountain, or Son of a Belly, reaffirms his indulgence in alcohol or food already suggested by his name. According to the widely held Late Antique view that the punishments in hell often correspond to the sin for which they are administered – the *lex talionis* – the thirsty man's tantalization with water confirms the audience's sense that one of his main vices must have been overindulging in drink.[55] Hence, both men, the student and the tax collector, received their

---

the halakhah, I am not aware of a single discussion regarding a transgression of their order (first arm, then head, following Deuteronomy 6.8) in the Mishna, Tosefta, or the Talmudim, adding to the oddity of the Yerushalmi's charge against the pious man (but see the later text *Song of Songs Rabbah* 4.6 and 6.17).

53 The trope that corpses do not feel shame or pain is attested in the Late Antique tradition about Diogenes, who asks for his body to be thrown over the city walls after his death. Since he would lack awareness, Diogenes argues that he certainly would not mind if the wild animals fed on him, see Cicero, *Tusculanae Disputationes* 1, 43. The Yerushalmi, in contrast, in the context of the covering of idolatrous pictures during a pious rabbis' burial procession, shows great concern for the fact that the deceased would have to see the pictures, since the main difference between the living and the dead is the latter's inability to move, and therefore to speak (Sanhedrin 3.1, 42c, 1–5).

54 The idea that the suffering of the righteous in this world exempts them of post-mortem punishment for minor transgressions, and that favourable ends in this world exempt the wicked from post-mortem rewards for minor good deeds, according to my knowledge, only occurs here in the Palestinian rabbinic literature. It is however very common in the Babylonian Talmud, see Elman Y., "Righteousness as Its Own Reward: An Inquiry into the Theologies of the Stam", *Proceedings of the American Academy for Jewish Research* 57 (1990) 35–67 and idem, "The Suffering of the Righteous in Palestinian and Babylonian Sources", *Jewish Quarterly Review* 80 (1990) 315–339, see also the similar doctrine in (Pseudo-)*Clementine Homilies*, where it is said to apply to Jews only, likely collectively (see ibid., 11.16.5).

55 Most punishments in late antique hells correspond to their sins; it is the combination of his name and his punishment that defines his identity as indulging in drink. On the *lex*

just deserts, entailing an inversion of the apparent unfairness of this-worldly social hierarchy.

Then, the Yerushalmi introduces another inmate of hell, a certain Mary, who is hanged by the nipples of her breast. The gruesome image of hanging is well attested as punishment for sexual transgression in many Christian and Jewish tours of hell.[56] The Yerushalmi, once more, can rely upon the audience to deduce from her punishment the sexual nature of Mary's sin. The torture of breasts as a punishment for sexual transgression, moreover, is attested in a Christian tradition contemporary to the Yerushalmi, the *Elijah Fragment*.[57] Finally, when the Yerushalmi calls her the daughter of 'Leaves of Onion,' it also implies that she had extra-matrimonial sexual intercourse which she seeks to hide like an onion that is hidden under its leaves – name and punishment, as in the case of the Son of a Fountain, both again specify the sin.[58]

Finally, the Yerushalmi brings a second, varying opinion for the nature of Mary's punishment, the placement of the hinge of the door of hell in her ear, an image known from slightly later rabbinic texts and a well-known punishment in the later Jewish tours of hell.[59] From this change in punishment, a shift in Mary's sin is to be deduced, which the Yerushalmi this time explicates. Her alternative, or second, sin, other than adultery, was to have publicized her fasting, or having deducted two sins for one fast day. Calculating rewards and

---

talionis and tantalization in hell see Himmelfarb, *Tours of Hell* esp. 75–105; Lieberman, "On Sins and Their Punishment."

56   See Himmelfarb, *Tours of Hell* 82–92.
57   The Christian *Elijah Fragment* describes women being tortured in their breasts; the Jewish, though not datable *Isaiah Fragment* (which may well depend on the Yerushalmi), describes hanging from the breasts (not from the nipples, as in the Yerushalmi) see Himmelfarb, *Tours of Hell* 35; 86–89. These are the two texts Himmelfarb posits as among the plausible source of the Yerushalmi, positing an inner-Jewish transmission for the *Elijah Fragment*, see note 20 above. While the *Elijah Fragment* clearly constitutes an originally Jewish composition, there is no evidence for such Jewish transmission history.
58   *Bereshit Rabbah* (82.12), a Palestinian rabbinic text with which the Yerushalmi stands in close dialogue, renders the verse from Jeremiah 49.10 'I revealed (Esau's) mysteries' to mean 'I peeled (Esau's) onion,' (*qlpyt bṣlyh*), which then is explained as uncovering his bastard (*mmzr*) offspring. See also Lieberman, "On Sins and Their Punishment" 35–36. Esau, in the period of the Yerushalmi, had become the rabbinic metonymy for Late (Christianizing) Rome, see Yuval I.J., *Two Nations in Your Womb: Perceptions of Jews and Christians in Late Antiquity and the Middle Ages* (Berkeley: 2006) 1–30.
59   The image of a pivot punishment as a metaphor for pain in the present world appears in texts post-dating – and likely familiar with – the Yerushalmi, such as *Avot DeRabbi Natan* (ed. Schechter, Appendix B, 156), *Yalkut Shimoni* (*Vayelekh* 940, eye under the pivot), and *Midrash Tehilim* (104:26, tongue under the pivot); it also appears in the later Jewish texts clearly dependent on the Yerushalmi such as *Darkhei Teshuvah*; see Himmelfarb, *Tours of Hell* 93f. For the pivot punishment in *Setme Kamwas* see below.

punishments for certain deeds falls partially into the Yerushalmi's criticism of false asceticism and works' righteousness.[60] Not attested here is the charge of ostentatious religious hypocrisy, to which I will return. Again, the Yerushalmi implies that the punishment also follows the *lex talionis*, for Mary is punished by being pinned down in the most public spot of Gehenna, its door. The sin of hypocrisy also leads to the introduction of Shimon ben Shetach: in a surprising turn, an unspecified voice now informs us that those in charge of hell will eventually release Mary from her torture, 'lifting' (*mrymyn*, a pun on *mrym*) the hinge of the gate of hell and placing it in the ear of Shimon ben Shetach – the person whose identity is at stake in the Yerushalmi's telling of the story.

The reason for Shimon's presence in hell, and his impending torture, is inadvertent hypocrisy: his neglect to follow through with a promise to kill witches made before he was elected patriarch. The student goes and warns him, equipped with instructions on how to impress Shimon by taking out and returning one of his eyes. In the story's sequel, as attested in Sanhedrin and Hagigah, the Yerushalmi reports how Shimon then hangs the witches.[61] Shimon hence eventually followed through with his promise to kill the witches; the Yerushalmi implies that Mary will be the one in whose ear the hinge of the gate of hell will for the time being.

What, then, can the audience learn from these stories of crimes and punishments, other than the identity of the patriarch in the first century BCE (which, moreover, is ultimately left unresolved)? The Yerushalmi's tour of the hereafter, experienced in form of a vision or a dream, like that of Virgil's *Aeneid*, seems to convey some concrete lessons about the nature of rabbinic paradise, hell, and the post-mortem rewards and punishments. Hell is a generally accepted idea whose details are astonishingly elusive in early Palestinian rabbinic sources,

---

[60] Mary's first sin seems to be a notion of work's righteousness which Lieberman explained with another Yerushalmi passage: Yerushalmi *Sotah* 5.7 (20c) describes a female 'bookkeeping Pharisee' (*prwš qyzy*) who thinks she can balance each sin through an ascetic deed. The Yerushalmi ridicules such a notion of works' righteousness when suggesting that Mary is punished in hell simply because she made a mistake in her calculations, hoping that her sins would outweigh her good deeds on the day of her death. In a similar vein, we should note that Yerushalmi *Sotah* also denounces a female false ascetic who claims to have lost her virginity due to intensive fasting (or self-affliction, she is called a *ṣyymnyt* in ibid. 3.4 19a), a transgression that falls within the same category of false asceticism which explains Mary's punishment, see Lieberman S., "Morsels: Yerushalmi amendments", *Tarbits* 5 (1934) 100–101 [Hebrew].

[61] For an attempt to contextualize the incident sociologically, and useful bibliography, see Ilan T., *Silencing the Queen: The Literary Histories of Shelamzion and Other Jewish Women* (Tübingen: 2006) 214–241; see also Hengel M., *Rabbinische Legende und frühpharisäische Geschichte. Schimeon b. Schetach und die achtzig Hexen von Askalon* (Heidelberg: 1984).

eschewing the intense Christian speculations on the topic.[62] Only in the Bavli do we find descriptions of the fate of select inmates of hell: Titus, Balaam, and Jesus (or 'the sinners of Israel' in some manuscripts) are depicted as suffering punishments commensurate to their respective crimes; Peter Schäfer has recently argued that Titus and Balaam have undergone a process of post factum Christianization.[63] In my view, the Yerushalmi constitutes not so much a tour of hell, inspired either by Jewish or Christian models, as a retelling of Christian monastic literature and a parody of gospel narratives, which the original rabbinic audience would have understood as such. For the Palestinian rabbis, Gehenna was real, but any tour of it would be have been associated with the Christian focus on the afterlife.

Illustrating intentional parody is a high bar to pass; we can approach it incrementally by considering how the Yerushalmi relates to popular discourse in fourth- and fifth-century Palestine. One of the most pertinent Christian texts that may us help explain the Yerushalmi is the dream vision of hell related by 'a very aged virgin advanced in the fear of God' in the so-called Systematic Collection of the *Sayings of the Desert Fathers*, a tradition the Egyptian monks from Scete brought to Palestine and translated from Coptic into Greek in their Judean settlements. As is the case in the Yerushalmi, the Greek text of the monastic collection, which was edited roughly contemporarily with the Yerushalmi and in proximity to the rabbis' centres of activity in the Galilee and in Caesarea, contains much older material which has been updated and reframed.[64] Both texts, however, should be assessed in the most accessible

---

62 One of the few early depictions of hell in Palestinian rabbinic literature of which I am aware is *Pesiqta deRav Kahana* 10.4 (parallels in *Tanhuma* (Buber) *Re'eh* 10 and Midrash *Mishle* 31.6). Here, the inmates of hell first misperceive the suffering as moderate, and are then soon corrected. Saul Lieberman already remarked that the earlier rabbinic sources 'do not mention the refined tortures of Gehenna, their minutiae, and the ramified penal code which governs Hades' in idem, "Some Aspects of After Life in Early Rabbinic Literature", in Lieberman S. (ed.), *Harry Austryn Wolfson Jubilee Volume* (Jerusalem: 1965), vol. 2, 496. Martha Himmelfarb, citing Lieberman, explains part of the rabbinic reluctance to describe hell by their exegetical focus; see eadem, *Tours of Hell* 77.

63 On the Christian overtones of Balaam in hell see Schäfer P., *Jesus in the Talmud* (Princeton: 2007) 82–94. On Titus' conversion to Christianity see Yuval, *Two Nations in Your Womb* 38–55. Needless to say, the Babylonian rabbinic material on hell is later than our story, and the Bavli's hell is much closer to Zoroastrian depictions of hell than of those in the Graeco-Roman world. Especially the *Dādestān Ī Dēnīg* (e.g. 31:4–5 and 40:4) and the *Ardā Wīrāz-nāmag* contain depictions very close to those of the Bavli, see also note 5 above.

64 See Guy J.-C., *Les Apophtegmes des pères: collection systématique* (Paris: 2005) 96–105 (18.45), translation according to Wortley, *Book of the Elders* 331–334, on the dating of the collection see note 21 above; for the full text see appendix II, 88–90 below.

layer of their redactional framework before attempting to reconstruct what earlier versions of the stories may have meant in an earlier context.

The monks' virgin speaking here is the daughter of a 'moderate, gentle, and well-tempered' father and of a mother who passes 'her time drunk with wine in the company of dissolute men.' Her father dies first, receiving a very poor burial, which is delayed by heavy rain, whereas the mother's eventual 'funeral and pomp,' as she later passes away, are such 'that you would think that even air was joining in burying her.' As the daughter, coming of age, wonders whether it is worth living a pious life, given that her father has received nothing in return in this life; she is drawn towards her mother's lifestyle. The following night, she has a dream vision in which a guide reprimands her, and in a tour of the afterlife she sees her father rewarded in paradise, and her mother tormented in hell. She decides to dedicate her life to God as a virgin.

The story of the pious virgin shares with the Yerushalmi many typical aspects of post-mortem social inversion stories: the juxtaposition of a good and a wicked character first in life and then in death, the rewards for the former and the punishment of the latter in the afterlife, the shabby burial of the righteous and the pompous interment for the wicked one, and of course the tour of hell itself all seem part of the stock inventory of such tales, known from examples such as Lucian, as well as the first- or second-century Demotic story of Setme Kamwas.

The Egyptian Demotic story of Setme Kamwas is far removed in time and place from the Jewish rabbinic and the Christian monastic narratives. A very brief comparison between the three stories, however, remains worthwhile, since it illustrates the common motifs shared by all Hellenistic cultures as much as the special relationship between the Yerushalmi and the Christian narrative. In the Demotic text, Horus son of Panashe, an Egyptian magician, returns from the underworld and becomes reincarnated as a prodigious and precocious child. One day his father sees the coffin of a rich man being carried out to the cemetery 'with (very loud) wailing ..., and great were the honours.... (In another moment) as he (i.e. the father) was looking down, he saw (the body of a poor man being carried out) wrapped (only) in a mat ... without anyone walking (behind him).'[65] After the father wrongly perceives the rich man as truly blessed, his prodigious son wishes for his father to share the poor man's fate in the underworld. In order then to appease the incredulous father, the son takes him on a tour of the netherworld composed of Hellenistic and Egyptian motifs. Here, father and son see a man in royal linen. It is the poor man whose burial they witnessed, who received the burial provisions of the rich man in

---

65   Griffith, *Stories of the High Priests of Memphis* 47.

the underworld and now stands near Osiris, holding a high rank. They also see 'the pivot of the door of the fifth hall was fixed in the right eye of a man who was pleading and lamenting loudly'; this man turns out to be the rich man whose burial they had witnessed. Other inmates of hell are punished for gluttony, tantalization with food and water equally occurs.[66]

The obvious similarity between Setme Kamwas, the story of the virgin, and the Yerushalmi's story are clear: the perception of two funerals of a rich and a poor man, the apparent intensification of the social hierarchy at the time of the funeral, the tour of hell that serves to reinforce the morals of the living, the torture which the rich man endures, and the honours bestowed upon the poor man. The numerous similarities between the Demotic text and the Yerushalmi, and especially the shared motif of the pivot punishment, the sin of gluttony, and the tantalization, have led Hugo Gressmann to believe that the Yerushalmi narrative is modelled on the Demotic one. Himmelfarb, however, has rightfully countered that the pivot punishment is more likely part of the 'common property of the Hellenistic Mediterranean', as is the entire motif of post-mortem social inversion.[67]

In turn, the more specific and exclusive overlaps between the Yerushalmi and the story of the Christian virgin, even if reconfigured to suit the respective storylines, reinforce our sense of a shared narrative and moral framework:
- In both the Yerushalmi ('Perhaps, for the Haters of Israel (i.e. Jews), there is no (reward)?') and in the Sayings of the Desert Fathers ('Is [the virgin's father] such an enemy of God that even the earth will not receive him in burial?' 'so if such a way of life was good in the sight of God, why was my father so tested?' …), the vision of hell comes in response to an acute religious crisis experienced after witnessing an improper burial for a pious person. (The Egyptian father is ignorant of the rich man's morality.)
- In both the Yerushalmi ('do not despise the sons of your Lord') and the Sayings of the Desert Fathers ('terrifying me by his appearance, he questioned me with an angry look and a harsh voice'), the guide reprimands the

---

66   Ibid. 49.
67   See Gressmann, *Vom reichen Mann* 59f., and Himmelfarb, *Tours of Hell* 81. Furthermore, the Demotic story is attested only once, on the verso of a slightly damaged papyrus which itself was written in 64 CE; the story itself is usually dated to Egypt of the first or second century CE. It thereby predates both the Yerushalmi and the Sayings of the Desert Fathers by centuries, and constitutes a direct intertext only to Luke's story of Lazarus and the Rich man which also shares most of the motifs here adduced (see below). The shared language and provenance of the original Coptic monastic literature and the Demotic narrative of Setme Kamwas is suggestive of a possibly closer literary relationship between these two texts, which unfortunately cannot be assessed in light of the loss of the original stories of the Desert Fathers.

surviving pious believer. (No such reprimand is uttered by Horus; albeit that the manuscript is defective here.)
- In the Yerushalmi, the name of the tax collector who is suffering in hell implies his indulgence in drink and food, likewise, the mother of the virgin is punished for 'drunkenness' and 'debauchery.' (The rich man is not charged with drunkenness or gluttony in the Egyptian story.)
- In the Yerushalmi, Mary is punished for sins in a way that implies her sexual transgressions; likewise, the mother of the virgin is described as being punished for 'adultery' and '*porneia*'.[68] (No sexual sins, or punishments for them, occur in the story of Setme Kamwas.)
- In the Yerushalmi the student sees his pious colleague 'between gardens, and orchards and fountains', whereas the virgin's father resides among 'many gardens, all sorts of fruits, and diverse trees of a beauty that defied description.' (Garden imagery is absent from the Egyptian story.)

In light of these shared elements, one is tempted to conclude that the story in the Yerushalmi and in the Sayings of the Desert Fathers seem almost identical in terms of ethics and narrative structure, and are both part of the larger moral and folkloristic repertoire of fifth century Palestine. While this may be true to a certain extent, the broad cultural overlap between the Yerushalmi and the Sayings of the Desert Fathers are but the shared background against which the Yerushalmi's parody of a Gospel narrative of post-mortem social inversion stands out sharply. The affinity of the Sayings of the Desert Fathers with the much earlier Lukan narrative suggest that the 'original' context of the story has been Christian since the first or second century, and that the rabbis, in this instance at least, are the colonized natives who mimic and subversively alienate the tales of the Christian colonizers of Palestine – all within a shared Hellenistic framework. While both narratives are modelled on the story of Lazarus and the rich man, the Yerushalmi engages the Gospel much more intimately than the patristic narrative.

2   Luke

The narrative of Lazarus and the rich man stems from the Gospel of Luke, a late first or early second-century Christian text that was continuously told, and retold, copied and translated, explained, and used throughout late antiquity – not least through stories such as that of the pious virgin. The Palestinian

---

[68]   On the varied meanings of the term cf. Jensen J., "Does *Porneia* mean Fornication? A Critique of Bruce Malina", *Novum Testamentum* 20 (1978) 161–184.

authors of the Yerushalmi would likely have been exposed to the Christian narrative, most likely orally, in Greek or Aramaic, as part of the story of Lazarus circulating among Palestinian Christians. In order to reconstruct the Gospel which the Rabbis may have heard in the fifth century, we need to turn to a number of witnesses.

The two witnesses closest to the way in which the rabbis would have heard the story of Lazarus are the Palestinian Christian Aramaic gospels and the Syriac Diatessaron. The Diatessaron's prominence among Eastern Christians, and its circulation in Palestine, suggest that the rabbis would have perceived all gospels as one text, as *the* Gospel, without differentiating between the various individual writings.[69] Sadly, both the Palestinian Christian Aramaic versions and the Diatessaron are mostly lost.[70] Therefore, I approach the likely form in which the author of the Yerushalmi heard the story with the help of several texts.

- First, the literary structure of the Diatessaron is preserved largely by the text's extant Arabic translation.[71]
- Secondly, I present the story according to its various translations into Syriac (mainly the Peshitta) as the one extant Aramaic source whose language is closest to the Palestinian Christian Aramaic the rabbis would have heard in all likelihood.[72] Needless to say, the Syriac gospels do not of course constitute historical evidence of the Palestinian Christian Aramaic gospels.

---

69 See Petersen W.L., *Tatian's Diatessaron: Its Creation, Dissemination, Significance, & History in Scholarship* (Leiden: 1994). For a broader exposition of my approach to the rabbis' oral exposure to key aspects of Gospel narratives see Zellentin, *Rabbinic Parodies* 142f.

70 For the fragments of the Palestinian Christian Aramaic gospels see Müller-Kessler C. – Sokoloff M. (eds.), *The Christian Palestinian Aramaic New Testament Version from the Early Period* (Groningen: 1998). The Diatessaron's wording can be partially reconstructed with help of the Syriac commentary on the Diatessaron by Ephrem. For an English translation see McCarthy C., *Saint Ephrem's Commentary on Tatian's Diatessaron: An English Translation of* Chester Beatty *Syriac MS 709 with Introduction and Notes*, Journal of Semitic Studies Supplement 2 (Oxford: 1993).

71 On the tradition of the Arabic Diatessaron see Euringer S., *Die Überlieferung der arabischen Übersetzung des Diatessarons* (Freiburg im Breisgau: 1912); Graf G., *Geschichte der christlichen arabischen Literatur* (The Vatican: 1944) 1, 150–155; and most recently Cook J.G., "A note on Tatian's Diatessaron, Luke, and the Arabic Harmony", *Zeitschrift für antikes Christentum* 10 (2006) 462–471. Petersen points out the enduring importance of the Arabic translations as the only complete Eastern witness of the Diatessaron. While the language of many of the Arabic readings seems to have been influenced by the Peshitta, the Arabic seems to preserve the original *sequence* of Tatian's work, which is of value to my considerations below; see Petersen, *Tatian's Diatessaron* 133–138; Baarda T., "An Archaic Element in the Arabic Diatessaron?", *Novum Testamentum* 17 (1975) 151–155.

72 I quote the translation of Lamsa G.M., *The Holy Bible From Ancient Eastern Manuscripts* (Philadelphia: 1957), with slight emendations. I consulted the Syriac edited by Kiraz G.A.,

Still, the lexical stability between Palestinian Jewish Aramaic, Palestinian Christian Aramaic, and Syriac allows us incrementally to approach a gospel version from the time of the Yerushalmi, in a closely related different dialect of the same language.

– Moreover, I also consult the story's patristic interpretation as indicative of the cultural context in which the rabbis would have encountered the story.

All these sources are chronologically, linguistically, or culturally removed from the Palestinian rabbis, but in their interplay they allow us a necessarily fuzzy, yet still the best approach to what would have been heard on the market place in fifth century Palestine. The Greek Gospels are of course best attested in Palestine Patristic literature; it is the Greek Gospels upon which the argument of this paper fully rests, whereas my suggestions for the pertinence of Christian Aramaic witnesses are illustrations of the claim. While always imperfect, improvable, and not provable, dismissing such an approach to the Aramaic Gospels would be commensurate with relinquishing any attempt to assess important literary and linguistic aspects of the most important narrative of the Late Roman historical context of the Yerushalmi.

To begin with, the Gospel of Luke has Jesus narrate as follows:

> There was a rich man, who used to wear purple and fine linen,
> And every day he made merry very lavishly.
> And there was a poor man (*wmskn'*) named Lazarus (*l'zr*),
> Who was laid down at that rich man's door, afflicted with boils.
> He longed to fill his stomach with the crumbs that fell (*dnplyn*) from the rich man's table;
> the dogs also came and licked his boils.
> Now it happened that the poor man died (*wmyt*)
> And the angels carried him into Abraham's bosom.
> And the rich man also died (*myt*) and was buried;
> And while he was tormented in Sheol, he lifted up his eyes from a distance,
> And saw Abraham with Lazarus in his bosom.
> And he called out in a loud voice, saying,
> 'O my father Abraham, have mercy on me,
>   and send Lazarus to dip the tip of his finger in water (*bmy'*) and wet my tongue (*lšny*);
>   for I am tormented in this flame.'

Comparative Edition of the Syriac Gospels: Aligning the Sinaiticus, Curetonianus, Peshitta and Harklean Versions (Piscataway, NJ: 2004).

> Abraham said to him, 'My son, remember you received your pleasures when you were living, and Lazarus his hardships;
> And behold now he is comfortable here, and you are suffering.
> Besides all these things, a great gulf is fixed between us and you,
> So that those who wish to cross over from here to you cannot,
> Neither from there to cross over to us.'
> He said to him: 'If this is so, I beseech you, O my father, to send him to my father's house;
> For I have five brothers; let him go (*n'zl*) and testify to them,
> So that they may not also come to this place of torment.'
> Abraham said to him: 'They have Moses and the prophets; let them hear them.'
> But he said to him: 'No, my father Abraham; but if only a man from the dead would go to them, they will repent.'
> Abraham said to him: 'If they will not hear Moses and the prophets, neither will they believe (*mhymnyn*) even if a man should rise for the dead.'[73]

The story sounds familiar in light of the motif of post-mortem social inversion. The rich man in purple and fine linen does not share his wealth with the poor man agonizing at his doorstep. Their fates are inversed in the afterlife, as we saw it happening in Lucian, in the story of Setme Kamwas, in the Sayings of the Desert Fathers, and of course in the Yerushalmi. The rich man asks to return to the world, in order to warn his brothers. The request is denied: Abraham emphasizes that following the precepts of Moses and the prophets is sufficient for a moral life, if the brothers do not hear them, he would not believe even someone returning from the dead.

The Church Fathers read Luke's story as *the* tour of hell, and as a faithful depiction of the hereafter. While stories such as that of the Christian virgin in the Sayings of the Desert fathers makes no clear reference to Lazarus, in its very similarity it shows how the story had become naturalized as part of Christian ethical discourse. Especially, it is the reading of Luke among the Church Fathers that seems as pertinent to the Yerushalmi as the gospel version. Tracing the way in which Luke was read among Christians allows us to see how the rabbis simultaneously accommodated and resisted the growing dominance of Christian paradigms in fifth century Palestine. To give but one example, Jerome, the Yerushalmi's longtime temporal and geographic neighbour (who had been greatly interested in Virgil's depiction of the afterlife which he

---

[73] Luke 16:19–31. See also Arabic Diatessaron 29:14–26.

alleges to have lost after his conversion to Christianity) understands Luke's description of the afterlife as straightforward description of the pre-Christian heaven and hell:

> Even if Lazarus is seen in Abraham's bosom and a place of refreshment (*locoque refrigerii*), what similarity is there between the underworld (*infernus*) and the reign of heavens? Before Christ Abraham is among those below (*inferos*); after Christ, the robber is in paradise (*paradiso*).[74]

For Jerome, Lazarus rests in a pre-Christian netherworld, which houses both places of torture and bliss – the traditional layout of the Hellenistic underworld. In Jerome's view, Luke describes the geography of the underworld as it existed prior to Jesus' resurrection, after which heaven and hell were more thoroughly separated. Other Church Fathers equally understood Luke's depiction as a straightforward description of the afterlife. In contrast to Jerome, they saw the fate of Lazarus and the rich man as proof of eternal and unchanging truths about the afterlife, offering a tripartite geography of hell, purgatory, and heaven.[75] The story of Lazarus had become the epitome of patristic views of the afterlife, which will guide my reading of the Yerushalmi's gospel parody. By parodying this story, the Yerushalmi distances itself from the entirety of the Late Antique Christian hell; by imitating the basic imagery and moral landscape of Luke, it also has become part of the Christian thought world.

---

74 Jerome, *Letter to Heliodorus* (Letter 60), trans. J.H.D. Scourfield, in *Consoling Heliodorus: A Commentary on Jerome, Letter 60* (Oxford: 1993) 44–47. For Jerome's engagement of rabbinic thought see for example Baskin J.R., "Rabbinic-Patristic Exegetical Contacts in Late Antiquity: A Bibliographical Reappraisal", in Green W.S. (ed.), *Approaches to Ancient Judaism* vol. 5 (Altanta: 1985) 53–80. For Jerome's acquaintance with Virgil and other Latin classics see Hagendahl H., *Latin Fathers and the Classics: a Study on the Apologists, Jerome and other Christian Writers* (Gothenburg: 1958) esp. 321f.

75 Especially Augustine of Hippo, another contemporary of the Yerushalmi who wielded much influence also in Palestine, bases his entire concept of purgatory on the account of Lazarus and the rich man, see *The City of God*, Chapter XXI. It is Clement of Alexandria who, along with Origin, has been credited with the invention of the Christian purgatory, modelled after Platonic ideas of purification through fire. See Goff, *The Birth of Purgatory* 52. On the importance of Abraham's bosom see Merkt A., "Abrahams Schoss: Ursprung und Sinngehalt eines antiken christlichen Jenseitstopos", in Ameling W. (ed.), *Topographie des Jenseits: Studien zur Geschichte des Todes in Kaiserzeit und Spätantike* (Stuttgart: 2011) 83–102.

3 Lazarus

With the importance of Luke for the Christian geography of the afterlife in mind, a closer look at the conceptual similarities between the Yerushalmi and Luke, reinforced by the likely lexical overlap between the Yerushalmi and assumable oral retellings of the Gospel, is helpful – a full juxtaposition of all respective evidence can be found in appendix 1 (71–87 below):

- The tantalization of the rich man and the tax collector, while being part of the Hellenistic lore, is very similar. In both the Christian and the rabbinic narrative, the rich man is depicted as longing to reach for water (*bmy'*,[76] *my'*) with their tongue (*lšny, lšnw*).
- The Yerushalmi loosely imitates a cluster of images from the Lazarus story. Here, the poor man (*wmskn'*) Lazarus (*l'zr*) waits for what falls (*dnplyn*) from the rich man's table; then, they both die (*myt*). In the Yerushalmi, the tax collector dies (*wmyt*), and one of the possible good deeds he did was that he acquiesced to a poor man's (*mskn*) taking a bread that fell (*wnpl*). It is Rabbi Lazarus (*l'zr*) who suggest Mary's first punishment.[77]
- The rich man asks that he be let go (*n'zl*) and testify to his brothers, yet Abraham replies that they will not believe (*mhymnyn*) him. Likewise, the Yerushalmi instructs the student to go (*'yzyl*) and tell Shimon about his impending punishment, yet the student objects that the patriarch will not believe (*mhmnty*) him.

The similarity between the two narratives, reinforced by the affinity between some Aramaic terms used, suggests that the Yerushalmi not only shares with Luke the broader motif of post-mortem social inversion, but actually seeks to evoke the Gospel story in an oral version that is loosely yet clearly related to the extant written one. Most importantly, the Yerushalmi's many oddities often seem to be modelled precisely on motifs known from the Gospel, evoking a rather playful take on the Christian narratives. The odd fact, that the student anticipates Shimon ben Shetach not to believe his instructions from the netherworld, as a first example, repeats Luke's statement that the rich man's brothers will not believe a man returning from the dead. The Yerushalmi's bizarre solution, then, to convince Shimon with a sign, spoofs Jesus' teaching elsewhere in the Gospel, consistent with the Yerushalmi's approach to such methods in general:

---

[76] Following Curetonianus.
[77] The importance of the names of rabbinic figures for the narrative is a literary strategy illustrated by Jeffrey Rubenstein; see idem, *Talmudic Stories: Narrative Art, Composition, and Culture* (Baltimore: 1999) esp. 111.

- In the Yerushalmi the student is instructed to 'take out your eye (*'pyq* *'[y]nk*), and it will come on your hand (*ydk*).' This language is reminiscent of another gospel's narrative, where Jesus advocates that 'if your hand (*'ydk*) or your foot offends you, cut it off and throw it away [...] and if your eye (*'ynk*) offends you, remove it (*'pqyh*)[78] and throw it away from you; it is better for you to go through life with one eye rather than having two eyes and fall in to the Gehenna of fire'.[79] The student, who already is in Gehenna (albeit as a visitor), takes the Gospel's instruction to take out one's eye literally, in order to prevent Shimon ben Shetach from 'fall(ing) into the Gehenna.'
- In the Yerushalmi the student seeks to make the 'sign.' Miracles are a pervasive topic in the Gospels, despite the many miracles he wrings, Jesus is equally portrayed as denying signs.[80] Patristic literature, however, abounds with signs and miracles, and the Yerushalmi elsewhere, in *Mo'ed Qatan* 3.1 (81c–d), rejects miracles as an unacceptable 'Christian' method of establishing divine intent. The pertinence of this passage is marked by similarity of language: there, the miracle is also designated by the instruction of the miraculously moved object to return to its place, which it does (*hwzryn whzrt*), a phrase evoked by the eye which returns to its place in the present passage (*hzrh hzrh*).[81]
- Accordingly, Shimon dismisses both the necessity of verification by miraculous sign, as well as the method, which is thrice marked as Christian. Firstly, as an enactment of Jesus' saying to tear out one's eye, secondly, as a method to sort out the truth in general, thirdly, Shimon expresses his belief in the student's piety, stating oddly and out of context that 'I know (*yd'*) that you are a pious man. Even if I think (*hšbyt*) in my heart (*blby*), with my mouth (*bpmy*) I will not say.' Again, the Yerushalmi thereby negates another Gospel passage which warns the Pharisees (!) of their impending punishment: 'But Jesus knew (*yd'*) their thoughts (*mhšbthwn*) and said to them [...] the mouth (*pwm'*) speaks from the fullness of the heart (*lb'*). I tell you, on the Day of Judgment you will have to give an account for every careless word you utter [...]. Then some of the scribes and Pharisees said to him, "Teacher, we wish to see a sign from you."'[82] Jesus, in Matthew, denies giving a sign, which allows us to hear the entirety of Shimon's actions as a playful reenactment of Jesus' precepts whose incoherence but points to the perceived incoherence

---

78 Following the Harklean version. The Peshitta has *htsyh*.
79 Matthew 18:8–9.
80 See e.g. Luke 11:29; Matthew 12:38–9; 15:18–19.
81 On the Yerushalmi's rejection of 'Christian' miracles as signs of proof see Zellentin, *Rabbinic Parodies* 213–227.
82 Matthew 12:25–38. See also Luke 6:45.

of the gospel: While Jesus denies giving a sign, Shimon refuses to witness a sign; while Jesus claims to know the thoughts of the Pharisees and claims that the moth speaks from the heart, Shimon refuses to speak his mind and keeps his thoughts in his heart, likely in order to avoid being condemned!

The senselessness inherent to aspects of the rabbis' conversation, hence, constitutes part the Yerushalmi's message. The many inscrutable features of the Yerushalmi passage were intended to be as bizarre as they seem still to us. Upon closer examination, the entire Yerushalmi passage turns out to be an elaborate parodic pastiche of several gospel passages that ridicule the Christian narrative by enacting its solemn teachings. This also holds true for the deeds of the rich man (see also 79–80 below, # 26–29).

The first possible good deed of the tax collector, to reiterate, was to let a chance falling of a piece of bread go unnoticed; an image that imitates the crumbs falling of the rich man's table in Luke as I argued above. The tax collector's other possible good deed occurs after he has invited the council members of his city to a feast (*'ryṣṭwn*). They did not come, or at least did not eat and hence he fed the poor (*msknyy'*) in order to avoid wasting the food. This second good deed seems to parody another passage from Luke, depicting Jesus as instructing his audience to invite the poor in the first place:

> (Jesus) also said to the one who had invited him, 'When you give a luncheon (ἄριστον)[83] or a supper, do not invite your friends or your brothers or your relatives or your rich neighbours, lest they may invite you, and you will be repaid for this. But when you give a reception, invite the poor (*mskn'*), [...]' Jesus said [...], 'A man gave a great supper, and invited many. And he sent his servant at supper time to tell those who were invited, "Behold, everything is made ready for you, come." One and all, they began to make excuses [...]. Then the master of the house was angry, and said to his servant: Go out quickly to the streets and lanes of the city, and bring in here the poor (*lmskn'*) [...].'[84]

Jesus' message, according to the opening of this passage, is that one should invite the poor rather than the rich to one's banquets, to perform a real act of charity rather than gain favour among those who are able to return it. The second part turns the hermeneutical screw a bit further, and calls for replacing the poor for the rich entirely. The banquet of those who eat the bread in the Kingdom of God are the righteous ones.

---

83   Following the Greek. The Peshitta has *šrwt'*, 'dinner.'
84   Luke 14:12–24. See also the Arabic Diatessaron 30:6–30.

The Yerushalmi's tax collector seems modelled on this second Lucan passage. He organizes a luncheon, *ariston* in Luke's Greek, a full cognate of the rabbinic Aramaic *'rysṭwn* offered by the Yerushalmi's tax collector. As the rich and powerful did not attend, the man in Luke then gives the food to the poor (*mskn'*), likewise, the tax collector in the Yerushalmi, after his guests do not arrive, gives the food to the poor (*msknyyh*). Reading the Yerushalmi as parodying this story guides us to perceive of the tax collector as having fulfilled a precept that, while dovetailing with the rabbis' own view of charity, is clearly marked as Christian. Luke, of course, declares that those initially invited will not be part of God's messianic dinner; the Yerushalmi turns Luke's narrative upside down and turns the tax collector himself into the unrighteous rich man of Luke's story of Lazarus, attacking the enemy with his own weapons indeed.

An effective parody of the two gospel passages, the story of Lazarus and that of the rich man's banquet, presupposes that the Yerushalmi's rabbinic audience – it has no other in mind – would be able to identify effortlessly the imitated passages on Lazarus and the banquet from Luke without having to engage in detailed studies of the New Testament. Only if the imitated text is readily available to this audience does my argument for parody hold, a necessity complicated by the fact that we already speaking about two passages originally separated: the story of Lazarus and the parable of the banquet.

The patristic readings of Luke are therefore of primary importance for my argument. First, passages important to the Church Fathers – such as the story of Lazarus and the botched banquet – are those the Christian population would have heard most often, and also those to which the rabbinic audience would, in all likelihood, have been exposed. Secondly, the Church Fathers' understanding of *the* Gospel guides the Yerushalmi's parody in terms of structure and content. We should note the conflation of the two passages from Luke in Christian discourse; Clement of Alexandria, for example, contracts the two stories already in the late second century:

> Why is the parable of Lazarus showing the picture of the rich and poor? And why 'nobody can serve two masters, God and Mammon,' the love of money (φιλαργυρία) so being named by the Lord? For example, the covetous (φιλοκτήμονες), who were invited, did not respond to the call to the supper, not because of their possessing property, but of their passion for possessing.[85]

---

85   Clement of Alexandria, *Stromateis* IV.6.30.4–IV.6.31.1, according to Stählin O. – Früchtel L., *Clemens Alexandrinus, vol. 2: Stromata Buch I–IV* (Berlin: 1960) 261.

Clement's reading of the rich man's crime as greed is fairly typical of later interpretations and already conflates the Lazarus story with the parable of the banquet. Elsewhere, Clement makes the rich man of our story the epitome of luxury.[86]

The Yerushalmi, just like the Church Fathers, conflates the rich man at whose door Lazarus lingers with the host of the parable of the banquet. Heeding to patristic discourse equally explains why the Yerushalmi, through the choice of his name Son of a Fountain, or Son of a Belly, and through his punishment with thirst, depicts the tax collector as a drunkard and a glutton, as we saw above. While we already saw a similar association of the rich man as a glutton and a drunkard by his parallel with the virgin's gluttonous mother, also Athanasius of Alexandria, for example, writing slightly before the Yerushalmi, states the following in 338 CE:

> In the same manner those also who suffer temporal afflictions here, after having remained steadfast, go forth to a place of comfort; while those who here persecute are trodden under foot, and have no good end. For even the rich man, according to the Gospel, having lived in pleasure here for a little while, suffered hunger there; and having drunk largely here, he was there parched with thirst. But Lazarus, after being afflicted in worldly things, found rest in heaven; and having hungered for bread ground from corn, he was there satisfied with that which is better than manna, even the Lord who came down and said, 'I am the bread which came down from heaven, and giveth life to mankind.'[87]

For Athanasius, the rich man was a glutton and a drunkard, adding yet another layer to the Yerushalmi's imitation of the patristic Lazarus of the fifth century. The Yerushalmi imitates the Christian discourse and switches its players, it is the rich drunkard who follows one of Jesus' precepts (of feeding the poor) and receives great honours during his burial, yet the true pious ones are the two students who live and die just, poor, and discretely. It is the Church Fathers' *ascetic* and *combined* reading of both Lucan passages that permeated fourth- and fifth-century Palestinian discourse which the rabbis turned on its head.

---

[86] See Clement of Alexandria *Paedagogus* II.II.
[87] Athanasius of Alexandria, Letter 10.6, trans. in Historical Tracts of S. Athanasius, Archbishop of Alexandria (London: 1885) 74–75, quoting John 6:51. See also Cyprian of Carthage, *Epistle* 54.3, depicting the *lex talionis* punishment of the rich sinner.

4 Tax Collectors and Sinners

The topic that constitutes the axis of the Yerushalmi's entire narrative, then, is the ascetic and studious mode of life, mirroring one of the central debates of fourth and fifth century Palestine.[88] Indeed, as if he had chosen his life as a pauper, Lazarus had become a beacon to the ascetic impulses of the church in the time of the Yerushalmi. Lazarus now stands for asceticism in all its forms: continence, deprivation of food, drink, and clothing.[89] In effect, the Yerushalmi seems to have picked up on a tension permeating the Christian culture of its time: while anchorites and monks excruciated their bodies, the Gospels themselves depict Jesus as wining and dining; while Christians pursued complete righteousness, Jesus is depicted in the company of sinners. The Yerushalmi deals with this tension by adopting, on the one hand, the Christian affinity towards asceticism when depicting the two pious students as ascetics. On the other hand, inversely, the sins of the Yerushalmi's Mary spoof two issues it connects with Christianity: an exaggerated concern with false asceticism and the alleged forgiveness of sexual sins. Parody again guides the way to understand the rabbis.

Mary incurs her second punishment, the pivot of the door of hell, either because 'she fasted one day and deducted two (sins) for it', or because she 'fasted (*ṣyymh*) and made it public to her neighbour', adding an additional second and third sin to her licentiousness. As we have seen above, the second sin, to calculate one's merit, falls within the Yerushalmi's denunciation of works' righteousness. Hypocritical asceticism, however, is not typically an issue for the Yerushalmi, and Mary's third sin, to have 'fasted' and to have made it public to her neighbour instead imitates a sin expressed in another Gospel passage:

> When you fast (*dṣymyn*), do not look sad like the hypocrites; for they disfigure their faces, so that they may appear to men that they are fasting. Truly I say to you, that they have already received their reward. But you,

---

[88] For a discussion of Palestinian rabbinic asceticism see Satlow M., "'And on the Earth you shall sleep': 'Talmud Torah' and Rabbinic Asceticism", *Journal of Religion* 83 (2003) 204–225; for the Christian context see Zellentin, *Rabbinic Parodies* 51–94; 167–212. For Christian asceticism, see e.g. Binns J., *Ascetics and Ambassadors of Christ: The Monasteries of Palestine, 314–631* (Oxford: 1994).

[89] Jerome, again, sees Lazarus' poverty as tantamount to asceticism (idem, *Letter to Pamminus* (Letter 48) 21). Gregory of Nyssa in the late fourth century, to mention yet another example, summarizes the teaching of the sister of Saint Basil and emphasizes how free Lazarus is from this material world, whereas the rich man suffers through attachment to his past (Gregory of Nyssa, *On the Soul and the Resurrection*).

when you fast, wash your face and anoint your head; so that it may not appear to men that you are fasting, but to your Father who is in secret; and your Father who sees in secret, he will reward you.[90]

Mary's third transgression in the Yerushalmi, hence, playfully enacts Jesus' teachings in the same way in which the Yerushalmi created the tax collector's good deeds: publishing one's fasting is a transgression which is clearly marked as 'Christian', just as the tax collector's charity is marked as such. And indeed, Mary's first transgression in the Yerushalmi, the licentiousness implied by her name and breast hanging punishment, as well as the reason why Shimon ben Shetah is about to take her place, both stem from another Gospel passage about one Shimon and a licentious Mary. This becomes clear when considering, in Luke and in his later readers, the story of a female sinner who approaches Jesus in the house of one Shimon, the Pharisee:

> The Son of man came, eating (*'kl*) and drinking (*wšt'*); and you say, 'Behold, a glutton and a drunkard, and a friend of tax-collectors (*dmks'*) and sinners (*wdḥty'*)!' [...] Then one of the Pharisees came and asked him to eat with him. And he entered the house of that Pharisee and reclined as a guest. Now there was in that city a woman who was a sinner (*ḥtyt'*) [...] Jesus answered, saying to him: 'Shimon (*šm'wn*), I have something to tell you.' He said to him: 'Say it, Teacher (*rby*).' Jesus said to (Shimon): 'There were two men who were debtors (*ḥyb'*) to a certain creditor; one of them owed him five hundred pence, and the other fifty pence. And because they had nothing to pay, he forgave them both. Which one of them will love him more?' Shimon answered, saying: 'I think the one to whom he forgave more.' Jesus said to him, 'You have judged truly.' And he turned to the woman, and said to Shimon: 'Do you see this woman? When I entered your house, you did not give me even water for my feet; but she has wet my feet with her tears and wiped them with her hair. You did not kiss me; but she, since she entered, has not ceased to kiss my feet. You did not anoint my head with oil; but she has anointed my feet with perfume. For this reason, I say to you, her many sins are forgiven because she loved much; but he to whom little is forgiven, loves little.' And he said to the woman: 'Your sins are forgiven.'[91]

---

90 Matthew 6:16–18. See the Arabic Diatessaron 9:39. Obviously, the message here dovetails with rabbinic thought as expressed e.g. in Mishna *Avoth* 2:16; 4:1.

91 Luke 7:34–50. See also Arabic Diatessaron 14:45–15:14; see also 37:43–37:50; 39:1–39:8; Mark 2:14. Jesus, of course, is depicted as eating with tax collectors more than once (see

Here, Jesus eats and drinks with the tax collectors and sinners, and has physical contact with the sinful woman; those who need forgiveness the most. The Yerushalmi imitates the narrative and wording of this passage in order to turn it on its head. While Luke speaks of Jesus eating (*'kl*) and drinking (*wšt'*), and as a friend of tax-collectors (*dmks'*) and sinners (*wdḥty'*) in the house of Shimon, the Pharisee; the Yerushalmi depicts the two students as eating (*'klyn*) and drinking (*wštyyn*) moderately in order to mark the difference between them and Son of a Fountain, the thirsty tax collector (*mwks*), and the sinful Mary, daughter of the Leaves of Onions, who will take the place of Shimon, the Patriarch. While Jesus claims to forgive the debtors (*ḥyb'*) who are especially laden with debt, the Yerushalmi insists that to the contrary, it is the deceased student's minute sinful 'debt' (*ḥwb'*) to God that is erased from his record in this world as well – Torah study and a pious life, not Jesus, are the only means to attain reward. While the rabbinic audience surely needed no reminder of this, they surely appreciated the careful mimicry and eclipse of the Christian narrative that reestablished the rabbinic order.[92] Mary indeed must have miscalculated her sins.

Luke's Shimon, the Pharisee, eating with Jesus, the friend of tax collectors, may well have been peg to which the rabbis attached their parody featuring Shimon ben Shetach, the alleged Patriarch, who lingers in hell until Mary will take his place. The story here in effect continues the precise and playful employment of names we saw in the case of Rabbi 'Lazarus' discussing Gehanna. We should then note that the Christian tradition identifies the anonymous sinful woman tending to Jesus in Luke's gospel as Mary of Bethany, the sister of the resurrected Lazarus and of Martha, as is well attested in the Arabic Diatessaron:[93]

> Now there was a man who was sick, *'l'z'r* of the town of Bethany, the brother of Mary (*mry'm*) and Martha (*mrt'*). This is the Mary who anointed the feet of Jesus with perfume and wiped them with her hair. *'l'z'r* who was sick was her brother.

Matthew 9.9–9.10), and among his most famous disciples is Matthew the tax collector (*mty mks'*, ibid. 10.1, duly remembered in Bavli Sanhedrin 43a), to whom the authorship of a Gospel was firmly attributed in the fifth century.

92 'Eating' and 'drinking' are of course hardly restricted to polemical purposes in the Yerushalmi, see e.g. *Pea* 8.9 21b, 18, as well as Genesis Rabbah 35.3 and Leviticus Rabbah 7.4.

93 Ciasca A., *Tatiani Evangeliorum Harmoniae Arabica* (Rome: 1888) fol. 142; Arabic Diatessaron 37:46–37:48, trans. H.W. Hogg. The tradition of identifying this sinner with Martha reaches back to the Gospel of John (11:1–2); the Arabic names for *mrym* and *mrth'* are cognate with the Peshitta of John.

In the Christian tradition, Jesus eats and drinks with a tax collector many a times, and once with Shimon the Pharisee, and he is tended to by the sinful Mary. The Western Christian as well as the Babylonian rabbinic tradition both associate this Mary of Bethany, who tends to Jesus with her hair, with Mary Magdalene, allowing us to posit such a hybrid of Mary Magdalene and Mary of Bethany, the sinful woman, as the inmate of the Yerushalmi's hell. It is this woman called Mary who seeks to hide her sins like an onion in many peels. While Matthew posits that 'the tax-collectors and the whores are going into the kingdom of God ahead of you', the Yerushalmi takes exception from this view, and instead praises Mary's sister Martha in the prequel to the story, as we shall see.[94]

5 The Women in the Cave

The sequel of the Yerushalmi story relates the famous incident how Shimon, the Patriarch, manages to overpower eighty witches in a cave in Ashkelon. The basis of the story in Mishna Sanhedrin 6:4 only mentions that he hanged eighty women in Ashkelon, all of the Yerushalmi's embellishments hence call for interpretation. The scene, for example, is set on a day of a rainstorm, *bywm sgryr*, a rare Hebrew insertion in a mostly Aramaic text. The Yerushalmi thereby possibly transposes a motif from the story of the Christian virgin, whose father was buried on the day of a rain storm. At the same time, however, the Yerushalmi's term, *bywm sgryr*, is itself rare in Palestinian rabbinic literature, and in effect marks a playful reference to Proverbs 27:15: 'a constant dripping on a stormy day (*bywm sgryr*) is what a woman of disputes (*w'št mdwnym*)

---

[94] We should not imagine the rabbis as carefully distinguishing between various Christian women called Mary whom they *all* presented as engaging in illicit intercourse. Accordingly, Mary Magdalene (*mrym mgdl'*), is understood as plaiting (*mgdl'*) 'women('s hair)' in Bavli *Shabbat* 104b. The Bavli in turn fuses Mary Magdalene with Mary, the mother of Jesus (see also Sanhedrin 67a) and even makes a point about the confusion of various Marys in *Hagiga* 4b, a tendency also found in various Christian traditions: the Gospel's sinful Mary of Bethany is also fused with Mary Magdalene in the Western Christian tradition (attested since Gregory the Great), and Mary the Mother of Jesus is often indistinguishable from Mary Magdalene in some Gnostic traditions; see the important volume: Jones F.S. (ed.), *Which Mary?: The Marys of Early Christian Tradition* (Leiden: 2003). On Mary's fate in rabbinic literature see Schäfer, *Jesus in the Talmud* 15–24; esp. Visotzky B., *Fathers of the World: Essays in Rabbinic and Patristic Literature* (Tübingen: 1995) 85–92. Likewise, the two Gospel persona by the name of Lazarus, one the poor man who dies and one who is resurrected, are of course kept separate in the Christian tradition, the Yerushalmi may or may not have fused them in its allusions.

is like.'⁹⁵ When Shimon ben Shetach then answers to the women in the cave, who demand how he reached them on such a rainy, that he walked 'in between the raindrops,' we should most probably understand the scriptural allusion as a playful misogynous aside: he avoids these raindrops, and these women 'of disputes' (*mdwnym*, from the root *dyn*, "to judge"), are themselves about to be judged for their transgressions. The allusion to the Bible sets the scene for a richly painted intertextual gem.

The scene in general richly evokes the imagery of Greek mythology and Bacchic orgies. The Yerusahlmi depicts Shimon as promising the sexual encounters the women desire, but then instructing his young male helpers to 'embrace and lift (*ygwp*) the witches away from the earth (*m'r"*).' Once they do so, he asks the witches to repeat the miracle they wrought previously, but the witches do not succeed anymore 'in what she did', i.e. in producing miracles. Shimon has them crucified one by one (according to Sanhedrin, collectively in Hagiga). The scene quite closely evokes a common motif of Greek mythology, the battle between Heracles and the Libyan giant Antaeus, son of Gaia, the earth. As Ovid puts it, Heracles, by lifting Antaeus, deprived him 'of his parental nourishment' (*alimenta parentis*);⁹⁶ hitherto, the contact with earth had made Antaeus invincible. This also explains why the witches lost their powers when lifted. The myth's pertinence becomes most apparent when considering the Yerushalmi's rendering in light of the vivid depictions of the battle not only in art, but also throughout Greek literature, for example by Philostratus the Elder:

> So Herakles, at a loss how to deal with Gaia (Earth), *has caught Antaios by the middle just above the waist, where the ribs are*, and set him upright on his thigh, still gripping his arms about him; then pressing his own fore-arm against the pit of Antaios' stomach, now flabby and panting, he squeezes out his breath and slays him by forcing the points of his ribs into his liver. Doubtless you see Antaios groaning and looking to Gaia (Earth), who does not help him, while Herakles is strong and smiles at his achievement.⁹⁷

---

95 The term *bywm sgryr* is used, e.g., in Yerushalmi *Megillah* 1.11, 71d (23), paralleled in Bereshit Rabbah 1.11; the rabbis are portrayed as not assembling in the study house because of the storm.
96 Ovid, *Metamorphoses* 9.183.
97 Philostratus the Elder, *Imagines* 2.21 (trans. A. Fairbanks, my emphasis), cf. e.g. Apollodorus 2.5.11 and Diodorus Siculus 4.17.4.

The battle's motifs the Yerushalmi imitates – grabbing by the middle, lifting of the ground, losing miraculous powers, and finally, gruesome death by suffocation – clearly mark the Yerushalmi's play on Greek myth, presenting Shimon as the victor over witches and Christian Mary alike.

Indeed, the Yerushalmi's sustained literary play on Greek myth is again intricate, intimate, and pervasive in this part of the scene. Shimon demands entry by the cave by calling out *'wym 'wym!*', a formula that has rightfully been associated with Bacchic orgies by Esther Dvorjetski; the entry formula, and the orgiastic group sex promised by Shimon, indeed very closely corresponds to alleged Dionysiac practices.[98] Furthermore, Dvorjetski shows that the rabbis with good reason associated the coastal cities of Southern Palestine with gentile cultic activities deep into Late Roman times; she also points to the prominence of Bacchic imagery in many of the caves that have indeed been excavated in Ashkelon. One could add to her important insights that some of the caves discovered around Ashkelon were used by lovers who left graffito there, while others bear imagery of naked male youths, evoking even more immediately the erotic exploits promised by the young men employed by Shimon.[99]

Dionysiac paganism in coastal southern Palestine, of course, is not challenged for the first time in the Yerushalmi. Dvorjestki cites illuminating examples from contemporary patristic and pagan polemics against Bacchic festivals associated with the region. When the Yerushalmi hence employs pagan motifs in its mythical battle against the witches portrayed as Bacchantes, it both imitates and rejects Christian discourse. On the one hand, it partially adopts the Christian claim to battle against the pagans of the coastal cities of southern Palestine, as epitomized most dramatically perhaps in the stories about Porphyry of Gaza.[100] On the other hand, however, it portrays the Christians themselves as pagans by associating the Bacchantes with Christian women, as we shall see. Moreover, we should consider that the Yerushalmi's evocation of a Bacchic orgy has an illuminating parallel in Eusebius' *Praeparatio evangelica*:

---

98 See Dvorjetski E., "A Talmudic Reality in the Erotic Rituals of Dionysiac-Bacchic Cult", in Zinguer I. (ed.), *Dionysos: Origines et Résurgences* (Paris: 2001) 79–93, 84. Typical forms of the exclamation include εὐέν, εὐάν εὐοῖ, see Liddell H.G. – Scott R., *Greek-English Lexicon* (Oxford: 1996) 705; 711; 724; as well as the repeated 'εὐαν εὐαν!' (see below). The exclamation, hence, was a fluid one, and the shift from a final [n] to an [m] in Hebrew *'wym* should not distract us. On *'wyym* as plural of *'w*, 'or', see also Yerushalmi *Shevu'ot* 4.5, 35c (61–64).

99 See Dvorjetski, "A Talmudic Reality" 91; see also Ory J., "A Painted Tomb Near Ascalon", *Quarterly of the Department of Antiquities in Palestine* 8 (1938) 38–44; Kogan-Zehavi E., "A Painted Tomb of the Roman Period at Migdal Ashqelon", *'Atiqot* 37 (1999) 181–209 [Hebrew; English summary 179–181].

100 See Dvorjetski, "A Talmudic Reality" 88–89; Zellentin, *Rabbinic Parodies* 193–195.

The Bacchae celebrate in their orgies the frenzy of Dionysus, keeping their monthly holiday with a feast on raw flesh, and, in performing the distribution of the flesh of the slaughtered victims, are crowned with their wreaths of serpents, shouting: 'Eve, Eve!' (Εὐαν Εὐαν), she through whom the deception crept in: a consecrated serpent, too, is the symbol of the Bacchic orgies. Therefore, according to the exact pronunciation of the Hebrews, the name Eve (Εὐα), with an aspirate, is at once interpreted as the female serpent.[101]

Disregarding the difficult of equation of Eve and the snake linguistically, Eusebius' facile equation of the Bacchic orgy with womanhood per se, as epitomized by Eve, still helps us understand the Yerushalmi. Both the rabbis and the church fathers in effect construct autonomous females in terms of cultic licentiousness, as epitomized in turn by the Bacchantes. Paganism, in the fourth century had been fully infused with Judaeo-Christian language, and vice versa, and the Yerushalmi in turn uses the Bacchantes to turn on the church fathers.

Indeed, in order to assess the Yerushalmi's employment of anti-pagan language against the women, we should remember that it tells the story about the killing of the Bacchic witches with the help of young men in clean garments in order to explain not how Eve contracted the original sin, but why one very specific licentious woman, Mary, will not be replaced by Shimon ben Shetach. The charge that Christians were engaged in Bacchic banquets and magic, of course, is well attested since Celsus.[102] Hence, we should consider that the Yerushalmi's association of Mary and other women in a cave is closely connected to the gospel narrative: namely, Mary of Magdalene and Mary, the mother of Jesus and James, in the company of other women, are portrayed as encountering men in bright garments when entering Jesus' burial cave, which had been miraculously opened by the angels, in Luke:

> They came to the tomb [...]. And there were with them other women (nš'). And they found the stone rolled away from the tomb. And they entered in, but they did not find the body of Jesus. And it came to pass as they were confused about this, behold, two men (gbryn) stood above them, and their robes (lbwšhwn) were shining; And they were afraid and bowed

---

[101] Eusebius of Caesarea, *Praeparatio Evangelica*, trans. K. Mras, in *Eusebius Werke*, vol. 8 (Berlin: 1954–1956) TLG 2018.001; modified translation according to Gifford: Eusebius of Caesarea, *Praeparatio Evangelica*, trans. E.H. Gifford, in *Eusebius of Caesarea: Praeparatio Evangelica* (Oxford: 1903), ad loc; Eusebius in turn cites Clement of Alexandria, *Protrepticus* 2.12.2.

[102] For a useful summary see Visotzky, *Fathers of the World* 75–81.

their faces to the earth (*b'r'*), and they said to them, 'Why do you seek the living among the dead? He is not here, but has risen [...]' They were Mary (*mrym*) of Magdala, and Joanna, and Mary the mother of James, and the rest who were with them [...].[103]

Mark, moreover, portrays the angel as a *young* man, akin to the Yerushalmi's young men, and the variant description of clothing throughout the gospels allows us to comprehend why the Yerushalmi chooses 'clean' clothes:

> And they entered the tomb, and saw a young man, sitting on the right, covered with a white robe; and they were astonished. But he said to them: 'Do not be afraid. You seek Jesus the Nazarene, who was crucified (Harklean: *d'ṣtlb*); he has risen; he is not here.'[104]

The Yerushalmi, it seems, by placing Mary in hell and the women in a cave, constructs a neat inversion of the dramatic ending of the gospel, which becomes most apparent when we allow for a fuzzy reconstruction based on all the evidence:

– In the Gospel, the cave opens miraculously, and the women (*nš'*) enter; in the Yerushalmi, Shimon enters by deceit, finding the women (*nšym*) inside.
– In the Gospel, the women find young men (*gbryn*) whose shining clothes (*wšlbwnwn*) are a sign of their supernatural character; in the Yerushalmi, the 'young men' (*gwbryn bḥwryn*) are put in 'clean robes' (*lbwšwn nqyyn*) in order to deceive the women into thinking that they are indeed supernatural.[105]
– In the Gospel, they bow their faces to the earth (*b'r'*), in the Yerushalmi, they are lifted away from the earth (*m'r'*).
– In the Gospel, they look for the dead, crucified (*d'ṣtlb*) Jesus who in effect is alive; in the Yerushalmi, they find death themselves, when the young men crucify (*wšlbwnwn*) them.

The text is less keen on constructing a precise imitation of the Gospel, but rather explores the question which outfit for the young men, in the imagination of the Christian Other, would be especially suitable for the task of convincing the Bacchantes that they are supernatural beings. Mary is in hell already, and the rabbis hardly imagined Jesus' burial cave to be in Ashkelon. Rather, the

---

103 Luke 24:2–10.
104 Mark 16:4–6.
105 We find a similar story in Matthew 28:2–28:6, here, the appearance of the angels 'was like lightning, and his clothing (*wlbwšh*) white as snow.' Especially in light of the fluid depiction in the gospels, the Yerushalmi's 'clean' robes would certainly evoke the Gospel's 'white', 'shining', or 'bright' ropes.

Yerushalmi teaches us that since the gospel tells that young men in shining cloths have convinced Mary Magdalene before, the trick should work again. The side-effect of this strategy, of course, is to cast doubt on the Christian narrative claims to the supernatural in general. By engineering a magical deceit based on the building stones of the gospel narrative, the Yerushalmi leaves no doubt that the women in the gospel were, in effect, in delusion, as Luke portrays the disciples' reaction when they first hear about the resurrection.

Likewise, the miracles wrought by the women, the magical procurement of 'bread', 'cooked food' (*tbšylyn*), and 'wine,' as well as 'meat' in Hagiga, seeks to associate Christian miracle stories with magic, and with the Bacchic rites respectively, employing another long-standing polemical convention. The Bacchic rites as perceived in the fourth century, as we have seen in Eusebius, consist of the consumption of raw meat; intoxicating wine is of course part of their very essence. At the same time, the four items magically procured in Hagiga, bread, meat, cooked food, and wine, in conjunction with the vessels and baskets in which the young men are placed, puts us again squarely in the world of Jesus' culinary miracles. It is again not any single one of these miracles that the Yerushalmi addresses in any detail, the text rather summarily associates all of them with Shimon's deceptive employment of false magic, pointing to the fact that such miracles usually belong to the realm of charlatanry. While the Assis fragment does not provide the pristine text we possess for the rest of the narrative, the Yerushalmi's allusion to the gospel can still be recuperated as in line with its textual strategy to parody the gospels throughout this story:

– By procuring bread and cooked food, in both Hagiga and Sanhedrin, the Yerushalmi integrates the feeding of the thousands:[106] when Jesus' disciples suggest that the crowds go and buy food for themselves, Jesus takes 'five loaves and two fish' to feed them all. The fish have been explicitly understood as cooked by the church fathers.[107]
– When the witches magically procure wine, in both tractates, the Yerushalmi evokes the Wedding of Cana, where Jesus miraculously produces wine.[108]

---

106 Matthew 14:16–21. See also Matthew 15:32–8; Mark 8:1–9; John 6:1–14; Diatessaron 18:22–46; 23.5–12.
107 Clement of Alexandria, for example, builds his model of frugality on 'the bread [...] and the cooked fish (τοὺς ἰχθύας τοὺς ὀπτούς)' with which Jesus feasted his disciples, *Pedagogus* 2.1.13.2; Clément d'Alexandrie, *Le pedagogue*, ed. and trans. Harl M. – Marrou H.-I. – Matray C. – Mondésert C. (Paris: 1960–1970) TLG 0555.002.
108 John 2:1–11; Diatessaron 5:22–35.

- Especially by adding meat, in Hagiga, the Yerushalmi fuses the Bacchic rites and the Eucharist, during which bread and wine transform into Jesus' blood and flesh.[109]
- The Yerushalmi tells how Shimon takes the eighty young men, procures them with clean robes, places them in pots, and covers their heads with baskets (*wkpwnwn*, a loanword from Greek pl. κόφινοι). We already saw how the 'young men' and the 'clean robes' parody elements from the resurrection narratives. Now we see that *all* of the props employed by Shimon point to the gospels' miracles: after feeding the thousands, the disciples take the leftovers and fill twelve baskets (*qwpynyn*, equally a loanword from Greek pl. κόφινοι, κοφίνους in the Greek gospels), and Jesus, while Jesus' magical production of wine occurs in large stone jars.

All of the Yerushalmi's imitations in this passage, to reiterate, are programmatically fuzzy: fish is more specific than food, pots are not jars, clean robes are neither necessarily white nor shiny, and so on. None of the Yerushalmi's 'parallels' with the gospel narratives are intended to be 'striking,' there certainly is no 'smoking gun' that would force the Yerushalmi's audience to consider the Christian intertexts. Instead, the Yerushalmi portrays the women in the cave by evoke the general aura of Christian magic as perceived by its sense of Christian myth. Yet the intertextuality is rich, and the deictic threshold accordingly low, and once the rabbinic audience grasps that the Bacchic witches stand for Christian magic and morals, the text avails itself of its freedom to defamiliarize the resurrection narrative to even greater polemical effect. Celsus would have rejoiced.

The execution of the witches, hence, is a playful illustration of how broadly the rabbis levelled the charge of magic against Jesus and his followers, as of course the Christians did against the Jews.[110] As summarized in appendix 1, the entire Yerushalmi passage is indeed a parodic pastiche of Gospel passages, as understood in the fifth century. We can now turn to the Yerushalmi's preceding narrative about the alternative identity of the patriarch, which is connected not only by halakhic inquiry, but also by its continuous parody of the *same* gospel passages: we will actually encounter not only one Yehuda, but also the other female protagonist of Luke's story, Martha, Mary's sister, who in the Yerushalmi took centre stage as the pious hostess of Yehuda ben Tabai and his lewd disciple. The Yerushalmi's redactional surface as well as its components hence deeply engage their Late Roman context.

---

109   John 6:46–56; Matthew 26:29–9; Mark 14:22–5; Luke 22:17–20; Diatessaron 19:46; 45:10–22.
110   See Schäfer, *Jesus in the Talmud* 35–39; 102–106; for the Christian countercharge see e.g. Epiphanius, *Panarion* II.30.12.4–5.

6   Out of Egypt: Jesus and the Lewd Disciple

To reiterate, just before relating the incident in Ashkelon that leads to an argument for the patriarchate of Shimon ben Shetach, the Yerushalmi first tells a story to argue that not Shimon, but Yehuda ben Tabai held this office. The incident is set in Alexandria and, according to Sanhedrin, on the road back to Jerusalem. Hagiga imagines a sea journey; Ashkelon is a likely stop in both cases. Yet beyond the geographic proximity, the narrative appears at first to be unconnected to the following one about the tour of hell – the only apparent continuity is the fact that this incident presupposes the patriarchate of one of the two officials under discussion. Both passages, however, hold the key for each other through their respective tacit engagement with elements of Christian narratives, illustrating that the Yerushalmi here structures both the separate stories and its redactional surface around its polemical engagement of Late Roman discourse:

> The one who said that Yehuda ben Tabai was Patriarch: the event in Alexandria supports him [...].
> The sons of Jerusalem[111] wanted to appoint Yehuda ben Tabai Patriarch in Jerusalem, and he did not accept it.[112]
> He fled (*'rq*) and went (*w"zl*) to Alexandria.
> And the sons of Jerusalem wrote: 'From Jerusalem the Great to Alexandria the Small, How long should my betrothed (*'rwsy*) sit with you,[113] and I sit (as a) deserted wife (*'gwmh*) in my house?'[114]
> (Yehuda) left and went (*myyty*) on a street.[115] He said: 'Do you remember the landlady (*mrth*) of the house who received us (*qbltn*, i.e. well) and was pious (*whsydh*)?'[116]
> Said to him one of his students (*'m(r) l(yh) ḥd mn tlmydwy*): 'Her eye (*'yynh*) was protruding (*šwwrh*).'
> He said to him: 'Two (sins) are upon you!

---

111   'The sons of Jerusalem' is missing in manuscript Leiden of Hagigah, yet added by a later hand.
112   'And he did not accept it' is missing in Sanhedrin and Hagigah.
113   According to Hagigah and the Assis fragment of Sanhedrin. Sanhedrin has: 'How long should my husband (*b'l*) dwell in you?'
114   Sanhedrin then continues with the narrative about Yehuda ben Tabai (see below), only Hagigah and the Assis fragment record the subsequent incident of the lewd disciple. Since the parallel of the narrative in the Babylonian Talmud was censored, medieval censorship may equally be the reason for its conspicuous excision in Sanhedrin as well.
115   Hagigah has 'boat.'
116   Following the Assis fragment, Hagigah is garbled here.

> First, that you looked at her,
> And second, that you suspected me to have looked at her!
> Did I speak about looks? No, I only spoke about her service (*bʿwbdh*)!'
> And (Yehuda) was angry at (the student),[117] and (the student) died.[118]

We learn that Yehuda ben Tabai tried to avoid being drafted into the office of Patriarch, perhaps in response to the tumultuousness of his times.[119] He flees to Alexandria, whereupon the Jerusalemites engage in strikingly matrimonial language in order to express the urgency of their desire to make him patriarch. Yehuda finally heeds their request and returns, delayed by a tragicomical incident of an ogling disciple.

Yehuda inquires whether his students remember a certain landlady, whom he describes as having received them with great piety. One student misunderstands his question as inquiring not about the woman's service or her piety, but about her attractiveness, which he subsequently denies because one of her eyes was 'protruding', or even 'jutted out', using a Syriac rather than rabbinic Aramaic term, and already thereby de-familiarizing the story for its rabbinic audience.[120] Enraged, Yehuda accuses the student of having ogled the woman, and of assuming his teacher to have done likewise. The student then 'departs', or more likely dies, as a result of Yehuda's anger; apparently, the student has sinned so egregiously that there seems to be no chance for atonement. The punishment is harsh given that ogling, while certainly not encouraged, is to the best of

---

[117] Hagigah has *wkʿs ʿlwy*, the Assis fragment has *wʿqpd*.

[118] Following the Assis fragment. Hagigah has 'and he went,' meaning that either Yehuda or the student left, or euphemistically that the student died.

[119] For an historical contextualization of this story see Schäfer P., "'From Jerusalem the Great to Alexandria the Small': The Relationship between Palestine and Egypt in the Graeco-Roman Period", in: Schäfer P. (ed.), *The Talmud Yerushalmi and Graeco-Roman Culture* (Tübingen: 1998) I, 129–140.

[120] Following Stephen Gero's reading 'a blind eye which is literally hanging out of its socket'; see idem, "The Stern Master and his Wayward Disciple: A 'Jesus' Story in the Talmud and in Christian Historiography", *Journal for the Study of Judaism* 25 (1994) 287–311, 300 n. 34. The root *š-w-w-r* (or *š-b-r*) is a hapax legomenon in rabbinic literature, and perhaps intentionally evoking a non-rabbinic form of Aramaic – it is indeed a Syriac word, clearly employed to evoke the narrative's Christian context! Michael Sokoloff's translation of the cognate Syriac term of the more accurate spelling *šwwrh* in manuscript Assis, or *šbrh* in Hagigah, is 'to jump out, leap', 'to be expelled, burst forth', or, for an eye, to 'bulge' in idem, *A Syriac Lexicon* (Piscataway: 2009), s.v., (ignoring the even more graphic Syriac examples Gero suggests). In his *Dictionary of Jewish Palestinian Aramaic*, however, Sokoloff translates the eyes in the Yerushalmi passage at hand as 'protruding' (ibid. 540), effectively glossing over the likely intentionally grotesque image of the eye jutted out.

my knowledge not attested as a sin in early rabbinic literature.[121] Sexual coveting, however, is a central theme in Christian ethics; accordingly, Stephen Gero's seminal study of the passage has long established that the Yerushalmi's narrative of the lewd disciple shares a Christian narrative and moral framework.[122]

The most important example demonstrating the Christian context of the story are the sixth century *Lives of the Monks of Palestine* by Cyril of Scythopolis. Here, the Christian Saint Sabas travels with one of his disciples. Upon meeting a pretty young woman, he asks the disciple: 'Look how excellent is the maiden who passed by – even though she is one-eyed (μονόφθαλμος).'[123] The disciple denies this, stating that she did in fact have two eyes (τοὺς δύο ὀφθαλμοὺς ἔχει), and in fact has very good eyes, whereupon Sabas reprimands the disciple for having ogled the woman and (temporarily) banishes him.[124] The fact that the earliest attestation of this particular version of the story post-dates the Yerushalmi should not detract us from its relevance here since a very similar story is already attested in the fifth century *Epic Histories Attributed to P'awstos Buzand*.[125] The Yerushalmi's story of Yehuda and his disciple, like that of Sabas and his disciple, are very similar indeed. A master alleges that a woman they encountered while traveling was 'pretty' and 'delectable' and a student insists that she was in effect one-eyed. In his answer the student reveals that he has ogled the woman, and the master reprimands him.

Gero argues that the Yerushalmi lacks 'awareness of the Christian (or Christianized) character of the adopted anecdote', and I agree that the Yerushalmi once again fully absorbs the Christian narrative and moral framework.[126] Yet, contrary to Gero's claim, I argue that the Yerushalmi does show full awareness of the Christian character of the story. This becomes clear when

---

121 Cf. Bavli *Nedarim* 20a and Brodsky D., *A Bride Without a Blessing: a Study in the Redaction and Content of Massekhet Kallah and its Gemara*, Texts and Studies in Ancient Judaism 118 (Tübingen: 2006) 127. For the dangers of lustful gazing in biblical discourse see Proverbs 5–7.
122 Gero, "The Stern Master" 287–311.
123 See Gero's discussion of the translation 'excellent' in idem, "The Stern Master" 296 n. 23.
124 See Schwartz E., *Kyrillos von Skythopolis* (Leipzig: 1939) IL.2, 85f. On the history of Saba see the excellent volume edited by Patrich J., *The Sabaite Heritage in the Orthodox Church from the Fifth Century to the Present* (Leuven: 2001).
125 Garsoïan N.G., *The Epic Histories attributed to P'awstos Buzand (Buzandaran Patmut'iwnk')* (Cambridge, MA: 1989) 207; discussed by Gero, "The Stern Master" 292–294.
126 See Gero, "The Stern Master" 296. Gero rightly concludes that 'the fact that there is a close relationship among the several versions of the story, Christian and Jewish, is evident. That the names of the protagonists are changed, along with other variations of detail, in the course of the repeated telling of what basically is the same moralizing anecdote has many parallels, in particular in hagiographic literature, and occasions no difficulty'; ibid., 297.

considering that the Yerushalmi, when retelling this story, parodies several Gospel passages, among them those it also engages in the subsequent narrative about the two pious disciples of Ashkelon.

The most important Gospel passage in the Yerushalmi's parody also purports the fact that the story originated in a Christian framework – it can only be understood in its exegetical context of Matthew 18:8–9. Cyril's story, namely, depicts a two-eyed woman whom the master presents as one-eyed, whereas the story attributed to P'awstos Buzand, much like the rabbinic story, depicts a student as insisting that a woman was truly one-eyed in response to his master's ambiguous praise for her. As Gero noted, both Christian stories are inspired by the Gospel of Matthew, especially the Greek for 'one-eyed', μονόφθαλμος, and 'having two eyes' τοὺς δύο ὀφθαλμοὺς ἔχει in Cyril, are indeed Gospel citations.[127] The story of Saba is indeed modeled precisely on the Gospel passage quoted above (47): 'if your hand or your foot offends you, cut it off and throw it away [...] and if your eye offends you, remove it and throw it away from you; it is better for you to go through life with one eye (μονόφθαλμος) rather than having two eyes and fall in to the Gehenna of fire.'[128] And this is precisely the passage the Yerushalmi spoofs when the pious disciple, in the subsequent story, seeks to impress Shimon ben Shetach, by literally removing his eye. Hence, the same passage from Matthew, exhorting one to take out one's eye, perpetuated in Christian ascetic discourse, is also the very passage the Yerushalmi will re-enact as a spoof in the subsequent story discussed above, when the pious student in hell is instructed to 'take out your eye, and it will come on your hand' in order to prevent Shimon ben Shetach from falling into the Gehenna.[129]

The Yerushalmi hence evokes the passage known from Matthew twice in an ascetic context, once in each of the two stories about the identity of the patriarch. Once it does so in the story about Shimon ben Shetach, as described above. Again it does so in the story about Yehudah, where it portrays the woman's eye as 'jutting out' in a context of ogling, akin to the story of Sabas. Here, it enacts the Gospel's moral maxim: 'But I say to you, that whoever looks at a woman with the desire to covet her, has already committed adultery with her in his heart.'[130] Now we understand the double indignation of Yehudah ben

---

[127] See Gero, "The Stern Master" 296 n. 24.
[128] Matthew 18:8–9.
[129] While Matthew depicts Gehenna as fiery, fire as an ingredient of hell does not enter the rabbinic tradition prior to the Bavli, see Himmelfarb, *Tours of Hell* 111f.
[130] Matthew 5.27–5.30 repeats the full saying: 'You have heard that it is said, "You shall not commit adultery." But I say to you, that whoever looks at a woman with the desire to covet her, has already committed adultery with her in her heart. If your right eye causes you to sin, tear it out and throw it away; it is better for you to lose one of your members than for your whole body to be thrown into hell. And if your right hand causes you to sin, cut it

Tabai in the Yerushalmi as a Gospel parody, when he scolds the student for having looked at a woman with the desire to covet her: 'first that you looked at her and second, that you suspected me of having looked at her!'

Already now we can see the coherence of the Yerushalmi's two passages, and their consistent parody of Christian texts, in fuller light. Both passages retell Christian monastic hagiographical material, known from the Sayings of the Desert Fathers and from the Lives of the Monks of Palestine respectively, and integrate it into a rabbinic framework, fully participating in the Christian narrative and moral paradigm. At the same time, both Yerushalmi passages focus on aspects of the Gospel that are central to patristic discourse and reenact them as a spoof, clearly distancing themselves from the Christian baggage of the narratives – they eat the date while throwing away the stone. As we will see, moreover, the entire story of the master and his lewd disciple, in effect, prepares the parodic pastiche of further Gospel passages which the second passage will continue.[131]

To begin with, the Yerushalmi, when parodically engaging the image of Jesus' friendship with tax collectors and sinners, evokes the above quotes narrative in Luke 7:33–50 about a certain woman who had wiped Jesus' feet with her hair. The woman's name had become Mary, the sister of Martha, long before the time of the Yerushalmi. Mary, the Yerushalmi argues, was not forgiven her sins in the slightest, as the pious student can see for himself when visiting hell. We now can appreciate the Yerushalmi's story about the piety and service of the landlady – *mrth* in rabbinic Aramaic – in light of a cognate story about the piety and service of the sisters Mary and Martha in Luke:

> And it came to pass while (Jesus and his disciples) were on the road (*b'wrh'*) to a certain village; and a woman named Martha (*mrt'*) received him (*qblth*, i.e. Jesus) into her house. And she had a sister whose name was Mary, and she came and sat at the feet of our Lord and listened to his words. But Martha was busy with much service (*btšmšt'*), and she came and said to him: 'My Lord, you do not seem to care that my sister has left me to serve (*lmšmšh*) alone? Tell her to help me.' Jesus answered and said to her: 'Martha, Martha, you are worried and excited about many things; but one thing is more important; and Mary has chosen the good portion (*tbt'*) for herself, which shall not be taken away from her.'[132]

---

off and throw it away; it is better for you to lose one of your members than for your whole body to go into hell.' See also Arabic Diatessaron 8:58–8.61.
131 The texts are juxtaposed in appendix 1, 71–87 below.
132 Luke 10:38–42. See the Arabic Diatessaron 13:30–13:35.

In order to appreciate the Yerushalmi's parody about the service of a certain *mrt'* who received (*qbltn*) Yehuda ben Tabai and his disciples, we should note that in the Gospel of John, the same story includes another Yehuda:

> Six days before the Passover Jesus came to Bethany, where Lazarus was, whom Jesus had raised from the dead. And they gave him a banquet there; Martha served, but Lazarus was one of the guests who were with him. Mary took a cruse containing pure and expensive nard, anointed the feet of Jesus, and wiped his feet with her hair, and the house was filled with the fragrance of the perfume. And Yehuda (*yhwd'*) Iscariot, one of his disciples (*ḥd mn tlmydwhy*) who was about to betray him, said (*w'mr*), 'Why was not this oil sold for three hundred pennies and given to the poor (*lmskn'*)?'[133]

John, of course, suspects Yehuda of ill intent; yet in the version of Mark, Jesus simply answers 'Let her alone; why do you trouble her? She has performed a good service for me' (*'bd' špyr' 'bdt lwty*).[134] While we cannot be certain how the Yerushalmi's audience had heard this narrative, we now can, if we allow for the usual fuzziness, appreciate how the entire Yerushalmi story is populated by people re-enacting scenes and bearing names from the Gospels:

– In the Gospel, Jesus and his disciples are on the *road*, among them is *Yehuda* Iscariot; hence, the Yerushalmi sends Yehuda ben Tabai and his students on the road.
– Martha (*mrt'*) receives (*qblth*) Jesus into her house; the Yerushalmi lets a certain 'landlady', *mrth* in rabbinic Aramaic, receive (*qbltn*) the rabbis.
– Yehuda, one of Jesus' students (*ḥd mn tlmydwhy*), speaks (*w'mr*) to criticize him; the Yerushalmi introduces the Christian story about the bulging eye by having one of Yehuda's disciples (*ḥd mn tlmydwy*) speak (*'mr*) to him.
– Jesus rejects Yehuda's argument, insisting that Martha has indeed performed a good service for him (*'bd' špyr' 'bdt*); the Yerushalmi has Yehuda give the same answer in order to reject his student's argument: 'No, I only spoke about her service (*b'wbdh*)!'
– Yehuda Iscariot, of course, dies prematurely,[135] as does Yehuda's disciple in the Yerushalmi.

In effect, the Yerushalmi turns the table on the two sisters, praising 'Martha' whom Jesus scolds, and soon thereafter consigning 'Mary', whose identity as

---

133 John 12:1–5.
134 Mark 14:6.
135 Matthew 27:5; Diatessaron 51:7–8.

a sinner is well established, to hell: she will be tortured in hell for her sins, and just as the tax-collector's good deed (*tybh*) has been taken away in the Yerushalmi, so will the good portion (*tbt'*) Luke had assigned to Mary accordingly be taken away. The Yerushalmi seeks to demolish the Gospel's narrative while sharing many, yet clearly not all, of its ethics.

The parodic gathering of gospel figures may only have one parallel in the fifth century: akin to the Christian *Cena Cypriani*, an early fifth century Latin text that parodically assembles a multitude of biblical figures at a freely retold wedding of Cana, the Yerushalmi's entire narrative is populated by gospel figures: on the left, Simon the Pharisee, Judas Iscariot, and the overzealous Martha, on the right, Mary and Lazarus. In the Yerushalmi, Shimon and Yehuda become patriarchs, Martha a pious hostess, and Rabbi Lazarus states that Mary hangs in hell.[136] The Yerushalmi here clearly suspects its rabbinic audience to know some Gospel passages as well as the Christian texts expects its own audience to know them!

In ever widening circles, the Yerushalmi's parody casts its own nets, and what some scholars have long suspected now turns out to be demonstrable as well: the flight of Yehuda ben Tabai and his return to Jerusalem are indeed closely related to the Gospel stories about the flight to Egypt.[137] Yet the relationship between the Yerushalmi and the gospel tradition is closer and more deeply parodic than has been realized. To reiterate, the Yerushalmi narrates this story as an argument that Yehuda ben Tabai was the patriarch. The men of Jerusalem want to appoint him, seemingly against his will: he fled (*'rq*), and went (*w'zl*) to Alexandria in Egypt, whereupon he is called back. The Yerushalmi here evokes another central passage in the Gospel of Matthew:

> The angel of the Lord appeared (*'thzy*) to Joseph in a dream (*bhlm'*), and said to him, 'Arise, take the infant boy and his mother, and flee (*w'rwq*) to Egypt, and stay there until I tell you [...]' Then Joseph rose up, took the infant boy and his mother in the night, and went (*w'zl*)[138] to Egypt. And he remained there until the death of Herod, so that what was said by the Lord through the prophet might be fulfilled, "I have called my son from Egypt" (Hosea 11.1). When King Herod died, the angel of the Lord appeared (*'thzy*) in a dream (*bhlm'*) to Joseph in Egypt. And he said to him, Arise, take the boy and his mother, and go to the land of Israel, for those

---

136 On the remarkable *Cena Cyprian* see Bayless M., *Parody in The Middle Ages: The Latin Tradition* (Ann Arbor: 1996).
137 See Gero, "The Stern Master" 291f. n. 11; Schäfer, *Jesus in the Talmud* 20.
138 Following the Sinaiticus and the Curetonianus, the Peshitta here repeats *'rq*, he fled.

who were seeking the boy's life are dead. So Joseph rose, took the boy and his mother, and he came to the land of Israel.[139]

It is in all likelihood the dream of the Christian virgin in the Sayings of the Desert Fathers that inspires the Yerushalmi to have the deceased student appear (*'thmy*) to his friend in a dream (*bhylm'*) in the sequel of the Yerushalmi, yet the imagery of a dream vision in this highly pertinent gospel passage adds to the sense of the Talmud's broad engagement with the same gospel narratives in both stories about potential patriarchs. One may even think that Yose(ph) ben Hanina was chosen to announce Mary's punishment to evoke his namesake here. Regardless, the path of Yehuda ben Tabai follows that of Jesus very closely. Both flee (*'rq* in the Yerushalmi, *w'rwq* in the Gospel) from Jerusalem, both go (*w'zl, w'zl*) to Egypt, both are being called back as family members, as son or as betrothed respectively, and both return.[140] Again, Yehudah here shouldn't be identified with Jesus or with his father Joseph, the Yerushalmi merely evokes the passage in order to eclipse its messianic portent – and to play a little more with the Other's text for the purpose, no less, to stablize the rabbis' moral universe.

We can now also make sense of the remarkable language the Yerushalmi uses to describe Jerusalem as a deserted wife, and Yehuda as her betrothed (*'rwsy* in Assis and Hagigah, or, more logically, as her husband, *b'l*, in Sanhedrin). Matrimonial language between Jerusalem and God is of course prevalent in prophetic language. In the Hebrew Bible, however, the groom or betrothed often is God rather than a human being.[141] The Gospels, in turn, depict Jesus throughout as the long awaited bridegroom, indicating such a marker of Christianity for the Yerushalmi's 'bridegroom' or 'husband', as well. For example, the Gospel of Luke also connects the image of Christ as bridegroom in connection with the highly pertinent imagery of 'eating and drinking with tax

---

139   Matthew 2:13–21. See Arabic Diatessaron 3:13–3:19.
140   Regarding Yehuda's odd flying (*'rq*) from his appointment as patriarch, and his return in a boat (*ylp'*), rather than on the street, in Hagigah, with his disciples (*tlmydwy*), we should also consider the following passage from the Gospel of John (6:15–6.21). 'But Jesus knew that they were ready to come and seize him to make him a king (*mlk'*), so he fled (Curetonianus: *'rq*) to the mountain alone. And when evening came, his disciples (*tlmydwhy*) went down to the sea and entered into a boat (Harklean: *l'lp'*), and were going to the port of Capernaum.' See also Arabic Diatessaron 18:47–19:13; here, Jesus *does* enter the boat. This tradition seems much less pertinent than the flight to Egypt, but it may help us understand the Yerushalmi's portrayal of Yehuda as refusing his election in the first place, and perhaps even the alternate means of transportation in Hagigah. The parallels, however, are too few to pursue this possibility.
141   See for example Isaiah 54. For the related question whether the woman in the Song of Songs is Israel or the Church see Hirshman M., *Rivalry of Genius: Jewish and Christian Biblical Interpretation in Late Antiquity* (Albany: 1996).

collectors and sinners', in opposition to those pious disciples of the Pharisees, who fast:

> Why do the disciples of John always fast and pray, and also those of the Pharisees; but yours eat and drink? He said to them, You cannot make the sons of the wedding feast fast so long as the bridegroom (*dḥtn'*) is with them. But the days will come when the bridegroom is taken from them; then they will fast in those days.[142]

The passage, like the ones discussed previously, associates the proclivity to eating, drinking, and the company of tax collectors of Jesus' disciples with the fact that Jesus is the bridegroom, the messianic betrothed of Luke's congregation. In the times of the Yerushalmi, Jesus' status as the bridegroom of church, or of the virgins, has become a central tenet in patristic discourse.[143] More specifically, the New Jerusalem in Revelation is a bride (*klt'*) for her husband (*b'l*) Jesus.[144] Hence, the Yerushalmi's choice to depict the patriarch Yehuda ben Tabai, the alleged patriarch, as the real husband (*b'l*) or bridegroom of Jerusalem, and the pious students Ashkelon as those who fast like the Pharisees' students in the gospels, makes most sense when understood as a response to these Christian claims about Jesus as the groom, again incorporating Christian imagery while imitating and eclipsing specific Gospel stories. It is not the written Gospel the Yerushalmi parodies, it is the free-floating association of motifs that marks the Gospel as lived by Christian neighbours, the holy men, and the Church Fathers of the time of its time. The main point of the Yerushalmi really *is* an argument for the identity of the patriarch, even if it remains unresolved, and perhaps offering some comic relief to a battered rabbinic audience.

It is paramount not to imagine the rabbis as studying the Gospels individually or in written form, but seeking to evoke the hearsay they had picked up from oral renderings. The rabbinic audiences' knowledge of these Gospel passages seems to have been clear enough for the parody to work, and vague

---

142   Luke 5:27–35. See the Arabic Diatessaron 7:9; 7:25–7:34, the imagery in Matthew 25, and the parallels in Mark 2:20 and Matthew 9:15.

143   The language is pervasive in Paul (e.g. 2 Corinthians 11:2), see also Methodius, *Banquet of the Ten Virgins* (Discourse 7), and Augustine, Sermon 55 "On the New Testament" 6. For a recent discussion see also Pagoulatos G., *Tracing the Bridegroom in Dura: The bridal Initiation Service of the Dura-Europos Christian Baptistery as Early Evidence of the Use of Images in Christian and Byzantine Worship* (Piscataway, NJ: 2008).

144   Revelation 21:2; cited according to Gwyn J., *The Revelation of John in Syriac Version Hitherto Unknown* (Piscataway, NJ: 2005) 26. The image of Jerusalem as a bride is not as widely discussed among the Church Fathers, but see Irenaeus, *Against Heresies* v.35.2.

enough to allow for the transgressions and inaccuracies that mark any polemical engagement. As is well known, only in the Bavli's retelling of the story of the stern master, the lewd disciple fully *becomes* Jesus of Nazareth. The Bavli sees his master's stern behaviour as the cause for Jesus' apostasy, for his turn to magic, and ultimately as the tragic cause of Christianity.[145] The authors of the Bavli are the only known historical audience of the Yerushalmi, and therefore, in the Bavli, we have historical evidence that part of the Yerushalmi's audience indeed grasped the Yerushalmi's tacit engagement of Christianity.

To be clear, the Yerushalmi's parody, in some ways does not go as far as the Bavli's explicit one, and while the text may well have identified Shimon ben Shetach with Simon the Pharisee, its lewd disciple should not be understood *as* Jesus, and Yehuda ben Tabai certainly not *as* Judas Iscariot. The Yerushalmi's parody is merely interested in creating an alter ego which can function as a vehicle for its anti-Christian polemics, and the unnamed disciple fulfils this task very well. The disciple, after, all, dies before re-entering Palestine, whereas Jesus returns from his own flight to Egypt. On the other hand, however, the Yerushalmi goes much further than the Bavli, in its engagement and re-enactment of a broad variety of Christian traditions, as I have argued that it does repeatedly.[146]

The Yerushalmi's intimacy with a number of Gospel passages in their patristic understanding should give us pause when considering how much Christianism there was in Jewish Palestine. The Christian intertexts of the long passage presented here span the entirety of the two Yerushalmi segments. The redactional layer of the Yerushalmi, as well as its narrative building blocks both engage their Late Roman context in a sustained way. In this instance at least, we cannot read the Yerushalmi on its own, we cannot derive any historical lessons about the first century BCE from it, and we cannot continue to understand classical rabbinic Judaism outside of history. The rabbis' chosen path to treat Christianity only tacitly includes a lot of noise beneath the halakhic surface. The Hellenistic genre of journeys to the underworld, and of comical inversion on the way, finds a worthy successor in the Yerushalmi, truly a Late Roman document.

---

145   *Sota* 47a; Sanhedrin 107b. The Bavli substitutes Joshua ben Perahiah for Shimon ben Shetach, and depicts the rabbinic disciple Jesus, as seeking to repent and as being rejected, akin to the temporary banishment, and in contrast to the eventual readmission, of Mar Saba's disciple. See Rubenstein J., *Stories of the Babylonian Talmud* (Baltimore: 2010) 116–149; Schäfer, *Jesus in the Talmud* 34–40.

146   See Zellentin, *Rabbinic Parodies* 137–236; now also Zellentin H., "Jerusalem Fell After Betar: The Christian Josephus and Rabbinic Memory", in Boustan R.S. – Herrmann K. – Leicht R. – Reed A.Y. – Veltri G. (eds.), *Envisioning Judaism: Studies in Honor of Peter Schäfer on the Occasion of his Seventieth Birthday* (Tübingen: 2013) I, 319–367.

Appendix 1
The Talmud Yerushalmi and its Palestinian and Babylonian Intertexts

All those who are stoned (to death) are hanged (afterwards, according to) the words of Rabbi Eli'ezer. And the sages said: Only the blasphemer and the idol worshipper is hanged.

A man is hanged with his face towards the people and a woman with her face towards the tree (according to) the words of Rabbi Eli'ezer, and the sages say that a man is hanged and a woman is not hanged.[147]

Yerushalmi Sanhedrin 6.9 (23c) according to the Assis fragment (see also Hagigah 2.2, 77d)	Palestinian Intertexts (Yerushalmi, Greek Gospels, and other rabbinic and Christian literature)	Babylonian Intertexts (Bavli, Peshitta, and other Christian literature)
1. What is the reason of Rabbi Eliezer (for his view in the Mishna that all those who are stoned to death are hanged afterwards)? 2. (He said): Just like the blasphemer (*mgdp*) who is stoned (to death) and hanged (afterwards) I bring you all the others who are that are stoned to death to be hanged. 3. What is the reason of the rabbanan (for their view)?	– Jesus is stoned and hanged in the Toldoth Yeshu tradition.[148] – Eliezer and Jesus traditions in Tosefta Hulin and Yerushalmi Mo'ed Qatan 3.1 (81c–d) – Judeans intend to stone Jesus for blasphemy. (John 10:33) – Jesus' blasphemy a pervasive topic in the Gospels. (Mattthew 9:3, 26:65, Luke 5:21)	On the eve of Passover, they hung Yeshu HaNotsri, and the herald went forth for forty days beforehand: Yeshu haNotsri will be stoned on the account of sorcery (*škyšp*, Sanhedrin 43a) The Jews answered, 'It is not for a good work that we are going to stone you, but because you are a blasphemer (*dmgdp*, John 10:33)

---

147 Mishna Sanhedrin 6.4.
148 According to T.-S. Misc. 35.88 and the two texts of ENA 2102 (Hillel Newman).

Yerushalmi Sanhedrin 6.9 (23c) according to the Assis fragment (see also Hagigah 2.2, 77d)	Palestinian Intertexts (Yerushalmi, Greek Gospels, and other rabbinic and Christian literature)	Babylonian Intertexts (Bavli, Peshitta, and other Christian literature)
4. (They said): Just like the blasphemer (*mgdp*) who stretched out his hands (*špšṭ ydw*) against the essence (i.e. God), is hanged, I include (only) all the rest of the those who stretch out their hands against the essence to be hanged. 5. Rabbi Li'ezer told them the incident of Shimon ben Shetach who hanged women in Ashkelon. 6. They told him: 'Eighty women he hanged and one does not judge two (capital cases) in one day'! 7. Some teach that Yehuda ben Tabai was Patriarch, and some teach that Shimon ben Shetach was Patriarch. 8. The one who said that Yehuda ben Tabai was Patriarch: the event in Alexandria supports him. 9. And the one who said Shimon ben Shetach was Patriarch: the even in Ashkelon supports him.	Jesus 'stretches out his hand' to perform miracles in the Gospels, a pervasive topic in later literature (e.g. Matthew 8:3, Luke 5:13, Acts of the Apostles 4:30, Acts of Philip, addition, Gospel of Nicodemus, 8 (24), Acts of Andrew and Mathias)	(Jesus) stretched out his hand (*wpšṭ 'ydh*) and touched him, saying, 'I do choose. Be made clean!' Immediately his leprosy was cleansed. (Matthew 8:3)

Yerushalmi Sanhedrin 6.9 (23c) according to the Assis fragment (see also Hagigah 2.2, 77d)	Palestinian Intertexts (Yerushalmi, Greek Gospels, and other rabbinic and Christian literature)	Babylonian Intertexts (Bavli, Peshitta, and other Christian literature)
10. The sons of Jerusalem wanted to appoint Yehuda ben Tabai Patriarch in Jerusalem, and he did not accept it. He fled (*'rq*) and went (*w'zl*) to Alexandria.	– Jesus to be made king, flees. (John 6:15) – Jesus flees to Egypt. (Matthew 2:13–4), see # 24.	– But Jesus knew that they were ready to come and seize him to make him a king, so he fled (c *'rq*) to the mountain alone. (John 6:15) – 'Escape (*w'rwq*) to Egypt, and stay there until I tell you [...]. Then Joseph rose up, took the infant boy and his mother in the night, and went (*w'zl*)[149] to Egypt. (Matthew 2:13–4, see # 11, 12 and 24) – King Jannai killed our rabbis, R. Joshua ben Perahia and Jesus fled to Alexandria of Egypt. (Sanhedrin 107b)

---

149 Following the Sinaiticus and the Curetonianus, the Peshitta has *'rq*, he fled.

Yerushalmi Sanhedrin 6.9 (23c) according to the Assis fragment (see also Hagigah 2.2, 77d)	Palestinian Intertexts (Yerushalmi, Greek Gospels, and other rabbinic and Christian literature)	Babylonian Intertexts (Bavli, Peshitta, and other Christian literature)
11. And the sons of Jerusalem wrote: 'From Jerusalem the Great to Alexandria the Small, How long should my betrothed (*'rwsy*) sit with you, and I sit (as a) deserted wife (*'gwmh*) in my house?'	– Jesus as bridegroom a pervasive optic in the Gospels. (Matthew 9:15, 25:1–10, Luke 5:34–35) – Jesus is called out of Egypt. (Matthew 2:14–15)	– As peace came, Shimon ben Shetah sent to him: 'From me, Jerusalem, the holy (*qdš*) city, to you, Alexandria of Egypt, my sister, my husband (*b'ly*) dwells in your midst, and sit desolately. (Sanhedrin 107b)[150] – And (Jesus) remained (in Egypt) until the death of Herod, so that what was said from the Lord by the prophet, might be fulfilled, I have called my son from Egypt. (Matthew 2:14–15, citing Hosea 11.1, see # 10, 12 and 24) – 'And I saw the holy city (*qdyšt'*), the new Jerusalem, [...] prepared as a bride adorned for her husband (*lb'lh*, Revelation 21:3)

---

150 Following the Vilna print, see also *Sotah* 47a. Manuscript Yad HaRav Herzog 1 has *'rq* instead of *'zl*.

Yerushalmi Sanhedrin 6.9 (23c) according to the Assis fragment (see also Hagigah 2.2, 77d)	Palestinian Intertexts (Yerushalmi, Greek Gospels, and other rabbinic and Christian literature)	Babylonian Intertexts (Bavli, Peshitta, and other Christian literature)
12. (Yehuda) left and went (*myyty*) on a street.	Jesus returns from Egypt. (Matthew 2:21)	So Joseph rose up, took the boy and his mother, and he went (*w't*') to the land of Israel. (Matthew 2:21, see #10, 11 and 24)
13. He said: 'Do you remember the landlady (*mrth*) of the house who had received us (*qbltn*) and was pious (*wḥsydh*)?'	Jesus is hosted attentively by the '*Martha*' and by the pious Mary (Luke 10:38–39), identified as the sinner of Luke 7:33–50 in later Christian tradition.	– [Joshua] said: I understand from this that there is peace. He stood up and found himself in a certain inn ('*wšpyz*'). They made him great honours ('*bdw lyh yqr' ṭwb*', Sanhedrin 107b)[151] – And it came to pass while they were on the way (*b'wrh'*) to a village, a woman named Martha (*mrth'*) received (*qblth*) (Jesus). And she had a sister whose name was Mary (*mrym*), and she came and sat at the feet of our Lord and listened to his words. (Luke 10:38–39, see #16, 20, 22, 32 and 33)

---

151 Following manuscript Yad HaRav Herzog 1, see also *Sotah* 47a.

Yerushalmi Sanhedrin 6.9 (23c) according to the Assis fragment (see also Hagigah 2.2, 77d)	Palestinian Intertexts (Yerushalmi, Greek Gospels, and other rabbinic and Christian literature)	Babylonian Intertexts (Bavli, Peshitta, and other Christian literature)
14. Said to him one of his students (*'mr lyh ḥd mn tlmydwy*): 'Rabbi, her eye (*'yynh*) was bulging (*šwwrh*).'	A student being attracted to a beautiful woman, depicted by his master as one-eyed, is a topic in Cyril of Scythopolis *Lives of the Monks of Palestine*	– He said: how nice is this inn (*'ksny'*). Said to him Jesus: Rabbi, here eyes (*'ynyh*) are narrow (*trwṭwt*, Sanhedrin 107b)[152] – Yehuda (*yhwd'*) Iscariot, one of his disciples (*ḥd mn tlmydwhy*) who was about to betray him, said (*w'mr*) [...] (John 12:4) – *šwwrh 'yynh* is a hapax legomenon, derived from Syriac (e.g. *wšwr 'ynwhy*)[153] – A student revealing a woman to be one eyed appears in *The Epic Histories Attributed to P'awstos Buzand*
15. He said to him: 'Two (sins) are upon you! First, that you looked at her, and second, that you suspected me to have looked at her!	Jesus prohibits looking at women. (Matthew 5.28)	You have heard that it is said, You shall not commit adultery. But I say to you, that whoever looks at a woman with the desire to covet her, has already committed adultery with her in his heart. (Matthew 5.28, see # 17, 36, 41)

152   Following manuscript Yad HaRav Herzog 1, see also *Sotah* 47a.
153   See Sokoloff, *A Syriac Lexicon* 1535.

Yerushalmi Sanhedrin 6.9 (23c) according to the Assis fragment (see also Hagigah 2.2, 77d)	Palestinian Intertexts (Yerushalmi, Greek Gospels, and other rabbinic and Christian literature)	Babylonian Intertexts (Bavli, Peshitta, and other Christian literature)
16. Did I speak about good looks? No, I only spoke about her service (*b'wbdh*)!	Martha provides service to Jesus, while Mary approaches him physically. (Luke 10:40–41)	– Martha has indeed performed a good service (*'bd' špyr' 'bdt*, Mark 14:6, see also Luke 10:40–41, and #13, 20, 22, 32 and 33)
17. And (Yehuda) was angry at (the student), and (the student) died (*w'qpd 'lwy wmyt*).	– Shmuel becomes angry with one of his diciples, who dies (*w'qpd 'lwy wmyt*), Yerushalmi *Mo'ed Qatan* 9.2, see also Bereshit Rabbah 100.7 and Yerushalmi *Berakhot* 19a – Jesus prohibits anger (Matthew 5:22)	– [Joshua] said: 'Wicked one! With these things do you busy yourself?' He sounded four hundred trumpets and excommunicated him. (Sanhedrin 107b)[154] – 'But I say to you that if you are angry (*dnrgz*) with a brother you will be liable to judgment.' (Matthew 5:22, see #15, 36, 41)
18. The one who said that Shimon ben Shetach was patriarch: the event in Ashkelon supports him.		
19. There were two students in Ashkelon.		

---

[154] Following manuscript Yad HaRav Herzog 1, see also *Sotah* 47a.

Yerushalmi Sanhedrin 6.9 (23c) according to the Assis fragment (see also Hagigah 2.2, 77d)	Palestinian Intertexts (Yerushalmi, Greek Gospels, and other rabbinic and Christian literature)	Babylonian Intertexts (Bavli, Peshitta, and other Christian literature)
20. Who ate like one (*'klyn khd'*), and drank (*wštyn*) like one, and labored Torah like one.	Jesus accused of overeating and drinking. (Luke 7:34 and Matthew 11:19)	For John the Baptist came. He did not eat (*'kl*) bread and did not drink (*št'*) wine [...] The son of Man came. He ate (*'kl*) and he drank (*wšt'*) [...] (Luke 7:33, see #13, 16, 22, 32 and 33)
21. One of them died, and (the townspeople) did not do piety to him (through mourning and burial rites).	– Poor man dies. (Luke 16:19–22) – The virgin's father dies and lies unburied for three days because of a rainstorm ... 'we gave him a burial in whatever way we could.'	There was a rich man [...]. And there was a poor man (*mskn'*) named *L'zr*, who was laid down at that rich man's door, [...] Now it happened that the poor man died (*wmyt*) (Luke 16:19–22, see # 22, 28, 30, 31, 39, 40)
22. Then *Son of a Fountain*, the tax collector (*mwks*) died (*wmyt*), and the entire town stopped working to do piety to him.	– Jesus a friend of the tax collectors a pervasive topic in the gospels. (Matthew 9:8–11, 11:19, 21:31, Luke 3:12, 5:27–30, 7:34, 15:1, 18:13) – Rich man dies. (Luke 16:22) – The virgin's mother days. 'She had such a funeral and pomp that you would think that even air was joining in burying her.'	– [...] and you say, 'Look, a glutton and a drinker of wine, a friend of tax-collectors (*dmks'*) and sinners (*wdhty'*)!' (Luke 7:34, see #13, 16, 20, 32 and 33) – And the rich man also died (*myt*) and was buried. (Luke 16:22 see # 21, 28, 30, 31, 39, 40)

Yerushalmi Sanhedrin 6.9 (23c) according to the Assis fragment (see also Hagigah 2.2, 77d)	Palestinian Intertexts (Yerushalmi, Greek Gospels, and other rabbinic and Christian literature)	Babylonian Intertexts (Bavli, Peshitta, and other Christian literature)
23. The (remaining) student began to be grieved and said: 'Vey! That the haters of Israel (i.e. Jews) do not have anything.'	'Is (the virgin's father) such an enemy of God that even the earth will not receive him in burial?'	'Haters of Israel' is common in the Bavli, but very rare in Palestinian Aramaic.[155]
24. (The deceased student) appeared (*'tḥmy*) (to his friend) in a dream (*bḥylm'*),[156] and he said to him: 'Do not despise the sons of your Lord. This one did one sin and got out of it, and this one did one good deed and got out of it.'	– Joseph, Jesus father, has a dream vision. – 'Sleep immediately overtook (the virgin)'; she has a dream vision showing her true justice.	The angel of the Lord appeared (*'tḥzy*) to Joseph in a dream (*bḥlm'*), [...] (Matthew 2:13–21, see # 10–12)
25. 'And what sin did this student commit?'		
26. 'Heaven forbid[157] he ever committed a sin, but one time he first put on the *Tefilin* of the head and then the *Tefilin* of the hands.'	Jesus does not appreciate care for Tefilin.	(The Pharisees) do all their deeds to be seen by others; for they make their *Tefilin* (*tpṭyhwn*) broad and their fringes long. (Matthew 23:5)
27. 'And what good deed did *Son of a Fountain*, the tax collector, do?'		

---

155 For the Bavli, see e.g. *Berakhot* 4b, 7a, 28a and 32a, *Shabbat* 33a, *Sukka* 29a, *Yoma* 72b and 75b, Sanhedrin 94a and 105b, and *Avodah Zarah* 4b). For Palestine, see e.g. *Wayiqra Rabbah* 25.1.

156 Assis lacks 'in a dream.'

157 Reading *ḥd* as *ḥs*, according to Hagigah and Sanhedrin.

Yerushalmi Sanhedrin 6.9 (23c) according to the Assis fragment (see also Hagigah 2.2, 77d)	Palestinian Intertexts (Yerushalmi, Greek Gospels, and other rabbinic and Christian literature)	Babylonian Intertexts (Bavli, Peshitta, and other Christian literature)
28. 'Heaven forbid he ever committed a good deed, but once he was walking in the market with bread in his hand [...], and it fell (*wnpl*) from him, and it was picked up by a poor man (*mskn*) taking it, but did not say anything to him so that (the poor man) would not blush.'	The poor Lazarus eats what falls from the rich man's table.	And there was a poor man (*mskn'*) named *L'zr* [...] he longed to fill his stomach with the crumbs that fell (*dnpl*) from the rich man's table. (Luke 16: 19–20 see # 21, 22, 30, 31, 39, 40)
29. And some say: He gave a feast (*'ryṣṭwn*) to the magistrates, but they did not come[158] to eat. He said: 'The poor ones (*msknyyh*) should come[159] and eat, so (the food) should not be thrown away.'	– Jesus suggests inviting the poor instead of the rich to an (Greek *ariston*). – Jesus tells a parable about the guests who did not come to an invitation, so the poor were invited. (Luke 14:12–24)	(Jesus) also said to the one who had invited him, 'When you give a luncheon or a supper, do not invite your [...] rich neighbors [...] But when you give a reception, invite the poor (*mskn'*) [...]' Jesus said to him, 'A man gave a great supper, and invited many.... (They do not come). Then the master of the house was angry, and said to his servant: "Go out quickly to the streets and lanes of the city, and bring in here the poor (*lmskn'*) [...]." (Luke 14:12–21)

---

158 'Come' is missing in the Assis fragment.
159 'Should come' is missing in the Assis fragment.

Yerushalmi Sanhedrin 6.9 (23c) according to the Assis fragment (see also Hagigah 2.2, 77d)	Palestinian Intertexts (Yerushalmi, Greek Gospels, and other rabbinic and Christian literature)	Babylonian Intertexts (Bavli, Peshitta, and other Christian literature)
30. After a few days, (the student) saw this student, his companion, promenading between gardens (*gnyn*), and orchards (*prdsyn*) and fountains (*mbw'yn dmwyy*).	– Lazarus is comforted in the afterworld. (Luke 16:22) – The virgin's father resides among 'many gardens, all sorts of fruits, and diverse trees of a beauty that defied description.'	And the angels carried him into Abraham's bosom. (Luke 16:22), see # 21, 22, 28, 31, 39, 40)
31. (The student) also saw the Son of a Fountain, the tax collector, his tongue (*lšwnw*) slavering (*šwtt*) next to a river, wanting to reach the water (*my'*), and not reaching it.	– The rich man is tantalized with water. (Luke 16:23–24) – The virgin sees her mother 'submerged up to her neck in the furnace [...] being burned by the fire.'	And while he was tormented in Sheol [...] he called out in a loud voice, saying, 'O my father Abraham, have mercy on me, and send Lazarus to dip his finger in water (*bmy'*) and wet my tongue (*lšny*); for I am tormented in this flame.' (Luke 16:23–24, see # 21, 22, 28, 30, 39, 40)
32. And (the student) also saw Mary (*mrym*), the daughter of *Leaves of Onions*.	Martha's sister Mary, who anointed Jesus and wiped him with her hair, used to be a loose woman. Jesus is accused of not knowing the woman's condition.	Mary wipes Jesus' feet with her hair. She used to be a sinner (*ḥthyt'*), but Jesus forgives her sins. (Luke 7:36–50, see # 13, 16, 20, 22, and 33)

Yerushalmi Sanhedrin 6.9 (23c) according to the Assis fragment (see also Hagigah 2.2, 77d)	Palestinian Intertexts (Yerushalmi, Greek Gospels, and other rabbinic and Christian literature)	Babylonian Intertexts (Bavli, Peshitta, and other Christian literature)
33. Rabbi Lazarus (*l'zr*) bar Yose said: 'She was hanging by the nipples of her breasts.'	– The Christian *Elijah Fragment* posits torture in breasts (cf. *Isaiah Fragment*) – Hanging a common punishment for sexual transgressions in Christian tours of hell (*Apocalypse of Peter, Apocalypse of Paul*). – Jesus depicts tax collectors and whores in the kingdom of heaven. (Matthew 21:31) – Mary's brother is called Lazarus. (Luke 11:2)	– 'Martha served, but Lazarus (*l'zr*) was one of the guests who were with him. Mary took a cruse containing pure and expensive nard, anointed the feet of Jesus, and wiped his feet with her hair, and the house was filled with the fragrance of the perfume. (John 12:1–5, see # 13, 16, 20, 22, and 32) – Mary Magdalene (*mrym mgdl'*) is understood as plaiting (*mgdl'*) 'women('s hair)' in Bavli *Shabbat* 104b and Hagigah 4b. – Truly I tell you, the tax-collectors and the whores are going into the kingdom of God ahead of you. (Matthew 21:31)
34. Rabbi Yose ben Hanina said: 'The hinge of the door of Gehenna was resting in her ear.'		

Yerushalmi Sanhedrin 6.9 (23c) according to the Assis fragment (see also Hagigah 2.2, 77d)	Palestinian Intertexts (Yerushalmi, Greek Gospels, and other rabbinic and Christian literature)	Babylonian Intertexts (Bavli, Peshitta, and other Christian literature)
35. (The student) said to them: 'Why is this?'		
36. They said to him: 'Since she fasted (ṣyymh) and made it public to her neighbors.' And there are some who say: 'Since she fasted one day, and deducted two (sins) for it.'	– Jesus prohibits to fast publicly. (Matthew 6:16–18) – Cf. Yerushalmi *Sotah* 5.7 (20c) on a woman who seeks to balance each sin through an ascetic deed, and ibid. 3.4 19a), on a female false ascetics who claims to have lost her virginity due to intensive self-affliction (ṣyymnyt)	When you fast (wṣymyn), do not look sad like the hypocrites; for they disfigure their faces, so that they may appear to men that they are fasting. […] so that it may not appear to men that you are fasting, but to your Father who is in secret; and your Father who sees in secret, he will reward you. (Matthew 6:16–18, see #15, 17, 41)
37. (The student) said to them: 'Until when will she be like this?'		
38. They said to him: 'Until Shimon ben Shetach comes, and we will lift it from (*Mary's*) ear and put it on his ear, because he said "If I will be made Patriarch, I will kill the witches." But as he was made patriarch, he did not kill the witches.		

Yerushalmi Sanhedrin 6.9 (23c) according to the Assis fragment (see also Hagigah 2.2, 77d)	Palestinian Intertexts (Yerushalmi, Greek Gospels, and other rabbinic and Christian literature)	Babylonian Intertexts (Bavli, Peshitta, and other Christian literature)
39. But go (*'yzyl*) and tell (*w'mwr*, i.e. Shimon about the witches and his impending punishment)!	The rich man wants to send Lazarus to warn his relatives about the impending punishment. (Luke 16:27–28)	He said to him: 'If this is so, I beseech you, O my father, to send Lazarus to my father's house; for I have five brothers; let him go (*n'zl*) and testify to them, so that they may not also come to this place of torment.' (Luke 16:27–28, see # 21, 22, 28, 30, 31, 40)
40. (The student) said to them: 'he is a great man, and will not believe (*mhymnty*) me.'	Relatives would not believe the emissary from Gehenna. (Luke 16:31)	But he said to him: 'No, my father Abraham; but if only a man from the dead go to them, they will repent.' Abraham said to him: 'If they will not hear Moses and the prophets, neither will they believe (*mhymnyn*) even if a man should rise for the dead.' (Luke 16:31, # 21, 22, 28, 30, 31, 39)

Yerushalmi Sanhedrin 6.9 (23c) according to the Assis fragment (see also Hagigah 2.2, 77d)	Palestinian Intertexts (Yerushalmi, Greek Gospels, and other rabbinic and Christian literature)	Babylonian Intertexts (Bavli, Peshitta, and other Christian literature)
41. They said to him: 'He will be very friendly and will believe you. And if he will not believe you, take out your eye (*'pyq 'ynk*), and it will come on your hand (*ydk*).' He took out his eye and it came to his hand.	Jesus advocates permanent removal of sinful eyes and hands. (Matthew 5:29, 18:8)	If your right eye (*'yny*) should cause you to stumble, pluck it out (*'pqyh*)[160] and throw it away from you [...]. And if your right hand (*'ydk*) causes you to sin, cut it off and throw it away. (Matthew 5:29, see # 15, 17, 36)
42. They said to him: 'Return it (*ḥzrh*)!' He returned it (*ḥzrh*), and it rejoined its companion.	Yerushalmi *Mo'ed Qatan* 3.1 (81c–d) for signs as unacceptable, 'Christian' form of proof: 'Return!' And it returned (*ḥwzryn wḥzrt*).	
43. (The student) went and said to (Shimon that there are witches). He wanted to make the sign before him.	Jesus' signs a pervasive topic in the gospels (Luke 11:29, Matthew 12:38–9, 15:18–19)	
44. (Shimon) said to him: 'You do not have to (do the sign); I know that you are a pious man. Even if I think (*ḥšbyt*) in my heart (*blby*), with my mouth (*bpmy*) I will not say.'	Jesus teaches that evil thoughts come from the heart and out of the mouth. (Matthew 9:33–34, 15:17–18)	But what comes out of the mouth (*pwm'*) proceeds from the heart (*lb'*), and this is what defiles. For out of the heart (*lb'*) come evil thoughts (*mḥšbt'*)... (Matthew 15:17–19)

---

160 Following the Harklean version. The Peshitta has *ḥtsyh*.

Yerushalmi Sanhedrin 6.9 (23c) according to the Assis fragment (see also Hagigah 2.2, 77d)	Palestinian Intertexts (Yerushalmi, Greek Gospels, and other rabbinic and Christian literature)	Babylonian Intertexts (Bavli, Peshitta, and other Christian literature)
45. At once Shimon ben Shetach went on a day of a rainstorm and he took with him eighty young men (*gwbryn*), and he gave them eighty clean robes (*lbwšwn nqyyn*) and he placed them in new pots (*bqdryn ḥdth*) and (placed) baskets (*wkpwnwn*) on their hea(ds)	– The virgin's father is buried 'even though the weather was still intemperate and the rain pouring down.' – Young men in shining robes await the women in Jesus' burial cave. – Jars and baskets feature in Jesus' food miracles.	– They came to the tomb [...]. And there were with them other women (*nš'*). And they found the stone rolled away from the tomb. And they entered in, but they did not find the body of Jesus. And it came to pass as they were confused about this, behold, two men (*gbryn*) stood above them, and their robes (*lbwšhwn*) were shining. (Luke 24:2–4) – The disciples take the leftovers and fill twelve baskets (*qwpynyn*, Matthew 14:16–21)
46. Shimon demands entry by the cave by calling out *"wym 'wym!"*	The Bacchae shout: 'Eve, Eve!' (Εὖαν Εὖαν, Eusebius, *Church History*, II.3.7–8)	
47. The witches miraculously procure bread, cooked food, and wine (as well as meat in Sanhedrin).	– Jesus miraculously procures wine, (cooked) fish, and bread. – Bread and wine are turned into Jesus' bread and flesh.	

Yerushalmi Sanhedrin 6.9 (23c) according to the Assis fragment (see also Hagigah 2.2, 77d)	Palestinian Intertexts (Yerushalmi, Greek Gospels, and other rabbinic and Christian literature)	Babylonian Intertexts (Bavli, Peshitta, and other Christian literature)
48. Shimon instructs his young male helpers to 'embrace and lift (*ygwp*) the witches away from the earth (*m'r''*).'	– Cutting of Antaios from the Earth cuts him of from the Earth's nourishment (Ovid, *Metamorphoses* 9. 183) – Herakles 'has caught Antaios by the middle just above the waist, where the ribs are,' Philostratus the Elder, *Imagines* 2. 21.	And they were afraid and bowed their faces to the earth (*b'r''*), and the(men) said to the (women), 'Why do you seek the living among the dead?(24:5)
49. The young men crucify (*wšlbwnwn*) the witches.	The women look for the crucified Jesus.	And they entered the tomb, and saw a young man, sitting on the right, covered with a white robe; and they were astonished. But he said to them: 'Do not be afraid. You seek Jesus the Nazarene, who was crucified (Harklean: *d'ṣṭlb*); he has risen; he is not here.' (Mark 16:4–6)

Appendix II
About the Daughter of the Good Father and the Evil Mother

An elder recounted, 'There was a very aged virgin advanced in the fear of God, and when she was asked by me about how she came to withdraw (from the world), she sighed and began to speak like this: "Oh wondrous fellow, it fell to me to be the child of a father who was of a kind and gentle disposition but weak and sickly of body. He lived so preoccupied with himself that he hardly ever came into contact with those living in the area. He remained on his land and passed his life there; if ever he was well, he would bring the fruits (of the earth) into the house, but for the most part he was confined to bed, nursing a disease. Such was his silence that he seemed to have no voice to those who did not know him. My mother was quite the opposite; she even busied herself with local affairs. She had so much conversation with everyone that her whole body seemed to be a tongue. Battle was often joined with everybody by her. She passed her time *drunk with wine* in the company of dissolute men. *Prostitute* that she was, she mismanaged the household so that our plentiful possessions could not suffice for us (the management had been handed over to her by my father). She used her body in such a way that few of the villagers were able to escape her licentiousness. Illness never approached her body; she did not experience pain, even a passing one, but from birth to death she kept her body intact and in good health. *Then it happened that my father died* after wrestling with chronic illness. Immediately the rain began pouring down; thunder and lightening filled the air. The rain did not let up for three days and three nights, *causing him to lie on the bed unburied*, so the villagers shook their heads, wondering what evil had secretly befallen them all. 'Is he such an *enemy of God* that even the earth will not receive him in burial?' Yet for fear that he would putrefy within and render the house inaccessible, even though the weather was still intemperate and the rain pouring down, we gave him burial in whatever way we could. My mother, now finding herself more at liberty, yet more shamelessly plied the debauchery of her body; she practically transformed the house into a brothel. She lived in such debauchery and profligacy that she left little for me in her abundance. But no sooner had death come upon her (with fear, as it seemed to me) than *she had such a funeral and pomp that you would think that even air was joining in burying her.* I was just passing out of childhood after her death and starting to be moved and titillated by physical desires such as usually occur. One evening I started to wonder what kind of life I would choose to live: would it be my father's, moderate, gentle, and well tempered? But then again I reckoned this: he achieved no good in life but departed this life having passed his whole time in sickness and affliction, and that not even the earth would receive him in burial. So if such a way of life was good in the sight of God, why was my father so tested, having chosen to live like that? Or would it be good to (live) like my mother? Should I devote my body to licentiousness, debauchery, and pleasure seeking? She abandoned none of her wicked doings and was *drunk all her life long*, yet she departed this life hale and hearty. So then," she said, "should I live like my mother? It is better to trust one's own eyes and not to go a step beyond what is plainly made known; and it seemed that she herself had established her worthless life for me. Night drew on and sleep immediately overtook me after these *logismoi*. There stood by me a person huge of body, fearful of countenance. Terrifying me by his appearance, he questioned me with an angry look and a harsh voice, 'Tell me, you: What are the thoughts of your heart?' I was so terrified by his appearance and the look of him that I did not dare glance at him. Raising his voice, he again commanded me to confess my opinions; but I was so paralyzed by fear that I forgot my *logismoi* and began saying I knew nothing. But even as I was denying it, that one caused me to remember everything that had been contemplated in my mind. Caught out and resorting to imploring, I begged to be worthy of forgiveness, and I explained the reason for this state of mind. He said, '*Come now to see them both, your father and your mother, and choose for yourself which life you wish from now on.*' He took my hand and led me to a *great plain with many gardens, all sorts of fruits, and diverse trees of a beauty that defied description*. He led me in there; my father met me, embraced me, and kissed me, calling me his child, and I, clinging to him, begged to remain with him. But he said, 'That is not possible at present; but if you want to follow in my footsteps, you will come here before long.' As I went on begging to stay with him, he who brought me there drew me again by the hand, saying, 'Come to see your own mother *burning in the fire* so that you may know to which way of life it is better to lean.' He set me in a dark and gloomy house filled with roaring and disturbance and showed me a furnace ablaze with fire and boiling pitch with some persons of fearful aspect standing at the furnace. When I looked down, I saw my own mother submerged up to her neck in the furnace, chattering and clamping her teeth, being burned by the fire, and becoming the fodder of many worms. When she saw me, she called out with lamentation, calling me her child, 'Ah me, my own deeds, child! Ah me, my doings! Everything to do with sobriety seemed nonsense to me. *I did not believe there were punishments for* porneia *and adultery; I did not hold there was torture for drunkenness and debauchery*. See what a great retribution and punishment I am receiving for a little pleasure; see what a severe sentence I receive for the smallest illicit delight; see how many are the wages I collect for despising God; all the immutable evils have caught up with me! Now is the time for helping, my child; recall now the nourishment you received from me. Do you now return the benefit if you derived any good from me. Have mercy on me as I burn in the fire and am consumed by it; have mercy on me who am being examined by such tortures. Have pity on me, my child; give me your hand and lead me away from here.' When I declined to do this on account of those standing by, again she called out with tears, 'Help, my child; child, help me! Do not turn away from the lamentation of your own mother; remember the days of my labour pains, and turn not away from her who is being lost in the *fire of Gehenna*.' Feeling some humane sentiment on account of her tears and the sound of her voice, I reached out my hand to draw her up, but the fire burned my hand, and I began to groan with weeping. They of the house arose, made fire, and asked the reason for my sighs. I explained to them what I had seen and that in fact I was resolved rather to follow the life of my father in the future, convinced by the unspeakable, tender, loving kindness of God what punishments lie ahead for those who want to live badly." Such were the things that blessed virgin announced from the vision: that great is the reward of the good, while the punishments for evil deeds and a disorderly life are enormous. So, by this counsel, let us improve ourselves in order to be found (among the) blessed.'[161]

Bibliography

Aristophanes, *The Frogs*, trans. J. Henderson, in *Aristophanes* (Cambridge, MA: 2002).
Assis M., "A Fragment of Yerushalmi Sanhedrin", *Tarbits* 46 (1977) 29–90 [Hebrew].
Athanasius of Alexandria, *Letter 10.6*, trans. in *Historical Tracts of S. Athanasius, Archbishop of Alexandria* (London: 1885) 74–75.
Augustine, *The City of God against the Pagans*, vol. 7, trans. G. E. McCracken and W.M. Green (Cambridge, MA: 1972).
Baarda T., "An Archaic Element in the Arabic Diatessaron?", *Novum Testamentum* 17 (1975) 151–155.
Baskin J.R., "Rabbinic-Patristic Exegetical Contacts in Late Antiquity: A Bibliographical Reappraisal", in Green W.S. (ed.), *Approaches to Ancient Judaism* vol. 5 (Atlanta: 1985) 53–80.
Bayless M., *Parody in The Middle Ages: The Latin Tradition* (Ann Arbor: 1996).
Becker A., "Positing a 'Cultural Relationship' between Plato and the Babylonian Talmud," *Jewish Quarterly Review* 101 (2011) 255–269.
Bernstein A.E., *The Formation of Hell: Death and Retribution in the Ancient and Early Christian Worlds* (Ithaca – London: 1993).
Binns J., *Ascetics and Ambassadors of Christ: The Monasteries of Palestine, 314–631* (Oxford: 1994).
Bonfil R. – Irshai O. – Stroumsa G.G. – Talgam R. (eds.), *Jews in Byzantium: Dialectics of Minority and Majority Cultures* (Leiden: 2011).
Boyain, D., *Socrates and the Fat Rabbis* (Chicago: 2009).
Brandon S.G.F., *The Judgment of the Dead: An Historical and Comparative Study of the Idea of a Post-Mortem Judgment in the Major Religions* (London: 1967).

---

[161] BHG 1322t, *de filia boni patris et malae matris*, cited according to Wortley, *Book of the Elders* 331–334, my emphases.

Bremmer J., "Tours of Hell: Greek, Jewish, Roman, and Early Christian", in Ameling W. (ed.), *Topographie des Jenseits: Studien zur Geschichte des Todes in Kaiserzeit und Spätantike* (Stuttgart: 2011) 13–34.

Brodsky D., *A Bride Without a Blessing: A Study in the Redaction and Content of Massekhet Kallah and its Gemara*, Texts and Studies in Ancient Judaism 118 (Tübingen: 2006).

Ciasca A., *Tatiani Evangeliorum Harmoniae Arabica* (Rome: 1888).

Clément d'Alexandrie, *Le pedagogue*, ed. and trans. Harl M. – Marrou H.-I. – Matray C. – Mondésert C. (Paris: 1960–1970).

Cohen Y., *Tangled up in Text: Tefillin and the Ancient World* (Providence: 2008).

Cook J.G., "A note on Tatian's Diatessaron, Luke, and the Arabic Harmony", *Zeitschrift für antikes Christentum* 10 (2006) 462–471.

Dvorjetski E., "A Talmudic Reality in the Erotic Rituals of Dionysiac-Bacchic Cult", in Zinguer I. (ed.), *Dionysos: Origines et Résurgences* (Paris: 2001) 79–93.

Elliot J.K., *The Apocryphal New Testament* (Oxford: 1993).

Elman Y., "Righteousness as Its Own Reward: An Inquiry into the Theologies of the Stam", *Proceedings of the American Academy for Jewish Research* 57 (1990) 35–67.

Elman Y., "The Suffering of the Righteous in Palestinian and Babylonian Sources", *Jewish Quarterly Review* 80 (1990) 315–339.

Euringer S., *Die Überlieferung der arabischen Übersetzung des Diatessarons* (Freiburg im Breisgau: 1912).

Eusebius of Caesarea, *Praeparatio Evangelica*, trans. E.H. Gifford, in *Eusebius of Caesarea: Praeparatio Evangelica* (Oxford: 1903).

Eusebius of Caesarea, *Praeparatio Evangelica*, trans. K. Mras, in *Eusebius Werke, vol. 8* (Berlin: 1954–1956).

Garsoïan N.G., *The Epic Histories attributed to P'awstos Buzand (Buzandaran Patmut'iwnk')* (Cambridge, MA: 1989).

Gero S., "The Stern Master and his Wayward Disciple: A 'Jesus' Story in the Talmud and in Christian Historiography", *Journal for the Study of Judaism* 25 (1994) 287–311.

Goff J. Le, *The Birth of Purgatory*, trans. A. Goldhammer (Chicago: 1984).

Graf G., *Geschichte der christlichen arabischen Literatur* (The Vatican: 1944).

Gressmann H., *Vom reichen Mann und armen Lazarus: Eine literaturgeschichtliche Studie* (Berlin: 1918).

Griffith F.L., *Stories of the High Priests of Memphis: The Sethon of Herodotus and the Demotic Tales of Khamuas* (Oxford: 1900).

Guy J.-C., *Les Apophtegmes des pères: collection systématique* (Paris: 2005).

Gwyn J., *The Revelation of John in Syriac Version Hitherto Unknown* (Piscataway, NJ: 2005).

Hagendahl H., *Latin Fathers and the Classics: A Study on the Apologists, Jerome and other Christian Writers* (Gothenburg: 1958).

Harmon A.M. (ed.), *Lucian in Seven Volumes* (New York: 1919).
Hengel M., *Rabbinische Legende und frühpharisäische Geschichte. Schimeon b. Schetach und die achtzig Hexen von Askalon* (Heidelberg: 1984).
Hezser C., "Apophthegmata Patrum and Apophthegmata of the Rabbis", in *La Narrativa Cristiana Antica. Codici Narrativi, Strutture Formali, Schemi Retorici*, Studia Ephemeridia Augustinianum 50 (Rome: 1995) 453–464.
Himmelfarb M., *Tours of Hell: An Apocalyptic Form in Jewish and Christian Literature* (Philadelphia: 1983).
Hirshman M., *Rivalry of Genius: Jewish and Christian Biblical Interpretation in Late Antiquity* (Albany: 1996).
Hutcheon L., *A Theory of Parody: The Teachings of Twentieth-Century Art Forms* (Urbana – Chicago: 2000).
Ilan T., *Silencing the Queen: The Literary Histories of Shelamzion and Other Jewish Women* (Tübingen: 2006).
Jensen J., "Does Porneia mean Fornication? A Critique of Bruce Malina", *Novum Testamentum* 20 (1978) 161–184.
Jerome, *Letter to Heliodorus* (Letter 60), trans. J.H.D. Scourfield, in *Consoling Heliodorus: A Commentary on Jerome, Letter 60* (Oxford: 1993) 44–47.
Jones F.S. (ed.), *Which Mary?: The Marys of Early Christian Tradition* (Leiden: 2003).
Kiperwasser R., "Rev. of Boyarin, Socrates and the Fat Rabbis", *Jewish History* 25 (2011) 377–397.
Kiraz G.A., *Comparative Edition of the Syriac Gospels: Aligning the Sinaiticus, Curetonianus, Peshitta and Harklean Versions* (Piscataway, NJ: 2004).
Kogan-Zehavi E., "A Painted Tomb of the Roman Period at Migdal Ashqelon", *'Atiqot* 37 (1999) 181–209 [Hebrew; English summary 179–81].
Kovacs M., *The Epic of Gilgamesh* (Stanford: 1989).
Lamsa G.M., *The Holy Bible From Ancient Eastern Manuscripts* (Philadelphia: 1957).
Langlois M., *Le premier manuscrit du livre d'Hénoch: Etude épigraphique et philologique des fragments araméens de 4Q201 à Qumrân* (Paris: 2008).
Liddell H.G. – Scott R., *Greek-English Lexicon* (Oxford: 1996).
Lieberman S., "Morsels: Yerushalmi amendments", *Tarbits* 5 (1934) 100–101 [Hebrew].
Lieberman, S., "Some Aspects of After Life in Early Rabbinic Literature", in Lieberman S. (ed.), *Harry Austryn Wolfson Jubilee Volume* (Jerusalem: 1965).
Lieberman, S., "On Sins and Their Punishment", in Lieberman, S., *Texts and Studies* (New York: 1974) 29–56.
Lieberman, S., "On the New Fragments of the Palestinian Talmud", *Tarbits* 46 (1977) 91–96 [Hebrew].
McCarthy C., *Saint Ephrem's Commentary on Tatian's Diatessaron: An English Translation of Chester Beatty Syriac MS 709 with Introduction and Notes*, Journal of Semitic Studies Supplement 2 (Oxford: 1993).

Merkt A., "Abrahams Schoss: Ursprung und Sinngehalt eines antiken christlichen Jenseitstopos", in Ameling W. (ed.), *Topographie des Jenseits: Studien zur Geschichte des Todes in Kaiserzeit und Spätantike* (Stuttgart: 2011) 83–102.

Müller-Kessler C., – Sokoloff M. (eds.), *The Christian Palestinian Aramaic New Testament Version from the Early Period* (Groningen: 1998).

Nickelsburg G.W.E. – VanderKam J.C., *1 Enoch: A New Translation* (Minneapolis: 2004).

Ory J., "A Painted Tomb Near Ascalon", *Quarterly of the Department of Antiquities in Palestine* 8 (1938) 38–44.

Pagoulatos G., *Tracing the Bridegroom in Dura: The bridal Initiation Service of the Dura-Europos Christian Baptistery as Early Evidence of the Use of Images in Christian and Byzantine Worship* (Piscataway, NJ: 2008).

Patrich J. (ed.), *The Sabaite Heritage in the Orthodox Church from the Fifth Century to the Present* (Leuven: 2001).

Petersen W.L., *Tatian's Diatessaron: Its Creation, Dissemination, Significance, & History in Scholarship* (Leiden: 1994).

Rubenstein J., *Talmudic Stories: Narrative Art, Composition, and Culture* (Baltimore: 1999).

Rubenstein J., *Stories of the Babylonian Talmud* (Baltimore: 2010).

Satlow M., "'And on the Earth you shall sleep': 'Talmud Torah' and Rabbinic Asceticism", *Journal of Religion* 83 (2003) 204–225.

Schäfer P., "'From Jerusalem the Great to Alexandria the Small': The Relationship between Palestine and Egypt in the Graeco-Roman Period", in: Schäfer P. (ed.), *The Talmud Yerushalmi and Graeco-Roman Culture* (Tübingen: 1998) I, 129–140.

Schäfer P., *Jesus in the Talmud* (Princeton: 2007).

Schäfer P., *The Origins of Jewish Mysticism* (Princeton: 2009).

Schäfer P., *The Jewish Jesus: How Judaism and Christianity Shaped Each Other* (Princeton: 2012).

Schremer A., *Brothers Estranged: Heresy, Christianity, and Jewish Identity in Late Antiquity* (Oxford: 2010) 101–120.

Schwartz E., *Kyrillos von Skythopolis* (Leipzig: 1939).

Siegal M.B.-A., *Literary Analogies in Rabbinic and Christian Monastic Sources*, Ph.D. dissertation (Yale University: 2010).

Siegal M.B.-A., "The Making of a Monk-Rabbi: the Background for the Creation of the Stories of R. Shimon bar Yohai in the Cave", *Zion* 76 (2011) 279–304.

Sokoloff M., *A Dictionary of Jewish Palestinian Aramaic of the Byzantine Period* (Ramat Gan: 2002).

Sokoloff M., *A Syriac Lexicon* (Piscataway, NJ: 2009).

Stählin O. – Früchtel L., *Clemens Alexandrinus, vol. 2: Stromata Buch I–IV* (Berlin: 1960).

Stausberg M., "Hell in Zoroastrian History", *Numen* 56 (2009) 217–253.

Visotzky B., "Prolegomena to the Study of Jewish-Christians in Rabbinic Literature", *AJS Review* 14 (1989) 47–70.

Visotzky B., *Fathers of the World: Essays in Rabbinic and Patristic Literature* (Tübingen: 1995).

Wimpfheimer B.S., *Narrating the Law: A Poetics of Talmudic Legal Stories* (Philadelphia: 2011).

Wortley J., *Book of the Elders: Sayings of the Desert Fathers: The Systematic Collection*, Cistercian Studies Series 240 (Collegeville: 2012).

Yuval I.J., *Two Nations in Your Womb: Perceptions of Jews and Christians in Late Antiquity and the Middle Ages* (Berkeley: 2006).

Zellentin H., *Rabbinic Parodies of Jewish and Christian Literature* (Tübingen: 2011).

Zellentin H., "Jerusalem Fell After Betar: The Christian Josephus and Rabbinic Memory", in Boustan R.S. – Herrmann K. – Leicht R. – Reed A.Y. – Veltri G. (eds.), *Envisioning Judaism: Studies in Honor of Peter Schäfer on the Occasion of his Seventieth Birthday* (Tübingen: 2013) I, 319–367.

CHAPTER 3

Cardinal Gabriele Paleotti's Call for Reform of Christian Art

Karl F. Morrison

1   Introduction: Paleotti and the Middle of the Road[1]

Taken in the broadest perspective, the entire history of iconoclasm in Christian culture, from the patristic age to the present day is an extended commentary on the difficulty of assimilating the Bible to the profane. The problem had an exact point of reference, indeed a test passage of Scripture. That is, how one verse, the second of the Ten Commandments (Exodus 20:4–6) was to be observed. As the never-ending controversy indicates, the practical difficulties spread beyond the horizons of historical confinement. Naturally, they arose from the familiar event of cultural borrowing: that is, importing wisdom from one world into an alien one, rather like pouring new wine into old skins. Yet, intellectual ambivalences in which iconoclasm and idolatry could become identical permanently blocked uniformly homogenized assimilation of Bible to word. That, together with the primordial authority of the Ten Commandments, created a permanently open and angry wound in the *communio sanctorum*.

In this paper, I consider one man's attempt to deliver the cult of sacred images, not only from suspicion of idolatry, but also from what he considered actual self-subversion by idolatry. He hoped thereby to legitimize compromising the letter of the biblical prohibition of images with their veneration. My focus is on a treatise by one of the most influential members of the College of Cardinals in the second half of the sixteenth century: Gabriele Paleotti (1522–1597), archbishop of Bologna. Paleotti, 'one of the key figures of the Tridentine Reform in Italy,'[2] wrote his long 'discourse' as a pastoral instruction to the people of his city and diocese. Unsurprisingly, he defended the use of religious images against Protestant iconoclasts. In that part of his polemic, he upheld the

---

1   I thank Dr. Ulrich Groetsch for kindly obtaining a microfilm copy of Paleotti's treatise for me from the Bavarian State Library, and the Erasmus Institute for the award of a Carey Senior Faculty Fellowship (2001–2002), when I first had the chance to study it in depth.

2   Jedin H., "Das Tridentinum und die bildenden Künste", *Zeitschrift für Kirchengeschichte* 74 (1963) 321–339, 331.

age-old connection between religious art and self-knowing. However, Paleotti went further. The exceptional aspect of his treatise is his sweeping denunciation of all art, including first and foremost, religious art as it was practiced in his day. In terms that could have given aid and comfort to his Protestant enemies, he wrote that religious art had become reprehensible, debased into the Devil's own tool. Art and religion had so far parted ways through the impieties blazoned on the walls and furnishings of churches, he thought, that he was able to quote a saying, known also to Martin Luther and circulated with several variations in Protestant England: 'There is no church without a chapel occupied by the Devil, and he has a place to sit wherever God's word is preached.'[3]

Paleotti's anxiety about art remained strong through the latter part of his life, as is indicated by a memorandum he wrote for the College of Cardinals in 1596, fourteen years after his treatise was published entitled 'A Most Recent Consideration of Removing Abuses of Images.' The labour of translating his enormous treatise into Latin for publication in the same year (1596) demonstrates the continued currency of his ideas.[4]

Two centuries later, the eighteenth-century polymath, Gotthold Ephraim Lessing was to pose the general question whether religious art were 'art'. Lessing reasoned that art, as such, allowed wide creative freedom to artists, while the cult functions of religious art required that images follow established conventions of representation and symbolism. In classical Greece, he observed, cult images of gods had to be laden with emblems and attributes identifying particular divinities. Paleotti's treatise is important, not least, because it marks a point of departure within the Church from which a trail leads to Lessing's exclusion of religious art from the realm of 'art'. In it one finds what came to be a point where the Church and its secular critics reached an amiable separation. The Cardinal intended to establish a common standard of representation and morality for all art. However, in developing his argument, he had to make one compromise after another. He realized that he could not control the rampaging autonomy of art. He demanded styles that remained 'true to life'

---

3 Paleotti Gabriele, *De Imaginibus Sacris et Profanis* (Ingolstadt, David Sartorius: 1594) 2.48 = p. 360. Paleotti originally published this book in Italian: *Discorso intorno alle imagine sacre et profane* (Bologna: 1582). The Italian text is published in Brocchi P. (ed.), *Trattati d'arte del Cinquecento*, vol. 2 (Bari: 1961) 117–562. One of the first objectives Paleotti set for himself when, as Cardinal Bishop of Albano, he was required to move to Rome was to arrange for the Latin translation of his *Discorso*. With its modest additions and embellishments, the translation represents a considered reaffirmation of views for the Latin-reading élite set forth a decade earlier in Italian for his whole diocese.

4 On Paleotti's ideas in general, and on his 1596 memorandum, see Feld H., *Der Ikonoklasmus des Westens* (Leiden: 1990) 203–208.

in verisimilitude; but he found the world around him full of artists exploring style after style, some extraordinarily bizarre, in attempts to lead viewers' eyes through labyrinths of, until then, unknown visual adventures. He demanded a morality in all art, domestic and public; but everywhere, even on the walls of churches, he found riotous immorality in representations of nudity and in flamboyant images taken from pagan mythology and its delights. Paleotti did not recognize that religion and 'art' were parting ways.[5] Still, this separation is latent in his admission that what he called 'diseases' afflicting art were beyond any cure known to him, and in his call for a censorship of religious art by officers and institutions of the Church, a kind of Index of forbidden styles and subjects.

It is worth stressing that the Devil was not a mere figure of speech for Paleotti, in his review of art's woes, but an actual, historical presence in the world. In 1576, a few years before his own treatise was first published (1582), a Franciscan friar, living in Bologna, dedicated to Paleotti what became a staple work in the literature of practical demonology. Among the evils of his day, the author, Girolamo Menghi, counted first and foremost the pernicious sickness in body and soul caused by 'very many' (*permulti*) people working by demons and sorcerers. As he wrote in his dedicatory letter to Paleotti, the art of the exorcist had been lost on the whole; few in their day knew how to counteract this wretched and accursed disease. Of those who knew the remedies, the fewest of the few wished to apply them. In his treatise, *The Scourge of Demons*, Menghi asserted that he upheld the age-old canonical tradition of the Church against those who had the key to casting out evil, but sealed it up in their hearts, refusing to share it with others out of some possessive zeal for empty glory. By publishing a detailed, how-to-do-it book of exorcism, he put in the hands of all what was needed to correct those who ignorantly and impiously walked in the paths of demons, taking refuge in the superstitions of old women.[6]

---

5   See Prodi P., "Ricerche sulla teorica delle arti figurative nella Riforma cattolica", *Archivio italiano per la Storia della pietà* 4 (1984) 123–212, 187: 'Mentre lo splendore dell'arte barocca sembra far risplendere una nuova epoca di espressione religiosa nell'arte, l'arte sacra si cristallizza in formule convenzionali e rigide, si sclerotizza.' See also Hecht C., *Katholische Bildertheologie im Zeitalter von Gegenreformation und Barock: Studien zu Traktaten von Johannes Molanus, Gabriele Paleotti und anderen Autoren* (Berlin: 1997) 332, on the distinction, which Paleotti did not regard, between theological and painterly concerns, and on the absence of a theological esthetic in the West, conditioning Paleotti's lack of that distinction. Dr. John Lupia kindly directed me to Hecht's book. In the twentieth century, that lack was still present to be addressed by Hans Urs von Balthasar valiantly and massively in the seven volumes of his study, *The Glory of the Lord: A Theological Aesthetics*.

6   Menghi Girolamo, *Flagellum daemonum … accessit postremo pars secunda quae Fustis Daemonum inscribitur* (Lyons, Pierre Landry: 1604) 1–4.

Such evils were abhorrent in Paleotti's eyes, he knew, and Menghi appealed for the Cardinal's favour in extirpating them. The exorcism of demons, as Menghi spelled it out in lurid step-by-step detail, gave Paleotti a practical guide related to his task of purging religious art of the filth that, he thought, deformed it and reforming art into a means of worshiping God in purity and innocence and, thereby, into a means of authentic self-knowing. The fixed point in Paleotti's argument for the reform of religious art was the familiar axiom, traditionally equivalent to 'know thyself,' 'nothing in excess.'

In the late eighth century, Theodulf of Orléans thought, mistakenly, that all Byzantines fell into one of two factions. They were all extremist zealots, either image-worshipers or image-smashers. Theodulf had found a safe, comfortable berth among the Franks, at Charlemagne's court. The Franks, he said, had found the right way, the way of moderation. They used religious images as memorials, teaching aids, and ornaments, while they recognized that there was nothing either necessary or harmful in images as such. The Franks fell into neither of the sacrilegious Byzantine errors; they lived by the proverb, 'nothing in excess'.[7]

Paleotti found himself righteously claiming the same middle ground in the terrifying, bitter war called 'Reformation.' Without citing Theodulf's treatise, Paleotti played variations on the same theme. Like Theodulf, Paleotti recognized that images were not essential, at least to the spiritually adept. Christ, Paleotti wrote, could be adored in essence and in person directly, rather than through the mediation of an image, even as members of strict religious orders, having reached more rarefied spiritual heights than others, could dispense with the music of organs and song in which the rest of the Church delighted.[8] One great difference in Paleotti's variation was that his enemies were not half a continent away, as Theodulf's had been. Paleotti's were close enough to be engaged in hand-to-hand combat. They were all extremists: on the one hand, pagans who worshiped images as though they were true gods; on the other, Jews, Muslims, and Protestant heretics and schismatics who cast out all religious images as idolatrous. Catholic Christians, Paleotti wrote, neither worshiped images nor spurned them. Taking their stand on the middle ground, 'the place where virtue resides,' they used images as instruments through which they transmitted reverence to God and the saints. Thus, they held to the moderation required by Church councils and canon law.[9] Lacking all pictures, the

---

7   Freeman A. with the collaboration of Meyvaert P. (ed.), *Opus Caroli Regis Contra Synodum* (*Libri Carolini*) (Hannover: 1998) prologue; 4.8; 100; 509.
8   Paleotti, *De Imaginibus* 1.32; 2.31 = 132; 275.
9   Ibid., 1.1 = 9.

synagogues of Jews, the mosques of Turks, and the recent *scholae* of heretics looked more like dwellings (*domicilia*) than churches. To look like a church, a building needed pictures.[10] At least, this is what Paleotti said before he began his inventory of demonically-inspired abuse in the Church.

After being entombed in archives for centuries, Theodulf's treatise little-by-little became generally known, as it had never been in his own time. At first cited from manuscript copies, it was printed in 1549, gaining authority among Protestants and, among Roman Catholics, derision as a Protestant forgery. The irony in Paleotti's argument from moderation lies in the fact that, while Theodulf and he played variations on the theme of moderation, he served on the Sacred Congregation of the Roman Inquisition responsible for placing and retaining Theodulf's work on the *Index of Forbidden Books*.[11]

2 Who was Paleotti?

Paleotti began his career as a member of the papal Curia under the stern reformer, Pope Paul IV (1555–1559).[12] At that point, the devotional revolution of the sixteenth century had passed through its initial, anarchic stages and entered a stage of consolidation, in counterpoint with extreme violence. A Bolognese, Paleotti continued traditions of his eminent family by studying law.[13] Pope Paul IV found in his mastery of canon and civil law and in his character, talents that he could use to advantage in reorganizing the papal bureaucracy. For forty years, under a series of nine popes – the very height of the Reformed Papacy – Paleotti fought tirelessly to defeat Protestantism and to purify the Roman Church.

In time, he became cardinal and bishop – later, archbishop – of his native city, Bologna. Bologna was not only a major Italian city and diocese, but also one of the greatest territories in the Papal States, the linchpin of papal

---

10   Ibid., 1.28 = 116.
11   On Theodulf's entry into the Reformation debates, see Freeman, *Opus Caroli Regis Contra Synodum* 12–13; 73–74; 77–79; Payton J.R. Jr., "Calvin and the *Libri Carolini*", *Sixteenth Century Journal* 28 (1997) 468–471.
12   See Prodi P., *Il cardinale Gabriele Paleotti (1522–1597)*, 2 vols. (Rome: 1959–1967). There is also a useful, and rather wide-ranging, doctoral dissertation on Paleotti by Hilbrich P.D., *The Aesthetic of the Counterreformation and Religious Painting and Music in Bologna, 1564–1615* (Ohio University: 1969).
13   On Paleotti's antecedents, going back to the twelfth century, see Prodi, *Il Cardinale Gabriele Paleotti* I, 17–40. A kinsman of a previous generation, Camillo Paleotti, figures in Castiglione's array of notable characters at the Court of Urbino. Castiglione Baldasar, *The Book of the Courtier*, ed. D. Javitch (New York: 2002) 2.62; 2.75 = 118; 125–126.

political, diplomatic, and military power in the North. Beginning from a position of strength, his influence and rank among the Cardinals steadily grew, and in at least two elections (1590, 1591), he fell only a few votes short of being elected pope. He might have been a candidate in 1585, had not the Sacred College grown weary of Bolognese during the long reign of Gregory XIII. When Paleotti entered the College of Cardinals (1565), he already moved in the circles of powerful reformers, including Filippo Neri (1515–1595) and Carlo Borromeo (1538–1584). Both Neri and Borromeo insisted that corruption had gone so far among professed believers that nothing less than the reconversion of Europe would restore the community of faith. Imposing on themselves lives of radical self-denial, they promoted concerted, sustained programmes aimed at nothing less than reconstituting the Church.[14]

Thus, Paleotti walked beside Neri as he became 'the second apostle of Rome,' producing a fundamental shift in public morals above all through the evangelistic work of the religious society he founded, the Oratorians. Paleotti walked with Borromeo, archbishop and cardinal, in the sweeping educational, administrative, and spiritual reforms he instituted in Milan, bringing his diocese into line with the laws enacted at the Council of Trent. Like Borromeo, Paleotti was tireless in advancing the Counter-Reformation in his diocese. On episcopal visitations he enforced the reform programme even in the most remote and inaccessible parishes. He preached and catechized. He established a seminary for the rigorous education of priests and exercised discipline over clergy and laity through diocesan synods.[15] As a member of the College of Cardinals, in collaboration with his spiritual allies, he contributed to bringing about an austere godliness among the Cardinals themselves, a reform of the Roman clergy, and imposition of the reform programme on all believers through the work

---

14   A sign of how closely Paleotti identified himself and his church with Rome is that he had a replica catacomb constructed in his episcopal church, which was dedicated to St. Peter. See Hecht, *Katholische Bildertheologie* 336.

15   On Paleotti's educational reforms, see Jones P.M., "Art Theory as Ideology: Gabriele Paleotti's Hierarchical Notion of Painting's Universality and Reception", in Farago C. (ed.), *Reframing the Renaissance: Visual Culture in Europe and Latin America, 1450–1650* (New Haven: 1995) 127–139, 137–138. Jones rightly stresses that Paleotti, who mistrusted social mobility, had no idea of raising the intellectual level of the illiterate majority in his diocese. It is difficult to tell how he could have hoped that his treatise on sacred and profane images would achieve the educational goals he intended for it, since, even to the author, it must have appeared, in Jones's words, 'ambiguous, repetitive, and prolix [...] by no means easily digestible.' (132) Despite these features, one contemporary found Paleotti's book so fundamental that, he wrote, no one could be a painter in future who had not read it carefully. Hecht, *Katholische Bildertheologie* 25. Dr John N. Lupia kindly directed me to Jones's article.

CARDINAL GABRIELE PALEOTTI'S CALL FOR REFORM OF CHRISTIAN ART 101

of several commissions (or 'congregations') including the Holy Office of the Inquisition, responsible for the *Index of Forbidden Books*.

Though now unknown, by comparison with others in his circle, Paleotti remained for forty years a tenacious and influential evangelist of reform. His strength lay in law and government, which is also to say in applying legal coercion. And yet, he had cultural horizons wide enough to enable his colleague, Cardinal Caesare Baronius (1538–1607) to engage him as an exalted proofreader for early instalments of Baronius's *Annales Ecclesiastici*, wide enough too for him to observe the visual arts in his society and in the churches around him, and to find in religious painting symptoms of spiritual corruption.[16] Originally published in Italian as a pastoral guide for his diocese, Paleotti's *Discourse on Sacred and Profane Images* is highly problematic in some respects. There were many painters of first importance in Paleotti's day (e.g., Titian), and, through the work of the three Carracci kinsmen, Bologna itself became the centre of an artistic revival, the first stage of Early Baroque art, which spread to Rome and began to flourish before the end of the century. Oscillating between his two spheres of power, Bologna and Rome, Paleotti himself inadvertently assisted in constructing the essential network of artists, workshops, and communication essential to the pre-eminence of Bolognese painters in Rome which began in his last years, a little before he became Cardinal Bishop of Albano and, as such, was required to take up residence in Rome (1589).[17]

At the same time, he began a general revision of his writings, and determined to prepare a Latin translation of his *Discorso*. Perhaps inspired by the preparation of Pope Clement VIII's revision of the *Index of Forbidden Books* (which was published in 1596), he delegated the actual work of translation to a member of his entourage. When published, the translation included some new supporting documentation and elaboration of a few passages, but no change of the original form or argument. For good measure, he composed a memorandum for the College of Cardinals on the urgency of removing abuses from the arts (1596). The demands of his offices as Archbishop of Bologna and Cardinal Bishop, first of Albano and then of Santa Sabina, came as with age his energy waned. Though he hoped to edit his entire *opera omnia*, this project came to nothing. For Paleotti allowed himself to be persuaded by 'wise men' not to

---

16 Baronius may have taken a hand in the artistic history of Counter-Reformation Rome by serving Pope Clement VIII as an advisor regarding the cycle of altarpieces to be painted for St. Peter's.
17 On Paleotti and Bolognese artists, see Prodi, *Il Cardinale Gabriele Paleotti* II, 543–549. Paleotti was transferred to from Albano to Santa Sabina (another of Rome's cardinal sees) in 1591.

undertake in the last stages of old age a demanding work when there was no great hope that his efforts would bear fruit.[18]

Yet, apart from rare allusions to unnamed artists, who made their art serve their piety,[19] Paleotti took no account of contemporary painters. He did not intend, he wrote, to compose a history of artists.[20] When he did name specific artists who deliberately used painting to express their personal devotion, he looked backward to painters of the fourteenth and fifteenth centuries and, most recently, to Albrecht Dürer (1471–1528), who died two generations before Paleotti wrote his book. He took no account of a revolution in the communication of visual images – printing – a medium much used, as it happens, by Dürer.[21]

3   Words and Images

Paleotti's preoccupation with literary traditions made it unnecessary for him to take visual evidence, actual pictures, into account. His exuberant praise of the pleasures of painting is a distinctly bookish philosophical essay on varieties of visual perception; it requires no graphic illustrations.[22] One would have no indication that he ever looked at pictures were it not for the multitude of examples he gave of how pictures accessible to him violated his norms of righteousness, respectability (*honestas*), and decorum. Likewise, what pass for theories of art in Paleotti's treatise come from literature, above all from the pagan classics of pre-Christian Antiquity and from theological texts written by authorities in the early Church, more than a thousand years before his time.

Paleotti's whole argument against the corruption of visual arts, and for their reform, rest on words. How did he justify this apparent inconsistency? We shall need to pay some attention to what he thought about the relationship between visual images and words as means of communication.

Whatever else may be said about it, that relationship was deeply antihistorical. Paleotti had no sense of history, or of style as a product and evidence

---

18   Prodi, *Il cardinale Gabriele Paleotti* II, 550–555. Paleotti Gabriele, "Novissima authoris consideratio in executione decreti Sacri Concilii Tridentini de tollendis Imaginum abusibus", in Prodi, "Ricerche sulla teorica" 196.
19   E.g., Paleotti, *De Imaginibus* 1.18; 2.21; 2.52 = 45; 223; 382.
20   Ibid., 1.18 = 45.
21   Ibid., 1.18 = 44–45. Aside from Dürer, Paleotti mentioned Pietro Cavallini (fl. 1308), a Roman, and two Florentine Dominicans, Fra Angelico (Giovanni da Fiesoli, ca. 1400–1455) and Bartolomeo di San Marco (1475–1517); Hecht, *Katholische Bildertheologie* 345.
22   Paleotti, *De Imaginibus* 1.22 = 92–96; Hecht, *Katholische Bildertheologie* 333–335.

of historical conditions and change.[23] He set forth no theory of stylistic development through periods, broken up by catastrophe and renewal, or of a nobler art in some age before his own degraded time, or, wistfully, of how art might be in better times to come. Corruption of style never occurred to him. At what moment did the corruption of morals that Paleotti laboured to reform fall upon the Church? He does not establish this point either. Corruption illustrated the general proposition that, in the general course of things, time devoured its own,[24] mocking people who, greedy for a kind of immortality, erected monuments to themselves without pausing to think that statues and memorials in churches, and great buildings, perished. Even the realms of the most powerful kings fell prey to time. The ways of Christian Antiquity, excluding anything but the sacred from churches, had fallen into disuse, and the lamentable state of painting was due to corruption brought about through time. In other regards, too, Paleotti's argument is deeply anti-historical. For example, astonishingly given his reliance on classical literature, Paleotti held that Christ came to cause pagan rulers (such as Alexander the Great) and the worship of ancient gods to be entirely forgotten. Heretics too – including Wycliffe, Luther, and others – burned in effigy by the Holy Office, should be erased from history.[25]

To say this is to raise a second aspect of Paleotti's ideas about the relationship between visual images and words: that is, what kinds of narratives Paleotti found being told in the visual arts of his day, and why he condemned them as abuses of a good and useful tool. At issue, beyond the narrative of Redemption, were the narratives by which the art-engendering classes in Paleotti's society imagined themselves, narratives that included classicism and pagan empires, not to mention obscenities and sacrilege as canonized in such venerable texts

---

23 On the absence of style from Paleotti's discussion, see Jones, "Art Theory as Ideology" 132; Hecht, *Katholische Bildertheologie* 60; 326.

24 E.g., Paleotti, *De Imaginibus* 2.18 = 208–209. However much one lusts by nature for immortality, death is the universal imperative; 2.18 = 207. The image of voracious time goes back to Ovid, *Metamorphoses* 15.234: *tempus edax rerum*. Paleotti alludes to this classical tag, 2.18 = 208–209: '*tempori edaci et invido*', a reflection on how great buildings, once impregnable, have been leveled to the ground and reduced to dust. Memorials in churches were swept away by refurbishment, to suit changed ideas of splendor: 1.32 = 134. See also 2.18; 2.47; 2.48; 2.50 = 207–208; 354; 358–359; 370. Portraits too were prey to time. Paleotti noted that many images of a house's forebears were called *fumosae* because, over the long run, they had become discolored and begrimed with smoke; 2.16 = 194.

25 Paleotti, *De Imaginibus* 1.24; 2.10 = 167; 202. Paleotti took from Roman Law his idea that heretics should fall under a sentence of oblivion. Still, he recognized that this was an impractical goal, and contented himself with describing how images of heretics were to be painted, using inscriptions and images to illustrate the deformities of monstrous wickedness and its punishment; 2.22 = 224–226.

as those of Boccaccio and Rabelais. Paleotti believed that how people communicated their imagined selves was of a piece with how they structured the selves they were. He knew that art and life reciprocally imitate each other and thereby change one another. How does society imagine and structure itself? Paleotti's argument identifies a deep hostility between the way approved by one leader of the Counter-Reformation and a multitude of other ways, perhaps the majority in a believing, aristocratic and condescendingly anti-clerical society, such as Castiglione had portrayed in *The Book of the Courtier*.

There were fault-lines in Paleotti's own arguments, where he realized that his moral attack on prevailing values could not win, and he sputtered into compromise for the time being, looking to gradual effects of tradition, law, and coercion for eventual victory.

Paleotti insisted that words and images were parallel means of communication, grounded in human nature. He always defined a subject by its goal, or end, and the end of human beings, he believed, was being held worthy of eternal happiness.[26] It was to be called to glory in what Paleotti imagined as 'the theatre of heaven.'[27]

By its ignorance and weakness, the frail nature people were born with seemed woefully incommensurate with this glorious destiny. However, God, the wise and benevolent Creator, had given ways to compensate for human frailty, and to overcome it. Above all, human beings, frail and insufficient as they were, were born for a social life, though Cicero had been right in saying that they were born for harsh toil, not for frivolity and play.[28] Sin had thwarted God's original blessing on the human race, though the Creator had, in mercy, sent a beam of eternal light – 'the light of nature' – into the hearts of all Adam's descendants. Some device using that light was needed for individuals to live as social creatures, to communicate with each other, to overcome the barrier to knowing things because they were absent. Art was needed to overcome the deficiencies of nature.[29]

Nature contained art's basic tools. The human body had a voice and moving limbs. Art came with the invention of signs, turning vocal sounds into articulate words and physical movements into meaningful gestures. Signs came into being by common consensus when the inherent desire to learn combined

---

26 Ibid., 1.18; 2.12 (ultimate happiness is enjoyment of the Trinity); 2.15 = 81; 175; 192; Jones, "Art Theory as Ideology" 127–131. See also Jones's application of Paleotti's theories to actual paintings; 131f.; 135f. On Paleotti's general teleological point of view, Hecht, *Katholische Bildertheologie* 333.
27 Paleotti, *De Imaginibus* 1.18; 2.50 = 81; 369: *theatrum caeli*.
28 Ibid., 2.31 = 277.
29 Ibid., 1.1; 1.4 = 6; 17–20.

with the desire to signify, to communicate, with others. By using signs, human societies compensated for individual ignorance and frailty. They learned how to provide food for themselves and for animals, and how to govern families, found cities, make tools. Like words, images enabled human beings to enlarge and preserve knowledge in all is branches and to make good again what age corrupted. In hundreds of ways, they served the common good.[30]

The visual arts, Paleotti thought, were among those inventions which sprang from the interior light of nature. He considered that God had given human beings the power of making images, depicting things and representing them to the eyes, and that this power – the power of *disegno* (*designatio*) – as prior to the power of words. It was the 'soul of painting and the first foundation of this art.' Except among the Hebrews, there were pictures before there were books; for the art of representation was more easily acquired than that of writing, and it was used in every corner of the world. Moreover, visual imagery entered the minds of deaf and mute persons, and there were many stories of how vision, having far more powerful impact than hearing, had changed physical reality, as when a white mother gave birth to an Ethiopian child, thanks to a picture of an Ethiopian in her bedroom, and as St. Francis of Assisi received the stigmata from his vision of a Seraph. Angels communicated, not by words, but by images transmitted to the mind.[31]

Paleotti considered the 'heretics' of his day enemies of the liberal arts, as Julian the Apostate had been in the late Roman Empire. They had, he wrote, destroyed schools, where the liberal arts were taught, and were intent on extinguishing knowledge of all sciences.[32] In his mind, the Protestant assaults against religious images were of a piece with this general attack on the mind, and they required Paleotti to defend images as a means of communication both normal in human society and essential to achieving he end of eternal blessedness for which the human race was made. Thus, he recognized both words and images as mediating knowledge with the objectives of pleasing and teaching minds, and moving, or winning hearts.[33] They were, in some sense, counterparts of one another. Sensing their mutuality, the ancient Greek lyric poet, Simonides of Chios (*ca* 556–*ca* 468 BCE) had referred to them in a paradox that became proverbial when he wrote that painting was 'mute poetry,' and poetry, 'talking pictures.'[34] To be sure, they represented things by different

---

30 Ibid., 1.4; 1.12; 1.17; 1.20 = 17–20; 54–56; 77; 87–88.
31 Ibid., 1.5; 1.26; 2.52 = 22–25; 107–109; 378.
32 Ibid., 2.12 = 176.
33 Ibid., 1.5 = 26.
34 Ibid., 1.5 = 25.

methods of imitation, and in media (words and colours) that had nothing in common. Though painters imitated what they found in books, many things in books could not be represented by the artist's brush.[35]

Painting and writing had the same end: to instruct. But painting served this end more generally and more effectively than writing, and, moreover, it fostered the still higher end for which the human race was made. Books were only for the learned. Pictures were accessible to every order of society and to every sort and condition of person. Tacitly discounting the power of preachers, Paleotti asked how, without images, the unlettered multitude would know the mysteries necessary to salvation.[36] Furthermore, verbal information conveyed meanings that had to be absorbed, parsed and digested by various mental faculties. A bridge of interpretation had to be crossed between the verbal sign and the thing it represented. No such bridge was needed with pictures. For viewers had from pictures a virtual experience of seeing the actual subjects represented, not signs that needed interpreting. Contemplating a picture of the Crucifixion, one could feel the sharpness of the spikes that fixed Christ to the Cross.[37] Consequently, painting had a direct and penetrating effect on the mind and heart.

4   The Power of Painting, and How It Went Wrong

When it joined spiritual beauty to images, painting enabled the human race to move toward its God-appointed goal, both because it conveyed knowledge essential to salvation to all, including the 'vulgar, illiterate multitude' excluded by books,[38] and also because pious images produced changes of heart more readily than books. They recalled the lapsed from evil by holding up dreadful punishments before their eyes. To the good, pictures stirred the passions to participate empathetically in the agonies and triumphs of the saints. Viewed with empathy, pictures stirred penitential grief for sin and terror-stricken devotion;

---

35   Ibid., 1.5 = 24–25. Paleotti frequently repeated his basic doctrine that painting was an art of imitation. Difficulties arose when painters imitated phantasies of their own minds, rather than being content with their art as an 'imitatio veri', meaning truths set forth in Scripture, common human decorum, or what was present to the eye in nature. See also 2.27; 2.41; 2.42; 2.52 = 252; 322–323; 328; 377.

36   Ibid., 1.18; 1.24 = 81–82; 101. See Jones, "Art Theory as Ideology" 127.

37   Paleotti, *De Imaginibus* 1.25 = 103. Cf. Prodi's reading of the connections Paleotti drew between painting and rhetoric. Prodi, "Ricerche sulla teorica" 198f.

38   Paleotti, *De Imaginibus* 2.49 = 363. On the illiterate multitude as the main audience for painting, and on the capacity of the illiterate for spiritual perception and, eventually, salvation, see Jones, "Art Theory as Ideology" 134; 137f.

they caused the soul to burn with hatred of the evil and with fiery zeal to imitate the saints.[39] Venerating in one action the image and its holy subject, believers moved from things apprehended by the senses to things inaccessible to the senses.[40] Miracles confirmed how God used images to advance his mercies toward the human race, interrupting or reversing the course of nature as when, through miraculous images, the sick recovered from incurable diseases and cities were saved from raging fires and besieging armies.[41]

Amid the opulence of Renaissance Rome, Paleotti knew very well that works of art were collected with 'great toil and great cost.'[42] When dedicated for rites and rituals of worship, they were sacrifices to God. By them, donors expressed their complete dependence on and obedience to God. From them, they derived the immense happiness; for, through their offerings, outward signs rendered by paintbrush and colours, they beheld inwardly the reality of God's majesty.[43]

And yet, Paleotti wrote his book precisely because, in his judgment, painting had gone wrong; it had left the straight and narrow path of religion. His treatise is a polemic. It was the Devil's own work, Paleotti wrote, that Protestants denounced and rejected the sacred functions of images, and that abuses among Roman Catholics, even in the adornment of churches, had gone so far as to bring mind the proverb: 'There isn't a church where the Devil doesn't occupy a shrine.'[44] The state of religious art demonstrated the Devil's handiwork in the holy of holies.

Paleotti was able to trace the legitimacy of religious images back to the Creation, when God himself made images. Moreover, under the Law, God had commanded images to be made and used in true religion by the Hebrews. God's sanction of images in sacred history was basic to Paleotti's rebuttal of Protestant charges that the Roman Church had fallen into idolatry; and he took meticulous care to explain how far the veneration of images, which he approved, differed from the diabolic lusts and superstitions of authentic idolatry.[45] He realized that there was truth in what the Protestants said.

---

39 Paleotti, *De Imaginibus* 1.18; 1.25 = 81–83; 103–105.
40 Ibid., 1.30 = 123.
41 Ibid., 1.26 = 106. Paleotti also mentioned images regarded as miraculous because they wept or bled, or because they were made by supernatural action (e.g., Veronica's handkerchief, the Holy Shroud, and the Holy House of Loretto); 1.16 = 73f.
42 Ibid., 2.15 = 191, referring to collections of (putatively) ancient coins, painting, and sculpture.
43 Ibid., 1.20 = 88.
44 Ibid., 2.48 = 360.
45 See ibid., 1.1; 1.4 (Moses's Tabernacle and Solomon's Temple); 1.15 (Moses wrote, but he also used images); 1.17; 1.31–32 = 6–7; 18; 23–24; 31–32; 128–138; Hecht, *Katholische Bildertheologie* 193–204; 222f.; 226f.

In all ages Satan had intruded subversively into the house of God. Paleotti was sure that, with remarkable versatility, the Devil had seduced others, even the Jews, into worshiping images as though they were true gods, that, in Paleotti's own day, the Devil had pushed the Protestants to the opposite extreme of abolishing images, spewing their venom on all and sundry, and that he laughed at the new idolatry with which he had hurled Roman Catholics into insane abuses.[46]

The making and reading of analogies was notoriously disputatious, and spawned idolatrous and superstitious abuses of images. Leaving aside false analogies, which were common as dust, Paleotti's argument required accurate making of correct visual analogies. For this reason, he insisted on verisimilitude – and kind of visual literalism – in paintings.[47] The Devil was in the understanding of images more than in their making.

Even so, reading analogies was by no means uniform. Like all signs, a picture was morally indifferent, neither good nor bad in itself, but balanced between virtue and vice.[48] Not only might viewers make of a picture something quite different from what the painter had in mind, but viewers themselves could take their analogical readings in quite opposite ways.[49] Some, Paleotti wrote, considered the brazen serpent Moses erected in the desert a sacred image, representing a mystery. Others found it an idol made for pleasure. The philosophers, he wrote, had a saying that everything is received, or not, according to the measure of the recipient, and not according to the measure of what is received or rejected, an awkward version of 'beauty is in the eye of the beholder.' Thus, he wryly commented, bees make the nectar of flowers into honey, and spiders turn it into lethal poison.[50] The story of sacred images was particularly complex. For, while it was true that the light of nature implanted by God made religion more truly characteristic of human being than reason – no one could be counted a human being without some awareness of God – the light of nature was dim. False principles arose from ignorance of God, and from them false religion arose with idol-worship. There were many theories about when the cult of idols first appeared, thanks to false readings of the analogies of art.[51]

Impelled by his consuming envy and ancient hatred of God, the Devil stirred up evil feeling and twisted desires in those whose ignorance of authentic

---

46 Paleotti, *De Imaginibus* 1.15; 1.24; 1.27; 2.3, 2.10 = 68–69; 71; 111; 147; 162; 168.
47 On Paleotti's ideas about verisimilitude, see Prodi, *Ricerche* 154–156.
48 Paleotti, *De Imaginibus* 2.17; 2.19; 2.50 = 197; 210; 369.
49 See ibid., 2.31 = 271: People who see a well-made painting for the first time may laugh at it, though the owner sees nothing novel or improvised in it.
50 Ibid., 1.10 = 49–50. See also 2.52 = 381.
51 Ibid., 1.14–1.15 = 60–66.

interpretation had overtaken them. Making the most of misunderstandings, he induced the susceptible to set up images in wood or marble in God's place, and to render to the Angel of Darkness the worship due to God alone. Thus, all used images; but some, under God's protection, followed correctly the light of nature and cultivated justice, innocence and piety, while others fell into the crime of superstition.[52]

Though Paleotti believed that his warfare was against powers of spiritual darkness, he intended to incite reform in human minds and hearts. Wide as his range generally was, his concern lay with his own Church. He did not have anything to say about unbelievers in distant, new-found continents, or indeed about Jewish idolaters long before in Sacred History. Without God's help, virtuous pagans died in sin and perished, condemned to eternal punishments.[53]

Paleotti even dismissed his contemporary enemies, the Protestant iconoclasts, with a perfunctory gesture. What did they mean, arguing that religious images were not holy because their materials and colours, and the artists who painted them, were not holy? They missed the point, Paleotti argued. Scripture was not holy because of the materials with which it was written (parchment, ink, and pen), or because of the Scribe's hand.[54] These enemies of the faith also absurdly argued that users of images fell into the ancient heresy of anthropomorphism, representing God – though he was incorporeal, uncircumscribed, and indescribable – complete with human physique, eyes, hands, face, and all the other body parts, not to mention portraying angels and the souls of the blessed also in bodies.[55] A moment's reflection, he wrote, unmasked the stupidity behind this charge of anthropomorphism. No one could think that material objects, such as paint, could convey divinity, or that the divine nature could be expressed in visual form.

To be sure, Scripture and the holy Fathers alluded to spiritual beings with material metaphors and similitudes in words, as when they spoke of God's face, or of the Holy Spirit as a dove, or of angels as young men wearing diadems and other appropriate insignia. But we know that spiritual realities are far from physical ones, and that these allusions were only imitations or analogues of things we can see with our physical sight.[56] Animals could sometimes be

---

52   Ibid., 1.1 = 6f. See also 1.14–1.15 = 60–66.
53   Ibid., 2.16 = 195.
54   Ibid., 1.16 = 76.
55   Ibid., 1.30; 1.33 = 122f.; 126; 136; 137. For Paleotti, the representation of spiritual beings in pictures was doubly a paradox of representing absent subjects: first, because all painting represents absent subjects, and, secondly, because the material portrayals of spiritual beings brought to mind the fact that they actually lacked bodies.
56   Ibid., 1.30 = 123.

deceived into reacting to images as though they were, or expressed, realities. Hating men, panthers could be teased into towering rages if, for a joke, the image of a man were stood up in front of them. But, not all animals were so gullible. When rustics put up scarecrows to fend off birds, the smarter birds were not long deceived and came and fed and built their nests among the ragtag manikins. With their charge of anthropomorphism, do the Protestants mean that a Christian, endowed with reason and nourished by the milk of Holy Church, is less perceptive than brute animals?[57]

Paleotti took no note of the Protestants' consuming zeal to translate Scripture and liturgy into vernacular languages, and to establish schools that would curtail illiteracy and enable every ploughboy to read the Scriptures, once a copy was in his hands.[58] He could not anticipate that the lines dividing the literate elite and the illiterate, unskilled, and rustic multitude would change. He held to the argument that, by attacking images, Protestants deprived the illiterate multitude of the mysteries of salvation. He was on firmer ground when he argued that, by abolishing spiritual contemplation through veneration of images, Protestants dissolved the communion of saints, the sacramental bond between believers on earth and those in heaven.

However, Paleotti's chief enemies were not Protestants, outside his own communion, but members of his own Church. There, the Devil's work was most troubling of all. Abuses by painting, he wrote, could be more deadly than iconoclasm which swept away images altogether.[59] Up to a point, he and the Protestant iconoclasts had the same enemies, though for different reasons. Ironically, some parts of his argument had much in common with Protestant polemics, which he derided as heretical iconoclasm.

The end of Christian painting, Paleotti wrote, was not pleasure alone, which might satisfy the purposes of pagan art, but utility joined together with pleasure – utility in advancing human salvation.[60] Painting was a morally neutral means. Its power as a sign, expressing something by way of likeness,[61] could be used to serve the end for which God created humanity. The power of *disegno* could also be turned by content and circumstance to reprehensible objectives, as had happened in Catholic churches.

What was wrong? Paleotti's startling agreement with Protestants begins with his argument that, abusing their freedom of choice, his fellow Catholics

---

57   Ibid., 1.33 = 137.
58   Cf. Paleotti's reference to *libri populares* spreading heretical poison; 2.7 = 156.
59   Ibid., 2.1 = 143.
60   Ibid., 2.30 = 264.
61   Ibid., 1.19 = 85. On Paleotti's conception of God-given hierarchic structures of the universe and society, see Jones, "Art Theory as Ideology" 138.

had confused means with end, making the use and enjoyment of paintings ends in themselves. God's infinite providence created everything in the world good. Giving human beings the means to pursue and obtain those goods, God also left them free choice, to use the rest of creation rightly or to abuse it. But, mistaking the means for the end, they tore apart the admirable hierarchic order God created. He had brought the world into being as though it were a clock, with all its works – the weights, movements (*momenta*), and wheels – set to perform the separate functions for the smooth running of the whole. But human abuses had disrupted that order, hurling arts, sciences, virtues, and all human ventures – into turmoil and confusion.[62] If the tide could be turned at all, it would take many years for people to abandon the dark shadows in which they lived, embrace piety, and restore dignity to sacred images. Paleotti hoped that his book would mark a beginning of the turn.[63]

Like his Protestant enemies, he found the use of images in his Church deeply contaminated by superstition. There were countless superstitions associated with images. Paleotti had a book recording administrative rulings against them in the Church of Bologna. From Scripture and writers of the patristic era, he culled a small, but chilling array of practices. Though severely punished by law, diabolic acts entailing the use of sacred images continued in his own day. He knew that images of saints were carried in procession through fields, with a riotous cacophony. The louder the racket, people believed, the richer the harvest. Images of the Apostle Paul were cast into rivers on the feast of his Conversion to produce good weather. Paleotti also knew of rituals in which saints were humiliated by way of their images. From records of the Second Council of Lyons (1274), if not from direct observations, he knew irreligious and nefarious acts of humiliation, in which images of the Cross, the Blessed Virgin, or other saints were cast down and smothered in nettles and thorns. By comparison, Paleotti seems to move into a tamer category of superstition when he notes that, through demonic tricks, people insisted that holy images be made with divinatory practices – that an image of St. Peter always be made after cock-crow; that an artist wear a veil made by a virgin when painting the Blessed Virgin, that colours be used appropriate to the liturgical day, that the painter's brush always have a fixed number of hairs.[64] Paleotti condemned such superstitions, but he found greater evils, which corrupted the production

---

62 Paleotti, *De Imaginibus* 2.12 = 174–176.
63 Ibid., 1. proem. = 3.
64 Ibid., 2.8 = 159–161. On the humiliation of the saints, see Geary P., *Living with the Dead in the Middle Ages* (Ithaca: 1994) 95–115, "Humiliation of the Saints"; 116–124, "Coercion of Saints in Medieval Religious Practice".

of art at the source. The malign influence of the Devil fades into the background as Paleotti turns to human agency.

The abuses that so alarmed him came about through the moral failings of patrons and painters. Paleotti laid his heaviest charge against patrons; painters only did their bidding.[65] In the commissions they parcelled out among their artistic hangers-on, the great were driven by craving for immortality, love of ostentation, and lust for praise without measure.[66] Paleotti found the vainglory of their 'Pharisaical arrogance'[67] in the armorials which they emblazoned flamboyantly on the walls and furnishings of churches, often lying about distinctions that never were. Their cult of ancestry, with its heraldic imagery, introduced a new idolatry into the Church.[68]

The same vices impelled them to commission portraits of themselves hoping to display their nobility, virtue, and beauty to general applause, yearning for praise that would continue to be rendered to them, through the portraits, after their deaths. Paleotti recognized that portraits commissioned by persons other than the subject could have laudable objectives, as, for example, in bridging the pain of separation by distance or death, or proving kinship in litigation through physical resemblance (e. g., paternity suits),[69] giving eligible bridegrooms in arranged marriages previews of spouses chosen for them sight unseen, or providing models of virtue, especially for the instruction of children. Yet, the general run of portraits came from vainglory, and human love of ostentation led painters to cater to their patron's vanity by tricking out their pictures with luxurious accessories, such as dogs, flowers, fans, parrots, and monkeys, not to mention opulent costumes, all extravagances that detracted from the dignity of the person. Of course, painters took advantage of artistic licence to efface deformities and to depict subjects, even lightheaded young women, more beautiful than they were.[70]

As he looked around him, Paleotti found portraits of reprobates, paintings that should be thrown out because of the shame and infamy attached to their subjects. These included portraits of people who were enemies of the faith, of those whose illicit acts vitiated their title to be called 'Christian,' those who intended their portraits to outrage others or cause them to fall into lechery.[71]

---

65 Paelotti, *De Imaginibus* 1. proem. = 4.
66 Cf. ibid., 2.18; 2.46 = 207; 209; 347.
67 Ibid., 2.46 = 347.
68 Ibid., 2.10; 2.48; 2.49 = 168; 348f.; 360f.; 363.
69 Ibid., 2.7; 2.19; 2.20 = 213; 215f.; 217f.; 218f.
70 Ibid., 2.20–2.21 = 218f.; 223.
71 Ibid., 2.20; 2.21 = 214; 222. Enemies of the faith included heretics, idolaters, tyrants, and rapists of virgins. Those who have lost their title to be called Christian included whores and other women of impure lives, charlatans, actors, mercenaries, and parasites.

Even those untainted by dishonour could find that portraits delivered unwelcome returns. By commissioning portraits of themselves, patrons could open the door to being mocked for inflated views of their own importance. Who could tell how the experiment in public relations would turn out? It all depended on what abilities artists could muster for the three or four hours needed to complete a portrait. Paleotti was quite sure that, by commissioning their own portraits, patrons succumbed to self-love, self-worship, captivated by their own Narcissistic blindness. He was quite sure that, contrary to patron's desire that their portraits would garner praise and undying fame, a portrait was in fact nothing but a *memento mori*, presenting the likeness of a body that would soon perish and be reduced to contemptible dust, and, he might have added, in a medium far more perishable than stone or bronze.[72] Indeed, if they were intended to present the reality of a person, portraits were exercises in futility. For they delivered only the image of the body, the prison-house of the invisible soul. Correspondingly, they moved only viewers who could be moved by external appearances, rather than by living, inward realities.[73] What was it to put these signs of worldly arrogance – heraldic emblems and images of living persons, up onto churches – except to foist human baseness onto the sanctuary of God, where the powers of heaven trembled with awe? What else was it but to mingle dung and ashes with gold?[74] He reserved his comments on tombs, epitaphs, and funerary insignia to the (unpublished) fourth book of his treatise.[75] Paleotti rebuked patrons for versions of self-worship when they plastered church buildings and furnishings with their armorials, and when they commissioned portraits of themselves, above all when they intended to ensconce their portraits in churches. He had other censures for their love of pre-Christian Antiquity. At this point, the Devil returned to Paleotti's argument.

Protestants considered Roman Catholics' use of religious images a later stage of pre-Christian pagan practice, and Paleotti admitted that, aided and abetted by archaeologists, painters and sculptors, the Protestants had a point. Remains of ancient idols, long buried in the earth, had been uncovered and restored by painters and sculptors, who were also busy making new images of ancient gods to adorn the dwellings of the rich. Images of pagan gods and goddesses crowded the entryways of princes' libraries, so full of pagan books too that there was no room for a holy writer.[76] In the early Church, martyrs burned with rage against the pagan gods, hurled their images down, and banished them

---

72 Ibid., 2.19 = 211f.
73 Ibid., 2.19 = 211–213.
74 Ibid., 2.28 = 360.
75 Ibid., 2.28 = 362.
76 Ibid., 2.12 = 178.

from sight.[77] By contrast, in his day, Paleotti found the houses and storehouses of the rich stuffed to overflowing with mythological figures, accumulated with great toil and expense over two or more generations.[78] Artists produced more and more every day, misled into thinking that nothing was elegant or conspicuously above the normal run without the impiety of a figure of Venus or Jupiter added, together with a few sacrifices. They alleged that the images were made just for pleasure, not for worship, and that the ingenuity of a painter and the technical excellence of a painting justified the image. But they offended the eyes of the faithful; the Devil laughed to see the flood of new gods and goddesses introduced into churches, his weapons installed in the houses of God as trophies of his demonic victory.[79] As consumers and propagators of pagan myth, patrons and artists allied with Satan and his henchmen, attempting to undermine Truth and therefore, nature itself.[80] For this very reason, Paleotti recalled, Moses had cast sculptors and painters, liars all, out of his republic.[81]

Their zeal for classical Antiquity allied patrons and artists with the Devil in another way. For multiplying images of pagan gods meant nudity, and Satan's prime objective had been to proliferate nudes, overflowing with wantonness and license. One function of art, Paleotti wrote in another connection was to cover those things that are sordid.[82] No evangelist relates whether the parts of the crucified Lord which, for modesty's sake (*pudoris causa*) are usually, and ought to be, covered were in fact covered by a cloth. But, Paleotti commented, depicting the Crucified's private parts covered was a centuries-old custom accepted by all Christians. If anyone painted this subject differently, it would seem to be the greatest impiety. Apparently, Paleotti did not know the marble

77   Ibid., 2.10; 2.15 = 107; 170.
78   Ibid., 2.15 = 190f.
79   Ibid., 2.10; 2.15 = 168–170; 189.
80   Ibid., 1.27 = 112.
81   Ibid., 2.41 = 323f., with a lapse of the pen substituting 'Moses' for 'Plato.' See Plato, *Republic* 10. 595a–602a.
82   Paleotti, *De Imaginibus* 1.20; p. 88. There is no indication that Paleotti knew of nude portraits, including nude self-portraits by Dürer, his model of a modern Christian painter, inoffensive at least in that they conceal the *pudenda*. Among the other nude portraits of Paleotti's era, one can mention Bronzino's portrait of Cosimo I de' Medici as Orpheus (c. 1538–1540; Philadelphia Museum of Art), and two French works, François Clouet's portrait of Diane de Poitiers (c. 1571; National Gallery of Art, Washington, D.C.), and, from the 'School of Fontainebleau', a portrait of Gabrielle d'Estrées and one of her sisters (late sixteenth century; Louvre). None of these paintings depict the *pudenda*.

crucifix made by Benvenuto Cellini for his own tomb, depicting Christ completely nude.[83]

Turning from the collaboration of patrons and artists specifically to artists, Paleotti found much to censure. The business of painters, after all, was to gratify the wills of their patrons, whether inspired by the Devil or by run-of-the-mill human aspirations. In their own ways, quite apart from patrons, artists deflected painting from its proper, religious end, making it pernicious for the artists themselves and for viewers (whom Paleotti here calls 'us').[84] Patrons allowed themselves to use art as a means to achieve praise through ostentation, and undying fame through their monuments, to present themselves as models to be admired and imitated by later generations, and to arouse their sensual desires. For their part, artists used painting to make money, to gain praise and esteem, to win favour by pandering to others' pleasures. Paleotti admonished artists to turn from their greed and ambition, and to practice their art in integrity and innocence. They should, he said, keep to the moral high road, and cast their eyes on nothing abject or base. They should never sell out their high spiritual hopes for payment or advantage. Their calling, he insisted, was to pursue God with love and industry, to fix their minds on the holiness they painted in its visible manifestations, and always to keep their eyes firmly set on eternal rewards.[85]

The Council of Trent had forbidden the use of 'unaccustomed images' and, with an eye to artists, Paleotti interpreted that prohibition widely against experimentation in painting. Long-standing abuse had to be condemned as firmly as innovation that ran contrary to Scripture or ecclesiastical tradition. The diseases of religious painting had come about, Paleotti wrote, because painters had abused their freedom and violated the norms of probability, decorum, and utility. They had failed in its task of verisimilitude, which, for Paleotti, meant 'imitating truth,' corresponding with 'the truth of a matter and an action' (*veritati rei et facti*).[86] They did not portray things as the eye saw, knew, and recognized them, yielding all too often to the phantasies of their own minds, hostile to truth and to art. They introduced elements not sanctioned by Scripture or normal human usage. They meddled with high matters that should be left

---

83   Ibid., 2.9 = 164. See also 2.26 = 247: Some pictures of the Crucifixion depict apostles semi-nude. Paleotti here objects to the representation on grounds of plausibility, rather than of piety. The crucifixion took place in winter, he wrote, but the stripped apostles are undressed as though for summer.
84   Ibid., 2.1 = 143. See 1.5 = 27: Artists should make paintings that correspond with mankind's high and glorious end.
85   Ibid., 1.19 = 84f.
86   Ibid., 2.25; 2.26; 2.27; 2.41; 2.42; 2.52 = 238; 243f.; 246; 252 (*ars est veri imitatrix*); 322f.; 328; 377.

to theologians and teachers. Paleotti wished to clip the wings of artistic licence with prudence and truth, constraining painters to abide by the common judgment of the learned and to form images approved by holy bishops for use in churches. Unfettered innovations, contrary to reason, truth, and nature itself, were on Paleotti's list for censoring.[87]

In their ignorance and infidelity to verisimilitude, artists intruded absurdities into representations of the most sacred subjects, as when they represented the Blessed Virgin as a young woman about twenty-five years old, holding the body of her thirty-year-old son, and depicted John the Baptist as a boy and Jesus as a bearded man, although they were only three months apart in age – his comment on representations of a mother younger than her son must have reminded contemporary readers of Michelangelo's *Pietà* (Rome, St Peter's), new and very celebrated in Paleotti's day.[88] Given the brutality of Christ's Passion, how could painters depict Jesus on the Cross with a full, white, delicate body, without wounds, lash-marks, or bruises? Errors of proportion in representing a human body, or relationships among figures in a painting, would make it untrue to life. There were many other ways in which painter's ignorance or lack of skill destroyed verisimilitude (the *imitationis norma*), and therefore the analogy between what was in the picture and what people saw around them.[89]

Under the momentum of the classical revival, filth deformed even the images of the holiest. In this regard, Paleotti detected the Devil's work most plainly. Pandering to classicism, artists painted Christ as though he were Apollo, and portrayed martyrdom as though it were a metamorphosis in pagan mythology. Yet worse, the Devil intruded himself into their portrayals of saints. Though, in life, the saints may have been the most severe ascetics, wasting their bodies with fasting and penitential tears, painters depicted them, not skeletal, but with full and luscious faces, bedecked with ornaments and lewd colours such as not even women of the fouler type, or actors, would dare put on. Painters were known to stoop so low as to use their mistresses as models or saints. More than the rule of decorum, which Paleotti cherished, was at issue.[90]

---

87   Ibid., 2.32; 2.41 = 278f.; 322–324.
88   Ibid., 2.28 = 256.
89   Ibid., 1.9; 2.21; 2.28 = 46–47; 223; 254–258. On idealized portrayals of the Crucified, see Prodi, *Ricerche sulla teorrica* 155. Cf. 2.48 = 362: It was an analogic offence to join family armorials to sacred things and divine worship. See also 1.19 = 19f.: Anyone would wish to see the true face of Christ, or of the Blessed Virgin, or the presence of the Apostles and their wonderful acts. Since we cannot do that in person, we compensate for our lack by the remedy of images.
90   On decorum, see, ibid., e.g., 2.27 = 253, on representations of the Blessed Virgin.

The Devil's promotion of nudity won here too, for, having taken the liberty of giving ascetic saints opulent bodies, painters did not flinch from displaying their robust physical endowments with indecently naked legs and shoulders. Though the saint's modesty and humility hardly ever allowed them to raise their eyes, artists depicted their eyes flashing with unbearable lewdness. Painters defended these abuses, Paleotti said, by saying that they took these liberties for the improvement of art and to display their ingenuity in imitating Antique masterworks. The truth of the matter, Paleotti added, was that they burned with excessive zeal for their own glory and celebrity, and he intended to tear this self-advertising abuse out of religious painting by the roots.

As he inventoried the stylistic defects of contemporary painters, Paleotti made it clear, chapter by chapter, exactly how brazenly artists had gone wrong by parting company with religion. Like patrons, they owed some corruptions to their own moral failings and some to the Devil. Paleotti took his stand against all the major directions art had taken in his day, human and demonic. As we have seen, he discountenanced classicism, not only because it idealized pagan religious myth, but also because it held up for emulation the deeds of ancient heroes and sages, completely outside the pale of Christian faith, even when they had not been its persecutors. He disapproved of pictures dense with allegory, symbol, and fantasy because, being hard to decipher, they failed to teach Christian truth directly and unambiguously. For the same reason, he censured paintings of obscure, recondite subjects and pictures painted in the surrealist styles of Mannerism, with disorienting focus or eccentric proportions, distorting spatial relations, and eye-dazzling *chiaroscuro*. Like improbable representations of Christ and the saints, such styles violated what Paleotti assumed to be the necessary analogy – verisimilitude, 'the rule of likeness' – between painting and forms of things made by God.[91]

He arraigned artists most consistently for their choices of subject. In subjects, one could see most clearly the degree to which painting had cut itself free from theology.[92] Impious and ignorant themselves, and driven by lust for wealth and celebrity, artists descended from right reason so far as to paint subjects that pandered, not only to vainglorious patrons, but, much worse, to the vicious, illiterate multitude – joke paintings of puerile and reprehensible subjects that impeached the painters' judgement, paintings of obscene riot,

---

[91] Ibid., 1.5; 2.51 = 26; 380.
[92] See ibid., 2.51 = 375: A picture is perfect in proportion to the degree in which it corresponds with theology; 2.3 = 147–149: Painters risk error when they expand the strict letter of Scripture by painting scenes that incorporate elements grounded in more or less doubtful hypotheses.

gluttony, and drunkenness, of social outcasts, most scandalously of prostitutes and other lewd women.[93] Painters no longer heeded the call to be 'mute theologians.'[94]

Together with patrons and compliant clergy, painters had made churches theatres of vanity instead of antechambers of heaven. Paleotti scorned their misplaced enthusiasm. It was one thing to represent heathen gods and pagans, but quite another to depict saints, firmly grounded in religion and piety. All the technical finesse and ingenuity artist displayed in these impious renditions of holy subjects were incitements to damnation and Satanic vainglory.[95] Painters, he wrote, should not turn to the Devil's ministry the art and talent they received from God.[96]

Paleotti did not underestimate the 'ineptitude, madness,' and depravity of painters.[97] Everywhere he saw systemic abuses, like multiple diseases. He knew that each disease required its own treatment. There could be, he said, no hard and fast rule for the reform of art, and he had no hope for a quick recovery.[98] Indeed, he realized that few, or none, could rise to the height he envisioned for painting, and he was filled with despair when, quite apart from Satan's malice, he considered that dearth, the universal corruption of the artist's discipline, and the (unspecified) losses of earlier masterworks suffered by his age.[99]

5 A Moderate's Proposals for Reform

And yet, even against such formidable odds, he felt able to set forth elements of a general remedy. His advice was not evenly distributed. He admonished patrons to serve the glory of God and purity of life, instead of vainglorious desires, and urged them to seek spiritual direction from pious and learned men. Beyond this, Paleotti offered little guidance for self-reform.[100]

By contrast, he had much improving practical advice for artists. He prayed that God would enlighten their minds, and that, illuminated by grace, they would turn from their errors.[101] Once fortified by grace, they would need to

---

93   Ibid., 1. proem.; 2.20; 2.21; 2.27; 2.31; 2.52 = 2f.; 214; 222; 254; 270–277; 373; 379.
94   Ibid., 2.51 = 375.
95   Ibid., 2.1; 2.11; 2.52 = 142; 173; 381.
96   Ibid., 2.21 = 221. See also 2.12 = 174.
97   Ibid., 2.27; 2.52 = 254; 382.
98   Ibid., 2.21 = 221.
99   Ibid., 2.51 = 374.
100 Ibid., 2.48–2.50 = 359f.; 366; 370.
101 Ibid., 2.1 = 145.

correct their ignorance by long years of study under the direction of the best masters. They would need, furthermore, to read widely – about plants and animals, about costumes and history, about theology and liturgy – to gain such knowledge as they had to have to portray their subjects accurately and in accord with sound doctrine. In considering their techniques and works, painters were to examine their consciences and, when plagued by doubt and suspicion, to do as their patrons were to do, seeking the godly direction of spiritual and learned men.[102] Indeed, Paleotti urged painters not to exploit the lascivious desires of patrons, but to find occasions to bring them to moral reform. When they suspected the motives behind a commission, they were to find out whether patrons had some morally destructive objective in view, such as seducing another man's wife. They must avoid becoming complicit in others' sins by nurturing lust. If painters found that patrons wished to use pictures as goads to lechery, they could evade complicity by not giving the customers what they wanted, but substituting for the image desired a pious image, say of Christ being beaten, or of a saint. He knew a painter in Bologna who had produced moral conversions by giving his customers more pious images than the ones they had ordered.[103]

In all these tactics for moral renewal, Paleotti took for granted that painting was a social artifact. Following this stance to its logical conclusion, Paleotti advised painters always to submit their works to judgment by consensus.[104] He frequently appealed to consensus, under such names as 'the common sense of all,' and the 'consensus of the Holy Catholic Church.' It was natural that he regarded consensus as a norm governing painting.[105]

He did not mean consensus of the majority. To be sure, he gave no credit to judgment by the unskilled and illiterate multitude, fallen away from right reason as it was, and given over to base desires. The multitude did not even look at pictures as *cognoscenti* did; for the masses were used to sweeping their eyes over clusters of paintings instead of looking at them one-by-one, and, apart from their taste for scenes of moral wantonness, they were easily and indiscriminatingly pleased.[106] He meant something like the *melior et sanior*

---

102   Ibid., 2.21 = 222.
103   Ibid., 2.21 = 222f. Paleotti also illustrated the power of paintings to produce righteous changes of heart with an anecdote about a Milanese nobleman, plotting murder, who was thrown into emotional turmoil at the sight of a crucifix. The nobleman, he wrote, fell at the foot of the crucifix and gave up his plot. Many others, he added, had had the same experience. 1.26 = 110.
104   E.g., ibid., 2.15; 2.20; 2.24; 2.46; 2.50; 2.51 = 141; 218; 230; 347; 372; 373.
105   Ibid., 2.51–2.52 = 375–382.
106   Ibid., 2.31; 2.52 = 275f.; 373; 379.

pars privileged in ecclesiastical elections where the votes were weighed, not counted. Paleotti had members of higher social orders in mind, as well as the illiterate multitude, when he wrote that many never thought about anything beyond what they perceived by their bodily senses; they never imitated what Scripture calls 'clean animals,' ruminating their food.[107] Paleotti advised painters to let their pictures rest before applying the final touches. Like the ancient Greek painter Apelles, they would do well at that stage to exhibit their paintings to the scrutiny of men of discernment, the few who were used to artistic rumination, and heeding their observations; for so they would gain an earthly crown from men and a heavenly one from God.[108] Lawyer that he was, Paleotti included in his remedy another court beyond the court of social consensus. The Church was the final arbiter of morals and he looked ultimately to ecclesiastical authority to cure the diseases he found in art generally and religious art particularly. He wrote *On Sacred and Profane Images* as a bishop, acting on powers over Church art that the Council of Trent had delegated to bishops. He associated coercive discipline with the 'ancient norm of Holy Church,' 'the authority and judgment of the Church,' 'the authority of the Catholic and Apostolic Church.'[109] He anticipated censorship of paintings under papal supervision like that instituted by the Council of Trent in the *Index of Forbidden Books*, censorship enforced by interdict and anathema.[110]

6 Difficulties with the Remedy

Some measure of how detached Paleotti's ideal of religious art was from innovations in art, and how markedly he was swimming against the tide, is given by a brief sampling of works he would have censored. His hostile judgement against works that depicted the Blessed Virgin younger than her thirty-year-old son is a clear allusion to Michelangelo's *Pietà* (commissioned in 1498). Though one of the most celebrated works of art in Europe, and carefully moved from

---

107 Ibid., 2.52 = 382.
108 Ibid., 2.52 = 380.
109 Ibid., 1.24; 1.33; 2.7 = 102; 140; 158.
110 Ibid., 2.7 = 144f.; 157f. Cf. 2.15; 2.24 = 191; 233. In fact, the Council of Trent itself decreed in its last session (1564) that paintings in the papal chapel, and in other churches, were to be covered if they depicted anything obscene or false. The *Indices of Forbidden Books* issued by Popes Sixtus V (1590) and Clement VIII (1596) included prohibitions of certain categories of pictures. Hecht, *Katholische Bildertheologie* 93; 40f.; 178–182; 280. Paleotti repeated his proposal that pictures come under surveillance by the Index in his memorandum to the Cardinals on purging art of its abuses (1596). Paleotti Gabriele, "De Tollendis Imaginum Abusibus Novissima Consideratio", in Prodi, "Ricerche sulla teorica" 208.

the old St. Peter's into the new one, it was disparaged by others in Paleotti's day for exactly the improbability he mentioned and, indeed, as being, for that reason, 'Lutheran' or 'heretical.' For Romans, his judgement against portrayals of nudity can only have brought to mind, first and foremost, Michelangelo's *Last Judgment* in the Sistine Chapel (1536–1541). Criticized for its abundant, athletic nudity even while it was being painted, the *Last Judgment* was spared from demolition by Pope Pius IV (1559–1565), who commissioned Michelangelo's assistant, Daniele da Volterra (1509–1566), to repaint sections that especially offended modesty, the first of several attacks on the painting in the name of decency. His adjustments were still recent when Paleotti became a cardinal (1565). Naturally, his dislike of nudity in the portrayal of saints would have excluded Titian's *The Penitent Magdalene* (ca 1550)[111] and Rosso Fiorentino's *Dead Christ Supported by Angels* (1524–1527),[112] both with renderings of seductively opulent bodies. Bronzino's portrait of *Cosimo I de' Medici as Orpheus* (1538–1540)[113] would have offended both Paleotti's strictures against nudity and the other ways in which the ruling orders of Christian society identified themselves with pre-Christian paganism.

Other categories of representations censured by Paleotti also had distinguished examples, much in fashion. He did not like obscure allegories, such as Giorgione's *Three Philosophers*,[114] or even his *Self-Portrait as David*.[115] Paleotti did not like paintings ambiguously Christian and pagan, such as Parmigianino's picture of a woman with an infant, sometimes called *The Madonna of the Rose*, and sometimes *Venus and Cupid* (1529–1530).[116]

Paleotti's proposed reform was a structure of theology and discipline. Manifestly, this remedy was far from assured. Indeed, he lethally diluted his own argument; for aversion to extremes led him to compromise, rather than to absolute rules. Evidently, change of heart, seeking spiritual direction, and submitting to long and arduous education hinged on individual choice. They fell among the great number of things that Paleotti knew no laws could regulate.[117] Consensus, too, offered no settled direction; for, given the enormous number and variety of judgements in play, it was hardly possible to find consensus.[118] Moreover, if it could be found, consensus might mislead, through the variability

---

111 Museo Nazionale di Capodimonte, Naples.
112 Museum of Fine Arts, Boston.
113 Philadelphia Museum of Art.
114 Kunsthistorisches Museum, Vienna.
115 Herzog Anton Ulrich Museum, Brunswick.
116 Staatliche Kunstsammlungen, Dresden.
117 Cf. Paleotti, *De Imaginibus* 2.51 = 375.
118 Ibid., 2.51 = 393.

and weakness of human ignorance. After all, in the Church's earliest days majority consensus was solidly on the side of paganism. Even the perceptive and learned followed the stupid, empty religion of the gods.[119] Despite his normal and frequent appeal to consensus, Paleotti once urged painters to flee to solitude if, in the torrential outpouring of questionable images and judgments, they wished to serve those who defended the just cause of imitation and who ought to burn with zeal for the virtuous life.[120]

Like many who despair of sweet reason to produce reform, Paleotti placed his hope in coercion. Authority was the linchpin of his argument for social enforcement, but here, especially, Paleotti ran into another difficulty. For his comments would have given aid and comfort to his Protestant enemies. Though he invoked Church authority, he was far from maintaining its infallibility. In fact, he undermined his whole argument from authority by writing that, throughout the ages, bishops, councils, and secular rulers had embraced and enforced error. One of Satan's oldest deceptions was to pervert the meaning of Scripture, suffuse the counterfeit sense with poison, and administer it to the leaders of the Church. Age after age, councils had confirmed Satan's perversions of Scripture with their decrees, which secular rulers had enforced by the sword. Satan had raised prelates up in the Church to lead the faithful multitude into error. Thus, repeatedly, some emperors, patriarchs, and bishops had been warriors for the Prince of Darkness against righteous laws.[121] Strictly interpreted, this argument demolished the doctrine of the inerrancy of the Church. At least one contemporary criticized him for appearing to deny the continuity of apostolic tradition.[122]

Paleotti had inveighed against the powerful of the world for offering donations in exchange for the right to intrude their armorials into churches, but he knew that bishops and other clerical rulers not only failed to bridle the prideful lusts of secular donors, but, to the contrary, rushed themselves to be the first to blazon their own insignia over every available altar cover, vestment, and sacred vessel.[123] He hardly rehabilitated his claims for authority as a corrective of error, much less his own credit and that of the Council of Trent, when he wrote that, despite these repeated lapses into Satan's camp, the authority of the Fathers and the consensus of the whole church had always prevailed.[124]

---

119   Ibid., 1.15; 1.18 = 71; 82.
120   Ibid., 2.20 = 220.
121   Ibid., 1.27 = 111–113.
122   Hecht, *Katholische Bildertheologie* 147–149.
123   Paleotti, *De Imaginibus* 2.48 = 358.
124   Ibid., 1.27 = 113.

CARDINAL GABRIELE PALEOTTI'S CALL FOR REFORM OF CHRISTIAN ART 123

In the end Paleotti's own zeal for middle-of-the-road positions, with his openness to compromise, sapped the strength from his polemic most of all. Castiglione had praised moderation as a supreme virtue for courtiers. To his thinking moderation (*mediocrità*) was a survival tactic. It gave courtiers flexibility to adapt themselves to conditions, chameleon-like, calibrating what they thought and said and did to the moods of the prince, on whose favour everything depended, angling too through 'artful behaviour' for advantage in the ruthless competition among courtiers for the prince's good well.[125] Moderation gave courtiers the freedom to mask what they were with what they appeared to be.

Again and again, Paleotti used his rule of moderation to justify prudent flexibility, stepping back from hard and fast rules. Profane pictures fired his indignation but he remembered that the Church Father, Augustine of Hippo, had sanctioned Christian use of pagan literature. Christians, Augustine wrote, should read pagan books critically and retain what could be used for the service and worship of God, discarding what was unsuitable or dangerous. Correspondingly, Paleotti accepted a bowdlerized classicism. Profane pictures, he wrote, were not to be thrown out, but subjected to righteous assessment with a view to appropriating whatever promoted piety.[126]

Much the same principle lay behind the chaste and expurgated classicism that Paleotti's friend, Carlo Borromeo, established as canonical in Church architecture. Paleotti fulminated against the multiplication of armorials in churches, while he admitted that they could be legitimately installed in particular chapels.[127] Throughout his treatise, he attacked abuses only to assert that his objections had to do with the motive of a patron or artist, or with the circumstances under which particular works were used, and that works belonging to the same categories (e. g., portraits) were acceptable if they were produced with pious motives or under circumstances enhancing devotion. He approved portraits of saints.[128] Painting, he insisted, was neither good nor bad in itself; its goodness or badness depended on its content and circumstances.[129]

---

125 See especially, Cox V., "Castiglione's *Cortegiano*: The Dialogue as a Drama of Doubt" and Javitch D., "*Il Cortegiano* and the Constraints of Despotism" in Javitch D. (ed.), *Baldassar Castiglione: The Book of the Courtier, The Singleton Translation* (New York: 2001) 307–319; 319–328. See also ibid., 301.
126 Paleotti, *De Imaginibus* 2.12 = 178.
127 Ibid., 2.27; 2.28 = 357f.; 366.
128 Paleotti approved portraits of saints as admonitions to virtue, just as he rejected portraits of evil people as incentives to wrong-doing; ibid., 2.23 = 227–231; Hecht, *Katholische Bildertheologie* 316.
129 See Paleotti, *De Imaginibus* 2.19 = 210. For other exceptions: on installations of donor portraits in churches, see 2.13 = 183; on joke pictures, 2.31 = 274; 277; on displaying and

Of course, there were exceptions. Despite numerous compromises, Paleotti never found it necessary to relent in his categorical opposition to nudes, pictures of heretics and heretical motifs (apart from unequivocally damning portrayals), paintings of saints calculated to arouse sensual desires, and the display in churches of war scenes and events from pagan myth and history.[130]

Compromising right and left and denying the inerrancy of the Church, he failed to locate a firm theoretical centre for the reforms of which he dreamed, much less a practical method of implementing them. Paleotti's situational arguments may have come to him from the development of Renaissance casuistry, with its avoidance of universal rules of personal behaviour and its preoccupation with how, in the *fora* of their consciences, individuals reasoned through and applied moral law to their particular circumstances. However, in his treatise, Paleotti took only fleeting glances at the internal *forum* of conscience. The powerful, destabilizing force that kept him from crystallizing rules for religious painting did not arise from individualistic moral theories. Instead, it arose from an actual interplay between sacred and profane art, an interplay that, to Paleotti's eyes, had made religious art a subdivision of secular painting. It arose from the fact that professed Christians insisted on importing into sacred art opulent sensuality such as Paleotti thought came from classical myth, its gods and nudes, and unprecedented experiments with style as a manipulator of human perception. It arose from Satanic intrusion into every chapel, every place where God's Word was preached.

It was well and good for him to teach that in churches everything should be sacred and appropriate to Christian mysteries. But he knew that there were profane pictures in churches, scenes from Roman mythology and history, tapestries depicting the Trojan War, wild bacchantes dancing, nude saints with the flashing, seductive eyes of whores and opulent bodies made for lechery. He knew that such abuses as these were simply what patrons wanted to see and artists were willing to produce, and that they were hatched in private places, the bedchambers where owners hid pictures that aroused them to forbidden delights, the libraries of princes lavishly embellished with murals of pagan gods, the houses, villas and storerooms crammed full by several generations

---

honouring in public a portrait in the presence of the subject, 2.20 = 220; on installing portraits of private citizens in public places, 2.20; 2.29 = 210; 219f.

130 Paleotti did provide a loophole for the display of pagan art. Pagan works of art, he wrote, gave pleasure to few and offence to many. They ought to be shoved away from public view into some secure inner chamber, like deadly weapons; ibid., 2.15 = 189. Presumably, they could be seen in controlled environments.

with extravagant collections of pagan antiquities – paintings, Paleotti wrote, sculptures, and coins.[131]

He makes us aware of how widely painting was spread through the social spectrum, from vile hovels made elegant and respectable by being adorned with painting, to the libraries and palaces and storerooms of princes.[132] He was concerned to teach men and women what images honoured Christian homes and what images shamed them, in the hope that patrons would be persuaded to seek what was right and pious, whether they were adorning churches or decorating their own homes.[133] This was one regard in which he feared the illiterate multitude could be misled by the tastes and enthusiasms of superior orders in society.[134]

Powerless in so many other ways, he realized that purging the homes of the faithful was beyond his reach, and that that was so in part because of the anti-clericalism that gave a place in some households to salacious pictures of clergy in lewd acts, and even to pictures of Protestant origins, often obscene burlesques of clergy, saints, and sacraments.[135] Offensive as it was for Christian men to have images of pagans who had persecuted the Church in Antiquity, it was yet more offensive for heads of households to keep images of heretics and Protestant satires of Catholics and their practices under their roofs. Yet this was done.[136] Paleotti had preached against collections of pagan art, trying to teach his diocese, trying to persuade his flock to give up their treasures, even though the works of art might be adorned with gold and magnificent workmanship. He called on them to bridle lust and advance in virtue by divesting themselves of these costly, spiritually lethal possessions, thereby teaching others to spurn such useless things. Paleotti had witnessed the breath-taking moment when Pope Pius V divested himself of more than one hundred ancient statues in the papal collection (1566). There were rumours that Pius intended to destroy all the pagan survivals in Rome. This papal divestiture may have given Paleotti hope of inspiring imitation.

Still, Paleotti knew that flocks and pastors could be of different minds. He knew that the citizens of Rome, as well as cardinals and members of the Roman nobility, had joyfully snapped up the statues released by Pius V. To his pain, he knew that, despite long efforts by Church officials, the people of Bologna – for

---

131   Ibid., 2.10; 2.15; 2.20 = 166; 190–192; 215.
132   Ibid., 1.20; 2.20 = 89; 218. See note 99 above.
133   Ibid., 1. proem. = 3f.
134   Ibid., 1.27 = 111. The unlearned could also be led into error by pagan images and obscure paintings: 2.10; 2.41 = 168; 322f.
135   Ibid., 2.4; 2.7 = 150; 158.
136   Ibid., 2.22 = 224.

whom he wrote his long treatise about sacred and profane images – cheerfully persisted in the superstitious use of images.[137] When he preached the gospel of divestiture, he knew that Bolognese owners of pagan antiquities considered them evidence of upright, honourable, and discerning judgment, as well as tangible wealth, and that, if they sensed danger of losing their collections, they were likely either to fight to the bitter end or to hide their disputed, costly treasures away in some dark, safe, inner chambers of their houses, as people forbidden to bear arms or families denied the right to wear certain distinctive costumes concealed the contraband, waiting for better times.[138] They could turn on their Bishop the same indulgent smile of naughty amusement provoked in secret by their lascivious pictures. He had no great hope of persuading his flock to surrender any works of art he considered shameful and impious, including anti-clerical lampoons that delighted them, no expectation of paralleling, in Bologna, Savonarola's bonfire of vanities.

7   Summary

We have now reviewed Paleotti's effort to reconcile Catholic practice with biblical precepts. He lamented the degree to which the cult of images had been invaded and subverted by old and new idolatries – the old in indigenous superstition and devotion to pagan antiquity, and the new in arrogant self-worship by the mighty. He detested Protestant iconoclasm as the Devil's work. But he found the Devil at work, more subtlety and with equal glee, in the perversion of religious art among Roman Catholics. Paleotti's great task was to purge religious art of the filth that had covered its beauty among his co-religionists and made it an agent of spiritual ruin instead of eternal blessedness and churches, a theatre of vanity instead of heaven's antechamber.

Though he never drew the conclusion himself, Paleotti was struggling against the emancipation of art from theology, a conclusion that he did specifically identify when he lamented that painters were no longer content to be 'mute theologians.' Everywhere around him he found proof that compliant clergy had embraced the new styles, nudity, and paganism that he denounced as contrary to faith and morals, proof that, even among his clerical confrères what he idealized as Christian art was of marginal relevance to art.

Paleotti's comments on portraits are enlightening. To his mind, portraits, like any other painting, could be used for good or ill, depending on free human

---

137   See note 64 above.
138   Paleotti, *De Imaginibus* 2.15 = 190f.

choice. He recognized that portraits could be used for worthy practical objectives, as in portraying for a prospective bridegroom the bride who had been chosen for him, sight unseen, in an arranged marriage. They could also be used to nurture pious emotions, as they were used to mitigate the pain of absence through death or distance, or to hold up for emulation persons whose virtue was generally acknowledged. However, he characterized them as anything but instruments of religious devotion. In the general perversion of painting, they served as tools of self-display and advertisement, richly furbished with lies and ostentation, and the perishable monuments on which vainglorious people pathetically pinned their hopes to be remembered. As tools of self-display and memorialization, he wrote, portraits were likely to misfire. Others, sooner or later, could understand the portrait quite differently from the way a subject intended, and the subject, however virtuous in fact, could become a laughingstock because of the portrait. In painting generally, as in the specific case of portraiture, interpretation was everything, and interpretation led to authentic self-knowing only when it served the end for which human beings were made: eternal felicity.

It would be easy to dismiss Paleotti as a spokesman for a fleeting moment of Puritanism in Mannerist Italy. His attack on the cult of pagan Antiquity, with its signature of nudity, certainly ran him counter to a conspicuous current in humanist culture and allied him with schools of thought that refreshed themselves with prudery. Still, what set Paleotti apart from humanism intoxicated by Antiquity was, not prudery so much as hostility to experimentation in art. Both Paleotti and unbowdlerized classicists were retrospective. They looked to the past differently, Paleotti, narrowing and focusing what he considered the legitimate scope of visual imagination while unregenerate classicists widened its scope by the huge array of experiments in subject and style which Paleotti inventoried, condemned, and intended to censor out of the Church. Paleotti used a telling phrase to refer to paradise; he called it the 'theatre of heaven' (*caeli theatrum*).[139]

His exclusions indicate how close he, like contemporary Jesuits, came to regarding church buildings, and their artistic contents, as sacred theatres. Explaining away the great disability of painting – that is could not represent action, but only an event frozen at one instant – Paleotti wrote that we complete the action in our minds, as we do when we see the picture of a horse running, or a storm-battered ship crashing on the rocks.[140] His exclusions of styles and subjects of art which he considered inappropriate to the Church took for

---

139   See note 27 above.
140   See n. 147.

granted that religious art ought to illustrate narratives of Scripture, the lives of saints, and doctrine. Paintings portrayed instants in stories which viewers carried in their minds. What Paleotti attacked as abuses were intrusions of other narratives into the visual space which he believed should be reserved for sacred narratives. Thus, he attacked armorials, which intruded family narratives, portraits of private persons, which intruded civic histories, and, most severely of all, pagan myth and history, which intruded stories hostile to the faith. In the same way, he disapproved of embellishing portraits with accessories of luxury – such as fans and monkeys – because they detracted from the subject's worth (*dignitas*). His scorn for nudity as the Devil's great subversion of religious art arose because he saw a categorical confusion, especially in portrayals of saints, between narratives of which nudity was the signature and narratives of ascetic, self-denying piety.

Paleotti envisioned churches as controlled environments created and adorned, for better or worse, by human choice, contexts for the narrative of salvation. His reverence for tradition led him to look backward, rather than forward. Thus, in his view, the presentation of sacred narrative through art should follow the learning stored up in books, and styles conveyed through long apprenticeships in workshops of approved master artists. Bookish scholarship and tradition were safeguards of the narrative to be taught by religious art, though, Paleotti grieved, they had failed to avert almost universal corruption in its day. He did not take the step of realizing what his ancient doctrine of time as the universal destroyer meant for tradition: namely, that truths were true for the time being, grew old, and failed with time.

Apart from his general scorn for ecclesiastical art as diseased in head and members, two aspects of Paleotti's argument anticipated the course that religious painting eventually took. The first was Paleotti's stress on individual judgment; the second, his call for official action by the Church to cure art's many sicknesses.

Although he had no general theory of historical process or development, the very crux of his whole argument was historical. Paradoxical as this may sound, every road his debate took led to unique personal judgment in unique circumstances. Thus, how painters chose their subjects, plied their technical skills, manipulated artistic licence, and, above all, lived into art as a religious calling depended on choices painters made individually for themselves, each in a distinctive set of circumstances. Likewise, how clients and viewers interpreted and used pictures varied from one moment of choice to another, beauty being in the eye of the beholder, but changing from time to time even in the eye of one and the same beholder. Demonic trickery clouded, or overwhelmed, some judgments with lusts and superstitions.

Judgement was individual and situational; and this was one reason why Paleotti could not settle hard and fast rules. To be sure, Paleotti's rule that time devoured all its own gave him a simple way to explain how consensus changed through the years and centuries, understanding that old structures and ornaments would inevitably, meaninglessly, be swept away. Paleotti brought Church art, and theology itself, into the realm of obsolescence where even the good are good only for the time being. His argument that leaders of the Church had from time to time fallen into error, thereby breaking the perpetuity of apostolic tradition, indicated how shattering his ideas could be for any theory of universal truth.

Paleotti limited his ideas about free choice with a vision of official censorship. He foresaw a way in which the theatre of heaven could be simulated in churches: namely, to create an official art, cut to the pattern of theology and subject to discipline by ecclesiastical authority. Defenders of the Church's *Magisterium* – its authority to teach doctrine and enforce obedience – held that Christ himself had promised to stand guarantor for its truth. For, they said, when Christ conferred the *Magisterium* on St. Peter and his successors as bishop of Rome, he also promised: 'Simon, Simon [...] I have prayed for thee that thy faith fail not; and when thou art converted, strengthen thy brethren' (Luke 22:31–32). Defined by the *Magisterium*, official art as envisioned by Paleotti would be enforced by institutional sanctions that allowed into the sacred theatres of churches only what befitted the holiness of God's house. Where ecclesiastical sanctions ran, enforcement by civil authorities, the secular arm with its sword, might well follow. Defended by this sort of quarantine, churches would be secured against novelties hatched by prideful secular patrons, ignorant, impious and possibly insane artists, and sensual enthusiasm of the vagrant, lustful, illiterate multitude. Paleotti did not anticipate that official art in the Church, a compound of theology and discipline, could paralyze creative imagination and spell the death of self-knowing. The apparatus for control already existed in his day, thanks to the Council of Trent, which placed the building and decoration of all churches under surveillance of diocesan bishops. Its full weight came to be felt when additions to canon law gave bishops and superiors general of religious orders power to give or withhold permission to publish sacred images in any fashion, prohibiting images of Christ, saints, and angels that did not accord with Church doctrine.[141]

Paleotti seems to have expected little success for his reform project. In the short run, his restrictive ideas may have fought too much against the tide to convince others. Perhaps it is right to think of him in his last days, attending

---

141 *Corpus Iuris Canonici* (Westminster: 1951), canons 1385; 1399 = 475; 481.

to the Latin translation of his *Discorso*, writing a memorandum to the Sacred College on the urgency of purifying art of its abuses, and planning an edition of his works, an isolated figure out of step with his times and ignored 'to the advantage of free artistic creativity.'[142] But time was on his side, at least regarding his appeal to censoring authority. Art and religion continued to go their separate ways, ever more distinctly. As the magnificence of sacred theatre reached[143] its zenith in Baroque churches, some of them abounding in nudes, prudery was still there to force Bernini to cover the exposed female bosoms on his monuments to Popes Urban VIII and Alexander VII (both in St Peter's, Rome).[144] Even in Paleotti's day the career of official art took significant victims in the churches cleared and reconfigured according to St. Carlo Borromeo's mercilessly detailed handbook of Church architecture and decor. Paleotti's suspicion of innovation in religious art as demonically inspired and contrary to sound faith also had a long career, together with restrictions of decorum which he valued. Whole new worlds were opening to Paleotti and his contemporaries. The magnificent arts of central and south America suddenly became known in all their awesome strangeness. Yet, they were beyond the pale allowed for the imitation of truth. Paleotti dismissed them with a reference to a passing curiosity that had caught his eye, images made with feathers, iridescent and changing in different lights.[145] Indeed, hostility to innovation and to alien arts has continued to mature until the present day, though the *Magisterium*'s official art has long since been isolated from areas in which creative experimenta-

---

142 Prodi, *Il cardinale Gabriele Paleotti* II, 561f. Jedin, "Das Tridentinum und die bildenden Künste" 339.
143 Paleotti, *De Imaginibus* 2.52 = 376f.
144 At some stage, probably 'in the late seventeenth century,' a stucco drapery was applied to the figure of *Charity Suckling a Child*, on Urban VIII's tomb. Pope Innocent XI required Bernini to cast, and paint, a bronze cover for the figure of *Truth*, on Alexander VII's tomb, and he may also have been responsible for covering the nakedness of *Charity*; Wittkower R., *Bernini: The Sculptor of the Roman Baroque* (London: 1997⁴) 253; 296.
145 Paleotti, *De Imaginibus* 2.52 = 376. In his account of the Spanish conquest of Mexico, Bernal Diaz del Castillo makes many admiring references to mantles, shields, state canopies, and other luxurious articles woven of feathers. Such materials were frequently shared out among soldiers as part of their loot. See, especially Diaz's mention of pictures in feathers of little birds covered with pearl-shells; Diaz del Castillo Bernal, *The Discovery and Conquest of Mexico, 1517–1521*, trans. A.P. Maudslay (New York: 1956) cc. 62; 63; 73 = 189; 193; 204f.; 249. Some articles made of feathers and taken from the Spanish conquests to Europe in the sixteenth century survive. E.g., shields in the Württembergisches Landesmuseum, Stuttgart, pictured in Pollig H. (ed.), *Exotische Welten. Europäische Phantasien*, exh. cat., Württembergisches Landesmuseum (Stuttgart: 1987) 297. A jade figure of the Aztec god, Xolotl, known to have been owned by the early seventeenth-century collector, Philipp Hainhofer, in Augsburg, is pictured and described in ibid., 305.

tion and discovery were pursued. There is an echo of Paleotti's demonism, too, in the anguished complaints of twentieth-century Roman Catholics against perceived deficiencies of Church art, as demonic, and as a 'wonderfully flexible and effective means' used by the Father of Lies to repel people from the Christian life.[146]

There was something ominous in the degree to which Paleotti's theology of pictures did undoubtedly form the theoretical background for all Church art.[147]

Bibliography

Balthasar H.U. von, *The Glory of the Lord: A Theological Aesthetics*, 7 vols. (New York: 1983–1991).

Castiglione Baldassar, *The Book of the Courtier, The Singleton Translation*, ed. Javitch D. (New York: 2002).

Cox V., "Castiglione's Cortegiano: The Dialogue as a Drama of Doubt", in Javitch D. (ed.), *Baldassar Castiglione: The Book of the Courtier, The Singleton Translation* (New York: 2002) 307–319.

Diaz del Castillo Bernal, *The Discovery and Conquest of Mexico, 1517–1521*, trans. A.P. Maudslay (New York: 1956).

Egenter R., *The Desecration of Christ*, trans. E. Quinn (Chicago: 1967).

Feld H., *Der Ikonoklasmus des Westens* (Leiden: 1990) 203–208.

Freeman A. with the collaboration of Meyvaert P. (ed.), *Opus Caroli Regis Contra Synodum* (*Libri Carolini*) (Hannover: 1998).

Geary P., *Living with the Dead in the Middle Ages* (Ithaca: 1994).

Hecht C., *Katholische Bildertheologie im Zeitalter von Gegenreformation und Barock: Studien zu Traktaten von Johannes Molanus, Gabriele Paleotti und anderen Autoren* (Berlin: 1997).

Hilbrich P.D., *The Aesthetic of the Counterreformation and Religious Painting and Music in Bologna, 1564–1615*, Ph.D. dissertation (Ohio University: 1969).

Javitch D., "Il Cortegiano and the Constraints of Despotism" in Javitch D. (ed.), *Baldassar Castiglione: The Book of the Courtier, The Singleton Translation* (New York: 2002) 319–328.

Jedin H., "Das Tridentinum und die bildenden Künste", *Zeitschrift für Kirchengeschichte* 74 (1963) 321–339.

---

146 See Egenter R., *The Desecration of Christ*, trans. E. Quinn (Chicago: 1967) 13f.
147 Hecht, *Katholische Bildertheologie* 331.

Jones P.M., "Art Theory as Ideology: Gabriele Paleotti's Hierarchical Notion of Painting's Universality and Reception", in Farago C. (ed.), *Reframing the Renaissance: Visual Culture in Europe and Latin America, 1450–1650* (New Haven: 1995) 127–139.

Menghi Girolamo, *Flagellum daemonum ... accessit postremo pars secunda quae Fustis Daemonum inscribitur* (Lyons, Pierre Landry: 1604).

Paleotti Gabriele, *Discorso intorno alle imagine sacre et profane* (Bologna: 1582), in *Trattati d'arte del Cinquecento, vol.* 2, ed. P. Brocchi (Bari: 1961) 117–562.

Paleotti Gabriele, *De Imaginibus Sacris et Profanis* (Ingolstadt, David Sartorius: 1594).

Payton J.R. Jr., "Calvin and the Libri Carolini", *Sixteenth Century Journal* 28 (1997) 468–471.

Pollig H. (ed.), Exotische Welten. Europäische Phantasien, exh. cat., Württembergisches Landesmuseum (Stuttgart: 1987).

Prodi P., *Il cardinale Gabriele Paleotti (1522–1597)*, 2 vols. (Rome: 1959–1967).

Prodi P., "Ricerche sulla teorica delle arti figurative nella Riforma cattolica", *Archivio italiano per la Storia della pietà* 4 (1984) 123–212.

Wittkower R., *Bernini: The Sculptor of the Roman Baroque* (London: 1997[4]).

CHAPTER 4

The Sacred Becomes Profane – The Profane Becomes Sacred: Observations on the Desubstantialisation of Religious Discourse in the Early Modern Age

Andreas Mahler

1

The following remarks are not to be seen as presenting a historical development, but merely as comments on a symptom. They are based on the theory that in England in the early modern age we can observe a process in the course of which religious discourse loses its unassailable position as absolute truth. The first phase of this process consists in real-life society appropriating the carnivalisation of the sacred, and occasionally also of religious discourse. (This was already common in the Middle Ages.) Their destabilisations increasingly tended to extend beyond the carnival period itself. A second phase of this secularisation or profanisation of the sacred is accompanied by the opposite phenomenon, in which non-sacred objects and topics are seized on by the sacred. This was due to the start of the loss of authority of religious discourse, which resulted in its pluralisation and meant that it could be functionalised. This in turn meant that what had previously been profane could increasingly be made sacred. Hand in hand with the weakening of its claim to be the only fount of truth went a loss of substance of religious discourse. It could be seen as a function not strictly bound to institutions and therefore applicable wherever desired. In a third and last phase an attempt is made to compensate for this by rescuing it from the area of public discredit and leading it into the private world of the individual subject. The privatisation and interiorisation of the sacred led in the upheavals of the early modern age to the creation of a new foundation for articulating religious authenticity, in which the sacred has admittedly lost its absolute validity, but in which it can, after a period of pluralising uncertainty, come to terms with itself again in the private field. A very popular place for this attempt to find new stability is the meditative poetry of the seventeenth century.

This theory will be illustrated primarily by three English literary texts from around 1600. That this is a selective choice is not for a moment disputed, nor do these texts form the cornerstones of the respective changes in direction in a historical process that might well be conceived of as linear. They are, however, eminently suitable as symptoms to describe the process of desacralisation and resacralisation, which raged with particular virulence around the threshold of the new century. The trend towards the profanation of the sacred in all areas can be seen vividly in the carnivalisation of religious discourse in Ben Jonson's *The Alchemist* (1610) and *Bartholmew Fair* (1614). In these plays it reaches its carnivalesque climax and at the same time marks the final conclusion of the first phase. In contrast the constructive countermovement, rescuing the sacred and leading it into the private world by sacralising the profane, can already be seen in John Donne's third satire (c. 1594/95); there, in the guise of the secular genre of the *satyre*, we see a tendency towards individual, meditative speech that was to characterise English poetry in the seventeenth century.[1]

The theoretical frame of reference for the following observations is formed by the works of Mikhail M. Bakhtin and the theories of Michel Foucault concerning the carnival and the question of the term 'discourse' respectively; the research by Robert Weimann into the way authority was regarded and dealt with in England in the early modern age is considered definitive; and the works of Norbert Elias, Philippe Ariès and Peter Burke form the basis as regards the general historical developments of society and people's mentality within the framework of the process of civilisation in Europe.

2

The term 'discourse' signifies typified forms of coherent linguistic expression, with the help of which the participants in the discourse record parts of their

---

[1] Accordingly, within the framework of the present structure, textual examples which could be read as documents of the second phase of the ideologically interested, sacralising appropriation of in themselves non-sacral objects have been deliberately omitted. Their function was primarily to legitimise the rule of government and theologically stabilise temporal royal authority following the loss of a sacramental concept of monarchy; this function has been depicted in a number of recent publications, in particular with reference to Shakespeare's history plays, for example, from the point of view of 'subversion' and 'containment', in Greenblatt S., "Invisible Bullets: Renaissance Authority and its subversion, *Henry IV* and *Henry V*", in Dollimore J. – Sinfield A. (eds.), *Political Shakespeare: New Essays in cultural materialism* (Manchester: 1985) 18–47; or, with reference to Shakespeare's rather ambivalent role in the creation of the 'Tudor Myth', in Zimmermann H., "Die ideologische Krise in *King Richard II*", *Shakespeare Jahrbuch West* (1988) 103–122.

reality in hypothetical form and order them in a homogenising way. Discourse can be recorded by means of texts; they are characterised by the significant recurrences in the lexemes describing the relevant area of reality, their function is to provide sense. Because of this function of interpretation and the claim to totalisation which is latently bound up with it, they are continually vying with each other. According to Foucault every society attempts to keep such rivalry in check by subjecting the discourses to control by institutions and interests and by forcing them into hierarchical order and in this way

> simultaneously controls, selects, organises and canalises the production of discourse by means of certain processes, whose purpose is to master the forces and dangers of the discourse, to ward off its unpredictable eventfulness, to circumvent its difficult and threatening materiality.[2]

Foucault includes three possibilities of control among the processes of mastering discourse. First there are processes of exclusion, such as prohibiting it, relegating it to the realms of inanity, or disqualifying by means of the boundaries drawn by society between truth and falsehood; these processes make what can be said impossible to say, unsaid or unspeakable. A second form consists of processes of limitation, such as commentaries, binding the discourse to the author's intention, and subjecting it to the framework and rules of specified disciplines; these processes regulate the utterances from the inside, as it were, by means of interpretative or authorising repetition or advance limitation. Finally there are processes that reduce the number of subjects, such as strictly distributing the speaking roles in a ritual, restricting the discourse to circles specially reserved for it, or committing it to underlying doctrines; these processes control and limit the number of people who can participate in the discourse. This wide variety of forms of subjugation clearly points to the close connection between discourse and power: 'discourse [...] is [...] the object of desire; [...] it was what people fight for and what they fight with; it is the power which people attempt to get hold of.'[3] Accordingly there is a closely guarded border between the participants in the discourse and those excluded from it, and crossing this border can be seen as the eventful acquisition of a hitherto inaccessible language, in accordance with Jurij M. Lotman's model of

---

2 '[J]e suppose que dans toute la société la production du discours est à la fois contrôlée, sélectionnée, organisée et redistribuée par un certain nombre de procédures qui ont pour rôle d'en conjurer les pouvoirs et les dangers, d'en maîtriser l'événement aléatoire, d'en esquiver la lourde, la redoutable matérialité.' Foucault M., *L'Ordre du discours* (Paris: 1971) 10f.

3 'Le discours [...] est aussi ce qui est l'objet du désir; [...] ce pour quoi, ce par quoi on lutte, le pouvoir dont on cherche à s'emparer.' Foucault, *Discours* 12.

plot, which is to be understood culturally and typologically.[4] Discourses are thus informed by a dialectic that determines them: they are an 'appropriated language [...] which adopts certain interests, purposes and aims, at the same time necessarily excluding, suppressing and expropriating other interests and purposes.'[5]

For the Middle Ages religious discourse is the privileged discourse of unlimited authority. It controls the hierarchy of discourse as the unassailable location of truth, in which constructions of meaning that make the world plausible are valid as a sign of the divine will, and, in this way given legitimacy, it forms the centre of discursive power, from which the processes of control set out to delineate a border between it and other discourses, a border that in principle cannot be crossed. Religious discourse prohibits as unfitting, rejects as insane, condemns as false; it controls from inside the authority of God's word, the repetition of exegesis, its division into fields of what can be said; it determines the distribution of the speech roles, limits and regulates active access to its use, tethers those admitted to it to dogmas declared to be binding. Delineating such a border separates what is acceptable and what is to be accepted from the threat of what consequently is to be excluded, it defines the areas of what is true and what is false, what can be heard and what is to go unheeded: 'It is always possible to speak the truth in the sphere of the wild outside; but you are only in the realm of truth if you obey the rules of a discursive "police force" [...].'[6]

The Reformation saw the start of a process in which the authority of religious discourse was slowly corroded, in the course of which the control mechanism of reducing the subjects in particular was increasingly destabilised:

> As never before, people were forced to pass judgement on truth and falsehood, on the correct and the incorrect meaning of literacy, judgements that were new or at least had to be passed without the help of the permanently valid authority of a universal church.[7]

---

4 Lotman Ju., *The Structure of the Artistic Text*, trans. R. Vroon (Ann Arbor: 1977) 231ff.
5 Weimann R., *Shakespeare und die Macht der Mimesis: Autorität und Repräsentation im elisabethanischen Theater* (Berlin – Weimar: 1988) 13f.; for an English translation of decisive parts of this book see Weimann R., *Authority and Representation in Early Modern Discourse*, ed. D. Hillman (Baltimore: 1996).
6 'Il se peut toujours qu'on dise le vrai dans l'espace d'une extériorité sauvage; mais on n'est dans le vrai qu'en obéissant aux règles d'une 'police' discursive qu'on doit réactiver en chacun de ses discours.' Foucault, *Discours* 37.
7 Weimann, *Mimesis* 57.

This tendency to increase the number of subjects is reinforced by the enhancement of the status of the vernacular as against Latin, to be seen in the demands for 'vernacular versions of the scriptures',[8] demands that could be heard in England too. Unauthorised outsiders who should have been excluded started to be admitted, and an authority that could have redrawn the old discursive frontier was not established; these two factors led to a 'process of secularising and ideologising discourse'[9] in England. Around the middle of the sixteenth century this process began to develop a momentum that was too strong to be put into its old place again. The relativising of religious discourse, a discourse that had previously been absolute, was reflected in the juxtaposition of points of view with equal validity. This juxtaposition had up till now only been conceivable in carnival, but not in the normative serious world of reality, and was repeatedly deplored, but nothing could now remedy the situation. At the same time, by placing the exegesis of the word of God, now raised to the rank of the sole standard, in the hands of the individual, it makes it a place of far-reaching 'politizing': 'As never before in the Catholic Middle Ages, the Word of the Bible was now transformed to suit the demands of divergent needs and to convey worldly purposes.'[10]

The development of the way people dealt with religious discourse in England in the course of the sixteenth century is to be understood as a transition from a discourse activity that was anchored in substance to one that uses the discourse functionally; accordingly it fits into the larger-scale process of macro-social development from the Middle Ages to the Modern Age, which Niklas Luhmann described as the transition from a stratified form of society to a functionally differentiated one, in the course of which it increasingly becomes clear that subsystems in society, such as the church, for example, could no longer be determined substantially by what was inherently inalienable about them, but only differentially by their lack of identity with other

---

[8] Burke P., "*Heu domine, adsunt Turcae!*: A Sketch for a Social History of Post-medieval Latin", in Burke P. (ed.), *Language, Self and Society* (Cambridge: 1995) 23–50, 25; Burke there shows above all how the areas where Latin was used (in church, in academia, in 'pragmatic' secular fields) multiplied in the early modern age and follows this up by describing how it was slowly replaced by the national languages.

[9] Weimann, *Mimesis* 59; for the relationship between the appropriation of the world in an increasingly individually determined fashion and the resulting undermining of authority hitherto regarded as given, cf. Weimann R., "Towards a literary theory of ideology: mimesis, representation, authority", in Howard J.E. – O'Connor M.F. (eds.), *Shakespeare Reproduced: The Text in History and Ideology* (London: 1987) 265–272.

[10] Weimann, *Mimesis* 68.

subsystems.[11] That other uses of religious discourse were possible is a sign of an irreversible instrumentalisation, functionalisation, and dynamisation, which in the present context is to be summarised in the term 'desubstantialisation' and which Robert Weimann aptly described as follows:

> Once [...] the religious word – not to mention the work of the church – had become an instrument of the new 'politizing', discourse assumed a larger spectrum of social functions. [...] The word, hitherto to a great extent the privilege of a minority, became available to many hitherto speechless activities in life [...]. This triggered an irreversible process: a radical change in the relationship between 'debate' and authority, between 'meere talke' and consciousness had started, with the result that authority and consciousness were not simply given and present at the start, but appeared increasingly also at the end *as a product of discursive activity*.[12]

Moreover this tendency towards the desubstantialisation of religious discourse corresponds to the separation of the sacred from the material, as is to be observed in the early Modern Age, and its transfer to an exclusively transcendental category.[13]

3

The origins of the profanation of the sacred can be found in the limited timeslot of the carnival. According to Bakhtin it contrasts with the authority of the normative world, which is only suspended for a limited period of time by the relativising cheerfulness of the hustle and bustle of the carnival. When it is over, the norms of life take over again. From this Bakhtin derives his theory of the two lives: 'In the Middle Ages people lived two lives simultaneously, an

---

11   Luhmann N., "Das Problem der Epochenbildung und die Evolutionstheorie", in Gumbrecht H.-U. – Link-Heer U. (eds.), *Epochenschwellen und Epochenstrukturen im Diskurs der Literatur- und Sprachhistorie* (Frankfurt: 1985) 11–33, esp. 22 ff.
12   Weimann, *Mimesis* 69.
13   The desubstantialising separation of the sacred from the material can be seen at the same time in the loss of basic forms of hierophany, as has been described by Eliade M., *The Sacred and the Profane*, trans. W.R. Trusk (New York: 1959) 11ff.; and thus forms part of the increasingly apparent 'conflict between sign and meaning' (Weimann, *Mimesis* 191) of signification in the early modern age; when the sacred no longer manifests itself unambiguously in the objects, but instead becomes worldly in secondary uses, it loses not only its certain significance but above all its 'palpable' concrete nature and substance.

official life and a carnival life. Their existence was determined by two aspects of the world: one devout and serious, the other laughing.'[14] Elsewhere he formulates it even more clearly:

> It could be said (with certain reservations, of course) that a person in the Middle Ages lived, as it were, *two lives*: one was the *official* life, monolithically serious and gloomy, subjugated to a strict hierarchical order, full of terror, dogmatism, reverence, and piety, the other was the *life of the carnival square*, free and unrestricted, full of ambivalent laughter, blasphemy, the profanation of everything sacred, full of debasing obscenities, familiar contact with everyone and everything. Both these lives were legitimate, but separated by strict temporal boundaries.[15]

In the light of Foucault's theories the carnival can accordingly be seen as a temporarily licensed place of a savage exterior, or more accurately, a sort of enclave for a savage interior. The carnival categories of familiarisation, misalliances, eccentricity and profanation[16] topple hierarchies and annul order, and in this way its topsy-turvy world inverts the normative world of discourse and also permits language to cross boundaries too. But because they are suspended in the carnivalesque enclave, they can from the outset not achieve the status of eventfulness that affects the serious world.

The carnival is the home of utopia, ambivalence and cathartic laughter; it is not in the first instance a place of serious criticism where alternative life projects of a new, normative serious nature can be worked out, but a place where everything is relativised, and the potential to disquiet is neutralised in the calming time-slot that surrounds it.[17] Accordingly the carnival does not exchange the substance of one truth for another truth, but it 'celebrates the shift itself, the very process of replaceability, and not the precise item that is

---

14   Bakhtin M.M., "Grundzüge der Lachkultur", in *Literatur und Karneval: Zur Romantheorie und Lachkultur*, trans. A. Kaempfe (Frankfurt – Berlin – Vienna: 1985) 32–46, 41. This is an extract from: Bakhtin M.M., *Rabelais and His World*, trans. H. Iswolsky (Bloomington, IN: 1984). Cf. also Eliade's theory 'that the *sacred* and *profane* are two modes of being in the world, two existential situations assumed by man in the course of his history'; Eliade, *The Sacred and the Profane* 14.
15   Bakhtin M.M., *Problems of Dostoevsky's Poetics*, ed. C. Emerson (Manchester: 1984) 129f. (italics in the original).
16   Cf. Bakhtin, *Problems* 123ff.
17   The conclusions reached by Barber C.L., *Shakespeare's Festive Comedy: A Study of Dramatic Form and its Relation to Social Custom* (Princeton: 1972) are also to be seen in this context. His well-known phrase 'through release to clarification' (4) finally leads to the acceptance of social inclusion: 'the misrule works […] to consolidate rule.' (205).

replaced. Carnival is, so to speak, functional and not substantive. It absolutizes nothing, but rather proclaims the joyful relativity of everything.'[18] Accordingly the ambivalent laughter of carnival cannot be seen as mockery and criticism, socially directed, of institutions of the normative world; it does not show two alternative truths, one of which is more correct than the other; rather it shows the other side of the one truth which serious life always has to conform to.

> We cannot turn laughter into something serious without destroying or at least distorting the contents of the truth that is opened up by the laughter. Laughter liberates people not only from external censorship, but above all from the great internal censorship, from the fear of the sacred, the prohibition by authority, the past and power, a fear that has been instilled into people in the course of thousands of years.[19]

The fundamental ambivalence of carnival lies rooted in the inclusion of the excluded,[20] in the syncretistic juxtaposition of the excluded and the excluding element; this dual nature of carnival is destroyed as soon as what has been included itself begins to develop a tendency to exclude: 'If carnivalistic ambivalence should happen to be distinguished in the images of decrowning, they degenerated into a purely negative *exposé* of a moral or socio-political sort, they became single-leveled, lost their artistic character, and were transformed into naked journalism.'[21] However, what Bakhtin here describes regretfully with reference to the carnival as an aesthetic celebration of cheerful relativity, seems to be of great importance for the process of civilisation[22] in the early Modern Age; the carnival enables a comic 'positivisation of negativity'[23] to take place, which in the turbulences of the Renaissance threatens through social identification to tip over into a revolutionary negativisation of positivity. In this way, apart from the celebrations of carnivalistic traditions,

---

18 Bakhtin, *Problems* 125.
19 Bakhtin, "Lachkultur" 38f.
20 Cf. also Ritter J., "Über das Lachen", *Blätter für Deutsche Philosophie* 14 (1940/1941) 1–21.
21 Bakhtin, *Problems* 126 (italics in the original).
22 For the concept of the process of civilisation and its relevance for the chronicling of history in the early modern age, see Elias N., *The Civilising Process: Sociogenetic and Psychogenetic Investigations*, trans. E. Jephcott (London: 2000).
23 For this phrase, coined with reference to Ritter's theories of the comic, see Warning R., "Komik und Komödie als Positivierung von Negativität (am Beispiel Molière und Marivaux)", in Weinrich H. (ed.), *Positionen der Negativität*, Poetik und Hermeneutik 6 (Munich: 1975) 341–366, esp. 344.

rituals of revolt did coexist with serious questioning of the social, political and religious order, and the one sometimes turned into the other. [...] The excitement of the occasion and the heavy consumption of alcohol meant that inhibitions against expressing hostility to the authorities or private individuals would be at their weakest. Add to this a bad harvest, an increase in taxes, an attempt to introduce, or to forbid, the Reformation; the resulting mixture could be explosive. There might be a 'switching' of codes, from the language of ritual to the language of rebellion.[24]

Such a secondary using of the forms of the carnival, the eventful overstepping of the enclave of the carnival, represent 'attempts at direct action, not symbolic action';[25] within the framework of the process of fundamental 'changes in the relationships of communication *and* the shaping of ideologies'[26] in the early Modern Age, they enable wider sections of society to take part in discourses they had hitherto been carefully barred from. Accordingly, from a socio-historical perspective, the loss of carnivalesque ambivalence contrasts with an increase in discursive power;[27] instead of the cheerful celebration of change can be seen an actual change, in the course of which authority of the Word shifts from an unquestioned anonymous given to a process in which the individual starts to 'search, examine and experiment':

> The existence of a fixed significance given by the early church is replaced by the principle (to a much higher degree determined by the individual) of becoming familiar with the text by constantly searching oneself for the correct meaning of the text, pleasing in the sight of God.[28]

This change from reading the predetermined significance of the world to an interpretative assertion of the self, guided by the intellect,[29] is based on the irreversible functionalisation of religious discourse which arises from the

---

24 Burke P., *Popular Culture in Early Modern Europe* (Aldershot: 1988) 203.
25 Burke, *Popular Culture* 204.
26 Weimann, *Mimesis* 80.
27 For a deep socio-historical depiction of the individual appropriation of religion, which in the 16th century and above all in the 17th affected more and more parts of the population, see Reay B., "Popular Religion", in Reay B. (ed.), *Popular Culture in Seventeenth-Century England* (London – Sydney: 1985) 91–128; for a general description of the transformation of popular attitudes in the early modern age under the headings of 'profanation' and 'politising', see Burke, *Popular Culture* 207ff.
28 Weimann, *Mimesis* 79.
29 See also Blumenberg H., *The Legitimacy of the Modern Age*, trans. R.M. Wallace (Cambridge, MA: 1986) 142ff.

experience of carnival that transcends boundaries and the concomitant destruction of its guarantee of homogeneity: 'discourse becomes a factor of the authorising of heterogeneous thought and action; it serves as an instrument to appropriate or expropriate natural and social relationships.'[30]

The process of gradually overstepping the time-limits of the carnival finds its instruments above all in the genres of carnivalised literature or rather in the carnivalisation of serious genres. The initial complaint about the decline in the absoluteness of religious discourse increasingly gives way in the early sixteenth century to an appropriating, secondary, propagandistic use, and finally results in a relativising portrayal of its functions and users that can no longer be suspended; Skelton's Collyn Clout still sees the problem as the abuse of language by the corrupt clergy, an abuse that can be rectified:

> With language thus poluted
> Holy churche is bruted
> And shamefully confuted.[31]

However, with the emergence of the 'expression of the "plurality of the worlds"'[32] and the concomitant pluralisation of discourses, a stage is soon reached when a re-monologising recuperation no longer seems possible, but an opportunity to actively take part in the discourse has at the same time been created; this can be seen in numerous examples, most strikingly in the Martin Marprelate controversy,[33] and is evident in the language itself in a new surge in the use of formerly religious terms in secularising contexts.[34] From 1590 onwards the theatre increasingly becomes the place where not only is such a secularising use tested and thus expressed[35] but where above all discourses in monologue form, such as religious discourse, are collected, presented and broken up into dialogues: 'The theatre at that time was at a crossroads where the whole range of functions of pamphlet, poem, chronicle, prose, translation, sermon, ballad,

---

30   Weimann, *Mimesis* 81.
31   Skelton John, *Collyn Clout*, in Skelton John, *The Complete English Poems*, ed. J. Scattergood (Harmondsworth: 1983) 246–278, l. 486–488.
32   Blumenberg, *The Legitimacy of the Modern Age* 180.
33   Cf. the description by Lecocq L., *La Satire en Angleterre de 1588 à 1603*, Études anglaises 32 (Paris: 1969) 109ff.; and also the more detailed account by Pierce W., *An Historical Introduction to the Marprelate Tracts: A Chapter in the Evolution of Religious and Civil Liberty in England* (New York: 1908).
34   Hughes G., *Words in Time: A Social History of the English Vocabulary* (Oxford: 1989) 49ff.
35   E.g. 'sermon' in *The Taming of the Shrew* IV.1.169. Edition used: Shakespeare William, *The Complete Works*, ed. S. Wells – G. Taylor (Oxford: 1988).

THE SACRED BECOMES PROFANE – THE PROFANE BECOMES SACRED 143

newspaper, and anecdote were integrated.'[36] Accordingly it becomes a place not only of the 'representing word', but also of the *represented* word',[37] where the authoritative word from outside, as well as those who purvey it, can be questioned and tested for the truth they contain. In this way the theatre as a place of fundamental bilingualism ranks before the narrative genres as far as the constant display of mutually relativising plurality of speech is concerned.[38]

4

For Ben Jonson the display of the plurality of speech in drama is 'the centreless exchange of diverse language types',[39] an explicitly formulated programme: 'Language most shows a man: speak that I may see thee.'[40] He examines religious discourse from the point of view of the Puritan variant; accordingly, what he depicts is already a stage of discursive fragmentation, where it is no longer a question of the one religious discourse but of a large number of competing religious discourses, amongst which the discourse of Puritanism is preparing to become the focal point in the name of a new authenticity and seriousness. In *The Alchemist* he depicts this movement in the characters of the two Puritans Tribulation Wholesome and Ananias. By including them in the collection of swindlers themselves swindled because of their greed, he already signalises their predominantly worldly interest, which Subtle formulates clearly immediately before Ananias's first entrance:

> This fellow is sent, from one negotiates with me
> About the stone, too; for the holy Brethren

---

36 Weimann, *Mimesis* 86; for an account of the correlation in the early modern age between the 'professionalisation of entertainment' on the stage and the contrary trend in the field of religion ('popular religion [...] was becoming de-professionalised'), see Burke P., "Popular Culture in Seventeenth-Century London", in Reay B. (ed.), *Popular Culture in Seventeenth-Century England* (London – Sydney: 1985) 31–58, esp. 41.
37 Bakhtin, *Problems* 108 (italics in the original).
38 For an illuminating discussion of Shakespeare's dramas as a site of Elizabethan dialogicity directed against Bakhtin's concentration on the novel, see Pfister M., "Comic Subversion: A Bakhtinian View of the Comic in Shakespeare", *Shakespeare Jahrbuch West* (1987) 27–43, esp. 32f.
39 Womack P., *Ben Jonson* (London: 1986) 80.
40 Jonson Ben, *Timber, or Discoveries*, in Jonson Ben, *The Complete Poems*, ed. G. Parfitt (Harmondsworth: 1975) 373–458, l. 2525f.

> Of Amsterdam, the exiled saints: that hope
> To raise their discipline, by it.
>> *Alch.*, II.4.28–4.31[41]

The confrontation of the Puritan with the alchemistic discourse is sparked off by the comic double meaning of the word 'faithful' (*Alch.*, II.5.7) and immediately places Ananias in the powerless role of a supplicant, who despite contrary morality ('I understand no heathen language, truly'; *Alch.*, II.5.12) has to accept, for reasons of worldly interest, the authoritative claim of the reprehensible alien discourse and the relativity of his own. The relativisation of the Puritan goes hand in hand with two other elements. On the one hand there is the carnivalisation of the contents, replete with satirical references; when Ananias can finally introduce himself as 'a servant of the exiled Brethren,/ That deal with widows; and with orphans' goods' (*Alch.*, II.5.46f.). This immediately conveys to the audience the accusation levelled against the Puritans at the time that they were legacy-hunters and greedily exploited wards. On the other hand the relativisation can be seen in the carnivalisation of the names; Ananias, baptised in the awareness that mankind is ineluctably sinful, is not merely the sinner per se, but at the same time as 'the varlet/That cozened the Apostles' (*Alch.*, II.5.72f.) he is a potential swindler, who is chased away by Subtle.

In contrast to Ananias, who is a fundamentalist believer, Tribulation represents a more functional point of view: 'Good Brother, we must bend unto all means,/ That may give furtherance, to the holy cause.' (*Alch.* II.1.11f.) He propagates a principle of adaptation, which is justified by the promise of future authority and which therefore demands adjustments in behaviour which contradict basic Puritan beliefs. He demands that Ananias ignore his view of the world and thus also the discourse governing it (cf. the discussion concerning 'Christmas'/'Christ-tide'; *Alch.*, III.2.43) in order to get closer to their goal. In this way, however, the Puritans' discourse is revealed to be no more than a flexible discourse, deprived of substance and used purely functionally to acquire power unscrupulously: 'We may be temporal lords, ourselves, I take it.' (*Alch.*, III.2.52) When the alchemistic and the Puritan discourses collide, it is the alchemistic one that keeps the upper hand; it can distinguish between truth and falsehood, between that which can and that which cannot be said, it pronounces prohibitions, it determines the discipline in which speech takes place, apportions the speakers' roles and imposes on those involved in the discourse a commitment to its dogmas and doctrines. As the discourse of truth

---

41 Edition used: Jonson Ben, *The Alchemist*, ed. D. Brown (London: 1976[4]); abbreviated: *Alch.*

occupying the central place in the fictional world of *The Alchemist* it discloses in play that the Puritan discourse of the world is seriously thirsting for power. It occupies the place the supporters of the Puritan discourse claim as their own and for which they are 'now, being toward the stone' (*Alch.*, III.2.68) even prepared to pay the price of their own truth. For this reason Tribulation admits that the catalogue of common accusations levelled at the Puritans, which Subtle now puts forward (*Alch.*, III.2.69–2.82; 2.86–2.97), is justified:

> Truly, sir, they are
> Ways, that the godly Brethren have invented,
> For propagation of the glorious cause.
> *Alch.*, III.2.97–2.99

However, at the moment of the explosion, when the alchemistic discourse collapses as the object of desire and thus ceases to be relevant, the Puritans are deprived of the orientation towards the centre that promises them power and can now only deny their own truth. Tribulation, the functional player, realises this bitterly; the fundamentalist Ananias on the other hand loses control of his discourse, which tips over into its opposite, powerless, profane cursing:

> I will pray there,
> Against thy house: may dogs defile thy walls,
> And wasps, and hornets breed beneath thy roof,
> This seat of falsehood, and this cave of cozenage.
> *Alch.*, V.5.112–5.115

By juxtaposing in a carnivalistic manner two discourses in *The Alchemist* Jonson reveals both their lack of substance and their unconditional thirst for power. By initially giving precedence to the alchemistic discourse, the Puritans' discourse undermines and dispossesses itself; by then letting the alchemistic discourse explode, he silences the Puritan and reveals the true core behind the 'holy vizard' (*Alch.*, III.2.69) of his religious discourse.

5

In *Bartholmew Fair* the Puritans' religious discourse appears as a mere empty shell, without substance, as a discourse of unconditional flexibility, which changes its truth by constant adaptation and consequently possesses neither fixed principles and values nor moral or ethical norms. In the character of

Zeal-of-the-Land Busy Jonson shows that the constancy of Puritan speech is now merely formal and its contents arbitrary. In the argument whether Win, who is pregnant, can give in to her insatiable desire for pork despite her mother's puritanical principles and go to the fair to satisfy this desire, Busy is called in to give advice. He immediately begins in the typical style of a Puritan sermon, whose structure is characterised by incremental repetition:

> Verily, for the disease of longing, it is a disease, a carnal disease, or appetite, incident to women; and as it is carnal, and incident, it is natural, very natural. Now pig, it is a meat, and a meat that is nourishing, and may be longed for, and so consequently eaten; it may be eaten; very exceedingly well eaten. But in the fair, and as a Bartholmew-pig, it cannot be eaten, for the very calling it a Bartholmew-pig, and to eat it so, is a spice of idolatry, and you make the Fair no better than one of the high places. This, I take it, is the state of the question. A high place.
> *BF*, 1.6.44–1.6.53[42]

This is the starting-point for the following variations of his religious discourse. When Dame Purecraft begs him 'to make it as lawful as you can' (*BF*, 1.6.56f.), Busy finds an argumentative solution:

> Surely, it may be otherwise, but it is subject to construction, subject, and hath a face of offence with the weak, a great face, a foul face, but that face may have a veil put over it, and be shadowed, as it were; it may be eaten, and in the Fair, I take it, in a booth, the tents of the wicked. The place is not much, not very much; we may be religious in the midst of the profane, so it be eaten with a reformed mouth, with sobriety and humbleness; not gorged in with gluttony, or greediness; there's the fear, for, should she go there as taking pride in the place, or delight in the unclean dressing, to feed the vanity of the eye, or the lust of the palate, it were not well, it were not fit, it were abominable, and not good.
> *BF*, 1.6.62–1.6.73

The Puritan discourse thus constructs its truth according to the demands of each new or changing situation. What seemed in principle wrong now becomes admissible for Win because Dame Purecraft desires it and in the end even becomes an exemplary demonstration of duty for Busy:

---

[42] Edition used: Jonson Ben, *Bartholmew Fair*, ed. G. R. Hibbard (London: 1977); abbreviated: *BF*.

> In the way of comfort to the weak, I will go and eat. I will eat exceedingly, and prophesy. There may be a good use made of it, too, now I think on't: by the public eating of swine's flesh, to profess our hate and loathing of Judaism, whereof the brethren stand taxed. I will therefore eat, yea I will eat exceedingly.
>
> BF, 1.6.86–1.6.91

The shift in the argumentation from absolute prohibition to moral duty shows the Puritan's discourse to be flexible, pragmatic and functional, in contrast to its authoritative and moral pretensions. By letting Busy himself break up his speech into dialogue form, Jonson undermines its substance as a monologue and reveals how it can be adapted for use in differing situations.

The shifting in the Puritan's speech from serious criticism of other people's cravings to the egoistical satisfying of his own, its carnivalisation by means of the motif of the 'affirmation of the body against the denying spirit',[43] can be found a second time when they enter the Fair. Win is admonished to close her senses in order to resist the temptations:

> Look not toward them, hearken not. The place is Smithfield, or the field of Smiths, the grove of hobby-horses and trinkets. The wares are the wares of devils; and the whole Fair is the shop of Satan! They are hooks and baits, very baits, that are hung out on every side to catch you, and to hold you, as it were, by the gills, and by the nostrils, as the fisher doth; therefore, you must not look, nor turn toward them – the heathen man could stop his ears with wax against the harlot o' the sea; do you the like, with your fingers, against the bells of the Beast.
>
> BF, III.2.35–III.2.44

However, the place where the pig is roasted cannot be discovered without making use of the senses, and as the Fair is no 'Lubberland' (BF, III.2.70), where the roasted pigs fly into people's mouths by themselves, Busy suggests using the sense of smell in the search for the roasted pig.

> No, but your mother, religiously wise, conceiveth it may offer itself by other means to the sense, as by way of steam, which I think it doth, here in this place. Huh, Huh!
>
> BUSY *scents after it like a hound* (BF, III.2.71–III.2.73)

---

43 Womack, *Ben Jonson* 146.

The discrepancy between the uplifting words and the greedy sniffing for the scent of roasted pig again marks the characteristic movement of breaking up the dialogue; in the speech itself it occurs straightaway in Busy's next, ambivalent statement: 'We scape so much of the other vanities by our early entering.' (*BF*, III.2.83f.) We would expect a Puritan to utter such a sentence with a sigh of relief; in the ideology that Busy constructed initially that it represents a test of his own steadfastness it seems to be rather a sign of sincere regret; for the audience, however, who are already familiar with Busy's greediness, it at the same time indicates the hypocrisy of this regret. And the fairground character Knockem recognises him as such: 'Good guests, I say, right hypocrites, good gluttons.' (*BF*, III.2.107f.) When Knockem a little later pretends to let himself be converted by Busy, the arbitrary and contradictory nature of the Puritan discourse can be seen most clearly; When Busy excludes pork from the list of prohibitions for reasons of self-interest, Knockem includes it again: 'Sir, I will take your counsel, and cut my hair, and leave vapours. I see that tobacco, and bottle-ale, and pig, and Whit, and very Ursla herself, is all vanity.' (*BF*, III.6.23–III.6.25) Busy, on the other hand, insists that pork is legitimate:

> Only pig was not comprehended in my admonition, the rest were. For long hair, it is an ensign of pride, a banner, and the world is full of those banners. And bottle-ale is a drink of Satan's, a diet-drink of Satan's, designed to puff us up, and make us swell in this latter age of vanity, as the smoke of tobacco to keep us in mist and error. But the fleshly woman, which you call Ursla, is above all to be avoided, having the marks upon her of the three enemies of man: the World, as being in the Fair; the Devil, as being in the fire; and the Flesh, as being herself.
> *BF*, III.6.26–III.6.35

But the pork roasting on the fire in the Fair contains the marks of the three archenemies of the Puritan, just as Ursla does; thus in the discursive climax of what is to be avoided Busy contradicts himself. His discourse is revealed self-contradictory, inconstant, unscrupulous discourse, not bound to any truth, which changes whenever the situation does: 'Now his belly is full, he falls a-railing and kicking, the jade.' (*BF*, III.6.44f.)

In this way the Puritan discourse here again proves to be a discourse of power, of exclusion, and of intolerance:

> No, minister of darkness, no, thou canst not rule my tongue; my tongue it is mine own, and with it I will both knock and mock down your

Bartholmew-abhominations, till you be made a hissing to the neighbour parishes round about.

BF, IV.1.84–IV.1.87

At the same time, however, this pretension is carnivalised by the author's strategies of 'semantic gravitation',[44] such as smuggling in a wrong etymology of the word 'abhominations', as if it were derived from 'ab homine'. Busy's incorrect pronunciation of the word reveals his ignorance and undermines the serious nature of the speeches for the audience. The carnivalisation of the Puritan discourse reaches its climax in the subsequent quarrel about the puppet-show. Busy storms onto the stage with a tirade that propels the materiality of the language into the foreground:

> I will remove Dagon there, I say, that idol, that heathenish idol, that remains, as I may say, a beam, a very beam, not a beam of the sun, nor a beam of the moon, nor a beam of the balance, neither a house-beam, not a weaver's beam, but a beam in the eye, in the eye of the brethren; a very great beam, an exceeding great beam; such as are your stage-players, rhymers, and morris-dancers, who have walked hand in hand, in contempt of the brethren, and the cause, and been borne out by instruments of no mean countenance.
>
> *BF*, V.5.6–V.5.12

However, his eloquence, rhetorically inflated by his passion, immediately collapses and reduces itself to accusing the puppet-show of profanity. In the course of his debate with the puppet of Dionysius he can find fewer and fewer arguments, until in the end the two of them, Busy and the puppet, confront each other in a 'Punch and Judy' style dialogue on a minimal level: 'It is profane. / *It is not profane.* / It is profane. / *It is not profane.*' (*BF*, V.5.63–V.5.66) Then the puppet strikes back; Busy does not succeed in filling the accusation of profanity with substance without the puppet being able to prove that the Puritans have always been profane in the sense Busy suggests (*BF*, V.5.72ff.) In the end Busy uses a fact that to him seems undeniable to underpin his discourse: 'Yes, and my main argument against you is that you are an abomination; for the male among you putteth on the apparel of the female, and the female of the male.' (*BF*, V.5.87–V.5.89) The puppet, however, lifts its dress and

---

44 See also Bentley J., "Semantic Gravitation. An Essay on Satiric Reduction", *Modern Language Quarterly* 30 (1969) 3–19.

proves to be without gender; Busy's main argument is thus merely a discursive assertion that can be empirically disproved. His discourse proves to be hollow; it is stripped bare step by step, robbed of its arguments and its premises: 'I am confuted, the cause hath failed me.' (*BF*, v.5.102) There is no sacred core behind the tirade of discursive self-profanation; nothing remains that could be re-established as normative, holy Puritan seriousness after the temporary enclave of carnivalesque play; the Puritan discourse is seen to be an arbitrary discourse without any substance.

6

Side by side with the trend towards the pluralisation and desubstantialisation of religious discourse, a contrary development can be seen around 1600, in which the attempt is made to express religious feeling in a new, authentic and individual way, but without at the same time linking it to a direct claim to power over others. This development shows the tendency to the 'internalisation of the word',[45] which can be understood as a sign of privatisation and interiorisation within the process of European civilisation, as evidence of a new 'piété intérieure', whose quality Philippe Ariès has described as follows:

> With lay people, prayers now more often than not seem to take on the form of a solitary meditation in a private oratory, or simply in the corner of the sleeping-room, on a piece of furniture especially adapted for that kind of usage, the *prie-dieu*.[46]

Religion's retreat into the private sphere, into the interior of the house, or into keeping a *journal intime* does not abolish forms of collective worship; but it shows that at least in certain circles there was now a need to understand faith as a question of subjective self-searching and self-assertion.

John Donne's third satire, which is rightly described as 'a remarkable doctrine in the history of religious tolerance',[47] gives particular expression to the 'ideology of searching, examining and experimenting that is critical of authority'[48] in the early Modern Age. The text undermines the common expectations

---

45 Weimann, *Mimesis* 85.
46 Ariès P., "Pour une histoire de la vie privée", in Ariès P. – Duby G. (eds.), *Histoire de la vie privée*, 5 vols., vol. 3: Chartier R. (ed.), *De la Renaissance aux Lumières* (Paris: 1986) 7–19, 10.
47 Stein A., "Donne and the Satiric Spirit", *ELH* 11 (1944) 266–282, 268.
48 Weimann, *Mimesis* 87.

of the genre by the strict focussing of the *dispositio* on the pattern of the sermon, which is to be counted among the *genus deliberativum*; it is additionally characterised by the two essential functions of deliberative speech: 'persuasion and exhortation'.[49] From the start the speaker finds himself in a paradoxical situation which prevents him from acting in the way he would naturally do as a satirist; he feels both pity and anger towards the world. The pity prevents a sudden outburst of anger; the anger prevents his tears from flowing freely. Instead of immediately aggressively attacking a target, the speaker pauses and poses a question:

> Kinde pitty chokes my spleene; brave scorn forbids
> Those teares to issue which swell my eye-lids;
> I must not laugh, nor weepe sinnes, and be wise,
> Can railing then cure these worne maladies?
> *Sat.*, III.1–4[50]

This immediately raises the question of the positive foundation on which the satirical speaker builds up his apparently salutary criticism; if the norm of *virtus* provided the Roman satirists with a firm support, then the Christian analogy to this must be faith:

> Is not our Mistresse faire Religion,
> As worthy'of all our Soules devotion,
> As vertue was to the first blinded age?
> Are not heavens joyes as valiant to asswage
> Lusts, as earths honour was to them?
> *Sat.*, III.5–III.9

The question of religion as the legitimation of satirical speech is straightaway evidence of the reflective character of the third *satyre* and endows it with a basic meditative note; if only true faith can lead to salvation, true courage is to be seen as the sincere search for truth, which is not be taken over from others as a finished concept, but which must be found by each individual:

---

49   Sloan T.O., "The Persona as Rhetor: An Interpretation of Donne's *Satyre III*" (1965), now in Roberts J.R. (ed.), *Essential Articles for the Study of John Donne's Poetry* (Hamden, CT: 1975) 424–438, 426.

50   Edition used: Donne John, *The Satires, Epigrams and Verse Letters*, ed. W. Milgate (Oxford: 1967); abbreviated: *Sat*.

> Alas,
> As wee do them in means, shall they surpasse
> Us in the end, and shall thy fathers spirit
> Meete blinde Philosophers in heaven, whose merit
> Of strict life may be'imputed faith, and heare
> Thee, whom hee taught so easie wayes and neare
> To follow, damn'd? O if thou dar'st, feare this;
> This feare great courage, and high valour is.
>
> *Sat.*, III.9–III.16

In this way the genre of satire is increasingly occupied by a religious discourse whose main aim can be seen as justifying each individual's life on the day of the Last Judgement. This is demonstrated for example in the structurising function of the imperative exhortations that occur throughout the text: 'feare this' (*Sat.*, III.15), 'Know thy foes' (III.33), 'Seeke true religion' (III.43), 'aske thy father' (III.71), 'doubt wisely' (III.77), 'Keepe the truth which thou hast found' (III.89). Accordingly people truly searching for truth must be on their guard not only against confusing superficial bravery and true courage (*Sat.*, III.17–III.32), and against the temptations of the devil, the world and the flesh, which merely lead people astray (*Sat.*, III.33–III.42), but also against pre-defined paths whose promise of salvation is not to be trusted: Catholicism (*Sat.*, III.43–III.48), Calvinism (III.49–III.54), the path of the Anglican Church (III.55–III.62) and the models of atheism (III.62–III.64) or unconsidered tolerance (III.65–III.69). Nowhere there is the true faith to be found; it cannot be discovered by blindly adopting the seeming truths of someone else, but only by actively acquiring and discussing with those people whose authority lies in the fact they have themselves been on a long quest for truth:

> aske thy father which is shee [religion],
> Let him aske his; though truth and falsehood bee
> Neare twins, yet truth a little elder is;
> Be busie to seeke her, believe mee this,
> Hee's not of none, nor worst, that seekes the best.
> To'adore, or scorne an image, or protest,
> May all be bad; doubt wisely; in strange way
> To stand inquiring right, is not to stray;
> To sleepe, or runne wrong, is.
>
> *Sat.*, III.71–III.79

Truth is accordingly not conceived as the result of finding it, but as a process of searching that cannot be completed in this life and which is to be embarked upon early:

> On a huge hill,
> Cragged, and steep, Truth stands, and hee that will
> Reach her, about must, and about must goe;
> And what th'hills suddenness resists, winne so;
> Yet strive so, that before age, deaths twilight,
> Thy soule rest, for none can worke in that night.
> To will, implies delay, therefore now doe.
>   *Sat.*, III.79–III.85

This shows how authority shifts inwards; searching for the true faith on an unsure oath, constantly plagued by doubts, man is only responsible to himself and therefore need not submit to any other, worldly institution. The individual thus becomes the last authority of truth in this world; his main aim is to find it and maintain it:

> Foole and wretch, wilt thou let thy Soule be ty'd
> To mans lawes, by which she shall not be try'd
> At the last day? Will it boot thee
> To say a Philip, or a Gregory,
> A Harry, or a Martin taught thee this?
>   *Sat.*, III.93–III.97

The model of the individual's search for truth that is constructed in Donne's 'Satyre III' finds its guarantee in God, but this God can no longer be grasped by the things of this world, merely as an invisible 'third instance'. He is the 'guarantor of the reliability of human knowledge',[51] which must be found by each individual on his own responsibility. The final image of the stream of power, which becomes the more dangerous and violent, the further away it is from its roots, summarises this knowledge in an emblematic way:

> As streames are, Power is; those blest flowers that dwell
> At the rough streames calme head, thrive and prove well,

---

51 Blumenberg H., "The Concept of Reality and the Possibility of the Novel", in Amacher R.E. – Lange V. (eds.), *German Literary Criticism: A Collection of Essays* (Princeton, NJ: 1979) 29–48, 32.

> But having left their roots, and themselves given
> To the streames tyrannous rage, alas, are driven
> Through mills, and rocks, and woods, and at last, almost
> Consum'd in going, in the sea are lost:
>> So perish Soules, which more chuse mens unjust
>> Power from God claym'd, then God himselfe to trust.
>
> *Sat.*, III.103–III.110

The satirical speaker in John Donne's third satire, wondering about the foundation of his speech, thus finds his way in the course of the text to a religious discourse; this form of appropriating sacralisation of what used to be profane acquired by the active individual foreshadows Donne's later religious poetry and its successors in the seventeenth century.[52] In it there develops a type of subjective, individual discourse about religion, which acquires without dispossessing, which searches for truth without associating power with it, which again gives the religious word substance but without claiming validity beyond the individual.

Bibliography

Ariès P., "Pour une histoire de la vie privée", in Ariès P. – Duby G. (eds.), *Histoire de la vie privée*, 5 vols., vol. 3: Chartier R. (ed.), *De la Renaissance aux Lumières* (Paris: 1986) 7–19.

Bakhtin M.M., *Problems of Dostoevsky's Poetics*, ed. C. Emerson (Manchester: 1984).

Bakhtin M.M., *Rabelais and His World*, trans. H. Iswolsky (Bloomington, IN: 1984).

Bakhtin M.M., "Grundzüge der Lachkultur", in *Literatur und Karneval: Zur Romantheorie und Lachkultur*, trans. A. Kaempfe (Frankfurt – Berlin – Vienna: 1985) 32–46.

Barber C.L., *Shakespeare's Festive Comedy: A Study of Dramatic Form and its Relation to Social Custom* (Princeton: 1972).

Bentley J., "Semantic Gravitation. An Essay on Satiric Reduction", *Modern Language Quarterly* 30 (1969) 3–19.

---

[52] For further information cf. the short chapter by Esch A., "Die 'metaphysische' Lyrik", in Göller K.H. (ed.), *Epochen der englischen Lyrik* (Düsseldorf: 1970) 100–128, as well as the list of further reading contained there. – The present article was first published in German in *Shakespeare Jahrbuch West* (1991) 24–45; I would like to thank George J. Low for the translation.

Blumenberg H., "The Concept of Reality and the Possibility of the Novel", in Amacher R.E. – Lange V. (eds.), *German Literary Criticism: A Collection of Essays* (Princeton, NJ: 1979) 29–48.
Blumenberg H., *The Legitimacy of the Modern Age*, trans. R.M. Wallace (Cambridge, MA: 1986).
Burke P., "Popular Culture in Seventeenth-Century London", in Reay B. (ed.), *Popular Culture in Seventeenth-Century England* (London – Sydney: 1985) 31–58.
Burke P., *Popular Culture in Early Modern Europe* (Aldershot: 1988).
Burke P., "*Heu domine, adsunt Turcae!*: A Sketch for a Social History of Post-medieval Latin", in Burke P. (ed.), *Language, Self and Society* (Cambridge: 1995) 23–50.
Donne John, *The Satires, Epigrams and Verse Letters*, ed. W. Milgate (Oxford: 1967).
Eliade M., *The Sacred and the Profane*, trans. W.R. Trusk (New York: 1959).
Elias N., *The Civilising Process: Sociogenetic and Psychogenetic Investigations*, trans. E. Jephcott (London: 2000).
Esch A., "Die 'metaphysische' Lyrik", in Göller K.H. (ed.), *Epochen der englischen Lyrik* (Düsseldorf: 1970) 100–128.
Foucault M., *L'Ordre du discours* (Paris: 1971).
Greenblatt S., "Invisible Bullets: Renaissance Authority and its subversion, *Henry IV* and *Henry V*", in Dollimore J. – Sinfield A. (eds.), *Political Shakespeare: New Essays in cultural materialism* (Manchester: 1985) 18–47.
Hughes G., *Words in Time: A Social History of the English Vocabulary* (Oxford: 1989).
Jonson Ben, *Timber, or Discoveries*, in Jonson Ben, *The Complete Poems*, ed. G. Parfitt (Harmondsworth: 1975) 373–458.
Jonson Ben, *The Alchemist*, ed. D. Brown (London: 1976^4).
Jonson Ben, *Bartholmew Fair*, ed. G.R. Hibbard (London: 1977).
Lecocq L., *La Satire en Angleterre de 1588 à 1603*, Études anglaises 32 (Paris: 1969).
Lotman J., *The Structure of the Artistic Text*, trans. R. Vroon (Ann Arbor: 1977).
Luhmann N., "Das Problem der Epochenbildung und die Evolutionstheorie", in Gumbrecht H.-U. – Link-Heer U. (eds.), *Epochenenschwellen und Epochenstrukturen im Diskurs der Literatur- und Sprachhistorie* (Frankfurt: 1985) 11–33.
Pfister M., "Comic Subversion: A Bakhtinian View of the Comic in Shakespeare", *Shakespeare Jahrbuch West* (1987) 27–43.
Pierce W., *An Historical Introduction to the Marprelate Tracts: A Chapter in the Evolution of Religious and Civil Liberty in England* (New York: 1908).
Reay B., "Popular Religion", in Reay B. (ed.), *Popular Culture in Seventeenth-Century England* (London – Sydney: 1985) 91–128.
Ritter J., "Über das Lachen", *Blätter für Deutsche Philosophie* 14 (1940/1941) 1–21.
Shakespeare William, *The Complete Works*, ed. S. Wells – G. Taylor (Oxford: 1988).
Skelton John, *Collyn Clout*, in Skelton John, *The Complete English Poems*, ed. J. Scattergood (Harmondsworth: 1983) 246–278.

Sloan T.O., "The Persona as Rhetor: An Interpretation of Donne's *Satyre III*" (1965), now in Roberts J.R. (ed.), *Essential Articles for the Study of John Donne's Poetry* (Hamden, CT: 1975) 424–438.

Stein A., "Donne and the Satiric Spirit", *ELH* 11 (1944) 266–282.

Warning R., "Komik und Komödie als Positivierung von Negativität (am Beispiel Molière und Marivaux)", in Weinrich H. (ed.), *Positionen der Negativität*, Poetik und Hermeneutik 6 (Munich: 1975) 341–366.

Weimann R., "Towards a literary theory of ideology: mimesis, representation, authority", in Howard J.E. – O'Connor M.F. (eds.), *Shakespeare Reproduced: The Text in History and Ideology* (London: 1987) 265–272.

Weimann R., *Shakespeare und die Macht der Mimesis: Autorität und Repräsentation im elisabethanischen Theater* (Berlin – Weimar: 1988).

Weimann R., *Authority and Representation in Early Modern Discourse*, ed. D. Hillman (Baltimore: 1996).

Womack P., *Ben Jonson* (London: 1986).

Zimmermann H., "Die ideologische Krise in *King Richard II*", *Shakespeare Jahrbuch West* (1988) 103–122.

PART 2

Early Modern European Knowledge about Pagan Religion

∴

CHAPTER 5

The Seventeenth Century Confronts the Gods: Bishop Huet, Moses, and the Dangers of Comparison

Martin Mulsow

1

It is only a tiny step from comparison to blasphemy. Whenever the spheres of the sacred and the profane intertwine, the atmosphere becomes explosive. The eighteenth-century, which according to Frank Manuel confronted the Gods, ends with a blasphemous poem by the French author Évariste de Parny, entitled *La Guerre des Dieux* (1799).[1] De Parny delights in uniting the Olympic deities with the Christian Trinity in a pornographic banquet, where the Christian religion is obscenely mixed with the Pagan world. Such a confrontation between the sacred and the profane has of course earlier antecedents.[2] So when Giordano Bruno in his *Spaccio della bestia trionfante* presents a centaur in his revision of the celestial constellations, he is lampooning the dual nature of Christ and when Bonaventure des Périers has Mercury make an appearance in his *Cymbalum Mundi* of 1538 this needs to be understood as a satirical reference to Christ as God's messenger.[3] These were implicit comparisons, capable

---

1 Parny Évariste, *La Guerre des Dieux* (Paris, Didot: 1799). On the topic in general cf. Manuel F., *The Eighteenth Century Confronts the Gods* (Cambridge, MA: 1959). On this topic see also Mulsow M., "Die Thematisierung paganer Religionen in der Frühen Neuzeit", in Bultmann C. – Rüpke J. – Schmolinsky S. (eds.), *Religionen in Nachbarschaft: Pluralismus als Markenzeichen der europäischen Religionsgeschichte* (Münster: 2012) 109–123. – I am grateful to the Center for Theological Inquiry in Princeton where I was a fellow in the academic year 2007–2008, during which time I could carry out the research for this study.
2 On the division of sacred and profane see Eliade M., *The Sacred and the Profane: The Nature of Religion*, trans. W.R. Trask (San Diego: 1959); Sheehan J., "Sacred and Profane: Idolatry, Antiquarianism, and the Politics of Distinction in the Seventeenth Century", *Past and Present* 192 (2006) 35–66.
3 Bruno Giordano, *Spaccio della bestia trionfante*, in Bruno Giordano, *Dialoghi italiani*, ed. G. Gentile (Florence: 1958³) II, 549–831. Cf. Ingegno A., *Regia pazzia: Bruno lettore di Calvino* (Urbino: 1987). Périers Bonaventure des, *Cymbalum mundi* (n.p.: 1537); Cf. Boerner W., *Das "Cymbalum Mundi" des Bonaventure des Périers* (Munich: 1980).

© KONINKLIJKE BRILL NV, LEIDEN, 2019 | DOI:10.1163/9789004398931_007

of opening readers' eyes and stimulating them to ask critical questions, or occasionally, to provoke laughter.

Such scandalous allusions reveal the kind of difficulties a genuine science of comparison encountered when in the course of the seventeenth-century it set out to juxtapose different religions with increasing objectivity.[4] On the surface it happened always under the premise of a polemic, which contrasted the *vera religio* of Christianity with the *idololatria* of pagan religions, blighted by their *fabulae* and *errores*.[5] Yet at a certain point a sincere comparison could no longer be dismissed. Antiquarians in particular had cultivated this skill and established a culture of facts, which expanded in the footnotes of their scholarly publications and seeped from there into the consciousness of their readers.[6]

One example of this kind of antiquarian culture of facts is Ezechiel Spanheim's stupendous *De praestantia et usu numismatum antiquorum*, which was first published in 1664 and went through numerous expanded editions thereafter. Among other things, Spanheim talks in it about the golden apples from the garden of the Hesperides, which were famously stolen by Hercules, who had to fight the dragon Ladon in order to regain these apples, which which guaranteed eternal youth. Spanheim's book features antiquarian coins with images of the garden of the Hesperides with a tree and a snake that are astonishingly reminiscent of the paradise story.[7] Although Spanheim avoids

---

4 Cf. e.g. Rubiés J.-P., "Theology, Ethnography, and the Historicization of Idolatry", *Journal of the History of Ideas* 67, 4 (2006) 571–596; Sheehan J., "The Altars of the Idols: Religion, Sacrifice, and the Early Modern Polity", *Journal of the History of Ideas* 67, 4 (2006) 649–674; Schmidt F., "La discussion sur l'origine de l'idolatrie aux XVIIe et XVIIIe siècles", in *L'Idolâtrie. Rencontres de l'Ecole du Louvre* (Paris: 1990) 53–68. On the practice of comparing see Miller P.N., "The Antiquary's Art of Comparison: Peiresc and Abaxas", in Häfner R. (ed.), *Philologie und Erkenntnis. Zu Begriff und Problem frühneuzeitlicher 'Philologie'* (Tübingen: 2001) 57–94; on the theoretical problem of comparison between religions see Smith J.Z., *Drudgery Divine. On the Comparison of Early Christianities and the Religions of Late Antiquity* (Chicago: 1990).

5 Cf. Mulsow M., "Antiquarianism and Idolatry: The Historia of Religions in the Seventeenth Century", in Pomata G. – Siraisi N. (eds.), *Historia: Empiricism and Erudition in Early Modern Europe* (Cambridge, MA: 2005) 181–210; Häfner R., *Götter im Exil. Frühneuzeitliches Dichtungsverständnis im Spannungsfeld christlicher Apologetik und philologischer Kritik (ca. 1590–1736)* (Tübingen: 2003). On the notion of idolatry see Halbertal M. – Margalit A., *Idolatry*, trans. N. Goldblum (Cambridge, MA: 1992).

6 Cf. Shapiro B., *A Culture of Fact: England, 1550–1720* (Ithaca: 2000); on antiquarianism in general, see Momigliano A., "Ancient History and the Antiquarian", *Journal of the Warburg and Courtauld Institutes* 13 (1950) 285–315; Schnapp A., *The Discovery of the Past. The Origins of Archaeology* (London: 1996).

7 Spanheim Ezechiel, *De praestantia et usu numismatum antiquorum* (London, Richard Smith: 1706^3) I, 331. The coin that Spanheim refers to is from the time of emperor Antoninus Pius (138–161). Spanheim saw it in the royal coin cabinet in Paris.

noting this parallel, he nonetheless could not refrain from doing so in the footnotes of his commentary on the Hymns of Callimachus, published in 1697.[8]

The consequences of such comparisons were however by then already clear to almost every scholar. A bold libertine by the name of Adriaan Beverland – from the same milieu of Isaac Vossius, with whom Spanheim was in contact – had perceived such similarities as a license to apply the allegorical interpretations of the Greek myths to the paradise story as well.[9] As fictitious place of this publication from 1678 entitled *De peccato originali* Beverland indicated 'Typis Adami et Evae, in Horto Hesperidum.'[10] If Greek and Roman amorists talk of apples whenever they refer to testicles and of tree trunks whenever they allude to the phallus, Beverland asks, then why not interpret the story of Adam and Eve as sexual allegory?

In Beverland three entirely distinct traditions converge: late humanism with a profound knowledge of ancient authors such as Ovid, Propertius, Catullus, and Petronius, Dutch Spinozism, as it occurred in likeminded libertine authors such as Adriaan Koerbagh and his work *Bloemhof*, and finally a pornographic culture, which surfaced at exactly that time in Holland and which generated

---

8   Spanheim Ezechiel, *In Callimachi Hymnos observationes* (Utrecht, Halma: 1697) 671: 'Quum autem in explanatione hujus loci tradant inter alia veteres ibidem Critici, Atlantem, relicto tamdiu coeli, quod humeris sustinebat, onere, aurea illa ex eadem arbore poma ab ipsis Hesperidibus, serpentis proinde custodis permissu, pactum; quis non continuo agnoscit in veteri illa fabula, adumbratum primae parentis pomum ex arbore, serpentis suasu, in Paradiso decerpentis, idemque Adamo tradentis factum?' It would be interesting to know if Spanheim makes this hypothetical comparison (Quum …, continuo …) because he is already influenced by Huet. For Spanheim's contacts with Huet see his letters, e.g. the one from 8.2.1665, Biblioteca Laurenziana Firenze, Ash. 1866. I am grateful to April Shelford for the information about Huet's correspondence. – Even if other contemporary accounts of Paradise refer to other cultures such as the Persian or cite Roman and Greek authors, they do not dare to make a direct comparison. See e.g. Vorst Johannes, *De paradiso diatriba* (Rostock, Johann Richel: 1653); Morin Etienne, *Dissertatio de paradiso terrestri* (n.p.: 1692). Only in treatises of the mid-eighteenth century or later does it become natural to use comparisons. For paradise illustrations see Til Salomon van, *Tabula situm paradisi*, in *Malachias illustratus* (Leiden, Jordan Luchtmans: 1701); cf. Scafi A., *Mapping Paradise. A History of Heaven on Earth* (Chicago: 2006) 312; Poulouin C., *Le temps des origines: L'Eden, le déluge et 'les temps reculés' de Pascal à l'Encyclopédie* (Paris: 1998).

9   Beverland Adriaan, *Peccatum originale κατ' ἐξοχὴν sic nuncupatum* ([Leiden]: 1678). Cf. Smet R. de, *Hadrianus Beverlandus (1650–1716). Non unus e multis peccator. Studie over het leven en werk van Hadriaan Beverland* (Brussels: 1988); Mulsow M., *Die unanständige Gelehrtenrepublik. Wissen, Libertinage und Kommunikation in der Frühen Neuzeit* (Stuttgart: 2007) 11ff.; 40ff.

10 See Beverland's personal copy, in which he prepared the new edition: university library Munich W 8 Theol. 5678.

works such as *De Haagsche Lichtmis* or *De Leidsche Straatschender*, both published in 1679, as well as the *D'openhertige Juffrouw* from 1680.[11]

It becomes clear why contemporaries seemed agitated when the boundaries between the sacred and profane became blurred – for example, in the footnotes of Jean Le Clerc's Bible commentaries. This was due to spectres like Beverland which haunted honest theologians during their sleepless nights. Le Clerc's commentary on Genesis appeared in 1693, four years before Spanheim's observations on the Hymns of Callimachus.[12]

2

But the theologians' nightmares do not suffice to understand the kind of changes that occurred in the comparative study of religions in the course of the seventeenth century, in the main body of texts so to speak and not through the backdoor of footnotes. These changes were profound and they precede the period which Frank Manuel has treated. To evaluate them properly it seems helpful to survey the intellectual span between François La Mothe Le Vayer (1588–1672) and Pierre-Daniel Huet (1630–1721), which means the French Catholic milieu between 1641, when La Mothe's *La vertu des payens* was published and 1679, when Huet's *Demonstratio evangelica* appeared. We shall pay particular attention to how these two scholars referenced ancient texts, in which already both biblical and pagan culture were confronted.

Today La Mothe Le Vayer is often called a *libertin érudit*, which in fact obscures how much he mastered and participated in the discourse of French Catholicism.[13] His scepticism is part of the Catholic *machine de guerre* against Calvinism, just as Huet's anti-Cartesian scepticism will be an outgrowth of the same strategic orientation a little later.[14] In his *La vertu des payens* La Mothe attempts to polish the reputation of Graeco-Roman antiquity in regard to

---

11 On Koerbagh see Israel J., *Radical Enlightenment. Philosophy and the Making of Modernity 1650–1750* (Oxford: 2001) 190–196. On pornography in the Netherlands see Leemans I., *Het woord is aan de onderkant. Radicale ideeën in Nederlandse pornografische romans 1670–1700* (Utrecht: 2002).

12 Clerc J. Le, *Genesis sive Mosis prophetae liber primus* (Amsterdam, A. Wolfgang and J. Waesberge: 1693).

13 On La Mothe Le Vayer see Pintard R., *Le libertinage érudit dans la première moitié du XVIIe siècle* (Paris: 1943); Cavaillé J.-P.: *Dis/Simulations. Jules-César Vanini, F. La Mothe Le Vayer, Gabriel Naudé, Louis Machon et Torquato Accetto: Religon, Morale et Politique au XVIIe siècle* (Paris: 2002). The concept *libertinage érudit* is criticized in Delatour J., "Le cabinet des frères Dupuy", *Science et technique en perspective* 9 (2005) 287–328.

14 Cf. Popkin R.H., *The History of Scepticism from Erasmus to Spinoza* (Berkeley: 1979).

modern Christian culture. Its backdrop was of course the theological problem of whether pagans before Christ were automatically condemned to Hell and if that included even such virtuous men as Socrates or Plato.[15]

Interestingly La Mothe Le Vayer addresses the comparison between biblical subjects and pagan myths only indirectly. He quotes the second-century critic of Christianity Celsus, fragments of whose works had been transmitted by Origen and who had drawn a parallel between Sodom and Gomorrah and the Phaeton myth and between the fall of Lucifer and the one of Vulcan, emphasizing the secondary and unoriginal quality of the Bible.[16] La Mothe Le Vayer prudently presents such comparisons in the context of his argumentation seemingly only in order to show that the Church fathers had good reason to condemn the pagans. In regard to this they were, according to him, historically right but from the vantage point of modern European times it would no longer be essential to reproduce such a condemnation. In fact, in retrospect it becomes evident in La Mothe's eyes that Graeco-Roman antiquity produced several important men such as Plato, Aristotle, Cicero, Pyrrho or Epicurus, who could by all means be called virtuous.

'Ample was of course the ignorance of pagans', La Mothe Le Vayer sums up, 'and outrageous the wickedness of Satan, who wanted to disparage sacred history – if he had been able to – by putting pleasant fairy-tales in place of divine truths.'[17] The Greek myths are fairy-tales, *fables*, and the official Christian terminology for such myths was in fact *theologia fabulosa gentilium*.[18] Further in the text, however, the attentive reader quickly recognizes that something does not seem right with this official condemnation, when no other 'devilish' critic of Christianity other than Celsus is mentioned but most venerable Fathers of the Church:

> Car assez de personnes ont remarqué le rapport qu'il y a entre Samson et Hercule, Hélie et Phaéton, Joseph et Hippolyte, Nabuchodonosor et

---

15   La Mothe Le Vayer François, *La vertu des payens*, in J. Prévot (ed.), *Les libertins du XVII siècle* (Paris: 1641; reprint, Paris: 2004) II, 1–215.

16   Origen, *Contra Celsum libri VIII*, ed. M. Marcovich (Leiden: 2002). On Celsus see Pichler K., *Streit um das Christentum. Der Angriff des Kelsos und die Antwort des Origenes* (Frankfurt: 2005); Andresen C., *Logos und Nomos. Die Polemik des Kelsos wider das Christentum* (Berlin: 1955).

17   La Mothe Le Vayer, *La vertu des payens* 57: 'Certes l'ignorance païenne a été grande et la malice du diable extrême qui veut eût voulu rendre l'Histoire Sainte moins considérable s'il eût pu, en supposant des fables agréables au lieu de ses divines vérités.'

18   See e.g. Pomey F.A., *Pantheum mythicum seu Deorum gentilium fabulosa historia* (Lyon, Antoine Molin: 1659). On the problem of 'fables' see Ginzburg C., "Myth, Distance and Deceit", in Ginzburg C., *Wooden Eyes: Nine Reflections on Distance* (New York: 2001) 25–61.

Lycaon, la manne des Israélites et l'ambroisie des dieux. Saint Augustin met en parallèle sur cela Jonas et Arion. Saint Cyrille, archevêque d'Alexandrie, et depuis lui Théophylacte apparient le même Jonas à cet Hercule que Lycophron nomme τριέσπερον, Trinoctium, à cause qu'il fut trois jours et trois nuits dans le ventre d'une baleine d'ou il sortit avec la pelade. Saint Théodoret ne doute point que Platon n'eût ouï parler du fleuve de feu que Daniel représente au septième chapitre de ses prophéties, le Pyriphlegethon du Tartare en étant presque une copie dans le dialogue de l'immortalité de l'âme. Et je me souviens que Raphaël de Volterre trouve dans la boîte de Pandore le péché originel que nous tenons d'Ève.

For many men have seen the connection between Samson and Hercules, Elias and Phaeton, Joseph and Hippolytus, Nebuchadnezzar and Lycaon, the manna of the Israelites and the ambrosia of the Gods. Saint Augustine juxtaposes Jonah and Arion, Saint Cyrill, archbishop of Alexandria and later Theophylactus juxtapose the same Jonah and Hercules, whom Lycophron calls *triesperon*, Trinoctium, because he spent three nights in the stomach of a whale [...]. Saint Theodoretus did not doubt that Plato heard the same river of fire speak, which Daniel presents in the seventh chapter of his prophecies, because Tartarus's Pyriphlegethon in the dialogue about the immortality of the soul is almost a copy thereof. And I recall that Raphael Volaterranus encounters the Fall of Man, whom we ascribe to Eve, in Pandora's box.[19]

After this irritating interlude, La Mothe Le Vayer is quick to show that he lists all of these testimonies only *ex negativo*:

Or nous n'avons rapporté tout ceci que pour faire voir les raisons qu'ont eues quelques Pères de condamner avec chaleur le philosophe dont je parle et ses livres puisque les ethniques d'alors, contre qui ils étaient tous les jours aux prises, osaient bien les mettre au-dessus de ceux que le Saint-Esprit a dictés. À présent que cette considération cesse, vu qu'il n'y a rien à craindre de tel, que le paganisme n'est plus et qu'encore que le monde ne soit pas purgé d'impies ni d'athées, si est-ce qu'il ne se trouve personne que préfère aujourd'hui Sature à Dieu le Père, ni Socrate, Platon, ou quelque autre semblable, à Jésus-Christ, nous pouvons bien dans un temps si différent parler d'eux avec moins d'animosité et rendre à leur vertu aussi bien qu'à leur science l'honneur qu'elles méritent.

---

19   Mothe Le Vayer, *La vertu des payens* 57.

> But I have reported all of these things only in order to provide those reasons of some of the Fathers to condemn the philosopher I have mentioned before and to burn his books with fervour, because the pagans of their day, with whom they constantly had disputes, dared to value these books more than those which had been dictated by the Holy Spirit. But once such considerations ceases to exist, because it becomes clear that there is no longer anything to worry about, since there is no longer such a thing as paganism, we are able to talk about them with much less hostility and to grant their virtue and learning the honour they deserve.[20]

La Mothe Le Vayer offers thus comparison as a mode, which Sigmund Freud would have termed one of denial: something that has been suppressed is recovered and expressed, but it is denied at the same time in order to make it presentable.[21] Yet, the boundary had been crossed. La Mothe had provided a taste of the relativity and similarity of religions.

The Jansenist Antoine Arnauld recognized precisely this aspect of his work and wrote a book against *La vertu des payens*, entitled *La necesseté de la foy en Jesu Christ pour etre sauvé*.[22] It was published posthumously in 1701 by Louis Ellies Dupin, just as the dispute about the rites and the strategy of accommodation of the Jesuits in China had reached its peak.[23] Around that time, La Mothe Le Vayer, who had called Socrates and Confucius virtuous and redeemed pagans before Christ, was lumped together with the Jesuits and with Pierre-Daniel Huet, Bishop of Avranches, who likewise had dared to mix Chinese thought and Graeco-Roman antiquity with sacred history.[24]

3

Unlike La Mothe Le Vayer, Huet was certainly no libertine, but he shared much of his language and outlook.[25] Comparison and a scepticism in regard to the

---

20 Ibid.
21 Freud S., "Die Verneinung", *Imago* 11 (1925) 217–221.
22 Arnauld Antoine, *La necessité de la foy en Jesu-Christ pour être sauvé* (Paris, Charles Osmont: 1701).
23 See in general Mungello D.E. (ed.), *The Chinese Rites Controversy: Its History and Meaning* (Nettetal: 1994).
24 See Rapetti E., *Pierre-Danuel Huet: Erudizione, filosofia, apologetica* (Milan: 1999). On the history of the comparison with Confucius see Zoli S., *Europa libertina tra controriforma e illuminismo: l'oriente die libertini e l'origine dell' illuminismo* (Bologna: 1989).
25 On Huet see besides Rapetti, *Pierre-Danuel Huet*, Shelford A., *Transforming the Republic of Letters: Pierre-Daniel Huet and European Intellectual Life 1650–1720* (Rochester: 2007);

claims of reason are for him two sides of the same story but he does not compare biblical and pagan subjects in order to subvert Christianity, but rather in order to utilize tradition as proof for the truth of Christianity. According to Huet the Old Testament books were authentic and the prophetic evidence in them for the advent of Christ valid, which is confirmed by the postulate for the cultural superiority of the Mosaic tradition in the form – indicative of Cartesian times – of a historical-geometrical proof.[26]

Just as Eupolemus identified the Egyptian Mnevis – founder of state and religion[27] – as Moses, opposing Hecataeus, and just as Artapanus juxtaposed Musaeus and Moses, Huet now pursues a strategy of tracing back the pagan cultural heroes to the Jewish legislator, but on a much grander style: ultimately all pagan culture is a blurred memory of the original Hebrew culture and Moses hides behind Cecrops, Minos, Romulus, Zoroaster, Musaeus, Orpheus, Linus, Amphion, Bacchus, Apis, Hermes, Serapis, Anubis, Typhon, Silenus, Pan, and Adonis, to name but a few.[28] All pagan myths, including those from China and Japan, are in Huet's eyes a distorted echo of the Mosaic world. Already in his *Traité de l'origine des romans* from 1670 Huet had developed a theory about fictions, where he argues that fictional narratives originated in oriental cultures, from where they spread like floods over countries.[29] This kind of phe-

---

Dupront A., *Pierre Daniel Huet et l'exégèse comparatiste au XVIIe siècle* (Paris: 1930); Guellouz S. (ed.), *Pierre-Daniel Huet* (Paris: 1994); Ligota C., "Der apologetische Rahmen der Mythendeutung im Frankreich des 17. Jahrhunderts (P.D. Huet)", in Killy W. (ed.), *Mythographie der frühen Neuzeit. Ihre Anwendung in den Künsten* (Wiesbaden: 1984) 149–161; Boch J., *Les dieux désenchantés. La fable dans la pensée français de Huet à Voltaire* (Paris: 2002); Rapetti E., *Percorsi anticartesiani nelle lettere a Pierre-Daniel Huet* (Florence: 2003).

26 On this type of proof see Borghero C., *La certezza e la storia. Cartesianesimo, pirronismo e conoscenza storica* (Milan: 1983); Shelford A., "Thinking Geometrically in Pierre-Daniel Huet's *Demonstratio evangelica* (1679)", *Journal of the History of Ideas* 63, 4 (2002) 599–617.

27 See Assmann J., *Ägypten. Eine Sinngeschichte* (Munich: 1996) 54.

28 On Eupolemus and Artapanus see Droge A., *Homer or Moses? Early Christian Interpretation of the History of Culture* (Tübingen: 1989); Gager J., *Moses in Graeco-Roman Paganism* (Nashville: 1972).

29 Huet Pierre Daniel, *Traité de l'origine des romans* (Paris, Claude Barbin: 1670) 12f.: 'Aussi à peine est-il croyable combien tous ces peuples [especially the peoples of the orient] ont l'esprit poëtique, inventif, et amateur des fictions; tous leurs discours sont figurez; ils ne s'expliquent que par allegories; leur Theologie, leur Philosophie, et principalement leur Politique, et leur Morale, sont toutes enveloppées sous des fables et des paraboles.' A source for error in the process of diffusion is, according to Huet who refers to Strabo, the tendency in oriental authors to appropriate thinkers of other cultures as their own and to mingle history and fiction: 'que les Histoires de ces peuples sont pleines de mensonges, qu'ils sont peu exacts et peu fideles' (p. 18). He shows this p. 14f. by examining the history of the reception of Esop's fables, which the Arabs ascribe to a certain sage Locman and

nomenon he appears to observe in the transition from the Mosaic culture to various pagan ones.

In his attempt to prove just that, Huet displays in his 'Moses', as he calls his *Demonstratio* in his correspondence, a formidable level of erudition, citing the most obscure sources and listing an array of pagan Greek, Patristic, Rabbinic, Byzantine, and Islamic authors. In Foucauldian terms it is an unleashed frantic episteme of similarity: in disregard of all critical considerations, his enormous erudition notwithstanding, Huet views every instance of identifying one character with another as evidence. His apologetic motivations thus take the comparative approach to its extremes – an approach that had already been hinted at in parts of the works of Duplessis-Mornay, Scaliger, Gerardus Vossius and Grotius, and had been expanded by Bochart and Dickinson.[30] But in the eyes of his contemporary critics – including Leibniz – he carries these comparisons *ad absurdum*, similar to the way Jean Hardouin had carried historical pyrrhonism to its absurd logical conclusions.[31] Huet's frenzy of identification does not even shy away from obscene deities such as Priapus, whom Huet mentions along with the other disguises of Moses, since Phornutus equates Priapus with Pan, whom Huet had already accepted in his line of obscured Mosaic characters.[32] One can only imagine how amused someone like Beverland must have been by the identification of the phallic deity as Moses. Even John Toland, like

---

the Iranians to Mirkond. This little treatise foreshadows already Huet's similar thoughts about the appropriation of Biblical persons under different names among other peoples. Compare also Huet's early theory of translation; cf. DeLater J.A., *Translation Theory in the Age of Louis XIV: The 1683 De optimo genere interpretandi of Pierre-Daniel Huet* (Manchester: 2002). In his later years Huet combines his theory of knowledge and myth diffusion with the topics of seafaring and commerce. See his *Histoire du commerce et de la navigation des anciens* (Paris, François Fournier: 1716). See Mulsow M., "Muskatnüsse und Paradiesvögelfüße", *Frankfurter Allgemeine Zeitung* 04.06.2008, "Geisteswissenschaften".

30 See Bochart Samuel, *Geographia sacra*, vol. 1: *Phaleg* (Caen, Pierre Cardonelle: 1646) ch. 11; I cite from the edition Frankfurt/Main 1681; there pp. 11ff. On Bochart see Stroumsa G., "Noah's Sons and the Religious Conquest of the Earth: Samuel Bochart and his Followers", in Mulsow M. – Assmann J. (eds.), *Sintflut und Gedächtnis* (Munich: 2006) 307–320; Shalev Z., *Sacred Words and Worlds. Geography, Religion and Scholarship, 1550–1700* (Leiden: 2011); Dickinson Edmund, *Delphi Phoenicizantes* (Oxford, H. Hall: 1655).

31 See Dascal M., *Leibniz – The Art of Controversies* (Dordrecht: 2008) xlf. On Hardouin see Grafton A., "Jean Hardouin: The Antiquary as pariah", in Grafton A., *Bring out your Dead. The Past as Revelation* (Cambridge, MA: 2001) 181–207.

32 Huet Pierre Daniel, *Demonstratio evangelica* (Paris, Étienne Michallet: 1679). I cite from the edition Amsterdam 1680.

Voltaire later, was surprised that Huet went so far as to derive the deities of the underworld from Moses.[33]

It was Arnauld again who established a connection between La Mothe Le Vayer and Huet and complained: It is scarcely possible to compose a more blasphemous book and one 'that would be more suitable to convince young free spirits that, although religion is important, all are equally good and that even paganism is a match for Christianity.'[34] It is then the relativity of an array of different world views which Arnauld adduces and which he perceives as a threat to Christianity's claim of uniqueness. What was originally well-intended as an apology against paganism and Spinoza's *Tractatus* had become a boomerang.

Interestingly, this allegation originated in the Jansenist camp. From their point of view Huet, in creating unsound links to paganism, was just like the Jesuits and Arminians. The Jansenists themselves, however, like orthodox Calvinists and the Lutherans in Germany, were very careful to keep sacred history and sacred hermeneutics separate from pagan material. Hence one may wonder what role the doctrine of grace played in the exclusion of the profane from the sacred.[35]

But how does Huet create such links? He uses Eusebius and his *Praeparatio* as well as his *Demonstratio Evangelica* as his models – not just in the title for his work. The latter had demonstrated in them the superiority of Jewish-Christian revelation vis-à-vis pagan beliefs and traditions. Thus, as a Christian, he continued the tradition of Jewish respondents to the challenge of Hellenistic culture, a tradition which included writers such as Artapanus of Alexandria, Eupolemus, and Josephus.[36] In some cases the response turned into the extreme claim that Moses had perfectly mastered all sciences and was the founder of all arts. During the early modern period such claims fell on fertile soil as for example in 'Mosaic physics' or in many other 'sacred' disciplines and

---

33   Toland John, *Origines judaicae* (London, Thomas Johnson: 1709) § 4; Voltaire, *Dictionnaire philosophique* ('Londres': 1764) Art. Bacchus.

34   Antoine Arnauld's letter to Dodart in *Lettres de Messire Antoine Arnauld, vol. 3* (Paris, Sigismond d'Arney: 1775) 400–403, 400f.: 'ce sont horribles choses, et capables d'inspirer à de jeunes libertins, qu'il faut avoir une religion; mais qu'elles sont toutes bonnes, et que le Paganisme même peut entrer en parallele avec le Christianisme.'

35   On the role of the Jansenists see Momigliano A., *La formazione della moderna storiografia sull'Imperio Romano* (Turin: 1938); Kley D. van, *The Religious Origins of the French Revolution: From Calvin to the Civil Constitution, 1560–1791* (New Haven: 1999²).

36   Eusebius, *Praeparatio evangelica*, ed. K. Mras (Berlin: 1954). On Eusebius' use of Jewish authors see Inowlocki S., *Eusebius and the Jewish Authors: His Citation Technique in an Apologetic Context* (Leiden: 2006); Johnson A.P., *Ethnicity and Argument in Eusebius' Praeparatio Evangelica* (Oxford: 2006).

eventually developed a prosperous afterlife.[37] Huet's *Demonstratio evangelica* is a strange historical-philological branch within this tradition.

4

Traces of such earlier Moses-exaltations become evident in the details of Huet's line of argument. This is clear, for example, when we take a look at the small portion of the twelve-hundred-page work which discusses the various names by which Moses was worshiped in Egypt. One of the many traces, according to Huet, leads to Mercury or Hermes, whom the Egyptians worshiped as Thot (or Taaut). Huet points out that already Martianus Capella in *De nuptiis philologiae et Mercurii* had implicitly observed this identification when he had Philology before the wedding ceremony inquire in some kind of gematric procedure if her future spouse Mercury would be a proper match.[38] This Thot was, according to Huet, none else than Moses, who due to his deeds, had been deified in Egypt.[39] Numerous parallels that were associated with both figures suggested such a conclusion. Huet bases his judgment on the work *Chanaan* by his teacher Samuel Bochart, whom he had accompanied on a trip to Sweden in 1652.[40] *Chanaan* is a work about the Phoenician language. Bochart had pointed

---

37   Blair A., "Mosaic Physics and the Search for a Pious Natural Philosophy in the Late Renaissance", *Isis* 91 (2000) 32–58; Mulsow M., "Moses omniscius oder Moses politicus? Moses-Deutungen des 17. Jahrhunderts zwischen sakraler Enzyklopädik und libertinistischer Kritik", in Kilcher A.B. – Theisohn P. (eds.), *Die Enzyklopädik der Esoterik. Allwissenheitsmythen und universalwissenschaftliche Modelle in der Esoterik der Neuzeit* (Munich: 2010) 177–202.

38   Martianus Capella, *De nuptiis philologiae et Mercurii*. See Stahl W.H. – Burge E.L. (eds.), *Martianus Capella and the Seven Liberal Arts, vol. 2: The Marriage of Philology and Mercury* (New York: 1977) 35. Huet may have received the hint that Thot was being alluded to from Hugo Grotius' commentary, *Satyricon, in quo de nuptiis philologiae et Mercurii libri duo et de septem artibus liberalibus libri singularis* (Leiden, Christophorus Raphelengius: 1599).

39   *Demonstratio evangelica*, 100f.: 'Aegypti regem fuisse Taautum narrat ibidem Philo: Mosem paterni regni succesorem destinaverat Thermuthis Aegyptiorum regis filia; eique rex ipse diadema suum imposuerat, ut legitur apud Josephum: atque hunc etiam σοφὸν, βασιλέα, νομοθέτην Clemens appellat. Sapientia inter Phoenices praestitisse Taautum tradit Porphyrius in libro de Judaeis: eruditum fuisse Mosem omni sapientia Aegyptiorum Acta Apostolorum indicant. Literarum repertor Taautus creditus est: idem de Mose tradiderunt Eupolemus, Theodoretus, et Isodorus, ut iam a me notatum est.'

40   See Huet's report on this voyage – in verses: Huet Pierre Daniel, *Iter Suecicum*, in Huet Pierre Daniel, *Huetiana ou pensées diverses de M. Huet, eveque d'Avranches* (Amsterdam, Herman Uytwerf: 1723) 438–449. See also the extensive correspondence between Huet and Bochart from 1650 to 1666, the year of Bochart's death, which is preserved in the Biblioteca Laurenziana Firenze, Ash. 1866. On both men's relationship see Shelford A.,

out that according to the fragments on cosmogony from Sanchuniathon, preserved in Eusebius, there were parallels to the Mosaic creation account, especially when it came to the description of a spirit that was hovering over the surface of the water, the deep.[41] The Phoenician account of Creation also starts with chaos and the spirit. Since this cosmogony can be derived, according to Sanchuniathon, from Taaut (whom already Philos of Byblos, his 'translator', had identified as Thot), Huet concluded that it was originally written on the columns of Phoenician temples, on which Thot, the inventor of script, had inscribed his knowledge, which had been copied by Hierombalus and eventually ended up with Sanchuniathon. The very same Thot, Huet points out, was, however, none other than Moses, whom Eupolemus and others likewise record as the inventor of writing. Already Porphyry had observed that Sanchuniathon had recorded the genuine history of the Jews.[42]

It is important to note that these original teachings of wisdom have a cosmogony as their subject, which, as is the case in Hesiod, is a theogony. Already Philo had noticed this similarity to Hesiod and accused the Greeks of having produced a poor copy of Phoenician culture. A succession of natural forces is presented as mythological descent of the Gods. According to Huet, this description reflects traces from the history of the patriarchs of ancient Israel, which Sanchuniathon had taken from Thot's tablets and had reproduced a somewhat distorted version thereof. It is the story of Abraham, Sarah, Isaac, which Sanchuniathon presents as Saturn/Kronos, the nymph Anobret, and Jehud.[43] Saturn too fathered a son, who would later be sacrificed. Philo of Byblos had already identified figures such as El in Sanchuniathon's work as Kronos. Joseph Scaliger was then the first to suggest in his commentary on the

---

"Amitié et animosité dans la République des Lettres: La Querelle entre Bochart et Huet", in Guellouz S. (ed.), *Pierre-Daniel Huet (1630–1721): Actes du colloque de Caen, 12–13 novembre 1993* (Paris: 1994) 99–108.

41 Bochart Samuel, *Geographia sacra, vol. 2: Chanaan* (Caen, Pierre Cardonelle: 1646). I cite again from the edition Frankfurt/Main 1681, p. 783; the reference is to Gen. 1,2.; Baumgarten A.I., *The Phoenician History of Philo of Byblos: a Commentary* (Leiden: 1981) 96f.

42 Eusebius, *Praeparatio evangelica* IX, 10, 413, cites from Porphyry's *De philosophia ex oraculis haurienda*.

43 Philo of Byblos in Eusebius, *Praeparatio evangelica* I, 10, 40: 'Kronos then, whom the Phoenicians call Elus, who was king of the country and subsequently, after his decease, was deified as the star Saturn, had by a nymph of the country named Anobret an only begotten son, whom they on this account called Iedud, the only begotten being still so called among the Phoenicians; and when very great dangers from war had beset the country, he arrayed his son in royal apparel, and prepared an altar, and sacrificed him.' I cite the translation by Edwin Hamilton Gifford, *Eusebius: Preparation of the Gospel* (Oxford: 1903) 45.

Babylonian fragments of Berosus, which he appended to his *De emendatione temporum*, that Kronos must in fact be identified as Abraham and Anobret as Sarah, mainly due to the epithet of the sacrifice of their 'only' son. The term 'only' – יחיד (*yeḥid*) – must then refer to Isaac.[44] Bochart further elaborated on the insight[45] and Huet incorporated this interpretation in his overall portrayal which he developed from Moses.

Philo had already written that the Phoenician king Kronos (El) was immortalized as a planet after his death. That was Philo's euhemeristic interpretation of the myth, an interpretation which Eusebius adopted for apologetic reasons. Accordingly, these Phoenician kings were apotheosized and their names were applied to stars and the forces of nature. Huet adopts this point of view, which fits seamlessly into his theory that the Phoenician names were in fact alternative names for biblical figures from the Mosaic account. Hence the transformation into deities in pagan myths was a secondary phenomenon. This secondary process also produced a number of translation mistakes and distortions *in interpretando* from 'Thot' to Sanchuniathon.[46] They had to be corrected to find out the true story.

In addition Huet suggests to correct also those mistakes which ancient interpreters made, when they were trying to solve these complex problems of translation. Varro for example confused, according to Huet, in his work *De lingua latina* the Phoenician God Taaut with Coelus and Saturn, failing to recognize that Taaut was in fact Moses and Coelus/Saturn Abraham.

But how did it happen that Moses was all of a sudden called *Thot* or *Thoyth*? Huet explains this with a speculation that he took from his knowledge of the practices of transmission. Since names of authors were sometimes derived from the opening words of a written piece, the name *Thoyth* must have been created from a word in the second sentence of the Genesis account of Creation,

---

44   Scaliger Joseph Justus, *De emendatione temporum* (Geneva, Rover: 1629), Appendix: *Veterum Graecorum Fragmenta Selecta*, 48: 'Hic vides primum Isacum, non autem Abrahamum μονογη sive יחיד dictum: deinde adumbratam, vel potius depravatam immolandi Isaci historiam, et caussam penitus dissimulatam, immolationem ementitam. Sed et nomen Sarae in Anobreth mutatum.' The discussion in Scaliger leads to the result that the term "only begotten" was supposed to refer not to Abraham but to his son.

45   Bochart, *Geograhia sacra: Chanaan* 790.

46   Eusebius, *Demonstratio evangelica* 101f.: 'Minime porro credendum est, Mosis libros ita fuisse assectatum Sachoniathonem, ut rerum principia describens nusquam ab iis recesserit. Ea excerpsit duntaxat, quae cum gentis suae religionibus, et receptis dogmatis consentirent. Neque vero, quae a Sanchoniathone scripta erant, fideliter retulit interpres Philo Byblius. Ex iis quae extant apud Eusebium facile agnoscas, quam multa sibi in interpretando permiserit. Mosem itaque Sanchoniathon, Sanchoniathonem Philo Byblius interpolavit.'

the term *Tohu*.⁴⁷ 'The name of the author came from his writings', Huet explained.⁴⁸ He tried to support this bold theory with a reference to Scaliger, who made a reference to *Thoyth* in his commentary on the fragments of Varro's *De lingua latina*. Scaliger, however, does not make a reference to the Bible there.⁴⁹

Whatever may be the case, Huet has already moved on in the chain of proofs. According to Julian the Apostate, *Monimus* was worshiped along with *Azizus* and the sun in Edessa.⁵⁰ In a conjecture Huet corrects this by pointing out that it must be a reference to Emesa in Phoenicia.⁵¹ Thus he is back at Phoecician religion. Iamblichus, on the other hand, had claimed that Monimus was Mercury. Huet takes this information and combines it with a passage, which he had discovered in the writings of the twelfth-century Jewish Bible commentator Ibn Ezra, who had quoted from Ibn Waḥshiyya's mysterious *Nabatean Agriculture*, which plays an important role in Maimonides' *Guide for the Perplexed*. It came allegedly from the quill of the Chaldean sage Kothami and had been translated into Arabic and was believed to reflect the ancient Sabean world view.⁵² There, a passage suggests that Moses was also called *Monios*. If it was in fact true that *Monios* was a Sabean term, then it must, in Huet's eyes, refer back to a very early phase of human history, when first traces of a subversion of Mosaic religion could be noticed.

This means that Huet is in need of some evidence that would show that the Sabeans were actually dissenters. Again, he believed to have found linguistic evidence, namely once he consulted the edition of Abulpharagius' *History of*

---

47   Gen. 1,1.
48   Eusebius, *Demonstratio evangelica* 106: 'Ad nomen Thoyth quod spectat, persuasum fuit Scaligero, et aliis, factum illud est ex *tahu*, quae dictio inter primas Geneseos Mosaicae dictiones occurrit. Nempe Auctori de scriptione sua nomen finxerunt.'
49   Varro, *Opera quae supersunt*, ed. J.J. Scaliger (Paris, Henri Estienne: 1573), *Conjectanea* (separate pagination), 25f. (on p. 14 of the Varro edition): 'ut etiam addam, Taautem illum, non Phoenicum sed Aegyptiorum numen fuisse, quem alii Theuth vocant, ut Cicero in libris de Natura Deorum.' Already Adrien Turnebe had written in his commentary to the same passage in Varro (printed in the same edition, separate pagination, 31): 'Taautem Eusebius (sic enim vocat) dicit esse apud Phoenicos Mercurium, qui ab Aegyptis Thot vocetur.'
50   Julianus Apostata, *Hym to king Helios*, in Julianus Apostata, *The Works of the Emperor Julian, vol. 1*, trans. W.C. Wright (Oxford: 1913) 358–362. See Zuntz G., *Griechische philosophische Hymnen* (Tübingen: 2005); Dillon J., "The Theology of Julian's Hymn to King Helios", Itaca 14/15 (2000) 103–115.
51   See however Drijvers H.J.W., "The Cult of Azizos and Monimos at Edessa", in Bergman J. (ed.), *Ex Orbe Religionum. Studia Widengren* (Leiden: 1972) 355–371.
52   See Hämeen-Anttila J., *The Last Pagans of Iraq. Ibn Washiyya and his Nabatean Agriculture* (Leiden: 2006).

the Dynasties, published in 1663 by the Oxford orientalist Edward Pococke.⁵³ Abulpharagius (the latinized form of Abu al-Faraj) – the Syrian Christian Bar Hebraeus – had written an Arab history. In his commentary Pococke points out that the Arabic verb *tseba*, which was a reference to the Sabeans, should be translated as 'to abandon an original cult of God by admitting new ones.' Thus the veracity of *Monios* as an early denomination – albeit corrupt – is established.⁵⁴

Using the *Monios* passage from Ibn Ezra, Huet corrects the term *Honios* in the *Catena Cabalae* (*Shalshelet ha-Qabbalah*) by Rabbi Gedalia ibn Yaḥya.⁵⁵ From this *Catena* he had already quoted all the various names that Moses had received from his sister, his mother, and others. He likewise adduced the eighth-century work *Pirke de Rabbi Eliezer* that was ascribed to the Tannaite Rabbi Eliezer ben Hurcanus (fl. ca. 100 CE) as well as the Rabbinic pseudepigraphic work *Liber de vita et morte Mosis* (*Divre ha-yamim u-ftirato shel Moseh*).⁵⁶ Byzantine chronologists such as Cedrenus and George Syncellus supplied him with additional material for other names for Moses.⁵⁷ Huet had been collecting such material for years.

In Ibn Ezra's commentary on Exodus there are already speculations whether there could be any connection between *Monios* or *Monimos* and various Greek terms – because it sounds so Greek.⁵⁸ Huet consults the fifteenth-century

---

53   Abulpharagius Gregorius, *Historia compendiosa dynastiarum*, ed. E. Pococke (Oxford, H. Hall: 1663).
54   Ibid., 108: 'Velut illa, quae nomen arcessit ab Arabico verbo, Tseba, quod est, pristinos Die cultus novis admissis relinquere.'
55   Eusebius, *Demonstratio evangelica* 105. Gedalya Ibn-Yahyâ Ben-Yôsef, *Sefer Shalshelet ha-Qabbalah* (Venice, Giovanni di Gara: 1587). On this book see David A., "Gedalia Ibn Yahia, auteur de Shalshelet ha-Qabbalah", *Revue des Études Juives* 154 (1995) 101–132.
56   Eusebius, *Demonstratio evangelica* 105f. On Pirke see Friedlander G., *Pirke de Rabbi Eliezer* (London: 1916); Kister M., "Ancient Material in Pirqe de-Rabbi Eli'ezer: Basilides, Qumran, the Book of Jubilees", in Maeir A.M. et al. (eds.), *'Go Out And Study the Land'* (*Judges 18:2*) *Archeological, Historical, and Textual Studies in Honor of Hanan Eshel* (Leiden: 2012) 69–94; on Moses' names cf. especially 84–89. Gaulmin Gilbert (ed.), *De vita et morte Mosis libri III* (Paris, Tussnaus du Bray: 1629). On the names of Moses there, see pp. 8f. On Moses' names from today's point of view see also Duke R., "Moses' Hebrew Name: The Evidence of the Visions of Amram", *Dead Sea Discoveries* 14 (2007) 34–48.
57   On Moses in Byzantine Chronicles see Magdalino P. – Nelson R. (eds.), *The Old Testament in Byzantium* (Dumbarton Oaks: 2010); Milikowsky C., "Justus of Tiberias and the Synchronistic Chronology of Israel", in Cohen S.J.D. – Schwartz J.J. (eds.), *Studies in Josephus and the Varieties of Ancient Judaism* (Leiden: 2006) 103–126.
58   Ibn Ezra, *Commentary on The Pentateuch: Exodus* (*Shemot*), trans. and annot. H.N. Strickman – A.M. Silver (New York: 1996) 44: 'Moshe (Moses) is a Hebrew form of an Egyptian name. Moses was called Monyos in Egyptian. The name is so written in a book on agriculture which was translated from Egyptian into Arabic. This is also recorded in

Portuguese Jewish Bible commentator Isaac Abravanel to clarify this point.[59] He adopts the latter's speculations that the name of Moses had been corrupted in the course of its translation from the Hebrew into Egyptian, then into Arabic and then finally into Greek. But he rejects other speculations such as a supposed connection between the term *Monios* and the Latin *magnus*.

The relation of *Monios* to Greek was rather tenuous then. This result enables Huet to push his argument further. He speculates that there was an early time, when *Monios* was derived from a epithet of Mercury. Mercury, as we may recall, was the Roman term for *Thot*, who was eventually identical with Moses. Bochart had suggested in his theory of corruption and of mythological translation that Mercury was actually Noah's son Cham (Canaan), whereas Noah was mistakenly viewed as Jupiter.[60] Huet did not adopt this theory, partly because, unlike Bochart, who focused on Noah and his sons, he was himself focused in his theory on Moses. Mercury-Thot, according to Huet, once had the epithet *Nemios*. To understand the meaning of this surname, Huet draws from the commentary of Gilbert Gaulmin to the above-mentioned rabbinic *Liber de vita et morte Mosis*, which the latter had edited in 1629[61] and in which he asserted that the syllables *mo* and *ni* were 'even today' used by Copts in Egypt and mean 'out of' (ni) 'the water' (mo).[62] Huet verified this assertion by looking into the so-called *Scala Magna* of the Coptic priest Barakat Ibn Kabar, a Coptic

---

the books of the Greek scholars. Perhaps the daughter of Pharaoh learned our language, or she asked some one for its Hebrew version. Do not be perplexed as to why moshe was not called mashuy, as nouns do not keep their forms as verbs do.'

59 Eusebius, *Demonstratio evangelica* 107. Abravanel Isaac, *Perush ha-Torah* (Venice, Bragadini: 1579). See Lawee E., "Isaac Abrabanel: From Medieval to Renaissance Jewish Biblical Scholarship", in Sæbø M. (ed.), *Hebrew Bible / Old Testament. The History of its Interpretation, vol. 2: From the Renaissance to the Enlightenment* (Göttingen: 2008) 190–214.
60 Bochart, *Geographia sacra: Chanaan*, 12: "Chanaan idem qui Mercurius".
61 Gaulmin, *De vita et morte Mosis*. Gaulmin's notes on book III are on pp. 192–199; 195f.: 'Obiter doctos monebimus hunc librum etiam hodie apud [196] Cophitas asservari, sed de illo alibi plenius. ΜΩ certe Aegyptiace *aqua*, NI est ex Monios; igitur est ex aqua. Nam quod ὑσῆς liberatim vult significare τὸ הושע linguae suae in mente habuit. Hinc Graecis ὑδογενής. ὡς φάτις ἀρχαίων, ὡς ὑδογενής διέτεξεν. In Spurio Orphei versu. De aliis eius nominibus Melchi, Ioachim, Adamosi, Tethmosi et sexcentis similibus apud Eusebium Cedren. Clement. Alexandr. nihil quaerimus. Sed Manetho et ipse Aegyptius etiam a popularibus suis *Osarseph* dictum scripserat, ad verbum est πύρσος quo etiam nomine dictus Achilles apud Lycophronis scholiasten si bene memini.' See Fabricius Johann Albert, *Codex pseudepigraphus veteris testamenti* (Hamburg, Christian Liebezeit: 1713) 833–835. On the designation of Moses as Osarsiphus see note 93 below.
62 It is right that 'Moses' is an Egyptian word (as suffix), but it means in fact 'child of'. See Griffiths J.G., "The Egyptian Derivation of the Name Moses", *Journal of Near Eastern Studies* 12 (1953) 225–231. But indeed "mooy" is water in Coptic. See Spiegelberg W., *Koptisches Handwörterbuch* (Heidelberg: 1912) 68.

dictionary which Athanasius Kircher had made accessible to the public.[63] Gaulmin had – if we read his account – used his etymology in order to explain *Monios*, not *Nemios*, and to verify the very meaning which was usually given to the name *Moses* by a pseudo-Hebrew etymology. Huet, however, seems to have tried to improve Gaulmin's argument in keeping the right sequence of the words *ni* and *mo*, which is closer to *Nemios* than to *Monios*. In this way he managed to give an elegant if complex deduction of Moses as the one who was pulled out of the Nile, derived from the ancient Egyptian and Phoenician distortions of his name.

5

Slowly we get a sense of how Huet precedes and what kind of books he pulls from the shelves. But above all we recognize that Huet's argument stretches over extremely long chains of conclusions, the single parts of which often seem speculative and at times unsubstantiated, and he utilizes a large array of diverse sources: Greek authors from late antiquity, Jewish commentators, as well as recently published Arabic, Coptic, and Byzantine texts. But what Huet barely does is subject these texts to a source-critical analysis. If we, however, attempt such an analysis now, it becomes clear that his sources reflect three ancient tendencies: the exaltation of Moses that can be found in Jewish-Hellenistic and early Christian apologetic writings; a multiplication of the name of Moses from mostly Rabbinical sources, which were a mode of raising the status and to reveal an array of characteristics and virtues; finally the complex pattern of the cultural translation of pagan religions of late antiquity into each other. Ancient polytheistic religions were not concerned about the identification of their deities with similar deities from other cultures and so made translation possible. In this respect, syncretistic religious practice is reflected in numerous theoretical texts, where Hermes is then identified with Thot or Isis with Diana. Within these translations attempts had already been made in antiquity to place the name Moses next to other names and to recognize derivations.

We can first consider the authors exalting Moses. If one follows Erich Gruen's interpretation of Artapanus and similar authors, then their unabashed

---

63 *Scala Magna*, in Kircher Athanasius, *Lingua Aegyptiaca restituta* (Rome, Hermann Scheus: 1643). The text had been brought to Europe by Pietro della Valle. On Barakat ibn Kabar see Meinardus O., *Two Thousand Years of Coptic Christianity* (Cairo: 1999) 60; Hamilton A., *The Copts and the West, 1439–1822: The European Discovery of the Egyptian Church* (Oxford: 2006) 201; El-Daly O., *Egyptology: The Missing Millennium. Ancient Egypt in Medieval Arabic Writings* (London: 2005) 58.

habit of attributing cultural achievements to Moses was not really syncretistic or a genuine attempt to convince non-Jews of the superiority of Jewish culture. Rather it represented the ingenious appropriation of non-Jewish heroes for the local audience.[64] Thus Huet falls victim to an almost frivolous game played by Hellenic-Jewish authors who with a wink of the eye allow Moses, and not Thot, to invent writing. The detailed arguments constructed by Huet, such as the one which cites the numerous characteristics shared by Moses and Thot in order to insist that they are one and the same figure, accepted at face-value what was actually meant as a provocative joke.[65]

With regard to the Rabbinic sources, the situation – seen from our current perspective – is not much better. The *Liber de vita et morte Mosis* is the amalgamation of two Midrashim, the *Dibre ha-yamim shel Moshe* (*The history of Moses*) and the *Midrash Petirat Moshe* (*The Midrah of Moses' death*). The first belongs to the genre of the 'rewritten Bible' and is written in pseudo-biblical Hebrew. It uses Exodus Rabba and the Josippon, two works from the tenth and eleventh centuries, and therefore originated itself in all likelihood in the eleventh century.[66] It is therefore a very late product and can hardly be considered a reliable source for the names given to Moses by his family. A late dating is also justified for the second Midrash. It exists in various recensions which can be dated to the period between the seventh and eleventh centuries.[67] In the Rabbinic literature the replications of the name Moses often have to do with the belief that repeated naming enhances status and makes numerous characteristics and virtues manifest. Huet, however, was searching in these names for references to other cultures.

---

64 Gruen E.S., *Heritage and Hellenism. The Reinvention of Jewish Tradition* (Berkeley: 1998) 153–160. See esp. p. 160: The Jewish-Hellenistic writers 'did not enlist in a deadly serious encounter to advance Jewish values against the claims of competing nations and cultures. Rather, they could exhibit a light touch, occasionally discerned in Pseudo-Eupolemus and Cleodemus Malchus, but readily obvious in Artapanus, a caprice and whimsy that tampered liberally with the Scriptures and inverted or transposed Gentile traditions to place the figures of Jewish legend in the center. The humor is mischievous rather than malicious. It sets the author in a superior posture of detachment, disengaged from ideological battle, and thereby augments the authority of his judgment. What stands out is not so much polemics as inventive imagination.'

65 See Mussies G., "The Interpretatio Judaica of Thot-Hermes", in Voss, M.H. van et al. (eds.), *Studies in Egyptian Religion* (Leiden: 1982) 87–120.

66 See Stemberger G., *Einleitung in Talmud und Midrasch* (Munich: 1982[8]) 328; Dan J., "Moses, Chronicles of", in *Encyclopaedia Judaica* (Jerusalem: 1971) XII, 413.

67 Cf. Stemberger, *Einleitung in Talmud und Midrasch* 328.

A third group of sources for Huet was provided, as we have seen, by the Christian chroniclers of the Byzantine Empire.[68] They first became accessible in the late sixteenth century when Hieronymus Wolf, Wilhelm Xylander and Johann Löwenklau edited and translated authors such as John Zonaras or Michael Glycas. Joseph Scaliger then used numerous old sources that were transmitted through the work of George Syncellus.[69] From Scaliger and Selden onwards such sources became fully integrated into the research on the history of the old religions of the Orient. In the works of the chronographers fragments of Jewish Pseudepigrapha (for example the First Book of Enoch, the so-called Book of the Watchers) have been passed down, including those whose survival was linked to their use of Eusebius' Chronicle such as fragments from Berosus and Manetho, which were contained in the text by Alexander Polyhistor and others used by Eusebius. Admittedly the Byzantine authors adopted and extended the Christianization of oriental chronicles made available to them by Eusebius. Thus, Xisuthrus is, for example, identified as Noah.[70] The Byzantines thus continue the interpretative 're-translation', which Hellenistic Jews had begun and which the Church Fathers had adapted to their own ends.

A critique of the sources of all these various syncretisms fashioned at various times for various purposes was far from Huet's mind. Yet one should also recognize that the fact that Huet had been duped by later fabrications is only one side of the coin. The other side comes into view if one considers how, since the archaeological discoveries of the twentieth century, the tendency that written testimonies were almost always treated as subsequent fabrication has on occasion been reversed. Meanwhile a greater sensitivity for the possible influences of old oriental sources upon Greek culture has come to the fore. We can take Huet's reference to the Sanchuniathon fragments as an example. In the light of the most recent research Huet's interpretation is not so far off the truth. Since the discovery of the Ugaritic archives in 1929 onwards is has become clear

---

68 See in general Hunger H., *Die hochsprachliche profane Literatur der Byzantiner*, vol. 1: *Philosophie – Rhetorik – Epistelographie – Geschichtsschreibung – Geographie* (Munich: 1978).

69 Glykas Michael, *Annales, qui Byzantinam historiam universalem exhibent* (Basel, Episcopius: 1572); on Löwenklau see Ben-Tov A., "Infamie und historische Wahrheit: Johannes Löwenklaus Apologia pro Zosimo", in Multhammer M. (ed.), *Verteidigung als Angriff. Apologie und Vindicatio als Möglichkeiten der Positionierung im gelehrten Diskurs* (Berlin: 2015) 9–25; Metzler D., "Johannes Löwenklau", in Stupperich R. (ed.), *Westfälische Lebensbilder* 13 (Münster: 1985) 19–44. Scaliger Joseph Justus, *Thesaurus Temporum* (Leiden, Thomas Basson: 1606). See Grafton A., *Joseph Scaliger: A Study in the History of Classical Scholarship*, 2 vols. (Oxford: 1983–1993).

70 See Adler W., *Time Immemorial. Archaic History and its Sources in Christian Chronography from Julius Africanus to George Syncellus* (Dumbarton Oaks: 1989) 34.

that the Phoenician cosmogony, passed down to us by Philo, does indeed date back in parts to the Late Bronze Age and is related to the Old Israelite world of Gods.[71] And since the discovery of the Hittite Kumarbi myth in Boghazköi (Boğazkale) in 1936 it has been realized that Hesiod's Theogony, as asserted by Philo, is indeed not free of West Asian influences.[72] Huet's project of detecting a pale reflection of biblical text in pagan mythology is not thereby rehabilitated, but it can now be re-considered with a new context which not only highlights deficiencies and shortcomings.

Huet adopted all of these lines of argument, consciously or subconsciously, and utilized them in his own project. If we draw on the parallel to psychoanalysis, then we discover that the comparative approach is used here not in the mode of denial, but in the mode of indifferent associativity, in which everything that plays a possible role in a multiplication of the Moses figure, comes to the fore.

It is not easy to answer the question why this mode of association assumed such a dominant position in Huet's scholarship. On the one hand it gives the scholar the opportunity to display his virtuosity and, as we have seen, to unveil relations and affinities with a wave of the magic wand. April Shelford has recently demonstrated how central this criterion was for Huet in assessing the erudition of scholars. Only after it had been met was Huet ready to debate serious questions with someone.[73] A further key word might be elegance. The magic of parallelisms possesses an almost musical elegance, achieved in ever new variations upon a single theme.[74] Behind all this one can discern the deeply Catholic conviction which found exemplary expression in Giovanni Pico della Mirandola's words that all traditions of humanity can only diverge

---

[71] Eissfeldt O., *Sanchunjaton von Berut und Ilumilku von Ugarit* (Halle: 1952); idem, *Taautos und Sanchuniathon* (Berlin: 1952); Baumgarten, *Phoenician History of Philo of Byblos*; Ebach J., *Weltentstehung und Kulturentwicklung bei Philo von Byblos. Ein Beitrag zur Überlieferung der Biblischen Urgeschichte im Rahmen des altorientalischen und antiken Schöpfungsglaubens* (Stuttgart: 1979). On the relationship of the Ugarit pantheon and the gods of Ancient Israel see Smith M.S., *The Origins of Biblical Monotheism: Israel's Polytheistic Background and the Ugaritic Texts* (Oxford: 2001).

[72] See West M.L., *The East Face of Helicon: West Asiatic Elements in Greek Poetry and Myth* (Oxford: 1997) 283–286.

[73] Shelford, *Transforming the Republic of Letters* 153ff.

[74] This aspect is emphasized by Ralph Häfner in the similar case of Edmund Dickinson's *Delphi Phoenicizantes*. See Häfner R., "Noah, Deukalion und das fossile Seepferdchen. Spurensuche im Schwemmland frühneuzeitlicher Komparatistik", in Mulsow M. – Assmann J. (eds.), *Sintflut und Gedächtnis* (Munich: 2006) 225–258, esp. 245–248. On the importance of the model of Second Sophistic polymathy for early modern "elegant" scholarship see Häfner, *Götter im Exil*.

so much from each other because they are different parts of a general revealed truth.[75] They can only be a priori differently sounding manifestations of the same truth. Huet transplanted this conviction from the Renaissance into the age of critical philology, and this essentially suspended his critical faculty, at least when judged by contemporary standards. Yet his strategy yielded a high return in apologetic arguments; all religions of humanity could be consulted in order to prove the truth of Christianity. The *Alnetanae Quaestiones* of 1692 demonstrate particularly well how Huet sought to reap the benefits of his approach.[76] Thanks to the dark and distorted myths contained in pagan religions he can corroborate, illuminate, and perhaps even elaborate upon the text of the Bible. When he speaks of the Babylonian confusion, he can substantiate the Biblical account of this event with the testimonies provided by Alexander Polyhistor and Plato;[77] Moses receives the Commandments from God, and this story is confirmed by similar accounts relating to the legislator in pagan society;[78] the oracle Urim and Thummim carried by Aaron on his breast takes on new meaning in view of the related custom observed by the high priest in Egypt.[79]

---

75   See Pico della Mirandola Giovanni, *Oratio de hominis dignitate*, ed. E. Garin (Pordenone: 1994). See Farmer S.A. (ed.), *Syncretism in the West: Pico's 900 Theses (1486)* (Tempe: 1998); see also the introduction to Pico della Mirandola Giovanni, *Über das Seiende und das Eine*, ed. P.R. Blum – G. Damschen – D. Kaegi – M. Mulsow – E. Rudolph – A.G. Vigo (Hamburg: 2006) IX–LXXIV.

76   Huet Pierre Daniel, *Alnetanae quaestiones de concordia rationis et fidei* (Leipzig, Johann Grosse: 1692). See for later additions of the *Demonstratio Evangelica* Huet's personal copy: Bibliothèque Nationale, Paris, Rèserve D.870.

77   Huet, *Alnetanae Quaestiones* 190. I cite from the Leipzig edition of 1692: 'Addidit Abydenus apud Eusebium et Cyrillum, facinoris auctores fuisse viros robustos et proceros, Deorum contemptores; locum fuisse Babylonem, sic dictam a Babel, quod confusionem sonat, ob confusam illic hominum loquelam. Idem ex Eupolemo prodidit Alexander Polyhistor, qui hinc disperses fuisse in varias muni plagas ait Gigantes operis inceptores, Diluvio superstites. Hoc linguae unius olim ab universis hominibus usurpatae in plurae linguas dissidium, praeter eos quos nominavi Scriptores, exprimit fabula vetus a Platone et Philone exposita, de lingua hominibus omnibus communi Saturni temporibus: quo munere cum in lasciviam abuterentur, fuisse ajunt eo multatos, discrete in plures sermone.'

78   Ibid., 214: 'Quod de Lege Mosi a Deo tradita, sacra et verax memorat historia, idem ad auctoritatem conciliandam plerique de se legumlatores inter Ethnicos jactarunt. Et suas quidem leges Jovi acceptas Minos referebat, suas Apollini Delphico Lycurgus, suas Minervae Zaleucus, suas Egeriae Numa, suas Dianae ejusque interpreti cervae Sertorius.'

79   Ibid., 215: 'Mirifici illius oraculi, Urim et Thummin, quod ad pectus applicitum ferebat summus Pontifex, per idque Dei voluntatem cognoscebat, simile fuit simulacrum sapphirinum, quod summus Aegyptiorum sacerdos atque judex de collo suspendum gestabat, et Veritas dicebatur. An ut per id admoneretur judex veritatis et aequitatis in judiciis ferendis retinendae? an ut per id persuaderetur populus veritatis eum esse compotem et veracem? an ut in rebus dubiis et obscuris simulacrum id consuleret, tanquam divinum aliquod oraculum, ut a Judaeorum Pontifice fiebat?' On the Urim and Thummim cf. Dam,

Huet does not probe into his sources too deeply for all these reasons. But when we now contrast indifferent utilization of Moses exaltations to our observation in La Mothe Le Vayer that in his work the late antique degradation of Moses played an important role, then it becomes clear that the Hellenistic dialectic between Moses exaltation and Moses degradation returns in a subtle way time and again during the seventeenth-century and influences profoundly the emerging discourse of a comparative history of religion. Artapanus and Celsus, Eusebius and Porphyry were not gone – they haunted the halls of the towers of theory, whether they were erected by honourable apologists or by astute libertines.[80]

6

As we have become increasingly aware today of how subtle the interaction between pagans, who had read the Bible, and rabbis, who were conversant with the philosophical currents of the pagan world – some of them henotheistic – was in antiquity, this should make us consider the early modern debates more carefully.[81] Here too each side displays the same profound knowledge of the other's views: orthodox theologians had studied the works of freethinkers, who in turn had supplemented their arsenal with texts from orthodox writings. Deists such as Herbert of Cherbury rely on pagan late antique conceptions of sun worship in order to discover in them an umbrageous version of a Judeo-Christian monotheism, and to demand the abolition of a condemnation of pagan culture, just as La Mothe Le Vayer had done in his *La vertu des payans*.[82]

Arnauld's warning that all this would lead to Free Thinking turned out to be right. This is illustrated in several cases. Delicate were especially those cases, where a criticism of religion and an interplay of religion and politics

---

C. van: *The Urim and Thummim: A Means of Revelation in Ancient Israel* (Winona Lake, IN: 1997).

80 See Schröder W., *Athen und Jerusalem. Die philosophische Kritik am Christentum in Antike und Neuzeit* (Stuttgart: 2011); Kinzig W., "Polemics reheated? The reception of ancient anti-Christian writings in the Enlightenment", *Zeitschrift für Antikes Christentum* 13 (2009) 316–350.

81 See e.g. Yadin A., "Rabban Gamliel, Aphrodite's Bath, and the Question of Pagan Monotheism", *Jewish Quarterly Review* 96 (2006) 149–179.

82 Herbert of Cherbury, *De religione gentilium errorumque apud eos causis* (Amsterdam, Blaeu: 1663). See Walker D.P., *The Ancient Theology. Studies in Christian Platonism from the fifteenth to the eighteenth century* (London: 1972) 164–193; Mulsow, "Antiquarianism and Idolatry".

had been expressed in the realm of profane history. That holds for example for Machiavelli's analysis of the actions of the early Roman King Numa Pompilius, who had alleged conversations with a divine being – a nymph – in order to endow his laws for the people with authority.[83] Although such analyses partly suggested parallels to the sacred sphere – Moses on Mount Sinai – this suggestion was usually not uttered.

La Mothe Le Vayer's comparative ventures pushed this connotation a small step further. He writes at one point:

> Escrire des fables pour des veritez, donner des contes à la posterité pour des histoires, c'est le fait d'un imposteur, ou d'un autheur leger et de nulle consideration; escrire des caprices pour des revelations divines, et des resveries pour les loix venues du Ciel, c'est à Minos, à Numa, à Mahomet, et à leurs semblables, ester grands Prophetes, et les propres fils de Iupiter.

> Telling fables as if they were true and passing down fairy-tales to posterity as if they were history is common to a swindler or a frivolous and very insignificant author; spreading bizarre laws as divine revelation and phantasms as divinely given laws and presenting oneself as great prophets and true sons of Jupiter is common to a Minos, a Numa, a Muhammad, and there like.[84]

La Mothe Le Vayer still carefully refrains from mentioning the name of Moses, but the cases he enumerates are already suggestive enough for the reader to supplement the 'and there likes' with Moses. Later, especially readers who were influenced by Huet's comparisons, were inclined to make such a supplementation.

Antoine Lancelot for example, the editor of Gabriel Naudé's *Apologie pour les grands hommes soupçonnés de magie* of 1712, added in a footnote to one

---

83 Machiavelli Niccolò, *Discorsi sopra la prima deca di Tito Livio*, in Machiavelli Niccolò, *Tutte le opere*, ed. M. Martelli (Florence: 1971) I, 11 = 94: 'E si vede che a Romolo, per ordinare il senato, e per fare altri ordini civili e military, non gli fu necessario dell' autorità di Dio; ma fu bene necessario a Numa, il quale simulò di avere domestichezza con una Ninfa, la quale lo consigliava di quello ch'egli avesse a consigliare il popolo: e tutto nasceva perché voleva mettere ordini nuovi ed inusitati in quella città, e dubitava che la sua autorità non bastasse.' For later developments see Stroumsa G., "Enlightenment Perceptions of Roman Religion", in Auffarth C. – Rüpke J. (eds.): *Studien zur antiken Religion in Antike und Neuzeit* (Stuttgart: 2002) 193–202.

84 Tubero Oratius [La Mothe Le Vayer François de], *De la philosophie sceptique*, in Tubero Oratius, *Dialogues faits a l'imitation des anciens*, reprint ed. A. Pessel (Paris: 1988) 41. See Ginzburg, "Myth, Distance and Deceit".

of Naudé's remarks about Numa Pompilius: 'Monsieur Huet and others believe that Numa took the kind of teachings and rituals, which the author discuses here, from Moses.'[85] This was insidious, because it cemented the link, at which La Mothe had only hinted. The result of this – which Huet had never intended – was a the thesis that was then put forward in the *Traité des trois imposteurs*, whose origins date back to around that time: Moses was, just like Jesus and Muhammad, an impostor. What in Huet had been said in the context of a general tracing of all cultures to Moses, was in the imposture-book given a destructive twist, so that Moses became a suspect of religious fraud.[86]

The derivation of the teachings of Numa Pompilius from those of Moses does indeed appear in the *Demonstratio evangelica*, where Huet states that the teachings of Pythagoras overlap with those of Numa, 'which are evidently derived from the Mosaic law.'[87] One must look very carefully indeed to see that what is important for Huet are not any similarities in religious politics or even the tactics of imposture, but only in the concept of the divinity shared by both Moses and Numa and that this similarity is legitimated through the comparison of the teachings about God by Numa and Pythagoras, which Plutarch had undertaken. It is rather Lancelot's little addition of the word 'rituals', which creates the short-circuit that leads to the libertine explosion.

---

85 Naudé Gabriel: *Apologie pour* les grands hommes soupçonnés de magie, ed. Antoine Lancelot (Amsterdam, Pierre Humbert: 1712) 184: 'M. Huet & autres croient que Numa Pompilius avoit puisé chez Moise les dogmes & les rites dont l'auteur fait ici mention.' The first edition of Naudé's book was 1625. See also Silk M., "Numa Pompilius and the Idea of Civil Religion in the West", in Filoramo G. (ed.), *Teologie politiche: Modelli a confronto* (Brescia: 2005) 335–356; Spini G., *Ricerca dei libertini. La teoria dell'impostura delle religioni nel Seicento italiano* (Florence: 1983²).

86 [anon.], *Traktat über die drei Betrüger. Französisch – Deutsch*, ed. W. Schröder (Hamburg: 1992); Charles-Daubert F. (ed.), *Le traité des trois imposteurs et l'esprit de Spinoza: philosophie clandestine entre 1678 et 1768* (Oxford: 1999). On this treatise see also Schröder W., *Ursprünge des Atheismus. Untersuchungen zur Metaphysik- und Religionskritik des 17. und 18. Jahrhunderts* (Stuttgart: 1998). On the topic in general: Niewöhner F., *Veritas sive Varietas. Lessings Toleranzparabel und das Buch von den drei Betrügern* (Heidelberg: 1988).

87 Eusebius, *Demonstratio evangelica* 79: 'Idem alibi pleraque Pythagorae dogmata, Numae Pompilii dogmata consentanea profert; quae ex Mosaicis legibus expressa esse manifestum est.'

7

A further identification of Moses by Huet is perhaps even more explosive than the one involving Numa's laws or the obscenity of Priapus: the identification with Osarseph, an Egyptian priest, which occurs in Manetho's Egyptian History.

Huet mentions Osarseph in the context of his thesis that the Egyptian God Osiris was none other than Moses: accordingly, Osarseph as a name was derived from Osiris and therefore Manetho had equated him with Moses.[88] Thus, Huet incorporates Manetho – from the transmission in Josephus's *Contra Apionem* – into his long list of non-biblical witnesses for the Old Testament, in proposition IV of his overall demonstration, and evidence for the variation of the Mosaic archetype.[89] Of course he fails to mention that Manetho only claims that Osarseph came from Heliopolis, a place where Osiris was worshipped and thus carried his name. But Huet again moves on dangerous terrain here. With Manetho we are confronted with the reverse side of the ancient Mosaic exaltation, the counter-attack of non-Jews against the Jewish claim to exceptionality. This was spearheaded by authors such as Hecataeus of Abdera or Manetho and later the anti-Christian polemicists.[90] In the case of La Mothe Le Vayer we have already seen how these bible-critical comparisons had an impact in the early modern period.

Osarseph was, according to Manetho, a priest among leprous Egyptians, who had been confined to stone pits, but revolted and ruled ruthlessly over Egypt for over thirteen years – Osarseph called himself then Moses – until they were expelled again to the 'borders of Syria.' This story is loosely connected with another one from five hundred years earlier, which Manetho tells us, namely about the Hyksos, a herdsmen people, who had likewise exercised a reign of terror over Egypt. After their expulsion, they supposedly founded the city of Jerusalem and thus become plausible ancestors of the Jews. According to Martin Bernal's speculation, they even exercised an influence on the Minoic culture of Crete and were decisive in the cultural transfer from 'Africa' to Greece.[91] Be that as it may, in Manetho both stories are intertwined, because Osarseph travels to Jerusalem and invites the Hyksos to become his allies and

---

88   Eusebius, *Demonstratio evangelica* 113. See also p. 87 and 105.
89   Flavius Josephus, *Contra Apionem* I, 26. See: Flavius Josephus, *Against Apion*, trans. and comment. J.M.G. Barclay (Leiden: 2013).
90   On Hecataeus see Dillery J., "Hecataeus of Abdera: Hyperboreans, Egypt and the Interpretatio Graeca", *Historia* 47 (1998) 255–275. On the anti-Christian Polemics see Schröder, *Athen und Jerusalem*.
91   Bernal M., *Black Athena. The Afroasiatic Roots of Classical Civilization*, vol. 2: *The Archeological and Documentary Evidence* (New Brunswick: 1991) 336–345.

lead them back to their old capital Avaris. That is the city to which the leprous Egyptians were banished by pharaoh Amenophis and from where the lepers and descendants of the Hyksos set out to conquer Egypt.

According to Peter Schäfer, the connection between the Egyptian and anti-Jewish strata of this story is undertaken by Manetho himself rather than later writers, and Jan Assmann discovers in these stories the memory traces of the trauma of Akhenaton's revolutionary Armana religion – traces which were responsible for the association of the horror scenario of a rule of lepers and foreigners with the Jews, who also worshipped only one God.[92] In Huet's naively positive identification of Moses as Osarseph or Osiris this very complex amalgam of Egyptian and anti-Jewish motivations has gotten lost. All the more freethinkers were able to take his identification of the two figures for granted. If they added to it their view of Moses as an impostor who only pretends to have a covenant with God, they could brew an explosive mixture.

During the 1750s for example, the German freethinker Johann Christian Edelmann in his handwritten commentary to the clandestine Latin treatise *De tribus impostoribus* was to base his claim that the leprosy of the Egyptians around Osarseph was caused by an excessive consumption of pork on the work of Huet. This theory makes it possible to connect the story of the Hyksos and the lepers and at the same time justifies Osarseph's injunction to his people 'not to spare any of the venerated animals of Egypt, but to slaughter them all and to consume them.'[93] Then this prohibition or command would become a dietary law given to avoid the causes of leprosy.

---

[92] Schäfer P., *Judeophobia: Attitudes Toward the Jews in the Ancient World* (Cambridge, MA: 1997) 17–21; Assmann J., *Moses the Egyptian. The Memory of Egypt* in Western Monotheism (Cambridge, MA: 1998).

[93] Manetho in Josephus, *Contra Apionem* I,26. Edelmann Johann Christian, *Extract aus einer von Euander übersetzten und mit Anmerkungen herausgegebenen Handschrift unter dem Titel Von den Betrügereyen der Religionen* (Berlin: 1761), in [anon.] [Müller Johann Joachim], *De imposturis religionum (De tribus impostoribus). Von den Betrügereyen der Religionen. Dokumente*, ed. and comment. W. Schröder (Stuttgart: 1999) 143–229 = Ms. 6728 of the University Library Wroclaw. On Osarsiph there 207–211. 207f.: 'Die Vorfahren der Juden waren aller historischen Wahrscheinlichkeit nach vom Aegyptischen Schweinehirtengeschlechte entsprossen, und durch den übermäßigen Genuß des Fleisches dieser Thiere mit der Krätze behaftet, die von dem Morgenländer Aussatz genannt wird.' This theory had already been developped in *La vie et l'esprit de Mr. Benoit de Spinosa* (s.l.: 1719) 89f., a specific version of the French treatise on the Three Impostors, printed in just a few copies. Edelmann continues: 'Die Egypter waren bekanntlich sehr reinlich: weil nun die Krankheit jener Hirten ansteckend war, so faßten sie den Entschluß, sie auf die Grenzen von Aegypten zu schaffen, um sich zu curiren und da zu wohnen. Sie räumten ihnen zu dem Ende nicht nur die Grenzfestung Pelusium ein, sondern sie gaben ihnen auch einen in den natürlichen Wissenschaften sehr erfahrnen Priester,

Edelmann reads Manetho's report parallel to the Exodus account and asks himself why the Jerusalemites and the lepers did not retreat immediately after their expulsion from Egypt to Jerusalem, but why the second group of them (the lepers who were led by Moses-Osarseph) first wandered in the desert for forty years. Edelmann's answer to this: Obviously the groups had separated and the lepers who were numerically weaker (despite the large number of 600,000 men given in the Exodus story) and Moses-Osarseph both had to wait for a full generation (forty years) until his dietary laws as a precaution to leprosy started to take effect.[94] Aside from that – and this is where Edelmann's reconstruction

    Namens Osarsyphus, mit, der hernach den Namen Moses annahm.' See also Edelmann Johann Christian, *Moses mit aufgedecktem Angesichte, 5. Anblick*, in Edelmann Johann Christian, *Gesammelte Schriften*, vol. 7/2, ed. M. Ammermann-Estermann (Stuttgart: 1987) 67ff. 68: '['Lichtlieb' speaks:] Ich gebe dir aber zu bedenken, ob die Egipter nicht gleiches Recht haben zu sagen, der Esra habe als ein gefräßiger Juden-Pfaffe, seine ohnedem voller Unwahrscheinlichkeiten steckende Juden-Historie, aus bittern Haß gegen die unschuldigen Egipter geschrieben, daß die Juden denn [dem?] Aussatz in den vorigen Zeiten sehr stark unterworfen gewesen seyn müßen, gestehet ja Esra selbst in seinen dem Mosi beygelegten Schriften, indem er denselben nicht Gesetze genug gegen diese Erb-Krankheit zu ihrer gänzlichen Vertreibung stellen laßen kann, ist es dann nun nicht weit wahrscheinlicher, daß die Egipter als eine der Reinlichkeit ergebene Nation, diese, unter ihnen wohnende, und sie nur ansteckende Schabe-Hälse von freyen Stücken aus dem Lande haben jagen können, als daß man dem gar zu verdächtigen Juden-Pfaffen Esra zu gefallen glauben soll, es habe sich sogar der König zu Egipten bis zum eußersten Ruins seines Landes geweigert, sie auf ihr anhalten ausziehen zu laßen? Und wann dieses allen Umständen nach im höchsten Grade unwahrscheinlich ist, und sie bey ihrer Verstoßung einen gewissen Mann namens Mosi zum Führer gehabt hätten, so hatte ja Manethon der zur Beschreibung seiner Historie die Urkunden seines Landes vor sich hatte, die den Esra fehleten, nicht den geringsten Nuzen oder Schaden davon, wenn er anstatt des Moses[,] denn [dem?] Esra den Juden zum Heerführer giebet, den Osarsyphum zu ihrem General machen wolte.'

94   Edelmann, *Extract* 208ff.: 'Hier müssen sich die Solymitaner von den Aussätzigen getrennt haben, weil man sonst nicht absehen kann, warum nicht Osarsyphus, der sich nun Moses nannte, mit ihnen nach Palaestina, sondern nach der arabischen Wüste gegangen ist. Vermuthlich mochten sie auch unter diesen nicht mehr gelitten werden, und Moses mußte diesen Weg nehmen, weil ihm kein anderer übrig blieb. Nun mußte es ihm freylich an allem fehlen, und sehr übel gehen, obgleich dieser Haufe nicht so groß gewesen seyn kann, als er im 2. B. Mos. c. 12, v. 37, angegeben wird, denn sonst hätte er mit den Solymitanern wohl fertig werden können. Von dem allen melden zwar die Bücher Mosis nicht das geringste, aber es ist aus dem Manethone klar, den unsere Gelehrten für den aufrichtigsten Egyptischen Geschichtsschreiber erkennen, und aus dem uns Josephus einige Brocken aufgehoben hat. Es ist auch in der That auffallend, daß Moses, wenn er nach den Büchern Mosis triumphirend mit 600000 Mann ausgeruhten und mit allem nothwendigen versehenen Leuten aus Aegypten gezogen, nicht gleich Palaestina eingenommen haben sollte, als sich mit ihnen nach einer sandigen Wüste zu wenden. [...] Ihm scheinet fürs erste genug gewesen zu seyn, das Volk glauben zu machen, er habe Umgang mit dem

connects with Machiavelli's reflection about Numa Pompilius – he needed to look for an opportunity to feign a conversation with God.[95]

Edelmann interprets then the 'normative inversion' of Jewish ceremonial law vis-à-vis the Egyptian as a change of menu aimed at getting rid of leprosy.[96] He is able to do so because John Spencer had in the meantime applied Maimonides's theory of the Jewish ceremonial laws as an inversion of the laws of the Sabeans, to the Egyptians.[97] In addition John Marsham had changed the parameters of chronology and established the primacy of Egyptian culture over that of the Hebrews. This alone already changes the premises, which were still binding for Huet, and makes speculations such as Edelmann's possible.

Both Spencer and Marsham were writing during Heut's lifetime, precisely in those years in which the *Demonstratio evangelica* was being written. John Spencer had begun in 1669 his research with a detailed study on *Urim* and *Thummim* and he had asserted for the Thummin a derivation from Egypt, in stark contrast to Huet's tendency to see in the Egyptian parallel confirmation of the Bible. Likewise, John Marsham had uncovered aspects of Hebrew culture which evinced a dependency upon Egyptian culture. These are the authors considered by Jan Assmann when he describes the re-orientation to a primacy of Egypt in the early modern period. Only when Huet finds his place in the picture does this turn in the history of the memory of Moses make sense, according to which Moses was an Egyptian who led the Jews to monotheism. The reason for this is that it was first Huet's identification of Moses with Osarsiphus – interpreted as the distorted echo of Moses in the Egyptian context – which made it possible for the generations after Spencer and Marsham to understand Moses as a figure who was first called Osarsiphus before renaming himself. In this manner Huet's intention was turned on its head.

Gott Jehova, und dieser habe versprochen, sie in ein gesegnetes Land zu führen, wenn sie sich vorher durch ihn von ihrem Aussatz würden haben reinigen lassen. Dieß ist die wahre Ursache ihres 40jährigen Aufenthalts in diesen Gegenden, denn es mußte vorher ein ganzes Geschlecht aussterben, ehe seine Cur an den Nachkommen fruchten konnte. Er verboth ihnen daher die Speisen, die den Aussatz theils zu Wege bringen, theils vermehren; und man sieht dies an seinen Gesetzen, die bey reinen Völkern nicht angetroffen werden.'

95 Machiavelli, *Discorsi*.
96 I take the term 'normative inversion' from Assmann, *Moses the Egyptian* chapter III, 1.
97 Spencer John, *De legibus Hebraeorum ritualibus, et earum rationibus* (London, Richard Chiswel: 1685). See Assmann, *Moses the Egyptian*; Stroumsa G., *A New Science. The Discovery of Religion in the Age of Reason* (Cambridge, MA: 2010) 95–99; Levitin D., "John Spencer's 'De legibus Hebraeorum' (1683–85) and 'enlightened' sacred history: a new interpretation", *Journal of the Warburg and Courtauld Institutes* 76 (2013) 49–92.

A potential effect of the change of chronology was the temptation for later, critical thinkers, now to draw rather from the Moses degradations than from the Moses exaltations like Huet had still done. When Edelmann cites Huet,[98] this should no longer be viewed as a true reference – he quotes only what was available through Manetho anyway – but more as an indicator that Huet remained the famous bishop, who had encouraged all of what was now happening.

8

Edelmann's rationalist interpretation of the Bible marks a certain final point in the profanization of sacred history, comparable to the biblical criticism of Hermann Samuel Reimarus from around the same time.[99] Both approach the biblical narrative with profane hermeneutics, which leaves no room for the miraculous or the inexplicable. The sphere of the profane had completely swallowed the sphere of the sacred, just as vice versa in Huet the sphere of the sacred, though to different extents, could ultimately be extended to all profane cultures, because they represent variations of a single sacred history.

It remains to be noted that the rationalization of events recorded in the Bible appear in both Edelmann and Reimarus as a different form of victory of the profane as for example the interpretation of the account of the Fall of mankind by Beverland. While they struggle for historical lucidity, Beverland's interpretation is characterized by a declared intention to transgress, to cross to the obscene and to antinomianism. He is interested the misalliance of the sacred and the profane, blasphemy and not just rational explanation.[100]

From this point of view, it would in fact probably have saddened Beverland were the world to be thoroughly profanized. And it is by no means entirely clear, if a rational exegesis of the Bible would in fact have marked an endpoint to profane view of history. Still by the end of the Enlightenment, tendencies of

---

98   Edelmann, *Extract* 208: 'Endlich nötigten sie so gar, nach Huetii Bericht in Demonstr. Evangel. p.m. 97 den Osarsyphum, der auch mit unter den Aussätzigen gewesen seyn soll, mit den benachbarten Solymitanern ein Bündniß wider die Aegypter einzugehen, worauf sie die Aegypter unversehens überfielen, und den König Amenophis nöthigten, sich nach Aethiopien zu ziehen.'

99   On Reimarus see Klein D., *Hermann Samuel Reimarus (1694–1768). Das theologische Werk* (Tübingen: 2009); Mulsow M. (ed.), *Between Philology and Radical Enlightenment. Hermann Samuel Reimarus (1694–1768)* (Leiden: 2011); Groetsch U., *Hermann Samuel Reimarus (1694–1768): Classicist, Hebraist, Enlightenment Radical in Disguise* (Leiden: 2015).

100 On the notion of misalliance ('mésalliance') see Bakhtin M., *Rabelais and His World* (Cambridge, MA: 1968).

a resacralization appeared and the call for a new mythology – a mythology of reason – soon employs a Huet-kind of parallelization again, for example when Christ is equated with Dionysius and as it was the case in Hölderlin and later in Nietzsche.[101] But this could be pushed even further if one views the entirely profanized world of Enlightened reason as some form of negative religion, whose cults are monetary and consumerist. That is Walter Benjamin's version of the dialectic of Enlightenment.[102] Such a world cannot be profanized, a fact which has animated Giorgio Agamben to call for a profanization of the 'unprofanizable' in order to return affairs to a free utilization by humankind.[103]

(*Translated from German by Ulrich Groetsch and Andrew McKenzie-McHarg*)

Bibliography

[anon.], *Traktat über die drei Betrüger. Französisch – Deutsch*, ed. W. Schröder (Hamburg: 1992).
Abravanel Isaac, *Perush ha-Torah* (Venice, Bragadini: 1579).
Abulpharagius Gregorius, *Historia compendiosa dynastiarum*, ed. E. Pococke (Oxford, H. Hall: 1663).
Adler W., *Time Immemorial. Archaic History and its Sources in Christian Chronography from Julius Africanus to George Syncellus* (Dumbarton Oaks: 1989).
Agamben G., *Profanations* (New York: 2007).
Andresen C., *Logos und Nomos. Die Polemik des Kelsos wider das Christentum* (Berlin: 1955).
Arnauld Antoine, *La necessité de la foy en Jesu-Christ pour être sauvé* (Paris, Charles Osmont: 1701).
Arnauld Antoine, *Lettres de Messire Antoine Arnauld, vol. 3* (Paris, Sigismond d'Arney: 1775).
Assmann J., *Ägypten. Eine Sinngeschichte* (Munich: 1996).
Assmann J., *Moses the Egyptian. The Memory of Egypt in Western Monotheism* (Cambridge, MA: 1998).

---

101 Frank M., *Der kommende Gott. Vorlesungen über die Neue Mythologie, vol. 1* (Frankfurt: 1982); idem, *Gott im Exil. Vorlesungen über die Neue Mythologie, vol. 2* (Frankfurt: 1988).
102 Benjamin W., *Kapitalismus als Religion*, in Benjamin W., *Gesammelte Schriften*, ed. R. Tiedemann – H. Schweppenhäuser, 7 vols. (Frankfurt: 1991) VI, 100–102.
103 Agamben G., *Profanations* (New York: 2007).

Bakhtin M., *Rabelais and His World* (Cambridge, MA: 1968).

Baumgarten A.I., *The Phoenician History of Philo of Byblos: a Commentary* (Leiden: 1981).

Benjamin W., *Kapitalismus als Religion*, in Benjamin W., *Gesammelte Schriften*, ed. R. Tiedemann – H. Schweppenhäuser, 7 vols. (Frankfurt: 1991).

Ben-Tov A., "Infamie und historische Wahrheit: Johannes Löwenklaus Apologia pro Zosimo", in Multhammer M. (ed)., *Verteidigung als Angriff. Apologie und Vindicatio als Möglichkeiten der Positionierung im gelehrten Diskurs* (Berlin: 2015) 9–25.

Bernal M., *Black Athena. The Afroasiatic Roots of Classical Civilization, vol. 2: The Archeological and Documentary Evidence* (New Brunswick: 1991) 336–345.

Beverland Adriaan, *Peccatum originale κατ' ἐξοχὴν sic nuncupatum* ([Leiden]: 1678).

Blair A., "Mosaic Physics and the Search for a Pious Natural Philosophy in the Late Renaissance", *Isis* 91 (2000) 32–58.

Boch J., *Les dieux désenchantés. La fable dans la pensée français de Huet à Voltaire* (Paris: 2002).

Bochart Samuel, *Geographia sacra, vol. 1: Phaleg* (Caen, Pierre Cardonelle: 1646).

Bochart Samuel, *Geographia sacra, vol. 2: Chanaan* (Caen, Pierre Cardonelle: 1646).

Boerner W., *Das "Cymbalum Mundi" des Bonaventure des Périers* (Munich: 1980).

Borghero C., *La certezza e la storia. Cartesianesimo, pirronismo e conoscenza storica* (Milan: 1983).

Bruno Giordano, *Spaccio della bestia trionfante*, in Bruno Giordano, *Dialoghi italiani*, ed. G. Gentile (Florence: 1958³) II, 549–831.

Cavaillé J.-P.: *Dis/Simulations. Jules-César Vanini, F. La Mothe Le Vayer, Gabriel Naudé, Louis Machon et Torquato Accetto: Religon, Morale et Politique au XVIIᵉ siècle* (Paris: 2002).

Charles-Daubert F. (ed.), *Le traité des trois imposteurs et l'esprit de Spinoza: philosophie clandestine entre 1678 et 1768* (Oxford: 1999).

Clerc J. Le, *Genesis sive Mosis prophetae liber primus* (Amsterdam, A. Wolfgang and J. Waesberge: 1693).

Dam, C. van, *The Urim and Thummim: A Means of Revelation in Ancient Israel* (Winona Lake, IN: 1997).

Dan J., "Moses, Chronicles of", in *Encyclopaedia Judaica* (Jerusalem: 1971) XII, 413.

Dascal M., *Leibniz – The Art of Controversies* (Dordrecht: 2008).

David A., "Gedalia Ibn Yahia, auteur de Shalshelet ha-Qabbalah", *Revue des Études Juives* 154 (1995) 101–132.

DeLater J.A., *Translation Theory in the Age of Louis XIV: The 1683 De optimo genere interpretandi of Pierre-Daniel Huet* (Manchester: 2002).

Delatour J., "Le cabinet des frères Dupuy", *Science et technique en perspective* 9 (2005) 287–328.

Dickinson Edmund, *Delphi Phoenicizantes* (Oxford, H. Hall: 1655).

Dillery J., "Hecataeus of Abdera: Hyperboreans, Egypt and the Interpretatio Graeca", *Historia* 47 (1998) 255–275.

Dillon J., "The Theology of Julian's Hymn to King Helios", *Itaca* 14/15 (2000) 103–115.

Drijvers H.J.W., "The Cult of Azizos and Monimos at Edessa", in Bergman J. (ed.), *Ex Orbe Religionum. Studia Widengren* (Leiden: 1972) 355–371.

Droge A., *Homer or Moses? Early Christian Interpretation of the History of Culture* (Tübingen: 1989).

Duke R., "Moses' Hebrew Name: The Evidence of the Visions of Amram", *Dead Sea Discoveries* 14 (2007) 34–48.

Dupront A., *Pierre Daniel Huet et l'exégèse comparatiste au XVIIe siècle* (Paris: 1930).

Ebach J., *Weltentstehung und Kulturentwicklung bei Philo von Byblos. Ein Beitrag zur Überlieferung der Biblischen Urgeschichte im Rahmen des altorientalischen und antiken Schöpfungsglaubens* (Stuttgart: 1979).

Edelmann Johann Christian, *Moses mit aufgedecktem Angesichte, 5. Anblick*, in Edelmann Johann Christian, *Gesammelte Schriften*, vol. 7/2, ed. M. Ammermann-Estermann (Stuttgart: 1987) 67ff.

Edelmann Johann Christian, *Extract aus einer von Euander übersetzten und mit Anmerkungen herausgegebenen Handschrift unter dem Titel Von den Betrügereyen der Religionen* (Berlin: 1761), in [anon.] [Müller Johann Joachim], *De imposturis religionum (De tribus impostoribus). Von den Betrügereyen der Religionen. Dokumente*, ed. and comment. W. Schröder (Stuttgart: 1999) 143–229.

Eissfeldt O., *Sanchunjaton von Berut und Ilumilku von Ugarit* (Halle: 1952).

Eissfeldt O., *Taautos und Sanchuniathon* (Berlin: 1952).

El-Daly O., *Egyptology: The Missing Millennium. Ancient Egypt in Medieval Arabic Writings* (London: 2005).

Eliade M., *The Sacred and the Profane: The Nature of Religion*, trans. W.R. Trask (San Diego: 1959).

Eusebius, *Preparation of the Gospel*, ed. and trans. E.H. Gifford (Oxford: 1903).

Eusebius, *Praeparatio evangelica*, ed. K. Mras (Berlin: 1954).

Fabricius Johann Albert, *Codex pseudepigraphus veteris testamenti* (Hamburg, Christian Liebezeit: 1713).

Farmer S.A. (ed.), *Syncretism in the West: Pico's 900 Theses (1486)* (Tempe: 1998).

Flavius Josephus, *Against Apion*, trans. and comment. J.M.G. Barclay (Leiden: 2013).

Frank M., *Der kommende Gott. Vorlesungen über die Neue Mythologie*, vol. 1 (Frankfurt: 1982).

Frank M., *Gott im Exil. Vorlesungen über die Neue Mythologie*, vol. 2 (Frankfurt: 1988).

Freud S., "Die Verneinung", *Imago* 11 (1925) 217–221.

Friedlander G., *Pirke de Rabbi Eliezer* (London: 1916).

Gager J., *Moses in Graeco-Roman Paganism* (Nashville: 1972).

Gaulmin Gilbert (ed.), *De vita et morte Mosis libri III* (Paris, Tussnaus du Bray: 1629).
Gedalya Ibn-Yahyâ Ben-Yôsef, *Sefer Shalshelet ha-Qabbalah* (Venice, Giovanni di Gara: 1587).
Ginzburg C., "Myth, Distance and Deceit", in Ginzburg C., *Wooden Eyes: Nine Reflections on Distance* (New York: 2001) 25–61.
Glykas Michael, *Annales, qui Byzantinam historiam universalem exhibent* (Basel, Episcopius: 1572).
Grafton A., *Joseph Scaliger: A Study in the History of Classical Scholarship*, 2 vols. (Oxford: 1983–1993).
Grafton A., "Jean Hardouin: The Antiquary as pariah", in Grafton A., *Bring out your Dead. The Past as Revelation* (Cambridge, MA: 2001) 181–207.
Griffiths J.G., "The Egyptian Derivation of the Name Moses", *Journal of Near Eastern Studies* 12 (1953) 225–231.
Groetsch U., *Hermann Samuel Reimarus (1694–1768): Classicist, Hebraist, Enlightenment Radical in Disguise* (Leiden: 2015).
Grotius Hugo, *Satyricon, in quo de nuptiis philologiae et Mercurii libri duo et de septem artibus liberalibus libri singularis* (Leiden, Christophorus Raphelengius: 1599).
Gruen E.S., *Heritage and Hellenism. The Reinvention of Jewish Tradition* (Berkeley: 1998).
Guellouz S. (ed.), *Pierre-Daniel Huet* (Paris: 1994).
Häfner R., *Götter im Exil. Frühneuzeitliches Dichtungsverständnis im Spannungsfeld christlicher Apologetik und philologischer Kritik (ca. 1590–1736)* (Tübingen: 2003).
Häfner R., "Noah, Deukalion und das fossile Seepferdchen. Spurensuche im Schwemmland frühneuzeitlicher Komparatistik", in Mulsow M. – Assmann J. (eds.), *Sintflut und Gedächtnis* (Munich: 2006) 225–258.
Hämeen-Anttila J., *The Last Pagans of Iraq. Ibn Washiyya and his Nabatean Agriculture* (Leiden: 2006).
Halbertal M. – Margalit A., *Idolatry*, trans. N. Goldblum (Cambridge, MA: 1992).
Hamilton A., *The Copts and the West, 1439–1822: The European Discovery of the Egyptian Church* (Oxford: 2006).
Herbert of Cherbury, *De religione gentilium errorumque apud eos causis* (Amsterdam, Blaeu: 1663).
Huet Pierre Daniel, *Traité de l'origine des romans* (Paris, Claude Barbin: 1670).
Huet Pierre Daniel, *Demonstratio evangelica* (Paris, Étienne Michallet: 1679).
Huet Pierre Daniel, *Alnetanae quaestiones de concordia rationis et fidei* (Leipzig, Johann Grosse: 1692).
Huet Pierre Daniel, *Histoire du commerce et de la navigation des anciens* (Paris, François Fournier: 1716).
Huet Pierre Daniel, *Iter Suecicum*, in Huet Pierre Daniel, *Huetiana ou pensées diverses de M. Huet, eveque d'Avranches* (Amsterdam, Herman Uytwerf: 1723) 438–449.

Hunger H., *Die hochsprachliche profane Literatur der Byzantiner, vol. 1: Philosophie – Rhetorik – Epistelographie – Geschichtsschreibung – Geographie* (Munich: 1978).

Ibn Ezra, *Commentary on The Pentateuch: Exodus (Shemot)*, trans. and annot. H.N. Strickman – A.M. Silver (New York: 1996).

Ingegno A., *Regia pazzia: Bruno lettore di Calvino* (Urbino: 1987).

Inowlocki S., *Eusebius and the Jewish Authors: His Citation Technique in an Apologetic Context* (Leiden: 2006).

Israel J., *Radical Enlightenment. Philosophy and the Making of Modernity 1650–1750* (Oxford: 2001) 190–196.

Johnson A.P., *Ethnicity and Argument in Eusebius' Praeparatio Evangelica* (Oxford: 2006).

Julianus Apostata, *Hym to king Helios*, in Julianus Apostata, *The Works of the Emperor Julian, vol. 1*, trans. W.C. Wright (Oxford: 1913) 358–362.

Kinzig W., "Polemics reheated? The reception of ancient anti-Christian writings in the Enlightenment", *Zeitschrift für Antikes Christentum* 13 (2009) 316–350.

Kircher Athanasius, *Lingua Aegyptiaca restituta* (Rome, Hermann Scheus: 1643).

Kister M., "Ancient Material in Pirqe de-Rabbi Eli'ezer: Basilides, Qumran, the Book of Jubilees", in Maeir A.M. et al. (eds.), *'Go Out And Study the Land' (Judges 18:2) Archeological, Historical, and Textual Studies in Honor of Hanan Eshel* (Leiden: 2012) 69–94.

Klein D., *Hermann Samuel Reimarus (1694–1768). Das theologische Werk* (Tübingen: 2009).

Kley D. van, *The Religious Origins of the French Revolution: From Calvin to the Civil Constitution, 1560–1791* (New Haven: 1999[2]).

La Mothe Le Vayer François, *La vertu des payens*, in J. Prévot (ed.), *Les libertins du XVII siècle* (Paris: 1641; reprint, Paris: 2004) II, 1–215.

Lawee E., "Isaac Abrabanel: From Medieval to Renaissance Jewish Biblical Scholarship", in Sæbø M. (ed.), *Hebrew Bible / Old Testament. The History of its Interpretation, vol. 2: From the Renaissance to the Enlightenment* (Göttingen: 2008) 190–214.

Leemans I., *Het woord is aan de onderkant. Radicale ideeën in Nederlandse pornografische romans 1670–1700* (Utrecht: 2002).

Levitin D., "John Spencer's 'De legibus Hebraeorum' (1683–85) and 'enlightened' sacred history: a new interpretation", *Journal of the Warburg and Courtauld Institutes* 76 (2013) 49–92.

Ligota C., "Der apologetische Rahmen der Mythendeutung im Frankreich des 17. Jahrhunderts (P.D. Huet)", in Killy W. (ed.), *Mythographie der frühen Neuzeit. Ihre Anwendung in den Künsten* (Wiesbaden: 1984) 149–161.

Machiavelli Niccolò, *Discorsi sopra la prima deca di Tito Livio*, in Machiavelli Niccolò, *Tutte le opere*, ed. M. Martelli (Florence: 1971).

Magdalino P. – Nelson R. (eds.), *The Old Testament in Byzantium* (Dumbarton Oaks: 2010).

Manuel F., *The Eighteenth Century Confronts the Gods* (Cambridge, MA: 1959).

Meinardus O., *Two Thousand Years of Coptic Christianity* (Cairo: 1999).

Metzler D., "Johannes Löwenklau", in Stupperich R. (ed.), *Westfälische Lebensbilder* 13 (Münster: 1985) 19–44.

Milikowsky C., "Justus of Tiberias and the Synchronistic Chronology of Israel", in Cohen S.J.D. – Schwartz J.J. (eds.), *Studies in Josephus and the Varieties of Ancient Judaism* (Leiden: 2006) 103–126.

Miller P.N., "The Antiquary's Art of Comparison: Peiresc and Abaxas", in Häfner R. (ed.), *Philologie und Erkenntnis. Zu Begriff und Problem frühneuzeitlicher 'Philologie'* (Tübingen: 2001) 57–94.

Momigliano A., *La formazione della moderna storiografia sull'Imperio Romano* (Turin: 1938).

Momigliano A., "Ancient History and the Antiquarian", *Journal of the Warburg and Courtauld Institutes* 13 (1950) 285–315.

Morin Etienne, *Dissertatio de paradiso terrestri* (n.p.: 1692).

Mulsow M., "Antiquarianism and Idolatry: The Historia of Religions in the Seventeenth Century", in Pomata G. – Siraisi N. (eds.), *Historia: Empiricism and Erudition in Early Modern Europe* (Cambridge, MA: 2005) 181–210.

Mulsow M., *Die unanständige Gelehrtenrepublik. Wissen, Libertinage und Kommunikation in der Frühen Neuzeit* (Stuttgart: 2007).

Mulsow M., "Muskatnüsse und Paradiesvögelfüße", *Frankfurter Allgemeine Zeitung* 04.06.2008, "Geisteswissenschaften".

Mulsow M., "Moses omniscius oder Moses politicus? Moses-Deutungen des 17. Jahrhunderts zwischen sakraler Enzyklopädik und libertinistischer Kritik", in Kilcher A.B. – Theisohn P. (eds.), *Die Enzyklopädik der Esoterik. Allwissenheitsmythen und universalwissenschaftliche Modelle in der Esoterik der Neuzeit* (Munich: 2010) 177–202.

Mulsow M., "Die Thematisierung paganer Religionen in der Frühen Neuzeit", in Bultmann C. – Rüpke J. – Schmolinsky S. (eds.), *Religionen in Nachbarschaft: Pluralismus als Markenzeichen der europäischen Religionsgeschichte* (Münster: 2012) 109–123.

Mulsow M., (ed.), *Between Philology and Radical Enlightenment. Hermann Samuel Reimarus (1694–1768)* (Leiden: 2011).

Mungello D.E. (ed.), *The Chinese Rites Controversy: Its History and Meaning* (Nettetal: 1994).

Mussies G., "The Interpretatio Judaica of Thot-Hermes", in Voss, M.H. van et al. (eds.), *Studies in Egyptian Religion* (Leiden: 1982) 87–120.

Naudé Gabriel, *Apologie pour les grands hommes soupçonnés de magie*, ed. Antoine Lancelot (Amsterdam, Pierre Humbert: 1712).

Niewöhner F., *Veritas sive Varietas. Lessings Toleranzparabel und das Buch von den drei Betrügern* (Heidelberg: 1988).

Origen, *Contra Celsum libri VIII*, ed. M. Marcovich (Leiden: 2002).

Parny Évariste, *La Guerre des Dieux* (Paris, Didot: 1799).

Périers Bonaventure des, *Cymbalum mundi* (n.p.: 1537).

Pichler K., *Streit um das Christentum. Der Angriff des Kelsos und die Antwort des Origenes* (Frankfurt: 2005).

Pico della Mirandola Giovanni, *Oratio de hominis dignitate*, ed. E. Garin (Pordenone: 1994).

Pico della Mirandola Giovanni, *Über das Seiende und das Eine*, ed. P.R. Blum – G. Damschen – D. Kaegi – M. Mulsow – E. Rudolph – A.G. Vigo (Hamburg: 2006).

Pintard R., *Le libertinage érudit dans la première moitié du XVIIe siècle* (Paris: 1943).

Pomey F.A., *Pantheum mythicum seu Deorum gentilium fabulosa historia* (Lyon, Antoine Molin: 1659).

Popkin R.H., *The History of Scepticism from Erasmus to Spinoza* (Berkeley: 1979).

Poulouin C., *Le temps des origines: L'Eden, le déluge et 'les temps reculés' de Pascal à l'Encyclopédie* (Paris: 1998).

Rapetti E., *Pierre-Danuel Huet: Erudizione, filosofia, apologetica* (Milan: 1999).

Rapetti E., *Percorsi anticartesiani nelle lettere a Pierre-Daniel Huet* (Florence: 2003).

Rubiés J.-P., "Theology, Ethnography, and the Historicization of Idolatry", *Journal of the History of Ideas* 67, 4 (2006) 571–596.

Périers Bonaventure des, *Cymbalum mundi* (n.p.: 1537).

Scafi A., *Mapping Paradise. A History of Heaven on Earth* (Chicago: 2006).

Scaliger Joseph Justus, *Thesaurus Temporum* (Leiden, Thomas Basson: 1606).

Scaliger Joseph Justus, *De emendatione temporum* (Geneva, Rover: 1629).

Schäfer P., *Judeophobia: Attitudes Toward the Jews in the Ancient World* (Cambridge, MA: 1997).

Schmidt F., "La discussion sur l'origine de l'idolatrie aux XVIIe et XVIIIe siècles", in *L'Idolâtrie. Rencontres de l'Ecole du Louvre* (Paris: 1990) 53–68.

Schnapp A., *The Discovery of the Past. The Origins of Archaeology* (London: 1996).

Schröder W., *Ursprünge des Atheismus. Untersuchungen zur Metaphysik- und Religionskritik des 17. und 18. Jahrhunderts* (Stuttgart: 1998).

Schröder W., *Athen und Jerusalem. Die philosophische Kritik am Christentum in Antike und Neuzeit* (Stuttgart: 2011).

Shalev Z., *Sacred Words and Worlds. Geography, Religion and Scholarship, 1550–1700* (Leiden: 2011).

Shapiro B., *A Culture of Fact: England, 1550–1720* (Ithaca: 2000).

Sheehan J., "Sacred and Profane: Idolatry, Antiquarianism, and the Politics of Distinction in the Seventeenth Century", *Past and Present* 192 (2006) 35–66.

Sheehan J., "The Altars of the Idols: Religion, Sacrifice, and the Early Modern Polity", *Journal of the History of Ideas* 67, 4 (2006) 649–674.

Shelford A., "Amitié et animosité dans la République des Lettres: La Querelle entre Bochart et Huet", in Guellouz S. (ed.), *Pierre-Daniel Huet (1630–1721): Actes du colloque de Caen, 12–13 novembre 1993* (Paris: 1994) 99–108.

Shelford A., "Thinking Geometrically in Pierre-Daniel Huet's Demonstratio evangelica (1679)", *Journal of the History of Ideas* 63, 4 (2002) 599–617.

Shelford A., *Transforming the Republic of Letters: Pierre-Daniel Huet and European Intellectual Life 1650–1720* (Rochester: 2007).

Silk M., "Numa Pompilius and the Idea of Civil Religion in the West", in Filoramo G. (ed.), *Teologie politiche: Modelli a confronto* (Brescia: 2005) 335–356.

Smet R. de, *Hadrianus Beverlandus (1650–1716). Non unus e multis peccator. Studie over het leven en werk van Hadriaan Beverland* (Brussels: 1988).

Smith M.S., *The Origins of Biblical Monotheism: Israel's Polytheistic Background and the Ugaritic Texts* (Oxford: 2001).

Smith J.Z., *Drudgery Divine. On the Comparison of Early Christianities and the Religions of Late Antiquity* (Chicago: 1990).

Spanheim Ezechiel, *In Callimachi Hymnos observationes* (Utrecht, Halma: 1697).

Spanheim Ezechiel, *De praestantia et usu numismatum antiquorum* (London, Richard Smith: 1706³).

Spencer John, *De legibus Hebraeorum ritualibus, et earum rationibus* (London, Richard Chiswel: 1685).

Spiegelberg W., *Koptisches Handwörterbuch* (Heidelberg: 1912).

Spini G., *Ricerca dei libertini. La teoria dell'impostura delle religioni nel Seicento italiano* (Florence: 1983²).

Stahl W.H. – Burge E.L. (eds.), *Martianus Capella and the Seven Liberal Arts, vol. 2: The Marriage of Philology and Mercury* (New York: 1977).

Stemberger G., *Einleitung in Talmud und Midrasch* (Munich: 1982⁸).

Stroumsa G., "Enlightenment Perceptions of Roman Religion", in Auffarth C. – Rüpke J. (eds.): *Studien zur antiken Religion in Antike und Neuzeit* (Stuttgart: 2002) 193–202.

Stroumsa G., "Noah's Sons and the Religious Conquest of the Earth: Samuel Bochart and his Followers", in Mulsow M. – Assmann J. (eds.), *Sintflut und Gedächtnis* (Munich: 2006) 307–320.

Stroumsa G., *A New Science. The Discovery of Religion in the Age of Reason* (Cambridge, MA: 2010).

Til Salomon van, *Tabula situm paradisi*, in *Malachias illustratus* (Leiden, Jordan Luchtmans: 1701).

Toland John, *Origines judaicae* (London, Thomas Johnson: 1709).
Tubero Oratius [La Mothe Le Vayer François de], *De la philosophie sceptique*, in Tubero Oratius, *Dialogues faits a l'imitation des anciens*, reprint ed. A. Pessel (Paris: 1988).
Varro, *Opera quae supersunt*, ed. J.J. Scaliger (Paris, Henri Estienne: 1573).
Voltaire, *Dictionnaire philosophique* ('Londres': 1764) Art. Bacchus.
Vorst Johannes, *De paradiso diatriba* (Rostock, Johann Richel: 1653).
Walker D.P., *The Ancient Theology. Studies in Christian Platonism from the fifteenth to the eighteenth century* (London: 1972).
West M.L., *The East Face of Helicon: West Asiatic Elements in Greek Poetry and Myth* (Oxford: 1997).
Yadin A., "Rabban Gamliel, Aphrodite's Bath, and the Question of Pagan Monotheism", *Jewish Quarterly Review* 96 (2006) 149–179.
Zoli S., *Europa libertina tra controriforma e illuminismo: l'oriente die libertini e l'origine dell' illuminismo* (Bologna: 1989).
Zuntz G., *Griechische philosophische Hymnen* (Tübingen: 2005).

CHAPTER 6

The Eleusinian Mysteries in the Age of Reason

Asaph Ben-Tov

> Odi profanum vulgus et arceo
> favete linguis: carmina non prius
> audita Musarum sacerdos
> virginibus puerisque canto.
>
> I loathe the profane crowd and ward it off.
> Keep still. I, the Muses' priest
> shall sing to [you], virgins and boys,
> songs yet unheard.
>
> HORACE, *Odes* 3.1.1–3.1.4

∴

The opening stanza of Horace's third book of odes would have been familiar to any alumnus of an early modern Latin-school.[1] Though the ode soon shifts from a lofty sacerdotal tone to one more humble and personal,[2] it succinctly portrays the solemnity and thrill of being initiated. Whatever the *poeta doctus* has to impart on his hearers is tinged with exclusivity. The *profanum vulgus*, i.e. the overwhelming majority of fellow humans an educated Roman or an early modern European of sufficient Latinity were likely to encounter, were excluded. These must remain profane in the literal sense of being denied entry to the *fanum*.[3] The second component is silence – though in Horace meant as

---

1 I am grateful to Jan Bremmer for his instructive comments on an earlier draft of this paper.
2 It should be noted, however, as Eduard Fraenkel has pointed out, that Horace's adaptation of the sacerdotal formula, meant to remove all profane persons who might render the religious act void, is itself markedly personalised. No real officiating Roman priest would use the first person singular (*odi, arceo*) and thus presume to talk on his own behalf; Fraenkel E., *Horace* (Oxford: 1957) 264.
3 On the etymology of *profanum*, and its meaning as 'away from the *fanum*', rather than a place 'in front of the *fanum*' see Wagenvoort H., "Profānus, profānāre", *Mnemosyne* 2, 4 (1949) 319–332; in the context of Horace's ode see Nisbet R.G.M. – Rudd N., *A Commentary on Horace: Odes Book III* (Oxford: 2003), *ad loc.* suggest that *profanum* may mean 'away from the temple'

a poetic borrowing from the reverent silence at religious offices rather than the hush of secrecy;[4] and finally, a promise of great reward for those who are allowed to cross the threshold. In Horace's case the reward of rare poetic beauty. For Horace's Roman audience the allurements (and perils) of secret cults would have required no further explanation.[5]

The present article examines the later seventeenth- and eighteenth-century learned fascination with one of the ancient world's most successful mystery cults, the Eleusinian Mysteries. Based in the small Attic town of Eleusis, the autumnal celebration of the mysteries of Demeter and Persephone, the 'two goddesses', was to last for over a millennium from archaic times to the close of the fourth century AD.[6] The intriguing revelation to initiates, and to them alone, of the *hiera* (the sacred objects) at the culmination of the festivities and the mysteries' evocative mythological background made the Eleusinian Mysteries a source of fascination, speculation, and polemical profanation for centuries after their last initiate had ventured to the realm of Pluto and Persephone. Apart from their intrinsic interest as a chapter in the Classical tradition, the early modern fortunes of the Eleusinian Mysteries offer an instructive case of early modern knowledge of religion and its profanating potential. To make my intention clear, a short explanation as to my understanding of profanation may be useful.

'Profane' in modern English and its equivalents in several other languages, is often used to designate the opposite of holy.[7] Whatever the definition and qualities of 'the holy' in different religious contexts may be, the existence of

---

rather than in front of it, and point out the strong sense of space of ancient religion, quoting, among others, Virgil, *Aen*eid 6. 258 'procul o procul este profani'.

4 West D., *Horace Odes III. Dulce Periculum* (Oxford: 2002) 15, sees these lines within the context of post civil-war Augustan ideology and its religious revival.

5 For the thrill of ancient mystery cults in general see Burkert W., "Der geheime Reiz des Verborgenen: Antike Mysterienkulte", in Kippenberg H.G. – Stroumsa G. (eds.), *Secrecy and Concealment. Studies in the History of Mediterranean and Near Eastern Religions* (Leiden: 1995) 79–100.

6 Bremmer J.N., "Initiation into the Eleusinian Mysteries: a 'thin' description", in Bull C.H. – Lied L.I. – Turner J.D. (eds.), *Mystery and Secrecy in the Nag Hammadi Collection and other Ancient Literature: Ideas and Practices. Festschrift for Einar Thomassen* (Leiden: 2011) 375–397; Burkert W., *Griechische Religion der archaischen und klassischen Epoche* (Stuttgart: 2011²) 425f.

7 See Wagenvoort, "Profānus, profānāre"; Welchering P., "Profan. Materialien zur Geschichte eines wenig beachteten und erforschten Begriffs", *Archiv für Begriffsgeschichte* 28 (1984) 63–99; Welchering's concise version of this account: Welchering P., "Profan, das Profane, Profanität" *Historisches Wörterbuch der Philosophie*, vol. 7 (Basel: 1989) 1442–1446; Mühling-Schlapkohl M., "Profanität", *Religion in Geschichte und Gegenwart* (Tübingen: 1998–2007⁴); Bremmer J.N., "'Religion', 'Ritual' and the Opposition 'Sacred vs. Profane'. Notes towards a terminological

a holy place, person, text, occurrence etc. requires a demarcation – physical, mental, stylistic or other – to distinguish it from the surrounding world of non-holy phenomena. It is here that the well known etymology of *profanum* offers a useful metaphor, indicating that which is outside the sanctuary. Profanation in the present context should be distinguished from any profane, sacrilegious, irreverent or irreligious act or utterance. If a holy phenomenon requires a demarcation distinguishing it from that which is not holy, profanation is here understood as the subversion of this division, running the gamut from drilling a hole in the sanctuary's outer wall to demolishing it altogether. It should be noted that acts of profanation in a historical context do not require a universal or even systematic objection to such demarcations. Some of the Eleusinian Mysteries' most vehement parofanisers were profoundly religious men eager to demolish what they understood to be a false sanctuary in order to fortify their own lines of sacral demarcation. In a sense, all external knowledge of religion, i.e. knowledge of religion based on criteria external to the theological, mythological, or sacral framework, has a profanating potential. Thus, explicating ancient Jewish Temple sacrificial laws in the context of ancient Near Eastern practices rather than biblical precepts, or Jesus' actions in light of antique pagan magical traditions,[8] are cases of profanation as they encroach, as outsiders, into the realm which, according to its own claim to validity, has an exclusively internal explanation. Mockery or even the use of profanities does not necessarily have that effect. Thus, as Johan Huizinga pointed out almost a century ago, medieval church goers chanting hymns to the tune of profane songs, and countless documented cases of late medieval blasphemy and extreme bawdiness in church are often manifestations of intimacy with the sacred. This late medieval misbehaviour is not without it complexities, and seems rooted in the ubiquity of the holy, and offers an intriguing case of porous boundaries between the holy and the profane, but does not constitute the critical profanation in the sense used here.[9] While these general observations are true of religious phenomena as a whole, mystery cults offer the study of knowledge and profanation a further twist. At the core of ancient mystery cults lies the revelation to the initiated of a great secret. The *profani* are here quite literally debarred from the sanctuary, and the demarcating line is also a physical obstruction. This offers a more concrete form of profanation, i.e. either the

---

Genealogy", in Graf F. (ed.), *Ansichten griechischer Rituale. Geburtstags-Symposium für Walter Burkert* (Berlin: 1998) 9–32, esp. 24–31.
8 Smith M., *Jesus the Magician: Charlatan or Son of God?* (London: 1978).
9 Huizinga J., *The Autumn of the Middle Ages*, trans. R.J. Payton – U. Mammitzsch (Chicago: 1996) ch. 6, esp. 183–186.

illicit entry of the uninitiated into the sanctuary or the sacrilegious revelation of the cult's secret from without the sanctuary's walls. Both these options were possible (and perilous) in antiquity. What concerns us here are not contemporary profanations, be it by mockery, betrayal of the Mysteries' secrets, or illicit presence at their celebration, nor even the polemical onslaught by Early Christian apologists (though these will play a crucial role behind the scenes) but the themes of knowledge and profanation of early modern encounters with the Mysteries. While profanation in the sense of physical encroachment or illicit revelations of the Mysteries were known to the ancients, a study of later seventeenth- and eighteenth-century approaches to the matter offers a case study of profanation which would have baffled ancient celebrants in Eleusis: an approach to knowledge about this religious phenomenon, and eventually the lack thereof, in distinctly non-Christian terms. In other words, early modern musings on the Mysteries of Eleusis offer a case of a second profanation, the explication of an ancient religious rite and belief not merely outside their original pagan framework, but from without the Christian framework and, more concretely, from without that of confessionalized Christian humanism. In other words, some early modern treatments of a long extinguished Attic mystery cult bear witness to the profanation of some Christian 'intellectual sanctuaries'.

1 Demeter and Persephone

The most important source for the myth of Demeter and Persephone is also its earliest literary testimony, the Homeric Hymn to Demeter. Composed in all likelihood sometime during the first half of the sixth century BCE[10] it is closely linked to the cult of Demeter and Persephone in Eleusis and seems to have been composed when the latter was at a relatively late stage of its development, with several elements in the Hymn meant to strengthen Eleusinian claims to an affinity with the cult.[11] The young Persephone or Korē (maiden), daughter of the corn goddess Demeter and Zeus, was abducted by Hades, god of the Underworld, by consent of her Olympian father, while gathering flowers on the plain of Nysa.[12] Her distraught mother roamed the earth by the

---

10   Richardson N.J., *The Homeric Hymn to Demeter* (Oxford: 1974) 10f.
11   Ibid., 12f.
12   There are several locations bearing this name. It is not clear which, if any of them, was meant by the poet. With later sources Sicily is identified as the place of abduction. For early modern readers among the most obvious reference would have been Diodorus

light of torches for nine days, fasting and searching in vain. On the tenth day Demeter discovered the fate of her daughter through Hecate and Helios, who had witnessed Persephone's abduction. In her anger Demeter abandoned the Olympus and roamed the earth disguised as an old woman. Arriving at Eleusis she is met by four of king Celeus' daughters. The goddess, still in disguise, is admitted into the royal household as a nurse to the king's infant son Demophon. On entering the palace the disguised goddess is met by the maid Iambe who offers her a stool and succeeds in making the goddess laugh.[13] Refusing to drink the sweet wine offered her by the queen Metanira, Demeter requests instead a simple barley drink (*kykeon*), which was later solemnly drunk by celebrants of the Eleusinian Mysteries. The goddess nursed the infant Demophon, anointing him with ambrosia, breathing on him, and placing him in a fire every night to cleanse him of his mortal elements and thus make him immortal. This, however, was not to be. The queen, Metanira caught sight one night of her infant son amid the flames and cried out in horror. The goddess then at last appeared in her true formidable form, and castigated mankind for its folly. Demophen would have to forgo immortality. Demeter instructs the Eleusinians to build a temple and altar for her, which they promptly do, and instructs them in her rites. She resides in her Eleusinian temple and laments her daughter while inflicting a terrible famine on the world; no seed sprouted, mankind was on the verge of extinction, and worst yet, from an Olympian point of view, with the extinction of mortals the gods would be deprived of sacrifices. Refusing to be placated by her fellow gods, Demeter remained aloof in her temple until finally Zeus asked his infernal brother to return Persephone to her mother. Hades cunningly forcing her to eat a pomegranate seed before leaving, Persephone is consigned to return to the Underworld for the third part of each year. Demeter and Persephone are reunited, at least for two thirds of each year, and the earth, recalled to life, once again brings forth nourishment. During her stay in Eleusis

---

Siculus, v. 3.1–3.2; Cicero, *In Verrem* IV, 106; Ovid, *Metamorphoses* v. 409. Cf. Richardson, *The Homeric Hymn to Demeter* 76f.

[13] [anon.], *Hymn to Demeter*, in *Homeric Hymns, Homeric Apocrypha, Lives of Homer*, trans. M. West (Cambridge, MA: 2003) ll. 200–205, 'She greeted no one with word or movement, but sat there unsmiling, tasting neither food nor drink, pining for her deep-girt daughter, until at last dutiful Iambe with ribaldry and many a jest diverted the holy lady so that she smiled and laughed and became benevolent – Iambe who ever since has found favor with her moods.' Whether Iambic poetry is named after Iambe, as has often been claimed, or vice versa, the mythological maid is thus named following an already existent iambic genre (and the episode thus not being an aetiological myth for iambic poetry but rather for the later Eleusinian *aischrologia*) is considered, with a decision for the latter in Rotstein A., *The Idea of Iambos* (Oxford: 2010) 167–182.

the goddess bestowed two great benefits on its inhabitants, and indirectly on mankind as a whole: agriculture and her secret rite:

> She went to the lawgiver kings, Triptolemos and horse-goading Diocles, strong Eumolpos and Keleos leader of hosts, and taught them the service, and showed the beautiful mysteries which one cannot depart from or enquire about or broadcast, for great awe of the gods retains us from speaking. Blessed is he of men on earth who has beheld them, whereas he that is uninitiated in the rites, or he that has had no part in them, never enjoys similar lot down in the musty dark when he is dead.[14]

Cycles of life, death, and resurrection in humans, nature, and agricultural are patent in this myth, as well as their mystical ramifications.[15] The myth itself has its structural peculiarities, especially in regard to the relation, and in some senses identity, of the mother and daughter goddesses.[16] Despite the agricultural background of the myth, it cannot, as Richardson points out, be assumed that it is a later personalized and eschatological graft on the primitive agricultural base. The two elements seem inseparable from the start.[17] What is important here is the Eleusinian context of the myth as an aetiological background to the mystery cult. Demeter is said to have bestowed two great benefits on the Eleusinians: the secret of agriculture, which also marks the passage from savagery to civilisation, hence Demeter's role as divine law-giver and the Athenian celebration of the *Thesmophoria*, preserved through mockery in Aristophanes' *Thesmophoriazusae,* and the goddess' mythological institution in Eleusis of her mystery-cult, the Eleusinian Mysteries, the beneficiaries of which, as the hymn avows, were promised a blissful existence in the netherworld. At first a local mystery cult, the Eleusinian Mysteries were eventually to attract followers from throughout the *oecumene* who would gather to be initiated at the Minor Mysteries, celebrated in the spring, and the Great Mysteries, celebrated in processions and sacrifices in Athens and Eleusis in the autumn month of *Boedromion*, culminating in Demeter's sanctuary in Eleusis, the *telesterion*, where the officiating priest (*hierophantēs*) would reveal to the

---

14 [anon.], *Hymn to Demeter*, trans. West, 473–482.
15 See Burkert W., *Ancient Mystery Cults* (Cambridge, MA: 1987); Kerényi K., *Die Mysterien von Eleusis* (Zurich: 1962).
16 Cf. Burkert W., *Structure and History in Greek Mythology and Ritual* (Berkeley: 1979) 138–142.
17 Richardson, *The Homeric Hymn to Demeter* 15.

initiates, and to them alone, the *hiera*, the sacred objects, and with them a great realisation which would promise them a blissful existence in the netherworld.[18]

Half a century ago George Mylonas published a study of Eleusis and the Eleusinian Mysteries,[19] the fruit of decades of archaeological work at Eleusis itself. Meticulous and circumspect throughout, Mylonas dismissed various ancient and modern conjectures about the Eleusinian Mysteries on the firm basis of archaeological evidence and a critical examination of texts. Toward the end of his book he considered the tantalising question of the content of the Eleusinian Mysteries: what was it that was actually being revealed to the initiates? Here the critical scholar waxed lyrical, and wistful:

> [...] A thick, impenetrable veil indeed still covers securely the rites of Demeter and protects them from the curious eye of modern students. [...] How many nights I have spent standing on the steps of the Telesterion, flooded with the magic silver light of a Mediterranean moon, hoping to catch the mood of the initiates, hoping that the human soul might get a glimpse of what the rational mind could not investigate! All in vain – the ancient world has kept its secret well and the Mysteries of Eleusis remain unrevealed.[20]

The ancients, according to Mylonas and others,[21] had guarded their secret well. It should be noted that among modern scholars the impenetrability of the Eleusinian Mysteries is not universally accepted. Thus Walter Burkert argues forcefully, that this total rejection of the possibility of knowledge about the hierophants' revelation to the initiates is informed more by pious rhetoric than fact, that a cult with such broad following could not have realistically remained secret, and that some of the ancient profanating sources (especially a passage in the third-century Church Father Hippolytus of Rome) contain at least some reliable information about the revelation within the Eleusinian sanctuary.[22]

---

18   Reconstructing the course of the Mysteries celebrated in Eleusis and, even more so, determining their meaning(s) for celebrants has proven a most complex task, with scholars differing of various points. See Parker R., *Polytheism and Society in Athens* (Oxford: 2005) 327–368; for a recent attempt at a diachronic reconstruction of the festivities and their meaning Bremmer, "Initiation into the Eleusinian Mysteries".

19   Mylonas G., *Eleusis and the Eleusinian Mysteries* (Princeton: 1961).

20   Mylonas, *Eleusis* 281. See also Walter Burkert's verdict on the intrinsic elusiveness of antique mystery cults in *Ancient Mystery Cults* ch. IV.

21   E.g. Eliade M., *A History of Religious Ideas, vol. 1: From the Stone Age to the Eleusinian Mysteries*, trans. W.R. Trask (Chicago: 1978) 296; Kerényi, *Die Mysterien von Eleusis*.

22   Burkert W., *Homo Necans. Interpretationen altgriechischer Opferriten und Mythen* (Berlin: 1997²) 283.

Central components of the celebration were public[23] and are well attested in ancient art and literature. Yet the Mysteries themselves, that is, the sacred objects revealed to the initiates and the content of the Mysteries were guarded. Anyone unsullied by murder could be initiated into these Mysteries, be they man or woman, Greek or 'barbarian', free or enslaved. Non-initiates, however, who entered the sanctuary, or initiates who divulged its secrets did so at their own peril. Even if the sacral content of the Mysteries was known to many in Antiquity, profanating them by illicitly entering the sanctuary could be a fatal mistake. Thus, as Livy tells us,[24] two shepherds of Acarnania who accidentally entered Demeter's sanctuary during celebration in the second century BCE were put to death by the Athenians, despite their innocence and the dire political consequences of this execution. Such harshness was not reserved for foreigners. The prohibition on those sullied with murder to partake in the Mysteries was, according to Suetonius, enough to cause no less a matricide than the emperor Nero to avoid initiation while travelling through Greece.[25]

2   Early Christian views of the Mysteries

Early Christian writers were, needless to say, hardly awe struck by the ancient injunction to secrecy and only too eager to expose the Eleusinian Mysteries for what they believed them to be – a pagan abomination. In their heated polemics against the various pagan practices and beliefs about them, early Christian writers saw in the secrecy shrouding the Mysteries nothing more than a cover for luridness and criminality. Elements of the Demeter myth were taken as proof that the secrets revealed to the initiates were at best mere obscenities. One of the best known instances of early Christian 'unveiling' of the Eleusinian Mysteries is offered by Clement of Alexandria (c. 150–c. 215) in his *Protrepticus* (Exhortation to the Greeks) where he attempts to convince the pagans of the absurdity of their religion. The myth of Demeter and Persephone is presented in a grotesque light. In attempting to demolish the Mysteries and their mythological background with devastating mockery, Clement was unintentionally also preserving, however distortedly, several clues about the Eleusinian Mysteries, for which modern scholars would later

---

23   For a consideration of the civic aspects of the Eleusinian Mysteries see Bruit Zaidman L. – Schmitt Pantel P., *Religion in the ancient Greek city*, trans. P. Cartledge (Cambridge: 1992) 132–140.
24   Livy, xxxi, 14.
25   Suetonius, *Nero* 34.

be grateful. Clement, however, was no antiquarian, and his aim was not the preservation but demolition of a still living pagan practice. His retelling of the myth spares no means to ridicule the pagan cult. A point, which will reverberate in early modern scholarship is what Clement saw as the pinnacle of depravity: instead of being greeted inside Celeus' palace by the dutiful Iambe, a myth itself involving bawdiness, Clement prefers the Orphic version where Baubo takes her place and reveals her genitalia to the grieving goddess, who is heartily amused by this unseemly gesture 'Demeter is pleased at the sight, and now at last receives the draught, delighted with the spectacle! These are the secret mysteries of the Athenians!'[26] The same tale was repeated a century later by Arnobius (died c. 330) in his polemical *Adversus nationes* (Against the Heathens).[27] The content of the sacred basket is enumerated: sesame and various other cakes, an assortment of symbolic artefacts, among them a woman's comb – euphemistic symbol used in the mysteries for the female genitalia.[28] That modern scholars find Clement's inventory unconvincing is, in the present context, unimportant. What is important is the assumption that in revealing their myth and cultic secret Clement was, to his mind, exposing their absurdity and helping render them harmless. Arnobius, for his part, assures readers that his portrayal of the cult of Demeter is not in the least slanderous. The Eleusinian mysteries are damned by the very pagan sources wishing to extol them.[29]

Since none the of the Church Fathers, not even those who had converted to Christianity, had formally been Eleusinian initiates, the following argument from Tertullian's *Apologeticus* of 197 is worth quoting. Refuting pagan accusations of criminality aimed at Christians' secret rites, Tertullian pointed out an inherent paradox of attributing criminality to a secret cult of which one is not an initiate:

> By whom then are [the fictitious Christian crimes] to be betrayed. Surely not by the culprits themselves, as by definition the guaranty of silence is owed to mysteries. The Samothracian and Eleusinian [mysteries] are kept in silence, how much more so is the case with such [mysteries] which revealed will occasionally provoke human chastisement while divine chastisement lies in store? If then they themselves did not betray

---

26 Clement of Alexandria, *Protrepticus*, trans. G.W. Butterworth (Cambridge, MA: 1979) 17P. See Edmonds R.G. III, *Redefining ancient Orphism: A Study in Greek Religion* (Cambridge: 2013) 174f.
27 Arnobius, *Adversus nationes* v. 25.
28 Clement, *Protrepticus* 19P.
29 Arnobius, *Adversus nationes* v. 26.

themselves, it follows that it must have been outsiders. And whence did they obtain their knowledge, when the profane are always excluded from participation in these rites, which shun spectators. Unless [you mean to suggest that] the impious are less fearful.[30]

And yet, ironically, when writing against the Gnostic Valentinians about a decade later Tertullian draws a parallel between the Valentinans' and Eleusians' secrecy – in both cases a mark of depravity and unsound teaching. For Tertullian too the revelation at the Eleusinian Mysteries was nothing but an obscenity – this time the likeness of a phallus, and the Mysteries' secrecy nothing more than a thin veil behind which initiated pagans vainly attempted to conceal their depravity.[31] Small wonder then that the Eleusinian Mysteries had a nasty reputation in Early Modern Europe. Thus, to cite but one example among many, the broad minded sixteenth-century pedagogue, Michael Neander (1527–1595) in his compendium on universal geography first printed in 1582, could state as a matter of course, that the town of Eleusis is known for its 'shameful rites and mysteries of Demeter'.[32] He was speaking on good authority.

3   Some Early Modern Approaches to the Mysteries

As far as early modern scholarship is concerned, one can trace an advancement of knowledge about the external celebration of the Eleusinian Mysteries, but the story to be told about early modern approaches to the Mysteries themselves is not one of an advancement of knowledge but rather its changing context, and, on occasion, a coming to terms with its absence. As the following will attempt to show, shifting approaches to knowledge can be as revealing as the history of its attainment.

As far as the external evidence of the Eleusinian celebrations is concerned, an early modern mile-stone was the publication in 1619 of *Eleusinia* by the Dutch scholar Johannes Meursius (1579–1639).[33] Having been appointed professor of history and Greek in Leiden in 1610 he was to spend fourteen years there before moving to Sorø in 1625 where he would serve his remaining years as professor and court historiographer in the service of the Danish crown. His

---

[30] Tertullian, *Apolog*eticus 6.
[31] Tertullian, *Adversus Valentinianos* 1.1.
[32] Neander Michael, *Orbis Terrae Partium succincta Explicatio* (Eisleben, Gubisius: 1583) P8ʳ. Eleusis clara sacris & mysterijs turpibus Cereris, quae Eleusinia dicta fuere.
[33] Meursius Johannes, *Eleusinia sive de Cereris Eleusinae sacro, ac festo* (Leiden, Elzevier: 1619).

years in Leiden witnessed a prolific scholarly output: editions of Greek texts, learned lucubrations, and several works on Dutch history as official historiographer to the Estates-General, as well as a series of antiquarian treatises devoted mostly to Attica.[34] Among the latter is the *Eleusinia* (1619), which attempted to reconstruct the cultic framework of the Lesser and Greater Mysteries on the basis of textual evidence. Its very nature as a work of antiquarian scholarship lends Meursius' study a matter-of-fact dryness; it avoids both Patristic polemics as well as Christian-Humanist speculations about the 'true' identity of Demeter. The Church Fathers are utilised, but as fallible authorities for the nature and course of the celebrations, not their religious and moral soundness. Meursius does not hesitate to state that Tertullian was wrong in attributing to the Mysteries in his anti-Valentinian treatise the exhibition of phallus shaped objects to the initiated – the Church Father, Meursius claims, was confusing the Eleusinian with the Bacchic rites. The Eleusinian initiates, he states dryly, were shown replicas of female pudenda.[35] The polemical context of Tertullian and other patristic utterances on the Mysteries is ignored. The Fathers are treated as ancient testimonies from which the antiquarian picks pieces of information, which he is free to accept or reject. That this was by no means the standard attitude toward Demeter (or her Latin equivalent Ceres, as she is most commonly referred to) is demonstrated by Meursius' friend Gerard Vossius (1577–1649), who in his monumental *De theologia gentili* (On pagan theology), following Plutarch, dwells on Demeter's identity with the Egyptian Isis,[36] proving thus the primacy of Egypt over Greece in the introduction of agriculture, demonstrated, to his mind, by the migration of Israelite Patriarchs to Egypt when Canaan was afflicted by drought.[37] Though Vossius does not offer a Hebrew etymology and Old Testament prototype for Demeter, as he does for other pagan gods, thus demonstrating their derivative nature as pagan misunderstandings of Old Testament events and persons,[38] she is intrinsically linked, via her Egyptian prototype Isis, to Old Testament history. None of this seems to have been of interest to Meursius.

A similar approach was adopted a century later, once again in a work of antiquarian scholarship, by the Helmstedt professor of Greek and Oriental

---

34 Sandys J.E., *A History of Classical Scholarship*, vol. 2 (Cambridge: 1908) 311. See also Skovgaard-Petersen K., *Historiography at the Court of Christian IV* (Copenhagen: 2002) 61–68.
35 Meursius, *Eleusinia* 33.
36 Vossius Gerard, *De theologia gentili* (Amsterdam, Blaeu: 1668) I, 67; V, 119.
37 Ibid., I, 70.
38 E.g. Vossius' identification of Minerva with the marginal Old Testament figure Naamah, mentioned in Genesis 4:22. Vossius, *De theologia* I, xvii.129.

languages, Johann Gottfried Lakemacher (1695–1736) in his 1734 compendium *Antiquitates Graecorum Sacrae* (The Sacred Antiquities of the Greeks), in which he offered a detailed day-to-day account of the nine-day celebration of the Greater Mysteries. Both Lakemacher and Meursius would be consulted decades after Vossius' monumental work had been discarded. Their antiquarian indifference to Christian polemics, and indeed for 'cracking the code' of the Mysteries and their secret, was by no means an obvious choice.

The evocative nature of the Mysteries and their foundational myth is brought to mind by an unexpected source. In 1684 came the posthumous publication of a treatise by Werner Rolfinck (1599–1673) with the alluring title *Mysteria Eleusiniana patefacta* (The Mysteries of Eleusis revealed).[39] The first thing to come to the modern reader's attention is that this work has nothing to do with the Eleusinian Mysteries. For Rolfinck, a celebrated anatomist at the university of Jena,[40] the Eleusinian mysteries to be revealed and explicated in this anatomical study is the human reproductive system. The choice of title is, however, more than an attention-grabbing ploy. Rolfinck is referring to the Orphic tradition preserved, as we have seen, in Clement of Alexandria and Arnobius, whereby the Eleusinian servant Baubo (instead of Iambe of the Homeric Hymn) amuses Demeter by exposing her private parts.[41] Patristic detractors of the Mysteries were eager to conclude that the sacred objects revealed to the initiates were none other than images of male or female genitalia – demonstrating the obscene and rather foolish nature of the pagan Mysteries. The enthusiastic anatomist Rolfinck posits the Patristic slur on its head by un-ironically designating human genitalia as *Sacra Eleusinia*, a true anatomical understanding of which reveals God's wisdom in fashioning His creatures. While the Eleusinian Mysteries themselves play no role in Rolfinck's treatise, beyond the title, the work itself is pervaded by the pious anatomist's amazement at human anatomy and its remarkable aptness to procreation. Whatever thought Rolfinck may have given ancient traditions concerning the Eleusinian Mysteries, the title is neither derogatory nor ironic but an anatomist

---

39 Rolfinck, Werner, *Sacra Eleusinia patefacta, seu tractatus anatomicus novus de organorum generationi dicatorum structura admirabili in utroque sexu, veterum atque neotericorum hypothesibus et inventis adcommodatus* (Frankfurt, Oehrlingius: 1684).

40 For Rolfinck see Pagel J.L., "Rolfink, Werner", *Allgemeine Deutsche Biographie* 29 (1889) 74; Piesner C., "Rolfink, Werner", *Neue Deutsche Biographie* 22 (2005) 9–10. Piesner sees in Rolfinck a transitional figure between Renaissance and modern experimental medicine and chemistry.

41 *Orphica Fragmenta* 395, ed. A. Bernabé.

sharing with his readers one of God's mysteries, the revelation which is anything but profanation.[42]

A rather less charitable approach we find in Rolfinck's younger contemporary, Nikolaos Kalliakis. Born in Crete in 1645 Kalliakis taught Aristotelian philosophy and Greek in Padua.[43] Sometime between 1678 and 1707 he composed a dissertation on the Eleusinian Mystery cult.[44] From the start Kalliakis, unlike the more circumspect Meursius, betrays a curiosity about the very core of the Mysteries. Though the answer he offers is crudely polemical, he was aware of the centrality of secrecy to the lure of the Eleusinian cult. The starting point for him is Livy's account, mentioned above,[45] of the unfortunate Acarnanian herdsmen's accidental breach of the Mysteries secrecy.[46] After offering a concise account of the externals of the Eleusinian cult and the stages of initiation, Kalliakis turns to his readers: 'And yet, you may perhaps ask with curiosity, what then were those mysteries, which were guarded with such religious silence? I myself admit to have been somewhat overtly curious in this matter.'[47] Unlike level-headed antiquarians, Kalliakis is riveted by the concealed secret itself. The externals of the cult, of which he has a solid grasp, he realises, leave the post-antique reader together with the uninitiated of Antiquity standing outside the sanctuary. He decides to venture into the *telesterion*. If any of his Paduan students were expecting their professor's curiosity to be coupled with even qualified sympathy, they were soon corrected. Plutarch, he continues, had argued that the primary role of initiation was to inspire in men and women the fear of the gods.[48] Kalliakis begs to differ. Their very secrecy proves their shamefulness. Who would conceal upright sanctity and so harshly punish the promulgation of what is decent? An obvious charge of lewdness had attached itself since Antiquity to the tale of Baubo, as we have seen. For

---

42   It is worth noting that in 1659 Rolfinck composed a gratulatory poem celebrating the publication of *De Sacrificiis* by Johannes Saubert Jr. (1638–1688), who had studied in Jena briefly in 1657/8. The subject of ancient cults seems to have been neither alien nor disinteresting to Rolfinck.

43   See Jöcher Christian Gottlieb, *Allgemeines Gelehrten-Lexicon* (Leipzig, Gleditsch: 1750), s.v. Calliacus.

44   Calliachius Nicolas, *Dissertatio de Sacris Eleusinis*, in Poleno Giovanni (ed.), *Utriusque Thesauri Antiquitatum Romanarum Græcarumque nova supplementa, vol. 4* (Venice, Pasquali: 1737) 321–326.

45   Livy, xxxi. 14.

46   Ibid., 321.

47   Ibid., 323. Sed vos tamen curiosius fortasse perquiretis, quae tandem essent illa mysteria, quae adeo religioso silentio essent abvolvendum? Fateor, me quoque hac in re paulo curiosiorem extitisse.

48   Plutarch, *De liberis educandis*.

all his indignation, Kalliakis is fascinated by the patristic account of Baubo's alleged obscenity. He finds the story of Demeter being amused by the indecent exposure, as told by Clement and Arnobius unconvincing (there is, to his mind, nothing funny about indecency), which leads him to indulge in his own theory, making Baubo's exposure somewhat more creative.[49] Having protested curiosity about the very core of the Eleusinian Mysteries, all the Paduan professor finds at its very core is perversity and probable criminality. The short and learned dissertation opening with curiosity about an awe inspiring secret ends in an elaboration of patristic polemics and revulsion. What had seemed to be a mysterious secret turns out to have been common depravity.[50] Kalliakis' dissertation is lent a final twist in a brief posthumous epilogue. The dissertation was first published three decades after his death in a collection of learned treatises from the university of Padua edited by the mathematician and antiquarian Giovanni Poleni (1683–1761). Commenting on his predecessor's dissertation in 1739, i.e. some fifty years after its composition, Poleni dryly notes that objectionable as Pagan cults may have been, he fails to see how identifying the Eleusinian Mysteries with obscenity agrees with the strict chastity required of Eleusinian priests.[51] Poleni's reservations about the traditional Patristic argument, by casting doubt, and arguing from probability, though here a mere aside, betrays a broader and deeper shift in early eighteenth-century scholarship. We shall encounter a sophisticated and elaborate exercise in historical argument from probability in a Leipzig disputation penned a decade later. Before arriving there, a further university dissertation elucidates the point.

We turn now from Padua to the Republic of Letter's northern extremity, to a dissertation on the Eleusinian Mysteries composed in 1707 at the Swedish university of Uppsala by the Regius professor of poetry Hemming Forelius (1654–1708).[52] From the outset the conceptual framework within which Forelius construes ancient paganism in general, and the cult of Demeter in particular, is laid out.[53] The pagan gods came to being either through the Devil's attempts to lead mankind astray, or through an ill-advised emulation of the true religion by ignorant pagans. This pagan proclivity was exacerbated after the Deluge and

---

49   Ibid., 324. Suspicor proinde, Baubonem artefactum quidpiam inguinibus suis apposuisse, quod virilem, ac juvenilem potissimum sexum prae se ferret: atque illud proinde renudatis pudendis, ubi obscoene contrectare incepisset in risum atque hilaritatem Deam moerentem traxisse.
50   Ibid., 325.
51   Ibid., vi.
52   Forelius Hemming, *De Mysteriis Eleusiniis Dissertatio* (Uppsala, Werner: 1707).
53   Ibid., 1–5.

found its elaboration in various forms of idolatry.[54] This was a fairly standard Protestant line of argument in the seventeenth and early eighteenth centuries. A further typical approach to antiquity exemplified in Forelius' dissertation is the assumption that an understanding of an ancient phenomenon pivots on identifying its etymology. *Mysterium* (μυστήριον), he argues, is in all likelihood derived from the Hebrew root סתר (*str*) from which are derived מסתתר (*mistater*, hiding) and מסתור (*mistor*, hiding place).[55] This dissertation is also typical of its kind in taking Christian orthodoxy (in this case Lutheran) as its vantage point, and thus construing pagan practices through the prism of superstition and idolatry. Furthermore, Forelius' stress on definitions and etymologies of the concepts underlying his argument is typical of university scholarship on pagan antiquity, the above mentioned Vossius offering this mode of argumentation its quintessential and most elaborate form in his *De theologia gentili*.[56] Concerning the Mysteries themselves, while Forelius does not venture to guess what they actually were, he follows Cicero (*De legibus* II, 36) in arguing that their main benefit was to transfer initiates from a state of uncivilised barbarism (*ex agresti immanique vita*) to a state of *humanitas*, as well as keeping men and women in awe of the gods and instilling in them a hope of the after-life. And yet, even this sympathetic stance does not cause Forelius to forget that the mysteries, whatever pious hopes they may have engendered in their initiates, were nothing more than a diabolical deception.[57] He is nonetheless interested in the antiquarian side of the mystery cult and, without making any original contribution, does offer a summary of the essence of the Minor and Greater Mysteries and an account of the nine-day celebration of the Greater Mysteries, culling information from both the Church Fathers and Meursius. Even though, in the short section on the rites of initiation,[58] Forelius peers, as it were, over Clement of Alexandria's shoulder, gleaning information from the second book of the *Stromateis*, without the invective, his overall

---

54 This verdict is not restricted to the Eleusinian Mysteries. See e.g. Forelius' comment at the outset of his *Dissertatio de Sacris Vestae Romanae* (Uppsala, Keyser: 1697) 1. In veterum scriptorum monumentis ubi paganorum religionem intuemur, non sine stupendo horrore intelligimus, illam non aliam fuisse, quam qvalem cupiditas humana, coeco mentium errore, & maligni spiritus instinctu, effinxerit.

55 Forelius also acknowledges the possibility of a Greek etymology derived from μυειν or μυεσθαι; Forelius, *De Mysteriis Eleusiniis* 6.

56 See more generally Ben-Tov A., "Pagan Gods in Late Seventeenth- and Eighteenth-Century German Universities: a sketch", in Ben-Tov A. – Deutsch Y. – Herzig T. (eds.), *Knowledge and Religion in Early Modern Europe: Studies in Honor of Michael Heyd* (Leiden: 2013) 153–177.

57 Ibid., 13.

58 Ibid., 25–27.

verdict is much the same, and he concludes by thanking Providence for not being benighted as the hapless Eleusinian initiates. His interpretation pivots on the inherent idolatry of pagan cults – the secrecy itself, however, in which the ancient Mysteries were shrouded, and on which he dwells in his dissertation, is not in itself incriminating. The subjection of this ancient religious phenomenon to Christian criteria and a Protestant reproach to idolatry do not lead Forelius, like his southern contemporary Kalliakis (or indeed the Church Fathers on whom they both rely) to 'expose' the Mysteries and thus invalidate them by an exposing act of profanation.

An antiquarian approach to the Mysteries was not necessarily as detached as Meursius or Lakemacher's and could have subversive implications. One example can be found in a treatise *De cultu ac usu luminum antiquo* (On the ancient worship and use of torches)[59] by a certain Heinrich Christian Ludwig Stockhausen (died 1747/8),[60] printed in Utrecht in 1726. A mixture of detailed antiquarian scholarship and traditional Christian invectives, the author intends nothing less than exposing the ancient mysteries hitherto barely dealt with by scholars.[61] The Mysteries' intrinsic, albeit perverse, link to Christian monotheism is expressed by Stockhausen's humanist predilection for

---

59   Stockhausen Heinrich Christian Ludwig, *De cultu ac usu luminum antiquo. Qui qualis fuerit in omnibus antiquorum sacris, delubris, oraculorum antris, consecrationibus, auguriis, lustrationibus, bello, triumphis, puerperiis, nuptiis, funerumque processu, reliqua ex omni antiquitate ostenditur. Accedit ultrior de mysterio Cereris eleusiniae, raptuque Proserpinae accensis facibus quaesitae ac dein culta explicatio* (Utrecht, Kroon & Hofman: 1726).

60   Of Stockhausen himself very little is known. A play by him (presuming this is the same Heinrich Christian Ludwig Stockhausen) entitled *Zenobia von Palmyra* (Halle, s.n.: 1720), celebrating the marriage of Friedrich August of Saxony and Maria Josepha of Austria the previous year, is extant. There are also extant several funerary orations delivered in Magdeburg in the 1740s by a Heinrich Christian Ludwig Stockhausen. In the title of one of them, delivered in September 1747 but printed the following year, Stockhausen is said to have already died, and is cited as a Prussian functionary: *Königl. Preuß. Hof-Rath, Regierungs-und Lehns-Secretario im Hertzogthums Magdeburg*; see: *Standrede, bey feyerlichen Leichenbegrägniß der weyland Hochwohlgebohrnen Frau, Frau Helenen, verwittibter von Alvensleben, geb. von der Schulenburg, In der Kirche zu Eichenbarleben gehalten, Von dem nunmehr in GOtt selig ruhendem Herrn Henirch Christian Ludewig Stockhausen, Damals Königl. Preuß. Hof-Rath, Regierungs-und Lehns-Secretario im Hertzogthums Magdeburg: Genau nach des wohlseligen Herrn Hof-Raths eigener Handschrift heraus gegeben*, in Niemeier Heinrich Wilhelm, *Die Ruhe der Seelen in Gott, wie sie, bey der Unruhe dieses Lebens, rechtmäßig zu suchen, und, einem guten Anfange nach, wircklich zu finden ist, bis sie, der Vollendung nach, im ewigen Leben seliglich erlanget wird, Als die weyland Hochwohlgebohrne Frau, Frau Helene, geb. von der Schulenburg* … (Magdeburg, Faber: 1748) 78–88 (Herzog August Bibliothek shelfmark Ni 238).

61   Ibid., 2.

etymology – this time Proserpina's alleged Aramaic etymology,[62] and the assertion that various pagan sacral uses of torches are derived from Jewish custom.[63] Though couched in the terms of traditional scholarship and decrying pagan 'idolatry', Stockhausen's treatise has a more nuanced element. The torch processions of the Early Church marking the Purification of the Virgin Mary are a ceremonial (not doctrinal) borrowing from the pagans.[64] His stress on the prevalence of the custom in contemporary Rome is a typical Protestant-antiquarian snide of the period.[65] The myth itself, Stockhausen suggests, once stripped of its superstitious paraphernalia, is a symbolic tale of nature and agriculture at winter[66] – like numerous other interpreters, Stockhausen has a Northern European climate in mind, rather than the Mediterranean, with its mild winter and scorching summer. Acknowledging the psychological power of cultic secrecy as a veil protecting an absurdity derided by many educated pagans in Antiquity,[67] Stockhausen, betrays an interest in the *experience* of the initiates rather than the bare bones of the ceremonies' exterior, but nonetheless rejects the Mysteries scornfully as folly and pagan superstition.[68]

An interpretation of the Eleusinian Mysteries, which was as influential in the eighteenth century as it was controversial, was put forward by the churchman and literary critic William Warburton (1698–1779) in his monumental *The Divine Legation of Moses demonstrated, on the Principles of a religious Deist* (1737–1741).[69] As the title suggest, Warburton's aim was the learned elaboration of a counter-intuitive argument: Deists had often argued on the ostensible lack of concern for the afterlife in the Old Testament. As a doctrine of an afterlife (a future state of reward and punishment) was taken by the latter as an essential component of any religion, the Old Testament was clearly a work of human fancy, which could lay no claim to divine inspiration. Accepting the Deists' negation of a doctrine of the afterlife in the Old Testament (a concession which would outrage many of his orthodox readers), Warburton attempts to turn the

---

62 Ibid., 37. Pherephattam esse verum Proserpinae nomen. Verbum פיר-פתא *pherphete* idiomate Chaldaico denotat fructum abundantem, quod proxime accedit ad Graecum illud: φερέφαττα.
63 Ibid., 4.
64 Ibid., 9f.
65 Drawing parallels between paganism and contemporary Roman Catholicism was a common Protestant argument in the seventeenth and earlier eighteenth centuries. The best-known example is *A Letter from Rome* (1729) by the Cambridge librarian and clergyman Conyers Middleton (1683–1750).
66 Ibid., 99.
67 Ibid., 24.
68 Ibid., 188f.
69 I have consulted the third edition published in London in 1742.

Deist argument on its head: it is precisely the absence of this doctrine, necessary for the wellbeing of the commonwealth and fully elaborated in the New Testament, which is proof of Moses' divine legation.[70] In his consideration of ancient religions and their teaching about the afterlife, as part of a general doctrine of Providence fostered by ancient legislators, Warburton's interpretation of the ancient Mysteries is of particular importance. It should be noted that Warburton sees all the mystery cults of Graeco-Roman antiquity as essentially identical, their local differences notwithstanding. They all emerged from Egypt and all served the same religious/pedagogical aim. His focus on the Eleusinian Mysteries is, as he concedes, due to the fact that they are better documented, but the argument applies to all the ancient Mysteries.[71]

In attempting to make sense of the Eleusinian Mysteries and the revelations they divulged to the initiates, Warburton is unimpressed by attempts of preceding scholars. Not even Meursius got it right, though he acknowledges the usefulness of his antiquarian compilation.[72] The ancient gods had their public and secret worship, the latter being the Mysteries.[73] What was it then that was communicated to the initiates in the Mysteries and why were these communicated in secrecy in the first place? The latter, according to Warburton had two reasons: 'Because nothing stimulates our Curiosity like that which retires from our Observation, and seems to forbid our Search. [...] and They were kept secret from the Necessity of teaching some things to the Initiated, improper to be communicated to all.'[74] The psychological appeal of secrecy accounts for the innocuous revelations of the Lesser Mysteries, which must have been common knowledge, but what then, Warburton asks, was revealed to the initiated at the Great Mysteries? They were not the general doctrines of a providence and future state – these, Warburton points out, were taught openly. Nor could they have been metaphysical speculations about the gods – this would blur the difference between the open teaching of the philosophers and the secrets

---

70 On Warburton see Young B., *Religion and Enlightenment in Eighteenth-Century England: Theological Debate from Locke to Burke* (Oxford: 1998) ch. 5. See also Young B., "Warburton, William", *Oxford Dictionary of National Biography*. On Warburton's interpretation of the Eleusinian Mysteries see Assmann J., *Moses the Egyptian: The Memory of Egypt in Western Monotheism* (Cambridge, MA: 1998) ch. 4; idem, *Religio Duplex. Ägyptische Mysterien und europäische Aufklärung* (Berlin: 2010) 98–114.
71 Warburton, *The Divine Legation of Moses* I, 135.
72 Ibid., 131: The modern Writers on the Mysteries are altogether in the Dark concerning its End and Original; not excepting *Meursius* himself: to whom however I am much indebted, for abridging my Search into Antiquity for the Passages that make mention of the *Eleusinian Mysteries*, and for bringing the greatest Part of them together under one View.
73 Ibid., 131f.
74 Ibid., 142f.

of the Mysteries. And this, in any case, would have not been beneficial to the state.[75] Since the aim of the Mysteries was to restore the soul to a state of purity and since the very core of polytheistic religion was an obstacle to this, the gods setting such a dismal example:

> So that, such of the Initiated, as they judged capable, were made acquainted with the whole Delusion. The *Mystagogue* taught them that *Jupiter, Mercury, Venus, Mars*, and the whole Rabble of licentious Deities, were indeed only dead Mortals, subject, in Life, to the same Passions and Vices with themselves; but having been, on several Accounts, Benefactors of Mankind, grateful Posterity had deified them; and, with their Virtues, had indiscreetly canonized their Vices. The fabulous Gods being thus routes, the supreme Cause of all Things took their Place of Course. Him, they were taught to consider the Creator of the Universe, who pervaded all Things by his Virtue, and governed all by his Providence.[76]

This euhemeristic line of interpretation was to gain a considerable following in the course of the eighteenth century – often by thinkers with an agenda opposed to Warburton's. Voltaire in his *Philosophie de l'histoire* (1765) published under the pseudonym l'Abbé Bazin, though differing from Warburton on central points, openly embraced the idea of the Eleusinian Mysteries as an enlightened institution meant to wean intelligent pagans off the superstition of polytheism.

An instructive example of a variation on Warburton's line of interpretation is offered by the short-lived materialist philosopher Michael Hißmann (1752–1784) who in 1776, shortly after receiving his masters' degree in Göttingen, published a short treatise *Ueber die Eleusinischen Geheimnisse* (On the Eleusinian Mysteries).[77] Accepting the outlines of Warburton's interpretation of the division into Lesser and Greater Mysteries, the latter being an enlightened refutation of polytheism and its superstitions, Hißmann is conspicuously silent about the revealed monotheism Warburton and others expected to find

---

75   Ibid., 145.
76   Ibid., 148. Interestingly, Warburton here adds the following note 'But here it is to be observed, that the Discovery of the Supreme Cause of all Things was not made to the Destruction of the Notion of local tutelary Deities, Being superior to Men, and inferior to God, and by him set over the several Parts of his Creation. This was an Opinion universally held by Antiquity, and never brought into Question by any Theist. What the ἀπόρρητα overthrew, was the vulgar Polytheism of Worship of dead Men.'
77   Published in two issues of the *Hannoversches Magazin* (1776), now available in: *Michael Hißmann. Ausgewählte Schriften*, ed. U. Roth – G. Stiening (Berlin: 2013) 251–259.

in the Greater Mysteries. This, it has recently been pointed out, gave his succinct interpretation of the Eleusinian Mysteries an atheist twist, which would have horrified Warburton and which also differed markedly from his teacher in Göttingen, Christoph Meiner's[78] interpretation of the Eleusinian Mysteries, appearing in tandem with Hißmann's treatise.[79] Meiners' less radical variation on the theme was to exercise considerable influence on Freemason and Illuminati understanding of the ancient Mysteries and, more importantly, on their understanding and structuring of their own grades of initiation.[80]

4   *Pro mysteriis eleusiniis*

Perhaps the most striking academic treatise on the Eleusinian Mysteries before Hißmann and Meiners was composed in 1745 by the short-lived Leipzig professor of Roman Law, Johann August Bach (1721–1758). A work of neither antiquarian scholarship in any meaningful sense, nor a theological rebuttal of their 'superstition', it is a learned defence of the Mysteries from Patristic allegations. Bach's *Pro mysteriis eleusiniis disputatio* (A disputation *in favour* of the Eleusinian Mysteries)[81] has as its purpose the defence of the probity of the Mysteries as a sincere and morally sound form of worship.

This is one of Bach's first works; delivered and published in the year he attained his master's degree at Leipzig's philosophical faculty, and half a decade before obtaining the doctorate in the law faculty, where he was to serve as professor of legal history (extraordinarius) between 1752 and his untimely death. Bach's infrequent appearances in modern works of scholarship are usually due

---

[78] Meiners Christoph, "Ueber die Mysteries der Alten, besonders über die Eleusinischen Geheimnisse", in Meiners Christoph, *Vermischte philosophische Schriften* part iii (Leipzig, Weygand: 1776) 164–342.

[79] On Hißmann's interpretation of the Mysteries and its possible relation to Meiners' influential work on the subject see Mulsow M., "Michael Hißmann und Christoph Meiners über die eleusinischen Mysterien", in Klemme H.F. – Stiening G. – Wunderlich F. (eds.), *Michael Hißmann (1752–1784). Ein materialistischer Philosoph der deutschen Aufklärung* (Berlin: 2013) 149–156.

[80] A consideration of the vast filed of Freemason and Illuminati fascination with ancient mysteries and the Eleusinian Mysteries in particular lies beyond the scope of the present paper. On the topic see Neugebauer-Wölk M., *Esoterische Bünde und bürgerliche Gesellschaft: Entwicklungslinien zur modernen Welt im Geheimbundwesen des 18. Jahrhunderts* (Göttingen: 1995); Meumann M., "Zur Rezeption antiker Mysterien im Geheimbund der Illuminaten: Ignaz von Born, Karl Leonhard Reinhold und die Wiener Freimaurerloge 'Zur wahren Eintracht'", in Neugebauer-Wölk M. (ed.), *Aufklärung und Esoterik* (Hamburg: 1999) 288–234; Assmann, *Religio Duplex*, esp. part ii.

[81] Bach Johann August, *Pro Mysteriis Eleusiniis Disputatio* (Leipzig, Langenheim: 1745).

to his history of Roman law (1754) and as part of the philological-historical 'scene' in mid-century Leipzig. A student of the classical scholar Johann Friedrich Christ (1701–1756), Bach was one of Christian Gottlob Heyne's (1729–1812) teachers in Leipzig, who, in later years, was to recall with gratitude Bach's influence on his understanding of historical scholarship.[82] While his utterances on the Eleusinian Mysteries break away from the long tradition of Christian approaches to pagan phenomena – he in fact polemicizes against this tradition – there is nothing to suggest Bach was anything other than a reasonably conformant Lutheran of the mid eighteenth century. Though a legal historian by profession and a philologist (Bach edited Xenophon's *Oeconomicus* in 1749), as well as a Neo Latin poet,[83] rather than a theologian, it is worth noting that he was appointed an assessor on the Leipzig Consistory in 1753.[84]

Bach's audience in the Leipzig auditorium may have found his spirited defence of the moral probity of a pagan mystery cult striking, and his outright dismissal of a long line of revered patristic opinions on the matter, as he notes that none of them had any first-hand knowledge of the Eleusinian Mysteries, may have even seemed audacious. Bach writes with an avowed sympathy for his remote subject matter – a point of considerable interest in itself. The decisive point, however, lies elsewhere; it is made clear in the opening sentence of the disputation: 'In the religious rites (*sacra*) of ancient peoples, which some call pagans (*quos gentiles vocant*), those things, far removed from the ken of the common crowd and kept concealed in secrecy, no doubt possessed great sanctity.'[85] The contrast with scholars like Kalliakis, Forelius, Stockhausen, or even Warburton is in Bach's treatment of the Mystery cult completely from without the framework of Christian concepts. So much so that 'paganism' itself

---

82   Heidenreich M., *Christian Gottlob Heyne und die Alte Geschichte* (Munich – Leipzig: 2006) 46–50.
83   A slim volume of his Latin and Greek poems was published three decades after his death by the Leipzig law professor August Cornelius Stockmann, *Ioannis Augusti Bachii JCti quondam Lipsiensis Carmina* (Dresden – Leipzig, Breitkopf: 1787). The volume is prefaced by a short biography.
84   See Steffenhagen, "Bach, Johann August", *Allgemeine Deutsche Biographie* 1 (1875) 749–750; Franke A., "Bach, Johann August", *Neue Deutsche Biographie* 1 (1953) 291. Bach is also awarded a short laudatory mention in Bursian C., *Geschichte der classischen Philologie in Deutschland von den Anfängen bis zur Gegenwart*, vol. 1 (Munich – Leipzig: 1883) 406f.; Meusel J.G., "Bach, Johann August", in *Lexikon der vom Jahr 1750 bis 1800 verstorbenen teutschen Schriftsteller*, vol. 1 (Leipzig: 1802) 130–131; Harlesius Theophilius Christoph, *De Vitis Philologorum nostra aetate clarissimorum* vol. 1 (Bremen, Foerster: 1764) 73–82–a near contemporary source impressed by Bach's pro Eleusinian disputation (75).
85   Bach, *Pro mysteriis* 3. In sacris antiquorum populorum, quos gentiles vocant, sine dubio permagnam sanctitatem habuerunt ea, quae a vulgi notitia remota, in occulto abdita tenebantur.

at the very outset of the disputation is treated with parenthesis. As the opening statement, which is elaborated in the first section, Bach sees the Eleusinian Mysteries as a classic case of a *religio duplex*,[86] that is a religious ethos, and practice, which together with its concrete (in this case Attic polytheistic) character meant to keep the ignorant crowd in fear of the gods and in legal and moral conformity with society, had a more abstract philosophical content, comprehended only by the learned and wise who seek the truth. In agreement with Varro, quoted in book four of Augustine's *City of God*, Bach concedes that not all truths are suitable for all to know.[87] That Bach's interpretation of the Eleusinian Mysteries is far removed from that of modern scholarship is here beside the point. What is crucial is the attempt to reinterpret them wholly from without the framework of Patristic and Christian Humanist views and value judgement, in an acute exercise in historicising scholarship. This is coupled with a disregard for the time-honoured question of etymology – a favourite means, as we have seen, of linking pagan phenomena to Old Testament (i.e. Christian) origins, nor does Bach betray any of the traditional disputational concern for sets and subsets of definitions, preparing the ground in countless university disputations on various facets of Antiquity, for a series of deductive demonstrations, nor is he concerned with the rebuttal of 'Papism' or 'atheism'. The essentially inductive nature of his argument leads him to admit its relative nature as opposed to the closed certainty customarily assumed in disputations. One example is the *probable* probity of the Eleusinian Mysteries, set out in a section entitled *Defensio ab exemplis* (a defence from examples).[88] Bach puts forward *exempla* of great men of Antiquity (allegedly excluding mythical figures) who were either initiated, or sought initiation, among them Cicero, Atticus, and Hadrian. They would not have done so unless there was a consensus (*communis opinio*) that the Mysteries were laudable. They were certainly *unlikely* to partake in a morally offensive cult[89] – an argument much akin to Giovanni Poleni's note on Kalliakis six years earlier. An even stronger circumstantial argument is suggested, according to Bach, by the very antiquity of the

---

86   Bach himself does not use the term. On early modern interpretations of ancient religions in terms of a *religio duplex*, i.e. an interpretation of world religions as doubled-layered phenomena with the mythical 'superstitious' exterior meant to please the masses, and an internal philosophic religion, understood by cultural elites, and essentially the same in all societies, see Assmann, *Religio Duplex*.

87   Ibid.; Augustine, *City of God* IV, 31. Ego ista conicere putari debui, nisi euidenter alio loco ipse [Varro] diceret de religionibus loquens multa esse uera, quae non modo uulgo scire non sit utile, sed etiam, tametsi falsa sunt, aliter existimare populum expediat, et ideo Graecos teletas ac mysteria taciturnitate parietibusque clausisse.

88   Ibid., 5f.

89   Ibid., §. III, *Defensio ab exemplis* 5f.

Mysteries, instituted by king Erechtheus *anno mundi* 2620, i.e. about a century, according to his calculations, after the Israelites' exodus, to celebrate the polis' deliverance from starvation by agricultural import, expressed symbolically by the arrival of Demeter.[90] This chronological reliance on biblical mile-stones does not lead to any link with biblical history, but serves merely to stress the fact that the Attic material culture at the time must, in all probability, have been very modest. It is highly improbable that a primitive agrarian community should institute a mystery cult devoted to moral corruption, since vice depends on the possibility of luxury – a condition which cannot be met by primitive farming communities, never too far above subsistence level.[91]

The fact that the Eleusinian *sacra* were shrouded in symbolic imagery was not a means to conceal criminality. Furthermore, as several rites (especially the mass) and portions of Christianity's basic vocabulary are taken from ancient Mystery cults (μυστήρια, τελεταί etc.) these would not have been adopted by the Primitive Church had they been used by their non-Christian predecessors and contemporaries for reprehensible cults.[92] To these are added other similarities, such as degrees of initiation in the Early Church before participation in the mass as fully fledged Christians.

Patristic attacks on the Mysteries were a pious fraud.[93] Bach, though paying polite homage to the Fathers' piety and commitment to the promulgation of Christianity, insists that pious lies are lies nonetheless. The Fathers attacked the Mysteries since they recognised their prominence in Pagan religion. They also constituted a convenient target since the uninitiated were not in a position to refute Patristic denigration, and the initiated were bound by silence. The Fathers, he continues with rather less reverence, though wise and pious, were not necessarily most erudite. They allowed their hatred of Pagan superstition to get the better of them and when encountering something laudable in Pagan culture they interpreted it *in malam partem*.[94] Since none of them had ever been initiated, how, he asks, could they have known anything about the Mysteries' well kept secrets. Bach concludes by turning the tables on the Fathers themselves, Tertullian in particular, by citing the latter's defence of secretive Christian rites in his *Apologeticum* from their Pagan detractors, who knew nothing about them.[95] In other words, unlike many of his predecessors,

---

90 Ibid., 7f.
91 Ibid., 6f.
92 Ibid., 12.
93 Ibid., 14. Bach refers here, as elsewhere, to Casaubon's *Exercitatio adversus Baronium* 'ubi plura piarum fraudum exempla commemorantur.'
94 Ibid., 15.
95 Ibid., 16.

not only is Bach purposefully avoiding a Christian framework in construing the Mysteries, he is in fact trying to rescue them from the Christian tradition. A probable understanding of the Mysteries' significance, following the argument of a hidden stratum veiled by fables and popular myth, reveals to Bach's mind nothing other than an abstract monotheism, sound moral teaching, and a belief in the immortality of the soul.[96]

Bach, it will be remembered, was later to become a professor of law and to some extent his arguments may have been informed by the mode of legal argumentation. This disputation, in an oblique way, also confirms the role the Leipzig law faculty played in the first half of the eighteenth century in introducing new ideas, which we identify as part of the Enlightenment.[97]

5   The Mysteries and the Immortality of the Soul

In their capacity as ancient arguments for the soul's immortality, the Eleusinian Mysteries were in Bach's days on the threshold of a flourishing career. Thus, to mention just a few examples, Bach's contemporary, the Göttingen law professor, Georg Ludwig Böhmer (1717–1797),[98] delivered a funerary oration as the University's vice-chancellor on 22. December 1754 entitled *Dogma de perenni animorum natura per Eleusinia praecipue sacra propagatum* (The teaching of the perennial nature of souls, propagated by the Eleusinian Mysteries).[99] Occasioned by the death of Johanna Maria Ayrer, wife of his fellow Göttingen law professor and Guelf councillor Georg Heinrich Ayrer (1702–1774).[100]

> Viri igitur profecto prudentes fuere, & naturae humanae consulti, quicunque primum, vndecumque acceptam doctrinam de perenni animorum natura, non minus quam reliqua vitae ciuilis & honestae praecepta, mysteriis complexi sunt, in quibus antiquissimum suo merito locum

---

96   Ibid., 18–25.
97   See Hammerstein N., "Die Universität Leipzig im Zeichen der frühen Aufklärung" in Martens W. (ed.), *Leipzig. Aufklärung und Bürgerlichkeit* (Heidelberg: 1990) 125–140.
98   See Liermann H., "Böhmer, Georg Ludwig", *Neue Deutsche Biographie* 2 (1955) 391.
99   *Memoriam Matronae Promariae Iohannae Mariae e gente Dornfeldia in coniugio viri illustris Georgii Henrici Ayreri ... civibus ac posteritati commendant Academiae Georgiae Augustae Prorector Georgius Ludovicus Boehmer D. cum Cancellario et Senatu. Ostenditur etiam, dogma de perenni animorum natura per Eleusinia praecipue sacra propagatum* (Göttingen, Schultz: 1754).
100 See Steffenhagen, "Ayrer, Georg Heinrich", *Allgemeine Deutsche Biographie* 1 (1875) 708.

habebant illa Eleusinia. In his commendatam esse mystis animorum immortalitatem, & praemia ac poenas, in Hade s. apud inferos persoluenda, iam disertis idoneorum scriptorum testimoniis probandum est, ad qua reuocari homines interdum, cur opus sit, hic disserere nihil opus est.

There were of yore wise men, well-versed in human nature, whoever they may have been, who evolved the received teaching on the eternal nature of souls with mysteries, [...] among which those Eleusinian Mysteries had a most ancient place of honour. In them was the [doctrine of] the immortality of souls entrusted to the initiates, as well as that of their just reward and punishment in the afterlife (*Hades*).[101]

The founders of the Mysteries, shrouded in antique anonymity, are treated unequivocally (and unapologetically) as purveyors of perennial wisdom, and the very core of the Mysteries, revealed in Antiquity only to the initiate, are used by a respected member of Göttingen's academic community as a fitting source of comfort at the funeral of a colleague's wife.

A further instance of a late eighteenth-century use of the Eleusinian Mysteries is offered by Wilhelm Heinse (1749–1803), who as a young man in 1774 published the first volume of his *Laidion, oder die eleusinischen Geheimnisse* (Laidion or the Eleusinian Mysteries), in essence the posthumous address of a recently deceased (though talkative) Greek girl to her bucolic lover, relating her blissful existence in the after-world and thus proving the soul's immortality to her bereaved friend. Here too, the immortality of the soul has become the essence of the Eleusinian Mysteries (pace Warburton).

Twenty one years later, in 1795 appeared the novel *Paullus Septimius, oder das letzte Geheimnis des Eleusinischen Priesters* (Paullus Septimius or the Eleusinian Priest's last Secret) by Friedrich Bouterwek (1766–1828). At the time still a Kantian philosopher, the future Göttingen professor used the fictitious figure of a wise old Eleusinian priest to show a young Roman (Paullus Septimus) the way out of philosophical Pyrrhonism and into the light of Kantian philosophy. Here, as with Heinse, the Eleusinian Mystery cult has become a philosophical-literary mouthpiece and has drifted away from both its Greek contexts as well as the long and problematic reputation among premodern Christian thinkers.

---

101 Böhmer, *Dogma de perenni animorum natura per Eleusinia praecipue sacra propagatum* B^r.

6 An Antiquarian Conclusion

Tempting as it may be to conclude with the early Romantics, the true significance of the shift we have been tracing is best gauged by taking a step back and ending with a dissertation composed in 1772 at the university of Erfurt by Heinrich August Frank (1728–1802) with the title *De Sacris Eleusiniis cum Christianis non comparandis* (On the Eleusinian rites which are not to be compared to Christian rites).[102] Frank was the director of the municipal gymnasium in Erfurt, a professor at the university's philosophical faculty (extraordinarius) and a member of the Erfurt Academy.[103] The work of a late eighteenth-century conservative, it illustrates the tectonic shift in learned approaches to ancient religions. The dissertation aims at refuting Voltaire's arguments about the Eleusinian Mysteries made in his 1765 *La philosophie de l'histoire*, where in chapter thirty seven the *philosophe*[104] addressed the perennial question of the Mysteries' secrets.[105] They were, Voltaire concluded, a philosophic confession of the One abstract God, repeating with approval Warburton's statement that such distilled notions of monotheism often had to be concealed behind a mythical façade. While the core of rational monotheism at the heart the Mysteries was beyond reproach, their various ceremonies – a necessary concession to the superstitious masses – was a parallel to Christian customs and beliefs added as superstitious accretions to the true worship of God the Father. Voltaire's reshaping of the religion of an antique elite in his own likeness and image is as historically untenable as traditional approaches. What concerns us here, is Frank's conservative rebuttal of these arguments.

Accordingly the dissertation sets out to establish the source of the Mysteries and to discover their ceremonial and doctrinal content. Following Diodorus Siculus Frank too identifies them as an Egyptian import, that is (like Vossius a century earlier) as a Greek version of Isis. Like many before him, Frank too sees Demeter's myth as a symbolisation of the turn to agriculture and stresses its

---

102 Frank Heinrich August, *De sacris eleusiniis cum christianis non comparandis* (Erfurt, Nonnus: 1772).
103 See Kiefer J.D.K., *Bio-Biographisches Handbuch der Akademie gemeinnütziger Wissenschaften zu Erfurt 1754–2004* (Erfurt: 2004) s.v.
104 Under the pseudonym of a certain abbot Bazin, which Frank seems to have accepted at face value.
105 Voltaire, *La philosophie de l'histoire. Par feu l'abbé Bazin* (London(?), s.n.: 1765) 225–233.

civilisatory role. Interestingly, he notes that the shift to agriculture, as opposed to hunting and pasture, was the occasion for the rise of positive law, at the base of which lies the right to property.[106]

As to Patristic allegations, Frank finds an elegant middle way: the Fathers were relating to the Mysteries' degenerate state in their own days, and not to the earlier period.[107] Voltaire and Warburton's attempts to portray the Eleusinian Mysteries as pure rational monotheism fail to convince Frank.[108] True, there were some Christian borrowings of ceremonial paraphernalia, but these never went beyond the surface of externals. No society has ever existed, which did not, to some extent, echo past customs. There can, he insists, be no two things further from each other than the Christian and Eleusinian methods of improving mankind.[109] The Mysteries, though of considerable moral uprightness, belonged to a religious landscape firmly rooted in antique polytheism and are neither an esoteric form of Christian monotheism nor its harbinger.

Times had changed. Conservative though he may have been, eager to refute deism, pantheism, and Spinozism, Frank's appraisal of the Mysteries is probably closer to the mark than Voltaire's (or Johann August Bach's less celebrated) retrospective rationalisation of ancient elites. Relying greatly on the antiquarian work of earlier scholars, Meursius first and foremost, they are no longer the den of obscenity portrayed by the Church Fathers, nor harbingers of a timeless truth, but a time-bound religious phenomenon rooted in remote antiquity – fascinating, harmless, and dead. Both knowledge and profanation can come from unexpected quarters.

Bibliography

[anon.], *Hymn to Demeter*, in *Homeric Hymns, Homeric Apocrypha, Lives of Homer*, trans. M. West (Cambridge, MA: 2003).

Assmann J., *Moses the Egyptian: The Memory of Egypt in Western Monotheism* (Cambridge, MA: 1998).

Assmann J., *Religio Duplex. Ägyptische Mysterien und europäische Aufklärung* (Berlin: 2010).

Bach Johann August, *Pro Mysteriis Eleusiniis Disputatio* (Leipzig, Langenheim: 1745).

---

106   Frank, *De Sacris Eleusiniis* 8.
107   Ibid., 10.
108   E.g., ibid., 19.
109   Ibid., 26.

Bach Johann August, *Ioannis Augusti Bachii JCti quondam Lipsiensis Carmina*, ed. August Cornelius Stockmann (Dresden – Leipzig, Breitkopf: 1787).

Ben-Tov A., "Pagan Gods in Late Seventeenth- and Eighteenth-Century German Universities: a sketch", in Ben-Tov A. – Deutsch Y. – Herzig T. (eds.), *Knowledge and Religion in Early Modern Europe: Studies in Honor of Michael Heyd* (Leiden: 2013) 153–177.

Böhmer Georg Ludwig, *Memoriam Matronae Promariae Iohannae Mariae e gente Dornfeldia in coniugio viri illustris Georgii Henrici Ayreri ... civibus ac posteritati commendant Academiae Georgiae Augustae Prorector Georgius Ludovicus Boehmer D. cum Cancellario et Senatu. Ostenditur etiam, dogma de perenni animorum natura per Eleusinia praecipue sacra propagatum* (Göttingen, Schultz: 1754).

Bremmer J.N., "'Religion', 'Ritual' and the Opposition 'Sacred vs. Profane'. Notes towards a terminological Genealogy", in Graf F. (ed.), *Ansichten griechischer Rituale. Geburtstags-Symposium für Walter Burkert* (Berlin: 1998) 9–32.

Bremmer J.N., "Initiation into the Eleusinian Mysteries: a 'thin' description", in Bull C.H. – Lied L.I. – Turner J.D. (eds.), *Mystery and Secrecy in the Nag Hammadi Collection and other Ancient Literature: Ideas and Practices. Festschrift for Einar Thomassen* (Leiden: 2011) 375–397.

Bruit Zaidman L. – Schmitt Pantel P., *Religion in the ancient Greek city*, trans. P. Cartledge (Cambridge: 1992).

Burkert W., *Structure and History in Greek Mythology and Ritual* (Berkeley: 1979).

Burkert W., *Ancient Mystery Cults* (Cambridge, MA: 1987).

Burkert W., "Der geheime Reiz des Verborgenen: Antike Mysterienkulte", in Kippenberg H.G. – Stroumsa G. (eds.), *Secrecy and Concealment. Studies in the History of Mediterranean and Near Eastern Religions* (Leiden: 1995) 79–100.

Burkert W., *Homo Necans. Interpretationen altgriechischer Opferriten und Mythen* (Berlin: 1997^2).

Burkert W., *Griechische Religion der archaischen und klassischen Epoche* (Stuttgart: 2011^2).

Bursian C., *Geschichte der classischen Philologie in Deutschland von den Anfängen bis zur Gegenwart, vol. 1* (Munich – Leipzig: 1883).

Calliachius Nicolas, *Dissertatio de Sacris Eleusinis*, in Poleno Giovanni (ed.), *Utriusque Thesauri Antiquitatum Romanarum Græcarumque nova supplementa, vol. 4* (Venice, Pasquali: 1737) 321–326.

Clement of Alexandria, *Protrepticus*, trans. G.W. Butterworth (Cambridge, MA: 1979).

Edmonds R.G. III, *Redefining ancient Orphism: A Study in Greek Religion* (Cambridge: 2013).

Eliade M., *A History of Religious Ideas, vol. 1: From the Stone Age to the Eleusinian Mysteries*, trans. W.R. Trask (Chicago: 1978).

Forelius Hemming, *Dissertatio de Sacris Vestae Romanae* (Uppsala, Keyser: 1697).
Forelius Hemming, *De Mysteriis Eleusiniis Dissertatio* (Uppsala, Werner: 1707).
Fraenkel E., *Horace* (Oxford: 1957).
Frank Heinrich August, *De sacris eleusiniis cum christianis non comparandis* (Erfurt, Nonnus: 1772).
Franke A., "Bach, Johann August", *Neue Deutsche Biographie* 1 (1953) 291.
Hammerstein N., "Die Universität Leipzig im Zeichen der frühen Aufklärung" in Martens W. (ed.), *Leipzig. Aufklärung und Bürgerlichkeit* (Heidelberg: 1990) 125–140.
Harlesius Theophilius Christoph, *De Vitis Philologorum nostra aetate clarissimorum*, vol. 1 (Bremen, Foerster: 1764).
Heidenreich M., *Christian Gottlob Heyne und die Alte Geschichte* (Munich – Leipzig: 2006) 46–50.
Hißmann Michael, "Ueber die Eleusinischen Geheimnisse", in Hißmann Michael, *Ausgewählte Schriften*, ed. U. Roth – G. Stiening (Berlin: 2013) 251–259.
Huizinga J., *The Autumn of the Middle Ages*, trans. R.J. Payton – U. Mammitzsch (Chicago: 1996).
Jöcher Christian Gottlieb, *Allgemeines Gelehrten-Lexicon* (Leipzig, Gleditsch: 1750).
Kerényi K., *Die Mysterien von Eleusis* (Zurich: 1962).
Kiefer J.D.K., *Bio-Biographisches Handbuch der Akademie gemeinnütziger Wissenschaften zu Erfurt 1754–2004* (Erfurt: 2004).
Liermann H., "Böhmer, Georg Ludwig", *Neue Deutsche Biographie* 2 (1955) 391.
Meiners Christoph, "Ueber die Mysteries der Alten, besonders über die Eleusinischen Geheimnisse", in Meiners Christoph, *Vermischte philosophische Schriften* part iii (Leipzig, Weygand: 1776) 164–342.
Meumann M., "Zur Rezeption antiker Mysterien im Geheimbund der Illuminaten: Ignaz von Born, Karl Leonhard Reinhold und die Wiener Freimaurerloge 'Zur wahren Eintracht'", in Neugebauer-Wölk M. (ed.), *Aufklärung und Esoterik* (Hamburg: 1999) 288–234.
Meursius Johannes, *Eleusinia sive de Cereris Eleusinae sacro, ac festo* (Leiden, Elzevir: 1619).
Meusel J.G., "Bach, Johann August", in *Lexikon der vom Jahr 1750 bis 1800 verstorbenen teutschen Schriftsteller*, vol. 1 (Leipzig: 1802) 130–131.
Mühling-Schlapkohl M., "Profanität", *Religion in Geschichte und Gegenwart* (Tübingen: 1998–2007[4]).
Mulsow M., "Michael Hißmann und Christoph Meiners über die eleusinischen Mysterien", in Klemme H.F. – Stiening G. – Wunderlich F. (eds.), *Michael Hißmann (1752–1784). Ein materialistischer Philosoph der deutschen Aufklärung* (Berlin: 2013) 149–156.
Mylonas G., *Eleusis and the Eleusinian Mysteries* (Princeton: 1961).

Neander Michael, *Orbis Terrae Partium succincta Explicatio* (Eisleben, Gubisius: 1583).
Neugebauer-Wölk M., *Esoterische Bünde und bürgerliche Gesellschaft: Entwicklungslinien zur modernen Welt im Geheimbundwesen des 18. Jahrhunderts* (Göttingen: 1995).
Nisbet R.G.M. – Rudd N., *A Commentary on Horace: Odes Book III* (Oxford: 2003).
Pagel J.L., "Rolfink, Werner", *Allgemeine Deutsche Biographie* 29 (1889) 74.
Parker R., *Polytheism and Society in Athens* (Oxford: 2005).
Piesner C., "Rolfink, Werner", *Neue Deutsche Biographie* 22 (2005) 9–10.
Richardson N.J., *The Homeric Hymn to Demeter* (Oxford: 1974).
Rolfinck, Werner, *Sacra Eleusinia patefacta, seu tractatus anatomicus novus de organorum generationi dicatorum structura admirabili in utroque sexu, veterum atque neotericorum hypothesibus et inventis adcommodatus* (Frankfurt, Oehrlingius: 1684).
Rotstein A., *The Idea of Iambos* (Oxford: 2010).
Sandys J.E., *A History of Classical Scholarship, vol. 2* (Cambridge: 1908).
Skovgaard-Petersen K., *Historiography at the Court of Christian IV* (Copenhagen: 2002).
Smith M., *Jesus the Magician: Charlatan or Son of God?* (London: 1978).
Steffenhagen, "Ayrer, Georg Heinrich", *Allgemeine Deutsche Biographie* 1 (1875) 708.
Steffenhagen, "Bach, Johann August", *Allgemeine Deutsche Biographie* 1 (1875) 749–750.
Stockhausen Heinrich Christian Ludwig, *Zenobia von Palmyra* (Halle, s.n.: 1720).
Stockhausen Heinrich Christian Ludwig, *De cultu ac usu luminum antiquo. Qui qualis fuerit in omnibus antiquorum sacris, delubris, oraculorum antris, consecrationibus, auguriis, lustrationibus, bello, triumphis, puerperiis, nuptiis, funerumque processu, reliqua ex omni antiquitate ostenditur. Accedit ultrior de mysterio Cereris eleusiniae, raptuque Proserpinae accensis facibus quaesitae ac dein culta explicatio* (Utrecht, Kroon & Hofman: 1726).
Stockhausen Heinrich Christian Ludwig, *Zenobia von Palmyra* (Halle, s.n.: 1720).
Stockhausen Heinrich Christian Ludwig, *Standrede, bey feyerlichen Leichenbegrägniß der weyland Hochwohlgebohrnen Frau, Frau Helenen, verwittibter von Alvensleben, geb. von der Schulenburg, In der Kirche zu Eichenbarleben gehalten, Von dem nunmehr in GOtt selig ruhendem Herrn Henirch Christian Ludewig Stockhausen, Damals Königl. Preuß. Hof-Rath, Regierungs-und Lehns-Secretario im Hertzogthums Magdeburg: Genau nach des wohlseligen Herrn Hof-Raths eigener Handschrift heraus gegeben*, in Niemeier Heinrich Wilhelm, *Die Ruhe der Seelen in Gott, wie sie, bey der Unruhe dieses Lebens, rechtmäßig zu suchen, und, einem guten Anfange nach, wircklich zu finden ist, bis sie, der Vollendung nach, im ewigen Leben seliglich erlanget wird, Als die weyland Hochwohlgebohrne Frau, Frau Helene, geb. von der Schulenburg ...* (Magdeburg, Faber: 1748) 78–88.
Voltaire, *La philosophie de l'histoire. Par feu l'abbé Bazin* (London(?), s.n.: 1765).
Vossius Gerard, *De theologia gentili* (Amsterdam, Blaeu: 1668).
Wagenvoort H., "Profānus, profānāre", *Mnemosyne* 2, 4 (1949) 319–332.

Warburton William, *The Divine Legation of Moses demonstrated, on the Principles of a religious Deist* (London: Gyles: 1742³).

Welchering P., "Profan. Materialien zur Geschichte eines wenig beachteten und erforschten Begriffs", *Archiv für Begriffsgeschichte* 28 (1984) 63–99.

Welchering P., "Profan, das Profane, Profanität" *Historisches Wörterbuch der Philosophie*, vol. 7 (Basel: 1989) 1442–1446.

West D., *Horace Odes III. Dulce Periculum* (Oxford: 2002).

Young B., *Religion and Enlightenment in Eighteenth-Century England: Theological Debate from Locke to Burke* (Oxford: 1998).

Young B., "Warburton, William", *Oxford Dictionary of National Biography*.

PART 3

Crossing the Boundaries in Biblical Scholarship: Ancient Preconditions and Early Modern Conflict

∴

CHAPTER 7

Athens and Jerusalem? Early Jewish Biblical Scholarship and the Pagan World

Azzan Yadin-Israel

> Those of you who have read the Book of Numbers know what I mean
> JULIAN, Emperor of Rome

⋮

'What has Athens to do with Jerusalem?' Tertullian famously asked, and lest he be misunderstood, appended two clarifying questions and an explanatory discussion: 'What has the [philosophical] academy to do with the church? What have heretics to do with Christians?'[1] Tertullian's criticism is aimed at what we might call (using 'Judaizing' as a paradigm) 'platonizing' and 'stoicizing' Christian heretics, who after accepting Christ essay to produce 'a Stoic or Platonic or dialectic Christianity.'[2] The passage, then, is concerned with the misguided – so Tertullian – application of philosophic principles and modes of argument to the gospel, and, taken on its own, is easily reconciled with a positive view of philosophy, provided it keep its distance from Christian teachings. As often happens, Tertullian was misunderstood all the same, and the Athens-Jerusalem contrast came to demarcate two incommensurable worldviews: the Christian (in more ecumenical times, Judeo-Christian/monotheistic) and the Pagan, or in broader and less historically grounded terms, reason and faith – the profane and the sacred.[3]

Sweeping dichotomies should be viewed with suspicion, and this one is no exception. Pagan antiquity was, in Keith Hopkins' phrase, a world full of gods, and many of the institutions that are today understood as secular had strong

---

1   Tertullian, *Against the Heretics* (*De praescriptione haereticorum*) ch. 7.
2   Translation follows Greenslade S.L., *Early Latin Theology: Selections from Tertullian, Cyprian, Ambrose, and Jerome* (Philadelphia – London: 1956) 36.
3   For a remarkable analysis of the phrase, its meaning for Tertullian and its later reception, see Leonard M., *Socrates and the Jews: Hellenism and Hebraism from Moses Mendelssohn to Sigmund Freud* (Chicago – London: 2012) 1–16.

religious overtones in antiquity.[4] Historical veracity notwithstanding, the association of Paganism with the profane is by now firmly established and manifested in the ongoing marginalization of Paganism from scholarly analysis of ancient Jewish biblical interpretation.[5] Let me offer a brief example, more striking for the fact that it does not involve the Palestinian or Babylonian rabbis, but the acculturated Jewish community of Alexandria. James Porter opens his fascinating study of Aristarchus and Crates, the great second-century BCE Homeric critics of Alexandria and Pergamum, respectively, with a summary of the classical tradition concerning the formation of the Homeric texts:

> According to the scholia of Dionysius Thrax (the learned Alexandrian grammarian of the mid-second century BC), the first critical edition of Homer came into existence in the following way. Homer's poems, scattered over time by floods, earthquakes and fire, resurfaced again, but in random quantities. It fell to Peisistratus to rescue the epics from almost certain oblivion [...] Seventy-two experts (γραμματικοί) were then appointed to the task of individually (κατ' ἰδίαν) reassembling Homer's poems, each according to his own lights and a wage that befitted learned men and connoisseurs of poems (κριταὶ ποιήματων).[6]

These seventy-two reconstructions of the Homeric epic were then placed before the group of scholars and that of Aristarchus was eventually crowned victorious. Much discussed in classical scholarship,[7] I cite it here because of its patent similarity to the account of the first translation of the Hebrew Bible, the Greek Septuagint, in the *Letter of Aristeas*, according to which, King Ptolemy commissioned Demetrius of Phalerum, his chief librarian, to collect all the books of the world, and the latter proposed that the law books of the Jews be included in the collection. The king wrote Eleazar, the High Priest in Jerusalem, and after some negotiation, six translators from each of the twelve Israelite tribes are sent to Alexandria. There

> they set to completing their several tasks, reaching agreement among themselves on each by comparing versions. The result of their agreement

---

[4] Some of these include theater, sports, and, in a sense, the city itself.
[5] Unless otherwise noted, 'Bible' and 'biblical' refer to the Hebrew Bible/Old Testament.
[6] Porter J.I., "Hermeneutic Lines and Circles: Aristarchus and Crates on the Exegesis of Homer", in Lamberton R. – Keaney J.J. (eds.), *Homer's Ancient Readers: The Hermeneutics of Greek Epic's Earliest Exegetes* (Princeton: 1992) 67–114, 67.
[7] On the field's initial acceptance and subsequent rejection of the historicity of the tale see Pfeiffer R., *History of Classical Scholarship: From the Beginnings to the End of the Hellenistic Age* (Oxford: 1968) 6–8.

thus was made into a fair copy by Demetrius. The business of their meeting occupied them until the ninth hour, after which they were free for bodily rest and relaxation, everything which they desired being furnished on a lavish scale [...] the outcome was such that in seventy-two days the business of translation was completed, just as if such a result was achieved by some deliberate design.[8]

The similarity between the two narratives is unmistakable. A king invites a group of seventy-two scholars to help establish a definitive version of the national epic of a community, furnishes them with handsome payment and/or a lavish work environment, and they produce a version that receives the group's collective blessing. Indeed, the Septuagint scholars are tasked not only with translating the Torah, but with establishing a precise recension of the biblical text, since existing copies 'have been transcribed somewhat carelessly and not as they should be, according to the report of the experts, because they have not received royal patronage.'[9] Whether the copies in question are of a pre-LXX Greek translation or of the Hebrew manuscripts available in Alexandria is a matter of considerable controversy.[10] In either case, the Septuagint's foundation-narrative, like that of the Homeric epic, involves the establishment of a reliable critical (inasmuch as it is the work of κριταί, 'experts') edition.

The points of similarity between these foundation narratives have not gone altogether unnoticed by ancient[11] or modern authors.[12] Still, the Peisistratus

---

8   [Aristeas], *The Letter of Aristeas*, trans. R.H. Shutt, in Charlesworth J.H. (ed.), *The Old Testament Pseudepigrapha* (New York: 1985) §§302–307 = 2.32–2.33.

9   [Aristeas], *Letter of Aristeas* §30 = 14–15.

10 For a recent discussion see Niehoff M., *Jewish Exegesis and Homeric Scholarship in Alexandria* (Cambridge: 2011). The Greek word Shutt renders 'transcribed,' *sesēmantai*, has been at the centre of a vigorous scholarly debate that reaches back to the nineteenth century, briefly summarized in Shutt's footnote (p. 14). Niehoff offers strong comparative evidence from the terminology of Homeric scholarship to suggest that the term refers to text critical markings (*Jewish Exegesis and Homeric Scholarship* 33–35).

11 See the fascinating discussion of Giannozzo Manetti's biography of Pope Nicholas V, the founder of the 'Alexandrian' project of collecting and translating codices and manuscripts in Greek and Latin – the foundation for the Vatican Library. Manetti, who knew the pope, connects the Peisistratus and Septuagint narratives in order 'to question the divine inspiration of the Septuagint, while at the same time asserting that both the secular and the sacred enterprises were remarkable feats of learning with tremendous cultural consequences'; Smith C. – O'Connor J.F., "What Do Athens and Jerusalem Have to Do with Rome? Giannozzo Manetti on the Library of Nicholas V", in Marino J. – Schlitt M.W. (eds.), *Perspectives on Early Modern and Modern Intellectual History: Essays in Honor of Nancy S. Struever* (Rochester, NY: 2001) 88–115, 101.

12 See McDonald L.M., *Forgotten Scriptures: The Selection and Rejection of Early Religious Texts* (Louisville: 2009) 87–88 who is agnostic as to the historical relationship between the two narratives; Wyrick J., *The Ascension of Authorship: Attribution and Canon Formation*

narrative is absent from many contemporary scholarly discussions of the Septuagint, including introductory surveys of the translation,[13] studies of the interaction between Homeric scholarship and Alexandrian Jewish Bible interpretation,[14] and even monographs on the Septuagint legend itself.[15] Casting a broader net, the intersection of the terms 'Septuagint' and 'Homer' in the American Theological Library Association (ATLA) database identifies a single source, while the intersection of 'Septuagint' and 'Peisistratus' (including the variant spellings Peisistratos, Pisistratus, and Pisistratos) not even one, a meagre – and altogether typical – yield. Nonetheless, it is clear that the marginalization of the 'profane' Pagan sources is untenable, both in terms of the overt engagement with the Bible on the part of Pagan intellectuals, and in terms of what is increasingly coming to be seen as a shared set of interpretive terms and assumptions governing late antique Homeric and Biblical scholarship.

1   Pagan Readers of the Bible

The Pagan engagement of the Hebrew Bible in late antiquity was substantive. As John Granger Cook has shown in detail,[16] and the copious Bible quotations in Menahem Stern's collection of Pagan sources on Jews and Judaism already indicated,[17] there are hundreds of references to the Hebrew Bible in Pagan sources, with a number of Pagan scholars consistently integrating biblical scholarship into their writings, chief among them Porphyry and Julian.

---

in Jewish, Hellenistic, and Christian Traditions (Cambridge, MA: 2004), argues for the priority of the Septuagint story and its influence on the Peisistratus account, but without considering the relative prestige of the two works within Alexandrian society and the likelihood that the leading intellectual figures of the Hellenistic world would feel compelled to borrow from the Letter of Aristeas. See also Giuseppe Veltri's discussion of the two narratives as part of a dynamic of canonization and decanonization in his *Libraries, Translations, and 'Canonic' Text: The Septuagint, Aquila and Ben Sira in the Jewish and Christian Traditions* (Leiden: 2006) 78–90.

13   See, e.g., Fernández Marcos N., *The Septuagint in Context: Introduction to the Greek Versions of the Bible*, trans. W.G.E. Watson (Leiden: 2000).

14   Niehoff, *Jewish Exegesis and Homeric Scholarship in Alexandria*.

15   Wasserstein A. – Wasserstein D.J., *The Legend of the Septuagint: From Classical Antiquity to Today* (Cambridge: 2006), especially the discussion of the Letter of Aristeas at 19–26.

16   Cook J.G., *The Interpretation of the Old Testament in Greco-Roman Paganism*, Studien und Texte zu Antike und Christentum 23 (Tübingen: 2004).

17   Stern M., *Greek and Latin Authors on Jews and Judaism*, 3 vols. (Jerusalem: 1974–1984).

Porphyry (c. 234–310 CE), a native of Tyre and the outstanding disciple of Plotinus, was perhaps the preeminent Pagan intellectual of his day. Before studying under Plotinus, Porphyry spent several years in Athens studying with Cassius Longinus, the rhetor and critic, writing extensively on the *Iliad* (his *Homeric Questions* date to this period) and he employed his philological training in service of his anti-Christian attack. And while this may not have been the primary point of his anti-Christian rhetoric (Pagan criticism of Christianity tended to focus on the latter's novelty), Porphyry produced an impressive body of Hebrew Bible and New Testament philology. Unfortunately, many of his biblical discussions appeared in his *Against the Christians*, a work that was declared illegal and burned by several Christian emperors, and is preserved mostly in citations from Christian responses to it.[18] Still, his undeniable brilliance is visible in the twelfth book of *Against the Christians*, where Porphyry was the first to argue that the Book of Daniel was not of Persian provenance (as indicated by its narrative framework), but rather a later Hellenistic book, even identifying the prophecies as *ex eventu* descriptions of events from the reign of Antiochus Epiphanes.[19] Julian, who reigned briefly as emperor (361–363 CE), wrote extensively on the Hebrew Bible, most prominently in his anti-Christian work *Against the Galileans*.

Given the breadth and depth of these Pagan authors' engagement with the Hebrew Bible, one might expect them to be more fully integrated into scholarship on late antique biblical interpretation. But most scholars appear not to be aware of these sources, while those that are more often than not marginalize their significance. Thus, the Israeli scholar David Rokeach has argued that Pagan bible scholarship should be viewed exclusively through the prism of the Pagan-Christian polemic, of which Jews were in no way a part: 'Careful reading of the pagan, Christian and Jewish sources related to the [interreligious conflict in the Roman Empire] led me to the conclusion that the Jews were no party to it',[20] their role being limited to mediation between the warring parties, or in Rokeach's terminology, 'the Jews were a sort of "middlemen" in

---

18 On the fate of *Against the Christians* see Cook J.G., *The Interpretation of the New Testament in Greco-Roman Paganism*, Studien und Texte zu Antike und Christentum 3 (Tübingen: 2000) 125.

19 According to Jerome, who wrote an extensive commentary on the Book of Daniel, Porphyry considered the story of Susanna (in the apocryphal chapter 13) to have been originally written in Greek since it contains a play on words: ἀπὸ τοῦ σχίνου σχίσαι and ἀπὸ τοῦ πρίνου πρίναι ('to split from the mastic tree' and 'to saw from the evergreen oak', respectively), 'a word-play appropriate to Greek rather than to Hebrew' (Stern, *Greek and Latin Authors* II, §464b).

20 Rokeach D., *Jews, Pagans and Christians in Conflict* (Leiden: 1982) 9.

the polemic between the pagans and the Christians.'[21] But the claim that Jews played no real part in the interreligious dynamics (in Rokeach's terms: conflict) of late antiquity is untenable.

For one thing, engagement with the Hebrew Bible was not always yoked to his anti-Christian polemic. To cite one example, in his allegorical exposition of the Cave of the Nymphs narrative,[22] Porphyry explains that Homer links the cave to water nymphs, the Naiades, in order to hint at the spiritual meaning embedded in this image:

> We [Porphyry] say that the Naiads are nymphs and in particular the powers which preside over the waters; they [the theologians] use the term generally of all souls that descend into generation. For they consider, as Numenius says, that the souls rest on divinely blown water; therefore, he says, the prophet said that the spirit of God was borne over the water.[23]

As Gager notes,[24] the theological and philosophical force of Numenius' original statement is hard to divine from this brief citation. Still, the passage is remarkable for the nonchalance with which Porphyry cites Genesis and tacitly endorses Numenius' characterization of Moses as 'the prophet,' and the implicit assumption that his readers will recognize the reference.

Moreover, even if all Pagan interpretations of the Hebrew Bible were motivated by anti-Christian animus, they remain part of the history of biblical interpretation and should be integrated into it on their own merit. Indeed, several of the readings offered by Porphyry and Julian map nicely onto the Jewish interpretive tradition. One fascinating example, discussed at length by Pieter van der Horst,[25] is the interpretation of Exodus 22:27 (LXX 22:28) in Julian:

---

21 Rokeach, *Jews, Pagans and Christians* 78. At one point, Rokeach resorts to a psychological explanation of Julian's position: 'In order to deal with the innate contradiction [of the simultaneous praise and denigration of the Jews], we must have recourse to the assumption that Julian's words were not intended for the Jews and not meant to disclose his real feelings towards them, but only to amplify with their help the momentum of his attack on the hated and dangerous Christians' (59–60). But the explanatory value of Emperor Julian's 'real feelings' is negligible.
22 Homer, *Odyssey* 13.102–13.112.
23 Porphyry, *On the Cave of the Nymphs*, trans. J. Gager, in *Moses in Greco-Roman Paganism* (Atlanta: 1989) §10 = 65; see Stern, *Greek and Latin Authors* II, §456b.
24 Gager, *Moses in Greco-Roman Paganism* 65–66.
25 Horst P.W. van der, "'Thou Shalt Not Revile the Gods': The LXX Translation of Ex. 22:28 (27), its Background and Influence", *Studia Philonica Annual* 5 (1993) 1–8.

But though their lawgiver forbade them to serve all the gods save only that one, whose 'portion is Jacob, and Israel an allotment of his inheritance' (Deut. 32:9); though he did not say this only, but methinks added also 'Thou shalt not revile the gods' (Exod. 22:27).[26]

The Masoretic text instructs 'You shall not revile *'elohim*, or curse a leader of your people.' Though *'elohim* is a standard biblical word for the God of Israel and is regularly rendered in the singular, here the Septuagint preserves the grammatical plurality of the Hebrew, *theous ou kakologēseis* ('you shall not revile Gods'). As van der Horst shows in his study on the topic, the Septuagint translation gives rise to – and may itself be the result of – a Hellenistic Jewish argument for religious pluralism that finds later expression in the writings of Philo:

> Why does (Scripture) say, "gods thou shalt not revile"? Do they then still accuse the divine Law of breaking down the customs of others? For, behold, not only does it offer support to those of different opinion by accepting and honoring those whom they have from the beginning believed to be gods, but it also muzzles and restrains its own disciples, not permitting them to revile these with a loose tongue.[27]

The similarity between Philo's interpretation and Julian's is unmistakable, and likely an indication that Julian's Christian education included Philo's writings. But other biblical interpretations cannot be so easily located in earlier Jewish or Christian writings. Here is Julian's interpretation of the Tower of Babel:

> Furthermore, Moses also consciously drew a veil over this sort of enquiry, and did not assign the confusion of dialects to God alone. For he says that God did not descend alone, but that there descended with him not one but several, and he did not say who these were. But it is evident that he assumed that the beings who descended with God resembled him [...]

---

26   Julian, *Against the Galileans* 238c, in Stern, *Greek and Latin Authors* II, §481a = 540.
27   Philo, *Quaestiones in Exodum* 2.5, trans. R. Marcus, in the Loeb Supplement Volume 2, 40–41. See also Philo, *De Specialibus Legibus* 1.9.53, which does not quote the verse in question but appears to refer to it: 'Yet he counsels them that they must not [...] deal in idle talk or revile with an unbridled tongue the gods whom other acknowledge, lest they on their part be moved to utter profane words against Him Who truly is' (trans. F.H. Colson, Loeb vol. 7, 128–129); Philo, *De Vita Mosis* 2.203; Josephus, *Contra Apionem* 2.237.

> [and] would reasonably be considered responsible for this division [...] If [then] the immediate creator of the universe be he who is proclaimed by Moses, then we hold nobler beliefs concerning him, in as much as we consider him to be master of all things in general, but that there are besides national gods who are subordinate to him [...] But if Moses first pays honour to a sectional god, and then makes the lordship of the whole universe contrast with his power, then it is better to believe as we do [...] than to honour one what has been assigned the lordship over a very small portion, instead of the creator of all things.[28]

As this extended quote makes clear, Julian utilizes a crux in the biblical account of the Tower of Babel to introduce a motif found throughout his work. The crux in question is God's cohortative address: 'Come, let us go down, and confuse their language there, so that they will not understand one another's speech',[29] with its clear implication of additional divine agents accompanying God in the confusion of human languages, agents Julian identifies with the national Gods that govern each people. All of which leads to the conclusion that Moses is unsuccessfully trying to juggle contrasting theologies of a God most high and a national god. Philo too notes the plural form, but explains it otherwise: 'God, being one, has about him an unspeakable number of powers, all of which are defenders and preservers of every thing that is created; and among these powers those also which are conversant with punishment are involved.'[30] Here the cohortative indicates that God is speaking to His powers, and particularly the power to punish, not to the national gods, as in Julian.

Julian's interpretation is paralleled elsewhere. The Aramaic translation of Genesis, Targum Pseudo-Jonathan (also known as Targum Yerushalmi) renders Genesis 11:7–8

> And the Lord said to the seventy angels which stand before Him, Come, we will descend and will there commingle their language, that a man shall not understand the speech of his neighbour. And the Word of the Lord was revealed against the city, and with Him seventy angels, having reference to seventy nations, each having its own language.[31]

---

28 Julian, *Against the Galileans* 146A–148C = §481a = 534–535.
29 Gen. 11:7.
30 Philo, *De Confusione Linguarum* §171.
31 Etheridge J.W., *The Targums of Onkelos and Jonathan Ben Uzziel On the Pentateuch With The Fragments of the Jerusalem Targum From the Chaldee* (London: 1862) 190.

A very similar account is found in the midrashic *Pirke de-Rabbi Eliezer*, in which 'The Holy One, blessed be He, descended with the seventy angels, who surround the throne of His glory, and they confused their speech into seventy nations and seventy languages [...] and He appointed an angel over each people.'[32] David Flusser notes these similarities and, characteristically, frames them in a way that accords the rabbinic (or para-rabbinic) sources self-evident primacy: 'Did this interpretive tradition reach Julian in writing, or orally? From a Jewish source or perhaps a Christian source dependent on rabbinic midrash?' And shortly thereafter he refers to 'the Jewish tradition that reached Julian.'[33] But Flusser is on shaky historical grounds. *Pirke de-Rabbi Eliezer* post-dates the Islamic conquests and is generally dated to the eighth or ninth century CE, while Targum Pseudo-Jonathan is likely later still. To be sure, these sources incorporated earlier traditions, but absent firm evidence that the Tower of Babel interpretation was one of them, the fact remains that the identification of God's cohort in the descent to the tower with the national deities governing each people appears first in the writings of the Pagan emperor, and only half a millennium later in Jewish sources.[34] Historical priority aside, Flusser's comments also reveal a deeply problematic tendency to cast Pagan authors as transmitters of traditions that invariably originate in rabbinic sources, perhaps mediated by 'a Christian source dependent on rabbinic midrash.' Excluded (without argument or justification) is the possibility that Julian (like Porphyry before him) was a creative interpreter of the Hebrew Bible.

2   Pagan and Rabbinic Interpretive Practices

Many scholars have discussed Greek analogues to rabbinic interpretive practices, perhaps most prominent among them Saul Lieberman and David Daube.[35] Still, it is telling that more than half a century after the publication of

32   [anon.], *Pirke de Rabbi Eliezer*, trans. G. Friedlander (New York: 1965) 177.
33   Flusser D., "The Image of the Masada Martyrs in Their Own Eyes and in the Eyes of the Their Contemporaries", in Flusser D., *Judaism of the Second Temple Period, vol. 2: The Jewish Sages and Their Literature*, trans. A. Yadin (Grand Rapids: 2009) 76–112, 109.
34   See Niehoff's discussion of Philo's *On the Confusion of Tongues* and its preservation of other Jewish Alexandrian interpretations of the Tower of Babel; *Jewish Exegesis and Homeric Scholarship* 77–92. None of these interpretations contain the motif in question, but their existence raises the possibility that Julian's writings draw from non-Philonic Alexandrian Jewish traditions.
35   Lieberman S., *Hellenism in Jewish Palestine* (New York: 1950); Daube D., "Rabbinic Methods of Interpretation and Hellenistic Rhetoric", *Hebrew Union College Annual* 22 (1949) 239–264; idem, "Alexandrian Methods of Interpretation and the Rabbis", in *Festschrift Hans*

Hellenism in Jewish Palestine, Philip Alexander finds it necessary to cite shared Greek-Rabbinic interpretive assumptions as evidence that 'Rabbinic Judaism is at home in the world of late antiquity; it is not untypical of its time and of its place.'[36] The need for such an argument is due in part to waning scholarly interest in the Hellenistic context of rabbinic hermeneutics in the latter decades of the twentieth century, and in part to the fact that Alexander is after something a little different and more fundamental than the scholars who preceded him, namely, the relationship between a canonic text (Homer and the Torah) and the community of interpreters that forms around it.[37]

Recent years have witnessed an increased awareness of the overlaps between Homeric and rabbinic interpretation. Yakir Paz offers a fascinating comparison of the formulas used by Homer's scholiasts and early rabbis to link a word or passage in the canonic text to a later written or oral tradition.[38] Paz surveys different types of traditions linked by the scholiasts to Homer – mythological motifs, literary works, philosophical themes, proverbs, legal pronouncements – and juxtaposes them with the early rabbinic phrases *mikan* and *mikan amru* ('from this [verse]' and 'from this [verse] they said'), which identify biblical verses as the source of proverbs and legal traditions.[39]

René Nünlist's study of Aristarchan hermeneutic principles paves the way for another fascinating parallel.[40] One of the principles he explores designates

---

  Lewald (Basel: 1953) 27–44. On the different approaches of these scholars see Moss Y., "Noblest Obelus: Rabbinic Appropriations of Late Antique Literary Criticism", in Niehoff M. (ed.), *Homer and the Bible in the Eyes of Ancient Interpreters* (Leiden: 2012) 245–268.

36 Alexander P.S., "'Homer the Prophet of All' and 'Moses our Teacher': Late Antique Exegesis of the Homeric Epics and of the Torah of Moses", in Rutgers L.V., – Horst P.W. van der – Havelaar H.W. – Teugels L. (eds.), *The Use of Sacred Books in the Ancient World* (Leuven: 1998) 127–142, 141.

37 Recognizing that the contours of canonicity vary for each of these texts, and for different sub-communities *among* late antique readers of Homer and the Bible, respectively.

38 Paz Y., "Re-Scripturizing Traditions: Designating Dependence in Rabbinic Halakhic Midrashim and Homeric Scholarship", in Niehoff M. (ed.), *Homer and the Bible in the Eyes of Ancient Interpreters* (Leiden: 2012) 269–298. This study is part of Paz's doctoral dissertation, which 'compares the Alexandrian Homeric commentaries and the rabbinic biblical exegesis' (269, footnote marked by asterisk).

39 This is not the place for a detailed discussion, but Paz's comparison is wanting in one critical respect. Namely, many of the legal traditions 'scripturized' by *mikan amru* are originally represented as anchored in a consciously extra-scriptural oral tradition, understood by proponents and opponents alike as an alternative to written Torah. Very different cultural dynamics are at work in the assertion that an ancient authority (Hesiod, Sophocles) was dependent on Homer, and the claim that apodictic Mishnah traditions are in fact scriptural.

40 Nünlist R., "*Topos Didaskalikos* and *Anaphora* – Two Interrelated Principles in Aristarchus' Commentaries", in Niehoff M. (ed.), *Homer and the Bible in the Eyes of Ancient Interpreters* (Leiden: 2012) 113–126.

a *topos didaskalikos*, 'an instructive verse'. For example, Aristarchus mobilizes this principle in the passage describing how Diomedes hurls his spear at the war god Ares and, guided by Athena, the spear penetrates 'into the depth of the belly where the war belt girt him.'[41] Since the precise location of the belt was a matter of controversy and could not be determined with certainty from other passages, Aristarchus marks this verse as a *topos didaskalikos* as its explicit nature 'can be applied to all cases that are doubtful or disputed.'[42] Nünlist provides numerous examples of this principle, including verses that clarify the meanings of words, spellings, and more. To the reader familiar with rabbinic legal interpretation, two points of similarity stand out. The first involves the scholiast's assertion that Homer teaches (*didaskei*)[43] and uses other activities to clarify the meaning of his own text, e.g., differentiating between different words,[44] stating a matter clearly,[45] and so on. This language, and the attendant notion of a pedagogically focused text, is reminiscent of the midrashic terminology found in the works of the school of Rabbi Ishmael,[46] which portray Scripture as teaching (*ba' ha-katuv lelemdekha*) or actively illuminating the meaning of the text through more specific actions: drawing an analogy, distinguishing between different legal cases, identifying analogous cases, and so on.[47] The second point of similarity is the holistic approach that allows a verse to be singled out as instructive regarding an issue that elsewhere defies dispositive resolution. Consider a similar argument from the Mekhilta of Rabbi Ishmael:

> '[A]n oath of YHWH shall be between the two of them' (Exod. 22:10): An oath by the Tetragrammaton. From this you can conclude with regard to all the oaths in the Torah. Since all the oaths in the Torah were stated without specification and Scripture (*ha-katuv*) specifies for you with regard to

---

41 Homer, *Iliad* 5.857, trans. Lattimore.
42 Nünlist, "*Topos Didaskalikos*" 114.
43 See the scholion to *Iliad* 6.418, discussed in Nünlist, "*Topos Didaskalikos*" 114.
44 Scholion to *Iliad* 15.437–15.438, discussed in Nünlist, "*Topos Didaskalikos*" 115–116.
45 Scholion to *Iliad* 1.50, discussed in Nünlist, "*Topos Didaskalikos*" 124–125.
46 Since the late nineteenth century, scholars have recognized that these midrashic works or, to use the Hebrew plural form, midrashim, make up two groups: the Mekhilta of Rabbi Ishmael and the Sifre Numbers belong to one group, associated with the figure of Rabbi Ishmael, while the Mekhilta of Rabbi Shimon ber Yohai, the Sifra, and Sifre Deuteronomy make up another, associated with that of Rabbi Akiva. For a survey of the literature in question see Kahana M., "The Halakhic Midrashim", in Safrai S. – Safrai Z. – Schwartz J. – Tomson P. (eds.), *The Literature of the Sages*, vol. 2 (Assen: 2006) 3–105. On the legal hermeneutics of the Rabbi Ishmael midrashim, see Yadin A., *Scripture as Logos: Rabbi Ishmael and the Origins of Midrash* (Philadelphia: 2004).
47 For a fuller list and more detailed discussion, see Yadin, *Scripture as Logos* 50–55.

one that it must be by the Tetragrammaton, so too I specify with regard to all the oaths in the Torah that they must be by the Tetragrammaton.[48]

Though oaths are mentioned many time in the Bible, Exodus 22:10 specifies that, in the case of a man entrusted with the possessions of another that go inexplicably missing, both must take an 'oath of YHWH.' The explicit mention of the name of God – singular in the Torah,[49] allows the reader to properly identify the nature of the other oaths in the Bible, even though they are stated in a hermeneutically opaque manner (*stam*): 'Scripture specifies [...] so too I specify.' The verse, in Aristarchus's terminology, is a *topos didaskalikos*.

Similar terminological and hermeneutic parallels are found in interpretive texts other than the scholia, such as the *Homeric Problems*, an allegorical tract attributed to the Hellenistic author Heraclitus.[50] Very little is known of Heraclitus, though David Konstan, the co-editor of the most recent edition of the *Homeric Problems*, suggests he 'may have been composing his work as early as the end of the first century AD',[51] though this cannot be proven with certainty.

Heraclitus belongs to a tradition of Homeric interpreters that offer allegorical readings of the *Iliad* by which they defend Homer against charges of impiety for his allegedly immoral representation of the Gods. In the course of his interpretation, Heraclitus clarifies a number of obscure terms in the Homeric text, e.g., the adjective *thoē* which appears in the phrase *thoē nux* ('*thoē* night') in a number of *Iliad* passages. Heraclitus begins his discussion with the statement *Hē te 'thoē nux' ouk allo ti sēmainei plēn*, which Russel and Konstan render '*Thoē* as an epithet of night denotes simply [...]' and is more literally rendered '*Thoē nux* denotes nothing other than [...]'.[52] This is a near literal parallel to the rabbinic *'ein* [lexeme] *'ella'* [meaning] ... ('[lexeme] is nothing other than [meaning]'), as in the following:

> When I see the blood I will '*pasaḥ*' over you (Exod. 12:13): *Pesiḥa* is nothing except 'protecting', as it is said 'Like birds hovering overhead, so the Lord of hosts will protect Jerusalem; he will protect and deliver it, he will spare (*pasoaḥ*) and rescue it' (Isaiah 31:5).[53]

---

48 Mekhilta of Rabbi Ishmael, Neziqin 16; Horovitz-Rabin edition, 303.
49 The phrase does appear in 2 Samuel 21:7 and 1 Kings 2:43.
50 Heraclitus, *Homeric Problems*, trans. D. Konstan – D.A. Russell (Atlanta: 2005).
51 Konstan D., "Introduction", in Heraclitus, *Homeric Problems* xiii.
52 Heraclitus, *Homeric Problems* §45.
53 Mekhilta Pisḥa 7; Horovitz-Rabin edition, 24.

In Exodus 12:13 God, having instructed the Israelite slaves to put blood on their doorposts, states that he will '*pasaḥ*' (in the *vav conversum* imperfect form) over them. The Mekhilta seeks to clarify the term by drawing on another verse, Isaiah 31:5, where the same root appears alongside a synonym that unambiguously means 'protect.' Interestingly, '*ella*' generally means 'but' or 'however,' and its employment in the rabbinic phrase '[the word] is nothing except [*'ella'*]' may be due to its phonetic similarity with the Greek *allo* in 'it is nothing except [*allo*].'

Of course, the terminological similarity mirrors the analogous hermeneutic procedure: just as the Mekhilta derives the meaning of *pasaḥ* from other verses in which it appears, so too Heraclitus divines the possible senses of *thoē* from *Iliad* 8.485–8.486 and *Odyssey* 15.299.

> Homer makes [the meaning of the word] quite clear in another passage: 'And into ocean fell the sun's bright light, drawing black night over the fertile land' (Il. 8.485–6). For he draws night behind him, as though she were tied to him, and she keeps pace with the suns' speed. So Homer very properly calls her *thoē*, 'swift.' However, one may, perhaps more convincingly argue that *thoē* is to be taken metaleptically, not of sharp movement but of sharpness of shape. Homer says elsewhere: 'From there I headed towards sharp-pointed [*thoēisin*] islands' (Od. 15.299) […].[54]

The *Homeric Problems* also employ a principle – familiar to some of the rabbinic interpreters – according to which self-explication is a conscious goal of the canonical text.[55] Consider the language of *Odyssey* 4.456–4.458, which describes the transformations of the Old Man of the Sea, a maritime deity who changes shapes in an attempt to avoid capture: 'First he became a lion with a fine mane/ a snake next, then a panther, and a mighty boar/ and liquid water he became, and a tall green tree.' Heraclitus offers a series of characteristically scientific interpretations, identifying each form with one of the elements: the lion is aether, the snake earth, and the tree growing aloft – air. But one of the transformations does not require allegorical interpretation, since it is identified from the outset as one of the elements, an aberration that Heraclitus attributes to Homer's pedagogical sensitivity: 'When he comes to water, he gives a more transparent statement, so as to assure us of the meaning of the preceding riddles: "and liquid water he became".'[56] Viewed from the perspective

---

54   Heraclites, *Homeric Problems* §45.1–45.7.
55   This principle is a more robust, intentional version of Aristarchus' *topos didaskalikos*.
56   Heraclitus, *Homeric Problems* §66.6.

of the author, Homer intended the account of the transformations to be read according to the *technē physiologikē*, as Heraclitus does, identifying each with a natural element. But he was aware that the language of the *Odyssey* is ambiguous and readers might fail to recognize the *hyponoia* underlying the narrative, so he offered them a hermeneutic signpost – an explicit reference to a natural element, that sheds light on the other, obscure statements. A single statement offered 'so as to assure us of the meaning of the preceding riddles.'

The Rabbi Ishmael midrashim offer a similar approach, casting lexical irregularities as intentional attempts on the part of Scripture to clarify its own meaning:

> 'Upon entering the land to which I am taking you' (Num. 15:18): Rabbi Ishmael says, Scripture (*ha-katuv*) altered this instance of entering (*biy'ah*) in comparison to all the other enterings (*biy'ot*) in the Torah [...] in order to teach you that when they entered the Land [of Israel] they were immediately obligated to observe the commandment of *ḥallah* [setting aside a loaf from the first yield].[57]

The Bible consistently introduces laws that take effect in Israel with the phrase 'when you enter (*ki tavo'u*) into the Land', but Numbers 15:18, which instructs regarding the agricultural commandment of *ḥallah*, deviates from the standard formula. The command takes effect 'upon entering' (*bevo'akhem*) the Land of Israel, rather than 'when you enter the Land.' Though prima facie a minor, stylistic irregularity, the Sifre understands it as an intentional, pedagogic act: 'Scripture (*ha-katuv*) altered this instance of entering (*biy'ah*) in comparison to all the other enterings (*biy'ot*) in the Torah [...] in order to teach you [...]' Like Heraclitus' interpretation of *Odyssey* 4.456–4.458, the Sifre assumes the Hebrew Bible offers its readers clues to help guide them toward a proper understanding.

3 Interpretive Foreknowledge

The idea that a text actively guides its own interpretation represents something of a conundrum, since it entails some degree of foresight on the part of the text itself regarding its own reception history. Phrased differently, a reader attributing to a text the kind of self-elucidation Heraclitus (and perhaps Aristarchus) attributes to Homeric epic and the Rabbi Ishmael midrashim to

---

57   Sifre Numbers §110; Horovitz edition, 113. See Yadin, *Scripture as Logos* 51.

the Torah, must also assume that the corpus in question is engaged in proleptic dialogue with its future interpreters. Though doubtless odd to contemporary readers, the idea seems to be shared by Pagan and Jewish readers alike.

An example of the former is Heraclitus' interpretation of Zeus' indecorous binding of Hera in *Iliad* 15.12–15.33. In typical fashion, Heraclitus explains the act as a scientific allegory of the creation of the world, one that involves the doctrine of the four elements – a doctrine of which Homer is the original author. As support for this view Heraclitus refers to the oath of Agamemnon in Book Three of the *Iliad*:

> Zeus, mighty god of storm clouds, heaven-dwelling;
> O Sun, who seest and hearest everything;
> O rivers, earth, and ye who dwell below
> and punish the dead, if any man swears falsely.[58]

According to Heraclitus, Agamemnon here allegorically invokes the four elements: Zeus corresponds to fiery ether, the rivers to water, earth to earth, and Hades to air.[59] But Agamemnon's oath also invokes the Sun, prompting Heraclitus to explain its presence as follows:

> Then why is there a fifth witness, the Sun? Homer has invoked him also in order to do a favor to the Peripatetic philosophers, who claim that the substance which they call 'rotational' is distinct from fire; they regard it as a fifth element.[60]

The fifth element or essence (*quinta essentia* or the quintessence) is part of the Peripatetic physics of the supernal world: an element that does not bear any of the traits of the earthly elements (hot, cold, wet, and dry) and is subject to neither change nor corruption. Homer includes the invocation of the sun *hina ... kharisētai*, 'in order to bestow a favor [on the Peripatetics].' Since Heraclitus knows full well that Homer predates Aristotle by centuries, it follows from his explanation that Homer knows the identity of his future interpreters, is familiar with the scientific-theoretical debates that will occupy their thought, and intentionally includes a reference to the sun in Agamemnon's oath in order to

---

58   Homer, *Iliad* 3.277–3.279, trans. Russel – Konstan.
59   Heraclitus, *Homeric Problems* §23.4–11. The last of these correspondences is based on the phonetic similarity between the Greek *Aidēs* (an alternate spelling of *Haidēs*) and *aides*, 'invisible'.
60   Heraclitus, *Homeric Problems* §23.12.

tip the scales in favour of one scientific-interpretive approach. As Heracltius states elsewhere, 'Homer has, by using allegory, passed down to his successors the power of drawing from him, piece by piece, all the philosophy he was the first to discover.'[61]

On the Jewish side we find a number of genres in which divine revelation addresses from the outset a future reader. This is certainly a common motif in later prophecy, which is often communicated in a purposely obscure manner so that its true meaning will only be made clear to a future reader. Thus in the last chapter of the Book of Daniel, a heavenly figure informs Daniel of a future time of great knowledge, but Daniel cannot grasp the meaning of these words:

> I heard but did not understand, so I said, 'My lord, what will be the outcome of these things?' He said, 'Go, Daniel, for these words are to remain secret and sealed to the time of the end' [...] none of the wicked will understand, but the knowledgeable will understand.
> DANIEL 12:8–10

As the divine figure makes clear, the prophet is not qualified to understand the prophecy, so it is 'to remain secret and sealed', inscrutable to contemporary readers. In a future time, however, there will arise an interpreter (or community of interpreters) that will be able to understand the true meaning of Daniel's prophecy, and he or they are the true addressee of God's words. A similar view is espoused in some of the Dead Sea Scrolls, particularly in the *pesharim*, which claim to extract from the biblical text esoteric information not known to prophets to whom the original revelation was made known. Thus we find in Pesher Habakkuk: "'So that my run the one who reads it" (Hab. 2:2). Its interpretation concerns the Teacher of Righteousness, to whom God has made known all the mysteries of the words of his servants the prophets.'[62] As Bilhah Nitzan notes:

> This pesher suggests that the authors of the *pesharim* considered the prophecies recorded in Scripture to be divine communications that contain mysterious secrets concerning their realization in 'the final generation'. But their interpretation as pertaining to these distant events was not given to the prophets at that time, but rather will be revealed to the

---

61   Heraclitus, *Homeric Problems* §34.8.
62   1QpHab 7.3–5.

reader selected for this task by God in the final generation, with their realization imminent.[63]

To this list we may add – with some necessary qualifications – Paul's praise of Abraham in Galatians:

> Just as Abraham 'believed God, and it was reckoned to him as righteousness,' so, you see, those who believe are the descendants of Abraham. And Scripture, foreseeing that God would justify the nations by faith, declared the gospel beforehand to Abraham, saying: 'All the nations shall be blessed in you.' For this reason, those who believe are blessed with Abraham who believed.
>
> GAL. 3:6–9; NRSV slightly revised

Setting aside its theological content – Paul's attempt to establish a covenantal genealogy that circumvents Sinai and effectively replaces Moses with the figure of Abraham – the key issue for the present discussion is Paul's characterization of Scripture declaring the gospel to Abraham because it *foresaw* the emergence of nations or gentiles being justified by faith. The statement in question is part of God's original covenant with Abraham: 'Go from your country to the land that I will show you […] I will make of you a great nation […] and in you all the families of the earth shall be blessed.'[64] The promise, then, is tripartite: it has a geographic component (the land), and national component (Abraham's descendants), and a universal component (all the nations). The first two are directly relevant to Abraham, since he must physically set off toward the promised land, and produce a son through whom the future nation will be constituted. Not so the universal component, whose realization will only begin many generations after Abraham's death when – so Paul – Christ appears on earth. This passage constitutes a divine promise and as such is forward-looking by nature, but Paul does not claim here that the nations'

---

63 Nitzan B., "The *Pesahrim* Scrolls from Qumran", in Kister M. (ed.), *The Qumran Scrolls and their World*, vol. 1 (Jerusalem: 2009) 169–190, 169. See also Nitzan B., "Pesher and Midrash in the Qumran Scrolls", *Meghillot* 7 (2009) 99–128. Brownlee makes a similar point in his edition of Pesher Habakkuk: 'That which was not made known [to Habakkuk] was the entire content to which the enigmatic words really relate, for they contain mysteries not disclosed. Knowledge of these was reserved for the Righteous Teacher. It was not mere chronological knowledge which Habakkuk lacked […] but it was an understanding of the specific events to which his words made veiled and enigmatic allusion.' Brownlee W.H., *The Midrash Pesher of Habakkuk* (Missoula: 1979) 110.

64 Gen. 12:1–3.

justification by faith is the fulfilment of God's promise to Abraham (though it is that too). Instead, he emphasizes the foreknowledge of Scripture in speaking to a reality still millennia removed from Abraham's time: the statement was made, in other words, because Scripture foresaw this future development (*proidousa hē graphē* ...).

Finally, consider the more elaborate scriptural foresight embedded in the legal interpretation of the following passage from the Mekhilta of Rabbi Ishmael:

> 'When a man opens a pit [or digs a pit and does not cover it ... the one responsible for the pit must make restitution]' (Exod. 21:33): I thus know only about one who opens a pit. How about one who digs a pit? [Scripture] teaches, saying: 'Or digs a pit.' But even before it said this, I could have reasoned: If the one who opens a pit is responsible, shall the one who digs a pit not be responsible? But if you say so, you would be decreeing punishment merely on the basis of reasoned argument. Therefore it is said: 'Or digs a pit,' to teach you that punishment cannot be decreed on the basis of a reasoned argument.[65]

Exodus 21:33 discusses the legal culpability of an individual in two scenarios: 'When a man opens a pit' and '[when a man] digs a pit and does not cover it' and, in either case, some damage occurs as a result of the action. However, the juxtaposition of the two scenarios is problematic since the liability of the digger of the pit can be derived from the liability of the one who opens a pit. After all, the Mekhilta reasons, if a person is liable when he uncovers an existing pit and neglects to return the cover to its place, surely the person who digs a pit and leaves it uncovered is liable. Why, then, would Scripture state the liability of the more serious case when it has established that of the less serious one? The Mekhilta's remarkable answer is that the liability of the more serious transgression indeed does *not* need to be stated – it is redundant and the reader is right to recognize it as such. Broken down to its constitutive elements, the argument thus far runs as follows:

a. Scripture fashions Exodus 21:33 such that the second part of the verse (the guilt of the digger) can be derived from the first part (the guilt of the uncoverer) by reasoned argument.
b. Scripture crafts the verse as outlined in (a) with the expectation that the reader will recognize the redundancy of the second part of the verse.
c. The reader indeed recognizes the redundancy.

---

65   Mekhilta Neziqin 11; Horovitz-Rabin edition, 288.

d. The reader further recognizes (b), that is, that the redundancy is the result of Scripture's desire to lead the reader to (c).

In other words, Scripture has provided a legally correct but hermeneutically redundant statement in order to lead the reader to recognize the redundancy, and to further recognize that Scripture set the redundancy up for that very purpose. All of which leads to the final conclusion:

e. 'Therefore it is said: "or digs a pit," to teach you that punishment cannot be decreed on the basis of reasoned argument.' In other words, the explicit (and redundant) statement of the digger's liability is meant to 'counter' the notion that a punishment can be established via reasoned argument, not because such an argument is flawed (it is not), but because such arguments are not admissible if they result in punishment. In other words, the liability of the one digging the pit is stated explicitly in order to teach the reader that such prohibitions must be stated *even when they can be derived by reasoned argument*.

Stepping back from the details of this passage, we find what amounts to a dialogue between Scripture and the later interpreter, predicated on the assumption that the Torah intentionally guides the reader to certain conclusions, and then further responds ('presponds') to these interpretations.

The sources discussed are by no means identical. For the Second Temple interpreters (Daniel, Qumran, Paul), proper understanding of Scripture is historically conditioned, as certain prophetic sayings are addressed to readers that will emerge only after certain conditions are met (the spread of wisdom, the birth of the Teacher of Righteousness, the advent of Christ); the Rabbi Ishmael midrashim assume a very elaborate dialogue between interpreter and text; while Heraclitus represents the Homeric statement that provides an anchor for the Peripatetics as generously bestowed by Homer – that is, free of historical or interpretive determinism. Still, and without minimizing these differences, they remain examples of textual *pronoia* in which the canonic text is aware of its future reception and 'leapfrogs' its contemporary readers so as to communicate with future generations of interpreters. Though I cannot enter into a detailed discussion of this point, it is clear that this approach is an attempt to overcome the temporal gap between the composition of a text and its later interpretation – a gap that is seen as problematic only when the text in question comes to represent a singular occurrence whose ongoing relevance is at once assumed and constituted by these interpretive practices.

Let me briefly elaborate for the different figures. Heraclitus would not assert that Homer is graciously supporting the Peripatetics if he did not consider the *Iliad* and the *Odyssey* the foundation of the totality of Greek knowledge; a closed corpus in that its content cannot be expanded (to say nothing of legitimately contravened) by later generations; the Book of Daniel and the Qumran Pesharim must establish elaborate proleptic narratives about the advent of future interpreters who reveal the meaning of prophetic visions, because bygone visions are the only legitimate material – contemporary prophecy is no longer a tenable proposition; as for the scriptural-rabbinic 'dialogue' of the Sifre Numbers, it seems to arise from the need to represent the rabbinic interpretation as wholly grounded in Scripture, even as the existence of a commentary bespeaks the need to add to the canonical text in order to illuminate its meaning. The authority of the commentary lies in its fidelity to Scripture, but the belatedness of the composition indicates that Scripture cannot stand alone. All of which is to say that our Pagan and Jewish authors are working within a conceptual framework that can, in a broad sense, be called 'canonic.'

This last statement represents the most fundamental argument offered in this essay for a revision of the traditional views that mark the Bible as sacred and the Pagan world as its profane other. As discussed above, the first involves a scholarly reorientation vis-à-vis the well-documented historical tradition of Pagan biblical interpretation, and in particular the recognition that Pagan authors could function as creative and insightful readers of the Hebrew Bible. The second argument hinges on the growing body of evidence pointing to substantive parallels in the terminology and interpretive techniques of the rabbis and the Hellenistic interpreters of Homer, be they scholiasts or allegorical commentators. The third argument is that the core conceptual underpinnings of the Homeric and biblical corpora – their temporal constitution as an object of interpretation – are closely affiliated. I cannot say whether this affiliation is the result of contact and influence (mutual or otherwise) in the earliest constitution of Homeric and biblical canonicity, but it is at least possible that the 'profane' was intimately and constitutively tied with the Bible from very early on.

Bibliography

Alexander P.S., "'Homer the Prophet of All' and 'Moses our Teacher': Late Antique Exegesis of the Homeric Epics and of the Torah of Moses", in Rutgers L.V., – Horst P.W. van der – Havelaar H.W. – Teugels L. (eds.), *The Use of Sacred Books in the Ancient World* (Leuven: 1998) 127–142.

[Anon.], *Pirke de Rabbi Eliezer*, trans. G. Friedlander (New York: 1965).

[Aristeas], *The Letter of Aristeas*, trans. R.H. Shutt, in Charlesworth J.H. (ed.), *The Old Testament Pseudepigrapha* (New York: 1985).

Brownlee W.H., *The Midrash Pesher of Habakkuk* (Missoula: 1979).

Cook J.G., *The Interpretation of the New Testament in Greco-Roman Paganism*, Studien und Texte zu Antike und Christentum 3 (Tübingen: 2000).

Cook J.G., *The Interpretation of the Old Testament in Greco-Roman Paganism*, Studien und Texte zu Antike und Christentum 23 (Tübingen: 2004).

Daube D., "Rabbinic Methods of Interpretation and Hellenistic Rhetoric", *Hebrew Union College Annual* 22 (1949) 239–264.

Daube D., "Alexandrian Methods of Interpretation and the Rabbis", in *Festschrift Hans Lewald* (Basel: 1953) 27–44.

Etheridge J.W., *The Targums of Onkelos and Jonathan Ben Uzziel On the Pentateuch With The Fragments of the Jerusalem Targum From the Chaldee* (London: 1862).

Fernández Marcos N., *The Septuagint in Context: Introduction to the Greek Versions of the Bible*, trans. W.G.E. Watson (Leiden: 2000).

Flusser D., "The Image of the Masada Martyrs in Their Own Eyes and in the Eyes of the Their Contemporaries", in Flusser D., *Judaism of the Second Temple Period, vol. 2: The Jewish Sages and Their Literature*, trans. A. Yadin (Grand Rapids: 2009) 76–112.

Gager J., *Moses in Greco-Roman Paganism* (Atlanta: 1989).

Greenslade S.L., *Early Latin Theology: Selections from Tertullian, Cyprian, Ambrose, and Jerome* (Philadelphia – London: 1956).

Heraclitus, *Homeric Problems*, trans. D. Konstan – D.A. Russell (Atlanta: 2005).

Horst P.W. van der, "'Thou Shalt Not Revile the Gods': The LXX Translation of Ex. 22:28 (27), its Background and Influence", *Studia Philonica Annual* 5 (1993) 1–8.

Julian, *Against the Galileans*, trans. W.C. Wright, in Stern M., *Greek and Latin Authors on Jews and Judaism*, 3 vols. (Jerusalem: 1974–1984).

Kahana M., "The Halakhic Midrashim", in Safrai S. – Safrai Z. – Schwartz J. – Tomson P. (eds.), *The Literature of the Sages, vol. 2* (Assen: 2006) 3–105.

Leonard M., *Socrates and the Jews: Hellenism and Hebraism from Moses Mendelssohn to Sigmund Freud* (Chicago – London: 2012).

Lieberman S., *Hellenism in Jewish Palestine* (New York: 1950).

McDonald L.M., *Forgotten Scriptures: The Selection and Rejection of Early Religious Texts* (Louisville: 2009).

Moss Y., "Noblest Obelus: Rabbinic Appropriations of Late Antique Literary Criticism", in Niehoff M. (ed.), *Homer and the Bible in the Eyes of Ancient Interpreters* (Leiden: 2012) 245–268.

Niehoff M., *Jewish Exegesis and Homeric Scholarship in Alexandria* (Cambridge: 2011).

Nitzan B., "Pesher and Midrash in the Qumran Scrolls", *Meghillot* 7 (2009) 99–128.

Nitzan B., "The Pesahrim Scrolls from Qumran", in Kister M. (ed.), *The Qumran Scrolls and their World*, vol. 1 (Jerusalem: 2009) 169–190.

Nünlist R., "Topos Didaskalikos and Anaphora – Two Interrelated Principles in Aristarchus' Commentaries", in Niehoff M. (ed.), *Homer and the Bible in the Eyes of Ancient Interpreters* (Leiden: 2012) 113–126.

Paz Y., "Re-Scripturizing Traditions: Designating Dependence in Rabbinic Halakhic Midrashim and Homeric Scholarship", in Niehoff M. (ed.), *Homer and the Bible in the Eyes of Ancient Interpreters* (Leiden: 2012) 269–298.

Pfeiffer R., *History of Classical Scholarship: From the Beginnings to the End of the Hellenistic Age* (Oxford: 1968).

Porphyry, *On the Cave of the Nymphs*, trans. J. Gager, in *Moses in Greco-Roman Paganism* (Atlanta: 1989).

Porter J.I., "Hermeneutic Lines and Circles: Aristarchus and Crates on the Exegesis of Homer", in Lamberton R. – Keaney J.J. (eds.), *Homer's Ancient Readers: The Hermeneutics of Greek Epic's Earliest Exegetes* (Princeton: 1992) 67–114.

Rokeach D., *Jews, Pagans and Christians in Conflict* (Leiden: 1982).

Smith C. – O'Connor J.F., "What Do Athens and Jerusalem Have to Do with Rome? Giannozzo Manetti on the Library of Nicholas V", in Marino J. – Schlitt M.W. (eds.), *Perspectives on Early Modern and Modern Intellectual History: Essays in Honor of Nancy S. Struever* (Rochester, NY: 2001) 88–115.

Stern M., *Greek and Latin Authors on Jews and Judaism*, 3 vols. (Jerusalem: 1974–1984).

Veltri, G., *Libraries, Translations, and 'Canonic' Text: The Septuagint, Aquila and Ben Sira in the Jewish and Christian Traditions* (Leiden: 2006).

Wasserstein A. – Wasserstein D.J., *The Legend of the Septuagint: From Classical Antiquity to Today* (Cambridge: 2006).

Wyrick J., *The Ascension of Authorship: Attribution and Canon Formation in Jewish, Hellenistic, and Christian Traditions* (Cambridge, MA: 2004).

Yadin A., *Scripture as Logos: Rabbi Ishmael and the Origins of Midrash* (Philadelphia: 2004).

CHAPTER 8

Richard Simon and the Charenton Bible Project: The Quest for 'Perfect Neutrality' in Interpreting Scripture

John Woodbridge

After the Peace of Nijmegen (1678–1679), Louis XIV, the 'Very Christian' King of France, emerged with pretensions of being the 'arbiter of Europe'. Though very powerful, Louis XIV still faced a serious competitor in the Holy Roman Emperor Leopold I who, supported by Pope Innocent XI, had plans to 'reunify' Christians of Europe, especially after the siege of Vienna by the Turks had been 'miraculously' lifted in 1683. Louis XIV believed that in fact the duty of 'reunifying' the Christian confessions fell on his royal shoulders. One goal of the King's 'grand design' was apparently to establish a universal monarchy and a uniform religion. In this light, was it not a necessary political and religious calculation to bolster Roman Catholicism as the sole religion in his own Kingdom? Would not this decisive stroke satisfy the demands of his Clergy, create a unified France and finally honor and fulfill the premise, *une foi, une loi, un roi*?[1] On October 17, 1685, Louis XIV revoked the Edict of Nantes, thereby depriving French Calvinists, or Huguenots, in his Kingdom of their religious and civil rights.[2] By 1685, however, so many rights had already been taken away from the Huguenots, so many of their churches destroyed, and so many of their pastors forbidden to lead worship services, that the Revocation seemed much more a confirmation of a royal policy already in place than a new legislative initiative.

During the two decades preceding the Revocation of the Edict of Nantes, Pastor Jean Claude of Charenton [Paris] served as the principal spokesperson and apologist for the Huguenot cause. He exercised his sometimes heavy-handed leadership in very trying circumstances. In great detail Elisabeth Labrousse analyzed the surging wave of new laws which restricted the social, economic and religious lives of Protestants. She proposed that from 1661, the beginning of Louis XIV's personal rule until the '*Paix de l'Eglise* (Peace of the Church)' (1669–1679), the government's harassment of Huguenots was often

---

1 Wolf J.B., *Louis XIV* (New York: 1968) 379–401.
2 Labrousse E., *La Révocation de l'Edit de Nantes* (Geneva: 1985).

quite intense. Between 1669 until 1678, the time-frame of particular interest for us, it was less so and the Huguenots regained a certain sense of cautious optimism about their future existence in France. After 1679, however, with Louis XIV's emergence as *'l'arbitre de l'Europe* (the arbiter of Europe)', a period of 'agony' engulfed the Protestants of France.[3] During the horrific *dragonnades*, booted missionary minded soldiers brutally forced many to convert to Catholicism. Others like Pierre Bayle sought 'refuge' outside the Kingdom's borders.

Before 1679, Pastor Claude had attempted to bolster the sagging spirits of the Protestants in whatever ways he could. In the mid-1670s, for example, Claude, along with his colleague Pierre Allix and other pastors of Charenton, decided to create a new translation of the Bible to serve the Reformed Churches of France. At the time, these churches primarily used the Genevan Bible, initially drafted by Olivetan (1535) and revised by Calvin (1540, 1545, 1551, 1560), Budé and Bertram (1588). They also employed versions by Diodati (1644) and Desmarets (1669).

For Pastor Claude and his colleagues, the Genevan Bible's deficiencies were becoming only too obvious. A number of its verbal expressions appeared outmoded. Moreover, many Parisian readers placed a premium on a pleasing literary style. But the Genevan Bible lacked the clarity and elegance evident in the hugely popular French version of portions of the Bible recently published by the Jansenist, Isaac-Louis Le Maître de Sacy (*Psaumes*, 1665; 1666; *Le Nouveau Testament de Mons*, 1667, *La Sainte Bible*, 1672–1693). Le Maître de Sacy hoped his work would foster a new type of spiritual devotion for the laity. He sought to translate Scripture in an uncomplicated manner which would help readers to understand more easily the meaning of the text. But perhaps more importantly, he wanted the faithful to know they had an obligation to read Scripture before sacramental communion.[4] Pastors Jean Claude, Pierre Allix and other Protestant leaders wanted to produce a new Protestant version of the Bible which would meet the spiritual needs of the Reformed churches of France, while simultaneously competing favorably with Le Maître de Sacy's popular version of the Bible. Their efforts to create this new version of the Bible have been designated the 'Charenton Bible' project.

Interestingly enough, Pastors Claude and Allix believed their version of the Bible could be crafted in such a way to make it acceptable and useful for both

---

[3] Ibid.
[4] Chédozeau B., "Les grandes étapes de la publication de la Bible catholique en français du concile de Trente au XVIIIe siècle", in Armogathe J.-R. (ed.), *Le Grande Siècle et la Bible, Bible de tous les temps* (Paris: 1989) 341–360, 351.

the Reformed and Roman Catholic communions of France. Upon first glance, their desire to give the version an inter-confessional allure appears puzzling. The deteriorating religious, economic and social situation of the Huguenots did not seem conducive to an ecumenical initiative. Moreover, Pastor Jean Claude was still caught up in the throes of the long-running Eucharistic controversy pitting the Protestants against the Jansenists, Arnauld and Nicole. The Jansenists claimed that the doctrine of transubstantiation had been a 'perpetual' belief of the Roman Catholic Church. They defended this thesis in a series of small and large tomes, especially the 'Grande' *Perpetuité de la foi de l'Eglise catholique touchant l'Eucharistie defendue contre le livre du sieur Claude...* (Paris, 1669; ...). In his apologetic rejoinders Pastor Claude argued quite the contrary that 'transubstantiation' was a doctrinal innovation and not a belief of the early Christian churches.[5]

Adding a different wrinkle to the debate, both Pastor Claude and the Jansenists temporarily agreed that the beliefs of Eastern Christians regarding the Eucharist could serve as a standard for determining which communion represented true Christian orthodoxy. If the Eastern Christians' view of the Eucharist mirrored the teachings of one of the churches, then the latter western church could claim to be the winner in the debate. In play apparently was Vincent of Lerins' famous dictum that what has been 'believed everywhere, always and by all' represented authentic Catholic tradition. The disputants threw themselves into a furious manuscript hunt. The diplomats of Louis XIV's government provided help to the Jansenists' efforts to collect documents. Some English Anglicans discussed privately their great worry that Jean Claude would lose the contest. They despaired that his defeat would signal a devastating defeat for the Reformed Churches of Europe. How could the beleaguered pastor of Charenton be rescued?[6]

History has its stunning surprises. Enter stage center Richard Simon (1638–1712), an Oratorian priest, into the apologetic fracas.[7] Simon played a central role in the Charenton Bible project and in the Protestant efforts to fend off the attacks of the Jansenists in the Eucharistic controversy. By studying the

---

5   Woodbridge J., "La 'grande chasse aux manuscrits,' la controverse eucharistique, et Richard Simon", in Elyade O. – Brun J. Le (eds.), *Conflits Politiques, Controverses Religieux, Essais d'histoire européenne aux XVIᵉ–XVIIIᵉ siècles* (Paris: 2002) 143–176.
6   Ibid.
7   Concerning Richard Simon, see: Brun J. Le – Simon S., *Supplément au Dictionnaire de la Bible XII* (Paris: 1996); Auvray P., *Etude bio-bibliographique avec des textes inédits* (Paris: 1974); Steinman J., *Richard Simon et les origines d'exégèse biblique* (Paris: 1960); Margival H., *Essai sur Richard Simon et la critique au XVIIᵉ siècle* (Geneva: 1970); Bernus A., *Richard Simon et son histoire critique du Vieux Testament* (Geneva: 1969).

sinuous, covert relations of Simon, the renowned biblical critic, with the Reformed Pastors Claude and Pastor Allix, we may come to a fuller understanding of the reason the Charenton Bible Project possessed the 'inter-confessional' allure that it did. We may also gain insights regarding what Simon meant when he indicated that he translated and commented on Scripture with 'perfect neutrality'.

The discovery of Simon's translation and notes on the Pentateuch, a manuscript integrally related to the Charenton Bible Project, affords us with previously unavailable resources with which to advance our basic understanding of the Charenton Bible project. In 1985, this manuscript came to the attention of scholars. Its whereabouts had been generally unknown for more than two centuries. A reference to the manuscript does appear in a book catalogue (1765) drawn up for the sale of the library of the German theologian, Siegmund Jacob Baumgarten. To this day the manuscript remains unpublished. It is an essential document in the history of biblical criticism.

In a first segment we will recount the basic story of the Charenton Bible Project. In a second segment, we will consider the criticisms of Bossuet, one of the leading Roman Catholic prelates of France, regarding Richard Simon's sub rosa involvement in the Protestant Charenton Bible project. Bossuet was particularly vexed by Richard Simon's advocacy of the stance of 'perfect neutrality' for the translator and commentator on Holy Scripture. Bossuet claimed that Simon's approach sowed 'indifference in religions'. In a third section, we will consider Simon's attempt to defend 'perfect neutrality' as a worthy scholarly trait. We will also reflect upon his rationale for the creation of an inter-confessional Bible acceptable to both Protestants and Roman Catholics.

1   The Story of the Charenton Bible Project

Towards 1672, or four years before Pastors Jean Claude and Pierre Allix of Charenton decided to create a new French version of the Bible, Reformed theologians in Geneva had begun contemplating the same task.[8] Relatively little progress was made on the Genevan Bible project due to other concerns pre-occupying the scholars assigned to its accomplishment. The years 1675–1676, however, seemed particularly propitious for completing the project. A wealthy Genevan named Olivier Fatio was disposed to fund the publishing

---

8   For the following account of the creation of the Charenton Bible Project, see: Simon Richard, *Additions aux Recherches curieuses sur la diversité des langues et religions d'Edward Brerewood*, ed. J. Le Brun – J. Woodbridge (Paris: 1983) 20–29.

of the translation in folio to the tune of 60,000 livres. In time, the pastors of Charenton and the Genevan professors became aware of the respective plans for the two Bible projects. They entered into correspondence regarding what progress they were making with their respective translation efforts. They also considered the possibility of combining their efforts in a joint French-Swiss Bible project. Jean Hermann Widerhold, a *libraire* and printer of Geneva, on occasion carried secret messages between the Parisian and Genevan correspondents. Widerhold sometimes worked for Olivier Fatio and was in relatively good standing with the Genevan theologians.

Undoubtedly, the Reformed pastors of Charenton did need help with their project. In the mid-1670s, the Reformed pastors did not find themselves in an especially promising context for undertaking the creation of a new version of the Bible. They were hard-pressed to answer the weighty polemical volumes of the Jansenists, Arnauld and Nicole. Owing to increased economic restrictions placed on the Huguenot community, they did not have large sums of money to finance a Bible project. Nor did they count in their midst biblical scholars who demonstrated a level of expertise in the biblical languages equal to that of Roman Catholics scholars such as Daniel Huet and Richard Simon.

Apparently aware of these limitations, towards 1675–1676, two Reformed men of letters, Henri Justel and Fremont d'Ablancourt, spoke with the Oratorian Richard Simon, one of their close friends. They asked him if he might lend a hand in helping the Protestant pastors create a translation with notes of the Bible. Simon regularly attended erudite discussions at the home of Henri Justel, a remarkable scholar in his own right. Justel kept abreast of news of the Republic of Letters through extensive correspondence with scholars throughout Europe. Moreover, with an openness of spirit, Justel welcomed a number of Roman Catholics to his meetings, including as noted the young priest, Richard Simon, a brilliant but irascible scholar.

That the Protestants Justel and d'Ablancourt in 1675–1676 should secretly discuss with the Roman Catholic Richard Simon the possibility of his covert involvement in a Protestant translation project is not quite as surprising as it would first appear. By the mid-1670s Simon had already established himself as one of the most knowledgeable biblical scholars in Paris. He had published *Cérémonies et coutumes qui s'observent aujourd'hui parmi les Juifs* (Paris, 1674) and Jerome Dandini's *Voyage du Mont-Liban* (Paris, 1675). His knowledge of biblical languages and versions of the Bible had been expanded dramatically through his work as the librarian for the Oratorian house, rue St. Honoré, Paris.

Of particular import for our story, in 1671, Simon had published *Fides Ecclesiae orientalis* (*The Faith of the Eastern Church*) of Gabriel Severe, arch-bishop of Philadelphie. In this work Simon criticized the scholarship of both the Reformed pastor Jean Claude and the Jansenists, Arnauld and Nicole in the Eucharistic controversy. Simon argued that a proper interpretation of the Eastern Christians' attestations gathered by both sides in the Eucharistic controversy was not evident in the writings of the disputants. Neither the Jansenists, nor Pastor Claude demonstrated a sufficient knowledge of Eastern oriental languages, nor a sufficient awareness of the religious and cultural influences which helped shape the documents. Simon's study demonstrated a remarkable expertise in oriental languages and a sophisticated understanding of the history and cultures of the Eastern Christians living under Turkish rule. It also revealed the Oratorian's willingness to criticize the Jansenists, Arnauld and Nicole, Catholics though they were. Simon had received a Jesuit Molinist education and did not fancy certain interpretations of Augustinian theology the Jansenists embraced. For many Roman Catholics, Simon's attack on the Jansenists' 'Grande' *Perpetuité* ..., a much talked about and esteemed apologetic work, seemed insolent if not downright traitorous. How could Simon, a priest, dare criticize an apologetic enterprise that had contributed significantly to the conversion of notable Protestants to Roman Catholicism?

In 1674, Arnauld and Nicole published volume III of the 'Grande' *Perpetuité* ... This huge volume was chock full of numerous attestations from Eastern Christians which purported to prove that the latter upheld the doctrine of transubstantiation. Once again, Pastor Claude and the Reformed pastors of Charenton were rocked. They were thrown on the defensive and hard pressed to answer this work.

In consequence, when Justel and d'Ablancourt approached Simon seeking his aid, they apparently understood that the Oratorian might assist them in fending off their mutual enemies the Jansenists, as well as provide the biblical expertise so desperately needed by Pastors Claude and Allix in the creation of a new French version of the Bible.

It is likely Henri Justel knew that Simon, his close friend, had been working on a translation of the Bible for some time. Moreover, for many years the Oratorian had been preparing a manuscript which would eventually become his epochal *Histoire critique du Vieux Testament* (1678). He proposed the highly controversial 'public scribes hypothesis' according to which unnamed inspired writers, or 'public scribes' along with Moses, wrote the Pentateuch. Not only did he challenge Moses's singular role as the Pentateuch's author, he argued that the Bible, given the way it was put together, offered no infallible chronology of human history. These provocative theses greatly disturbed Bossuet, the Jansenist Arnauld, fellow Oratorians, and many other Christian scholars in the Republic of Letters. For some, the suspicion began to grow that Simon might be a Spinozist in priest's garb.[9] But in 1675–1676, this suspicion had not fully ripened. Justel was pleased that his friend Simon was willing to pursue negotiations with the Protestant pastors of Charenton regarding his participation in their Bible translation project.

According to his own witness, Simon presented to Pastor Claude a plan regarding the principles to follow for the creation of an inter-confessional translation of the Bible. Simon also indicated that he gave to Claude, through the good auspices of d'Ablancourt, a manuscript copy of his own translation with notes on much of the Pentateuch. Pastor Claude had been assigned the responsibility to translate the Pentateuch for the Charenton Bible project. Simon later praised Pastors Claude and Allix for allegedly accepting the principles he had proposed to guide the translation efforts. Simon eventually placed his plan and principles for the Charenton Bible project in his *Histoire critique du Vieux Testament* (1678).

Seeking to demonstrate to the Protestants the depth of his good will and that he could genuinely help their cause, Simon also provided them with a manuscript, *Additions aux Recherches curieuses sur la diversité des langues et religions d'Edward Brerewood*, a manuscript which Professor Jacques Le Brun and I edited and published in 1983 (Presses universitaires de France). In this work, Simon took direct aim and fired at the Jansenists' essential accusation that the Protestants were doctrinal innovators regarding their view of the Eucharist.

In the preface to the *Brerewood Additions* Simon assumed the guise of an Anglican priest. He argued that the beliefs of the Reformed churches of Europe regarding the doctrine of the Eucharist were closer to the beliefs of the Eastern Christians than the teaching of the Roman Catholic Church about transubstantiation:

> Ce qui trompe la plupart des théologiens, c'est qu'ils s'imaginent que les Orientaux conviennent bien plus avec ceux de l'Eglise romaine qu'avec les Protestants dans tout ce qui regarde la matière des sacrements; mais ils se trompent, car, si les Chrétiens du Levant reconnaissent sept sacrements, ce n'est pas à la façon des nouveaux théologiens de Rome, qui prétendent qu'ils sont tous également sacrements et fondés sur la parole de Dieu.

---

9   For Simon's interaction with Spinoza, consult: Woodbridge J., "Richard Simon's Reaction to Spinoza's *Tractatus Theologico Politicus*", in Gründer K. – Schmidt Biggemann W. (eds.), *Spinoza in der Frühzeit seiner religiösen Wirkung* (Heidelberg: 1984) 201–226.

> What misleads most theologians is that they imagine that Eastern Christians agree more with those of the Roman Church than with the Protestants regarding all that has to do with the sacraments; but they are mistaken, for if the Christians of the East recognize seven sacraments, it is not in the same way as the new theologians of Rome who assert the sacraments are all equally sacraments and founded upon the word of God.[10]

Once again, Simon criticized sharply the scholarship of the Jansenists:

> Monsieur Arnauld est encore, à mon avis, plus blâmable en cela que Baronius; et il y a lieu d'être surprise que ce docteur ait entrepris d'écrire de gros volumes touchant la créance des Eglises du Levant, sans avoir la connaissance des langues orientales.
>
> Monseiur Arnauld is again, in my opinion, more blameable in that than Baronius; there is reason to be surprised that this doctor undertook to write large volumes concerning the beliefs of the Churches of the East without having knowledge of oriental languages.[11]

The pastors of Charenton apparently hoped to pass off the *Brerewood Additions* as a 'Huguenot' response to the latest volume of the Jansenists' 'Grande' *Perpetuité* ... Madame de Varennes, a Protestant printer in Paris, began taking steps to publish the work.

Knowing that Simon's own translation of portions of the Bible was available to them, the pastors of Charenton asked the theologians of Geneva if they would join with them in creating a joint Bible project. They informed the Genevans that a talented though unnamed scholar [Simon] was prepared to help with the joint project, provided appropriate monies were forthcoming. In responding to this proposal, the Genevan theologian Louis Tronchin indicated that the Genevans would accept this offer 'as much owing to the utility of the work as well as to bond together even more tightly our union with the churches of France.'[12] The Bible project, then, was perceived as potentially fostering greater unity between the French Protestants and the Genevan Protestants at a critical juncture when the French Protestants were in perilous straits. But the Genevans wanted to know what plan would be pursued in the creation of

---

10 Simon, *Additions aux Recherches curieuses sur la diversité des langues et religions d'Edward Brerewood*, ed. J. Le Brun – J. Woodbridge (Paris, 1983), 46.
11 Ibid., 61.
12 Ibid., 23.

the new version before they would provide the monies to purchase the manuscript. Regarding the anonymous scholar, the Genevan Tronchin wrote:

> Avant que de conseiller l'achat de la Bible de celui qui s'est occupé l'espace de dix ans à cette correction, il serait nécessaire d'en voir une feuille ou deux des endroits les plus considérables pour juger du mérite de son travail. Et si l'on est persuadé de l'utilité de cette correction, on conduira les libraires de Genève à payer ce qu'il faudra à l'Auteur; et l'on traitera avec eux pour l'impression de la correction que l'on désire de faire.

> Before advising the purchase of the Bible from the person who spent ten years regarding this correction, it would be necessary to see a page or two of the more considerable passages in order to judge the merit of his work. And if one is persuaded of the utility of this correction, one will have the book dealers [*libraires*] of Geneva pay what is necessary to the author; and it will be arranged with the book dealers to print the correction one desires to make.[13]

As requested, Simon provided the Genevans with samples of his work, a chapter of Job and a chapter of Proverbs. Jean Le Clerc, the Remonstrant man of letters, later claimed that the Genevans rejected these samples. In fact, they retorted that the author of the samples had plagiarized them from Samuel Bochart, a Reformed theologian.

Towards the very end of the year 1676, the Genevans sent their own plans for a translation of the Bible to the Parisian pastors. A number of Genevans would translate the Bible and use with care notes from the Diodati version as well as from the Desmaret version. The French pastors would have only a consultative role in this translation process. The Genevans sent samples of a translation by Michel Turretini, one of their theologians, to the French pastors for their assessment. Henri Justel gave these samples regarding Genesis 3 and II Corinthians 7 to Simon. The Oratorian quickly drew up an evaluation in which he severely criticized the quality of Turretini's work.

On January 15, 1677, Fremont d'Ablancourt wrote to Micheli, a Genevan, about the judgment of 'Notre Docteur' [Simon's name still not noted]: 'Regarding the sample of your project, I have just learned that one has sent to you the critique that M. Justel and I have had made by one of the most skillful men [Simon] that we have here.' Then on February 1, 1677, Jean Daille, representing the pastors of Charenton, wrote to François Turrettini in Geneva:

---

13   Genève, BUP, Archives Tronchin 38, fol. 146.

> Je ne sais s'ils seront satisfaits des mémoires qu'on leur a envoyés, non pas tant sur l'essai, que M. Widerhold nous a fait voir, que sur le général du dessein de la nouvelle edition. Mais à moins que de cela, vous jugez bien, Monsieur, qu'ils ne doivent pas s'attendre qu'on leur fournisse rien de ce côté-ci.
>
> I do not know if they [the Genevans] will be any more satisfied by the memoirs that were sent to them regarding the essay that M. Widerhold had us look at, as regarding the general plan for the new edition. But less than that, you will judge well, Monsieur, that they should not expect that one will furnish anything from this side.[14]

The Parisian pastors apparently believed they held the upper hand in negotiations with the Genevans. The Parisian Protestant pastors could now proceed with their own project following Simon's guidelines and using his translation because Widerhold, the printer, during a stay in Paris, had become convinced of the superiority of their project over that of the Genevans. Moreover, Widerhold had apparently convinced Olivier Fatio, the wealthy Genevan who was to fund the project, to support the Charenton Bible project.

The hopes of the pastors of Charenton, however, were soon dashed. By April 1677 the Genevans learned that the unnamed scholar helping the pastors of Charenton was a Roman Catholic. The Genevan theologians informed Olivier Fatio, the wealthy financial backer, of this astounding fact. He immediately abandoned the Charenton Bible project. Simon later wrote about this startling turn-about: 'But those of Geneva survived this affair; they represented to [the person] who was the master of the monies that their brothers of Charenton had become Papists.'[15] Any further co-operation with the pastors of Charenton on a joint-Bible project based on purchasing a 'Bible' from an unknown scholar was simply out of the question. Now the scholar's Roman Catholic religion was revealed. No monies would be forthcoming to pay for the purchase of a translation of a Bible with notes from Simon, a 'papist.' Likewise, no greater union between French and Swiss Protestants would be fostered due to their joint project.

When news of the collapse of the project reached Simon, the priest felt obliged to rush to Madame Varennes' printing house to retrieve the Brerewood Additions. After all, his manuscript was larded with pro-Protestant sentiments. Madame de Varennes returned the original manuscript copy of the work to

---

14   BPU Genève, ms. fr. 486, fol. 270.
15   Simon Richard, *Lettres choisies, vol. 3, Supplément* (Amsterdam, Pierre Mortier: 1730) 287.

Simon. What she did not tell him, was this: without his permission, she had another copy of the manuscript made. This copy came into the possession of the Reformed pastor, Jacques Basnage.

For his part, Simon excised the pro-Protestant sentiments from the *Brerewood Additions* and used portions of the text in his *Histoire critique de la créance et des coutumes des nations du Levant* (1684) and in other works including the *Histoire critique du Vieux Testament*. After the Revocation of the Edict of Nantes (1685) Bayle complained that Simon, like an 'enraged dog', also attacked the French Protestants in print.

Jacques Basnage, now a Reformed pastor in exile, found Simon's public criticism of the Huguenots rude and unbelievably hypocritical. He compared his copy of the *Brerewood Additions* with Simon's new publications that were in part based on that manuscript. Basnage wrote that this comparison had revealed 'multiple omissions, multiple changes, even many parts obliterated.' Basnage continued, 'I saw this with my own eyes.'[16] Basnage wanted the Republic of Letters to know that Simon, an arch critic of the Huguenots in 1685, had earlier expressed and defended pro-Protestant sentiments.

As for the Genevan Bible, it was eventually published. On November 26, 1678, Pierre Bayle wrote about the circumstances of its publication:

> Mrs de Geneve se sont determinez à faire imprimer leur Bible sans avoir regard au travail de Mrs de Charenton qui n'a pas encore passé le Pentateuque, de sorte que la presse roule dessus, ils n'ont pas voulu laisser echapper la belle disposition où se trouvoit un bon marchand de leur ville nommé Mr Fatio, d'avancer 15 m[ille] livres pour les frais de l'impression.

> Messieurs of Geneva are determined to have their Bible printed without regard to the work of the Messieurs de Charenton, which has not yet gotten beyond the Pentateuch, and the press is now rolling; they did not want to miss out on the good disposition of a well-to-do merchant of their city, named M. Fatio, to advance fifteen thousand livres for the cost of the printing.[17]

---

16   Basnage Jacques, *Divi Chrysostomi Epistola ad Caesarium monacham juxta Exemplar C. L.V. Emerici Bigot* (Utrecht, Acher: 1687) 203.

17   Geneva, Archives d'Etat, Compagnie des Pasteurs, R 13, fol. 698, printed in: Labrousse Elizabeth, McKenna Antony, Bergon Laurence, Bost Hubert, Bunge Wiep van, and James Edward (eds.), *Correspondance de Pierre Bayle*, vol. iii (Oxford, 2004), no. 160, p. 94.

But what was the fate of the Charenton Bible project? It never saw the light of day. The Protestant pastors of Charenton did not apparently have the ability, the money or the time necessary to complete the translation work. After the revocation of the Edict of Nantesin 1685, the participants in the project felt obliged to leave France.

2 Bossuet's Charge that the Alleged 'Perfect Neutrality' of Simon's Translation and Notes of the Bible Sowed 'Indifference of Religions'

In 1704, Bossuet once again went on the attack against Richard Simon. He had earlier condemned Simon's *Histoire critique du Vieux Testament* in 1678 and more recently the priest's *Nouveau Testament de Trévoux* in 1702.[18] Now he excoriated Simon's involvement once again in the Charenton Bible project. In many regards, Bossuet's criticisms of 1704 were not new. They echoed Jean Le Clerc's claims and those of a number of Roman Catholic clerics. Not only did Bossuet score Simon's alleged willingness to sell himself as a mercenary pen, he was disturbed by the alleged 'perfect neutrality' of the Oratorian's guidelines for Bible translation and notes.

According to Bossuet, Simon's guidelines promoted religious indifference; Bossuet's assessment dripped with sarcasm.

> Voilà sans doute un beau projet pour un Prêtre Catholique: c'est de faire une Bible propre à contenter tous les partis, c'est-à-dire, à entretenir l'indifférence des Religions, & qui dans nos controverses ne décide rien, ni pour ni contre la Vérité: le plan & le modèle d'un si bel ouvrage est donné par M. Simon, & le travail est partagé avec un Ministre. Au reste, on eût fait des Notes: sans notes M. Simon convient encore aujourd'hui qu'on ne peut traduire la Bible, & il eût été curieux de voir, comme on eût gardé dans ces Notes la parfait neutralité, qu'on avoit promise entre l'Eglise & l'Hérésie, entre Jesus-Christ & Bélial. [...] c'est ce que M. Simon désavoue, & il soutient qu'on ne parla jamais des douze mille livres: Car aussi, comment avouer qu'il ait vendu aux Protestants sa plume mercenaire? Mais cependant ce qu'il avoue, n'est guère meilleur. Il raconte quelque démêlé entre Genève & Charenton: Le plus fort de leur dispute, dit-il, rouloit sur un fond de soixante mille livres, qu'un bon Suisse avoit destine à cet Ouvrage; &, continue-t-il, il se peut bien faire, que si ces Messieurs

---

[18] Woodbridge J., "Censure Royale et Censure episcopale: le confit de 1702", *Dix-huitième siècle* 8 (1976) 333–355.

de Charenton en étoient devenus les Maîtres, ils auroient reconnu les bons services que le Prieur de Bolleville (c'est un des noms de M. Simon) leur auroient rendu pour attire ce fonds à Paris. Voilà donc ce Prieur de Bolleville devenu arbitre & médiateur entre Charenton & Genève, & leur homme de confiance: il favorisoit ceux de Charenton dans le dessein qu'ils avoient de s'attirer les soixante mille livres, & il espéroit partager le butin avec eux. Ne disons rien davantage, déplorons l'aveuglement de celui, qui semble ne sentir pas la honte d'un tel marché, & déplorons en même temps la nécessité où nous sommes de faire conoître un Auteur, qui voudroit être l'interprète de l'Eglise catholique, après s'être livré aux Protestants, pour mériter auprès d'eux cette qualité.

Voila without doubt a beautiful project for a catholic priest: it is to make a Bible designed to please all parties, that is to say, to uphold the indifference of religions, and that in our controversies decide nothing, neither for or against the truth. It has been curious to see how one guarded in these notes the 'perfect neutrality' which one promised between the church and heresy, between Jesus Christ and Belial [...] Monsieur Simon maintains that one never spoke about 12,000 livres: for how could he confess he had sold his mercenary pen to the Protestants. But, however, what he does confess is scarcely better. Voila, then, the prior of Bolleville [Simon] become the arbiter and mediator between Charenton and Geneva, and their man of confidence; he favoured those of Charenton in the plan they had to attract sixty thousand livres, and he hoped to share the booty with them. Let us not say more; let us deplore the blinding of him who does not seem to feel the shame of such bargaining.[19]

From Bossuet's point of view, the 'ecumenical' character of the Charenton project was due to Simon's reliance upon a method of 'perfect neutrality' as a means to placate both 'heretics' and Roman Catholics. The priest espoused this method, allegedly stimulated by mercenary motivations. Bossuet wanted to warn other Roman Catholics that Simon was a 'suspect' priest.

Earlier, in 1699, Jean Martianay had made similar charges in his *Défense de la Bible de S. Jerome contre la critique de M. Simon ci devant prestre de l'Oratoire*

---

19   Bossuet Jacques Benigne, *Instructions sur la version du Nouveau Testament imprimé a Trevoux en l'année M. DCC. II. Avec une ordonnance publiée à Meaux* (Paris, Anisson: 1702), 274–7.

(pp. 67–68–109).[20] The monks for whom Martianay said he spoke believed Simon had engaged in creating a Bible that was neither Roman Catholic, nor Calvinist and this kind of Bible could promote 'the indifference of religions'. From the monks' point of view, such a project 'was unworthy of a Catholic priest'.

These charges appear nearly identical to those made later by Bossuet. In fact, the charges and Simon's response to them may have stimulated Bossuet to launch his own vitriolic verbal assault against Simon in 1704. The very same year Bossuet died.

3 Simon's Defense of 'Perfect Neutrality' As a Worthy Scholarly Trait

In 1699, Simon responded to Martianay's accusations by writing several lengthy letters to a Monsieur Hamel. In these letters the priest defended his engagement with the pastors of Charenton and his concept of 'perfect neutrality'. He also explained his rationale for proposing the kinds of guidelines for Bible translation he had advocated. Simon boldly proclaimed that he could not be anything less than an orthodox Roman Catholic because none other than Bossuet in the mid-1680s had approved his involvement in the Charenton Bible project. Simon wrote:

> Loin d'en être scandalisé, il témoigna approuver ma réponse, parce qu'il paroissoit manifestement que je n'avois eû d'autre dessein que de rendre service à l'Eglise, & d'empêcher que ceux de Geneve ne publiassent une Bible pleine de fausses notes, dont ils avoient ennvoïé la premiere feüille imprimée à leurs freres de Paris avec leurs projet. Ce qui causa de la division entr'eux, parce que ceux-ci ne pûrent approuver le projet de ceux de Geneve.
>
> Far from being scandalized, he (Bossuet) evidenced approval of my response, because it seemed clear that I had no other goal than to render service to the Church and to stop those of Geneva from publishing a Bible full of false notes […] they had sent the first printed page to their brothers

---

20 Printed in Martianay Jean, *Réponse aux difficultez qu'on a faites contre le Traité de la Verité & de la Connoissance de Livres de la Sainte Ecriture. Avec La défense de la Bible de Saint Jerôme, contre la Critique de Mr Simon, ci-devant Prestre de l'Oratoire* (Paris, Pierre Witte, 1703).

in Paris with their project. This caused a division among them, because those (in Paris) were not able to approve the project of those in Geneva.[21]

Simon claimed this his valiant efforts had been intended to prevent the pastors from Charenton from creating a Bible that would have been filled with interpretations contrary to the teachings of the Roman Catholic Church. In doing this, he proposed that the Charenton Bible project would have been 'very orthodox and very favourable to the Catholic Religion'.[22] He averred:

> Vous remarquez que cette Bible auroit été également utile aux Catholiques & aux Protestans, parce qu'on en bannissoit toutes les fausses notes qui ne servent qu'à rendre ceux-ci opiniâtres dans leur Religion, & à éloigner les Catholiques de la lecture de ces sortes de Versions. C'étoit avoir gagné beaucoup sur l'esprit des Ministres de Charenton, que d'obtenir d'eux, qu'on ôteroit de leur Bible un grand nombre de remarques contraires à la Religion Catholique, & de leur avoir fait goûter un projet qui étoit entierement à l'avantage des Catholiques.
>
> You will observe that this Bible would have been equally useful to Catholics and to Protestants because one banished all false notes from it which would have only made them [the Protestants] obstinate in their religion and distanced Catholics from the reading of these kinds of versions. It was to have gained much influence over the Ministers of Charenton, to have obtained from them that one would remove from their Bible a great number of remarks contrary to the Catholic religion and to have had them appreciate a project which was entirely oriented towards the advantage of Catholics.[23]

Simon likewise proposed that Roman Catholic exegetes were not indemnified from introducing their own theological prejudices into their notes for Bibles. For example, he cited his old foes, the Messieurs de Port-Royal [the Jansenists], as those who included notes in their version of the New Testament to justify their particular theological sentiments.[24] Simon argued that his guidelines for translation would have created a Bible acceptable to both Protestants and

---

21 Simon, *Lettres choisies* Lettre 2, 240.
22 Ibid., 241.
23 Ibid. 270.
24 Ibid., 248.

Catholics without it encompassing anything contrary to Roman Catholic orthodoxy. Moreover, the priest observed:

> On y auroit évité avec soin toutes les partialitez qui viennent des Traducteurs & des faiseurs de notes, lesquels interpretent l'Ecriture plûtôt par raport à leurs préjugez, que par raport aux termes du texte sacré: ce qui entretient de perpetuelles disputes dans l'Eglise & dans l'Etat. Il ne s'agit pas de décider en controversiste, mais de bien décider & conformément à la signification propre des mots qui sont dans l'Ecriture.

> [...] one would have avoided with care all the partialities which come from translators and makers of notes who interpret Scripture more in accord with their prejudices than in accord with the terms of the Holy text: this introduces perpetual disputes into the Church and into States. The point is not to decide matters as a controversialist, but to decide well and in conformity with the proper meaning of the words which are in Scripture.[25]

By stipulating that a translator and commentator on Scripture should let the words of Scripture determine their meanings rather than the translator's or commentator's theological presuppositions, Simon had proposed guidelines for the translation and commenting on the Bible that may have resulted in a more 'neutral' understanding of Scriptural texts. But the premise that the translator or commentator should not allow personal theological convictions to influence the understanding of the actual meaning of the words of the text was genuinely offensive to many of Simon's contemporaries. The translations and notes of many Protestant and Roman Catholic Bibles of the day seemed designed to agree with or bolster the beliefs of the respective religious communities from which they were issued.

The task of assessing Simon's application of his own principles in the translation and commenting upon the Pentateuch is facilitated by a letter dated 1699 in which the priest characterized the way his translation efforts would have advanced if the Charenton Bible Project had been allowed to come to fruition. The letter is addressed to Monsieur 'H' [Hamel] and is prefaced with this description: '[...] one exposes the nature of the notes which would have entered into the French Bible, about which one reported the project in the preceding letter.'[26]

---

25 Ibid., 247–248.
26 Simon, *Lettres choisies* Lettre 3, 252.

Simon explained why he was willing to provide examples of what his 'perfect neutrality' would have signified in the Charenton Bible project: 'Because your friends wished to know how I would have guarded in my Notes the perfect neutrality which I proposed in my project, I wish to satisfy them [...]'[27]

For the priest, 'perfect neutrality' signified seeking the natural meaning of the words of Scripture without reference to a party spirit or theological prejudices. In his mind this approach was associated with a sincere quest for 'truth'. Moreover, when he encountered Hebrew words with equivocal meanings, he was determined to provide his readers with notes that indicated the range of possible meanings for the words. Simon claimed that his guidelines did not have sceptical entailments for Roman Catholics. The latter could refer to Catholic traditions to give necessary guidance in seeking to understand the 'unclear' passages. Simon did admit, however, that a translator of Scripture could never affirm that he had created a 'perfect translation' of the Bible. Too many factors complicated the task of translation to allow such an affirmation.

Simon claimed that his translation and note on Genesis 1: 1, for example, proffered a clear model of what he understood 'perfect neutrality' to represent. In his notes he indicated that the verse should not be cited as a warrant for the doctrine of the Trinity. The verse did not philologically sustain the Trinitarian teaching as Christians with vested interests were inclined to argue. They would have to look to other passages of Scripture to find warrant for the doctrine.[28]

Interestingly enough, Simon cited the authority of 'notre Vulgate' in his notes on Gen. 1.1. For that matter Simon referenced the authority of Saint Jerome and the Vulgate in numerous other notes of the Pentateuch manuscript. How these references comport with the priest's announced quest to translate and comment with 'perfect neutrality' remains a puzzling enigma. Did not these appeals to the authority of the Vulgate compromise his program? Was he possibly attempting to shield himself from aggressive Roman Catholic critics?

Simon specifically responded to Bossuet's charge that his 'perfect neutrality' could sow anything other than 'indifference of religions.' He denied Bossuet's accusation that he had taken theological stances equidistant between Protestant heretics and Roman Catholics:

> Voilà à-peu-près le plan des Notes qui auroient entré dans la Bible Françoise dont i lest question. Jugez maintenant, si l'on peut dire que ces Notes garderoient une parfait neutralité entre les Heretiques & les Catholiques; ou si l'on ne doit pas plûtôt dire, que cette neutralité ne tend

---

27   Ibid.
28   Ibid., 283.

qu'à ne pas donner pour certain ce qui ne l'est pas, & qu'à marquer l'equivoque des mots Hebreaux, lors qu'ils sont en effet équivoques.

Voila more or less the plan of the Notes which would have been in the French Bible [...] Judge now, if one is able to say that these Notes keep a perfect neutrality between Heretics and Catholics; or if one ought rather to say, that this neutrality only tends not to give for certain that which is not so and that it marks that which is equivocal in Hebrew words when they are in effect equivocal.[29]

4 Conclusions

The teasing out of the sinuous relations between the Oratorian priest Richard Simon and Pastor Claude and other Huguenot ministers in the Charenton Bible project helps us to understand better the reasons the project took on its interconfessional traits. That Simon associated his principles of biblical criticism with an advocacy of 'perfect neutrality' in translation and making notes on the biblical texts is an intriguing aspect of the story of the Charenton Bible project. Simon may have underestimated just how controversial his elusive program of working towards 'perfect neutrality' could be for Confessional Christians. In the *Brerewood Additions* Simon described the ideal scholar as an 'honest man' who was judicious, 'free from prejudices', 'enlightened' and a searcher after truth.[30] Professor Le Brun has suggested that Simon's advocacy of these traits may stem from his attraction to diffused forms of Cartesian thought.

By no means did Richard Simon act like a shrinking violet when it came to extolling his own abilities and worth. Simon possessed the self-confidence (some might say hubris) to propose that his quest for 'perfect neutrality' contributed to making him the first scholar in Christian history to engage in creating a 'veritable' (his term) translation of the Bible. After all, from his point of view, he was the first scholar in Christendom's history to understand fully the principles of Bible translation and how to draft notes designed to explain the meaning of Scriptural texts. Simon also assured his readers that he was the first savant to apply the French word critique to the study of the Bible. For him, criticism encompassed among other things the art of judging texts and discerning what within them was authentic.

---

29 Ibid., 284.
30 Simon, *Additions*, Préface, 47.

Often hailed as the 'Father of Modem Biblical Criticism' (competing with Spinoza for this title), Richard Simon participated in a series of heated controversies that agitated what Paul Hazard so famously called, 'The Crisis of the European Mind' (1680–1715). He sparred not only with Bossuet, a persistent critic, but with Jean Le Clerc and a host of other scholars. Quite simply, Simon possessed a genuine knack for making enemies.

The story of Richard Simon's involvement in the Charenton Bible project, an inter-confessional enterprise with French Huguenot pastors, creates the context in which several facets of the priest's innovative program of biblical criticism emerged. The story, then, encompasses more than a poignant tale of the collapse of a surprising 'ecumenical' venture-surprising due to the rank hatred and suspicions that Huguenots and Roman Catholics on occasion exhibited towards each other in Louis XIV's France. The story of the Charenton Bible project also constitutes a neglected chapter of considerable import for our understanding of the origins of what becomes known as higher biblical criticism.

Bibliography

Auvray P., *Etude bio-bibliographique avec des textes inédits* (Paris: 1974).

Basnage Jacques, *Divi Chrysostomi Epistola ad Caesarium monacham juxta Exemplar C. L.V. Emerici Bigot* (Utrecht, Acher: 1687).

Bernus A., *Richard Simon et son histoire critique du Vieux Testament* (Geneva: 1969).

Bossuet J. B., *Instructions sur la version du Nouveau Testament imprimé a Trevoux en l'année M. DCC. II. Avec une ordonnance publiée à Meaux* (Paris, Anisson: 1702).

Brun J. Le – Simon S., *Supplément au Dictionnaire de la Bible XII* (Paris: 1996).

Chédozeau B., "Les grandes étapes de la publication de la Bible catholique en français du concile de Trente au XVIIIe siècle", in Armogathe J.-R. (ed.), *Le Grande Siècle et la Bible, Bible de tous les temps* (Paris: 1989) 341–360.

Labrousse E., *La Révocation de l'Edit de Nantes* (Geneva: 1985).

Margival H., *Essai sur Richard Simon et la critique au XVIIe siècle* (Geneva: 1970).

Martianay J., *Réponse aux difficultez qu'on a faites contre le Traité de la Verité & de la Connoissance de Livres de la Sainte Ecriture. Avec La défense de la Bible de Saint Jerôme, contre la Critique de Mr Simon, ci-devant Prestre de l'Oratoire* (Paris, Pierre Witte, 1703).

Simon Richard, *Lettres choisies, vol. 3, Supplèment* (Amsterdam, Pierre Mortier: 1730).

Simon Richard, *Additions aux Recherches curieuses sur la diversité des langues et religions d'Edward Brerewood*, ed. J. Le Brun – J. Woodbridge (Paris: 1983).

Steinman J., *Richard Simon et les origines d'exégèse biblique* (Paris: 1960).

Wolf J.B., *Louis XIV* (New York: 1968).

Woodbridge J., "Censure Royale et Censure episcopale: le confit de 1702", *Dix-huitième siècle* 8 (1976) 333–355.

Woodbridge J., "Richard Simon's Reaction to Spinoza's Tractatus Theologico Politicus", in Gründer K. – Schmidt Biggemann W. (eds.), *Spinoza in der Frühzeit seiner religiösen Wirkung* (Heidelberg: 1984) 201–226.

Woodbridge J., "La 'grande chasse aux manuscrits,' la controverse eucharistique, et Richard Simon", in Elyade O. – Brun J. Le (eds.), *Conflits Politiques, Controverses Religieux, Essais d'histoire européenne aux XVIe–XVIIIe siècles* (Paris: 2002) 143–176.

CHAPTER 9

The Devil in the Details: The Case of Hermann Samuel Reimarus (1694–1768)

Ulrich Groetsch

In 1720 during his *peregrinatio academica* through Holland and on his way to Oxford, a young university graduate from Wittenberg visited the famous Geneva-born, Arminian theologian Jean Le Clerc (1657–1736),[1] who was living in self-imposed exile in Amsterdam. Next to Pierre Bayle, Le Clerc was one of the foremost scholars of his time. Although his excellent critical skills were widely acknowledged and his works were discussed in classrooms and lecture halls beyond the confines of European academia – his *Ars Critica* (first published in 1697) remained a standard text for students at Harvard Divinity School well into the nineteenth century – Le Clerc had fallen into disrepute among orthodox theologians already early in his career.[2] The accusations were almost always the same: Le Clerc does not recognize the sacred and exceptional status of the Hebrew language;[3] he is an inveterate admirer of Louis Cappel and Hugo Grotius and follows their claim that the sacred text was faulty and corrupted;[4] he is a judaizer, because he asserts that the pronouncements of the Prophets need to be understood in their own context

---

[1] On Jean Le Clerc in general see; Barnes A., *Jean Le Clerc (1657–1736) et la République des Lettres* (Paris: 1938); Golden S., *Jean Le Clerc* (New York : 1972); Brun J. Le, "Jean Le Clerc", in Schobinger J.-P. (ed.), *Die Philosophie des 17. Jahrhunderts* (*Grundriss der Geschichte der Philosophie*), vol. 2 (Basel: 1993) 1018–1024; Pitassi M.C., *Entre croire et savoir: le problème de la méthode chez Jean Le Clerc* (Leiden: 1987); more specifically Reventlow H. Graf, "Bibelexegese als Aufklärung. Die Bibel im Denken des Johannes Clericus (1657–1736)", in Reventlow H. Graf et al. (eds.), *Historische Kritik und biblischer Kanon in der deutschen Aufklärung* (Wiesbaden: 1988) 1–19.

[2] Even Pierre Bayle, himself not particularly afraid of confronting religious orthodoxy, voiced his concerns about some of Le Clerc's views. In a letter to the Calvinist minister Jacques Lenfant (1661–1728), Bayle writes: 'Mr. Le Clerc vient de faire un Livre contre Mr. Simon. Il y a de bonnes choses mais trop hardies […].' Quoted in Pitassi, *Entre croire et savoir* 19.

[3] Einem Johann Justus von, *Selectae Animadversiones ad Johannis Clerici Scripta* … (Magdeburg, Johann Siegler: 1735) 85: […] minus praeclare de lingua Ebraea sentit.

[4] Ibid. 88: […] familiare ipsi est, cum Capello & Grotio, cujus perpetuus est admirator, ut sana etiam ac integra scripturae loca corrupta & vitiata esse, sine ulla necessitate adferat.

rather than as references to a future Messiah;[5] and he values profane authors over sacred ones and employs them maliciously against the Holy Books rather than use them sparingly, as maidservants instead of overlords of the biblical θεόπνευστοι, the divinely inspired scribes.[6]

Our young graduate does not seem to have given such charges much thought, because his recollections of the meeting indicate that Le Clerc's unorthodox practices caught him still off-guard:

> [Le Clerc] judges and criticizes all people very freely. To me, it seemed a little bit profane when he claimed that he examined the Bible just as if he was reading Aristophanes. He is currently working on a commentary on the Prophets and on the book of Job.[7]

Such utterances may come as a surprise to us, once we reveal the identity of our young graduate: it was Hermann Samuel Reimarus (1694–1768)[8] of Hamburg, one of the most notorious biblical critics of his time, whose devastating attack on revelation had theological circles up in arms – the Richard Dawkins of his age, so to speak. But the young student who met the famous man of letters from Amsterdam was still a far cry from his later self. At Wittenberg, Reimarus's *alma mater*, the spirit of Abraham Calov (1612–1686), the archdeacon of Lutheran orthodoxy and Hugo Grotius's nemesis, was still haunting the corridors and even Reimarus's mentor in Hamburg, the Hebraist Johann Christoph

---

5 Ibid. 97f.: Nihilo minus Clericus *judaizat*, animi pendet, dubiusque hinc inde vacillat, nescius, in quam se potissimum partem interdum vertat [...] in V.T. non tantum esse vaticinia, quorum verba pertinent duntaxat ad res sub Messia futuras, sed & alterum genus vaticinorum, quae ita concepta sunt, ut respiciant quidem, si series orationis spectetur, res ante Messiam impletas [...].

6 Ibid. 100: Immo interdum plus profanis auctoribus, cumprimis historicis, plus auctoritatis tribuit, quam divinis, illosque male in S.S. usurpat. Cautela vero haec semper observanda est: textus sacer non est emendandus secundum relationem scriptorum profanorum; sed hi ubi discrepant, sunt corrigendi secundum scriptores sacros, quia hi sunt θεόπνευστοι, atque ita majorem fidem merentur, quam illi.

7 See Staats- und Universitätsbibliothek Hamburg Carl von Ossietzky (StUBH), *Reimarus Nachlaß* III b 4, "Tagebuch Notizen aus Holland": '[...] [Le Clerc] judicirt und critisirt sehr frei über alle Leute. Es schiene mir ein wenig profan, das er sagte, er critisirte die Bibel nicht anders, als ob er den Aristophanes vor sich hatte. Er schreibt jetzo einen Commentar über die Propheten und den Hiob.'

8 On Reimarus see Groetsch U., *Hermann Samuel Reimarus (1694–1768): Classicist, Hebraist, Enlightenment Radical in Disguise* (Leiden: 2015); Mulsow M., (ed.), *Between Philology and Radical Enlightenment: Hermann Samuel Reimarus (1694–1768)* (Leiden: 2011); see also Klein D., *Hermann Samuel Reimarus (1694–1768): Das theologische Werk* (Tübingen: 2009).

Wolf (1683–1739),[9] expressed subtle criticism of Le Clerc's *Ars Critica*,[10] which the latter countered with an overly harsh review of the second volume of Wolf's *Bibliotheca Hebraea*.[11] Both at Jena and Wittenberg – if not even already at the *Gymnasium Illustre* in Hamburg[12]–Reimarus had received thorough instruction in the principles of *hermeneutica sacra*,[13] which the Lutheran theologian Johann Jacob Rambach, likewise a graduate of Jena, would later codify in his *Institutiones Hermeneuticae Sacrae*,[14] a much-cherished manual of Lutheran orthodoxy. According to Rambach, the sacred style could not 'be expounded with the works of Aeschylus, Pindar, Terence, Cicero, Seneca [...] as Jean Le

---

9   On Wolf see Mulsow M., "Johann Christoph Wolf (1683–1739) und die verbotenen Bücher in Hamburg", in Steiger J.A. (ed.), *500 Jahre Theologie in Hamburg: Hamburg als Zentrum christlicher Theologie und Kultur zwischen Tradition und Zukunft* (New York: 2005) 81–111; also idem, "Mikrogramme des Orients. Johann Christoph Wolfs Notizhefte und seine Cudworth-Lektüre", in Thouard D. – Vollhardt F. – Mariani Zini F. (eds.), *Philologie als Wissensmodell* (Berlin: 2010) 345–396.

10 Wolf Johann Christoph, *Bibliotheca Hebraea, vol. 2* (Hamburg, Felginer: 1721) 263: Io. Clericus, Prof. Theologus Arminianorum Amsteldamensis, variis libris hoc argumentum, quamvis non ubique aeque recte feliciterque illustravit [...].

11 For Le Clerc's review of Wolf's *Bibliotheca Hebraea, vol. 2*, see *Bibliotheque Ancienne et Moderne* 16 (1721) 332–365, esp. 339, where Le Clerc writes: Mr. Wolf trouve qu'à cet égard, je n'ai pas également réüssi par tout, *non aeque recte feliciterque*. Personne ne le fait mieux, que moi-même; mais si j'avois suivi les idées de nôtre Auteur en tout, ou en partie; je craindrois, qu'une autre forte de gens ne fissent le mêma jugement de ce que j'aurois écrit.

12 Shortly after arriving at the University of Jena, Reimarus wrote a detailed letter to his mentor Johann Christoph Wolf, informing him about his progress. Both Salomon Glassius and August Pfeiffer are among the authors Reimarus specifically refers to: Hinc et factum est, ut ex quo Hamburgum reliqui, eadem non intermisserim, nec de manibus unque deposuerim, siquidem integrum hunc annum vel in perscrutando utriusque foederis instrumento, vel in iis ipsis Auctoribus, qui Critices praecepta tradiderunt, Glassio, Pfeiffero, Hottingero aliisque perlegendis, vel in excolendo Rabbinismi notitia consumsi, et mox etiam Chaldaica atque Syriaca aggredi paro. Letter Reimarus to Johann Christoph Wolf, 23 March 1715, StUBH, Supellex 119, fol. 424r.

13 On the subject see Steiger J.A., *Philologia Sacra* (Neukirchen-Vluyn: 2011).

14 Rambach Johann Jacob, *Institutiones Hermeneuticae Sacrae* (Jena, Hartung: 1725). See also Herbers P., *Die hermeneutische Lehre Johann Jakob Rambachs*, Ph.D. dissertation (University of Heidelberg: 1952); on Rambach see in general Bister U. et al. (eds.), *Johann Jacob Rambach: Leben– Briefe – Schriften* (Basel: 1993); also Hug W., *Johann Jacob Rambach (1693–1735): Religionspädagoge zwischen den Zeiten* (Stuttgart: 2003); see also Stemmer P., *Weissagung und Kritik: Eine Studie zur Hermeneutik bei Hermann Samuel Reimarus* (Göttingen: 1983) 46f.; Sträter U., "Rambach, Johann Jakob", *Religion in Geschichte und Gegenwart* 7 (2004[4]) 31f.

Clerc does so preposterously.'[15] Mixing the sacred and the profane could lead to entirely untenable results, especially if profane sources are used to judge the veracity of the sacred text.[16] No matter what, Holy Scripture remained the sole βάσις ἐπιστήμης, 'the sole basis of knowledge', as Johann Gerhard's successor at Jena, the theologian Johann Michael Dilherr (1604–1669) expressed in his treatise *De usu lectionis scriptorum secularium et antiquitatis* (On the use of reading profane writers and of antiquarian knowledge).[17] A commentator was also no polyhistor[18] and should by all means avoid trying to be one.[19] Truth comes first of all from within Scripture and cannot be brought to it from outside. A *philosophia moralis*, a *scientia rerum naturalium, mathematicarum disciplinarum sive physicarum*, and *scientia medicinae* may only serve to disprove factual misconceptions, but these disciplines should not be used to destroy the truth of miracles or to dismiss the supernatural just because they lack the means to explain them.[20] These were roughly the principles that were preached from the pulpits in university lecture halls at Jena, Wittenberg, Helmstedt, Greifswald, or Halle and that had been hammered into Reimarus's mind when he was still a student himself.

But why was it necessary to hammer these principles into students' heads? What was it that put fear into young students' hearts once they saw that Le Clerc had quoted the Greek comedian Aristophanes in his Bible commentaries? We may just as well call the spectre by its name: secularization. If the Bible was profanized, if its status as sacred text was no longer preserved in its entire

---

15   Rambach, *Institutiones Hermeneuticae Sacrae* 285: Phrasis sacra, *legem cordi inscribere* EX AESCHYLI, PINDARI, TERENTII, CICERONIS, SENECAE monumentis exponi non potest, ut praepostere facit IO. CLERICUS [...].

16   Rambach, *Institutiones Hermeneuticae Sacrae* 284: Deinde observandum [...] *parallelismum profanorum auctorum* non semper esse tutum adminiculum, veram vocis significationem definiendi. Quo pertinet quando [...] CLERICUS, malae caussae patrocinaturus, in *art. Crit. Part. II. Sect. I. cap. VII. P. 210.* conquisitis multorum.

17   Brückner, "Dilherr, Johann Michael" *Allgemeine Deutsche Biographie* 5 (1912) 225; Dilherr Johann Michael, *De usu lectionis scriptorum secularium et antiquitatis* (Jena, Steinmann: 1635) 5.

18   On the term, see Mulsow M., "Polyhistorie", in Ueding G. (ed.), *Historisches Wörterbuch der Rhetorik, vol. 6* (Tübingen: 2003) 1521–1526; also Grafton A., "The World of the *Polyhistors*: Humanism and Encyclopedism", *Central European History* 18 (1985) 31–47; Jaumann H., "Was ist ein Polyhistor? Gehversuche auf einem verlassenen Terrain", *Studia Leibnitiana* 22 (1990) 76–89.

19   Rambach Johann Jacob, *Erläuterung über seine eigene Institutiones Hermeneuticae Sacrae* (Giessen: Krieger: 1738) 261: [...] man muß sich hüten, daß man sich nicht verwirre *in tanto adparatu eruditionis humanae*, oder auf die Gedancken komme, es könne niemand die heilige Schrift erklären, der nicht ein vollkommener polyhistor sey [...].

20   Rambach, *Institutiones* 456–498.

purity, then it could be hermeneutically treated like any other text of profane literature. It was then no longer automatically true and meaningful, because it was sacred, but it could as a document of human origins be erroneous and immoral. That was exactly the kind of rift which manifested itself in the tiniest footnotes by scholars such as Le Clerc, the rift of secularization. In the case of Reimarus, his rejection of revelation would ultimately lay the foundations for future research about the historical Jesus. Methodologically, this shift was influenced by the role both antiquarianism and philology assumed in scriptural exegesis. It becomes therefore only evident through a careful examination of the milieu of scholarship and the culture of footnoting, which Anthony Grafton has so lucidly described and which becomes ultimately a key for our understanding of early modern culture in general.[21] Footnotes will then also be guiding us through the work of Reimarus.

When our young Reimarus himself mounted the pulpit as Professor of Oriental languages at the *Gymnasium illlustre* in his native Hamburg in 1727, we can safely assume that he was still under the influence of Lutheran orthodoxy. Aside from teaching Hebrew grammar and Jewish antiquities, he was instructing future students of theology in the principles of a *hermeneutica sacra*.[22] His case, however, is particularly intriguing, because even once he had metamorphosed into an ardent critic of revelation, he kept publicly silent about it. Reimarus, so to speak, remained a closet radical throughout his life. Only the publication of portions of the explosive *Apology or Defense of the Reasonable Worshippers of God* by Lessing between 1774 and 1778 led to his somewhat involuntary posthumous 'coming out'.[23]

This does, however, not mean that we are entirely at the mercy of his disguise. In the preface to his radical *Apology* Reimarus claimed to have secretly worked on his *magnum opus* for about thirty years. This means that sometime during the 1730s he must have started to draft his subversive criticism, which would eventually culminate in his complete rejection of a *hermeneutica sacra* and a *de facto* convergence of the principles of *philologia sacra* and *philologia*

---

21 See, e.g. Grafton A., *Joseph Scaliger: A Study in the History of Classical Scholarship, vol. 1: Textual Criticism and Exegesis* (Oxford: 1983); idem, *Forgers and Critics: Creativity and Duplicity in Western Scholarship* (Princeton: 1990); idem, *The Footnote: A Curious History* (Cambridge, MA: 1999); idem, *Bring out your Dead: The Past as Revelation* (Cambridge, MA: 2001).

22 Reimarus Hermann Samuel, *Handschriftenverzeichnis und Bibliographie*, ed. W. Schmidt-Biggemann (Göttingen: 1979) 28f.

23 Reimarus Hermann Samuel, *Apologie oder Schutzschrift für die vernünftigen Verehrer Gottes*, ed. G. Alexander, 2 vols. (Frankfurt: 1972).

profana.[24] Since an exact dating of this shift is not possible, any of Reimarus's writings of the 1730s seem particularly intriguing.

It is with good reason then that the significance of his commentary on the book of Job has been duly noted,[25] which was anything but a labour of love for Reimarus, but rather a project thrown into his lap by his mentors Wolf and Fabricius.[26] Both his mentors were members of the *Patriotic Society*, a literary circle of writers, scholars, and lawyers. One of their fellow 'Patriots' was the devout and somewhat reclusive merchant-scholar Johann Adolf Hoffmann[27] who shortly before his death in 1731 had embarked on an edifying commentary on the book of Job. The unfinished manuscript must have fallen into Fabricius's hands, who passed it on to his talented son-in-law Reimarus to employ his philological skills and prepare Hoffmann's manuscript for publication. With these narrow perimeters already in place – on the one hand, there was little room for disobedience to his father-in-law or Wolf; on the other hand, his own contribution and creativity were seriously hampered by the preserved manuscript – Reimarus was anything but ecstatic about this work. His barely legible handwritten corrections and additions to the Hoffmann manuscript

---

24 An exact dating of Reimarus's shift from orthodoxy to heterodoxy seems futile. Based on his own account (StA HH, NL Reimarus 622:1, A 14b–in a later draft of his *Apology* Reimarus points out that he had worked on this project for about thirty years – we can assume that it occurred some time during the mid-1730s. See Alexander G., "Einleitung", in Reimarus, *Apologie* I, 23; see also Stemmer, *Weissagung und Kritik* 90f.; somewhat disagreeing with Stemmer is Günter Mühlpfordt in his review of the *Vindicatio dictorum Veteris Testamenti in Novo allegatorum*, Theologische Literaturzeitung 113, 3 (1988) 199–204, 203; see also Hübner H., "Die 'orthodoxe' hermeneutica sacra des Hermann Samuel Reimarus", in Beetz M. – Cacciatore G. (eds.), *Die Hermeneutik im Zeitalter der Aufklärung* (Cologne: 2000) 99–111.

25 Schmidt-Biggemann W., "Erbauliche versus rationale Hermeneutik: Hermann Samuel Reimarus' Bearbeitung von Johann Adolf Hoffmann's 'Neue Erklärung des Buchs Hiob'", in Walter W. (ed.), *Hermann Samuel Reimarus, 1694–1786: Beiträge zur Reimarus-Renaissance in der Gegenwart* (Göttingen: 1998) 23–52; Hoffmann Johann Adolf, *Neue Erklärung des Buchs Hiob, darin das Buch selbst aus der Grund-Sprache mit dem darin liegenden Nachdruck ins Teutsche übersetzet* (Hamburg, Felginer: 1734).

26 In his preface Reimarus admits that he was drawn into this project against his own will: Ich gestehe aber gleich Anfangs offenherzig, daß ich gantz wieder meine Absicht und Vermuthen hinein gezogen bin. See Reimarus Hermann Samuel, "Vorrede", in Hoffmann, *Neue Erklärung des Buchs Hiob* 13*.

27 On Hoffmann see Schröder H., "Hoffmann, Johann Adolf", in *Lexikon der hamburgischen Schriftsteller*, vol. 3 (Hamburg: 1857) 316–319. The most extensive biographical information about Hoffmann is still provided by the anonymous sketch ("Nachricht von dem Leben und den Schriften des Verfassers") appended to the tenth edition of Hoffmann Johann Adolf, *Zwey Bücher von der Zufriedenheit nach den Gründen der Vernunft und des Glaubens* (Hamburg, Bohn: 1745[10]) 603–640.

show that he was uncomfortable with the enterprise.[28] These tensions reveal themselves in the final work. Although Reimarus does not explicitly question the truth of the biblical account, the focus of his added commentary on philology, antiquarianism, polyhistory, as well as the applied sciences neutralizes Hoffmann's commentary. The theological content is almost entirely submerged and barely perceptible for the reader, a latent 'de-theologization' of Scripture.

So when Job asserts his godliness for not having succumbed to the worship of the sun and the moon[29] 'Have I looked up at the sun in its brightness or at the full moon in its movements, so that my heart was secretly enticed and I kissed my hand in worship'[30]–Hoffmann suggests that Job describes here the most ancient kind of idolatry, mainly because people then could not identify any other direct cause for the growth of crop and cattle. Above all, however, it showed that its protagonist did not set his heart on the merely mundane aspects of life. He remained a steadfast believer and did not lapse into the idolatrous practice of heathens to greet the sun with a kiss to his hand.[31] This bare-boned approach to what could have been a rich and most interesting interpretation should not come as a surprise. Hoffmann's work falls completely in line with most commentaries by Lutheran and Reformed luminaries. But none of them showed a particular inclination of moving beyond the fact that 'Job had abhorred this kind of ungodliness,' to which, as Ezekiel[32] tells us, 'at one point even the Israelites succumbed.'[33]

---

28 An incomplete portion of Hoffmann's manuscript with Reimarus's notes and corrections has survived and is catalogued under StUBH, Cod. Theol. 1295.

29 Job 31:26–27. I am using the notation of the *Biblia Hebraica Stuttgartensia* (BHS) throughout.

30 See Gordis R., *The Book of Job: Commentary, New Translation, and Special Studies* (New York: 1978) 342.

31 Hoffmann, *Neue Erklärung des Buchs Hiob* 814: Die erste Abgötterey fiel auf die Sonne und den Mond; und solches rührte daher, weil sie ihre Verehrung bloß richteten auf die äusserliche sichtbare Ursache des Wachsthums auf dem Felde und Gedeyens bey der Heerde. Da fiel ihnen denn nichts mehr in die Augen als die Sonne [...] Dieses mogte wohl noch zu Hiobs Zeiten die eintzige und bekannteste Abgötterey seyn; welches denn von dem Alterthum des Lebens und des Buches Hiob zeuget. Hiob sagt sich; weil sein Hertze nicht an dem irdischen geklebet, so sey sein Gemüth auch nicht bey denen äusserlichen Ursachen des irdischen Seegens stehen blieben [...] Daß sich mein Hertz heimlich verleiten lassen ; von der Gewohnheit so vieler Völcker in und um mein Vaterland; meine Hand zu einem Kuß an den Mund zu legen. D.i. Sonne und Mond als GOTT anzubeten [...].

32 Ezek. 8.

33 Mercier Jean, *Commentarii, in Iobum, et Salomonis Proverbia, Ecclesiasten, Canticum Canticorum* (Leiden, Hackius: 1651) 247: [...] in quam impietatem videmus & Israelitas aliquando prolapsos esse ut ex Ezech. videmus qui Israelitas reprehendit quod facies

In Reimarus' interpretation of the passage, in contrast, Job moves from the centre of a Lutheran *hermeneutica sacra* to the margins of a straightforward philological analysis, seasoned with sprinkles of antiquarian insights into the culture of the Near East. Reimarus first explains that the Hebrew אור (light) is commonly used as a metaphor not only for the sun, but for celestial bodies in general. This, however, is by no means peculiar to Hebrew. According to Reimarus, we find the same instance in Greek, where authors do not always write about the λαμπρὸν φάος ἠελίοιο (the bright light of the sun) but are often more succinct and just use the term φάος (light). In the *Odyssey* for example, during her and Telemachus's visit to Phylos, Athena, disguised as Mentor, urged the talkative Nestor to hold his tongue and make a sacrifice to the gods, because ἤδη γὰρ φάος οἴχεθ' ὑπὸ ζόφον (the light has already gone to the gloom of the world below).[34] Likewise the Egyptians, contends Reimarus, referred to the sun as Ὧρος (Horus), which is testified by both Plutarch and Macrobius, and without much reservation he signs on to Le Clerc's slightly adventurous theory that Herodotus's[35] reference to Οὐροτάλτ (Ourotalt), whom the Arabs worship, was equally an allusion to the sun.[36] Le Clerc had pointed out that a careful examination of the term revealed 'traces of the word אור', which means 'fire or heat,' and of 'the word תהלה', which means also 'radiance'. This makes then perfect sense, 'because the sun was the hottest and brightest of all celestial bodies.'[37] Just as the Huguenot theologian Pierre Jurieu had demonstrated, Reimarus points out, lunar and sun worship were widespread in antiquity,[38]

---

orientem solent versus converterent ejus adorandi causa. Ab hac impietate se hoc loco fatetur Iob abhorruisse [...].

34   Homer, *Odyssey* 3.335.
35   Herodotus, *The Histories* 3.8.3.
36   Hoffmann, *Neue Erklärung des Buchs Hiob* 820f.: 'Auch wird bey den Griechen die Sonne nicht allein λαμπρὸν φάος ἠελίοιο, sondern auch schlechthin φάος genannt. Hom. Od. γ. Ἤδη γὰρ φάος οἴχεθ' ὑπὸ ζόφον. Die Aegyptier hiessen die Sonne Ὧρος Macrob. Sat. I.21. adde Plut. de Jf. & Os. 366 a. Die Chaldäer und Perser ihre Oromazes gehöret auch gewisser massen hierher [...] Sonderlich der Araber ihr 'Οὐροτάλτ Herod. III. 8. welches Clericus billiger auf die Sonne zieht und von אור und תהלה solis splendore ableitet [...].'
37   Clerc Jean Le, *Veteris Testamenti Libri Hagiographi ...* (Amsterdam, Wetstein: 1731) 128: Si probe perpendamus nomen *Ourotalt*, in eo inveniemus vestigia vocis אור *or*, aut *our*, quae *ignem*, aut *calorem* significat, & vocis תהלה *thoholah*, quae est *splendor*; & quarum significatio optime consentit cum natura *Solis*, calidissimi & splendissimi omnium siderum.
38   Jurieu Pierre, *Histoire Critique des Dogmes et des Cultes ...* (Amsterdam, L'Honoré: 1704) 606f.: Nous supposons toûjours comme un principe, que sous chaque nom de Dieu sont cachez des Dieux Naturels [...]. On ne peut douter en façon du monde, que le Dieu Naturel, caché sous le nom de *Bahal*, ne soit le Soleil [...]. Le Belenus des Gaulois, & Achileïens, étoit, selon eux, Apollon [...]. Au reste le nome prouve que c'étoit le Soleil. *Hercule* est pur

because names such as Baal, Moloch, Astharoth, or Melechet were all references to the sun or moon.[39] Interpreting Job's plea as a reference to idolatry would also logically connect to the story's geographical setting. With the Chaldeans and Arabs as his neighbors, Job was basically surrounded by sun and moon worshippers. The latter were especially well-known for cultivating a particular devotion to what, according to Reimarus, Hesychius had called ἡλίου ἀνατολή (sunrise).

There is not much theology in all of this. In stark contrast to Hoffmann, Reimarus dives aggressively into a straightforward philological and antiquarian analysis, as it was practiced during the seventeenth and eighteenth centuries by erudites such as Gerard Vossius,[40] Adriaan Reland,[41] or Thomas Hyde[42] and that would ultimately find its monumental expression in such voluminous collections of scholarship as Johann Georg Graevius's *Thesaurus Antiquitatum Romanarum*,[43] Jacob Gronovius's *Thesaurus Graecarum Antiquitatum*,[44] or, somewhat later, Blasio Ugolino's *Thesaurus Antiquitatum Sacrarum*.[45] Although Hoffmann was not blind to the reference to idolatry, his mindset remained within the strict boundaries of a very conventional Lutheran *hermeneutica sacra*. Reimarus's on the other hand, ventures already outside of these boundaries. In fact, if we did not know beforehand that it was supposed to be a commentary on the Book of Job, we would not immediately realize that Reimarus was talking about the Bible. Not even the cross-references to other passages in Scripture, where instances of sun or lunar worship are mentioned, are of any great significance. They are basically treated as another historical source, just as Homer, Herodotus, and Plutarch are. At times Reimarus's

---

Phénicien, האיר כול *Heir coul*, signifie dans cette langue, *illuminat omnia*, il éclaire toutes choses [...]. Les Romains, dans le commerce qu'ils avoient avec Carthage, on pris connoissance de leur Theologie, & ont vû qu'ils donnoient à leur Bahal, le titre & l'éloge de *Heir cul*.

39 Ibid., 606: [...] *Astoreth* est assurément la Lune [...]. Bahal, Astoreth, & l'armée des cieux, qui font mis ensemble, signifient le Soleil, La Lune & les étoiles [...]. Les divers noms, que ce même Dieu a portez [sic.] dans la Syrie, font voir que c'est le Soleil. Les Assyriens Palmyreniens l'appelloient *Aglibelus* [...] Ils l'appelloient aussi *Malacbelus*, composé de Bahal & du mot *Melek* qui signifie Roi, parce qu'il est le Roi des Astres.

40 Vossius Gerard, *De theologia gentili et physiologia christiana* (Amsterdam, Blaeu: 1641).

41 Reland Adriaan, *Palaestina ex monumentis veteribus illustrata* (Utrecht, Broedelet: 1714).

42 Hyde Thomas, *Historia religionis veterum persarum* (Oxford, Theatrum Sheldonianum: 1700).

43 Graevius Johann Georg, *Thesaurus antiquitatum romanarum* (Utrecht, Halma: 1694–1699).

44 Gronovius Jacob, *Thesaurus graecarum antiquitatum* (Leiden, Van der Aa: 1697–1702).

45 Ugolinus Blasius, *Thesaurus antiquitatum sacrarum* (Venice, Herthz: 1744–1769).

commentary does not sound much different from his comments in his celebrated edition of Cassius Dio's *Historiae Romanae*, which he completed twenty years later.[46]

But this is only one part of the story. The Book of Job, with its abundance of critters and creatures, reveals another facet of Reimarus's erudition that would eventually be characteristic of the positivist dimension of his radical work and which will culminate close to thirty years later in the publication of his pioneering work of scholarship[47] on animal behaviour, the *Allgemeine Betrachtungen über die Triebe der Thiere* (General observations of animal instincts, 1762) as well as his *Vornehmsten Wahrheiten der natürlichen Religion* (The most excellent truths of natural religion, 1754). Reimarus's commentary is a testimony to his attempt to combine philology and antiquarianism with his broad scientific interest. During his travels in Holland he had been fascinated by the cutting of peat[48] and mesmerized by the magnetic demonstrations which the Dutch physicist and mathematician Nicolas Hartsoeker often performed for his visitors.[49] As a professor in Hamburg he pleaded[50] for a more active and hands-on approach to language instruction, where concrete objects and the natural surroundings became an integral part of the lesson, thus already anticipating the agenda of Johann Bernhard Basedow's *Philantropinum*.[51] He found joy and tranquility in nature, strolling through his garden, planting flowers and herbs, and he delighted in his exchanges with Peter Hinrich

---

46   Cassius Dio, *Historiae Romanae quae supersunt*, ed. Hermann Samuel Reimarus (Hamburg, Herold: 1750–1752).

47   See Mayr E., "Geleitwort", in Reimarus Hermann Samuel, *Allgemeine Betrachtungen über die Triebe der Thiere, hauptsächlich über ihre Kunsttriebe*, ed. J. von Kempski (Göttingen: 1982) 9.

48   See StUBH, *Reimarus Nachlaß* III b 4, "Tagebuch Notizen aus Holland", fol. 2: Der holländische Torft wird aus kostiger, schlammiger, und morastigter Erde gemacht, welche auf das feste Land aufgeschüttet, getrocknet, und alsdann abgestochen wird, ich habe probiret, das ein solche Torft über 24 Stunden Feuer halten kann.

49   Ibid., fol. 5.: Er [Hartsoeker] zeigte uns einen Magneten, der kugel rund gemacht war, ohngefehrt 2/3 Schuh im Diametro, konte 200 lb. ziehen, wenn er eine Nadel in der Hand über dessen Polen hielte, richtete sich dieselbe in der Hand perpendiculariter in die Höhe [...].

50   Reimarus Hermann Samuel, *De optima ratione discendi docendique elementa linguae latinae*, in *Kleine gelehrte Schriften. Vorstufen zur Apologie oder Schutzschrift für die vernünftigen Verehrer Gottes*, ed. W. Schmidt-Biggemann (Göttingen: 1994) 351–369.

51   Overhoff J., "Johann Bernhard Basedow als Hauslehrer auf Borghorst", *Jahrbuch für Historische Bildungsforschung* 8 (2002) 171f.

Tesdorpf,[52] a retired merchant and a distant relative of his from Lübeck, whose cabinet of natural marvels from his journeys around the globe fascinated him.[53]

Not surprisingly then, the interests of both Hoffmann and Reimarus diverge again when it comes to the natural world and the beautiful cosmological passages in the last three chapters of Job. So whereas the former views the Leviathan as Typhon, the mythical creature, which, as the source and sum of all evil, 'repeatedly clashes with the forces of divine grace'[54] and is ultimately as Satan responsible for 'all fear and torment',[55] Reimarus's analysis is a bit more entertaining and cheerful. For the most part, Reimarus becomes preoccupied with Theodor Hase's dissertation *De Liviathan Jobi*, in which the theologian from Bremen had argued that the Leviathan was a massive toothed fish and not, as Bochart had suggested,[56] a crocodile.[57] In his dissertation, Hase recounted his eye-opening experience of a whaling ship returning to Bremen from the Arctic[58] with such a monstrosity of a beast that the imagery of Leviathan immediately came to his mind.[59] The creature, which had been killed in the Barents Sea, measured approximately seventy feet,[60] exceeding

---

52 Peter Hinrich Tesdorpf III (1712–1778); Tesdorpf O.L., *Die Geschichte des Tesdorpf'schen Geschlechts bis 1920* (Munich: 1921) 66–80.

53 Mönckeberg C., *Hermann Samuel Reimarus und Johann Christian Edelmann* (Hamburg: 1867) 42.

54 Hoffmann, *Neue Erklärung des Buchs Hiob* 44: [...] als des Ursprungs alles Bösen anzudeuten. Absonderlich wurde diesen Typhon zugeschrieben, daß er die Natur, insbesondere die Lüffte vergiffte, und immer wieder die göttlichen Gnaden-Kräffte streite. Alles was schädlich sowohl in den Säfften und Seelen menschlicher Leiber, als auch in den Lüfften über der Erde, ward diesem Typhon als Urheber beygemessen.

55 Ibid., 953: [...] so ist Leviathan der Ursprung aller Angst und Quaal.

56 Bochart Samuel, *Hierozoicon sive Bipertitum opus de Animalibus S. Scripturae* (Frankfurt, Zunner: 1675) II, 770–795. Bochart argued that the Hebrew term תַּנִּין was a synoym of לִוְיָתָן.

57 Hase Theodor, *De Liviathan Jobi et Ceto Jonae Disquisitio* (Bremen, Grimm: 1723).

58 The term *Grönland* (Greenland – see following note) is misleading. The best whaling grounds were usually between Jan Mayen Island and Spitsbergen. See Feddersen B.H. – Asbach W., *Der historische Walfang der Nordfriesen* (Husum: 1991) 32.

59 Hase, *De Liviathan Jobi* 3: Hujus rei documentum haud leve superiori aestate (a. MDCCXXI.) exstitit, quando una XXV. Navium, quae a civibus meis in mare Hyperboreum, quod GROENLANDIAM alluit, piscatum balaenas allegatae fuerant. Vaegrandis alicujus, ac insoliti prorsus piscis, quem inter altos undarum frigore duratarum montes non sine Herculeo labore necaverant, exuvias ad nos apportavit. Ego, ut, quae de illo per ora vulgi circumferebantur, intellexi, ut in eas dilapsus fui cogitationes, hanc illam marinam esse belluam, quam sub nomine LEVIATHANIS magnificis adeo verbis describere apud Jobum capitibus XL. Inde a commate vicesimo & XLI [...].

60 Ibid., 6: Piscis illius, quem nautae nostri sub gradu circiter latitudinis septimo & septuagesimo cum semis jugularunt, *magnitudo* fuit pedum circiter LXX.

the common catch of the whalers in length by about twenty feet.[61] Unlike common whales, which had baleen plates to filter food, this monster had an arsenal of impressive and razor-sharp teeth that were, however, 'not unlike those of humans'[62] in their arrangement. According to Hase, this creature's habitat extended beyond the waters of the Arctic and it was 'by all means no stranger to the Red Sea'[63] and since this was just about the opportunity to kill two birds with a stone, Hase proclaims that the same beast was also responsible for the biblical Jonah's agonizing three days.[64]

The creature that engendered so much excitement in Hase was most likely a sperm whale, which does not have baleen plates, but does indeed roam most ocean waters. Since the whaling ships usually processed the cadaver already at sea, it was unlikely that Hase saw more than just its jaw-bone, and he had to rely on the recollections of the homecoming crew.[65] Whaling was undoubtedly a dangerous business, but add to that the cock-and-bull tales of the whalers and the creature may indeed have turned into something quite horrifying. Much of Hase's narrative, however, may not have sounded too unfamiliar to Reimarus. Each year around Easter the whaling ships left Hamburg, soon to return with barrels of whale blubber. All Reimarus needed to do is stroll down to the banks of the Elbe, where the returning ships unloaded their cargo and the blubber was heated to produce train-oil. The German traveller Zacharias

---

61   Ibid., 7: Unde constat, eos magnitudine aut anteire, aut aequare saltim vulgares baleanas, quae raro ultra pedes quinquaginta extenduntur, quamquam & sint, qui in longe majorem molem excrescant.

62   Ibid., 8: Os ejus non tam crassis grandibusque munitum est labiis, quibus gaudent balaenae, illas autem laminas longas, quae in balaenae ore magna copia reperiuntur, vulgo *Baarden* vocant, heic frustra quaesiveris [...]. Dentibus autem consitum est ferratis, grandibus, acutis, dentibus humanis non prorsus absimilibus [...].

63   Ibid., 39: In ipso etiam sinu Arabico non prorsus peregrinum esse suo loco ostendetur pluribus.

64   Ibid., 3: Pariter, cum, quae de horribilis magnitudinis ingluvie, ex qua inspectantibus, mirantibusque nautis ingentem alium piscem evomuit, narrabantur, audirem, cogitare coepi, anne hic ejusdem quoque generis cetus fuerit, quem post trium circiter dierum in ejus ventre moram divinum vatem JONAM, in terram ejecisse sacrarum literarum monimenta docent.

65   See also the first-hand account of Bullen Christian, *Eines Seefahrenden Journal oder Tag-register, Was auff der Schiffahrt nach der Nordt-See und denen Insuln Groenlandt und Spitsbergen täglich vorgefallen im Jahr Christi 1667. Worin ausfuhrlich der Wallfischfang, deren Arth und Natur, auch andere in der See vorgefallene wunderbare Sachen eygentlich und natürlich beschrieben werden* (Bremen, Wessel: 1668).

Conrad von Uffenbach describes this process vividly in his recollections of his visit to Hamburg.[66]

But Reimarus does not seem convinced by Hase's argument. Since, according to Scripture,[67] the Leviathan could not be domesticated like Lesbia's sparrow in Catullus's poem,[68] Reimarus is certain that Hase's theory must be wrong:

> Alone the comparison of the Leviathan with a bird illustrates that it could not have been a toothed fish. How difficult would it be to say about a monstrous fish, which could never live on land, that no maiden could play with it like a pet bird?[69]

Just imagine: a playful Lesbia relaxing on the banks of the Jordan river, playing with a whale on a leash. That just seemed too outlandish to be true. For Reimarus, the Leviathan could be nothing other than a crocodile. It takes him little effort to find the weakness in Hase's argument. According to Scripture, the Leviathan's 'pride are the channels of his shield shut up tight as with a seal.'[70] Since Hase concluded that the *cetus dentatus* had no scales, he was forced to find an alternative explanation for this passage. So he had interpreted it as a reference to the verse before, which described the Leviathan's teeth.[71] To Reimarus, however, this did not seem very plausible:

---

66 Uffenbach Zacharias Conrad von, *Merkwürdige Reisen durch Niedersachsen, Holland und Engelland. Zweyter Teil* (Frankfurt, Gaum: 1753) 84.

67 Job 40:29; 'Will you play with it as with a bird, or will you put it on a leash for your girls?'; see Gordis, *The Book of Job* 468.

68 Catullus, *Carmen 2*: Passer, deliciae meae puellae, quicum ludere, quem in sinu tenere, cui primum digitum dare appetenti et acris solet incitare morsus [...].

69 Hoffmann, *Neue Erklärung des Buchs Hiob* 959 (e): 'Wirst du ihn zahm machen, und mit ihm als einem Vogel spielen können? ותקשרנו לנערותיך aut ligabis eum puellis tuis i.e. alligatum funiculo dabis puellis tuis; verbum praegnans. Oder ihn an einem Faden gebunden deinen Mädchens [sic.] geben, sich damit zu erlustigen? Passer deliciae meae puellae quicum ludere. Catullus, init [...]. Allein aus eben der Vergleichung des Leviathans mit solchem Vogel erhellet, daß kein Zahn-Fisch könne gemeynet seyn. Denn wie hart wäre es nicht von einem ungeheuren Fisch der nimmer aufs Land kommen kan zu sagen, daß kein Mädchen mit ihm als wie einen Vogel spielen könne?'

70 Job 41:7.

71 Hase, *De Liviathan Jobi* 170–172: Hinc illi, qui balaena cogitarunt, magna se implicari difficultate animadverterunt. Squamis enim instructas esse nemo vidit [...]. Et sane fateor hanc rem meum animum diu ancipitem tenuisse, quod in eo pisci, quem tracto, squamas invenire potui nusquam [...] Quid enim, quaeso te, Lector, hic loci de SQUAMIS legitur? Vocantur illae Ebraice קשקשות vel קשקשים, sed nihil quidquam heic tale reperio [...]. Ita, ut nisi facto ingenti faltu omnem turbare velimus saepientissimi Oratoris ordinem, summaque imis miscere, heic loci non de cute, nedum squamis, sed de oris DENTIBUS cogitandum sit.

Hase is hard-pressed here, because the toothed fish does not have any scales. To save himself, he pulls this description together with half of the preceding verse [...]. But the usage among the poets, who call the teeth of an animal weapons, does not justify that the shields may also refer to its teeth.[72]

Reimarus, however, has no problem using the ancient military as a source of inspiration. The structure of the skin of the crocodile was, according to him, similar to the *testudo* or turtle formation of the Roman soldiers, which Lipsius had so meticulously described in his *Poliorceticon*.[73] The soldiers would be layering their shields over their heads and on the sides to protect themselves from arrows and missiles.[74] Even once the description of the creature becomes more outlandish – 'Its sneezes flash forth light and its eyes are like the eyelids of the dawn. From its mouth go flaming torches [...]'[75] – Reimarus still does not second guess his initial classification of the species. He argues that ancient poets in general such as Silius Italicus or Ovid often resorted to this kind of language whenever they referred to animals. According to Reimarus, such figurative language is not even completely out of place here, because crocodiles tend to 'hold their breath under water for such a long time that they have to release it afterwards much more forcefully, as Bochart had shown.'[76] Although Reimarus most likely had never seen a living crocodile, one should not automatically conclude that his knowledge was exclusively bookish, for that would mean underestimating the influence Reimarus's surroundings had on his worldview. Hamburg offered plenty of alternatives for a hands-on exploration. Reimarus

---

72 Hoffmann, *Neue Erklärung des Buchs Hiob* 996: Herr Hasaeus hat hier seine Noth, weil der Zahn-Fisch keine Schuppen hat. Also nimmer er um sich zu retten, die Hälffte des vorigen Verses mit zu dieser Beschreibung [...]. Allein die Loca der Poeten, da sie die Zähne der Thiere, Waffen nennen, wollen es noch nicht ausmachen, daß durch Schilde auch können Zähne verstanden werden.

73 Lipsius Justus, *Poliorceticon sive de machinis, tormentis, telis libri quinque* (Antwerp, Officina Plantiniana: 1596) 18–24.

74 Hoffmann, *Neue Erklärung des Buchs Hiob* 996: Es ist mir fast gar zu klar, daß auf die Art der Schilde gezielet werde, da die Soldaten bey Belagerung einer Stadt die Schilde so dichte über den Kopf musten an einander halten, daß kein Spieß, Pfeil oder Schleuder-Stein durchdringen konnte.

75 Job 41:18–19.

76 Hoffmann, *Neue Erklärung des Buchs Hiob*, 997 (q): Dies ist, sag ich, die Poetische Beschreibung [...] Es reden die Poeten so von dem Schnauben andrer Thiere. Silius L. VI. v. 242. *Frenoque teneri impatiens crebros exspirat naribus ignes*. Ovid. Metam. VII. 356. *Spiratque e pectore flamma* [...]. Allein bei dem Crocodil und Hippopotamo ist solches etwas eigentlich wahr, indem dieselben unter Wasser die Lufft so lange zurück halten, und folglich hernach desto stärcker von sich blasen, wie Bochartus zeiget.

THE DEVIL IN THE DETAILS: THE CASE OF HERMANN SAMUEL REIMARUS   287

probably also visited his relative Peter Hinrich Tesdorpf in Lübeck and marvelled at his impressive cabinet of curiosities. Among its most precious pieces were in fact the mounted heads of a crocodile and of a hippopotamus, the 'true and genuine Behemoth [...] from Job.'[77] Whenever Tesdorpf was in Hamburg Reimarus allowed him access to his library so that he could get his hands on the anatomical works by Bernhard Siegfried Albinus or Mark Catesby's books on birds, insects, and other critters.[78]

The auction catalogue of Reimarus's library is both testimony to and proof for his active pursuit of scientific interests. It lists a large arsenal of works not only on botany, the mathematical sciences (including applied mathematics), medicine, and mineralogy, but also on commerce and navigation, hunting and dendrology, not to mention all the theological and philological works. That this is no coincidence is illustrated by the outline of a lecture which Reimarus wrote towards the end of his life. It remained unpublished until only a few years later when one of his most talented students, the economist Johann Georg Büsch, decided to publish a greatly enlarged version of it. This lecture serves as an almost symbolic reflection of Reimarus's scholarly cosmos. It is designed as a broad survey of all the historical, philosophical, and mathematical sciences and presents natural history with an emphasis on the experimental and applied sciences alongside of anthropocentric universal history with its related disciplines. This perspective allows Reimarus to be viewed as a bridge between the world of the polyhistors, with its focus on philology and antiquarianism, and the curiosity and experimental spirit of the later Enlightenment, which would peak with the generation of the 'lunar men',[79] the generation of Reimarus's son, the physicist Johann Albert Heinrich Reimarus (1729–1814), also a close friend of Erasmus Darwin.

Reimarus's Job commentary is a reflection of this kind of learning. It illustrates how he fuses the philology and antiquarianism of scholars such as Jean Le Clerc or Grotius with an interest in the applied sciences. Although he does not show any of Le Clerc's inclination towards textual emendation, he also has no reservation about incorporating profane sources into his analysis. But he stretches beyond Le Clerc by drawing parallels to the world of applied and experimental sciences. This approach is already a radical departure from the *analogia fidei* of Lutheran faithfuls. In his Job commentary, however, Reimarus

---

77   Tesdorpf, *Die Geschichte des Tesdorpf'schen Geschlechts* 70.
78   Letter Peter Hinrich Tesdorpf to Reimarus, 26 July 1745, *StA HH, NL Reimarus* 622:1, A 23, vol. 2.
79   Uglow J., *The Lunar Men: Five Men whose Curiosity Changed the World* (New York: 2003).

does not yet use this erudition against the biblical text, but uses it parallel to it. That this would change only a few years later, is no longer a secret.

When Reimarus and Jean Le Clerc met again a few years later, the predicaments were markedly different. By then, Reimarus had evidently absorbed Le Clerc's work to a greater extent than the latter could have wished. Gone was the reservation about Le Clerc's profanization of Scripture. This 'imaginary encounter' occurred on the banks of the Red Sea, where God had so miraculously provided a dry passage for his chosen people. As an appendix to his Pentateuch commentary, Le Clerc contends that the crossing of the Red Sea was by no means as miraculous as generally assumed.[80] He attributed this mistaken belief to an 'excessive love of prophetic signs', according to which it is falsely believed that 'God changed the order of nature habitually'.[81] Le Clerc argues that a closer examination of the incident reveals that the Israelites' crossing was in fact entirely plausible, without supernatural forces carrying them over.[82]

According to Le Clerc, history proves that there are plenty of instances where skilled leadership took advantage of the forces of nature to overcome sheerly unsurmountable obstacles. To these belongs Alexander's passing of Mount Climax as well as Scipio's conquest of Carthage.[83] The natural condi-

---

80   See for example Stumpf Johann Ludwig, בקעת ים סוף *Seu de Divisione Rubri Maris Miraculosa* (Giessen, Müller: s.a.) 11: Certe non potest non sinistri ominis haberi labor ille, quando tam anxie id ostendere satagit, quomodo intra 4. vel 5. horarum spatium transire omnes potuerint [...]. Imo vero certum est, quicquid obvertatur tantum agmen intra tant illum tempus traduci non potuisse.

81   Clerc Jean Le, *Dissertatio de Maris Idumaei Trajectione*, in *Joannis Clerici Commentarius in Mosis Prophetae Libros Quinque* (Tübingen, Cotta: 1733) 613: Prodigorum amor nimius non raro, ut Deus ordinem naturae consuetum mutasse perperam crederetur, effecit.

82   Le Clerc has a very clear concept of what would constitute a miracle: Duo iterum sunt rerum genera, quae extra ordinem Deus ipse operatur. Aliae ejusmodi sunt, ut non possint naturalibus causis, hoc est vi humanae [...] tribui [...]. Aliae in se spectatae possent quidem effectus naturalium causarum haberi, qualis est vehementior ventus [...]. Hos possunt gignere causae naturae, & saepe gignunt [...]. Si, cum nullus ordine Naturae oriturus esset ventus [...], Deus singulari voluntate oriri ventum [...] haec miracula erunt. Though overall sceptical, Le Clerc has created a loophole which does not entirely exclude the possibility of a miraculous passage. For Le Clerc, howerver, the true miracle would in fact have been if God had revealed the impending events to Moses in detail beforehand: 'Si Deus revelasse haec Mosi dicatur, quod volumus habemus; sola enim revelatio summum erit miraculum.' This fully agrees with Le Clerc's overall high esteem for the Prophetic Books of the Bible. See Le Clerc, *Dissertatio de Maris Idumaei Trajectione* 620; see also Reventlow, "Bibelexegese als Aufklärung" 17.

83   Le Clerc, *Dissertatio de Maris Idumaei Trajectione* 621: Hinc quantum sit discrimen inter hunc transitum Alexandri per littus Pamphylii maris, & sinus Erythraei trajectionem satis liquet [...]. Non minus differt ab Hebraeorum trajectu Publii Africani militum ad Carthaginis murum accessus.

THE DEVIL IN THE DETAILS: THE CASE OF HERMANN SAMUEL REIMARUS 289

tions that the Israelites encountered certainly played to their advantage. At the point of their passage, the gulf was no wider than two Roman miles[84] - around 1.6 miles – and it was thus no major obstacle even for such a myriad of people to cross within just a few hours. Le Clerc also has a solution for the apparent conflict between the magic of the strong wind, which pushed the sea back throughout the night, and the Israelite's tight schedule to make it across before the morning in order to be able to watch the spectacle of drowning Egyptians:

> The Israelites were in no necessity to flee in a long military column. After the wind dried a very wide space, they could cross with a broad front, just like the Egyptians who were chasing them; if only a few [Egyptians] had advanced at the same time, the entire army could not have drowned, because the following ranks would have been severed from the leading portion of the long column.[85]

Such a formation would allow for a much swifter progress. Apart from that, continues Le Clerc, the Israelites must have started their transit already once the main body of water had been pushed away. The Bible's וַיָּבֹאוּ בְנֵי־יִשְׂרָאֵל בְּתוֹךְ הַיָּם בַּיַּבָּשָׁה (And the Israelites walked through the midst of the Sea on dry ground)[86] should not be understood too literally. Of course there were still deeper patches and puddles, but בַּיַּבָּשָׁה (on dry ground) means ultimately that 'there is no longer any water on top of the ocean floor'.[87] The rooks, reeds, and the mud on the ocean floor was then, according to Le Clerc, what sealed the Egyptians' fate. This was certainly no easy terrain for the Egyptian chariots and horsemen. When some of them eventually crashed they added to the amalgam of natural obstacles for those following behind them, making the Egyptian defeat ultimately inevitable.[88]

---

84   Ibid., 615: Primum est eum sinum qua desinit, arctissimum esse, ut omnes testantur, qui de eo egerunt [...]. Haec circiter duobus milliaribus a se invicem distant.
85   Ibid., 615: [...] Israelitas ordine militari & longo agmine necesse non habuisse fugere. Latissimo spatio vento exsiccato, lata fronte trajicere potuerunt, quemadmodum tentarunt post eos Aegyptii; totus enim exercitus Aegyptius submersus non fuisset si pauci simul processissent, cum longi agminis postrema acies multum fuisset a fronte abfututa.
86   Ex. 14:22.
87   Le Clerc, *Dissertatio de Maris Idumaei Trajectione* 618: [...] neque enim hoc ita intelligendum, quasi ne humida quidem ac lutosa fuerit. *Sicca* dicitur humus, supra quam non sunt undae, opponiturque non ulgini, sed aquae [...]
88   Ibid., 618f.: Hisce sine dubio multum Aegyptiorum currus & equos tardari necesse fuit [...]. Fundum maris inaequale, rupibusque & fruticibus variis inlocis asperum non facile curribus peragrabatur [...]. Eversi autem, aut fracti aliquot currus totum agmen turbabant,

Not surprisingly, the Reimarus of the *Apology* was not impressed. With all due respect for Le Clerc's erudition,[89] his analysis – beginning with the selective use of his sources – seemed outright biased. According to Reimarus, Le Clerc had based his analysis solely on a passage in Diodorus Siculus, who had estimated the distance between the two shores to be around sixteen *stadia* [~1.6 miles]. But since many other ancient writers such as Strabo, Arrian, or Pliny the Elder provided a far larger number – sixty *stadia* to be precise [~6 miles]–Clerc should by all means have known better. Reimarus explains:

> I am also well-aware of a passage in Diodorus Siculus, which calculates the width as sixteen stadia. But the passage is undoubtedly corrupt, because it disagrees with the unanimous judgement of all other ancient sources and the scribe could in his mind easily have confused sixteen and sixty (ἑκκαίδεκα and ἑξήκοντα), when he heard it. [Le Clerc] appears to have been not entirely unbiased if he bases his judgement upon this single corrupt passage in Diodorus and at the same time conceals the opposite views of all other ancient writers.[90]

This criticism would have been an especially painful slap in Le Clerc's face. Reimarus triumphs here on Le Clerc's home turf. In the second volume of his *Ars Critica* Le Clerc had written extensively on exactly these kinds of mistakes where scribes accidentally wrote down what they happened to have in their heads or what they believed to have heard when a passage was dictated to them.[91]

---

confusisque ordinibus, concitatisque quantum licebat equis, dum quisque antevertere alios nititur, lentius sine dubio exercitum procedere necesse fuit.

89 Reimarus, *Apologie* I, 326: Es ist hier bey Clerico nicht Unbedachtsamkeit, nicht Unwissenheit, Unbelesenheit und dergleichen, Ursache an der mangelhaften und verkehrten Vorstellung, sondern eine grobe Partheylichkeit. Konnte aber wohl was elenderes von einem sonst geschickten Manne zur Rettung des Israelitischen Durchganges vorgebracht werden?

90 Ibid., 318: Ich weis auch wohl, daß eine Stelle bey dem Diodoro Siculo die Breite nur auf 16 Stadia rechnet. Aber die Stelle ist ohne Zweiffel verdorben: weil sie wieder das einmühtige Zeugniß aller Alten läufft, und weil sechzehn mit sechzig (ἑκκαίδεκα mit ἑξήκοντα) leicht in Gedanken oder im Hören, von dem Abschreiber haben vertauscht. Le Clerc [...] scheinet nicht gar unpartheyisch gehandelt zu haben, wenn er sich auf diese eintzige verdorbene Stelle des Diodori berufft, und die gegenseitigen Zeugnisse der Alten verschweigt.

91 Clerc Jean Le, *Ars Critica*, vol. 2 (Amsterdam, Van Waesberge: 1712[4]) 88: Certe cum qui scribit aliud agit, quod saepe potuit contingere, facile fit ut quae cogitat, non quae dictantur, scribat [...]. Scribentes enim non modo verba, sed etiam sensum adtendunt, & in longa scriptione, saepe fit ut sententiae ratio major habeatur, quam verborum. Si praesertim qui dictabant, lucri causa, quam maxime poterant festinarent, ut sine dubio saepe factum est;

But even if the distance was as short as Le Clerc had assumed, Reimarus asserts, his analysis is nonetheless clouded by the desire to bring the Israelites across swiftly. Apart from the fact that it would have been impossible to position approximately three million people in a broad line along the coast ready to set over, the pace Le Clerc assumes does not take the substantial number of disabled and elderly people into account, who must equally have been part of such a multitude, not to mention the cattle and carriages with their belongings. Ancient scholars such as Strabo had already noted the extremely inaccessible terrain, and more recently, the sixteenth-century French traveller Pierre Belon concluded that 'the frequent cliffs made a navigation [of this part of the Red Sea] very difficult and dangerous',[92] and there was obviously a reasons for its name יָם סוּף (Sea of Reeds), because of the many reeds and moss that grew in the muddy soil.[93] Yet, Reimarus argues, Le Clerc had only chosen to acknowledge these factors once it was time for the Egyptians to meet their fate:

> But once poor Pharaoh must drown, [Le Clerc] includes the untraversable ocean floor. All of a sudden, there is deep mudd in many places and quick sand, into which the wheels [of the chariots] sink [...]. The chariots collide [...], they crash on the cliffs, the wheels break, get turned upside down [...]. Did the wind carry all the sand and mud there? Did the cliffs and coral reefs grow during the last night-watch, just like fungus?[94]

---

    nihil mirum si voculae saepe minus necessariae a Scribentibus omittebantur, aut miscebantur synonymae.

[92] Belon Pierre, *Les observations de plusieurs singularitez et choses memorables, trouvées en Grece, Asie, Judée, Egypte, Arabie, & autres pays estranges, redigées en trois liures* (Paris, Marnef: 1588).

[93] Reimarus, *Apologie* I, 319f.: Strabo schreibt: daß auf dem rothen Meere schlimm zu schiffen sey [...] so bezeugt es noch in neueren Zeiten Petrus Bellonius: Man kann auf dem rothen Meere, nicht anders als mit Beschwerden und grosser Gefahr schiffen, wegen der häuffigen Felßklippen [...]. Es kommt aber ein neues Hinderniß für Fußgänger hinzu, daß auch der Boden mit vielem Moose, Schilf und Grünigkeit bedeckt ist. Denn es heist nicht umsonst Schilfmeer [...]. ja die angrenzenden Fischer pflegten sich am Strande von dem ausgeworffenen Seemose Hütten, oder wenigstens Dächer ihrer Gruben, zu machen. Das hat Bochart mit vielen Zeugnissen der Alten bewiesen [...].

[94] Ibid., 324f.: Nun aber soll der arme Pharao ersauffen. Jetzt läst er die Unwegsamkeit des Seebodens einfließen. Da ist an vielen Orten ein häuffiger tieffer Schlamm: dort ist ein tieffer Sand, da die Räder stark hinein schneiden [...]. so kommen die Wagen in einander, und halten sich auf, fahren an die Klippen hinan, zerbrechen die Räder, werffen um [...]. Hat der Wind nun erst so vielen Sand und Schlamm dahin geführt? Sind die Klippen und Corallen-Stauden, wie die Schämme, in der letzten Nachtwache hervorgewachsen?

Reimarus's criticism is not entirely unjustified. If Le Clerc had shown the same rigor that he was advocating in his initial meeting with Reimarus and consistenly applied it to the passage, he would have had to acknowledge the obvious discrepancies in the biblical account. In spite of his notoriety as a profanizer, he is not putting his principles into practice with the same perseverance, because he would have to sacrifice revelation. Reimarus, not without disappointment,[95] recognizes this and faults Le Clerc for it. Although both men basically use a very comparable range of sources – classical works and travel accounts – Reimarus in fact is the one who has taken Le Clerc's principles fully to heart and 'examined the Bible just as if he read Aristophanes'. With the reverberations of their meeting in our ears, we may wonder who would have been more shocked had it occurred thirty years later.

Reimarus never published his radical work during his lifetime. Only after his death, the German dramatist and critic Lessing published portions of it from 1774 until 1778, which sent shockwaves through Germany and created one of the most important public debates of the Enlightenment.[96] During these years, Germany made a leap forward into modernity. Many of Reimarus's ideas and his criticism had already found hosts in people's minds and fragmentary copies of portions of the radical work had already circulated clandestinely. So Lessing's decision to put these issues out in the open triggered a confrontation with orthodoxy and sparked a public debate about such questions as revelation, the role of the Apostles, and the historical Jesus. Not without justification have people such as Albert Schweitzer emphasized the significance of Reimarus's work for future theological scholarship about the life of Jesus,[97] and during the nineteenth century, Reimarus's work found an enthusiastic reception among Young Hegelians such as David Friedrich Strauss and Bruno Bauer.[98] This is also a testimony that Reimarus's work could not simply be dismissed as the destructive work of a rationalist deist philosopher. In fact, much of his argument builds on a long tradition of philological and antiquarian scholarship that has its roots in the works of the humanists and reformers. Reimarus towers on the

---

95 Ibid., 323: Aber einem so belesenen und vernünftigen Manne, als Clericus war, ist seine Partheylichkeit, in der Behauptung der Möglichkeit dieses Durchgangs durchs Rothe Meer, kaum zu verzeihen.

96 On the subject of the *Fragmentenstreit* see Boehart W., *Politik und Religion. Studien zum Fragmentenstreit (Reimarus, Goeze, Lessing)* (Schwarzenbek: 1988); Nisbet H.B., *Lessing: Eine Biographie* (Munich: 2008) 705–744.

97 Schweitzer A., *The Quest of the Historical Jesus* (London: 1911) 13–26.

98 Strauss D.F., *Hermann Samuel Reimarus und seine Schutzschrift für die vernünftigen Verehrer Gottes* (Leipzig: 1862); Kempski J. von, "Spinoza, Reimarus, Bruno Bauer: Drei Paradigmen radikaler Bibelkritik", in *Hermann Samuel Reimarus (1694–1768): ein 'bekannter Unbekannter' der Aufklärung in Hamburg* (Göttingen: 1973) 96–112.

shoulders of these giants of learning and erudition and is able to look further ahead than they. His skilful mind combines and processes this legacy with the experimental curiosity of the intellectual of a port city, who is continuously exposed to new discoveries and a culture of exchange.[99] Only if we acknowledge this tremendous complexity of learning and scholarship will we be able to add another piece into the puzzle of Germany's drive towards secularization during the eighteenth century.

Bibliography

Barnes A., *Jean Le Clerc (1657–1736) et la République des Lettres* (Paris: 1938).

Belon Pierre, *Les observations de plusieurs singularitez et choses memorables, trouvées en Grece, Asie, Judée, Egypte, Arabie, & autres pays estranges, redigées en trois liures* (Paris, Marnef: 1588).

Bister U. et al. (eds.), *Johann Jacob Rambach: Leben– Briefe – Schriften* (Basel: 1993).

Bochart Samuel, *Hierozoicon sive Bipertitum opus de Animalibus S. Scripturae* (Frankfurt, Zunner: 1675).

Boehart W., *Politik und Religion. Studien zum Fragmentenstreit (Reimarus, Goeze, Lessing)* (Schwarzenbek: 1988).

Brückner, "Dilherr, Johann Michael" *Allgemeine Deutsche Biographie* 5 (1912) 225.

Brun J. Le, "Jean Le Clerc", in Schobinger J.-P. (ed.), *Die Philosophie des 17. Jahrhunderts (Grundriss der Geschichte der Philosophie)*, vol. 2 (Basel: 1993) 1018–1024.

Bullen Christian, *Eines Seefahrenden Journal oder Tag-register, Was auff der Schiffahrt nach der Nordt-See und denen Insuln Groenlandt und Spitsbergen täglich vorgefallen im Jahr Christi 1667. Worin ausfuhrlich der Wallfischfang, deren Arth und Natur, auch andere in der See vorgefallene wunderbare Sachen eygentlich und natürlich beschrieben werden* (Bremen, Wessel: 1668).

Cassius Dio, *Historiae Romanae quae supersunt*, ed. Hermann Samuel Reimarus (Hamburg, Herold: 1750–1752).

Clerc Jean Le, *Ars Critica, vol. 2* (Amsterdam, Van Waesberge: 1712⁴).

Clerc Jean Le, "Rev. of Wolf, Bibliotheca Hebraea, vol. 2", *Bibliotheque Ancienne et Moderne* 16 (1721) 332–365.

Clerc Jean Le, *Veteris Testamenti Libri Hagiographi …* (Amsterdam, Wetstein: 1731).

Clerc Jean Le, *Dissertatio de Maris Idumaei Trajectione*, in *Joannis Clerici Commentarius in Mosis Prophetae Libros Quinque* (Tübingen, Cotta: 1733).

---

99 On the significance of port cities in this context see, for instance, Cook H., *Matters of Exchange: Commerce, Medicine, and Science in the Dutch Golden Age* (New Haven, CT: 2008).

Cook H., *Matters of Exchange: Commerce, Medicine, and Science in the Dutch Golden Age* (New Haven, CT: 2008).

Dilherr Johann Michael, *De usu lectionis scriptorum secularium et antiquitatis* (Jena, Steinmann: 1635).

Einem Johann Justus von, *Selectae Animadversiones ad Johannis Clerici Scripta ...* (Magdeburg, Siegler: 1735).

Feddersen B.H. – Asbach W., *Der historische Walfang der Nordfriesen* (Husum: 1991).

Golden S., *Jean Le Clerc* (New York: 1972).

Gordis R., *The Book of Job: Commentary, New Translation, and Special Studies* (New York: 1978).

Graevius Johann Georg, *Thesaurus antiquitatum romanarum* (Utrecht, Halma: 1694–1699).

Grafton A., *Joseph Scaliger: A Study in the History of Classical Scholarship, vol. 1: Textual Criticism and Exegesis* (Oxford: 1983).

Grafton A., "The World of the Polyhistors: Humanism and Encyclopedism", *Central European History* 18 (1985) 31–47.

Grafton A., *Forgers and Critics: Creativity and Duplicity in Western Scholarship* (Princeton: 1990).

Grafton A., *The Footnote: A Curious History* (Cambridge, MA: 1999).

Grafton A., *Bring out your Dead: The Past as Revelation* (Cambridge, MA: 2001).

Groetsch U., *Hermann Samuel Reimarus (1694–1768): Classicist, Hebraist, Enlightenment Radical in Disguise* (Leiden: 2015).

Gronovius Jacob, *Thesaurus graecarum antiquitatum* (Leiden, Van der Aa: 1697–1702).

Hase Theodor, *De Liviathan Jobi et Ceto Jonae Disquisitio* (Bremen, Grimm: 1723).

Herbers P., *Die hermeneutische Lehre Johann Jakob Rambachs*, Ph.D. dissertation (University of Heidelberg: 1952).

Hoffmann Johann Adolf, *Neue Erklärung des Buchs Hiob, darin das Buch selbst aus der Grund-Sprache mit dem darin liegenden Nachdruck ins Teutsche übersetzet* (Hamburg, Felginer: 1734).

Hoffmann Johann Adolf, *Zwey Bücher von der Zufriedenheit nach den Gründen der Vernunft und des Glaubens* (Hamburg, Bohn: 1745[10]).

Hübner H., "Die 'orthodoxe' hermeneutica sacra des Hermann Samuel Reimarus", in Beetz M. – Cacciatore G. (eds.), *Die Hermeneutik im Zeitalter der Aufklärung* (Cologne: 2000) 99–111.

Hug W., *Johann Jacob Rambach (1693–1735): Religionspädagoge zwischen den Zeiten* (Stuttgart: 2003).

Hyde Thomas, *Historia religionis veterum persarum* (Oxford, Theatrum Sheldonianum: 1700).

Jaumann H., "Was ist ein Polyhistor? Gehversuche auf einem verlassenen Terrain", *Studia Leibnitiana* 22 (1990) 76–89.

Jurieu Pierre, *Histoire Critique des Dogmes et des Cultes ...* (Amsterdam, L'Honoré: 1704).

Kempski J. von, "Spinoza, Reimarus, Bruno Bauer: Drei Paradigmen radikaler Bibelkritik", in *Hermann Samuel Reimarus (1694–1768): ein 'bekannter Unbekannter' der Aufklärung in Hamburg* (Göttingen: 1973) 96–112.

Klein D., *Hermann Samuel Reimarus (1694–1768): Das theologische Werk* (Tübingen: 2009).

Lipsius Justus, *Poliorceticon sive de machinis, tormentis, telis libri quinque* (Antwerp, Officina Plantiniana: 1596).

Mercier Jean, *Commentarii, in Iobum, et Salomonis Proverbia, Ecclesiasten, Canticum Canticorum* (Leiden, Hackius: 1651).

Mönckeberg C., *Hermann Samuel Reimarus und Johann Christian Edelmann* (Hamburg: 1867).

Mühlpfordt G., "Rev. of Reimarus, Vindicatio dictorum Veteris Testamenti in Novo allegatorum", ed. P. Stemmer, *Theologische Literaturzeitung* 113, 3 (1988) 199–204.

Mulsow M., "Polyhistorie", in Ueding G. (ed.), *Historisches Wörterbuch der Rhetorik*, vol. 6 (Tübingen: 2003) 1521–1526.

Mulsow M., "Johann Christoph Wolf (1683–1739) und die verbotenen Bücher in Hamburg", in Steiger J.A. (ed.), *500 Jahre Theologie in Hamburg: Hamburg als Zentrum christlicher Theologie und Kultur zwischen Tradition und Zukunft* (New York: 2005) 81–111.

Mulsow M., "Mikrogramme des Orients. Johann Christoph Wolfs Notizhefte und seine Cudworth-Lektüre", in Thouard D. – Vollhardt F. – Mariani Zini F. (eds.), *Philologie als Wissensmodell* (Berlin: 2010) 345–396.

Mulsow M., (ed.), *Between Philology and Radical Enlightenment: Hermann Samuel Reimarus (1694–1768)* (Leiden: 2011).

Nisbet H.B., *Lessing: Eine Biographie* (Munich: 2008).

Overhoff J., "Johann Bernhard Basedow als Hauslehrer auf Borghorst", *Jahrbuch für Historische Bildungsforschung* 8 (2002) 171f.

Pitassi M.C., *Entre croire et savoir: le problème de la méthode chez Jean Le Clerc* (Leiden: 1987).

Rambach Johann Jacob, *Institutiones Hermeneuticae Sacrae* (Jena, Hartung: 1725).

Rambach Johann Jacob, *Erläuterung über seine eigene Institutiones Hermeneuticae Sacrae* (Giessen, Krieger: 1738).

Reimarus Hermann Samuel, *Apologie oder Schutzschrift für die vernünftigen Verehrer Gottes*, ed. G. Alexander, 2 vols. (Frankfurt: 1972).

Reimarus Hermann Samuel, *Handschriftenverzeichnis und Bibliographie*, ed. W. Schmidt-Biggemann (Göttingen: 1979).

Reimarus Hermann Samuel, *Allgemeine Betrachtungen über die Triebe der Thiere, hauptsächlich über ihre Kunsttriebe*, ed. J. von Kempski (Göttingen: 1982).

Reimarus Hermann Samuel, *De optima ratione discendi docendique elementa linguae latinae*, in *Kleine gelehrte Schriften. Vorstufen zur Apologie oder Schutzschrift für die vernünftigen Verehrer Gottes*, ed. W. Schmidt-Biggemann (Göttingen: 1994) 351–369.

Reland Adriaan, *Palaestina ex monumentis veteribus illustrata* (Utrecht, Broedelet: 1714).

Reventlow H. Graf, "Bibelexegese als Aufklärung. Die Bibel im Denken des Johannes Clericus (1657–1736)", in Reventlow H. Graf et al. (eds.), *Historische Kritik und biblischer Kanon in der deutschen Aufklärung* (Wiesbaden: 1988) 1–19.

Schmidt-Biggemann W., "Erbauliche versus rationale Hermeneutik: Hermann Samuel Reimarus' Bearbeitung von Johann Adolf Hoffmann's 'Neue Erklärung des Buchs Hiob'", in Walter W. (ed.), *Hermann Samuel Reimarus, 1694–1786: Beiträge zur Reimarus-Renaissance in der Gegenwart* (Göttingen: 1998) 23–52.

Schröder H., "Hoffmann, Johann Adolf", in *Lexikon der hamburgischen Schriftsteller*, vol. 3 (Hamburg: 1857) 316–319.

Schweitzer A., *The Quest of the Historical Jesus* (London: 1911).

Steiger J.A., *Philologia Sacra* (Neukirchen-Vluyn: 2011).

Stemmer P., *Weissagung und Kritik: Eine Studie zur Hermeneutik bei Hermann Samuel Reimarus* (Göttingen: 1983).

Sträter U., "Rambach, Johann Jakob", *Religion in Geschichte und Gegenwart* 7 (2004[4]).

Strauss D.F., *Hermann Samuel Reimarus und seine Schutzschrift für die vernünftigen Verehrer Gottes* (Leipzig: 1862).

Stumpf Johann Ludwig, בקעת ים סוף *Seu de Divisione Rubri Maris Miraculosa* (Giessen, Müller: undated).

Tesdorpf O.L., *Die Geschichte des Tesdorpf'schen Geschlechts bis 1920* (Munich: 1921).

Uffenbach Zacharias Conrad von, *Merkwürdige Reisen durch Niedersachsen, Holland und Engelland. Zweyter Teil* (Frankfurt, Gaum: 1753).

Uglow J., *The Lunar Men: Five Men whose Curiosity Changed the World* (New York: 2003).

Ugolinus Blasius, *Thesaurus antiquitatum sacrarum* (Venice, Herthz: 1744–1769).

Vossius Gerard, *De theologia gentili et physiologia christiana* (Amsterdam, Blaeu: 1641).

Wolf Johann Christoph, *Bibliotheca Hebraea*, vol. 2 (Hamburg, Felginer: 1721).

PART 4

Scientific Knowledge and Religion

CHAPTER 10

Cry Me a Relic: The Holy Tear of Vendôme and Early Modern Lipsanomachy

Anthony Ossa-Richardson

> plus une relique est fausse, plus elle intéressera l'historien
> PHILIPPE GEORGE[1]

∴

No movement in the history of ideas is instantaneous or final. One movement allows another: the refuted belief of old returns as a thought entertained for the sake of the soul – a truth not literal but symbolic – and its refutation as an act of pedantry and barbarism. In this little historical quadrille, more than one step may be called a profanation, for each partner sees profanity in the stance of the other. Profanation is perceived only in relation to what is held true, or *most* true.

In 1699, Jean-Baptiste Thiers (1636–1703), the learned curé of Vibraye, launched an attack on one of the most celebrated relics in France: the Holy Tear of Vendôme, 'Madame Sainte-Larme', supposedly one of those shed by Christ for the death of Lazarus,[2] and preserved in the local abbey of Sainte Trinité.[3] Thiers was already infamous for his *Traité des superstitions*, a compendious assault on folk-beliefs of the French provinces, which had begun appearing in

---

* My utmost thanks to Jean-Louis Quantin for his comments on this article.
1 George P., "Les reliques des saints: un nouvel objet historique", in: Bozóky E. – Helvétius A.-M. (eds.), *Les reliques: objets, cultes, symboles: Actes du colloque international de l'Université du Littoral Côte d'Opale 4–6 septembre 1997* (Turnhout: 1999) 229–237, 236.
2 John 11:35.
3 The Vendôme piece was one of a number of tear relics venerated across France from the eleventh century onwards, on which see the erudite and beautifully-illustrated article by Knight K.-J., "Droplets of Heaven: Tears Relics in the High and Later Middle Ages", *The Mediaeval Journal* 6 (2016), 45–80. On the relic in relation to the history of emotions, see now Hickey H.M., "Capturing Christ's Tears: *La Sainte Larme* in Medieval and Early Modern France", in Downes S. and Randles S. (eds.) *Feeling Things: Objects and Emotions through History* (Oxford: 2018), 58–71.

a revised edition of four volumes in 1697; but in his 1699 *Dissertation* he took a microscope to the Tear.[4] It was a case of personal interest, as he later admitted; every year his own flock would desert the parish in droves for the Festival of the Holy Tear in Vendôme.[5] The focus of his critique was a rather old book on the relic, the *Histoire véritable*, first published in 1641 by the Vendômois monks;[6] this little work had supported the Tear's authenticity with a long history of its provenance, excerpts of mediaeval testimonies, and a list of its curative miracles – each of which Thiers demolished in turn. Predictably, the monks were none too happy at this verbal profanation of their most venerable relic; they sent Thiers pseudonymous Latin hate-mail, arranged for a preacher to denounce him in the pulpit, and finally commissioned a pamphlet in the Tear's defence.[7] The author of this pamphlet, not named in print, was soon revealed as an old friend of Thiers – the brilliant Maurist scholar Jean Mabillon (1632–1707). Mabillon had already acquired fame for his innovative philology, and notoriety for his critique of folk saints; he was therefore the last man anyone might have expected to defend the authenticity of an untraceable relic. Thiers replied in turn, more stinging than ever.[8] Mabillon remained silent.

This episode illustrates a period when the 'lipsanomachy', the dispute over relics, had shifted away from the Protestants to within the Catholic Church.[9] It has attracted some notice from modern historians, although biographers of Mabillon are embarrassed about it, when they are not entirely silent.[10] But it

---

4   Thiers Jean-Baptiste, *Dissertation sur la Sainte Larme de Vendôme* (Paris, Thiboust and Esclassan: 1699).

5   Thiers Jean-Baptiste, *Réponse à la lettre du Père Mabillon touchant la pretendue Sainte Larme du Vendôme* (Cologne, Heirs of Cornelis van Egmond: 1700).

6   The *Histoire* was evidently written (at least in part) in 1633; see Montaiglon A. de (ed.), *Recueil de poésies françoises des XVe et XVIe siècles*, 12 vols. (Paris: 1855–1877) I, 43n.

7   [Mabillon Jean], *Lettre d'un benedictin à Monsieur L'Evesque de Blois, touchant le discernement des anciennes reliques* (Paris, Pierre de Bats: 1700). On the other circumstances, see Thiers, *Réponse* 132–134. According to Rochambeau A. de, *Voyage à la Sainte-Larme de Vendôme: étude historique et critique sur cet antique pélérinage* (Vendôme: 1874) 58, Alexandre Pinevoise, curé of Moisy, wrote another response to Thiers in 1702.

8   Thiers, *Réponse*.

9   I coin the term 'lipsanomachy' from the early modern Latin neologism, *lipsanomac'hi*, 'relic-deniers', itself from the Greek λείψανον, 'relic', and μάχ-ομαι, 'to fight'. Also spotted in the period is *lipsanomastiges*, 'relic-scourges'.

10 The most ample discussions are Daniel-Odon Hurel, "Jean Mabillon, Jean-Baptiste Thiers et la congrégation de Saint-Maur", in *Dom Jean Mabillon: figure majeure de l'Europe des lettres. Actes des deux colloques du tricentenaire de la mort de dom Mabillon*, eds Jean Leclant et al. (Paris: 2010), 59–76; and Patrice Boussel, *Des reliques et de leur bon usage* (Paris: 1971), 113–22. It is briefly treated in Hickey, "Capturing Christ's Tears", 67–9. See also Jean-Louis Quantin, *Le catholicisme classique et les pères de l'Église: un retour aux sources (1669–1713)* (Paris: 1999), 490–3. Among Mabillon's biographers, Léon Deries and

is worth taking up again, this time with a long view: controversy over the Tear, as we shall see, illuminated religious dispositions not only between Thiers and Mabillon, but long after them, and long after the disappearance of the relic itself, with its translation into legend. In particular, it brought to the surface a latent tension between two fundamentally different ways of understanding just what a relic was, how it functioned within religious worship, and how it ought to be evaluated.

1   The Tear

Whether suppositious or not, a tear, in and of itself, isn't much of a relic; after the first flush of moisture on a hot cheek, one's tears are almost imperceptible. What a pilgrim to Sainte Trinité *saw*, and perhaps handled, was something else. The 1641 *Histoire véritable* describes the relic as follows:

> Le premier vase qui paroît aux yeux de ceux qui adorent ce divin Reliquaire, semble estre de couleur de corne, et le second qui est enfermé dans celuy-cy, paroît de couleur bleuë: mais tous deux sont d'une nature si exquise, que les Lapidaires les plus experts, aprés les avoir long-temps considerez, ont confessé ingenuëment, qu'ils ne connoissoient point la matiere dont ils étoient faits, et qu'elle avoit esté prise dans le Ciel et non dans la terre. En effet ce n'est ny verre, ny crystal, ny pierre, ny aucun metal; et ce qui rend la chose plus admirable, c'est qu'on ne decouvre au premier Vase ny vestige, ny fracture par où l'on puisse s'imaginer que le petit Vase contenant la Sainte Larme ait esté mis dedans.

> The first vessel which will appear to the eyes of those who adore this divine reliquary, seems to be the colour of horn, and the second, enclosed in the first, appears blue: but both are of a nature so exquisite that the most expert lapidaries, after long consideration, have honestly admitted that they do not recognise at all the material of which the vessels are made, and that it has been taken from heaven, not from the earth. For it is neither glass, nor crystal, nor stone, nor any metal, and what makes it even more remarkable is that one cannot see in the first vessel any vestige

---

Gall Heer ignore the episode; Henri Leclercq, *Mabillon*, 2 vols (Paris: 1953–7), II, 738–50, is unimpressed by his subject's contribution, and his account, like Boussel's, relies heavily on quotation; Blandine Barret-Kriegel, *Jean Mabillon* (Paris: 1988), 155–6, gives it a single line, attributing Mabillon's involvement to political expedience.

or fracture through which one could imagine that the smaller vessel, containing the Holy Tear, was placed therein.[11]

Another account describes the outer vessel as an 'espéce de Verre', and the inner as a 'petite Phiole'.[12] The key point is the absence of any opening or join in the object: this was not a man-made bottle or phial, not a lachrymatory, but a natural object, a gem enclosing a drop of water or other liquid with enough room to move about within.[13] Such was the view of Joseph Addison, who compared the Tear to a stone he had seen in the Settala Wunderkammer in Milan: 'a piece of Crystal, that enclos'd a couple of Drops, which look'd like Water when they were shaken, tho' perhaps they are nothing but Bubbles of Air.'[14] Antonio Gavin, a Spanish priest converted to Anglicanism, and a strong critic of Catholic superstitions, had visited Vendôme fifteen or so years earlier, and perceived still less:

> These Fathers, who are Reformed *Benedictins*, told us, That now for so many Hundred years, that is to say, since the time of our Saviour, the said Tear had been preserved so fresh, as a Tear that actually drops from the Eye. We viewed this Crystal very attentively holding it up against the Light, and afterwards took a review of it at the Light of a Wax-Taper, but we could discover nothing of what they were pleased to tell us.[15]

---

11   *Histoire véritable de la Sainte Larme que N. Seigneur pleura sur le Lazare* (Vendôme, Hyp: 1641 [1669]) 14.
12   "Mémoires", in [Mabillon] *Lettre* 54.
13   This phenomenon, now known as a 'fluid inclusion', is caused by the cooling, and shrinking within its cavity, of hydrothermal fluid trapped in a crystal as it grows. The majority of examples are microscopic, but we may presume that the Holy Tear was a rare – and, indeed, spectacular – specimen of those large enough to see, a bubble of perhaps 1–2 cm, and presumably in quartz, by far the most common material for such an inclusion. The *Histoire*'s description of the relic as two vessels of varying colour suggests the interior presence of a 'phantom' crystal, caused by an interruption in the period of the mineral's growth. My thanks to Peter Tandy of the Natural History Museum, London, for his assistance on these subjects.
14   Addison Joseph, *Remarks on Several Parts of Italy &c. in the Years 1701, 1702, 1703* (London, Tonson: 1705) 37. Cf. the items listed in Paulo Maria Terzago's catalogue of the Wunderkammer, *Musaeum Septalianum* (Dertona, Viola: 1664) 24, nos. 27–31. Fluid inclusions had earlier been described by Robert Boyle, *Essay about the Origine and Virtues of Gems* (London, Godbid: 1672) 43, for whom they were evidence that crystal had once been liquid.
15   [Gavin Antonio], *Observations on a Journy to Naples, wherein the Frauds of Romish Monks and Priests are Farther Discover'd* (London, Roycroft: 1691) 97f.

Nineteenth-century historians were in agreement: the Holy Tear, now lost, had only been 'one of those transparent quartz crystals whose interior encloses a mobile drop of water', or perhaps 'a bit of matter resembling a few grains of dust'.[16] A basic grasp of mineralogy was all that was needed to explain and desacralise the relic. But this was a late, profane assessment. For the *Histoire*, and the mediaeval tradition it encapsulated, the Tear was otherworldly, of a material unknown to any lapidary, 'prise dans le Ciel'. Its inner chamber was blue, as if celestial. Recent scholarship has identified the mediaeval anxiety over relics as a question of materiality: how could a spark of divinity remain immanent in fluid, perishable matter?[17] Indeed, of all forms of matter, a tear might be thought the most evanescent; 'nothing dries more quickly'.[18] But the Vendôme relic perfectly enacts the material paradox, for it both contains (and displays) the divine 'tear', and at the same time refigures it as a hard, idealised body, a blue crystal chased in gold – a fragment of immutable heaven.

The crystal was stored in an elaborate reliquary, four golden coffers one inside the other, and this in turn was kept behind an even more elaborate stone screen carved as a Gothic portal in miniature.[19] The Holy Tear was well hidden from the eyes of the faithful; as one later pen put it, the coffers formed a 'rempart, comme pour la protéger contre les regards profanateurs'.[20] These larger objects, with their own complex iconographies, were first represented on the page in the seventeenth century, and given serious interpretation only in the nineteenth, long after their disappearance. The screen, probably from around 1200, portrayed the legendary provenance of the Tear, as described in the 1641 *Histoire*: after being collected by an angel, it was given to Mary Magdalene, who, fleeing from the Jews to Provence with her family, bequeathed it to St Maximin at Aix-en-Provence. From there it was at some time brought to Constantinople, where, in 1040, Michael IV the Paphlagonian awarded it to the

---

16 Pétigny J. de, *Histoire archéologique du Vendômois* (Vendôme: 1849) 191: 'un de ces cristaux transparents de quartz dont l'intérieur renferme une goutte d'eau mobile [...] un peu de matière semblable à quelques grains de poussière', in the second place quoting Ferdinand Camille Duchemin de La Chesnaye. Cf. Rochambeau, *Voyage à la Sainte-Larme* 60.

17 See, especially, Bynum C.W., *Christian Materiality: An Essay on Religion in Late Medieval Europe* (Cambridge, MA: 2011).

18 Ferrand Jean, *Disquisitio reliquiaria, sive, De suspicienda et suspecta earumdem numero reliquiarium quae in diversis Ecclesiis servantur multitudine* (Lyon, Anisson: 1647) 72: lacrymas Servatoris (quibus nihil arescit citius). Cf. Erasmus, *Adagia*, 1147.

19 On the screen, see Crozet R., "Le monument de la sainte larme à La Trinité de Vendôme", *Bulletin monumental* 121 (1963) 171–180. Crozet estimates the screen at 2.3 m tall. Cf. Isnard I., *L'abbatiale de la Trinité de Vendôme* (Rennes: 2007) 90f.

20 Pottier A., *Histoire du précieux sang de Notre Seigneur Jésus-Christ conservé en l'abbaye de la Sainte Trinité de Fécamp* (Rouen: 1838) 2.

Count of Anjou, Geoffroy Martel, for his military assistance in Sicily against the Saracens. Martel brought it home to Vendôme, where he had recently founded the abbey of Sainte Trinité; the Tear remained there ever since.[21] Peter Brown notes the central importance of provenance to the authenticity of translated relics in mediaeval Constantinople, and we see the same here – the value and miraculous power of the Tear depended on its metonymic attachment to the divinity, and so it was essential to establish a continuous history between Christ and Vendôme.[22]

If the Tear's actual origin is obscure, it certainly had a popular fame outside Vendôme by the mid-thirteenth century, for it appears as common knowledge in the *Chronique rimée* of Philippe Mouskes.[23] Our earliest proper description of it is by the historian François de Belleforest in 1575, and outside France it is mentioned by the Jesuit scholar Giovanni Battista Segni in 1610.[24] In the seventeenth century appear references in printed correspondence to an old tradition: the exchange of pilgrim souvenirs from the site. Visitors would collect water from the Loire or elsewhere near the abbey in metal *ampoules* decorated with symbols of the Holy Tear, and send them to pious associates, demonstrating the full extension of the relic's metonymic power.[25] Letters by François de Sales, the Port-Royal abbess Marie Angelique Arnauld, and even the Cartesian philosopher Jacques Rohault either enclose, or thank their addressee for sending, what they call 'larmes de Vendôme'.[26] In a much-cited passage, Francis identifies the 'larme' he is about to send as

> une goutte de l'eau dans laquelle on a trempé la phiole, dans laquelle est, ainsi qu'on tient par la tradition ancienne des habitans de Vendôme, de la terre sur laquelle tombèrent les larmes de Notre-Seigneur, tandis qu'au

---

21   *Histoire véritable* 11–22. On the competing hypotheses of the relic's origin, see Knight, "Droplets of Heaven", 55.

22   Brown P., *The Cult of the Saints: Its Rise and Function in Latin Christianity* (London: 1981) 92f.

23   Mouskes Philippe, *Chronique rimée*, ed. Baron de Reiffenberg, 2 vols. (Brussels: 1836) I, 442 (l. 11470–11477).

24   Münster Sebastian, *Cosmographia*, trans. and rev. F. de Belleforest, 2 vols. (Paris, Sonnius: 1575) I, 322; Segni Giovanni Battista, *Reliquiarium, sive, De reliquiis et veneratione sanctorum* (Bologna, Rossius: 1610) 3.

25   Rochambeau, *Voyage à la Sainte-Larme* 7–23.

26   Sales François de, "Letter to an unknown woman, 7 June 1622", in Sales François de, *Lettres, vol. 3* (Paris: 1817) 60f.; Arnauld Marie Angelique, "Letter to the Queen of Poland, 11 Jan 1657", in Arnauld Marie Angelique, *Lettres, vol. 3* (Utrecht, s.n.: 1742) 33; Rohault Jacques, "Letter to Malebranche, 9 July 1671", in Malebranche Nicolas, *Fragments philosophiques inédits et correspondance*, ed. Vidgrain J. (Paris: 1923) 38.

> temps de sa mortalité et de ses peines il pria et adora son Père éternel pour la rémission de nos péchés.
>
> a drop of the water in which has been dipped the phial containing – according to the ancient tradition of the inhabitants of Vendôme – some of the earth on which fell the tears of our Saviour, during which, at the time of his death and his agony, he prayed and adored his eternal Father for the remission of our sins.[27]

Tradition was flexible, easily adapted, especially when the object itself remained so well hidden. For Jean-Baptiste Thiers, at the end of the century, this mystery was no accident:

> On voit bien à quel dessein on a pris tant de précautions pour cacher cette Larme. On a voulu par là réduire les Curieux à l'impossibilité de l'examiner, et leur ôter le moyen d'en découvrir la fausseté et l'illusion.
>
> We see well to what end so many precautions have been taken to hide this Tear. They have wanted by this method to make it impossible for the curious to examine it, and thus to remove their means of disclosing its falsity and illusion.[28]

Thiers was not the first to impugn the Holy Tear. Calvin scoffed at it, and at tear-relics in general, in the course of his famous catalogue of 1542, comparing them to the weeping idols of the pagans. Others, notably Pierre Jurieu, followed.[29] Jean Ferrand, swinging his lance in all directions against the Calvinists, defended the authenticity of the Tear in 1647; as he observed, 'tears were once collected by the heathens in phials as they fell from the eyes, originally mixed with the cinders of burnt bones for drinking, and, in later times, carefully preserved.' Christ's tears were gathered by Mary, and, since she was poor, only in glass; subsequently, as they attracted riches, they were enclosed in agate, alabaster and

---

27   Sales, "Letter" 60.
28   Thiers, *Dissertation* 28f.
29   Calvin Jean, *Traité des reliques*, in *Three French Treatises*, ed. F. Higman (London: 1970) 74; Person David, "A Treatise of Laughing and Mourning", in Person David, *Varieties, or, A Surveigh of Rare and Excellent Matters Necessary and Delectable for all Sorts of Persons* (London, Badger: 1635) 187f.; [Jurieu Pierre], *Suite de l'accomplissement des prophetes* (Rotterdam, Acher: 1687) 244f.

gold. For Ferrand this was a point of pious belief.[30] Antonio Gavin, who had actually seen the Tear, and could recount the local legends, was more specific in his condemnation. He wrote,

> They have recourse to this Relick in all Maladies of the Eyes, and upon this account, it brings a vast Income to these Fathers. Surely People had need to be Endowed with a great Stock of Simplicity and good Intention to adore things, which even according to humane Tradition are so uncertain and doubtful.[31]

This, in 1691, was Thiers's critique *in nuce*.

2   Thiers's Scepticism

By the time the *Dissertation* was published, Thiers had evidently been mulling it over for some time, since he mentioned it in the first volume (1697) of his revised *Traité des superstitions*; here, too, we find a *précis* of its argument.[32] For Thiers, the Holy Tear was a fraud, invented and preserved by mediaeval monks to attract pilgrim lucre; far from being a victimless crime, it propagated superstition, that is, 'undeserved worship', and profaned the genuine traditions of the Catholic Church.[33] He was no free-thinker; at the outset of his *Dissertation* he emphasised his belief in the authenticity of true relics.[34] What he wanted, rather, was to strip the spurious accretions from Catholic history. False relics and other superstitions were like counterfeit coinage, threatening the devaluation of the true. They also rendered the Church susceptible to the attacks of Protestants, who denied relics altogether. 'Falsehood', he intoned, quoting a letter of Innocent III, 'must not be tolerated under the pretext of piety.'[35]

---

30   Ferrand, *Disquisitio reliquiaria* 72f.: Lacrymas olim ex oculis cadentes phialis excipi ab Ethnicis, tum iis bibulam ossium exustorum fauillam perfundi, denique sedulo conservari consuevisse, testantibus Tibullo, Ovidio, Sitio, Statio, Virgilio, sexcentisque aliis scriptoribus paganis.
31   [Gavin], *Observations* 97f.
32   Thiers Jean-Baptiste, *Traité des superstitions qui regardent les sacremens*, 4 vols. (Paris, Dezallier: 1697–1704) I, 110–112 (on unowed worship and superstition); II, 452–460, in the context of false masses.
33   Thiers, *Dissertation* 5f.
34   Ibid., 3.
35   Thiers, *Dissertation* sig. ē1r: 'Falsitas tolerari non debet sub velamine pietatis.' Innocent's *mot* is also quoted on the title-page.

When he came to discuss the particulars of the Holy Tear, Thiers had no trouble pointing out the gaps, errors and unfounded assertions in the origin narrative of the *Histoire véritable*. It was, he said, like killing flies with a cannon.[36] The Gospels, of course, knew nothing of an angel collecting Christ's tears. Nor was it likely that Mary fled to Provence; in this matter Thiers drew quietly on an old controversy of the 1640s, incited by one of his predecessors, Jean de Launoy, labelled 'dénicheur des saints' for his assaults on the authenticity of local worship.[37] There was no St Maximin in the time of Mary, and so he could not have inherited the Tear from her. France itself was only Christianised later. Geoffroy Martel did not help the Byzantine emperor against the Saracens, and could not have visited Constantinople. The foundation charter of Sainte Trinité did not mention the Tear, nor did any other abbey document before the twelfth century. Thiers's battery of negative evidence went on and on without remorse. And his formidable handling of the documents, his acuity in producing knowledge as the situation demanded, went far beyond mere scepticism in uncloaking the relic's pretension to antiquity.

The 'evidence' brought forward in the *Histoire* was easily brushed aside: it was all ambiguous, or too recent to be given credence, or it proved only the existence of something believed to be Christ's tear. Likewise, the miracles supposedly worked by the relic were all suspect, found in the Benedictine register, or in old popular songs; even if they had happened, they could not be attributed with confidence to the Tear. Often it was faith itself, even misplaced, that gave rise to miracles.[38]

Above all, the authenticity of the Holy Tear was supported only by popular tradition, and not by any official proclamation of the Church.[39] Here was the crux of Thiers's complaint – and if elsewhere he reminds us of a Bayle, an enlightened sceptic, this comment must remind us of his true purpose: the grounding of religious practice in the authority of the ecclesiastical hierarchy. Thiers pointed to the decrees of previous Church councils, and above all Trent. He quotes from the decrees of the twenty-fifth session (1563) of Trent:

> Statuit sancta Synodus nulla admittenda esse nova miracula, nisi recognoscente et approbante Episcopo: qui simul atque de iis aliquid

---

36   Ibid., sig. ē1v: je tuë des mouches à coups de canon.
37   On the controversy, see Feuillas M., "La controverse magdalénienne au milieu du XVIIe siècle: ripostes provençales à Jean de Launoy", in Duperray È. et al. (eds.), *Marie Madeleine dans la mystique, les arts et les lettres* (Paris: 1989) 89–110.
38   Thiers, *Dissertation* 142.
39   Ibid., 121–126.

compertum habuerit, adhibitis in consilium Theologis et aliis piis viris, ea faciat quae veritati et pietati consentanea judicaverit.

The holy Synod states that no new miracles are to be admitted unless with the recognition and approval of the Bishop, who, as soon as he has acquired some experience of these matters, and has received the counsel of theologians and other pious men, will do what he has judged to be in agreement with truth and piety.[40]

This decree was evidently a counterblast to the Protestant critique of false worship among lay Catholics. Calvin, in addition to disapproving of relic-veneration as idolatry, had pointed out that the true remains of saints could hardly be distinguished from the false: how often had the bones of a criminal been passed off as holy?[41] In denying the faculty of discernment to private individuals, Trent sought to overcome the multiplicity of false claims, on which Calvin's complaint had rested. Catholics remained acutely conscious of the problem of false relics: in 1603 the curé Jean Belot deplored the 'infinite number of reliquaries' containing 'profane things made up to attract the simple people, and proved by false miracles', even as he also defended the existence of 'holy and august relics'.[42]

In explicit responses to the Protestant challenge, the Trent decree was a familiar passage: it had continued to serve its apologetic purpose. Segni and Ferrand both quoted it,[43] while in Thiers's era it fulfilled the same function in a 1685 dialogue on relics by Marin Grostête des Mahis, a convert from Calvinism now active at Orléans. Towards the end of this work, the Calvinist tells his Catholic friend, 'You revere these objects whose authenticity you cannot be

---

40   Ibid., 144f. The quotation is abridged; the original reads as follows: 'Haec ut fidelius observentur statuit sancta synodus nemini licere ullo in loco vel ecclesia etiam quomodolibet exempta ullam insolitam ponere vel ponendam curare imaginem nisi ab episcopo approbata fuerit. Nulla etiam admittenda esse nova miracula nec novas reliquias recipiendas nisi eodem recognoscente et approbante episcopo. Qui simulatque de his aliquid compertum habuerit adhibitis in consilium theologis et aliis piis viris ea faciat quae veritati et pietati consentanea iudicaverit.'
41   Calvin, *Traité* 96.
42   Belot Jean, *Les Fleurs de la philosophie chrestienne et morale* (Paris, Du Brueil: 1603) fol. 119r: Il y a un nombre infiny de reliquaires en beaucoup d'Eglises, que si on avoir la vraye cognoissance d'où ils procedent on y verroit beaucoup d'apostasie, et qui sont procedez de choses prophanes et inventees pour attirer les simples gens, et sont confirmez par faux prodiges: ie ne veux toutesfois par ces miennes paroles mespriser les sainctes et almes reliques que nous avons.
43   Segni, *Reliquiarium* 60; Ferrand, *Disquisitio reliquiaria* 386.

entirely certain of; it is a terrible obstacle.'[44] The Catholic replies that Trent has forbidden the unauthorised acceptance of new relics, and that 'the bishops should even remove old relics from the eyes of the common people, if they can recognise their falsity.'[45] These writers also provide historical examples of discerning holy men: Segni cites St Martin of Tours, and Grostête mentions St Charles Borromeo, both of whom had laboured against false relics and false worship. Both saints are named approvingly in Thiers's *Dissertation*.[46] Anti-Protestant apologetics was an important context for his work, but not the only one: he pointed to an older and still closer model: Guibert de Nogent's *De pigneribus* (or *pignoribus*) *sanctorum*, from the early twelfth century. This treatise had attacked the Benedictines of St Medard-de-Soissons for their superstitious worship of a tooth-relic, accusing them of impiety and avarice, and of failing to discern true from false relics, a task ultimately to be left to the Pope.[47] The parallel to Thiers's project was obvious.

The arrogation of discernment, in the matter of relics and other religious objects, to Church superiors and trained theologians had long been an important ballast for Catholics in defence of their worship. It was necessary, among other things, to prevent the chaos of private interests. As Thiers put it, 'if every individual were permitted to publish his miracles without the opinion of the bishops, one would often hear the cry of "miracle!" in churches with some relic or extraordinary image'.[48] The Holy Tear of Vendôme, he is at pains to observe, has never been authorised by the bishops of Chartres, under whose jurisdiction the abbey had been until 1697.[49] Thiers does not mention that other tear-relics did have episcopal sanction – for instance, that kept at

---

44 Grostête des Mahis Marin, *L'Entretien d'un Catholique et d'un Calviniste sur le sujet des reliques*, in Grostête des Mahis Marin, *Deux lettres* (Orléans, Boyer: 1685) 105.

45 Ibid., 107: les Evesques doivent même ôter de devant les yeux des peuples les anciennes Reliques, dont ils peuvent reconnoître la fausseté.

46 Thiers, *Dissertation* 174f. on St Martin; 181f. on St Charles.

47 Guibert de Nogent, *De sanctis et eorum pigneribus*, in [*Opera*], ed. R.B.C. Huygens (Turnhout: 1993); see, e.g., p. 157 on impiety and greed, and p. 89 on the authority of the Pope. Thiers invokes Guibert's authority several times in his *Dissertation*; for instance at pp. 142–3 against the significance of miracles. On Guibert's critique of relics, see, among other recent works, Jay Rubinstein, *Guibert of Nogent: Portrait of a Medieval Mind* (New York: 2002), 124–30, with some discussion of the book's composition; Karin Fuchs, *Zeichen und Wunder bei Guibert de Nogent: Kommunikation, Deutungen und Funktionalisierungen von Wunderzählungen im 12. Jahrhundert* (Munich: 2008); and Bynum, *Christian Materiality*, 188, in the context of her broader argument on relics.

48 Thiers, *Dissertation* 148: Car s'il étoit permis à chacun de publier des miracles sans l'aveu des Evêques, on entendroit souvent crier *miracle* dans les Eglises où il y a quelque Relique, ou quelque Image extraordinaire.

49 Ibid., 143.

St-Pierre-les-Selincourt, whose charter of permission would be proudly transcribed by the abbey canon Jacques le Merchier in his 1707 history of the relic.[50]

But from Vendôme, without doubt, one heard the unwarranted cry of 'miracle'. The only possible object of such confected mumbo-jumbo as the *Histoire véritable*, Thiers concluded, was financial. He later pointed out that the monks proferred a basin at the side of those coming to kiss the Tear, for the sole purpose of collecting oblations: this 'sordid' practice was in stark opposition to the dispassionate piety with which true relics should be displayed.[51] The same goal lay behind the Vendômois' bruiting about of their Tear's miracles. Earlier, more pious monks had kept the knowledge of their miracles to themselves, so as to discourage the commotion of foreign visitors; they had even sought to dissuade their patron saints from continuing to work miracles from the grave.[52] Thiers quotes a number of sources to support this claim, including the oration of Pierre de Limoges (fl. 1130s) at the tomb of his patriarch St Stephen of Grandmont, a passage too curious to be left on the pages of early modern scholarship:

> Serve Dei, tu ostendisti nobis paupertatis viam, et toto conamine docuisti nos per eam incedere. Nunc vero arcta via ad latam et spaciosam tuis nos vis miraculis revocare? Et qui praedicasti solitudinem, nunc in solitudine fora et nundinas vis congregare? Non curiositate ducimur, ut miracula videre velimus. Sanctitati tuae satis credimus. Caveas igitur ne decaetero ea miracula facias, quae tuam extollant sanctitatem et nostram humilitatem destituant. Non sic tuae provideas laudi, ut nostrae sis immemor salutis. Quod si aliter feceris, tibi dicimus, et per obedientiam, quam tibi promisimus, constanter asserimus, ossa tua hinc extrahemus, et in flumen spargemus.
>
> Servant of God, you have shown us the path of poverty, and taught us with every effort to tread that path. Would you now by your miracles call us back from the straight and narrow, towards the broad and spacious path [i.e., of worldly pleasure]? And would you, who have preached solitude, now assemble the courts and marketplaces in our solitude? We are not so led by curiosity that we wish to see miracles; we believe enough in

---

50 Merc[h]ier Jacques le, *Histoire de la larme sainte de NS Jesus-Christ reverée dans l'abbaye de Selincourt* (Amiens, Caron-Hubault: 1707) 38f.

51 Thiers, *Réponse* 129.

52 Thiers, *Dissertation* 148f. Monastic solitude was dear to Thiers, and he had treated this matter in his earlier monograph on the subject: see Thiers Jean-Baptiste, *Traité de la clôture des religieuses* (Paris, Dezallier: 1681) 469–74.

your holiness. Be careful, then, not to perform those miracles henceforth, which extol your holiness and undermine our humility. Do not look after your glory at the expense of our salvation. And if you should do otherwise, I tell you, and faithfully swear by the obedience I have promised you, that I will dig up your bones from this place, and scatter them in the river.[53]

St Stephen, it is said, did as he was told. Faced with a model of such severe piety, the Benedictines of Vendôme could only appear greedy and concupiscent. Their celebrations, moreover, verged on the blasphemous. According to the *Histoire véritable*, during the annual Festival of the Holy Tear, at which an imprisoned criminal was pardoned, the relic was carried in procession under a rich velvet canopy, 'with the same solemnity that one is accustomed to carry the holy Sacrament at Corpus Christi'.[54] Gavin had noted this with horror: the monks, he said, 'bestow upon it the Worship of *Latria*, even the same they give to Jesus Christ himself.'[55] Thiers felt the same. No Catholic, he argued, should treat any relic, even a genuine one, as equal to the Eucharistic Host. A tear was especially unworthy of reverence, since it was only a kind of sweat or saliva, a superfluity of the humours, and therefore not an essential part of Christ's sacred body – here Thiers could draw on an early modern Aristotelian conversation about the nature of tears and other corporal secretions.[56] Even if the Tear *had* been genuine, then, the Vendômois ceremony would be impious, a profanation of the Host. Still worse, Thiers had been informed that the monks carried the Tear in the Corpus Christi procession as well, although, when he sent an envoy to confirm the veracity of this allegation, it turned out to be false.[57]

---

53   Thiers, *Dissertation* 153, quoting Henriquez Crisóstomo, *Fasciculus sanctorum Ordinis Cisterciensis ... complectens liber secundus* (Cologne, Cholinus: 1631) 137 (II.11.4). Henriquez gives no source, although the passage derives from the anonymous *Vita Sancti Stephani Confessoris*; see *Patrologia Latina* CCIV, col. 1030. I translate above from Henriquez's Latin; Thiers quotes it in his own French version.
54   *Histoire véritable* 38: avec la même solemnité que l'on a accoûtumé de porter le saint Sacrament le jour de la Fête-Dieu.
55   [Gavin], *Observations* 97.
56   Thiers cites Pseudo-Aristotle, *Problemata* v.35, and Rhodiginus Ludovicus Caelius, *Lectionum antiquarum libri XXX* (Basel, Froben: 1542) XII.3 = 433f.; see also Petit Pierre, *De lacrymis libri tres* (Paris, Cramoisy: 1661) 39–45.
57   Thiers, *Réponse* 73–75.

3 Mabillon's Charity

Following Trent, Thiers placed authority over relic-worship with local bishops, and so he concludes his *Dissertation* with a request to the Bishop of Blois to investigate, and do away with, the Holy Tear.[58] Blois was a new seat: only two years before, the diocese had been created from parishes, including Vendôme, under the control of Chartres, with David-Nicolas de Berthier installed as bishop. Thiers's timing was excellent, seeking to convince the new authority to correct the oversight of his predecessors.

Jean Mabillon's reply to Thiers, which appeared in 1700, was written as an open *Lettre* to Berthier. According to Thiers's *Réponse*, also addressed to Berthier, Mabillon had told their mutual friend Louis de Tressan, the Bishop of Mans, that he would never defend the Holy Tear; it was strange, then, that he should change his mind upon reading the *Dissertation*.[59] Unsurprisingly, Thiers suspected an *esprit de corps*, if not the outright coercion of his superiors, behind Mabillon's defence. Indeed, Thiers had already come into conflict with the Maurists on the subject of monastic studies, behind which was an ongoing rivalry between the regular and secular clergy.[60] Even contemporaries ignorant of the Tressan story were astonished at the difference in outlook between the *Lettre* and Mabillon's other work, for instance his 1698 attack on the worship of unknown saints. It is telling that an *éloge* for the Maurist after his death in 1707 insisted that the *Lettre*, although he had been 'obliged to write it', shared the same spirit as his criticism; it was, said the *élogiste*, 'an exact and sincere piety, but one which would leave nothing to chance in its object.'[61] Others recognised a different purpose in the *Lettre*: not to establish the authenticity of the Holy Tear, but only to defend the good faith of the Benedictines.[62] Indeed, throughout the *Lettre*, Mabillon's attitude to the relic itself remains ambiguous.

The arguments of the *Lettre* in support of the Tear are entertainingly weak, for they largely amount to the claim that the relic *could*, theoretically, be genuine. It was certain, Mabillon remarked, that Christ shed tears at the resurrection

---

58   Thiers, *Dissertation* 184.
59   Thiers, *Réponse* 5.
60   Quantin, *Le catholicisme classique* 491 n. 114.
61   [Anon.], "Éloge de Dom Mabillon", *Histoire de l'académie royale des inscriptions et belles lettres* 1 (1717) 355–368, 365: 'une pieté exacte et sincére; mais qui ne veut rien de hazardé dans son object'. See also Ruinart Thierry, *Abrégé de la vie de dom Jean Mabillon* (1709), ed. T. Barbeau (La Froidfontaine: 2007) 128f., agreeing with the *éloge*.
62   Pin Louis-Ellie Du, *Bibliothèque des auteurs ecclésiastiques du dix-septième siècle*, 7 vols. (Paris, Pralard: 1708) v, 124; Cerf Philippe le, *Biblioteque historique et critique des auteurs de la congregation de St Maur* (The Hague, Grosse: 1726) 282.

of Lazarus. This was uncontentious: only a Strauss could deny it.[63] It was no less certain, continued Mabillon, jumping from recorded events to value-judgement, 'that these tears were worthy of being preserved, and that they deserved a respect proportionate to the infinite majesty of the Son of God.'[64] The logic is that if the tears were worthy of being saved, they *were* saved: implied is something like the principle of sufficient reason. And although the Gospels did not mention the angelic collection of the tears, we cannot reason from such a silence, for as St John explicitly states,[65] not all of Christ's deeds were written down.[66] Who are we to deny the possibility of such a miracle? In an attempt at quotemanship, Mabillon matches Thiers's scrap of Innocent III with another: 'It is better to leave everything in the hands of God than to settle a question rashly.'[67]

The force of the latter position – a pious fideism – rests entirely on a rejection of negative argument, that is, of *argumentum ex silentio*. It was this form of argument that had always underpinned sceptical critiques of historical claims, as in the work of Lorenzo Valla. Matthieu Bochart, a Calvinist pastor of Alençon, and the brother of the famous scholar Samuel, had relied on it in his 1656 treatise on relics, arguing that there was no evidence of their veneration before the fourth century AD.[68] The same was true of Thiers, whose assaults on the legends in the *Histoire véritable* largely depend on the lack of evidence for each link in the relic's back-story, from the Gospels forward.

But if Mabillon had no better means to support the Tear's authenticity than by denying the force of negative argument, he did at least have good reason to upbraid Thiers. Over thirty years before, Thiers had himself attacked negative argumentation, in response to a pamphlet by the 'dénicheur des saints', Jean de Launoy.[69] For Launoy, the argument *ex silentio* was the central plank of any

---

63 Strauss D.F., *Das Leben Jesu, kritisch bearbeitet*, 2 vols. (Tübingen: 1835–1836) II, 158: nichts Anderes übrig bleibt, als aus dieser Incongruenz des johanneischen Christus und des denkbar wirklichen [...] auf den unhistorischen Charackter der johanneischen Erzählung zu schliessen.

64 [Mabillon], *Lettre* 35: Il n'est pas moins certain que ces Larmes estoient dignes d'estre conservées, et qu'elles meritoient un respect proportionné à la Majesté infinie du Fils de Dieu.

65 John 21:25.

66 [Mabillon], *Lettre* 43.

67 Ibid., 12: Melius est Deo totum committere, quam aliud temere definire.

68 Bochart Matthieu, *Traité de l'origine du service des reliques, de l'invocation des saints, des images et du culte rendu aux images des saints* (Saumur, Lesnier: 1656).

69 On this dispute, see Grès-Gayer J.M., "'L'Aristarque de son siècle': Le docteur Jean de Launoy (1601–1678)", in Quantin J.-L. – Wacquet J.-C. (eds.), *Papes, princes et savants dans l'Europe moderne: Mélanges à la mémoire de Bruno Neveu* (Geneva: 2006) 269–285, 279f.

critical historiography, and he defended its validity in a 1662 dissertation on the subject, listing 150 examples of its use or acceptance, from Christ onwards.[70] The young Thiers, in opposition, insisted:

> nullum habebit robur abnutivum argumentum, ex omnium licet antiquiorum Auctorum silentio generali confectum quando ipsius conclusioni, vel unius gravis, docti, accurati et ingeniosi Scriptoris, quantumvis novitii, quantumvis neoterici adversabitur auctoritas.

> The negative argument, though it may rest on the general silence of all ancient authors, will have no force when the authority of even *one* serious, learned, accurate and intelligent writer, however recent, however modern, stands against its conclusion.[71]

In light of his part in the Holy Tear controversy, this statement may surprise us. But here as elsewhere, early modern scholars could take a flexible part in religious disputes: their commitment to critical rigour wavered with context. Of Thiers's 1662 view Mabillon approved – as it suited him to. But how, he demanded, could it be squared with the incredulity of the *Dissertation*?[72]

Further positive arguments, of a character rather like that of the *Histoire véritable*, could be found in an appendix to Mabillon's *Lettre*, entitled, 'Mémoires pour servir d'éclaircissement à l'Histoire de la Sainte Larme de Vendôme'. Thiers judged that this appendix could not have been written by Mabillon himself, since the standard of French was so poor.[73] The 'Mémoires' contained two kinds of evidence for the Tear's authenticity, which it labelled 'extant proofs' and 'literary proofs'. The latter consisted merely of further mediaeval documents attesting to the relic.[74] But the former were much more interesting, even if they were just as ineffective as evidence, for these 'extant proofs' were the material appurtenances of the relic, described here for the first time.[75] Later iconographers, writing long after the disappearance of the

---

70   Launoy Jean de, *De auctoritate negantis argumenti dissertatio* (Paris, Martin: 1662), with pp. 9–12 on Christ. His conclusion can be found on pp. 176–177. On Launoy and negative argument in the context of ecclesiastical erudition, see Quantin J.-L., "Reason and Reasonableness in French Ecclesiastical Scholarship", *Huntington Library Quarterly* 74 (2011) 401–436, 408–414.
71   Thiers Jean-Baptiste, *Exercitatio adversus Iohannis de Launoy Dissertationem de auctoritate negantis argumenti* (Paris, Le Sourd: 1662) 182f.
72   [Mabillon], *Lettre* 9f., and cf. Quantin, "Reason and Reasonableness" 412f.
73   Thiers, *Réponse* 155.
74   "Mémoires", in [Mabillon], *Lettre* 59–67.
75   Ibid., 49–59.

objects, all relied on the 'Mémoires', with its engravings of the golden reliquary coffer and the carved screen before it – as so often, a defence of the Middle Ages against sceptical modernity in fact served to recreate it in the subsequent historical imaginary. The piece was not without its difficulties, however. For one thing, it constructed a rather different genealogy for the Tear, based on a reading of the carved screen figures and the text on the coffer: by this account, Geoffroy is taken out of the equation, and the relic, along with its reliquary, passed instead through the hands of Nitker, Bishop of Freising, Emperor Henry III, his wife Agnes of Poitou, and her mother Agnes of Burgundy. Thiers wasted no time in underlining the inconsistency between these stories.[76] Still more problematic than this discrepancy was the writer's ignorance of iconography: as later scholars realised, many curious details had not been taken into this account, and neither the coffer nor the screen correctly dated or placed. If this was an attempt at new knowledge in the service of religion, a stronger effort would have to await the researches of the nineteenth century, drawing on a huge corpus of comparative material.

More than the authenticity of the Tear itself, Mabillon was concerned about Thiers's tone and attitude, and the implications of his rules for judging relics. If Thiers's style would be gently mocking in his *Réponse*, Mabillon was overtly hostile, even in his haughty terms of address to the curé.[77] He called the *Dissertation* a 'Satyre scandaleuse', and its author a 'Libertin' and a 'Bouffon'.[78] It was a work of impiety, he said, and it suggested a larger, more dangerous disbelief in religious matters. Thiers could have easily expressed doubt about the Holy Tear without being quite so rude about the Benedictines: and in this complaint we hear the stung pride of a pious man, not the disinterest of a critic.[79]

Beyond the *ad hominem* remarks, one of Mabillon's chief concerns was that Thiers's reasoning on the Holy Tear would apply equally well to all other relics: if one followed his rule, 'there would be few or almost no relics which could pass as genuine.'[80] This anxiety was not unjustified, and Thiers, in his *Réponse*, embraced its implications with a zeal that rather undermines his earlier profession of belief.[81]

Again and again in his lengthy reply, Thiers expressed bafflement that so great a scholar as Mabillon should demean himself by defending the Holy

---

76   Thiers, *Réponse* 144f.
77   A fact not lost on Thiers, who pointed it out in his *Réponse* 9.
78   [Mabillon], *Lettre* 5f.
79   Ibid., 36–9.
80   Ibid., 7f.: si l'on applique cette regle pour verifier les Reliques, il y en aura peu ou presque point qui puissent passer pour veritables.
81   Thiers, *Réponse* 22.

Tear. For one thing, he could point to the critical rules Mabillon had drawn up in his work on unknown saints.[82] In hindsight, these looked rather like a dry run for the principles of Thiers's own *Dissertation*: Mabillon had argued that saints should not be worshipped unless their holiness could be supported with valid proofs, and that authority in these matters rested with the Pope, who, before making a decision in a given case, must attentively consider its facts.[83] Furthermore, Mabillon had cited as an example the discernment of St Martin of Tours and St Gregory, both of whom appear in Thiers's *Dissertation*; he had even quoted Guibert, and observed that, far from trusting saints' bodies on the basis of miracles, the faith of the pious could effect miraculous cures even when mistaken as to the object of their belief.[84]

But if the *Lettre* disappointed Thiers in its quiet abandonment of Mabillon's earlier critical principles, something far more problematic lay within. If we should give up our ability to discern true relics from false, then it followed that we should tolerate those who mistakenly worship a false relic:

> quand on se tromperoit à l'égard de quelqu'une, je ne crois pas que ce soit un culte superstitieux, si l'objet que l'on tient de bonne foy pour averé, est digne de veneration, c'est-à-dire si l'on croit de bonne foy que cette Relique soit d'un Saint, qui est reconnu pour tel dans l'Eglise. [...] Car quand il seroit vray que ces Reliques ne seroient pas tout-à-fait certaines, elles peuvent meriter quelque honneur par rapport à la personne à qui on les attribuë, parce qu'encore qu'elles ne fussent pas en effet veritables, elles sont en quelque façon les mesmes choses que les veritables, au moins par representation. C'est sur ce fondement que l'on honore les Croix, quoyque faites d'une autre matiere que du bois de la vraye Croix, parce qu'elles en ont la figure et qu'elles la representent.

> When one is deceived about some relic, I do not think that it is a superstitious worship if the object that one holds in good faith for authentic is worthy of veneration, that is, if one believes in good faith that this relic is that of a saint, and is recognised as such by the Church [...] For even if it is true that these relics are not completely certain, they may deserve some honour by connection to the person to whom they are attributed,

---

82 Ibid., 65.
83 [Mabillon Jean], *Eusebii Romani ad Theophilum Gallum epistola de cultu SS ignotorum* (Paris, Robustel: 1705) 38–40 = Mabillon Jean, *Dissertation sur le culte des saints inconnnus* (Paris, Musier: 1698) 8f.
84 [Mabillon], *Epistola* 5f. (*Dissertation* 20f.) on St Martin; 60f. (29f.) on Gregory; 62f. (30f.) on Guibert.

because although they are not *actually* genuine, they are in some way the same as the genuine, at least by representation. It is on this basis that we worship crosses, although they are made of a different material than the wood of the True Cross, because they have the same form, and they represent it.[85]

What seems at first to be a principle of charity leads to a surprising conclusion about the nature of relic-worship, that is, about the way a relic signifies its original. We are inclined to think of relics as deriving their power, at least in the mediaeval mind, from their actual contact with the divine, a relation of metonymy. As one scholar has recently put it: 'The logic of the relic is metonymic rather than metaphoric: the holiness of the relic is a function of its contiguity with the world and the flesh, as well as the precise historical provenance of the material artifact.'[86] But this is precisely what Mabillon denies: in his analysis, the holiness of a relic is purely a function of its capacity to recall the divine, a relation of likeness, of metaphor. Provenance is irrelevant: all that matters is purpose. For Mabillon, the relic is thus conflated with the image. This was not entirely without precedent. The principle of charity was already present in Guibert's sceptical treatise on relics: if an unlettered member of the congregation should use the wrong words in prayer, or believe a false relic holy, so long as he acts 'praecordialiter et secundum fidem', he will be aided by God, who is concerned more with *intention* than with words.[87] In this claim can be seen a key example of Guibert's broader moral focus on intention, an innovation of the early twelfth century.[88]

This principle would remain standard, though not universal, after the Reformation.[89] Marin Grostête allowed that, if the bishops, after close examination of a relic, mistakenly deemed it genuine, God would not penalise

---

85 [Mabillon], *Lettre* 19, 20.
86 Kearney J., *The Incarnate Text: Imagining the Book in Reformation England* (Philadelphia: 2009) 58.
87 Guibert, "De sanctis et eorum pigneribus" 108f.: 'apud deum, qui causa et fructus est orationis, intentio deprecantis tota difigitur, quocumque modo animus per simplicitatem super suo intercessore errare videatur [...] auris divina intentiones potius quam verba metitur.' Cf. Platelle H., "Guibert de Nogent et le *De pignoribus sanctorum*. Richesses et limites d'une critique médiévale des reliques", in Bozóky É. – Helvétius A.-M. (eds.), *Les reliques. Objets, cultes, symboles. Actes du colloque international de l'Université du Littoral-Côte d'Opale (Boulogne-sur-Mer), 4–6 septembre 1997*, Hagiologia 1 (Turnhout: 1999) 109–121, 120.
88 On the importance of intention in this period, see Morris C., *The Discovery of the Individual, 1050–1200* (Toronto: 2004), 73–75.
89 Cf. Quantin, *Le catholicisme classique* 490, on Gabriel Vázquez.

worshippers for their belief: 'their devotion did not prevent them from being agreeable to God, and did not prevent God from mercifully according them the graces which they asked of him'.[90] The function of relics, after all, was 'to excite our zeal by the reminiscence of the saints to whom they belong' – in this is the germ of Mabillon's view.[91] What we see in the *Lettre*, under such pressure from Thiers's artillery, is the idea taken to its logical extreme, and so forcing a reevaluation of the nature and purpose of the relic.

Thiers was appalled. Mabillon had championed the value of 'good faith' in religious beliefs; but what was more easy to dissimulate than good faith? What better cover for abuse?[92] To agree with the Maurist would be to abandon the very notion of superstition, the worship of a false object. As always, Thiers had his Fathers, Doctors and Council minutes at the ready.[93] He also had his regular companion Guibert, who had warned of the dangers in honouring unproved relics.[94] Thiers exclaimed:

> Je prie le P. Mabillon de remarquer, que ce pieux Abé n'excuse point cet énorme sacrilege sur la bonne foi, parce qu'il suppose que celui qui le commet en honorant pour Saint ce qui n'est pas Saint, est dans la bonne foy, et qu'il ne le feroit pas, s'il ne croyoit de bonne foy, que c'est un veritable Saint qu'il honore.
>
> I pray Father Mabillon declare that this pious Abbé does not in any way excuse such terrible sacrilege on the basis of good faith, since he supposes that a man who commits that sacrilege in honouring as holy that which is not holy, is acting in good faith, and that if the belief were not in good faith, that man could not hold that it was a true saint whom he honoured.[95]

Although revering a false relic in error was only a material superstition, less serious than the formal superstition of false worship in full knowledge, it was nonetheless entirely censurable, 'for it is contrary to true religious worship, whose proper character is to have the spirit for one's principle, and the truth

---

90 Grostête, *Entretien* 108: leur devotion ne laisseroit pas d'estre agréable à Dieu, et de le porter à accorder misericordieusement les graces qu'ils luy demandent.
91 Ibid., 106f.: leur usage est d'exciter nôtre zéle par la commemoration des Saints dont elles sont les restes sacrés.
92 Thiers, *Réponse* 46f.
93 Ibid., 48–60.
94 Guibert, "De sanctis et eorum pigneribus" 103.
95 Thiers, *Réponse* 48f.

for one's object.'⁹⁶ Truth, for Thiers, trounced charity. Especially heinous was Mabillon's suggestion that it was acceptable to worship an unconsecrated host in error: this was nothing less than the blackest idolatry, and Thiers 'blushed with shame' that his old friend could sustain such blasphemy.⁹⁷

It is curious that Mabillon, no less than Thiers, could claim both Guibert and post-Tridentine polemics as intellectual precedents. It is as if a single tradition – one which united caution with a principle of charity, still present in, say, Grostête – was broken in two by the new demands of rigour and severity at the turn of the century. Thiers inherited the justice of that tradition, Mabillon the mercy. But there was piety in each position, and if the secular view of the Holy Tear after 1700 was a foregone conclusion, it would have been difficult to predict the reception of their clash among the good Catholics of later ages.

4 After Thiers and Mabillon

At his death in 1703, Thiers was satirised for his assault on the Holy Tear:

> A Vandôme tout rit, Prieur, Abbé, Convers;
> Et j'entens Frere Oignon, d'ici qui carillonne:
> Il est donc mort, dit-il, notre bon ami Thiers,
> Qui parloit librement et du quart et du tiers;
> Qui la Larme attaquant n'est pleuré de personne.⁹⁸

His dispute with Mabillon was famous among contemporaries. The more philosophical critics of the day stuck up for Thiers and ridiculed his opponent: these included the Catholic Richard Simon and the Huguenot Jacques Basnage de Beauval.⁹⁹ Conservative scholars, even if disinclined to reject Thiers's reasoning, disapproved of his tone, and underlined his own scholarly goofs.¹⁰⁰

---

96   Ibid., 49: parce qu'elle est contraire au veritable culte de la Religion, dont le caractere propre est d'avoir l'esprit pour principe et la verité pour objet *in spiritu et veritate*.
97   Ibid., 59.
98   Dreux du Radier Jean-François, *Eloges historiques des hommes illustres de la Province du Thymerais* (Paris, Berthier and De Poilly: 1749) 61.
99   'Sainjore Mr. de' [= Simon Richard], *Bibliothèque critique on recueil de diverses pieces critiques*, 4 vols. (Paris, De Lormes: 1708) III, 337; 355f.; Simon Richard, *Critique de la Bibliotheque des auteurs ecclesiastiques*, 4 vols. (Paris, Ganeau: 1730) II, 409f.; Basnage Jacques, *Entretiens sur la religion*, 2 vols. (Rotterdam, Acher: 1713³) I, 389f.
100   Du Pin, *Bibliothèque* V, 123–126; le Cerf, *Biblioteque historique* 279–284; Chalippe Candide, *La vie de Saint-François* (Paris, Prault: 1728) 642. Aside from Thiers's inconsistency on the validity of negative argument, his most infamous error, widely repeated as a comic *faux*

The controversy was also noticed by men of letters outside France – Caspar Sagittarius at Jena, and the *émigré* Michael de la Roche in England, both, as Protestants, predictably siding with Thiers.[101]

Few took the argument forward, although the Carmelite monk Honoré de Sainte-Marie, a reliable enemy of the *modernes*, devoted an entire article of his monumental *Réflexions* to the subject.[102] Like others, he condemned Thiers's impiety; but the damage had been done, and although he praised Mabillon's erudition and acumen, he could not bring himself to accept the Maurist's fantastical claims about the Holy Tear.[103] Sainte-Marie's own explanation aimed to do away with Thiers's qualms, and Calvin's; it also accounted for the silence of the early Middle Ages on the subject, and the concentration of tear-relics in France. He argued that these relics, including that of Vendôme, were not the natural tears of Christ at all, but miraculous tears shed by a crucifix in the church of St Pierre-le-Puellier, Orléans, at the end of the tenth century, and subsequently distributed throughout the provincial parishes. This was, of course, merely to substitute one miracle for another; but in redescribing the Holy Tear as distinctively French, the monk's account served more generally to defend the faith of local peoples against the critical savageries of Thiers's *Traité des superstitions*.

After about 1730, the Republic of Letters lost interest in the Holy Tear: it was no doubt felt that everything which could be said had already been said. Berthier himself never got involved. Pilgrims, indeed, continued to come, even after the relics had vanished. The loss occurred after the Revolution: local officials arrived at the abbey in October 1790, conducted a census of the relics and other valuables, and destroyed most, including the golden coffers of the Tear.[104] The carved portal survived until 1803, when it was demolished, allegedly to

---

  pas, was his misunderstanding of the title of Philo's essay *Quod omnis probus liber*, as meaning 'That every book is good', when in fact it meant, 'That every good man is free' (περὶ τοῦ σπουδαῖον εἶναι ἐλεύθερον). See Thiers, *Réponse* 115.

101 Sagittarius Caspar, *Introductio in historiam ecclesiasticam*, 2 vols. (Jena, Bielck: 1719²) II, 530; Roche Michael de la (ed.), *Memoirs of Literature*, 8 vols. (London, Vaillant: 1722) II, 149–151 (Article 35).

102 Sainte-Marie Honoré de, *Réflexions sur les règles et sur l'usage de la critique*, vol. 3 (Lyons, Molin: 1720) 338–55 (V.5.2). This work, a systematic defence of Catholic belief over 1,500 pages long, was translated into Latin as the *Animadversiones in regulas et usum critices*, 3 vols. (Venice: 1738–1739), and widely cited by contemporaries. Although it has since fallen into obscurity, it would well repay further study.

103 Sainte-Marie, *Réflexions* III, 348f.

104 de Pétigny, *Histoire archéologique* 187–190. Metais C., *L'Église et l'abbaye de la Trinité de Vendôme pendant la Révolution (1790–1802)* (Vendôme: 1886), quotes and discusses the extant summary of the census document in more detail; see p. 9 on the Holy Tear.

allow more light into the choir, but more probably to discourage any lingering interest in the old relic.[105] The crystal, meanwhile, had been saved, shorn of its accoutrements; it was taken to the district office and kept by a bureaucrat named Morin, where his children had it for a plaything. By 1803, it had passed back into Catholic hands: the Blois curate Mathurin Gallois, Etienne Bernier, Bishop of Orléans, and finally the Archbishop of Milan, Giovanni Battista Caprara.[106] Its subsequent history is lost.

As the crystal disappeared, the Holy Tear passed into legend, and in this state it would live again. Professional demystifiers continued to quote Thiers's critique with approval in the 1810s and 20s,[107] but at the same time, the idea of the relic resurfaced in poetry. At the start of Alfred de Vigny's 1824 epic *Éloa*, the angel of the title is born from the tear Christ shed for the dead Lazarus:

> Larme sainte à l'amitié donnée,
> Oh! vous ne fûtes points aux vents abandonnée!
> Des Séraphins penchés l'urne de diamant,
> Invisible aux mortels, vous reçut mollement,
> Et, comme une merveille au Ciel même étonnante,
> Aux pieds de l'Éternel vous porta rayonnante.[108]

We are not so far, in these verses, from the hymns to the Holy Tear transcribed at the end of the *Histoire véritable*: the apostrophes of the mediaeval poems are rendered here as Romantic exclamations, but the celestial imagery of the *Histoire* is very much in force again. In the following decades, the mood of these lines, and of this *genre*, extended to the scholars and historians of France: a new piety, or at least a new confidence in piety. Émile Chavin de Malan, then known chiefly for his work on the saints, produced a biography of Mabillon in 1843, in which the critic is not ridiculed or reproved for his defence of the Holy Tear, but rather consoled. The Tear is now a 'poétique légende' fabricated by the Middle Ages in its 'amour du merveilleux'.[109] Chavin de Malan, if he does not believe the relic's authenticity, nonetheless experiences a 'bonheur infini'

105　Rochambeau A. de, *Le vendomois épigraphie et iconographie*, 2 vols. (Paris: 1889–1894) I, 55.
106　Rochambeau, *Voyage à la Sainte-Larme* 55.
107　Salgues J.-B., *Des erreurs et des préjugés répandus dans la société*, 3 vols. (Paris: 1810–1813) II, 176–181; Collin de Plancy J.-A.-S., *Dictionnaire critique des reliques et des images miraculeuses*, 2 vols. (Paris: 1821) II, 55–58.
108　Vigny A. de, *Éloa, ou La soeur des Anges* (Paris: 1824) 5.
109　Chavin de Malan É., *Histoire de D. Mabillon et de la congrégation de Saint-Maur* (Paris: 1843) 438.

in speaking of it, for behind the legend stands Christ's love for mankind. The value of Christianity, he says, lies in its moral revolutions:

> Dans l'antiquité, les larmes étaient un MAL; dans le christianisme, elles sont spiritualisées, sanctifiées, divinisées, elles sont devenues un BIEN. En une seule de ces larmes consolables que forment la douleur et la foi en se mêlant ensemble, nous avance plus ici-bas que la recherche et la possession de toutes choses.
>
> In antiquity, tears had been an EVIL. In Christianity, they were spiritualised, sanctified, made divine: they became a GOOD. In a single one of these consolable tears, formed of grief and faith mixed together, we advance further than in the search and possession of all things.[110]

This passage represents an important shift in Catholic attitudes to the past. Crucially, its attitude to the Holy Tear is not susceptible to the criticism of a Thiers, because it locates value beyond the historical record. In such a way the merit of the relic could be sustained alongside a dispassionate investigation into its history, and while Chavin de Malan had no interest in such a study, his contemporaries did, even as they shared his affection for the mysterious crystal, now just an idea. Thus for the historian Jules de Pétigny, the relic was only a natural gemstone, and a trick of the Greeks on Geoffroy Martel; moreover, its golden coffers had been fashioned in Freising for Nitker, as an ornamental reliquary with no original connection to the Tear whatsoever.[111] Nonetheless, the popular belief in the relic's authenticity was not a contemptible superstition, but a 'touchante et poétique croyance'.[112] Similarly, the antiquary and numismatist Étienne Cartier, noting the Thiers – Mabillon episode in 1849, declined to adjudicate between them, preferring simply to recall 'une des plus belles légendes du moyen âge'. The relic-story is, again, 'touchant', because it symbolises 'l'affection la plus pure qui puisse unir les homes'; mediaeval belief in the Tear's divinity had consoled and alleviated distress.[113]

Cartier's comments appear in an article from the first volume of the *Mélanges d'archéologie, d'histoire et de littérature*, a journal edited by two Jesuit fathers, Charles Cahier and Arthur Martin. The pair belonged to the circle of

---

110 Ibid., 441.
111 de Pétigny, *Histoire archéologique* 187 n. 3.
112 Ibid., 189.
113 Cartier É., "Recherches sur l'origine du type des monnaies chartraines", in Cahier C. – Martin A. (eds.), *Mélanges d'archéologie, d'histoire et de littérature, vol. 1* (Paris: 1849) 51–73, 69.

FIGURE 10.1 [Unknown Illustrator], one end of the reliquary coffer of the Holy Tear, engraving from Jean Mabillon's *Lettre d'un Benedictin* [...] (Paris, Pierre and Imbert de Bats: 1700) plate facing p. 49.

Adolphe-Napoléon Didron, a prominent mediaevalist who had worked for the preservation of cathedral architecture with Viollet-le-Duc since the 1840s. It was in this setting that the study of mediaeval iconography was first nurtured in France, and its greatest exponent, Emile Mâle, would later pay tribute to Didron, Cahier and Martin.[114] Those scholars felt already the value of pre-Tridentine religion, and of the 'dear legends which had nourished Christianity for so many centuries'.[115]

In 1853 the new methods were applied to the Holy Tear. Arthur Martin, reviewing the antiquities of Freising Cathedral for an article in the *Mélanges*, digressed for a few pages on the gold coffers which had enclosed the Vendôme relic. The outermost coffer, engravings of which he found in Mabillon [Fig. 10.1], was full of eyes: a large one on the end, a Melchizedek with an eye for a head, and an Aaron standing on an eye. Mabillon, having no experience with iconography, had been unable to understand the imagery, but Martin himself recognised the theme from his studies: Melchizedek, the type of Christ, represented the Christian Church, with its eye open before heaven, while Aaron, a token of the Jews, stood for the blindness of their religion. The Vendômois monks who inherited the coffer from Freising had failed, like Mabillon, to grasp its symbolism; they had presumably interpreted the great eye as that of

---

114 Mâle É., *L'art religieux du XIIIe siècle en France* (Paris: 1898) vii – viii. For Mâle, too, 'touchant' is a key phrase; he applies it on p. i to the description of cathedrals as 'the Bible of the poor'.

115 Ibid., ii: L'Église rougit des chères légendes qui avaient bercé la chrétienté pendant tant de siècles. Le concile de Trente marque la fin des vieilles traditions artistiques.

Christ, and supposed the coffer to contain one of his tears, or else added the crystal themselves to complete the mystery.[116] The relic and its legend, then, rested entirely on a misunderstanding – it was an iconographical problem. But for Martin, as for his immediate predecessors, there was no issue of fraud:

> Si ces traditions ont été loin de produire la certitude, elles ont pu suffire à la bonne foi. Qu'il y ait eu erreur, l'erreur involontaire n'a pas été un crime. La vue pouvait être trompée, le coeur ne l'était pas. Ce que le fidèle vénérait, ce qu'il aimait à Vendôme, n'était-ce pas dans les larmes de Béthanie l'amitié divine de celui qui a été non seulement généreux jusqu'à verser son sang pour les hommes, mais *doux de coeur* jusqu'à répandre sur ses amis des larmes.

> If these traditions are far from producing certitude, they could at least suffice for good faith. Even if there was an error, involuntary error was not a crime. The sight could be deceived; the heart was not. What the faithful venerated, what they loved at Vendôme, lay in the tears of Bethany: the divine *amitié* of someone who was not only so generous that he gave his blood for mankind, but so gentle of heart that he shed tears for his friends.[117]

The tone was now set. Jacques Texier, in his 1857 dictionary of *orfévrerie*, disagreed with Martin on the iconographic *minutiae* of the coffer, preferring to follow François de Sales's notion of the Holy Tear; but like Martin he rejected imposture, and concluded by quoting Cartier's opinion of the relic's value.[118] In 1860 Maxime de Montrond expressed the same, denying the authenticity of the Tear while speaking of the 'traits aimables du génie tendre et chrétien du moyen âge'.[119] Arthur Forgeais, in an 1865 survey of pilgrim *ampoules* dredged from the Seine, thought Martin had the whole matter sewn up.[120] Achille de Rochambeau, finally, in his 1874 monograph on the Tear, gave his seal of approval to the position.[121]

---

116 Martin A., "Antiquités de la Cathédrale de Frisingue", in Cahier C. – Martin A. (eds.), *Mélanges d'archéologie, d'histoire et de littérature, vol. 3* (Paris: 1853) 63–94, 80–81n.
117 Martin, "Antiquités" 81n.
118 Texier J.R.A., *Dictionnaire d'orfévrerie, de gravure et de ciselure chrétiennes* (Paris: 1857) 1086–1107.
119 Montrond M. de, *Fleurs monastiques: souvenirs, études et pèlerinages* (Paris: 1860) 437.
120 Forgeais A., *Numismatiques des corporations parisiennes: collection de plombs historiés trouvés dans la seine* (Paris: 1865) 65–86.
121 Rochambeau, *Voyage à la Sainte-Larme* 60.

In all this was the ghost of Mabillon. The relic, he had said, was only the sign of something greater; to worship a false relic with a true heart was acceptable to God, who looked to intentions, to the directed will, not to the understanding. In that proposition, suggested by Guibert and reviled by Thiers, lay the critical faultline of enlightened Christianity. A piece of what is now called 'material culture', with all its celestial mysteriousness, had become the focus for a conversation about the most immaterial question imaginable. Mabillon's own formula was quoted with gusto by Montrond and Rochambeau, but the sentiment was already implicit among the antiquaries of the mid-century. To be saved was not the divine origin of a bit of quartz, a cabinet curio, but the 'affection' and 'amitié' which had given it life, and above all the 'bonne foi' which kept it alive: thus Thiers, in purifying the historical record, had profaned the spirit which gave that record meaning. If the Calvinists drew their strength from the individual faith, the freedom of personal interpretation, these Catholics drew it rather from the corporate unity of their history: no longer eager to shuck off the superstitious, they now embraced the pious peasants of the past, hardly concealing their nostalgia for the era of religious agreement – even agreement in error. To this end, the argument of Mabillon's *Lettre* was an invaluable response to Enlightenment criticism. Flies, it turned out, are difficult to kill with a cannon.

Bibliography

Addison Joseph, *Remarks on Several Parts of Italy &c. in the Years 1701, 1702, 1703* (London, Tonson: 1705).

[anon.], "Éloge de Dom Mabillon", *Histoire de l'académie royale des inscriptions et belles lettres* 1 (1717) 355–368.

Arnauld Marie Angelique, "Letter to the Queen of Poland, 11 Jan 1657", in Arnauld Marie Angelique, *Lettres, vol. 3* (Utrecht, s.n.: 1742) 33.

Barret-Kriegel B., *Jean Mabillon* (Paris: 1988).

Basnage Jacques, *Entretiens sur la religion*, 2 vols. (Rotterdam, Acher: 1713³).

Belot Jean, *Les Fleurs de la philosophie chrestienne et morale* (Paris, Du Brueil: 1603).

Bochart Matthieu, *Traité de l'origine du service des reliques, de l'invocation des saints, des images et du culte rendu aux images des saints* (Saumur, Lesnier: 1656).

Boussel P., *Des reliques et de leur bon usage* (Paris: 1971).

Boyle Robert, *Essay about the Origine and Virtues of Gems* (London, Godbid: 1672).

Brown P., *The Cult of the Saints: Its Rise and Function in Latin Christianity* (London: 1981).

Bynum C.W., *Christian Materiality: An Essay on Religion in Late Medieval Europe* (Cambridge, MA: 2011).

Calvin Jean, *Traité des reliques*, in *Three French Treatises*, ed. F. Higman (London: 1970).
Cartier É., "Recherches sur l'origine du type des monnaies chartraines", in Cahier C. – Martin A. (eds.), *Mélanges d'archéologie, d'histoire et de littérature, vol. 1* (Paris: 1849) 51–73.
Cerf Philippe le, *Biblioteque historique et critique des auteurs de la congregation de St Maur* (The Hague, Grosse: 1726).
Chalippe Candide, *La vie de Saint-François* (Paris, Prault: 1728).
Chavin de Malan É., *Histoire de D. Mabillon et de la congrégation de Saint-Maur* (Paris: 1843).
Collin de Plancy J.-A.-S., *Dictionnaire critique des reliques et des images miraculeuses*, 2 vols. (Paris: 1821).
Crozet R., "Le monument de la sainte larme à La Trinité de Vendôme", *Bulletin monumental* 121 (1963) 171–180.
Dreux du Radier Jean-François, *Eloges historiques des hommes illustres de la Province du Thymerais* (Paris, Berthier and De Poilly: 1749).
Ferrand Jean, *Disquisitio reliquiaria, sive, De suspicienda et suspecta earumdem numero reliquiarium quae in diversis Ecclesiis servantur multitudine* (Lyon, Anisson: 1647).
Feuillas M., "La controverse magdalénienne au milieu du XVIIe siècle: ripostes provençales à Jean de Launoy", in Duperray È. et al. (eds.), *Marie Madeleine dans la mystique, les arts et les lettres* (Paris: 1989) 89–110.
Forgeais A., *Numismatiques des corporations parisiennes: collection de plombs historiés trouvés dans la seine* (Paris: 1865).
Fuchs K., *Zeichen und Wunder bei Guibert de Nogent: Kommunikation, Deutungen und Funktionalisierungen von Wunderzählungen im 12. Jahrhundert* (Munich: 2008).
[Gavin Antonio], *Observations on a Journy to Naples, wherein the Frauds of Romish Monks and Priests are Farther Discover'd* (London, Roycroft: 1691).
George P., "Les reliques des saints: un nouvel objet historique", in: Bozóky E. – Helvétius A.-M. (eds.), *Les reliques: objets, cultes, symboles: Actes du colloque international de l'Université du Littoral Côte d'Opale 4–6 septembre 1997* (Turnhout: 1999) 229–237.
Grès-Gayer J.M., "'L'Aristarque de son siècle': Le docteur Jean de Launoy (1601–1678)", in Quantin J.-L. – Wacquet J.-C. (eds.), *Papes, princes et savants dans l'Europe moderne: Mélanges à la mémoire de Bruno Neveu* (Geneva: 2006) 269–285.
Grostête des Mahis Marin, *L'Entretien d'un Catholique et d'un Calviniste sur le sujet des reliques*, in Grostête des Mahis Marin, *Deux lettres* (Orléans, Boyer: 1685) 105.
Guibert de Nogent, "De sanctis et eorum pigneribus", in Guibert de Nogent, [*Opera*], ed. R.B.C. Huygens (Turnhout: 1993).
Henriquez Crisóstomo, *Fasciculus sanctorum Ordinis Cisterciensis … complectens liber secundus* (Cologne, Cholinus: 1631).
Hickey H.M., "Capturing Christ's Tears: La Sainte Larme in Medieval and Early Modern France", in Downes S. and Randles S. (eds.) *Feeling Things: Objects and Emotions through History* (Oxford: 2018) 58–71.

Histoire véritable de la Sainte Larme que N. Seigneur pleura sur le Lazare (Vendôme, Hyp: 1641 [1669]).

Hurel D.-O., "Jean Mabillon, Jean-Baptiste Thiers et la congrégation de Saint-Maur", in Leclant J. et al. (eds.), *Dom Jean Mabillon: figure majeure de l'Europe des lettres. Actes des deux colloques du tricentenaire de la mort de dom Mabillon* (Paris: 2010) 59–76.

Isnard I., *L'abbatiale de la Trinité de Vendôme* (Rennes: 2007).

[Jurieu Pierre], *Suite de l'accomplissement des prophetes* (Rotterdam, Acher: 1687).

Kearney J., *The Incarnate Text: Imagining the Book in Reformation England* (Philadelphia: 2009).

Knight K.-J., "Droplets of Heaven: Tears Relics in the High and Later Middle Ages", *The Mediaeval Journal* 6 (2016), 45–80.

Launoy Jean de, *De auctoritate negantis argumenti dissertatio* (Paris, Martin: 1662).

Leclercq H., *Mabillon*, 2 vols. (Paris: 1953–1957).

Mabillon Jean, *Dissertation sur le culte des saints inconnus* (Paris, Musier: 1698).

Mabillon Jean, *Lettre d'un benedictin à Monsieur L'Evesque de Blois, touchant le discernement des anciennes reliques* (Paris, De Bats: 1700).

Mabillon Jean, *Eusebii Romani ad Theophilum Gallum epistola de cultu SS ignotorum* (Paris, Robustel: 1705).

Mâle É., *L'art religieux du XIII[e] siècle en France* (Paris: 1898).

Martin A., "Antiquités de la Cathédrale de Frisingue", in Cahier C. – Martin A. (eds.), *Mélanges d'archéologie, d'histoire et de littérature, vol. 3* (Paris: 1853) 63–94.

Merc[h]ier Jacques le, *Histoire de la larme sainte de NS Jesus-Christ reverée dans l'abbaye de Selincourt* (Amiens, Caron-Hubault: 1707).

Metais C., *L'Église et l'abbaye de la Trinité de Vendôme pendant la Révolution (1790–1802)* (Vendôme: 1886).

Montaiglon A. de (ed.), *Recueil de poésies françoises des XVe et XVIe siècles*, 12 vols. (Paris: 1855–1877).

Montrond M. de, *Fleurs monastiques: souvenirs, études et pèlerinages* (Paris: 1860).

Morris C., *The Discovery of the Individual, 1050–1200* (Toronto: 2004).

Mouskes Philippe, *Chronique rimée*, ed. Baron de Reiffenberg, 2 vols. (Brussels: 1836).

Münster Sebastian, *Cosmographia*, trans. and rev. F. de Belleforest, 2 vols. (Paris, Sonnius: 1575).

Person David, "A Treatise of Laughing and Mourning", in Person David, *Varieties, or, A Surveigh of Rare and Excellent Matters Necessary and Delectable for all Sorts of Persons* (London, Badger: 1635) 187f.

Pétigny J. de, *Histoire archéologique du Vendômois* (Vendôme: 1849).

Petit Pierre, *De lacrymis libri tres* (Paris, Cramoisy: 1661).

Pin Louis-Ellie Du, *Bibliothèque des auteurs ecclésiastiques du dix-septième siècle*, 7 vols. (Paris, Pralard: 1708).

Platelle H., "Guibert de Nogent et le De pignoribus sanctorum. Richesses et limites d'une critique médiévale des reliques", in Bozóky É. – Helvétius A.-M. (eds.), *Les reliques. Objets, cultes, symboles. Actes du colloque international de l'Université du Littoral-Côte d'Opale (Boulogne-sur-Mer), 4–6 septembre 1997*, Hagiologia 1 (Turnhout: 1999) 109–21.

Pottier A., *Histoire du précieux sang de Notre Seigneur Jésus-Christ conservé en l'abbaye de la Sainte Trinité de Fécamp* (Rouen: 1838).

Quantin J.-L., *Le catholicisme classique et les pères de l'Église: un retour aux sources (1669–1713)* (Paris: 1999).

Quantin J.-L., "Reason and Reasonableness in French Ecclesiastical Scholarship", *Huntington Library Quarterly* 74 (2011) 401–436.

Rhodiginus Ludovicus Caelius, *Lectionum antiquarum libri XXX* (Basel, Froben: 1542).

Rochambeau A. de, *Voyage à la Sainte-Larme de Vendôme: étude historique et critique sur cet antique pélérinage* (Vendôme: 1874).

Rochambeau A. de, *Le vendomois épigraphie et iconographie*, 2 vols. (Paris: 1889–1894).

Roche Michael de la (ed.), *Memoirs of Literature*, 8 vols. (London, Vaillant: 1722).

Rohault Jacques, "Letter to Malebranche, 9 July 1671", in Malebranche Nicolas, *Fragments philosophiques inédits et correspondance*, ed. Vidgrain J. (Paris: s.a.) 38.

Rubinstein J., *Guibert of Nogent: Portrait of a Medieval Mind* (New York: 2002).

Ruinart Thierry, *Abrégé de la vie de dom Jean Mabillon* (1709), ed. T. Barbeau (La Froidfontaine: 2007).

Sagittarius Caspar, *Introductio in historiam ecclesiasticam*, 2 vols. (Jena, Bielck: 1719²).

'Sainjore Mr. de' [= Simon Richard], *Bibliothèque critique on recueil de diverses pieces critiques*, 4 vols. (Paris, De Lormes: 1708).

Sainte-Marie Honoré de, *Réflexions sur les règles et sur l'usage de la critique*, vol. 3 (Lyons, Molin: 1720).

Sales François de, "Letter to an unknown woman, 7 June 1622", in Sales François de, *Lettres, vol. 3* (Paris: 1817) 60f.

Salgues J.-B., *Des erreurs et des préjugés répandus dans la société*, 3 vols. (Paris: 1810–1813).

Segni Giovanni Battista, *Reliquiarium, sive, De reliquiis et veneratione sanctorum* (Bologna, Rossius: 1610).

Simon Richard, *Critique de la Bibliotheque des auteurs ecclesiastiques*, 4 vols. (Paris, Ganeau: 1730).

Strauss D.F., *Das Leben Jesu, kritisch bearbeitet*, 2 vols. (Tübingen: 1835–1836).

Terzago Paulo Maria, *Musaeum Septalianum* (Dertona, Viola: 1664).

Texier J.R.A., *Dictionnaire d'orfévrerie, de gravure et de ciselure chrétiennes* (Paris: 1857).

Thiers Jean-Baptiste, *Exercitatio adversus Iohannis de Launoy Dissertationem de auctoritate negantis argumenti* (Paris, Le Sourd: 1662).

Thiers Jean-Baptiste, *Traité de la clôture des religieuses* (Paris, Dezallier: 1681).

Thiers Jean-Baptiste, *Traité des superstitions qui regardent les sacremens*, 4 vols. (Paris, Dezallier: 1697–1704).

Thiers Jean-Baptiste, *Dissertation sur la Sainte Larme de Vendôme* (Paris, Thiboust and Esclassan: 1699).

Thiers Jean-Baptiste, *Réponse à la lettre du Père Mabillon touchant la pretendue Sainte Larme du Vendôme* (Cologne, Heirs of Cornelis van Egmond: 1700).

Vigny A. de, *Éloa, ou La soeur des Anges* (Paris: 1824).

CHAPTER 11

The Powerlessness of the Devil: Scientific Knowledge and Demonology in Clemente Baroni Cavalcabò (1726–1796)

Riccarda Suitner

1   Rovereto, 1749: The Outbreak of the Dispute Over Diabolical Power

In 1749, several years after completing the work, the abbot Girolamo Tartarotti finally received permission from the Inquisition to publish his *Congresso notturno delle lammie* (Nocturnal gathering of witches).[1] Describing gatherings of witches and pacts with the Devil as a mere product of human fantasy, in this work the Italian scholar attempted to re-evaluate the Devil's influence over the physical world. Even before its publication, the book had already triggered one of the last great controversies over witchcraft, a conflict which shook the Italian intellectual world of the mid eighteenth century.[2] The debate gravitated around the Accademia degli Agiati, an institution founded a year after the publication of the *Congresso notturno* in Rovereto, Tartarotti's birthplace, but it had repercussions well beyond the boundaries of this small town, at the time under Habsburg control, even reaching German-speaking territories.[3] In 1761 a

---

1   Tartarotti Girolamo, *Del congresso notturno delle lammie libri tre* (Rovereto, Pasquali: 1749). I am grateful to Hartmut Hecht, Eberhard Knobloch and Bernd Roling for their advice on several points.

2   For exhaustive reconstructions of the Rovereto dispute see Parinetto L., *I lumi e le streghe. Una polemica italiana intorno al 1750* (Paderno Dugnano: 1998); 1st ed. entitled *Magia e ragione: una polemica sulle streghe in Italia intorno al 1750* (Florence: 1974); Suitner R. (ed.), *Gli Illuministi e i demoni. Il dibattito su magia e stregoneria dal Trentino all'Europa* (Rome: 2019). Cf. also Provenzal D., *Una polemica diabolica nel secolo XVIII* (Rocca S. Casciano: 1901); Venturi F., *Settecento riformatore, vol. 1: Da Muratori a Beccaria* (Torino: 1998) 355–377; Israel J., *Radical Enlightenment. Philosophy and the Making of Modernity 1650–1750* (Oxford: 2001) 375–405. The dispute over the Devil's power was not the only one in which Tartarotti (1706–1761) was involved. A second controversy followed his denial of the sainthood and martyrdom of bishop Adalpreto; having fallen into disgrace with the bishop of Trent in 1762 his fellow citizens were even subjected to an interdict for having erected a bust in his honour.

3   For a history of the Roveretan Academy, founded in 1750, see Bonazza M., *L'Accademia Roveretana degli Agiati* (Rovereto: 1998); Ferrari S., "Una società 'confinante': la vicenda storica dell'Accademia degli Agiati", in Ferrari S. (ed.), *Cultura letteraria e sapere scientifico nelle Accademie tedesche e italiane del Settecento* (Rovereto: 2003) 91–126. On relations between

volume entitled *Das große welt-betrügende Nichts* (The great world-deceiving Nothing) was published under the Italian pseudonym of 'Ardoino Ubbidiente dell'O.S.A.'. Behind this fictitious name, perhaps an allusion to the Jesuit Jean Hardouin, was an eccentric figure by the name of Jordan Simon. A member of the order of the Hermits of St Augustine and from 1757 of the *Akademie nützlicher Wissenschaften* in Erfurt, Simon became dean of the Faculty of Theology at the local university in 1766. Seven years later he was forced to leave Erfurt under mysterious circumstances, fleeing the city suddenly by night; there followed years of wandering between Münnerstadt, Rome, Bohemia, Vienna, and Prague, where he was finally elected to a chair in polemics at the university.[4]

Magic is the 'nothingness' to which Simon refers in the title of his book, conceived with the aim of disseminating the theories of another participant in the Roveretan debate, the Veronese intellectual Scipione Maffei, in Germany. The latter, in the trilogy consisting of the *Arte magica dileguata, Arte magica distrutta* and *Arte magica annichilata* (1749–1754), had attempted to dissipate that magical world left intact by Tartarotti's approach.[5] The *Congresso notturno delle lammie* had in fact postulated a clear distinction between magic, seen as actually existing, and witchcraft, a phenomenon reduced to a mere mental disorder, the hallucinations of ignorant and easily deceived individuals. The arguments set out in Tartarotti's treatise did not explicitly refute the interaction between the sphere of separated spirits and the human world: the possibility of making a pact with the Devil was denied to witches but conceded to wizards, alone deemed capable of exerting a genuine power over the natural world.[6]

---

the Academy and German culture cf. idem, "L'Accademia Roveretana degli Agiati e la cultura di lingua tedesca (1750–1795)", in Ferrari S. (ed.), *Cultura letteraria e sapere scientifico nelle Accademie tedesche e italiane del Settecento* (Rovereto: 2003) 217–276; Spada A., "Scambi culturali tra Italia e Austria a metà del '700. Le Accademie di Salisburgo, Innsbruck e Rovereto", in Destro A. – Filippi P.M. (eds.), *La cultura tedesca in Italia 1750–1850* (Bologna: 1995) 191–216.

4 Ubbidiente dell'O.S.A. Ardoino [= Simon Jordan], *Das grosse Welt-betrügende Nichts oder die heutige Hexerey und Zauberkunst* (Frankfurt – Leipzig, s.n.: 1761). On Simon's adventurous life cf. Kleineidam E., *Universitas studii Erffordensis. Überblick über die Geschichte der Universität Erfurt, vol. IV* (Leipzig: 1981) 109–122; 124–127; 170–173; 313–315; Strüber S., *P. Jordan Simon aus dem Orden der Augustiner-Eremiten. Ein Lebensbild aus der Aufklärungszeit* (Würzburg: 1930).

5 Cf. Maffei Scipione, *Arte magica dileguata, lettera del signor marchese Maffei al padre Innocente Ansaldi dell'Ordine dei Predicatori* (Verona, Carattoni: 1749); Fiorio Antonio, *Arte magica distrutta. Risposta di don Antonio Fiorio veronese arciprete di Tignale, e Valvestino, vicario foraneo* (Trent, Brunati: 1750); idem, *Arte magica annichilata, libri tre. Con un'appendice* (Verona, Andreoni: 1754).

6 Cf. Tartarotti, *Del congresso notturno delle lammie* 159–168.

In the eyes of the 'Reformist' milieu in contact with the circles of the Accademia degli Agiati, represented by figures like Maffei and the Capodistrian Enlightenment thinker Gianrinaldo Carli, Tartarotti's treatise seemed to lack the courage needed to deal a definitive blow to the supernatural world; the theological faction, by contrast, had seen an increasingly irreconcilable conflict develop between 'Enlightenment' knowledge and religion since the outbreak of the dispute. Tartarotti, under attack from several quarters, was thus forced to publish an *Apologia del Congresso notturno* in 1751, complete with an appendix containing a letter in which his protégé Clemente Baroni Cavalcabò presented a selection of papers composed by numerous Italian intellectuals on their master's behalf.[7] Clemente Baroni Cavalcabò is a neglected figure in existing studies of the Italian debate over magic and witchcraft.[8] Clemente Baroni came from a family of merchants, probably not of noble origin as he implied by signing himself 'delli marchesi Cavalcabò'. His earliest published work was a translation from Latin of an anonymous Masonic text, the first of a vast number of historical studies, scientific and philosophical essays and the start of his active participation in the intellectual life of the Accademia degli Agiati, of which he was a member since its foundation.[9]

At the age of twenty-seven, two years after intervening on Tartarotti's behalf, Baroni Cavalcabò published a treatise with the unusual title *L'impotenza del demonio di trasportare a talento per l'aria da un luogo all'altro i corpi umani* (The Powerlessness of the Devil to Transport Human Bodies Through the Air from One Place to Another at Will).[10] 'Seeing that the issue of witchcraft,

---

7   Baroni Cavalcabò Clemente, *Lettera del Signor Clemente Baroni delli Marchesi Cavalcabò ad un giornalista oltramontano, sopra il Congresso Notturno delle Lammie del Sig. Abate Girolamo Tartarotti*, in Tartarotti Girolamo, *Apologia del Congresso notturno delle lammie, o sia Risposta di Girolamo Tartarotti all'Arte magica dileguata del sig. march. Scipione Maffei, ed all'opposizione del sig. assessore Bartolommeo Melchiori. S'aggiunge una lettera del Sig. Clemente Baroni di Cavalcabò* (Venice, Occhi: 1751) 223–268.

8   See Parinetto, *I lumi e le streghe* 245–269, and the essays published by Riccarda Suitner, Christian Zendri, and Antonio Trampus in Suitner (ed.), *Gli Illuministi e i demoni*. *L'impotenza del demonio* is also mentioned in Venturi, *Settecento riformatore* 374–375.

9   Baroni Cavalcabò Clemente, *Dichiarazione dell'instituto e scopo de' Liberi Muratori, dove si prende a confutare il candeliere acceso de' Liberi Muratori eretto di fresco* (Rovereto, Marchesani: 1749). For biographical information and a brief presentation of Baroni Cavalcabò's writings cf. Leonardi C., "Clemente Baroni Cavalcabò", in *Dizionario biografico degli italiani*, vol. 6 (Rome: 1964) 462–466; Mazzuchelli Giovanni M., *Gli scrittori d'Italia*, vol. 2 (Brescia, Bossini: 1758) 384–386; Rosmini Carlo, *Memorie intorno alla vita e agli scritti di Clemente Baroni Cavalcabò* (Rovereto, Marchesani: 1798).

10 Baroni Cavalcabò Clemente, *L'impotenza del demonio di trasportare a talento per l'aria da un luogo all'altro i corpi umani dimostrata da Clemente Baroni delli Marchesi Cavalcabò accademico di Rovereto, dove anche si dimostra l'impossibilità di volare con artifizio umano*

having exerted the pens of many renowned Intellectuals, had not yet been resolved', remarked an anonymous reviewer in the periodical *Memorie per servire all'istoria letteraria*,

> he aimed to put an end to it with a master-stroke; attempting to demonstrate that the Devil cannot carry human bodies through the air from one place to another at will; when this is conclusively proven witches and witchcraft will go up in smoke at once.

'I would have no fear of asserting', continued the anonymous reviewer, 'the fact that the Devil is powerless [...], did I not fear the Theologians.'[11] Could refuting the Devil's ability to transport a human body through the air really mean dealing a 'death blow' to his power, capable of making belief in the existence of witchcraft *tout court* go up in smoke? In a certain sense, yes: for instance, as we will see in greater detail below, one consequence of this theory might be to call into question the Devil's ability to convene witches on the Sabbath. However, to understand why intervening in discussions of this type in the mid-eighteenth century still meant venturing onto fairly slippery ground, we need to go back to the Amsterdam of over sixty years earlier and the scandal caused by the publication of the pastor Balthasar Bekker's *De Betoverde Weereld* (The Enchanted World).

From a philosophical point of view the publication of Bekker's treatise (1691–1693) had marked a major turning point in European demonological debate. This work presented a radical consequence of Descartes' substance dualism, applied to an issue on which Descartes had rarely taken a stance.[12] Bekker's starting premise was the consubstantiality of the human soul and the Devil, both finite spirits, created and completely heterogeneous with respect to the reality of *res extensae*. From the prerogative proper to our soul of acting exclusively on its own body and not on that of others, Bekker deduced that the Devil, a separated spirit lacking a body, was unable to exert any sort of influence over human beings. The Dutch pastor's objective was not to take his conclusions to the point of a radical denial of the existence of invisible spirits, but

---

(Rovereto, Marchesani: 1753). Now available also in reprint ed. and with an introduction by R. Suitner (Bologna: 2013).

11 *Memorie per servire all'istoria letteraria* 2 (1753) 51; 56.

12 It is mainly in his correspondence that Descartes makes some mention of the nature of separated spirits (but with exclusive reference to angels). Cf. for example the letter to Regius of January 1642: Charles Adam Paul Tannery (eds.), *Œuvres de Descartes* (Paris: 1897–1913), III, 491–510; the letter to More of August 1649, V, 402–405; the letter to Mersenne of 28 October 1640, III, 205–216); the letter to x*** of March 1637, I, 352–4.

merely to circumscribe their power: the Devil, as a corrupted spirit no longer equal to the angels, was relegated to the bottom of hell, in chains.[13]

The well-known accusations of Spinozism and atheism levelled at Bekker and the massive controversy which followed, counting over 300 interventions for and against, took place almost a century after witch hunts in the Netherlands had virtually ceased.[14] The Italian debate over the Devil's prerogatives, however, remained firmly grounded in what was still an extremely widespread practice, even on the far side of the German border. One of the most sensational cases occurred in the very same year that Tartarotti took an explicit stance in the debate over witchcraft. On 21 June 1749 a nun named Maria Renata Singer was burned at the stake at Würzburg. In his appendix to the *Congresso notturno* the abbot had published, and annotated with his refutation, an Italian translation of the speech given by the Jesuit Georg Gaar when the woman was pronounced guilty, centred on the apologetic need for the belief in the existence of witchcraft, as a divine expedient to persuade atheists 'who believe there is no other substance than the corporeal and material' of the existence of God and the Devil.[15]

It was common to come across speeches of this type, not only when listening to the sermons of the more reactionary preachers or leafing through the records of witch trials. Even an examination of the impact of Cartesian and Bekkerian theories in strictly philosophical circles reveals that the break was indeed a radical one, but insufficient to ensure the rapid disappearance of the idea of a world animated by supernatural powers largely beyond human control. The picture which emerges is a complex one: especially in Germany and Italy the process which saw the victory of the 'new philosophy' and of the scientific revolution over traditional demonology was slow and beset with

---

13　Bekker Balthasar, *De Betoverde Weereld, Zynde een Grondig Ondersoek Van't gemeen gevoelen aangaande de Geesten, derselver Aart en Vermogen, Bewind en Bedryf: als ook't gene de Menschen door derselver kraght en gemeenschap doen*, vol. 2 (Amsterdam, Van den Dalen: 1691) § VII.

14　Israel J., "The Bekker Controversies as a Turning Point in the History of Dutch Culture and Though", *Dutch Crossing. A Journal of Low Countries Studies* 2 (1996) 5–21; Fix A., *Fallen Angels. Balthasar Bekker, Spirit Belief, and Confessionalism in the Seventeenth Century Dutch Republic* (Dordrecht: 1999) 83–124.

15　Tartarotti Girolamo, *Ragionamento del padre Giorgio Gaar della Compagnia di Gesu fatto avanti al rogo di Maria Renata strega abbruciata in Erbipoli a' 21. di Giugno del corrente anno 1749. Tradotto dal tedesco nell'italiano dal Dr. F.A.T. con alcune annotazioni critiche dell'Ab. Girolamo Tartarotti* (Verona, Ramanzini: s.a.). On this event cf. Behringer W., *Witchcraft Persecutions in Bavaria. Popular Magic, Religious Zealotry and Reason of State in Early Modern Europe* (Cambridge: 1997) 357–359; Riezler S. von, *Geschichte der Hexenprozesse in Bayern. Im Lichte der allgemeinen Entwickelung dargestellt* (Stuttgart: 1896) 301f.

difficulties.[16] In Germany it was only from the early eighteenth century onwards that the demonological *querelle*, inextricably linked to the debate over atheism which already saw Cartesians and the opponents of Descartes on opposite sides, made the vexed question of the prerogatives of angels and demons a merely speculative one.

Two dissertations published a few years apart, Christian Thomasius's *De crimine magiae* (1701) and Friedrich Hoffmann's *De diaboli potentia in corpora* (1703) marked a decisive turning point in the debate, with the sudden appearance of the demonological issue in the philosophical debate of the early German Enlightenment. The two philosophers were united in their disagreement with Bekker's decided scepticism about the powers of the supernatural world. However, from the perspectives of legal history and medicine respectively these two essays immediately became the main models on the basis of which belief in the physical interaction between created spirits and the natural world began to be reconsidered in Germany on a purely philosophical level and in direct connection with developments in the post-Cartesian discussion of substance dualism. The result was the demolition of the so-called 'theory of the diabolical pact' (*Teufelspakttheorie*), which in the early eighteenth century still represented one of the legislative bases for witchcraft convictions.[17]

Over forty years later, when Baroni Cavalcabò published his *L'impotenza del demonio*, these arguments were still far from over, not only in Catholic Rovereto, but also in Protestant German territories. The existence of the Devil, his ways of interacting with the human soul and even the possibility that witches made pacts with him and were carnally possessed by him were still controversial and hotly debated issues. The repercussions of Hoffmann's and Thomasius's publications continued to make themselves felt and numerous contenders expressed their own opinions on the subject, rendering the demonological debate yet more complex. The dispute over the prerogatives of invisible spirits and their powers to affect the material world remained one of the many aspects of the debate on atheism within the *Aufklärung*, which

---

16   On demonology and the scientific revolution cf. Clark S., *Thinking With Demons. The Idea of Witchcraft in Early Modern Europe* (Oxford: 1997) 151–311; Easlea B., *Witch-Hunting, Magic and the New Philosophy. An Introduction to Debates of the Scientific Revolution 1450–1750* (Sussex, NY: 1980).

17   Thomasius Christian, *Theses inaugurales, de crimine magiae* (Halle, Salfeld: 1701); Hoffmann Friedrich, "De diaboli potentia in corpora, dissertatio physico-medica curiosa", in Hoffmann Friedrich, *Opera omnia, vol. 5* (Geneva, De Tournes: 1761) 94–103. Cf. Pott M., "Aufklärung und Hexenaberglaube. Philosophische Ansätze zur Überwindung der Teufelspakttheorie in der deutschen Frühaufklärung", in Lorenz S. – Bauer D.R. (eds.), *Das Ende der Hexenverfolgung* (Stuttgart: 1995) 183–202.

throughout the eighteenth century came up against the disruptive effects of the strict substance dualism defended by Bekker in his *Betoverde Weereld*.[18] In Italian-speaking areas, unlike in Germany, the only place which saw disputes over diabolical power was mid-eighteenth-century Rovereto, and Baroni Cavalcabò's treatise was the only intervention in the debate which set itself the ambitious aim of demonstrating philosophically that angels and demons were by nature 'limited substances',[19] thus attempting to draw a clear separation between separated spirits and the human world.

2 The Flight of the Witch

Baroni Cavalcabò's *L'impotenza del demonio*, while attacked by the more conservative clergy, also marked a break, at times in the form of an open disagreement, with Tartarotti's *Congresso notturno*. One of the many aspects in which this treatise differs fundamentally from previous interventions in the Roveretan dispute is the complete absence of social concerns. Baroni Cavalcabò does not seem particularly concerned about the issue of equity of witch trials; somewhat paradoxically, witches are never explicitly mentioned in the treatise, nor is the advisability or otherwise of applying the death penalty to them. Unlike most of the disputants in the Italian debate, Baroni Cavalcabò does not precede his arguments with an erudite historical reconstruction aimed at tracing the origins of witchcraft back to Judaic or pagan superstition.

The critique of the Jesuit Martin del Rio, investigations of the origins and development of witchcraft, the way in which Tartarotti dealt with the issue of witches' gatherings, we read in a manuscript note held at the Biblioteca Civica in Rovereto, are all insufficient elements to refute the nocturnal meetings of witches once the Devil's ability to transport them has been accepted [Fig. 11.1]. Baroni Cavalcabò thus sets out

> with all the force of which Philosophy appears to me to be capable, to demonstrate the intrinsic impossibility, and thus the falsity, of one of the

---

18 On post-Bekkerian demonological debate in Germany cf. Pott M., *Aufklärung und Aberglaube. Die deutsche Frühaufklärung im Spiegel ihrer Aberglaubenskritik* (Tübingen: 1992); Nooijen A., *"Unserm grossen Bekker ein Denkmal"? Balthasar Bekkers* Betoverde Weereld *in den deutschen Landen zwischen Orthodoxie und Aufklärung* (Münster: 2009); Bunge W. van, "Introduction to Balthasar Bekker", in Bekker Balthasar, *Die bezauberte Welt (1693)*, ed. W. van Bunge (Stuttgart: 1997) 43–54.

19 Baroni Cavalcabò, *L'impotenza del demonio* 135.

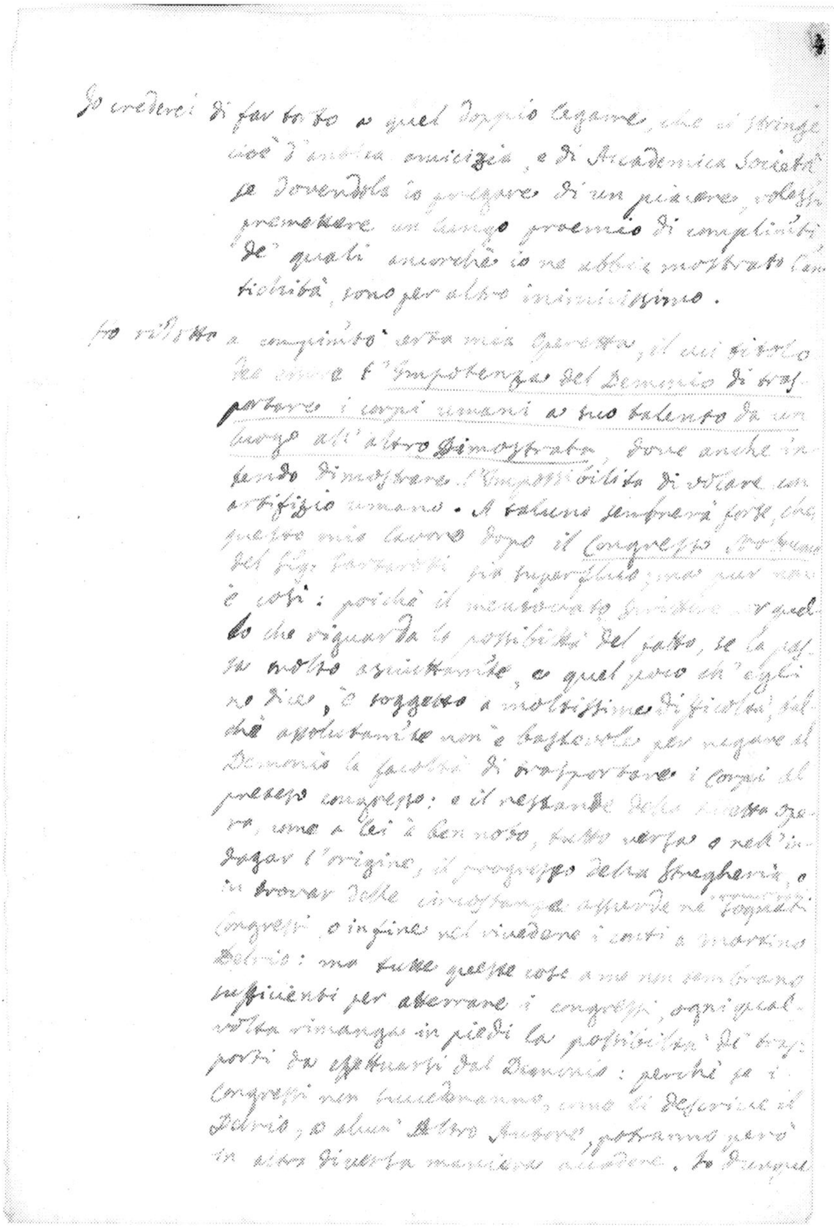

SCIENTIFIC KNOWLEDGE & DEMONOLOGY 337

FIGURE 11.1 Clemente Baroni Cavalcabò, *Lettere ed altri scritti meno importanti sopra oggetti letterari e filosofici*. Rovereto, Biblioteca Civica, Ms. 16.4-2, fol. 38 v.

many alleged works of the Devil, which is in any case one of the most amazing, the most difficult and which forms the basis for witchcraft.[20]

Leaving aside any explicit mention of some of the most widely debated topics in the discussions of the period, such as magic and pacts with the Devil, the philosopher thus decided to devote his refutation to just one of the many phenomena traditionally ascribed to demonic powers: human flight.

In the so-called *Canon episcopi*, a text of uncertain origin first attested in the abbot Regino of Prüm's *De Synodalibus causis et disciplinis* (906), belief in the nocturnal flights of devotees of the goddess Diana was branded a pagan superstition, to be punished with a charge of apostasy. The flight of witches was reduced to a mere illusion; the Devil was denied the capacity to exert any type of physical power over humans, except over their senses, which he was able to alter and influence during sleep. It was this theory which was passed down by medieval canon law, although on a popular level belief in the flight of witches never really died out. During the fifteenth century a new interpretation of the *Canon* increasingly led to the re-emergence of the theory that human flight was not a mere hallucination but an actual possibility. The gradual dissemination of the *Malleus maleficarum* (1486–7) and of the sixteenth- and seventeenth-century demonological literature deriving from it in European theology faculties (principally Jean Bodin, Peter Binsfeld, and Martin del Rio) led to a true 'canonization' of the concept of witchcraft, which even in the mid-eighteenth century entailed the concrete possibility of signing pacts with the Devil, the reality of witches' flight and their metamorphosis into animals.[21]

This is thus the scenario forming the backdrop to the refutation of the Devil's ability to move human bodies attempted by Baroni Cavalcabò in *L'impotenza del demonio*, a fairly rarefied text, completely devoid of non-philosophical references to the issue of witchcraft. The author's starting premise is that, despite the impossibility of demonstrating philosophically the existence of created spirits, it is entirely legitimate to investigate their prerogatives using the principles of the mechanics and dynamics of René Descartes, Gottfried Wilhelm Leibniz, Friedrich Hoffmann, and Christian Wolff.[22] Baroni Cavalcabò's stated mission is to free philosophy of the wrong generally done it of being considered incapable of settling the numerous controversies over the prerogatives of angels

---

20 Baroni Cavalcabò, Preface to *L'impotenza del demonio* XXI.
21 See Pott, *Aufklärung und Aberglaube* 195f.; Tschacher W., "Der Flug durch die Luft zwischen Illusionstheorie und Realitätsbeweis", *Zeitung der Savigny-Stiftung für Rechtgeschichte* 116 (1999) 225–276.
22 Baroni Cavalcabò, Preface to *L'impotenza del demonio* XVIII–XX.

and demons using its own powers; essentially, he did not wish to renounce the clearest and most evident notions which we possess of natural things.[23] A not dissimilar procedure can be seen in one of the philosopher's numerous unpublished manuscripts, currently held in the Biblioteca Civica at Rovereto. Among these we find, alongside demonological writings, treatises and fragments on legal matters, on the interactions between mind and body and on happiness,[24] a short piece presented to the members of the Accademia degli Agiati in 1763 entitled *Del naturale galleggiamento nell'acqua dei corpi umani viventi* (On the Natural Buoyancy in Water of Living Human Bodies). This very short text [Fig. 11.2] argues against the traditional 'trial by water', in other words the practice of plunging suspected witches into the water of a river or lake, with their left wrist tied to the right leg and vice versa. If the suspect floated this was thought to be proof of a pact with the Devil, able to intervene to help her; by contrast, sinking was proof of innocence. In the manuscript, Baroni Cavalcabò, who had written various essays on hydraulics, attempted to demonstrate that the buoyancy of the human body was compatible with the laws of hydrostatics, thus refuting the belief in the Devil's powers from a different angle.

Although he considered *De Betoverde Weereld* a fundamental text, Baroni Cavalcabò nonetheless distanced himself explicitly from many of the book's theories, starting with the rejection of Bekker's radical application of the dualism of *res cogitans* and *res extensa* to the demonological sphere. Although Baroni Cavalcabò himself postulated an explicit connection between the problem of the mind/body relationship and that of the interaction of any finite spirit with the material sphere in a manuscript entitled *Del commercio dell'anima col corpo*, in his most important work he refrained from taking a stance on the matter.[25] Girolamo Tartarotti had also fallen back on the analogy between the human soul and separated spirits, but from a somewhat different perspective. According to him, the interaction between two completely heterogeneous substances such as body and soul appeared to lay the foundations for the impossibility of a radical denial of the influence of invisible spirits over the human body; however, it would be contradictory to ascribe to the Devil a power over the physical world superior to that of the human soul over its body.

---

23   Baroni Cavalcabò Clemente, *Difesa dell'impotenza del demonio*, Rovereto, Biblioteca Civica, Ms. 16.6–1.

24   For a complete list of Baroni Cavalcabò's surviving manuscripts see Benvenuti E., *I manoscritti della Biblioteca Civica di Rovereto descritti*, vol. 2 (Rovereto: 1909) 12; 14–17; 22; 28; 30; 34–38; 42–44; 47; 49; 52.

25   Baroni Cavalcabò Clemente, *Del commercio dell'anima col corpo. Confutazione dei sistemi di Mallebranche e Leibnizio*, Rovereto, Biblioteca Civica, Ms. 16.6–3; Baroni Cavalcabò, *L'impotenza del demonio* 23.

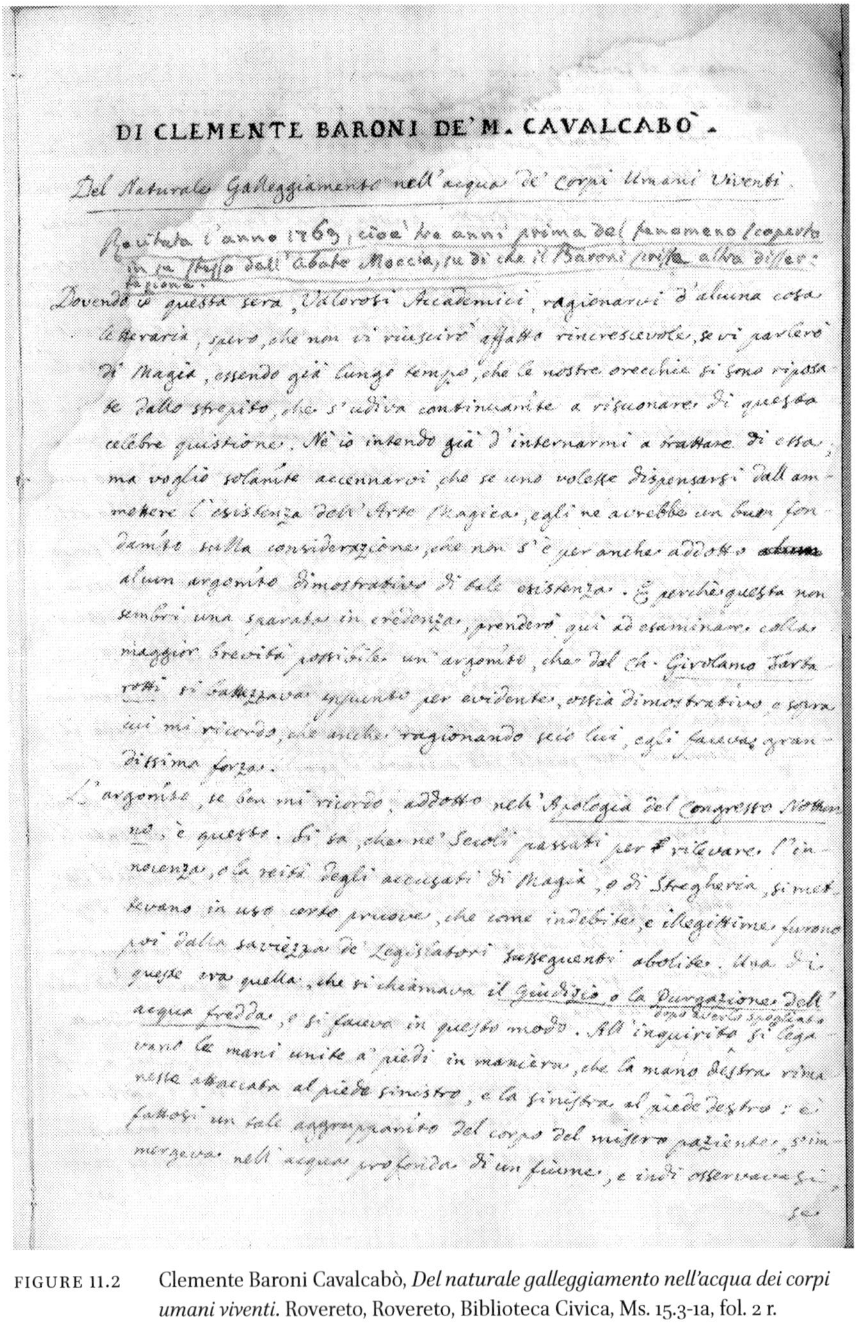
DI CLEMENTE BARONI DE' M. CAVALCABÒ.

Del Naturale Galleggiamento nell'acqua de' Corpi Umani Viventi.

Recitata l'anno 1763, cioè tre anni prima del fenomeno scoperto in se stesso dall'Abate Moccia, su di che il Baroni scrisse altra disser: tazione.

Dovendo io questa sera, Valorosi Accademici, ragionarvi d'alcuna cosa letteraria, spero, che non vi riuscirò affatto rincrescevole, se vi parlerò di Magia, essendo già lungo tempo, che le nostre orecchie si sono riposate dallo strepito, che s'udiva continuamente a risuonare di questa celebre quistione. Nè io intendo già d'internarmi a trattare di essa, ma voglio solamente accennarvi, che se uno volesse dispensarsi dall'ammettere l'esistenza dell'Arte Magica, egli ne avrebbe un buon fondamento sulla considerazione, che non s'è per anche addotto ~~alcun~~ alcun argomento dimostrativo di tale esistenza. E perchè questa non sembri una sparata in credenza, prenderò qui ad esaminare colla maggior brevità possibile un argomento, che dal Ch. Girolamo Tartarotti si battezzava appunto per evidente, ossia dimostrativo, e sopra cui mi ricordo, che anche ragionando seco lui, egli faceva grandissima forza.

L'argomento, se ben mi ricordo, addotto nell'Apologia del Congresso Notturno, è questo. Si sa, che ne' Secoli passati per rilevare l'innocenza, o la reità degli accusati di Magia, o di Stregheria, si mettevano in uso certe pruove, che come indebite, e illegittime, furono poi dalla saviezza de' Legislatori susseguenti abolite. Una di queste era quella, che si chiamava il Giudizio o la Purgazione dell'acqua fredda, e si faceva in questo modo. All'inquisito dopo averlo spogliato si legavano le mani unite a' piedi in maniera, che la mano destra rimanesse attaccata al piede sinistro, e la sinistra al piede destro: e fattosi un tale aggruppamento del corpo del misero paziente, s'immergeva nell'acqua profonda di un fiume, e indi osservavasi, se

FIGURE 11.2 Clemente Baroni Cavalcabò, *Del naturale galleggiamento nell'acqua dei corpi umani viventi.* Rovereto, Rovereto, Biblioteca Civica, Ms. 15.3-1a, fol. 2 r.

He thus attributed to the Devil only the ability to move fluids and influence the human mind, just as our soul is able to affect its body thanks to the mediation of the animal spirits.[26]

Tartarotti's stance essentially mirrored that taken by Friedrich Hoffmann in his 1703 dissertation *De diaboli potentia in corpora*, though lacking the rigorous physiological bases which had supported the latter's arguments. In his work Hoffmann categorically denied that the Devil could perform miracles such as transporting witches.[27] However, for the doctor from Halle Bekker's idea that 'nihil daemones in corpora possunt' was false: the Devil has some power to affect the material world, though limited and of a non-physical, merely spiritual nature. His power is exerted exclusively over subtle bodies and fluids, in the macrocosm over the substance composed of air and ether, in the microcosm over 'spiritual matter, which animates and controls all the members of our body'.[28] In *L'impotenza del demonio* Baroni Cavalcabò rejects the belief that these arguments by analogy can be of help in resolving the controversy over the relationship between mankind and separated substances: 'it is wrong to deduce a general consequence from a specific instance, and therefore we cannot infer from what happens to our soul what happens to created spirits in general'. On the other hand the *commercio* (interaction) between these two substances is *oscurissimo* (most obscure); not everyone believes in the existence of animal spirits and, though conceding their existence, in Baroni Cavalcabò's view Hoffmann's arguments would in any case not be credible since, even assuming that our soul had animal spirits, the theory limiting the powers of the Devil to the motion of fluids alone would be somewhat arbitrary.[29]

---

26   Tartarotti, *Del congresso notturno delle lammie* 77–79.
27   Hoffmann, "De diaboli potentia in corpora" § VI.
28   Ibid., § XVII: 'Ordine jam sequitur, postquam lustravimus ea, quae in macrocosmo diabolus perpetrare potest, ut haec etiam investigemus, quae in corpore humano fabricare possit. Dicimus itaque, cum in materiam fluidam tenuissimam, quae in macrocosmo est aër & aether, ipsi potestatem adscribamus, eodem modo quoque quoad microcosmum, in fluidum illum tenuissimum, animantium & corporis humani, potestatem ipsi esse concessam: idque maxime propterea, quoniam certo scimus, materiam spirituosam, quae movet & regit omnes nostri corporis artus, nonnisi aërem esse subtilissimum, tenuibus sanguinis sulphureis particulis mixtum'. On Hoffmann's demonology cf. Pott, *Aufklärung und Aberglaube* 387–396; Nooijen, "*Unserm grossen Bekker ein Denkmal*"? 241–245. More generally on his physiology: Duchesneau F., *La physiologie des Lumières. Empirisme, modèles et théories* (The Hague: 1982) 32–64; Geyer-Kordesch J., "Holistic Medicine and the Materialistic Sciences in the Enlightenment", in Bödeker H.E. (ed.), *Strukturen der deutschen Frühaufklärung 1680–1720* (Göttingen: 2008) 333–356.
29   Baroni Cavalcabò, *L'impotenza del demonio* 14f.

These premises introduced the demonstration of diabolical powerlessness proper, in which the author attempted to prove definitively the incompatibility between physical laws and some of the operations traditionally attributed to the Devil, prerogatives denied to inferior spirits and ascribable exclusively to God who otherwise 'would have had difficulty [...] in providing for the good order and conservation of the universe'.[30] The starting point is the analogy between fluids and air, and consequently between the condition of a body lying at the bottom of a body of water and a man on the earth's surface.[31] Given these presuppositions, for Baroni Cavalcabò the means by which the Devil could make a body fly from one place to another were reduced to five: 1) by impressing motion on it; 2) by means of whirlwinds; 3) through the condensation of air; 4) by depriving the human body of absolute gravity; 5) by teaching people to fly.[32] With the partial exception of a chapter devoted to clarifying how no passage of scripture, however ambiguous, admits of the faculty which he denies the Devil, Baroni Cavalcabò conducts his demonstration exclusively on the basis of the laws of the scientific revolution. The references deployed range from Descartes's laws of motion to those of Newton, from recent dissertations such as Ruggero Boscovich's *Sopra il turbine* (1749) to experiments with pneumatic pumps, whose rarefying effects on air are used as an analogy for the condition of a human being swept up by a vortex.[33]

However, it is the principle of conservation in the version proposed by Leibniz which represents the linchpin of the demonstration of diabolical powerlessness. The publication in the *Acta eruditorum* of the *Brevis demonstratio erroris memorabilis Cartesii et aliorum* (1686) marked Leibniz's first public stand against the laws of motion as set out by Descartes in his *Principia philosophiae* and in *Le Monde*, and the beginning of a long and well-known dispute with the Cartesians.[34] According to Leibniz, Descartes 'memorable error' was that of postulating, starting from the axiom of divine immutability, the conservation in the world of the same quantity of motion present since Creation, identifying

---

30   Ibid., 90.
31   Ibid., v. The analogy between air and water was topical in the scientific literature of the eighteenth century, in which gases were still considered fluids. For a fairly similar comparison between the condition of bodies at the bottom of a body of water and on the earth's surface, albeit in a very different context, cf. Pascal Blaise, *Traitez de l'equilibre des liqueurs, et de la pesanteur de la masse de l'air* (Paris, Desprez: 1663) 25–44.
32   Baroni Cavalcabò, *L'impotenza del demonio* 17–23.
33   See especially ch. 6 of *L'impotenza del demonio* (46–55), entitled *Si mostra, che il demonio non può trasportare i corpi umani arbitrariamente da un luogo all'altro per mezzo de' turbini*. ('It is demonstrated that the Devil cannot arbitrarily carry human bodies from one place to another by means of whirlwinds.')
34   Cf. Iltis C., "Leibniz and the *vis viva* Controversy", *Isis* 62 (1971) 21–35.

this with motive force, reducing the real world to a mere geometrical extension and failing to take sufficient account of the concept of *force*. The perpetual motion (*perpetuum mobile*) implied by Cartesian physics is impossible since no machine can increase its force without recourse to an external impulse: new force always originates from a loss of pre-existing force. When two bodies collide, every loss or gain in terms of force by one body corresponds to an equivalent loss or gain of force by the other. Leibniz's conclusion was thus that what remained constant was not the quantity of motion (*quantitas motus*), but the total motive force (*vis motrix*) present in a closed system, equivalent in every moving body to the product of its mass and the square of its velocity (mv^2).[35]

It is the principle of conservation in the concise formulation given by Leibniz in his brief note of 1686 which according to Baroni Cavalcabò precluded separated spirits from acting as extrinsic agents for the communication of motion, whatever means of setting a body in motion were postulated, even recourse to the compression of air. The Devil's impression of a force on a living being not already moving through the air, like a bird, would occur 'without a clash between the bodies' and would lead to an increase in the sum total of motive force, regardless of whether this was indicated by the factor mv^2 and thus identified with *vis viva*, or by mv, in other words *vis mortua*.[36] All this is not confined exclusively to the Devil. In contrast to Bekker, for whom the Devil's status, as a fallen spirit, is inferior to that of the angels, for Baroni Cavalcabò benign and malign substances are ontologically identical. This allows him a second argument: to refute earlier angelological models using the principle of the conservation of motive force. If angels – and therefore demons as well – lack a body (and in this Baroni Cavalcabò dissociates himself from Leibniz)

---

35 Leibniz Gottfried Wilhelm, "Brevis demonstratio erroris memorabilis Cartesii et aliorum circa legem naturae, secundum quam volunt a Deo eandem semper quantitatem motus conservari; qua et in re mechanica abuntur", *Acta Eruditorum* (March 1686) 161–163. On Leibniz's dynamics cf. Stammel H., *Der Kraftbegriff in Leibniz' Physik*, Ph.D. dissertation (University of Mannheim: 1982); Heinekamp A. (ed.), *Leibniz' Dynamica* (Stuttgart: 1984); Duchesneau F., *La dynamique de Leibniz* (Paris: 1994). The Cartesian version of the principle of conservation can be found in Descartes René, *Principia philosophiae* (1644) AT VIII, 53–54; idem, *Le Monde* (1664) AT XI, 439.

36 Baroni Cavalcabò, *L'impotenza del demonio* 62. The terms *vis viva* and *vis mortua* were first used by Leibniz in "Specimen dynamicum, pro admirandis naturae legibus circa corporum vires & mutuas actiones detegendis, & ad suas causas revocandis", *Acta Eruditorum* (April 1695) 145–157. *Dead force*, whose formula is mv (in other words the Cartesian formulation of the principle of conservation of motion) is a mere 'sollicitatio ad motum', unlike *living force*, which is a 'vis ordinaria, [...] cum motu actuali conjuncta', 'ex infinitis vis mortuae impressionibus continuatis nata' (149).

they cannot avail themselves of their own motive force. This is true both if you support Malebranchian occasionalism and if you support the model of *influxus physicus* or, like the Leibnizians, preestablished harmony and the corporeal nature of angels.[37]

By applying the principle of conservation to pneumatological problems, Baroni Cavalcabò turned it in a direction which was not genuinely Leibnizian: Leibniz had always upheld the distinction between the spheres of dynamics and angelology and – like Descartes – had never shown a particular interest in strictly demonological issues.[38] Seen from this angle it is understandable that Baroni Cavalcabò avoids quoting the more naive considerations of Tartarotti's *Congresso notturno*, one of the immediate precedents in which the flight of witches was discussed, restricting himself to dealing with this text directly only in relation to the issue of gravity.[39] In a treatise pervaded by the rationalistic claim to be using scientific knowledge in the service of demonology there was no room for topics such as the risk of suffocation run by witches due to their impact with air during flight, the incompatibility between the usual tranquillity of air and the violent whirlwinds potentially used for the same purpose by the Devil and the risk that the latter's incarnation in a material body to personally transport a witch might trigger a sort of *regressus ad infinitum*.[40]

3 Baroni Cavalcabò and His Adversaries: Post-Cartesian Psychology VS. Traditional Demonology

Baroni Cavalcabò's application of the law of conservation to demonological issues is undoubtedly naive in many ways. However, his arguments give his treatise a more speculative and entirely novel imprint compared to any

---

37 Baroni Cavalcabò, *L'impotenza del demonio* 23–31; 39–45. On Leibniz's angelology cf. Geretto M., *L'angelologia leibniziana* (Soveria Mannelli: 2010); Roling B., *Locutio angelica. Die Diskussion der Engelsprache als Antizipation einer Sprechakttheorie in Mittelalter und Früher Neuzeit* (Leiden: 2008) 666–673.

38 One of the most interesting contexts in which Leibniz tackles the issue of the Devil's prerogatives is the essay "De incarnatione Dei seu De unione hypostatica" (1669–1670). Here the philosopher denies the possibility of a 'hypostatic union'–in the peculiar sense which Leibniz attributes to this expression – between demons and the souls and bodies of the possessed and consequently the Devil's ability to penetrate the human mind. Cf. Leibniz Gottfried Wilhelm, "De incarnatione Dei seu De unione hypostatica", in Leibniz Gottfried Wilhelm, *Philosophische Schriften, vol. 1*, ed. Deutsche Akademie der Wissenschaften zu Berlin (Berlin: 1971) 532–535; Geretto, *L'angelologia leibniziana* 129–131.

39 Baroni Cavalcabò, *L'impotenza del demonio* 11–13.

40 Tartarotti, *Del congresso notturno delle lammie* 75f.; 80.

of the earlier interventions which appeared during the Italian demonological *querelle*. *L'impotenza del demonio* immediately attracted criticism from colleagues and reviewers, as is well documented by the author's manuscript legacy, in which transcriptions of the attacks on him alternate with continuous, heartfelt defences of his book.[41] The year of its publication an anonymous writer accused the author of 'rendering vain the holiest Scriptures, of declaring pointless the most ancient Rites of the universal Church of Christ, of opposing general opinion, and of going against the most constant, soundest, most venerable tradition'. The reviewer, the Dominican Gaetano Maria Locatelli, alongside some of the work's more strictly scientific aspects, also attacked the short section of *L'impotenza del demonio* devoted to demonstrating 'the harmony between reason and faith', certain that Scripture did not admit of 'any opinion favourable' to Baroni Cavalcabò. In Locatelli's view, the interpretation of some biblical episodes traditionally cited as confirmation of the Devil's ability to transport a human body through the air was particularly scandalous. The theory of diabolical powerlessness, as well as having implications which at the time were considered purely legal, calling into question the possibility of making pacts with the Devil or the Devil's ability to transport witches through the air, had equally subversive consequences for orthodoxy if used as an exegetical criterion. The theory lent itself to a denial of the literal meaning of some famous biblical episodes, such as the Devil's transport of Christ to the summit of the Temple of Jerusalem[42] or of the prophet Habakkuk by an angel.[43]

Tartarotti's interpretation of the episode related in the apocryphal addition to the book of Daniel that appears in the Septuagint, on the basis of which God was thought to have 'increased the powers of the Angel, as his agent, [...] and given strength and resistance to the body of the Prophet'[44] was refuted by Baroni Cavalcabò who stated, by contrast, that

> in many passages of the Old Testament which make reference to angels who appeared to men [...] in my opinion, these apparitions were often nothing more than signs with which God signalled his presence to men in a supernatural way: this allows us to reconcile the apparent discordances

---

41 The reviews of and attacks against *L'impotenza del demonio* and the author's defensive writings and notes are held at the Biblioteca Civica di Rovereto with the title *Difesa dell'impotenza del demonio* (cf. note 24 above).

42 Matthew 4:1.

43 Daniel XIV, 31–42; [Locatelli Gaetano M.], "Dissertazione contro l'operetta del Signor Clemente Baroni, intitolata L'impotenza del demonio di trasportare a talento per l'aria i corpi umani", *Raccolta nuova di opuscoli scientifici e filologici* 1 (1755) 129–191.

44 Tartarotti, *Del congresso notturno delle lammie* 81.

in the sacred Text in a marvellous way. But whatever the case, it is also certain that, in accordance with the views of many Holy Fathers and sound interpreters, it is not always clear in the Scriptures that the word Angel refers to an Angelic substance proper and that sometimes we should in fact interpret this word as referring to God himself.[45]

The second weapon used by Baroni Cavalcabò to refute Tartarotti's idea is far more interesting, and is provided by 'our Wolffian principles':[46] in other words, once again by the system of a philosopher who, like Leibniz, had never been particularly interested in problems of this kind. Why press the philosophy of Christian Wolff into service in a discussion about witches, angels, demons, and their power?

Many decades after the publication of Leibniz's *Brevis demonstratio*, Wolff dedicated some brief notes to defending the principle of conservation without introducing any significant differences with respect to the terms in which the question had already been posed by Leibniz.[47] Wolff's name is in fact not to be found in the pages of *L'impotenza del demonio* devoted to motive force; what does appear in Baroni Cavalcabò's treatise, however, is an aspect of his philosophy which did present some significant novelties with respect to its formulation in Leibniz, in other words, Wolff's version of the theory of the plurality of worlds:

> If we wish to suppose that the Angel carries out such a transport himself thanks to a force extraordinarily communicated to him, and actually put into effect this aforementioned possibility, we must also assume that another world and another order of things exists, since this is a consequence of Wolff's fine doctrine that *si quod intrinsece possibile actum*

---

45 Baroni Cavalcabò, *L'impotenza del demonio* 230.
46 Ibid., 85.
47 Wolff Christian, "Principia dynamica", *Commentarii academiae scientiarum petropolitanae* 1 (1728) 217–238; idem, *Vertheidigung der Meinung von der bewegenden Krafft, welche sich in den Cörpern befindet, gegen Hr. Muys Einwendungen*, in Wolff Christian, *Gesammelte Werke*, sec. 1, vol. 21.4 (1739; reprint, Hildesheim: 1981) 128–141. Wolff discusses the laws of motion in ch. 4 of sec. 2 of his *Cosmologia generalis, methodo scientifica pertractata, qua ad solidam, in primis Dei atque naturae, cognitionem via sternitur*, in Wolff Christian *Gesammelte Werke*, ed. J. École (Frankfurt – Leipzig: 1737²; reprint, Hildesheim: 1964). For a discussion of the originality of Wolff's stance on dynamics cf. École J., "Cosmologie wolffienne et dynamique leibnizienne. Essai sur les rapports de Wolff avec Leibniz" *Les études philosophiques* 19 (1964) 3–9; Rey A.-L., "La lecture wolffienne de la Dynamique leibnizienne. Un moyen d'identifier la spécificité de la notion de substance chez Wolff", in Stolzenberg J. (ed.), *Christian Wolff und die europäische Aufklärung*, part 2, in Wolff Christian, *Gesammelte Werke*, sec. 3, vol. 102 (Hildesheim: 2007) 237–258.

consequi deberet, quod in mundo aspectabili actualitatem non consequitur, alius existere deberet mundus.[48]

Wolff's system and in particular his *Cosmologia generalis*, from which Baroni Cavalcabò drew the quotation, postulates a mechanical universe governed by strict causal links. In it all things are reciprocally linked and each contains within itself the reason why the other is next to it or follows it. The modification of one thing follows or derives from a state of the other. Once God has created given bodies and subjected them to specific physical laws, the only possible movements are those which result from the essence of the bodies and the laws of motion. If God causes a change through a miracle, something else will subsequently happen that would not have occurred without this preceding change. As such, it is impossible to state that after a miracle the same series of causes and effects, i.e. the same world, persists. This is the theory of *nexus rerum* (in Wolff's writings also termed *series* or *successio rerum*) which led to Wolff being accused of Spinozism and fatalism, especially by the theologians Johann Franz Budde and Joachim Lange, with whom he was engaged in a long dispute.[49] This Wolffian 'framework' was particularly congenial to Baroni Cavalcabò for the purposes of his argument: the potential for an angel to enact the transportation of a body by means of a force impressed upon it from the outside would imply the violation of the normal concatenation of events and thus necessarily presupposed the existence of a different 'order of things'.

The presence of the *Cosmologia generalis* among the sources of *L'impotenza del demonio* is not in itself in any way surprising. The Accademia degli Agiati was one of the Italian Enlightenment institutions most open to German philosophical debate and Baroni Cavalcabò himself often reviewed the latest publications. Among the most recent and most widely accepted philosophical systems,

---

[48] 'Qualora si voglia supporre, che l'Angelo per forza a lui straordinariamente comunicata eseguisca da se un tal trasporto, e riduca all'atto la menzionata possibilità, conviene anche supporre, che un altro mondo, e un altro ordine di cose esista, essendo ciò una conseguenza della bella dottrina del Wolfio, che *si quod intrinsece possibile actum consequi deberet, quod in mundo aspectabili actualitatem non consequitur, alius existere deberet mundus.*' (Baroni Cavalcabò, *L'impotenza del demonio* 125–126) The quotation is taken from Wolff, *Cosmologia generalis* § 100.

[49] Cf. Ciafardone R., "La controversia tra Christian Wolff e i teologi di Halle Johann Christian Lange e Franz Budde", in Giordano G. (ed.), *Filosofia ed etica. Studi in onore di Girolamo Cotroneo* (Rubbettino: 2005) 77–99. For Wolff's concise presentation of the *nexus rerum* cf. *Der vernünfftigen Gedancken von Gott, der Welt und der Seele des Menschen, auch allen Dingen überhaupt, Anderer Theil, bestehend in ausführlichen Anmerckungen*, in Wolff Christian *Gesammelte Werke*, sec. 1, vol. 3, ed. C.A. Corr, (Frankfurt: 1740⁴; reprint, Hildesheim: 1983) § 176.

probably none was better suited than Wolff's rigorous mechanicism to a philosophical demolition of the belief in the powers of physical action of separated spirits, although there is no major development of this system in a demonological direction in the German philosopher's writings. In Germany, too, there were thinkers who dealt explicitly, though in very different ways, with these issues. Many were only indirectly pupils of Wolff. The Halle professor Christoph Andreas Büttner, in his *Diiudicatio Iudicii de non-existentia diaboli* (1734), attempted to refute disbelievers in the reality of diabolical powers on the basis of purely logical and psychological principles, drawn mainly from his own *Cursus philosophicus* and from texts by Wolff; Alexander Gottlieb Baumgarten's pupil, Georg Friedrich Meier, in his *Philosophische Gedanken von den Würkungen des Teufels auf dem Erdboden* (1760) went in the completely opposite direction, drawing a sceptical conclusion regarding the potential for proving the existence of the Devil philosophically.[50]

According to Medoro Rossi, one of Baroni Cavalcabò's many critics, one of the most scandalous features of *L'impotenza del demonio* was the use of excessively controversial authors as 'primary foundations for these modern philosophical flights' aimed at providing mathematical proof of the undemonstrable; this claim, specified Rossi, ran up against the author's failure to clarify the relationship between mind and body before attempting to measure the powers of the Devil. The treatise also contained an unforgivable profanation of the authority of St Augustine: Baroni Cavalcabò had opened *L'impotenza del demonio* by explicitly declaring 'false' the Augustinian maxim according to which

> It is difficult for man to discover what [demons] are capable of by nature, what they are incapable of by prohibition, and what the condition of their own nature does not allow for. It is in fact impossible without that divine gift.[51]

Against this new adversary Baroni Cavalcabò received the unexpected support of the Jesuit Francescantonio Zaccaria, who in his *Storia letteraria d'Italia* defended philosophy's right to oppose its own 'manifest doctrines' to the

---

50 Büttner Christoph A., *Diiudicatio Iudicii de non-existentia diaboli* (Halle, Grunert: 1734); Meier Georg F., *Philosophische Gedanken von den Würkungen des Teufels auf dem Erdboden* (Halle, Hemmerde: 1760).

51 'Quid autem possint [Daemones] per naturam, nec possint per prohibitionem, et quid per ipsius naturae suae conditionem facere non sinantur, homini explorare difficile est, immo vero impossibile, nisi per illud donum Dei'. Rossi's review was published anonymously in *Novelle della Repubblica letteraria* (1753) 260–262. The quotation from St. Augustine on p. 1 of *L'impotenza del demonio* comes from the *De trinitate* III,18.

'dubious doctrines' of theology in the matter of invisible spirits.[52] A few years later, Baroni Cavalcabò intervened personally on these issues in a rejoinder to Locatelli, taking this opportunity to clarify the apologetic benefits of his treatise for an adversary who was 'to be pitied because he so demonstrably lacks the good principles, not only of Physics and Metaphysics, but also of Dialectics'. Not only is it false that 'as common opinion claims, attempting to circumscribe the supposed power of the Devil is a task that can do harm to good religion.' Scientific knowledge, far from representing a danger to religion, is better suited than quotations from Scripture (as we have seen, relegated almost exclusively to a very short chapter of *L'impotenza del demonio*) to rendering credible to the infidel some specific aspects of Christian doctrine.[53]

4 Conclusion

The intellectual world gravitating around the Accademia degli Agiati never truly freed itself of what today we would call, to use John Pocock's well-known expression, a *conservative Enlightenment* stance.[54] Baroni Cavalcabò, Tartarotti and the other Italian intellectuals who, each in their own fashion, intervened in this dispute, nonetheless thought the persecution of witches a pointless anachronism; they considered it necessary to set more stringent limitations on the Devil's powers, though often vaunting the apologetic advantages of their own positions; they were all involved in lengthy disputes with those who saw any attempt at limiting diabolical powers as an unwarranted interference by reason and science in matters of faith. As Franco Venturi wrote in the opening paragraph of a chapter of his classic *Settecento riformatore*, in Italian-speaking intellectual circles the Rovereto dispute was the 'greatest effort made at that period to test the limits and value of human reason, putting it to the test against tradition, superstition and prejudices'. On this occasion 'the Cartesian

---

52 Zaccaria Francescantonio, *Storia letteraria d'Italia*, vol. 8 (Modena, s.n.: 1755) 72–76.
53 Cf. the letter published by Baroni Cavalcabò in the periodical *Novelle letterarie di Firenze* 17 (1756) 107–112. Baroni Cavalcabò is thinking in particular of the doctrine of miracles: cf. idem, *Dei miracoli. Estratti e materiali per l'opera meditata su tale argomento dal Baroni*, Rovereto, Biblioteca Civica, Ms. 16.6–2.
54 See Pocock J.G.A., "Conservative Enlightenment and Democratic Revolutions. The American and French Cases in British Perspective", *Government and Opposition* 24 (1989) 81–105; idem, "Clergy and Commerce: The Conservative Enlightenment in England", in Ajello R. (ed.), *L'età dei Lumi: studi storici sul Settecento europeo in onore di Franco Venturi*, vol. 1 (Naples: 1985) 523–562.

tradition, the art of criticism and the nascent modern scientific spirit came into conflict with a dark and oppressive world, at once popular and theological, attempting to penetrate it and annihilate it.'[55]

However the group formed by the antagonists of diabolical power was anything but compact, torn apart internally by suspicions of heresy and mutual accusations. Each of its representatives had to face not only a theological veto but also internal opposition which was perhaps even stronger. Girolamo Tartarotti, certain that the belief in witchcraft was a mere superstition, was forced for years to face the theological condemnations of his *Congresso notturno delle lammie*. Yet he in turn accused Gianrinaldo Carli of heresy for having made the opposing error, paving the way with the denial of magic, which he himself had not dared to suggest, for a repudiation of the Devil and of God; Tartarotti had always insisted that angelogical and demonological issues did not pertain to the sphere of science but to that of faith.[56] For the same reasons the abbot had criticised Baroni Cavalcabò's attempt, using the laws of dynamics, to demonstrate the Devil's inability to move human bodies, claiming that his one time protégé had ventured onto excessively slippery ground.[57]

The attacks which the contenders in this dispute levelled at one another are an indication of a dramatic epistemological impasse caused by the difficulty of reconciling scientific knowledge and religious orthodoxy, post-Cartesian psychology and traditional demonology. However, although cosmological constructs such as those of Leibniz and Wolff, postulating a universe in which forces governed by the laws of mechanics interacted, still met with significant resistance in theological circles, some novelties had by now nonetheless gone so deep as to penetrate even the most orthodox Italian milieux. Even ardent supporters of the reality of diabolical power were more or less consciously influenced, at least on a terminological level, by the image of the world drawn by the 'new philosophy' and did not hesitate to employ images drawn from post-Cartesian terminology. In 1750 the author of an anonymous attack on Scipione Maffei's *Arte magica dileguata* argued in favour of the powers of malign spirits, comparing the Devil's power over man to that of a builder of automata: just as a skilled craftsman, imitating the works of nature, succeeds in bringing to life a piece of bronze or metal by means of mechanisms, wheels and springs to the point that 'it will seem to many to have some sort of spirit informing it from

---

55 Venturi, *Settecento riformatore* 335.
56 On the Tartarotti-Carli *querelle* cf. Parinetto, *I lumi e le streghe* 143–168.
57 See Girolamo Tartarotti's letter to Ottolino Ottolini of 6 October 1753 held at the Biblioteca Capitolare di Verona (Cod. DCCCCLXXXI, VIII, 46).

within' so the Devil, with his profound knowledge of the 'intrinsic properties of things' must be able to affect humans physically.[58]

The Roveretan demonological dispute lasted only a few years. Its effects, however, can be traced in very different contexts from that in which it broke out and died down, and we find echoes of it not only in the writings of the Augustinian Jordan Simon alias 'Ardoino Ubbidiente', whom we met at the beginning of this survey, but also in Bavaria, where a few years after the events dealt with here a similar dispute took place. On 13 October 1766 the Theatine Ferdinand Sterzinger, pronouncing the *Akademische Rede von dem gemeinen Vorurtheil der wirkenden und thätigen Hexerey* (Academic Speech on the common Opinion concerning effective and active Witchcraft) during a meeting of the Academy of Sciences in Munich, triggered the outbreak of the so-called *Bayerischer Hexenkrieg*: the nature of witches and their destiny became the subject of heated debates among the customers of the city's beer parlours and even of barber's shops.[59] A year later he was forced to publish an apology to defend himself from the numerous charges of atheism levelled at him. The pamphlet, entitled *Betrügende Zauberkunst und träumende Hexerey*, comprised eleven paragraphs in which belief in the flight of witches, described as ridiculous and false, contrary to reason and to the laws of nature, was refuted in part through recourse to the authority of Clemente Baroni Cavalcabò, who thus found an unexpected champion in German territory.[60]

(Translated from Italian by Erika Milburn)

---

58   *Osservazioni sopra l'opuscolo che ha per titolo Arte magica dileguata, di un prete dell'oratorio* (Venice, Occhi: 1750) 4. The author of the pamphlet is Andrea Lugiato: cf. G.M. [i.e. Gaetano Melzi], *Dizionario di opere anonime e pseudonime di scrittori italiani o come che sia aventi relazione all'Italia*, vol. 2 (Milan: 1852) 297.

59   Sterzinger Ferdinand, *Akademische Rede von dem gemeinen Vorurtheil der wirkenden und thätigen Hexerey* (Munich, Mayr: 1766). For a reconstruction of the controversy see Behringer W., "Der 'Bayerische Hexenkrieg'. Die Debatte am Ende der Hexenprozesse", in Lorenz S. – Bauer D.R. (eds.), *Das Ende der Hexenverfolgung*, Hexenforschung 1 (Stuttgart: 1995) 287–313.

60   Sterzinger Ferdinand, *Betrügende Zauberkunst und träumende Hexerey, oder Vertheidigung der akademischen Rede, von dem gemeinen Vorurtheile der wirkenden und thätigen Hexerey, wider das Urtheil ohne Vorurtheil* (Munich, s.n.: 1767) §§ LII–LXII.

Bibliography

[Anon.], *Memorie per servire all'istoria letteraria* 2 (1753).

Baroni Cavalcabò Clemente, *Dichiarazione dell'instituto e scopo de' Liberi Muratori, dove si prende a confutare il candeliere acceso de' Liberi Muratori eretto di fresco* (Rovereto, Marchesani: 1749).

Baroni Cavalcabò Clemente, *Lettera del Signor Clemente Baroni delli Marchesi Cavalcabò ad un giornalista oltramontano, sopra il Congresso Notturno delle Lammie del Sig. Abate Girolamo Tartarotti*, in Tartarotti Girolamo, *Apologia del Congresso notturno delle lammie, o sia Risposta di Girolamo Tartarotti all'Arte magica dileguata del sig. march. Scipione Maffei, ed all'opposizione del sig. assessore Bartolommeo Melchiori. S'aggiunge una lettera del Sig. Clemente Baroni di Cavalcabò* (Venice, Occhi: 1751) 223–268.

Baroni Cavalcabò Clemente, *L'impotenza del demonio di trasportare a talento per l'aria da un luogo all'altro i corpi umani dimostrata da Clemente Baroni delli Marchesi Cavalcabò accademico di Rovereto, dove anche si dimostra l'impossibilità di volare con artifizio umano* (Rovereto, Marchesani: 1753).

Baroni Cavalcabò Clemente, "[Letter]", *Novelle letterarie di Firenze* 17 (1756) 107–112.

Behringer W., "Der 'Bayerische Hexenkrieg'. Die Debatte am Ende der Hexenprozesse", in Lorenz S. – Bauer D.R. (eds.), *Das Ende der Hexenverfolgung*, Hexenforschung 1 (Stuttgart: 1995) 287–313.

Behringer W., *Witchcraft Persecutions in Bavaria. Popular Magic, Religious Zealotry and Reason of State in Early Modern Europe* (Cambridge: 1997).

Bekker Balthasar, *De Betoverde Weereld, Zynde een Grondig Ondersoek Van't gemeen gevoelen aangaande de Geesten, derselver Aart en Vermogen, Bewind en Bedryf: als ook't gene de Menschen door derselver kraght en gemeenschap doen*, vol. 2 (Amsterdam, Van den Dalen: 1691).

Benvenuti E., *I manoscritti della Biblioteca Civica di Rovereto descritti*, vol. 2 (Rovereto: 1909).

Bonazza M., *L'Accademia Roveretana degli Agiati* (Rovereto: 1998).

Bunge W. van, "Introduction to Balthasar Bekker", in Bekker Balthasar, *Die bezauberte Welt (1693)*, ed. W. van Bunge (Stuttgart: 1997) 43–54.

Büttner Christoph A., *Diiudicatio Iudicii de non-existentia diaboli* (Halle, Grunert: 1734).

Ciafardone R., "La controversia tra Christian Wolff e i teologi di Halle Johann Christian Lange e Franz Budde", in Giordano G. (ed.), *Filosofia ed etica. Studi in onore di Girolamo Cotroneo* (Rubbettino: 2005) 77–99.

Clark S., *Thinking With Demons. The Idea of Witchcraft in Early Modern Europe* (Oxford: 1997).

Duchesneau F., *La physiologie des Lumières. Empirisme, modèles et théories* (The Hague: 1982).

Duchesneau F., *La dynamique de Leibniz* (Paris: 1994).
École J., "Cosmologie wolffienne et dynamique leibnizienne. Essai sur les rapports de Wolff avec Leibniz" *Les études philosophiques* 19 (1964) 3–9.
Easlea B., *Witch-Hunting, Magic and the New Philosophy. An Introduction to Debates of the Scientific Revolution 1450–1750* (Sussex, NY: 1980).
Ferrari S., "Una società 'confinante': la vicenda storica dell'Accademia degli Agiati", in Ferrari S. (ed.), *Cultura letteraria e sapere scientifico nelle Accademie tedesche e italiane del Settecento* (Rovereto: 2003) 91–126.
Ferrari S., "L'Accademia Roveretana degli Agiati e la cultura di lingua tedesca (1750–1795)", in Ferrari S. (ed.), *Cultura letteraria e sapere scientifico nelle Accademie tedesche e italiane del Settecento* (Rovereto: 2003) 217–276.
Fiorio Antonio, *Arte magica distrutta. Risposta di don Antonio Fiorio veronese arciprete di Tignale, e Valvestino, vicario foraneo* (Trent, Brunati: 1750).
Fiorio Antonio, *Arte magica annichilata, libri tre. Con un'appendice* (Verona, Andreoni: 1754).
Fix A., *Fallen Angels. Balthasar Bekker, Spirit Belief, and Confessionalism in the Seventeenth Century Dutch Republic* (Dordrecht: 1999).
Geretto M., *L'angelologia leibniziana* (Soveria Mannelli: 2010).
Geyer-Kordesch J., "Holistic Medicine and the Materialistic Sciences in the Enlightenment", in Bödeker H.E. (ed.), *Strukturen der deutschen Frühaufklärung 1680–1720* (Göttingen: 2008) 333–356.
Heinekamp A. (ed.), *Leibniz' Dynamica* (Stuttgart: 1984).
Hoffmann Friedrich, "De diaboli potentia in corpora, dissertatio physico-medica curiosa", in Hoffmann Friedrich, *Opera omnia, vol. 5* (Geneva, De Tournes: 1761) 94–103.
Iltis C., "Leibniz and the vis viva Controversy", *Isis* 62 (1971) 21–35.
Israel J., "The Bekker Controversies as a Turning Point in the History of Dutch Culture and Though", *Dutch Crossing. A Journal of Low Countries Studies* 2 (1996) 5–21.
Israel J., *Radical Enlightenment. Philosophy and the Making of Modernity 1650–1750* (Oxford: 2001).
Kleineidam E., *Universitas studii Erffordensis. Überblick über die Geschichte der Universität Erfurt, VOL. IV* (Leipzig: 1981).
[Locatelli Gaetano M.], "Dissertazione contro l'operetta del Signor Clemente Baroni, intitolata L'impotenza del demonio di trasportare a talento per l'aria i corpi umani", *Raccolta nuova di opuscoli scientifici e filologici* 1 (1755) 129–191.
Leibniz Gottfried Wilhelm, "Brevis demonstratio erroris memorabilis Cartesii et aliorum circa legem naturae, secundum quam volunt a Deo eandem semper quantitatem motus conservari; qua et in re mechanica abuntur", *Acta Eruditorum* (March 1686) 161–163.

Leibniz Gottfried Wilhelm, "Specimen dynamicum, pro admirandis naturae legibus circa corporum vires & mutuas actiones detegendis, & ad suas causas revocandis", *Acta Eruditorum* (April 1695) 145–157.

Leibniz Gottfried Wilhelm, "De incarnatione Dei seu De unione hypostatica", in Leibniz Gottfried Wilhelm, *Philosophische Schriften, vol. 1*, ed. Deutsche Akademie der Wissenschaften zu Berlin (Berlin: 1971) 532–535.

Leonardi C., "Clemente Baroni Cavalcabò", in *Dizionario biografico degli italiani, vol. 6* (Rome: 1964) 462–466.

[Lugiato Andrea], *Osservazioni sopra l'opuscolo che ha per titolo Arte magica dileguata, di un prete dell'oratorio* (Venice, Occhi: 1750).

Maffei Scipione, *Arte magica dileguata, lettera del signor marchese Maffei al padre Innocente Ansaldi dell'Ordine dei Predicatori* (Verona, Carattoni: 1749).

Mazzuchelli Giovanni M., *Gli scrittori d'Italia, vol. 2* (Brescia, Bossini: 1758).

Meier Georg F., *Philosophische Gedanken von den Würkungen des Teufels auf dem Erdboden* (Halle, Hemmerde: 1760).

Melzi G., *Dizionario di opere anonime e pseudonime di scrittori italiani o come che sia aventi relazione all'Italia, vol. 2* (Milan: 1852).

Nooijen A., "Unserm grossen Bekker ein Denkmal"? *Balthasar Bekkers* Betoverde Weereld *in den deutschen Landen zwischen Orthodoxie und Aufklärung* (Münster: 2009).

Parinetto L., *I lumi e le streghe. Una polemica italiana intorno al 1750* (Paderno Dugnano: 1998).

Pascal Blaise, *Traitez de l'equilibre des liqueurs, et de la pesanteur de la masse de l'air* (Paris, Desprez: 1663) 25–44.

Rey A.-L., "La lecture wolffienne de la Dynamique leibnizienne. Un moyen d'identifier la spécificité de la notion de substance chez Wolff", in Stolzenberg J. (ed.), *Christian Wolff und die europäische Aufklärung, part 2*, in Wolff Christian, *Gesammelte Werke, sec. 3, vol. 102* (Hildesheim: 2007) 237–258.

Pocock J.G.A., "Clergy and Commerce: The Conservative Enlightenment in England", in Ajello R. (ed.), *L'età dei Lumi: studi storici sul Settecento europeo in onore di Franco Venturi, vol. 1* (Naples: 1985) 523–562.

Pocock J.G.A., "Conservative Enlightenment and Democratic Revolutions. The American and French Cases in British Perspective", *Government and Opposition* 24 (1989) 81–105.

Pott M., *Aufklärung und Aberglaube. Die deutsche Frühaufklärung im Spiegel ihrer Aberglaubenskritik* (Tübingen: 1992).

Pott M., "Aufklärung und Hexenaberglaube. Philosophische Ansätze zur Überwindung der Teufelspakttheorie in der deutschen Frühaufklärung", in Lorenz S. – Bauer D.R. (eds.), *Das Ende der Hexenverfolgung* (Stuttgart: 1995) 183–202.

Provenzal D., *Una polemica diabolica nel secolo XVIII* (Rocca S. Casciano: 1901).
Riezler S. von, *Geschichte der Hexenprozesse in Bayern. Im Lichte der allgemeinen Entwickelung dargestellt* (Stuttgart: 1896).
Roling B., *Locutio angelica. Die Diskussion der Engelsprache als Antizipation einer Sprechakttheorie in Mittelalter und Früher Neuzeit* (Leiden: 2008).
Rosmini Carlo, *Memorie intorno alla vita e agli scritti di Clemente Baroni Cavalcabò* (Rovereto, Marchesani: 1798).
[Rossi Medoro], "Rev. of Cavalcabò, L'impotenza del demonio", *Novelle della Repubblica letteraria* (1753) 260–262.
Spada A., "Scambi culturali tra Italia e Austria a metà del '700. Le Accademie di Salisburgo, Innsbruck e Rovereto", in Destro A. – Filippi P.M. (eds.), *La cultura tedesca in Italia 1750–1850* (Bologna: 1995) 191–216.
Stammel H., *Der Kraftbegriff in Leibniz' Physik*, Ph.D. dissertation (University of Mannheim: 1982).
Sterzinger Ferdinand, *Akademische Rede von dem gemeinen Vorurtheil der wirkenden und thätigen Hexerey* (Munich, Mayr: 1766).
Sterzinger Ferdinand, *Betrügende Zauberkunst und träumende Hexerey, oder Vertheidigung der akademischen Rede, von dem gemeinen Vorurtheile der wirkenden und thätigen Hexerey, wider das Urtheil ohne Vorurtheil* (Munich, s.n.: 1767).
Strüber S., *P. Jordan Simon aus dem Orden der Augustiner-Eremiten. Ein Lebensbild aus der Aufklärungszeit* (Würzburg: 1930).
Tartarotti Girolamo, *Del congresso notturno delle lammie libri tre* (Rovereto, Pasquali: 1749).
Tartarotti Girolamo, *Ragionamento del padre Giorgio Gaar della Compagnia di Gesu fatto avanti al rogo di Maria Renata strega abbruciata in Erbipoli a' 21. di Giugno del corrente anno 1749. Tradotto dal tedesco nell'italiano dal Dr. F.A.T. con alcune annotazioni critiche dell'Ab. Girolamo Tartarotti* (Verona, Ramanzini: s.a.).
Thomasius Christian, *Theses inaugurales, de crimine magiae* (Halle, Salfeld: 1701).
Tschacher W., "Der Flug durch die Luft zwischen Illusionstheorie und Realitätsbeweis", *Zeitung der Savigny-Stiftung für Rechtgeschichte* 116 (1999) 225–276.
Ubbidiente dell'O.S.A. Ardoino [= Simon Jordan], *Das grosse Welt-betrügende Nichts oder die heutige Hexerey und Zauberkunst* (Frankfurt – Leipzig, s.n.: 1761).
Venturi F., *Settecento riformatore, vol. 1: Da Muratori a Beccaria* (Torino: 1998).
Wolff Christian, "Principia dynamica", *Commentarii academiae scientiarum petropolitanae* 1 (1728) 217–238.
Wolff Christian, *Cosmologia generalis, methodo scientifica pertractata, qua ad solidam, in primis Dei atque naturae, cognitionem via sternitur*, in Wolff Christian, *Gesammelte Werke*, ed. J. École (Frankfurt – Leipzig: 1737²; reprint, Hildesheim: 1964).

Wolff Christian, *Vertheidigung der Meinung von der bewegenden Krafft, welche sich in den Cörpern befindet, gegen Hr. Muys Einwendungen*, in Wolff Christian, *Gesammelte Werke, sec. 1, vol. 21.4* (1739; reprint, Hildesheim: 1981) 128–141.

Wolff Christian, *Der vernünfftigen Gedancken von Gott, der Welt und der Seele des Menschen, auch allen Dingen überhaupt, Anderer Theil, bestehend in ausfürlichen Anmerckungen*, in Wolff Christian *Gesammelte Werke, sec. 1, vol. 3*, ed. C.A. Corr, (Frankfurt: 1740[4]; reprint, Hildesheim: 1983).

Zaccaria Francescantonio, *Storia letteraria d'Italia, vol. 8* (Modena, s.n.: 1755).

Index Nominum

Aaron 179
Ablancourt, F. d' 257–259, 261
Abraham 43–46, 81, 84, 170–171, 247–248
Abravanel, I. 174
Abulpharagius 172–173
Adam 104, 161
Addison, J. 302
Adonis 166
Aeschylus 275
Agamben, G. 1 n.2, 188
Agnes of Poitou 315
Akhenaton 184
Albinus, Bernhard Siegfried 287
Alexander, P. 240
Amenophis 184, 187 n.98
Amphion 166
Anderson, G. 10
Anobret 170–171
Antaeus 55, 87
Antigonus 11
Antiochus Epiphanes 235
Antoninus Pius 160 n.7
Anubis 19, 166
Alexander of Abonoteichos 9, 18
Alexander, P.S. 240 n.36
Alexander Polyhistor 177, 179
Alexander the Great 17–19, 103, 288
Apelles 120
Apis 18, 166
Apollo 116, 280 n.38
Apollodorus 55 n.97
Apollonius of Tyana 15
Apuleius 20
Ares 241
Aries 13
Ariès, P. 134, 150
Arignotus 11–12
Arion 164
Aristarchus 232, 241–244
Aristophanes 24–26, 202, 274, 276
Aristotle 21, 163, 245, 311 n.56
Arnauld, Antoine 165, 168, 180, 188, 255, 257–258, 260
Arnauld, Marie-Angelique 304
Arnobius 205, 208, 210

Arrian 290
Artapanus 166, 168, 175, 176 n.64, 180
Artemis 16
Assmann, J. 166 n.27, 167 n.30, 184, 186, 214 n.70, 218 n.86
Astharoth 281
Athanasius of Alexandria 50
Atlas 14
Athena 241, 280
Augustine 27, 45 n.75, 69 n.143, 123, 164, 218, 348
Ayrer, Georg Heinrich 220
Azizus 172

Baal 281
Bacchus 166
Bach, Johann August 216–220, 223
Bakhtin, M. M. 134, 138–140, 143 n.37–38, 187 n.100
Balaam 38
Baldwin, B. 9 n.8, 10
Barakat Ibn Kabar 174
Barber, C.L. 139 n.17
Baroni Cavalcabò, Clemente 332, 335–351
Baronius, Caesar 101, 206
Basedow, J.B. 282
Basnage, Jacques 263, 319
Baubo 205, 208–210
Bauer, B. 292
Baumgarten, Alexander Gottlieb 348
Baumgarten, A.I. 170 n.41, 178 n.71
Baumgarten, Sigmund Jacob 256
Bayle, Pierre 254, 263, 273, 307
Bayless, M. 67 n.136
Becker, A. 26 n.10
Behringer, W. 334 n.15
Bekker, Balthasar 333–336, 339, 341, 343
Belial 265
Belleforest, François 304
Belon, Pierre 291
Belot, Jean 308
Ben Abuya, Elisha 29
Bendlin, A. 18 n.51
Benjamin, Walter 188

358　　　　　　　　　　　　　　　　　　　　　　　　　　　INDEX NOMINUM

Ben Shetach, Shimon   29–31, 33–34, 37, 46–47, 53, 55, 57, 61, 64, 70, 72, 77, 83, 86
Ben Tabai, Yehuda   29–30, 60–62, 64, 66–70, 72–73
Bentley, J.   149 n.44
Ben-Tov, A.   3, 177 n.69, 211 n.56
Berdozzo F.   10 n.10, 14 n.26
Bernal, D.   130 n.145
Bernal, Martin   183
Bernier, Etienne   321
Bernstein, A.E.   23 n.1, 24 n.3
Berosus   171, 177
Berthier, David-Nicolas de   312, 320
Bertram   254
Beverland, Adriaan   161–162, 167, 187
Binsfeld, Peter   338
Blair, A.   169 n.37
Boccaccio   104
Bochart, Matthieu   313
Bochart, Samuel   167, 169–171, 174, 261, 283, 286, 291 n.93, 313
Bodin, Jean   338
Boehart, W.   292 n.96
Böhmer, Georg Ludwig   220–221 n.101
Bompaire, J.   10
Borghero, C.   166 n.26
Borromeo, Carlo   100, 123, 130, 309
Boscovich, R.   342
Bossuet, Jacques Benigne   256, 258, 264–266, 269, 271
Bourgeaud, P.   1 n.1
Boussel, P.   300 n.10
Bouterwek, Friedrich   221
Brandon, S.G.F.   23 n.1, 24 n.4
Bremmer, J.   24 n.6, 27 n.20, 198 n.6–7, 203 n.18
Bronzino   121
Brown, P.   304
Bruit Zaidman, L.   204 n.23
Brun, J. Le   255 n.5,7, 259, 270, 273 n.1
Bruno, Giordano   159
Budde, Johann Franz   347
Budé   254
Bullen, Christian   284 n.65
Büsch, Johann Georg   287
Büttner, Christoph Andreas   348
Burke, P.   134, 137 n.8, 141 n.27

Burkert, W.   198 n.5, 202 n.15, 203
Bynum, C.W.   303 n.17

Cahier, Charles   322–323
Caprara, G. Battista   321
Carli, Gianrinaldo   332, 350
Cartier, Étienne   322, 324
Cassius Dio   282
Cham   174
Calov, Abraham   274
Calvin, Jean   254, 305, 308, 320
Capella, Martianus   169
Cappel, Louis   273
Cassius Longinus   235
Caster, M.   10 n.9, 20
Castiglione, Baldasar   99 n.13, 104, 123
Catesby, Mark   287
Catullus   161, 285
Cecrops   166
Cedrenus   173
Celeus   201, 205
Cellini, Benvenuto   115
Celsus   57, 60, 163, 180
Ciasca, A.   53 n.93
Cicero   13, 14 n.24, 20 n.65, 35 n.53, 104, 163, 201 n.12, 211
Charenton, Allix of   254, 256, 258–259
Charenton, J.C. of   253–256, 258–259, 270
Chavin de Malan, Émile   321–322
Chédozeau, B.   254 n.4
Christ, Johann Friedrich   217
Chrysis   17
Clement of Alexandria   45 n.75, 49–50, 57 n.101, 60 n.107, 174 n.61, 204–205, 208, 210–211
Clark, S.   335 n.16
Cleodemus Malchus   11, 176
Coelus   171
Cohen, Y.   34 n.52
Colpe, C.   1 n.1
Cook, J.G.   42 n.71, 234, 235 n.18
Confucius   2, 165
Cox, V.   123 n.125
Crates   232
Crozet, R.   303 n.19
Cyril of Scythopolis   63–64, 76
Cyrill of Alexandria   164, 179 n.77

INDEX NOMINUM

Daille, Jean 261
Damis 15
Dandini, Jerome 257
Daniel 164, 235, 246, 249–250, 345
Darwin, Erasmus 287
Dascal, M. 167 n.31
Daube, D. 239
Dawkins, R. 274
Del Rio, Martin 336, 338
Delatour, J. 162 n.13
Delz, J. 10
Demeter 198, 202–208, 210, 219, 223
Demetrius of Phalerum 232–233
Demonax 17–18
Descartes, René 333, 335, 338, 342, 343 n.35, 344
Desmarets 254
Devil 4, 96–97, 107–108, 110, 112–118, 126, 128, 147–148, 152, 210, 330–336, 338–339, 341–345, 348–351
  -Satan 108, 114, 118, 122, 147–148, 163, 283
Diana 175, 179 n.78, 338
Dickinson, Edmund 167, 178 n.74
Didron, Adolphe-Napoléon 323
Dihle, A. 1
Dilherr, Johann Michael 276
Dinomachus 11
Diocles 202
Diodati 254, 261
Diomedes 241
Dionysus 24, 57, 149, 188
Dionysus Thrax 232
Diogenes 18, 35 n.53
Donne, John 134, 150, 153–154
Dreux du Radier, Jean-François 319 n.98
Drijvers, H.J.W. 172 n.51
Droge, A. 166 n.28
Dryden, John 1
Duchesneau, F. 341 n.28
Dürer, Albrecht 102, 114 n.82
Duke, R. 173 n.56
Dupin, Louis Ellies 165, 312 n.62, 319 n.100
Duplessis-Mornay, Philippe 167
Dvorjetski, E. 56

Edelmann, Johann Ch. 184–187
Eissfeldt, O. 178 n.71

El 170–171
Eleazar 232
Eliade, M. 1 n.1, 138 n.13, 139 n.14, 159 n.2, 203 n.21
Elias (prophet) 164
Elias, N. 134, 140 n.22
Eli'ezer 71, 173
Elliot, J.K. 27 n.18
Enkidu 23
Enoch 27, 177
Epicurus 163
Erechtheus 219
Etheridge, J.W. 238 n.31
Eucrates 11–12, 16–17
Eumolpos 202
Eupolemus 166, 168–170, 176 n.64
Eusebius 56–57, 86, 168–174 n.59, 177, 180, 182 n.87–88
Ezekiel 279

Fabricius, Johann Albert 174 n.61, 278
Fatio, Olivier 256–257, 262–263
Feddersen, B.H. 283 n.58
Ferrand, Jean 303 n.18, 305–306, 308
Feuillas, M. 307 n.37
Fiorentino, Rosso 121
Flusser, D. 239
Forelius, Hemming 210–212, 217
Forgeais, Arthur 324
Foucault, M. 134–135, 136 n.6, 139
Fraenkel, E. 197 n.2
Francis of Assisi 105
Frank, Heinrich August 222–223
Frateantonio, C. 14
Freeman, A. 99 n.11
Freud, Sigmund 165

Gaar, Georg 334
Gager, J. 166 n.28, 236
Gaia 55
Gallois, Mathurin 321
Gaulmin, G. 174–175
Gavin, Antonio 302, 306, 311
Gedalia Ibn Yaḥya 173
George, Philippe 299
Gerhard, Johann 276
Geretto, M. 344 n.37

360 INDEX NOMINUM

Gero, S.   62 n.120, 63–64, 67 n.137
Geyer-Kordesch, J.   341 n.28
Gilgamesh   23–24
Ginzburg, C.   163 n.18, 181 n.84
Giorgione   121
Glycas, M.   177
Goff, J. Le   23 n.1, 45 n.75
Graevius, Johann Georg   281
Grafton, A.   167 n.31, 177 n.69, 276 n.18, 277
Greenblatt, S.   134 n.1
Gregory of Nyssa   51 n.89
Gregory the Great   54 n.94, 316
Gregory XIII   100
Grès-Gayer, J.M.   313 n.69
Gressmann, H.   34 n.51, 40
Griffith, F.L.   26 n.16, 174 n.62
Griffiths, J.G.   174 n.62
Groetsch, U.   4, 187 n.99
Gronovius, Jacob   281
Grotius, Hugo   167, 169 n.38, 273–274, 287
Gruen, E.   175, 176 n.64

Habakkuk   246, 247 n.62, 345
Hadrian   218
Häfner, R.   160 n.5, 178 n.74
Hämeen-Anttila, J.   172 n.52
Hammerstein, N.   220 n.97
Halbertal, M.   160 n.5
Hall, J.   10
Hardouin, Jean   167, 331
Hartsoeker, Nicolas   282
Hase, Theodor   283–286
Hazard, P.   5 n.4, 271
Hecataeus   166, 183
Hecate   16, 201
Heidenreich, M.   217 n.82
Heinse, Wilhelm   221
Helios   13, 201
Henry III   315
Hera   245
Heracles   9, 24–25, 55
Heraclitus   19, 242–246, 249
Herbert of Cherbury   180
Hercules   14, 160, 164, 280 n.38, 283 n.59
Hermes   15 n.34, 26, 166, 169, 175
Herod, King   67, 74
Herodotus   9, 13, 15 n.36, 18, 280–281
Hesychius   281

Heuß, A.   19 n.55
Heyne, Christian Gottlob   217
Hickey, H.M.   299 n.3
Hierombalus   170
Hieronymus Wolf   177
Himmelfarb, M.   27, 36 n.55–59, 38 n.62, 40, 64 n.129
Hirshman, M.   68 n.141
Hippocrates   11
Hippolytos   163
Hippolytus of Rome   203
Hißmann, Michael   215–216
Hoffmann, Friedrich   335, 338, 341
Hoffmann, Johann Adolf   278–279, 280 n.36, 281, 283, 285 n.69, 286 n.72
Homer   24 n.6, 232, 236, 240–246, 249–250, 280
Hopkins, Keith   231
Horace   197–198
Horst, P.W. van der   236C237
Horus   39, 41, 280
Hosea   67, 74
Huet, Pierre-Daniel   5, 159, 161 n.8, 162, 165–188, 257
Hughes, G.   142 n.34
Huizinga, J.   199
Hunger, H.   177 n.68
Hurel, D.-O.   300 n.10
Hutcheon, L.   24 n.7
Hyde, Thomas   281
Hölderlin   188

Iamblichus   172
Ibn Ezra   172–173
Ibn Waḥshiyya   172
Ilan, T.   37 n.61
Iltis, C.   342 n.34
Ion   11
Isaac   170–171
Isaiah   68 n.141, 142–143
Ishmael   241–242, 244, 248–249
Isis   12, 175, 207, 222
Israel, J.   330 n.2, 334 n.14
Italicus, Silius   286

James   57–58
Jannai, King   73
Jedin, H.   95 n.2, 130 n.142

Jehud 170
Jensen, J. 41 n.68
Jerome 44–45, 51 n.89, 235 n.19, 265, 269
Jesus 28, 31, 38, 45–48, 50–54, 57–60, 65–87,
    116, 182, 199, 265, 277, 292, 311
  –Christ 115–117, 119, 129, 159, 188, 247,
    249, 299, 304, 311–313, 320–323, 345
Job 261, 274, 278–283, 285 n.67, 287
Johnson, Ben 4, 134, 143, 145–147
Jonah 164, 284
Jones, F.S. 54 n.94
Jones, P.M. 100 n.15, 103 n.23, 104 n.26,
    110 n.61
Josepha of Austria, Maria 212 n.60
Joseph (Jesus' Father) 67–68, 73, 75, 79
Joseph (Son of Jacob) 164
Josephus 168, 169 n.39, 183, 185 n.94,
    237 n.27
Julian the Apostate 105, 172, 231, 234–239
Jupiter 114, 174, 181, 215
Jurieu, Pierre 280, 305
Justel, Henri 257–259, 261

Kalliakis, Nikolaos 209–210, 212, 217–218
Kearney, J. 317 n.86
Keleos 202
Klein, D. 187 n.99, 274 n.8
Knight, K.J. 299 n.3
Koerbagh, Adriaan 161, 162 n.11
Konstan, D. 242, 245 n.57
Kothami 172
Kovacs, M. 24 n.2
Kircher, A. 175
Kronos 170–171

Labrousse, E. 253
Lakemacher, J.G. 208, 212
La Mothe Le Vayer 5, 162–168, 180–181, 183
Lancelot, Antoine 181–182
Lange, Joachim 347
Langlois, M. 27 n.19
Launoy, Jean de 307, 313, 314 n.70
Lazarus, Rabbi 32, 53, 67, 82
Lazarus the poor 27, 40 n.67, 41–46, 49–51,
    54 n.94, 80–81, 84
Lazarus the resurrected 53–54 n.94, 66–67,
    82, 299, 313, 321
Le Clerc, Jean 162, 261, 264, 271, 273–277,
    280, 287–292

Leclerq, Henri 301
Lecocq, L. 142 n.33
Lehmann, R. G. 5 n.5
Leibniz, Gottfried Wilhelm 167, 338,
    342–344, 346, 350
Le Maître de Sacy, Isaac-Louis 254
Lenfant, Jacques 273 n.2
Leonard, M. 231 n.3
Leopold I 253
Lesbia 285
Lessing, Gotthold Ephraim 96, 277, 292
Leviathan 283, 285
Lieberman, S. 30 n.29–30, 34, 36 n.55–
    38 n.62, 239
Limoges, Pierre de 310
Linus 166
Lipsius, Justus 286
Livy 204, 209
Locatelli, Gaetano Maria 345, 349
Löwenklau, Johann 177
Lotman, J. M. 135, 136 n.4
Louis XIV 253–255, 271
Lucian of Samosata 3, 9–21, 25–26, 39, 44
Lucius Verus 9
Luhmann, N. 137, 138 n.11
Luke 27–28, 40–49, 52–53, 59–60, 65,
    67–69, 71–72, 74–75, 77–79, 80–82,
    84–86, 129
Luther, Martin 96, 103
Lycaon 164
Lycophron 164, 174 n.61

Mabillon, Jean 300–301, 312–325
Machiavelli 181, 186
Macleod, M. D. 10
Macrobius 280
Magdalino, P. 173 n.57
Mahis, Marin Grostête de 308, 309 n.44
Maffei, Scipione 331, 350
Mahler, A. 4
Maimonides 172, 186
Mâle, Emile 323
Manetho 174 n.61, 177, 183–185, 187
Manetti, Gianozzo 233 n.11
Manuel, F. 159, 162
Marcus Aurelius 9
Mark 58, 59 n.106, 60 n.109, 66, 77, 87
Marprelate, Martin 142
Mars 215

Marsham, John   186
Martel, Geoffroy   304, 307, 322
Martha   53–54, 60, 65–67, 75, 77, 81–82
Martianay, Jean   265–266
Martin, Arthur   322–324
Martin of Tours   309, 316
Mary (Magdalene)   32–33, 36–37, 41, 46, 51–54, 56–60, 65–68, 75, 77, 81–83, 303, 305, 307
Mary (Mother of Jesus)   57–58, 213
Matthew   23, 47, 52–60, 64, 67–69, 72–79, 82–83, 85–86, 345 n.42
McDonald, L.M.   233 n.12
Meier, Georg Friedrich   348
Meiners, Christoph   216
Melchizedek   323
Merchier, Jaques le   310
Melechet   281
Memnon   12
Menghi, Girolamo   97–98
Mennipus   13, 16
Mercier, Jean   279 n.33
Mercury   159, 169, 172, 174, 215
Merkt, A.   45 n.75
Meumann, M.   216 n.80
Meursius, Johannes   206–209, 211–212, 214, 223
Michael, Glykas   177 n.69
Michael IV the Paphlagonian   303
Michelangelo   116, 120–121
Middleton, Conyers   213 n.65
Miller, P.N.   160 n.4
Minerva   207 n.38
Minos   166, 179 n.78, 181
Mithrobazanes   16
Moloch   281
Montaiglon, A. de   300 n.6
Montrond, Maxime de   324–325
Mnevis   166
Möllendorf, P.   10 n.14
Monimus   172
Morris, C.   317 n.88
Morrison, K.   4
Morsimus   25
Moses   5, 44, 84, 107 n.45, 108, 114, 166–187, 214, 236–238, 247, 258, 288 n.82
Mouskes, Philippe   304
Münster, Sebastian   304 n.24

Muhammad   181–182
Mulsow, M.   5, 159–161 n.8, 167 n.29, 169 n.37, 180 n.82, 216 n.79, 275 n.9, 276 n.18
Mungello, D.E.   165 n.23
Musaeus   166
Mussies, G.   176 n.65
Mylonas, G.   203

Naudé, Gabriel   181–182
Neander, Michael   206
Nebuchadnezzar   164
Nemean lion   11
Neri, Filippo   100
Nero   19, 204
Nesselrath, H.-G.   9 n.8, 15 n.31, 17 n.47, 18, 19 n.56
Nestor   280
Neugebauer-Wölk, M.   216 n.80
Newton   342
Nicole, Pierre   255, 257–258
Niehoff, M.   233 n.10, 234 n.14, 239 n.34
Niemeier, Heinrich Wilhelm   212 n.60
Nietzsche   188
Nisbet, R.G.M.   197 n.3
Nitker   315, 322
Nitzan, B.   246, 247 n.62
Noah   174, 177
Nogent, Guibert de   309
Numa Pompilius   181–183, 186
Nünlist, R.   240–241

Octavian/Augustus   19
Oliver, J. H.   10
Olivetan   254
Orotalt   280
Orpheus   13–14, 20, 114 n.82, 121, 166
Osarseph   174 n.61, 183–185
Osiris   19, 40, 183–184
Ossa-Richardson, A.   4
Ovid   55, 87, 103 n.24, 161, 286, 306 n.30

Pancrates   12
Paleotti, Gabriele   95–131
Pan   166–167
Pandora   164
Parinetto, L.   330 n.2, 332 n.8, 350 n.56
Parker, R.   203 n.18
Parmigianino   121

INDEX NOMINUM

Parny, Evariste de 159
Paul 69 n.143, 82, 111, 247, 249
Pausanias 14–15, 20
Paz, Yakir 240
Peisistratus 232–234
Peregrinus Proteus 9, 18
Des Périers, Bonaventure 159
Persephone 16, 198, 200–201, 204
Peter 82, 111, 129
Pétigny, Jules de 322
Petronius 161
Pfeiffer, August 275 n.12
Pfeiffer, R. 232 n.7
Pfister, M. 143 n.38
Pico della Mirandola 178–179
Pierce, W. 142 n.33
Phaeton 13, 164
Phales 15
Philostratus, Lucius Flavius 15
Philos of Byblos 170–171
Philostratus the Elder 55, 87
Phornutus 167
Pichler, K. 163 n.16
Pindar 275
Pinevoise, Alexandre 300 n.7
Pintard, R. 162 n.13
Plato 19, 24, 114 n.81, 163–164, 179
Pliny the Elder 19, 290
Plotinus 235
Plutarch 182, 207, 209, 280–281
Pluto 198
Pococke, Edward 173
Pocock, John 349
Poleni, Giovanni 210, 218
Pope, Alexander 23
Pope Alexander VII 130
Pope Clement VIII 101, 120 n.110
Pope Innocent III 306, 313
Pope Innocent XI 130 n.144, 253
Pope Paul IV 99
Pope Pius IV 121
Pope Pius V 125
Pope Urban VIII 130
Popkin, R.H. 162 n.14
Porphyry of Gaza 56
Porphyry of Tyre 169 n.39, 170, 180, 235–236, 239
Porter, J. 232

Pottier, A. 303 n.20
Pott, M. 335 n.17–18
Poulouin, C. 161 n.8
Priapus 167, 183
Prodi, P. 97 n.5, 99 n.12, 101 n.17–18, 116 n.89, 130 n.142
Propertius 161
Prüm, Regino of 338
Ptolemy 19, 232
Pyrrho 163
Pythagoras 182

Quantin, J.-L. 317 n.89

Rabelais 104
Rambach, Johann Jacob 275–276 n.16
Reay, B. 141 n.27
Reimarus, Joh. Albert H. 287
Reimarus, Hermann Samuel 5, 187, 273–288, 290–292
Reland, Adriaan 281
Richardson, N.J. 200 n.10, 202
Rochambeau, Achille de 300 n.7, 303 n.16, 321 n.105–106, 324–325
Roche, Michael de la 320
Rohault, Jaques 304
Rokeach, D. 235–236
Rolfinck, Werner 208–209
Romulus 166
Rossi, Medoro 348
Rotstein, A. 201 n.13
Rubenstein, J. 46 n.77, 70 n.145
Rudd, N. 197 n.3
Russel 242, 245 n.57

Sabas 63–64
Sagittarius, Caspar 320
Sainte-Marie, Honoré 320
Sales, François de 304, 305 n.27, 324
Samson 164
Sanchuniathon 170–171, 177
Sandys, J.E. 207 n.34
Sarah 170–171
Satlow, M. 51 n.88
Saturn 164, 170–171, 179 n.77
Savonarola 126
Scafi, A. 161 n.8
Scaliger, Joseph 167, 170–172, 177

Schäfer, P.   28 n.22, 29 n.26, 54 n.94, 60 n.110, 62 n.119, 184
Schilling, R.   1
Schmidt-Biggemann, W.   278 n.25
Schmitt Pantel, P.   204 n.23
Schnapp, A.   160 n.6
Schremer, A.   28 n.22
Schröder, W.   180 n.80, 182 n.86, 184 n.93
Schweitzer, Albert   292
Scipio   288
Segni, Giovanni Battista   304, 308–309
Selden, John   177
Seneca   275
Serapis   166
Setme Kamwas   26, 39–41, 44
Severe, Gabriel   257
Shakespeare   134 n.1, 143 n.38
Shapiro, B.   160 n.6
Sheehan, J.   159 n.2, 160 n.4
Shelford, A.   161, 165 n.25, 166 n.26, 169 n.40, 178
Shimon ber Yohai   241 n.46
Siculus, Diodorus   55 n.97, 201 n.12, 222, 290
Siegal, M.B.-A.   27 n.21
Silenus   166
Simon, Jordan   331, 351
Simon, Richard   255–271, 273, 319
Simon the Pharisee   67, 70
Simonides of Chios   105
Singer, Maria Renata   334
Skelton, John   142
Skovgaard-Petersen, K.   207 n.34
Sloan, T.O.   151 n.49
Smith, C.   233 n.11
Smith, J.Z.   160 n.4
Smith, M.   199 n.8
Smith, M.S.   178 n.71
Socrates   163, 165
Sokoloff, M.   34 n.51, 62 n.120
Sophocles   19, 240 n.39
Spanheim, Ezechiel   160–162
Spencer, John   186
Spickermann, W.   3, 20 n.64
Spiegelberg, W.   174 n.62
Spinoza   168, 259, 271
Stammel, H.   343 n.35
Stausberg, M.   24 n.5
Stemberger, G.   176 n.66

Stephen of Grandmont   310
Stern, M.   234, 235 n.19, 236 n.23
Stockhausen, Heinrich Ch. L.   212–213, 217
Stockmann, August Cornelius   217 n.83
Strabo   166 n.29, 290–291
Strauss, David Friedrich   292, 313
Stumpf, Johann Ludwig   288 n.80
Suetonius   19, 204
Suitner, R.   4
Sybil   1
Syncellus   173, 177

Tag   15
Tantalus   24
Tartarotti, Girolamo   330–334, 336, 339, 341, 344–346, 349–350
Tartarus   17, 164
Terence   275
Tertullian   205–207, 219, 231
Tesdorpf, Peter Hinrich   283, 287
Texier, Jacques   324
Theodoretus   164, 169
Theodulf of Orléans   98–99
Theophylactus   164
Thiers, Jean-Baptiste   299–301, 305–316, 318–322, 325
Thomasius, Christian   335
Thot   169–171, 172 n.49, 174–176
Tiresias   13, 19
Titian   101, 121
Titus   38
Toland, John   167, 168 n.33
Tressan, Louis de   312
Triptolemos   202
Tronchin, Louis   260–261
Turretini, Michel   261
Typhon   166, 283

Uffenbach, Zacharias C. von   285
Uglow, J.   287 n.79
Ugolino, Blasio   281
Ulysses   13, 16

Valla, Lorenzo   313
Valle, Pietro della   175 n.63
Varennes, Mme de   260, 262
Varro   171–172, 218
Veltri, G.   234 n.12

Venturi, Franco   330 n.2, 332 n.8, 349, 350 n.55
Venus   114, 215
Veronese, Paolo   4
Vigny, Alfred de   321
Virgil   1, 5, 14 n.24, 24, 37, 44–45, 198 n.3
Visotzky, B.   28 n.23, 54 n.94, 57 n.102
Voltaire   166, 168, 215, 222–223
Volterra, Daniele da   121
Volterre, Raphaël de   164
Vossius, Gerardus   167, 207–208, 211, 222, 281
Vossius, Isaac   161
Vulcan   163

Wagenvoort, H.   197 n.3, 198 n.7
Warburton, William   213–217, 221–223
Warning, R.   140 n.23
Wasserstein, A.   234 n.15
Webb, E.   2 n.3
Weimann, R.   134, 136 n.5, 137 n.9, 138
Welchering, P.   198 n.7
West, D.   198 n.4
West, M.L.   178 n.72
Widerhold, Jan Hermann   257, 262
Wimpfheimer, B.S.   29 n.24

Wolf, J.B.   253 n.1
Wolf, Johann Christoph   275, 278, 338
Wolff, Christian   338, 346–48, 350
Woodbridge, J.   5, 255 n.5, 259 n.9, 264 n.18
Wortley, J.   27 n.21
Wycliffe, John   103

Xisuthrus   177
Xylander, Wilhelm   177

Yadin-Israel, A.   3, 180 n.81, 241 n.46, 244 n.56
Young, B.   214 n.70
Yuval, I.J.   36 n.58
Yose ben Hanina   32, 68, 82

Zaccaria, Francescantonio   348, 349 n.52
Zellentin, H.   4, 24 n.7, 26 n.10, 28 n.22, 34 n.51, 42 n.69, 47 n.81, 70 n.146
Zeus   15, 16, 18, 22, 200–201, 245
Zimmermann, H.   134 n.1
Zoli, S.   165 n.24
Zonaras, John   177
Zoroaster   166